Leadership and Innovation

Leadership and Innovation

A Biographical Perspective on Entrepreneurs in Government

edited by Jameson W. Doig and Erwin C. Hargrove

The Johns Hopkins University Press   Baltimore and London

The Johns Hopkins University Press
701 West 40th Street   Baltimore, Maryland 21211
The Johns Hopkins Press Ltd., London

The paper used in this publication meets the minimum requirements of American National Standard for Information Sciences—Permanence of Paper for Printed Library Materials, ANSI Z39.48-1984.

The first stanza from Emily Dickinson's poem *I dwell in Possibility—*, quoted in chapter 1, is reprinted from *The Complete Poems of Emily Dickinson*, edited by Thomas H. Johnson. Copyright by Martha Dickinson Bianchi; © renewed 1957 by Mary L. Hampson. Reprinted by permission of Little Brown and Company. Reprinted also by permission of the publishers and the Trustees of Amherst College from *The Poems of Emily Dickinson*, edited by Thomas H. Johnson, Cambridge, Mass.: The Belknap Press of Harvard University Press, Copyright 1951, © 1955, 1979, 1983 by The President and Fellows of Harvard College.

Library of Congress Cataloging-in-Publication Data

Leadership and innovation.

  Bibliography: p.
  Includes index.
  1. Government executives—United States—Biography.
I. Doig, Jameson W.   II. Hargrove, Erwin C.
JK723.E9L43   1987   353.07'4'0922 [B]   87-4155
ISBN 0-8018-3442-2 (alk. paper)

Contents

Foreword

This is a book about men and women who held posts of top authority in public organizations (and one comparative private one). From there each made a dent on the world, an innovative mark, actually affecting what his or her agency got done, and how—in short, turning formal authority into effective influence, exerting power in that special sense of personal impact on the work of one's associates. A quarter-century ago I tried to clarify the strategic problem of employing power in that sense from the most prominent position of authority our system affords: the federal presidency. This book takes the problem one and two levels down, into the executive branch, and deals with it illustratively, biographically, from person to person.

The results are illuminating. Despite diversity, common threads emerge, encouraging hypotheses for further study. Some are handily supplied by authors attentive to their task. Others a reader draws at will. These stories of real people caught in the act of exercising influence shed light especially on the complex, often mysterious connections among individuals, institutions, and environments. Authority figures *can* exercise personal leadership, personalities *can* make a difference. Organizational processes *cannot* account for everything. Occasionally they do not account for much! Yet there is a big *but*: from one situation to the next, the would-be leader's influence swells or diminishes depending on how personal operating style fits organizational needs and outside conditions.

The leader who succeeds in one agency at one time fails at another agency or in another time. If bosses can matter—and the stories here support the common notion that they do—then so do structures, missions, and settings as those alter over time. The stories support this too.

Interestingly, those things appear to alter faster than do operating styles of individuals; those styles are relative constants in grown-ups, it seems, and less changeable than are the institutional incentives playing on different associates. Not only do I read that, I have often seen it.

One of the most interesting leaders in this book is James E. Webb, who reshaped NASA to put a man on the moon. When I was young, I once served as his "water boy," the staff assistant at his door, minding his mail and his meetings, following up and fending off, fetching and carrying. At that time Webb was very influential in the Bureau of the Budget (now OMB), serving as director under Harry S. Truman, from August 1946 to January 1949. During Webb's first year there he invented, among other things, "Economic Indicators," a set of charts, updated monthly, which he later handed on to the then infant Council of Economic Advisers, which has produced them since. It was wonderful to watch Webb's use of his indicators. He would carry them around in a leather folder tucked under his arm, whipping them out at the slightest provocation to help him vivify a point: "You see what I mean, Mr. President. . . . Look at what's happened to unemployment, here . . . and to industrial production. See that . . . and notice farm production . . . and oh, see the demand for home mortgages? Here. Now what it all adds up to, sir, is this: we'd better. . . ." Webb talked with those charts the way some people talk with their hands. Truman ate it up.

Webb's next assignment, unhappily, was as under secretary of state, seconding Dean Acheson, supposedly to "run the department" while the secretary made and negotiated policy—always an illusory division of labor, bound to disappoint, especially at State, which scarcely ever has been "run" in the usual sense by anyone and certainly not by Webb. He had not been under secretary long when, lacking anything under his arm, he sought to invent "Foreign Policy Indicators." These he asked the career staff around him to prepare, and asked, and asked—at first insistent, ultimately querulous. He never got them. A senior career diplomat explained to one of Webb's own aides (brought over from BOB):

> He won't get these things. We'll see to it he doesn't. Can you imagine the under secretary bounding around the building (not to mention the White House!) brandishing his charts and saying, "OK, why's cold-war production down? Yugoslavia came over last month; why not Albania this month? And what's for next month?" Preposterous. It can't be allowed to happen.

Circumstances alter cases. Leadership in one context becomes frustration in another. The organizational context can be crucial, as can the policy context. Central to both is timing. Webb's innovative influence on many aspects of the Truman regime's policies and processes owed much to chronology. Before 1946 and after 1950, wars shaped the federal budget—and the president's attention, and his staffing, and the Bureau's—far more than the budget director did or could have hoped to do. Webb's time in office turns out to have been serendipitous for him. The preceding two and one-half years or the following two and one-half would not have yielded him an equal chance to found his reputation as an institutional leader.

Still, chancy as it may be, and time-bound as it surely is, to lead an institution from the top, to transform nominal powers into actual influence, is statecraft, a high calling when attempted nationally—and very much the same thing, as this book shows, when attempted in the many organizations of which our executive establishment consists. It is among the most challenging of human activities, stirring ambition, exciting admiration, arousing fear or pity (to one's taste), inspiring the dramatists since literature began, ignored by almost nobody in all of human history—until the coming of American political science.

There it has fared rather badly, for reasons that I think are deeply cultural, but there is no need to belabor the point. It is enough to say, with cheers, that this book contributes toward righting the balance. Also, I suppose not incidentally, it is fun to read. Stories about real people almost always are.

Richard E. Neustadt
Harvard University
Cambridge, Massachusetts

Preface

Our main task in this volume is to examine the strategies used by innovative government leaders, and their impact, using a biographical approach. We call these public leaders *entrepreneurs*, and we explain in chapter 1 why we believe this term aptly describes this class of public officials.

If our theme is entrepreneurial, the project itself has been collegial. We conceived the idea for a book during a telephone conversation and then convened several potential authors for an exploratory discussion at the meeting of the American Political Science Association in Chicago in 1983. The strong interest expressed at that meeting encouraged us to recruit other authors and begin the project. In some cases we sought authors and let them pick their subjects, using a set of guidelines that we had set out. In other cases we searched for authors who would write on public officials who we thought should be in the book.

A grant from the Alfred P. Sloan Foundation made the project possible, and we thank Arthur Singer, vice president, for his confidence in our idea.

A matching grant from the research division of the National Endowment for the Humanities supported a conference on entrepreneurial leadership at the Brookings Institution in May 1985. We thank John Williams of NEH and James Carroll and Lee Fritschler of Brookings.

The project was blessed with a small number of very astute advisers who agreed from the outset to read papers, chair panels at the conference, and provide general advice about the project. The effort began to come together as a book at the dinner meeting of authors and advisers at Brookings. The advisory group consisted of Alan Altshuler, James W. Fesler, Fred I. Greenstein, Matthew Holden, Jr., Herbert Kaufman, xii *Preface*

Laurence E. Lynn, Jr., Frederick C. Mosher, Richard E. Neustadt, Don K. Price, Harvey Sherman, and Robert C. Tucker. We thank each of these individuals for the help they gave us; at critical points their advice made a difference.

Additional comments on the papers were given by Vincent Davis, John DiIulio, Luther Gulick, Pendleton Herring, Edith Mosher, Dennis Palumbo, Bert Rockman, and Philip Selznick and by a perceptive reader for the Johns Hopkins University Press, who prefers to remain anonymous. Our thanks to Henry Tom, the senior social sciences editor at the Hopkins Press, for his helpful guidance and encouragement at every step.

The Institute for Public Policy Studies at Vanderbilt and the Woodrow Wilson School at Princeton provided administrative and secretarial support. We particularly wish to thank Lottie Strupp and Regina Perry at Vanderbilt and Alexis Faust and Julianne Bauer at Princeton. Vanderbilt University and the Woodrow Wilson School provided subventions toward the cost of publication of the volume, and we are grateful.

This was a good collaboration among scholars. We hope that the quality of that effort is reflected in the coherence and usefulness of the volume.

"Leadership" and Political Analysis

Jameson W. Doig and Erwin C. Hargrove

The history of what man has accomplished in this world," Carlyle argued, "is at bottom the History of the Great Men who have worked here. They were the leaders of men . . . the modellers, patterns, and in a wide sense creators, of whatsoever the general mass of men contrived to do or to attain."[1] Although Carlyle's enthusiasm is not shared by those who lived through the era of Hitler and Mussolini, great emphasis is still placed—in the study of the rise and fall of nations—on the actions and influence of powerful individuals: Julius Caesar and Elizabeth I, for example, V. I. Lenin and Mahatma Gandhi, Winston Churchill and Franklin D. Roosevelt.

In the field of business enterprise too, preeminently in the United States, great attention is given to the individuals who—often as heroes, sometimes as villains—create and shape empires of commerce and profit: the Carnegies, Fords, Rockefellers, and at least one Iacocca of the modern world.[2] Even in the more systematic and probing studies of corporate behavior, primary attention is often directed to the values, actions, and impact of chief executives and other business leaders.[3]

The tradition in the social sciences is quite different. Here, particularly in the study of American politics, the role of interest groups in shaping public policy is emphasized, together with the powerful impact of bureaucratic routine and institutional processes. Against the continuous pressures of these forces and other factors (such as disastrous events), the opportunities for conscious and sustained executive leadership—to redirect individual agencies and programs, to make an impact on the economy and society—appear to be highly limited. Even those agency leaders who "hurled themselves into the fray," Herbert Kaufman concludes in his recent study of federal executives, had very little impact on policies and programs. "They make their marks in inches, not miles," he argues, and their "modest incremental accomplishments" are probably "typical of public officials in the federal system, perhaps of public officials everywhere."[4] Kaufman's conclusions are more or less typical of the writings of political scientists during the past fifty years.[5]

There are, of course, exceptions. Those who study the American president and his counterparts in other nations often treat their subjects as central actors in reshaping programs and entire societies.[6] And a few individuals of lesser rank are occasionally singled out for close attention; Robert Moses and J. Edgar Hoover are prominent examples. These people have had an impact, it is widely agreed, but their careers and influence are highly unusual among the thousands who have held high executive (but nonelective) office in the United States. Moreover, their activities and impact are used to illustrate an important lesson: that power given to such individuals is likely to be power misused; that we are better off as a society when our appointed executives and our career officials are well shackled.[7]

The emphasis on systems of pressure and power and the limited attention given to the strategies and impact of particular leaders are the results of several factors. One is the effort of political scientists and their colleagues to be "scientific," that is, to search for regularities in the messy data of political life.[8] The role of specific leaders, or of "leadership" generally, appears more difficult to treat when the researcher's goal is generalization and prediction across a wide range of institutions and eras. Moreover, some scholars believe that leaders of government programs and agencies do, in fact, make very little difference, that structure and systemic patterns are in almost all situations determinative. If the emperor has no clothes, why should we attempt to study his style of dress?

Occasionally a social scientist has broken free from these traditions and searched fruitfully for generalizations that might apply to executive leadership at a variety of levels, in public as well as private institutions. One of the best of this genre is Philip Selznick's *Leadership in Administration*, and its fate is instructive. Largely disregarded by political scientists and sociologists since its publication by Harper and Row in 1957, Selznick's volume has been influential mainly in schools of business and in writings on leadership problems and strategies in the corporate world.[9]

Whether leaders in public agencies can and do make a difference should be a matter of interest not only to scholars, as they seek to understand the dynamics of governmental action and the sources of innovation. When the pessimistic view of Kaufman and his large band of colleagues dominates the scholarly literature, it also influences the texts and the teaching of public policy and is likely to convey a message to society's best potential leaders: if you are interested in using your talents and energies to accomplish challenging tasks, government service is not for you. Moreover, widespread acceptance of this "conventional wisdom" might suggest to those who do enter public service (as a career or for briefer periods) that the sophisticated course is to conserve their energies and emotional commitments for family and after-hours activities, since even vigorous and dedicated efforts on the job will yield few real achievements. Thus the position held by Kaufman and his fellow social scientists would tend to become a self-fulfilling hypothesis.[10]

James March expresses a similar concern in a recent essay on leadership. He argues that there are "two contending theories of how things happen in organizations." One, influenced by stories of Bismarck, Alfred Sloan, and other "heroic" figures, attributes "a large share of the variance in organizational outcomes to special properties of specific individual managers"; but careful research does not confirm that causal attribution. The second theory, "filled with metaphors of loose coupling [and] organized anarchy . . . seems to describe administrative reality better, but it appears uncomfortably pessimistic about the significance of administrators." "Indeed," he continues, "it seems potentially pernicious even if correct."[11]

But March does not conclude that the second theory is correct. Rather, he describes a third theory which "is probably closer to the truth than either of the others." According to this theory, the leaders of an organization do have an impact, but the crucial variable is not the quality of any one individual: "Administrators are vital as a class but not as individuals. . . . What makes an organization function well is the density of administrative competence."[12]

Reclaiming Individual Leadership as Important

Our own sense, as we reviewed the evidence in the early 1980s, was that March's third theory captured the reality of organizational behavior better than his second ("organized anarchy") theory. March's thesis also has the merit of encouraging people to try: if you can join an organization with a strong administrative team, you and your colleagues can make a difference.

However, March's understanding of how that "density of administrative competence" might arise, be nourished, or disintegrate seemed to us too mechanical: he found its sources in "selection procedures" that have weeded out the less able and in collegial motivations that reinforce the tendency of all members of the team to "push themselves to the limit." Moreover, his view seemed to undervalue the role that one or two individuals at the top—the department head or the program administrator, for example—can have in creating an environment for innovation, and in attracting and holding a team of able individuals, or (on the down side) in causing the best members to depart in frustration and in sadness. Indeed, March rejected the view that top leadership is an important factor in explaining why some organizations function at a high level of performance: "When an organizational system is working well, variations in outcomes will be due largely to variables unrelated to variations in attributes of top leaders. Where top leadership affects variation in outcomes, the system is probably not functioning well."[13]

In contrast to the dominant "second theory" tradition, and March's variant, scholars who have studied specific policy arenas often place great weight on the role of particular leaders. James Webb as head of the National Aeronautics and Space Administration in the 1960s, Nancy Hanks at the National Endowment for the Arts in the 1970s, David Lilienthal at the Tennessee Valley Authority in the 1930s—these were a few of the leaders who seemed to close observers to "make a difference."

We were intrigued. Were the students of NASA, TVA, and other specific agencies and programs in error, mistaking the rhetoric of leaders and the turbulence of political battle for the reality of influence? Or did individual leaders and their close associates sometimes have a significant impact on their organizations and the broader society? And if they did have an impact, how did they do it? What strategies did these leaders employ to break through the powerful forces of bureaucratic routine, interest group pressures, and narrow professional jealousies in order to reshape some portion of their political and policy worlds?

As we considered how to make headway in answering these questions, we thought that one useful stratagem might be to select a number of individuals who had held high-level government posts for several years, and who on first inspection appeared to have "made a difference" in the organization's behavior and impact, and then examine closely the reality of that provisional claim. If we could locate authors who were familiar with the policy arenas in which these executives operated, those observers might be able to sort out the influence of their chosen subjects from the myriad other factors that shape agency behavior and impact. Moreover, if these authors were willing to devote some attention to a "biographical perspective," they might combine their analysis of leadership strategies and influence with some consideration of the leader's early experiences, evolving social concerns and values, and motivations for action. With this mixture of ingredients, even if the impact of the leader's actions could not be precisely calibrated, the writer would have an interesting story to tell, offering suggestive lessons regarding the uses and dangers of power and perhaps some inspiration for those not yet ready to acquiesce in Herbert Kaufman's conclusion "that we should not overestimate what we can achieve. . . . People may perform better if they recognize how little they can do than if they approach their tasks believing the myth that they can impose their will on the world."[14]

In order to narrow the field of candidates, we decided to select our "sample" from the universe of individuals who had served at least five years in high-level executive positions in national, state, or local government in the United States. Within this large category, we did not make our selections in any rigorous way; our main aim was to include ten to fifteen individuals who held high-level positions during a period of years when their agencies had devised new programs or other significant innovations and who on first inspection appeared to be personally involved both in devising and in implementing those changes.[15]

In the American governmental system, both career and noncareer public officials hold high-level executive positions.[16] We thought that it would be advantageous to include representatives of both groups in our selection.

We then consulted with a number of people who were closely familiar with a wide range of program areas and with the executives who had held senior positions in those areas during periods of change. In 1983, several of these individuals agreed to take on the task of preparing biographical essays on some of the promising candidates. Others agreed to serve as advisers; they offered comments regarding the overall direction of the project, and they suggested for close study candidates whose life histories and leadership styles were particularly interesting.[17]

Here, then, are the individuals who emerged from these various consultations, and whose stories and influence are the subject of the chapters that follow. The government positions shown in italics are the main focus of our chapter essays.

Robert M. Ball. Born 1914. B.A. Wesleyan, 1935, M.A. 1936. Staff, U.S. Social Security Board, 1939–46; social security staff at American Council on Education, 1946–49, and at U.S. Senate, 1947–48. *Assistant director, U.S. Social Security Administration, 1949–52; deputy director, 1953–62; commissioner, 1962–73.* Senior scholar, National Academy of Sciences, 1973–81; visiting scholar, Center for the Study of Social Policy, 1981–.

Wilbur J. Cohen. Born 1913. Ph.B. Wisconsin, 1934. Staff, U.S. Social Security Board/Administration, 1935–56; professor, University of Michigan, 1956–83. *Assistant secretary, U.S. Department of Health, Education and Welfare, 1961–65; under secretary, 1965–68; secretary, 1968–69.* Professor, University of Texas, 1980–.

Mariner Eccles. Born 1890. High school in Utah. Business official, 1920–33; assistant secretary, U.S. Department of the Treasury, 1933–34. *Chairman, U.S. Federal Reserve Board, 1934–48.* Business executive, 1948–77. Died 1977.

James Forrestal. Born 1892. Dartmouth, 1911–12; Princeton, 1912–15. Dillon, Read & Company, 1916–40; Assistant to the President of the United States, 1940. *Under secretary of the navy, 1940–44; secretary, 1944–47; secretary of defense, 1947–49.* Died 1949.

Nancy Hanks. Born 1927. B.A. Duke, 1949. Federal government official, 1951–55; assistant to Nelson Rockefeller, 1956–59, and to Laurence Rockefeller, 1959–69 (and project coordinator, studies of the performing arts). *Chairman, National Endowment for the Arts, 1969–77.* Died 1983.

David E. Lilienthal. Born 1899. B.A. DePauw, 1920; LL.B. Harvard, 1923. Practice of law, 1923–31; member, Wisconsin Public Service Commission, 1931–33. *Director, Tennessee Valley Authority, 1933–41; chairman, 1941–46.* Chairman, Atomic Energy Commission, 1946–50; Development & Resources Corporation, 1955–79. Died 1981.

Robert S. McNamara. Born 1916. B.A. University of California, Berkeley, 1937; M.B.A. Harvard, 1939. Staff, Ford Motor Company, 1946–61 (vice president, 1955–60; president, 1960–61). *Secretary of defense, 1961–68.* President, World Bank, 1968–81.

Gifford Pinchot. Born 1865. B.A. Yale, 1889. *U.S. Chief Forester, 1898–1910.* Activist, Progressive party, 1910ff.; commissioner of forestry, Commonwealth of Pennsylvania, 1920–22; governor of Pennsylvania, 1923–27, 1931–35. Died 1946.

Hyman G. Rickover. Born 1900. B.S. U.S. Naval Academy, 1922; M.S. Columbia, 1929. Officer, U.S. Navy, 1922ff. *Director of atomic submarine development, 1947–81.* Died 1986.

Elmer B. Staats. Born 1914. B.A. McPherson College, Kansas, 1935; Ph.D. University of Minnesota, 1939. Staff, U.S. Bureau of the Budget, 1939ff., deputy director, 1950–53, 1958–66; National Security Council staff, 1953–58. *Comptroller general of the United States, 1966–81.*

Austin J. Tobin. Born 1903. B.A. Holy Cross, 1925; LL.B. Fordham, 1928. *Port of New York Authority*, legal staff, 1927–42; *executive director, 1942–72.* Died 1978.

James E. Webb. Born 1906. B.A. University of North Carolina, 1928; LL.B. George Washington, 1936. Staff, U.S. House of Representatives, 1932–34. With law firm and private business, 1934–43. Federal official, 1945–46; Director of the Budget, 1946–49; under secretary, Department of State, 1949–52; business executive, 1952–61. *Administrator, National Aeronautics and Space Administration, 1961–68.*

That is our selected dozen from the ranks of government officials.[18] And we add one more, whose experience suggests that the world of the private executive is at times quite similar to the terrain of the public official:

Bernard J. O'Keefe. Born 1919. B.E.E. Catholic University, 1941. U.S. Navy, 1943–46. Massachusetts Institute of Technology staff, 1946–47. *EG&G, Inc.,* 1947ff.: *executive vice president, 1960–65; president, 1965–78; chairman of the board, 1978–.*

There are here no Julius Caesars or others who believed that they could "impose their will on the world." But they are, certainly, a group of individuals who rejected the pessimism of Kaufman and the counsel of Henry Adams, who doubted that leaders made any difference in history.[19] These are individuals who sought and sometimes gained greater personal influence over events than March's "third theory" would suggest. By and large, the stories are promising, in illustrating that individuals and small teams of dedicated officials can make a difference, and instructive, in suggesting strategies that work and dangers to which all men and women in positions of high power may fall prey. We would not, of course, argue that *all* high-level officials—the motivated and the passive, those of active intelligence and the dull-witted—can make a significant difference. Only that those who attempt to understand the terrain of battle and use their resources with craft and guile can sometimes do so—if they treat difficulties not as insurmountable hurdles but as opportunities. Emily Dickinson rather than Henry Adams is the philosopher of our baker's dozen:

> I dwell in Possibility—
> A fairer House than Prose—
> More numerous of Windows—
> Superior—for Doors— (1862)

Entrepreneurial Executives

As the description of our search-and-selection procedure suggests, we were interested in individuals whose careers at managerial levels were linked to innovative ideas and to efforts to carry these ideas into effect, often attended by some risk to their organizations and to their own careers. Although the term *entrepreneur* has more commonly been applied to innovative activity in the world of business, *entrepreneurial leadership* seemed to us to suggest the main dimensions that we and our fellow authors wanted to explore in these biographical studies. In fact, a major line of research—from Schumpeter to Chandler—focuses on entrepreneurial behavior in much the way that we have approached our chosen executives.[20]

In order to provide a common focus or checklist of activities for our authors to examine in studying their thirteen subjects, we identified six dimensions that deserved attention. To what extent, and how, did our executives:

1. identify *new missions and programs* for their organizations;
2. develop and nourish *external constituencies* to support the new goals and programs, and to support the organization generally, while neutralizing existing and potential opposition;
3. create *internal constituencies* that supported the new goals (while eliminating opposition), through changes in organizational structures, in recruitment systems and key appointments, and in reward and penalty systems;
4. enhance the organization's *technical expertise* (through recruitment of skilled personnel and addition of new equipment) in order to improve its capacity to identify and develop interesting program options, and to implement new goals and programs;
5. *motivate and provide training for members* of the organization so that they would have the skills to work efficiently in old and new program areas and the desire to extend their efforts beyond standard or accepted levels of performance; and
6. systematically scan organizational routines, and points of internal and external pressure, in order to *identify areas of vulnerability* (to mismanagement and corruption and to loss of the leaders' own power and position), followed by remedial action.[21]

As the list suggests, innovative programs are important, but strategies of implementation are at least equally critical. Our hope, largely borne out by the essays in this volume, was that it would be possible to explore in some depth the range of "inside" and "outside" strategies used by our entrepreneurs in order to identify new opportunities and to attain the goals they believed were important. And when they failed to achieve important aims (and most of them did fail at times), we might be able to locate their difficulties by examining their efforts in relation to the strategies set forth above.

The ability of a government official to utilize some or all of these six strategies depends on a range of factors. Some of these are external elements that encourage or may restrict entrepreneurship, while others relate to a mix of personality and situation. In the following paragraphs, we describe several of these important variables, as suggested by our case studies and by other writings on political life.

External Factors

Among the important external variables that provide fertile ground for entrepreneurship are a governmental system characterized by fragmentation and overlap, a ground swell of public support for new social values, and the rise of new technologies. All of these are illustrated by the cases in this volume, and at this point we comment briefly on all three.

Students of the American political system, in particular, note that the fragmented structure of our tripartite and federal system is an important hurdle to sustained and coherent national leadership. Individual departments and bureaus at the national, state, and local levels seek their own allies and often resist central coordination.[22] However, this fragmentation also yields opportunities for policy experimentation and for initiative in building political coalitions that are not as readily available in a coherent and tightly run governmental system; and those possibilities attract men and women interested in that kind of "entrepreneurial opportunity." We see this, for example, in the way that Hyman Rickover, buried deep in the formal hierarchy of the Navy, was able to reach outside for allies and establish an independent power base within the tradition-bound military. The same point is illustrated by the grafting of new programs onto and around existing government structures: for example, a national program in the arts was created, not as a subordinate bureau in the U.S. Department of Commerce, but as a freestanding agency, to thrive or fail, depending on the strategic skills of its first leaders; and Nancy Hanks made effective use of that opportunity. Similarly, the independent administrative position of the Tennessee Valley Authority and the Federal Reserve Board provided opportunities for creative action, and such opportunities were grasped by David Lilienthal and Mariner Eccles in the 1930s.

That Lilienthal and Eccles had their greatest successes in the 1930s calls attention to the second external factor, the role of public opinion in providing opportunities for those who are entrepreneurially inclined. The expectation that government would be an active force in society was more widely accepted in that decade than it had been a decade earlier, and this public attitude was essential to broadening the range of initiatives that Lilienthal and Eccles could take. So, too, the increasing public concern for conservation at the end of the nineteenth century was crucial to Gifford Pinchot's effort to obtain support for his forestry activities.

As the chapters on Lilienthal, Eccles, and Pinchot illustrate, however, public opinion is not entirely an independent variable; the ground swell of public concern is often so vague as to provide little direction for the executive; and at times the entrepreneurs are actively involved in *creating* the "widespread" public demand to which they appear to be responding. For example, Lilienthal and his associates took an active role in creating the demand for home electrification in the Tennessee Valley; Tobin and his allies inspired (more than they responded to) the public demand for regional operation of the New York–New Jersey airports; and Nancy Hanks shaped the demand of both artists and the general public for a more active federal role in supporting regional orchestras and local museums.

Technology—and particularly the rise of a new technology that may require large public capital investment—is a third factor that yields opportunities for entrepreneurial executives. Thus, Rickover built his entrepreneurial career on nuclear power for naval ships; Tobin and his aides foresaw the likely impact of container shipping and developed massive new marine terminals to take advantage of what would later be known as the "container revolution"; Webb orchestrated the national program built on space technology (where public concern regarding the Russian space program was also essential to providing the financial support Webb needed); and Bernard O'Keefe also found some of his major opportunities in the relation of technology to public-service and commercial markets.

These are not the only external variables of importance in shaping the possibility of entrepreneurial success by government executives. At least one other factor deserves mention here, because of its significance to several of our thirteen entrepreneurs: the role of elected officials and their aides in providing political resources and active support. In the United States and other democratic systems of government, alliances with elected officials are essential to appointed executives, but the significance of these relationships varies greatly. Theodore Roosevelt's support for Pinchot was especially important, as was the encouragement of the White House for Nancy Hanks and congressional support for Admiral Rickover.

Personality and Skill

The opportunities available because of these external variables are grasped systematically and effectively by *some* men and women and not by others. Personal characteristics are significant in determining whether one can make use of these opportunities and employ the six dimensions of entrepreneurship listed above—defining new goals, organizing supporting constituencies, motivating staff, and so forth. There are three important characteristics that may be crucial to successful innovative action carried out in the complex environment of government office: a capacity to engage in systematic rational analysis; an ability to see new possibilities offered by the evolving historical situation; and a desire to "make a difference"—to throw one's energies and personal reputation into the fray in order to bring about changes.

As to the first, the six aspects of entrepreneurship suggest that entrepreneurial leaders are inevitably engaged in highly detailed calculations of probabilities and means-ends analysis, although not always systematically formulated. Of course, some of the entrepreneur's actions are based on hunch, or shaped by individual personality characteristics and unconscious acceptance of cultural and economic traditions. But Schumpeter's comments on this point remind us to search carefully for evidence of *uncommon rationality* when studying an entrepreneur:

> In one sense, he may indeed be called the most rational and the most egotistical of all. . . . Conscious rationality enters much more into the carrying out of new plans, which themselves have to be worked out before they can be acted upon, than into the mere running of an established business, which is largely a matter of routine. And the typical entrepreneur is more self-centered than other types, because he relies less than they do on tradition and connection and because his characteristic task—theoretically as well as historically—consists precisely in breaking up old, and creating new, tradition.[23]

Examples of such "uncommon rationality" are seen in Elmer Staats's approach to management analysis at the General Accounting Office (here the technique imported and the strategies of importation both illustrate the orientation toward rationality); Austin Tobin's strategies in adding airports and marine terminals to the Port Authority's domain in the 1940s; and Forrestal's approach to the problem of naval management.

The second faculty is the ability to see the political logic in an emerging historical situation and to act on that insight. This is, in part, a cognitive ability; one sees how one's goals may be reinforced by linking them to larger historical trends. However, a leader who would use such insight must also persuade others to accept his definitions of the situation and must set forth plausible strategies of action.[24]

For example, David Lilienthal sold the idea of electric power to rural people in the Tennessee Valley who had little understanding of what it could do for them. With the assistance of young engineers and lawyers, he invented new forms of municipal and rural power distributorships in which low prices were designed to boost consumption. This was an exercise of uncommon rationality, but it was also the expression of a political insight that the people of the valley could be mobilized as a constituency for TVA. His rhetoric, on courthouse steps and from the backs of trucks, tied TVA and cheap electric power to the New Deal and the sins of the private power companies. Technology was placed within a political and social context and became part of a popular movement. In much the same way, James Webb knew how to sell NASA as the harbinger of a new age, and Admiral Rickover understood how nuclear sea power could be dramatized not just as a technology but as the basis for a new Navy. Linking this capacity for missions to a larger context often served the uncommon rationality of our subjects.

The third element of personality suggested by our case studies is the desire to "make a difference." As these essays show, our thirteen entrepreneurs were strongly motivated to place their individual imprints on the complex world of public policy. For some, such as Nancy Hanks and Elmer Staats, the personal style was low-keyed but assertive. Others, such as Lilienthal and Rickover, were more overtly competitive, even combative, reminding us of Schumpeter's characterization of the entrepreneur as a person who has the "will to conquer: the impulse to fight, to prove oneself superior to others."[25] For all of our chosen leaders, probably, the "will to conquer" was there; some sought only to conquer challenging political and technical problems, while others were motivated as well by the need to dominate people inside and beyond their organizations.

The Puzzle of Success and Failure

In the pages above we have identified three attributes of skill and four historical conditions favorable to its exercise on behalf of entrepreneurial leadership. An individual who possessed all three attributes in optimally favorable historical conditions would very likely be effective in achieving entrepreneurial goals. Less than the full complement of attributes or favorable conditions may often suffice in particular instances, and individual success stories and specific cases can be analyzed and compared to infer the winning combination of variables in particular situations. But how does one account for failure after success has been achieved? Almost all of our thirteen subjects experienced significant reverses. In general, their talent did not erode. What happened? Pinchot had worked hand in hand with President Theodore Roosevelt, but his influence faltered and he was later dismissed by President William Howard Taft. Lilienthal attempted to use the strategies of leadership that he had developed at TVA when he was chairman of the

Atomic Energy Commission, but they did not work. Forrestal was an able leader of the Navy and played a crucial role in unifying the military establishment, but he then found that he was unable to exert effective leadership as secretary of defense. James Webb was highly effective both as a director of the Bureau of the Budget and at NASA, but his tenure as under secretary of state, which came between the two other jobs, was disappointing to him and to others.

The combinations of personal ability and historical situation that explain success may also be analyzed to account for mixed results or failure. Two generalizations about the relation of skill and circumstance to achievement are suggested by our studies:

1. Achievement is favored by a good match of individual skill and the organizational task attempted.

Such a match does not guarantee achievement; environmental factors are also important. But other things being equal, a match of skill and task—in which the individual is given an opportunity to play to his or her strengths—is often an important ingredient of entrepreneurial success. For example, Lilienthal's gift for making popular appeals was perfectly matched to the task of creating a public constituency for TVA in the Tennessee Valley, in the savage fight for survival against the private utilities. Robert McNamara had developed the skills of analytic management in the business world that were effective in imposing strategic analysis on the military services. Nancy Hanks had discovered ways to build supportive networks for her activities in the foundation world and put the lessons learned to good use in government. Elmer Staats had worked with Congress for years in the Bureau of the Budget and knew how to appeal to its members.

The tasks they assigned themselves matched their skills in most cases. They did play to their strengths, and to a great extent they invented their tasks within the general institutional roles they were asked to fill. Moreover, most of our thirteen executives sought associates who could provide strength where they perceived personal limitations, as illustrated by Webb's development of a multiple leadership team at NASA and Tobin's creation of a skilled public relations team to work with the press in the New York region.

By the same token, a poor match of individual skills and organizational task renders leadership less effective. The explanation of failure in talented people is sometimes a puzzle. One reason may be that they attempt assignments for which their skills are not appropriate. This can take the form of a simple mismatch, or it can be more subtle. A leader who uses all his energy to learn how best to be effective in one situation may fail because he applies the lessons learned from that success to a completely different situation. There are two different causes of failure, but they are sometimes hard to disentangle. The very passion that Pinchot invested in the creation of the Forest Service appeared to be crusading rigidity when attempted on the broad stage of conservation politics and policy. Forrestal was superb at collegial leadership as secretary of the navy, but was weak after he became head of the national military establishment, when the exercise of independent authority was needed. Lilienthal could not make popular leadership work at the AEC because he could not find a mission about which he could preach. McNamara discovered that his own methods of systematic management were misleading him about the conduct of the war in Vietnam.

2. The favorable match of skill to task must be reinforced by favorable historical conditions if there is to be significant achievement.

Friendly public opinion, timely technology, and alliances with politicians may reinforce skill. A creative leader who seeks entrepreneurial achievements on the basis of skill alone, in the absence of such reinforcements, will have a much harder time. Pinchot, for example, rode the wave of Progressive politics about conservation, and Eccles and Lilienthal were strengthened in their work by the reform politics of the New Deal. Webb drew on cold-war politics to persuade President Kennedy of the need for a mission to the moon. Staats remodeled the GAO in response to congressional criticisms of the narrowness of his agency and an incipient congressional market for evaluation information. The achievements of Cohen and Ball were part and parcel of Democratic electoral and policy politics. These are instances that illustrate the faculty of insight into the emerging historical situation and the ability to link programmatic goals to broader social trends favoring those goals.

Skill and politics can be reinforcing; both are important in explaining achievement. It is not a question of one being more or less important than the other. For example, political conditions that favor achievements do not create those achievements; someone must lead the way. Sidney Hook makes the distinction between eventful and event-making leaders.[26] The former preside over events of importance that probably would have occurred in any case. The latter add their individual contribution to the content and shape of events. For the most part, these entrepreneurial leaders were event-making. There would have been a TVA without Lilienthal, a Port Authority without Tobin, and a social security system without Cohen and Ball, but the calculations and insights of these individual leaders gave direction and content to those institutions and explain significant organizational achievements.

Almost all of these leaders had the personal support of elected executives as patrons. Theodore Roosevelt gave strength to Pinchot. Franklin Roosevelt was a constant helper to Eccles, Lilienthal, and, to a lesser extent, Forrestal. Presidents Kennedy and Johnson were vital for the successes of McNamara and Webb. Hanks could not have been an effective leader of the NEA without President Nixon behind her. Staats and Rickover relied continuously on congressional allies; indeed, Congress saved Rickover from the Navy.

Behind that support was the perception by elected leaders that these executives contributed to the leaders' own political strength. Webb's achievements at NASA redounded to the benefit of Kennedy and Johnson. Cohen devised social security programs that Johnson viewed as aiding his own reputation. Lilienthal and Tobin produced results for which politicians could take credit. Administrative entrepreneurs may thus generate political capital for their elected associates.

Failure is most often linked to a shift of political support away from the entrepreneur. There were two patterns here. Some leaders fell out of favor with their politician patrons or their successors. Thus, Taft and Pinchot did not get along. Truman lost confidence in Eccles and Forrestal, and McNamara suffered the same fate under Lyndon Johnson. However, the tides of politics also shifted in ways that made it more difficult for successful entrepreneurs to impose their will on events. Lilienthal faced a politics of secrecy, military security, and cold war at the AEC that frustrated all his efforts to nurture the international control and peaceful uses of atomic energy. McNamara did not embrace the political opposition to the war in Vietnam, but he permitted his own doubts about American capacity to win the war to undermine the effectiveness of his leadership so that his president eased him out of office.

Varieties of Leadership Strategies

Entrepreneurial leaders operate within the terrain provided by political support, individual skills, and other factors identified above. There they ply their trade—using the six strategies of goal setting and implementation in a sustained effort to make an impact on their own organizations and on the broader world. If we look only at our limited sample of thirteen executives, both administrative styles and preferred strategies varied greatly. However, as figure 1.1 suggests, there are some clusters worth noting in terms of two variables—coalition-building skills and the use of rhetoric and symbols.

Rhetorical Leadership

Some individuals are highly adept at using evocative symbols and language as political resources; they excel at what one might call *rhetorical leadership*. In some instances, the leader comes to personify the organization and its deeper values. For example, David Lilienthal created a myth for TVA around the ideal of "grass-roots democracy" which not

Figure 1.1

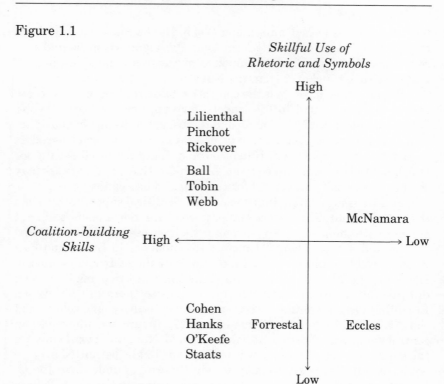

only rallied the organization's supporters and fended off its opponents but provided a sense of purpose for those within the organization and gave guidance for the conduct of TVA programs. Pinchot socialized an entire organization of young Forest Service professionals by creating organizational norms that were extensions of his own belief in the vigorous life; he was the organization incarnate.

Such leaders create myths for the organizations they lead, justifying specific programs in terms of some larger set of principles.[27] Moreover, as mythmakers these leaders may become independent political figures to whom elected politicians turn for help in their own work. Thus, TR used Pinchot's efforts to support his own image as a conservationist, and FDR used Lilienthal and TVA as a showpiece for the New Deal. Also, the charisma of these entrepreneurs contributes to the development of strong bureaucratic cultures in which the myth is institutionalized in operational practices. Leadership of this kind will often find its opportunities in the creation of new organizations with new missions, such as the development of a backward region or the development of nuclear technology.

In addition to Pinchot and Lilienthal, our chapters include four other executives who seem to us especially effective in using rhetorical leadership. Webb worked consciously and effectively at building the image of NASA as the best-managed agency in the federal government. Tobin took the reins at the Port of New York Authority and built on its existing reputation as an independent agency, emphasizing its "non-political" character and its use of "businesslike methods" as he led it into new fields of battle. Rickover was a skillful publicist for what was sometimes called "the Rickover Navy." And in social security, while Ball and Cohen were a team, it was Ball—the career civil servant—who was distinctively effective as a public figure who used rhetoric and symbolic language to cast the program in politically appealing terms.

As figure 1.1 indicates, we are inclined to place the other entrepreneurs in our sample somewhat lower in terms of this dimension. Gifted advocates and administrators generally, they relied far less on the evocative use of symbols and language. On this point the reader can, of course, reach her or his own judgment based on the chapters that follow.

Coalition-building Skills

In view of the fragmented nature of the American political system, leaders bent on innovation must gather support from private interest groups, other government agencies, the media, and elected officials. Attracting such support and shaping an effective coalition would seem to be almost a *sine qua non* of effective entrepreneurial leadership, and at least three of our six dimensions of entrepreneurship emphasize this political skill.

As figure 1.1 shows, then, most of the executives examined in this book were skilled at constructing and maintaining coalitions to support their aims. Nancy Hanks, for example, combined White House support with coalition formation throughout the arts world to give the NEA the political strength necessary for expansion. Wilbur Cohen was an active participant in the overlapping worlds of universities, interest groups, and government, and he knew how to create alliances among them. Elmer Staats drew on a generation of experience in working with Congress, and he made Congress his constituency as he transformed the GAO. Forrestal had a crucial role in creating the intragovernment coalition behind the National Security Act of 1947.

Bernard O'Keefe was not an executive in government, although much of the work of his company was for government. The more telling point, however, is that his style of administrative leadership of that corporation was politically skillful in the search for new missions, the development of external constituencies, and the nurturing of internal technology and institutional capacity. His political work as an executive was analogous to that of government executives. Just as Lilienthal and Tobin searched for new missions for their organizations in order to keep them responsive to and valued by their constituencies, so O'Keefe searched in the world of government for new missions for his firm. His management of the firm, in which he nurtured and protected the technological expertise of others, reminds one of Webb's role at NASA.

In our reading of the evidence, not all of our chosen thirteen ranked high on this dimension. We place Forrestal somewhat below the leading group, because of his greater difficulty when he shifted from the Navy to Defense, and we place two men—Marriner Eccles and Robert McNamara—near the other end of the continuum. Eccles and McNamara knew how to manage others to provide direction and drive to organizations, but they were not coalition builders. They were sustained by presidential support and made few efforts to build alliances either within or outside the organizations they led. Their earlier professional successes, in the business world, had been based mainly on other talents. It would be interesting to consider why Forrestal and O'Keefe appeared to have political skills denied two of the other businessmen, but evidence is too elusive for anything but speculation.

Conclusion

When biographies are "most successful," one writer observes, "they portray not only an individual but a whole society."[28] The twelve biographical essays in this volume may not quite reach that goal, but they do, perhaps, tell us a lot about how a society and its leaders search for and identify new opportunities for social action, allocate funds and talent to pursue these novel paths, and in time set firmly in place new programs and new strategies through which still further social invention may take place.

Thus, a national forest service is created and staffed by a "committed polity";[29] electricity comes to the rural homes of the impoverished Tennessee Valley; a system of social security and a program of space exploration are launched, each with reverberations that change the self-image and sense of opportunities for millions of Americans. In these and a dozen other innovations described in the following chapters, historical circumstances and public opinion are crucial elements. But so are the ideas, the personal motivations, the blood and sweat of particular men and women who lead the way. In his biographical analysis of business regulation in the United States, Thomas McCraw concluded that the four men he studied "achieved their goals only under certain conditions . . . and only through a good deal of administrative artistry on their own part. . . . [Yet they] clearly made an enormous difference" in regulatory policy and in the broader society.[30] In our wider canvass of American public leaders, we and our fellow authors reach the same conclusions—though perhaps some of us would substitute *significant* for enormous.

In reviewing these essays, we are struck by the importance of personal motivation in shaping organizational direction and the social agenda, and by recurrent themes of "the American character" as that character has been described by Commager and others.[31] Here we find, for example, sustained, single-minded motivation and the Puritan ethic embodied in the Catholic Tobin, in Rickover, of Jewish heritage, and in many of our other entrepreneurs; and irrepressible optimism—in the face of what others considered great obstacles—which was crucial to the actions and the success of Nancy Hanks, David Lilienthal, and most of the innovators in our catch.

In this opening chapter, we have identified several of the conditions under which entrepreneurial leaders have made, and can make, a difference and some of the diverse patterns of innovative leadership. A few of our authors use their own studies to suggest additional patterns and dimensions; see, for example, the discussions in the chapters on Rickover and on Cohen and Ball. Perhaps here we should note that our use of the phrase "to make a difference" is not intended to convey applause; we do not mean to imply that the "successful" entrepreneur is necessarily engaged in activities that are socially desirable.

Whether there should be a space program or a nuclear Navy, for example, and whether it is better to have (or abolish) such semi-independent agencies as TVA, the Federal Reserve Board, and port authorities are clearly matters for debate. Several of our authors express reservations about the general direction or about specific programs and strategies of "their" entrepreneurs. And for some of us, one of the important conditions encouraging successful entrepreneurship—fragmented governmental structures—raises significant problems of accountability in a democratic society. Perhaps, as others have argued, it might be desirable to try to institutionalize creative leadership to meet important social problems—and render such leadership more accountable to considered public opinion and democratic preference—through strengthened political parties, for example, or civil service reform, or improved instruments for citizen participation.[32] And possibly some of the desirable changes will, in time, turn out to be feasible. Meanwhile, as Eugene Bardach argues,[33] fragmentation and decentralization create checks and balances that obstruct "orderly" innovation, and there will be a need for talented men and women who can define new goals, build coalitions that knit together public and private interests, and carry out other entrepreneurial tasks required in this society of great diversity.

Notes

1. Thomas Carlyle, *On Heroes, Hero-Worship, and the Heroic in History* (1840), 1.
2. "The living embodiment of the American dream," according to the dust jacket of his autobiography, *Iacocca* (New York: Bantam Books, 1984), which topped the *New York Times* list of nonfiction best sellers for 1985.
3. "We can borrow from Emerson," concluded Kenneth R. Andrews in *The Concept of Corporate Strategy*, "and say that a corporation is essentially the lengthened shadow of a man" (Homewood, Ill.: Dow Jones–Irwin, 1971), 238. See also Thomas C. Cochran, *The American Business System* (Cambridge: Harvard University Press, 1957); Alfred D. Chandler, Jr., *The Visible Hand: The Managerial Revolution in American Business* (Cambridge: Harvard University Press, 1977); and the writings of Peter F. Drucker.
4. Herbert Kaufman, *The Administrative Behavior of Federal Bureau Chiefs* (Washington, D.C.: Brookings Institution, 1981), 135, 174.
5. See, for example, Pendleton Herring, *Public Administration and the Public Interest* (New York: McGraw-Hill, 1936); David B. Truman, *The Governmental Process* (New York: Knopf, 1951); Robert C. Wood, *1400 Governments* (Cambridge: Harvard University Press, 1961); Jeffrey L. Pressman and Aaron Wildavsky, *Implementation* (Berkeley and Los Angeles: University of California Press, 1973); and Hugh Heclo, *A Government of Strangers: Executive Politics in Washington* (Washington, D.C.: Brookings Institution, 1977).

On occasion, political scientists working in this tradition have touched on the role of individuals, but only briefly. For example, in *Essence of Decision* (Boston: Little, Brown, 1971), Graham T. Allison comments on page 166: "The hard core of the bureaucratic politics mix is personality." As Fred Greenstein has noted (in discussion with the authors), Allison does not develop that important point, leaving bureaucratic politics as the central theme of his analysis.

6. See, for example, Richard E. Neustadt, *Presidential Power* (New York: John Wiley, 1960); Fred I. Greenstein, *The Hidden-Hand Presidency* (New York: Basic Books, 1982); Valerie Bunce, *Do New Leaders Make a Difference?* (Princeton: Princeton University Press, 1981); S. E. Ayling, *Portraits of Power* (New York: Barnes & Noble, 1963); Ann Ruth Willner, *The Spellbinders* (New Haven: Yale University Press, 1984); and Robert C. Tucker, *Politics as Leadership* (Columbia: University of Missouri Press, 1981).
7. See Robert A. Caro, *The Power Broker: Robert Moses and the Fall of New York* (New York: Random House, 1974); and William W. Turner, *Hoover's FBI: The Men and the Myth* (New York: Dell, 1971). As Caro observes: "Power is not an instrument that its possessor can use with impunity. It is a drug that creates in the user a need for larger and larger dosages. And Moses was a user" (19).
8. See for example David M. Ricci, *The Tragedy of Political Science* (New Haven: Yale University Press, 1984), chap. 9 and passim.
9. Selznick's book was a major source for the argument put forward in Thomas J. Peters and Robert H. Waterman, Jr., *In Search of Excellence: Lessons from Amer-*

ica's Best-Run Companies (New York: Harper & Row, 1982); see pp. 85, 98–99, 281–82. It also influenced earlier business-school writings (such as Andrews, *Concept of Corporate Strategy*), which presented a less romanticized view of leadership than Peters and Waterman. In the early 1980s Selznick was viewed by some members of the Harvard Business School faculty as the guru for students of organizational leadership. His *Leadership in Administration* was reprinted in a paperback edition in 1984 (Berkeley and Los Angeles: University of California Press).

10. In his *Tragedy of Political Science*, David Ricci makes a related point regarding the dominant thrust of political-science empiricism: "It does gather great amounts of sheer information about political life. . . . But at the same time, it injects a measure of despair into political studies by highlighting the dreary or dangerous imperfections of democratic behavior. The risk here was foreshadowed by behavioralists themselves, when they observed that support for democratic government may be rooted in popular myths" (294).

11. "Consider two general types of errors a manager might make in assessing the importance of intentional actions in controlling organizational outcomes. A manager might come to believe in considerable personal control over outcomes when, in fact, that control does not exist. A 'false positive' error. Such a belief would lead to (futile) attempts to control events, but it would not otherwise affect results. Alternatively, a manager might come to believe that significant personal control is not possible when, in fact, it is. A 'false negative' error. Such a belief would lead to self-confirming withdrawal from efforts to be effective. . . . The social costs of the first seem small, relative to the second. Given a choice, we would generally prefer to err on the side of making false positive errors in assessing human significance, rather than false negative errors" (James G. March, "How We Talk and How We Act: Administrative Theory and Administrative Life," in *Leadership and Organizational Culture*, ed. T. J. Sergiovanni and J. E. Corbally [Urbana: University of Illinois Press, 1981], 28).

March carries this argument farther than we would. When an executive believes that he or she has considerable personal control over outcomes but that perception is mistaken, the leader may reach for unrealistic goals, wasting resources of money, materiel, and political support better applied to a more realistic target or to quite different programs. Some of the activities of Robert McNamara, Austin Tobin, and other executives whose efforts are analyzed in this volume illustrate this cautionary note.

12. Ibid., 29.

13. Ibid., 29, 33.

14. Kaufman, *Administrative Behavior of Federal Bureau Chiefs*, 196–97. Then and now, we would not underestimate the great difficulty of sorting out the impact of individual leaders from other factors, such as interest group pressures and fortuitous events, that shape organizational action, success, and failure. As the following chapters show, some of our authors have found it easier to isolate the impact of leadership than have others. For an excellent discussion of the problem of multiple causation and ways to examine the role of leaders see Fred I. Greenstein, *Personality and Politics: Problems of Evidence, Inference and Conceptualization* (Markham, 1969; New York: Norton, 1975), chap. 2. The problem of sorting out causation in our studies is discussed briefly in Jameson W. Doig, "Entrepreneurial Leadership in the 'Independent' Government Organization" (Paper prepared for the annual meeting of the American Political Science Association, Chicago, 1–4 September 1983), 2–7.

15. Our approach to selecting and studying high-level executives was quite different from Kaufman's. From a group of about eighty federal bureaus (Defense and

State excluded), he selected six for close scrutiny. Such variables as bureau size and age were used in selecting the six, but the question of whether the bureau (or bureau chief) had recently engaged in innovative efforts was not a relevant factor. Kaufman then studied the behavior and impact of the six bureau chiefs during a one-year period; for four of the six executives, this was only the first or second year in the top bureau post. His assessment of their impact was based on their influence in the bureau only during this year of study; whether their initiatives had a marginal or significant impact in later years was not examined. In contrast, by selecting individuals with a reputation for having strongly shaped innovative programs and then assessing the validity of that claim over a period of years—using the individual and his career as the unit of analysis—we were more likely to capture cases of significant leadership influence, as well as variations in influence depending on skill and circumstance.

On reading a draft of this chapter, Kaufman emphasized that he does not contend that bureau chiefs and other government executives have *no* impact. On pages 139–57 of his 1981 book, for example, he describes the chief's role in setting organizational tone, building agency prestige, and nudging agendas, priorities, and decisions. But the weight of his findings falls heavily on the side of limitations, and he concludes that "the continuities [in agency policies and practices] overshadow what the chiefs can accomplish" (161). As the comments just above suggest, his selection and study procedures would tend to lead him toward that conclusion.

16. See, for example, Heclo, *Government of Strangers.*

17. The advisers are listed in the Preface.

18. For those who are interested in the career/noncareer mix of our sample, we would label four of the twelve as career officials. Ball, Rickover, Staats, and Tobin all held career positions in government agencies for most of their active lives. Cohen had extensive government experience. The remaining seven—Eccles, Forrestal, Hanks, Lilienthal, McNamara, Pinchot, and Webb—had little or no government experience prior to their appointments to high government posts, but their government service after initial appointment continued for eight to twenty years.

19. "In history heroes have neutralysed each other, and the result is no more than would have been reached without them" (Adams to William James, 26 December 1882). "My own conclusion is that history is simply social development along the line of weakest resistance, and that in most cases the line of weakest resistance is found as unconsciously by society as by water" (Adams to Samuel Tilden, 24 January 1883). These letters are included in *The Letters of Henry Adams, Volume II: 1868–1885,* ed. J. C. Levenson et al. (Cambridge: Harvard University Press, 1982), chap 5.

20. See Joseph A. Schumpeter, *The Theory of Economic Development* (Cambridge: Harvard University Press, 1934), chap. 2; and Chandler, *The Visible Hand,* 201–3, 376, and passim. While this book was in production, we saw Arthur M. Schlesinger, Jr.'s *Cycles of American History* (Boston: Houghton Mifflin, 1986); in chapter 14 he uses Schumpeter's perspective and develops an argument on leadership which is in some respects similar to ours. For another approach to public entrepreneurship, see John W. Kingdon, *Agendas, Alternatives, and Public Policies* (Boston: Little, Brown, 1984), 188–93.

21. Note that each of the six categories can be subdivided so as to set out questions that might be examined in studying particular leaders. For example, under (1), one might explore such questions as these: To what extent was the selection of new goals and programs preceded by a *systematic* search for alternative program directions, with an analysis of the costs and benefits associated with each? What were the main criteria used in deciding upon new missions and programs? What time per-

spective was employed in evaluating alternative opportunities (how long a time horizon did the entrepreneur have)?

22. See, for example, Francis E. Rourke, ed., *Bureaucratic Power in National Politics*, 4th ed. (Boston: Little, Brown, 1986).

23. Schumpeter, *Theory of Economic Development*, 91–92. Edgar Schein also emphasizes the importance of rational analysis for effective leadership (see his *Organizational Culture and Leadership* [San Francisco: Jossey-Bass, 1985], 321ff.).

24. This point is discussed in Tucker, *Politics as Leadership*; and in Erwin C. Hargrove and Michael Nelson, *Presidents, Politics and Policy* (Baltimore: Johns Hopkins University Press, 1984), esp. chap. 4.

25. Schumpeter, *Theory of Economic Development*, 93.

26. Sidney Hook, *The Hero in History: A Study in Limitation and Possibility* (New York: John Day, 1943).

27. We use the term *myth* to mean a characterization of organizational purpose that contains elements of both aspiration and reality (see Murray Edelman, *Political Language* [New York: Academic Press, 1977] 102).

28. Iris Origo, *A Need To Testify* (New York: Harcourt Brace Jovanovich, 1984), 3.

29. The phrase is Philip Selznick's (*Leadership in Administration*, chap. 2) and refers to the psychological conversion of workers (who simply trade their labor for pay) into dedicated citizens of an institution whose broad values shape their lives. The chapters on Rickover, Tobin, and Pinchot emphasize this theme.

30. Thomas K. McCraw, *Prophets of Regulation* (Cambridge: Harvard University Press, 1984), viii.

31. Henry Steele Commager, *The American Mind* (New Haven: Yale University Press, 1950).

32. See, for example, Heclo, *Government of Strangers*, chap. 7; Hugh Heclo and Lester M. Salamon, eds., *The Illusion of Presidential Government* (Boulder, Colo.: Westview Press, 1981); and Joel L. Fleishman, ed., *The Future of American Political Parties* (Englewood Cliffs, N.J.: Prentice-Hall, 1982).

33. Eugene Bardach, *The Skill Factor in Politics* (Berkeley and Los Angeles: University of California Press, 1972).

Rhetorical Leaders

David Lilienthal and the Tennessee Valley Authority

Erwin C. Hargrove

David Lilienthal's style of leadership emphasized rhetoric, in speech and writing, as the chief means of winning support for and creating cohesion within the organizations he led. He also believed that organizational effectiveness depended upon public support and participation. The "grass-roots democracy" ideal, which Lilienthal developed at the Tennessee Valley Authority, required bureaucracy to carry out its missions with the support and participation of the people it was to serve. His rhetorical style of leadership was a means of articulating the ideal as a basis for support.

This chapter explores how Lilienthal developed his beliefs about organization and leadership and brought both to full expression in his leadership of TVA from 1933 to 1946. His inventiveness at critical junctures in the life of the new organization not only permitted TVA to survive but gave it a stable institutional identity. The TVA experience shaped him as well. He brought his rhetorical style and belief in participatory bureaucracy to the chairmanship of the Atomic Energy Commission, from 1946 to 1950, with disappointing results, because neither the organizational mission nor the politics surrounding that mission were congenial to his leadership. The AEC experience was, in some respects, a negative mirror image of the TVA years for Lilienthal. In the third major phase of his career, he invented an overseas development firm, the Development and Resources Corporation, which gave him the opportunity to repeat the TVA experience in developmental projects around the world. This chapter emphasizes the TVA years.

Lilienthal believed that organizations and publics could be mobilized by ideas. He was a creator of myths by which organizations could live. His books were vehicles for generalizing about such myths, and he always considered himself a writer as well as an administrator. He kept a regular journal for most of his adult life as a means for reflecting on his practical experience.[1] But he always sought to understand practical experience in terms of generalizations about effective leadership.

A very important part of Lilienthal's makeup was his desire to be unique. When he was eighty he recalled his inventiveness at TVA as an expression "of a creative impulse, wanting to do something that hadn't been done before."[2] His *Journals* make clear that throughout his life he sought recognition and respect for his uniqueness. He wished to stand apart as one who had made unusual contributions. And the way to do this was to be inventive and creative, in both words and actions.

Lilienthal's habit of keeping a journal gives us vivid clues to his personality as it formed and continued to develop throughout his life. The first entry, dated 17 May, 1917, made when he was a seventeen-year-old freshman at DePauw University in Indiana, records the advice of a young lawyer who "noticed how seriously I was looking at life" and suggested the "amusement and self-cultivation" of a diary as an antidote. But a year later, when he reread what he had written, he commented on its "seriousness."[3] One of the themes expressed in that first year was the desire to "write as a career" but also to do "social service" (2). These two ambitions were strong throughout his life. His journal was an intimate record of his activities and a source of reflection on the vocation of leadership.

When a DePauw professor offered to make any of his students a "great man or woman," Lilienthal challenged him to "try it on me" (4–5). He was consciously grooming himself to be a leader. After delivering a well-received talk at a DePauw chapel assembly, he recorded, "I had a taste this morning of what some day may be my customary diet." He had thrown himself into the preparation of the talk with great intensity, working on it for months (6–7). The writing of major speeches and books was to receive similarly intensive treatment. He became a college debator and won the Indiana state oratorical contest and the Midwest interstate contest and tied for second in the national contest in Topeka, Kansas. To his mind, this was preparation for the career ahead, "the expanding influence of the training, the trips, the meeting of people, getting up before every sort of audience from a Quaker congregation to a high school crowd" (7).

He also went out for football at DePauw and recorded his love of "the fighting spirit" (8). But he especially liked boxing. Many years later he told an interviewer that he would not have put himself in so many controversial positions in his career if he had not been a combative person. He recalled how he had learned to box in high school and how while in college he had boxed with a professional lightweight known as the Tacoma Tiger, whom he could never beat. He was also the boxing coach at DePauw while a student. Lilienthal did not regard boxing as an expression of combativeness for its own sake. "I think I considered competence at defending yourself a means of preserving your personal independence. I learned that from my father. 'Be your own man,' he used to say." Lilienthal went on to add that "there's something missing when you don't have a McKellar laying it on the line any more. The moral equivalent of that for me is taking on challenges, different kinds of McKellars or Tacoma Tigers—maybe the Minerals and Chemicals thing, the D. and R. thing—and trying to meet them."[4]

Ambition, rhetorical skill, and combativeness in behalf of independence served a developing idealism, derived in part from the New Freedom of Woodrow Wilson, which Lilienthal carried into the conservatism of the 1920s.[5] By 1919 he knew that he wished to be a lawyer in order to study the industrial conditions of labor, become an expert, and write on labor problems. He entered the Harvard Law School in 1920.

He had only been in law school a few months when he confided to his diary the wish that he "could get such a man as [Louis B.] Brandeis or [Frank P.] Walsh interested in me and my ambitions so that I could get some bit of personal guidance and encouragement from them" (13). And, indeed, in early 1921 he wrote Frank P. Walsh, a prominent industrial relations lawyer. His letter described his ambition to be an expert in labor law and led to an extended correspondence.[6] For the rest of his life Lilienthal was to cultivate important people. It became a vital resource for his leadership, because he had friends who knew of his work and who could help him in his fights, give him advice, persuade others, and give his causes publicity. This was not simply currying favor. One of his close TVA associates caught it: "His obvious qualities of mind impressed the people with whom he dealt. . . . Look at his career as combining idealism and opportunism. He impressed people of great discrimination—Brandeis, Frankfurter, FDR, Acheson. He could take a difficult task and carry it out."[7] He impressed people with his actions, but he used personal ties as a political resource.

After he graduated from Harvard in 1923, Lilienthal went to work for Chicago labor lawyer Donald Richberg, who was general counsel for the national railroad unions. Richberg was one of a number of labor leaders and lawyers Lilienthal had written and visited.[8] Felix Frankfurter, his teacher at Harvard, and Walsh had recommended him to Richberg. In the mid-twenties he worked on a number of important labor cases for the Richberg firm. But he also pursued his hopes for a "literary" career by writing articles for the *American Review*, *Outlook*, the *New Republic*, and the *Nation*. He formed his own Chicago firm, specializing in public utility law. As special counsel to the city of Chicago, Lilienthal helped the city win a refund of $20 million for telephone company customers. His law review articles on utility issues and his founding editorship of a national information service on utility regulation complemented his practice in bringing him national recognition as a public utility lawyer.[9]

In 1931 the new governor of Wisconsin, Phillip F. LaFollette, appointed Lilienthal to the Wisconsin Railroad Commission, which was renamed the Public Service Commission after Lilienthal, at the governor's request, drafted legislation that strengthened and expanded the commission's regulatory powers.[10] Lilienthal was an aggressive member of the commission who attracted national attention by his advocacy of public utility regulation. One student of regulation in Wisconsin wrote that the young commissioner's accomplishments "must be offset to a degree by the friction and animosity he created in the relations between the utilities and the Commission . . . such an attitude is not completely helpful in the negotiational procedure which characterizes much of the regulatory process."[11] Lilienthal's own belief was that too many public-service commissions were captives of the industries they regulated.[12]

References to Lilienthal's combativeness in Wisconsin are appropriate because he was combative at TVA. The few Wisconsin journal entries capture his awareness of his own intensity:

> My tendency to overwork and get all intense about phases of my work must be a nuisance [to his wife]. (21)

> It is the driving of others and yourself that seems to take the kink out of you. (26)

Lilienthal put heavy pressure on himself and others to get work done, and the intensity of his efforts would periodically bring him to the point of exhaustion, so that he would require rest and vacations. This pattern continued throughout his life.

One can see the elements of a developing leadership style in the young adult years. He was ambitious for achievement and recognition both for himself and for social and political reform. His administrative style involved intensive homework, the combative pressing of advantages and opportunities, and the cultivation of patrons and alliances. He had learned to use rhetoric to good effect in Wisconsin. His appointment to the first board of the new Tennessee Valley Authority would give him the opportunity to fully develop and express his style of leadership as a leader of the most innovative creation of the New Deal.

TVA

Legislation resembling the TVA Act of 1933 had been debated in the Congress for a decade before the election of Roosevelt guaranteed its passage into law. The two previous Republican presidents had vetoed more limited bills. There were two strands to the incipient TVA. The first was the longstanding desire of members of Congress from the Tennessee Valley states to assist the development of southern agriculture through the use of the government-owned nitrate plants at Muscle Shoals, Alabama, for the manufacture of fertilizer. The plants had been built in connection with the construction during World War I of Wilson Dam at Muscle Shoals for the manufacture of munitions. The second strand was the public power tradition represented by Senator George Norris, who hoped that a number of dams could be created along the Tennessee River for the production of electric power. Norris was an opponent of private utilities and an advocate of publicly owned power systems. TVA could have been strictly a power and fertilizer company on the basis of these two conceptions. President-elect Roosevelt added the vision of a multipurpose authority that would develop the natural resources of the region in a comprehensive manner.[13]

The TVA Act gave the authority specific powers to build dams, generate and sell power, improve navigation and flood control, manufacture fertilizer, and assist agricultural development. These were regarded as interrelated missions; for example, dams generate hydroelectric power and facilitate navigation and flood control. The assumption of a decentralized multipurpose authority for natural resource development permeates the Act. Section 22 of the act calls upon TVA to develop plans for regional development, and Section 23 provides that the president may introduce legislation to implement such plans. The mandate to prepare plans is not accompanied by statutory authority to carry them out.

The First TVA Board

President Roosevelt appointed Arthur E. Morgan, an accomplished conservation engineer and president of Antioch College, as chairman of the first TVA board. FDR stipulated that the other two members of the board be expert in the areas of agriculture and power and left it to Morgan to find nominees to recommend to him. In due course the name of Harcourt A. Morgan, president of the University of Tennessee, was submitted and approved. H. A. Morgan, an expert on the boll weevil, had spent his life working for improvements in southern agriculture. Supreme Court Justice Louis D. Brandeis suggested Lilienthal's name to A. E. Morgan. Lilienthal had used Felix Frankfurter's sponsorship to call on Brandeis in Washington, and the justice also had had favorable reports on the young reformer from his daughter, who lived in Madison, Wisconsin. After a brief meeting with Lilienthal in Chicago, Morgan sent his name to Roosevelt for nomination to the board.[14]

These three men, the two Morgans and Lilienthal, faced an extraordinary challenge. They were to create an organization and decide how it was to implement the language of the TVA Act. The character and mandate of the organization was stipulated only in the most general way. It was to be a government corporation and therefore was not placed under a department. The board was to report directly to the president. But, the most important questions about mission organization and mission were not spelled out. The act authorized TVA to distribute as well as generate hydroelectric power but was silent about the mode of distribution. The question of the relation of TVA to the private utilities of the region was left open. It was expected that TVA would help farmers improve their productivity, but the method for organizing such activities was not stipulated. Section 22 authorized the preparation of plans for the region, but the relation of such plans to the other activities of the authority was unclear. There was no blueprint in the act for the relation of TVA to other federal agencies and state and local governments.

Lilienthal was the articulator of the TVA myth of grass-roots democracy which was to both guide the organization and serve as a defense against opponents. This act of creativity grew, in part, out of his relationship with his two colleagues. They are therefore a key part of this story.

A. E. Morgan was an engineer who joined a belief in technological progress to a commitment to a cooperative society. As chief engineer for the construction of a series of dams on the Little Miami River in Ohio, he had combined extraordinary innovation in dam design with a social experiment that provided housing, schools, and adult education for construction workers and their families.[15] The twin themes of technology and grass-roots experimentation were implicit in his background and beliefs. The TVA statute provided for the appointment of a "chief engineer," and Morgan asked Roosevelt to appoint him to that position, which he used as a basis for insisting that TVA have its own construction force and personnel system, independent of the federal civil service. Two goals of Morgan's were thereby accomplished: (1) TVA engineering and construction could be held to his high technical standards, and (2) the principle of a nonpolitical organization that would not engage in patronage hiring was established.

Morgan also advanced the ideals of integration of functions in a multipurpose authority. For example, the chief TVA architect was lodged in the engineering department rather than the planning department, which had a positive effect on the aesthetic design of the dams. He also articulated at TVA a long-time practice in his engineering firm of decentralization of professional decisions within the organization, so that many decisions were made at the dam site by those responsible. Morgan's ideas about regional development and social planning were less than comprehensive and often difficult to decipher. He did not wish TVA to develop a master plan for the Valley. Rather, he conceived of the authority as a demonstration agency that would try small model experiments. A TVA engineer who talked often with Morgan remembered: "His conception was artistic and intellectual. TVA would act like a limited scope model that would be so perfect and idealized that the utilities would copy it. No need for large scope. One demonstration farm and one demonstration cooperative and one TVA municipal power company would be enough. The yardstick would exemplify the right way of doing things."[16]

Morgan wanted TVA to try experiments of various kinds, most of which were not carried out. The "new town" of Norris, Tennessee, became a reality as a planned community, and it survives in its simplicity today. Other ideas, such as the promotion of handicraft industries, the use of scrip for money in rural communities, that TVA refuse to deal with real estate firms that exploited land in order to raise the standards of real estate, and that the authority might take control of land abused by farmers, brought ridicule and undermined his credibility with his fellow directors.[17] Such ideas were tentative and were suggested by Morgan for discussions that never took place because the ideas were not taken seriously. Morgan also believed in the National Recovery Act hope for cooperation between government and industry, and he viewed the competition between TVA and the private utilities in the region as one of efficiency as measured by the yardstick principle. Under that principle, TVA would generate and distribute hydroelectric power to consumers more cheaply and efficiently than the private companies, and once this was realized, the utilities would follow TVA methods. Therefore, in Morgan's view, TVA did not need to displace the private companies in the Valley; it would simply have a distribution area of its own. He did not perceive a deep political struggle between the New Deal and the private companies, as embodied in the creation of TVA, the Rural Electrification Administration, and the Utility Holding Company Act.[18]

Morgan did not believe that relationships between principals in government were political. He felt that the three board members would be guided by the facts to agree upon the correct decisions. When they did not do so, he was inclined to attribute disagreement to bad motives on the part of the others.[19]

Morgan's experimentalism was rejected by his colleagues, but he left clear legacies, particularly the ideal of technical decision making in a nonpolitical organization with the rationality of professionals as a guiding force. This ideal permeated the TVA organization.

H. A. Morgan was a long-time land grant college administrator and dean of agriculture who had learned a great deal about introducing new ideas and techniques to farmers. He believed that change could not be imposed and that people learned by doing. He liked to stay in the background and encourage others to take initiatives. For example, although he was TVA chairman from 1938 to 1941, he permitted Lilienthal to have the national limelight and to be the organization's de facto leader.

He was a "modernizer" of southern agriculture. He believed that it was necessary to pull marginal farmers away from bad habits that were depleting the soil through the regular planting of row crops such as corn, tobacco, and cotton. In the judgment of southern agricultural experts, the nitrate fertilizers used year after year by farmers were injuring the land. Morgan was among those who believed in a change to phosphate fertilizer and greater reliance on clover, hay, grass, and livestock as means of conserving and strengthening the land. This was the progressive view in the southern land grant colleges and among extension service agents at the time.[20]

His tangible contribution to the development of TVA programs was his insistence that the TVA fertilizer demonstration program be administered by the land grant colleges through the extension service. He was opposed to the development of a system of TVA demonstration farms. Morgan did not idealize these local networks; indeed, he said that the agricultural faculties had "mediocre ideas."[21] But he thought that using existing institutional links with farmers was the most efficient way to modernize farms. He also favored using the more efficient, and therefore the more prosperous, farms as demonstration sites. Morgan did not justify this strategy on political grounds, although he surely must have realized the political import of his policy. TVA was working with the agricultural establishment of the Valley. In retrospect, Lilienthal suggested that Morgan was trying to avoid having to work directly with the Department of Agriculture bureaucracy in Washington. In Lilienthal's view, Morgan felt that if TVA had to take direction from the Washington bureaucracy, it would be encumbered in dealing directly with farmers.[22] So Morgan turned to the grass-roots institutions close at hand to do the job.

This strategy was consistent with Morgan's career-long belief that one could not plan for others but had to find ways to motivate them to change. The viewpoint was clearly expressed in a memorandum sent to his codirectors on 3 October 1933 in which he recommended that all

TVA planning activities undertaken under Section 22 of the TVA Act be carried out in cooperation with state and local governments in the region. TVA should not develop plans of its own for any part of the Valley unless there was no one else to do it. He argued that planning would not be effective without the active participation of agencies representing the people of the region. They would neither recommend nor implement with enthusiasm anything in which they had not had a part. The authority could be a catalyst to promote studies and to help states develop planning capacities, but it should not plan by itself.[23]

Morgan's recommendation to the board prevailed, and the precedent was set that in the future all TVA activities that fell broadly under Section 22 rather than under the specific statutory responsibilities of the authority would be conducted in cooperation with other federal agencies, state and local governments, and private groups. This was the basis of the original grass-roots principle. For example, TVA maintained a small forestry staff and sought to stimulate the development of state forestry programs and state park systems. Often such work was done under contract between TVA and other agencies.

H. A. Morgan's philosophy of grass-roots participation was usually couched in vague, general language about the "common mooring" shared by human beings in a world of nature. The idea of common mooring was the straightforward ecological notion that people are dependent upon nature for economic development and are obliged to respect its unity and limits. It was necessary for Lilienthal to extract the grass-roots idea and develop it into a general philosophy, for Morgan would never have done it himself.[24]

All three TVA board members accepted and implemented A. E. Morgan's conception of TVA as a nonpolitical, professional organization. This provided protection from politicians. They also accepted the logically derivable belief in the importance of interdisciplinary planning and discussions in a multipurpose authority. H. A. Morgan carried the day on the decentralization of the agricultural demonstration program and other programs of technical assistance to states and localities. "A.E." was opposed, but "H.A." had Lilienthal's vote. The chairman thought that TVA should work with subsistence farmers to help them stay on the land and foresaw that TVA reliance on the state agricultural colleges and the U.S. extension service would favor the larger, more efficient farmers.[25] H.A. disagreed. He wanted to modernize southern agriculture and thought of subsistence farming as perpetuating a "peasantry."[26] By the same token, both H.A. and Lilienthal were critical of A.E.'s ideas for social experiments. They were fearful that talk of reforming the real estate industry to make it more ethical or confiscating the land of farmers who neglected the soil would jeopardize the infant

TVA, which needed all the political support it could get. Lilienthal thought that A.E. was a paternalist who wished to plan for people. In a 1936 talk to TVA employees, Lilienthal ridiculed a number of his ideas, saying, "I have no confidence in progress that comes from plans concocted by supermen and imposed upon the rest of the community for its own good. . . . I don't have much faith in 'uplift.' "[27]

A gap developed in the first months between A. E. Morgan, on one side, and H. A. Morgan and Lilienthal, on the other. The two board members were concerned about A.E.'s inclination to reserve important decisions for himself as chairman, his somewhat haphazard style of management, and his utopian ideas.[28] H.A. and Lilienthal also found that despite an age difference of more than thirty years, they agreed on most things and particularly on the need for TVA to be practical. Their skepticism about A.E. lay behind their August 1933 recommendation that responsibility for the administration of specific TVA programs be divided among the three board members, with policy reserved for the entire board. A.E. would oversee engineering, construction, navigation and flood control, education, training, and housing. H.A would run the agriculture, fertilizer, and forestry programs. Lilienthal would have charge of the power program and the legal department.[29] The chairman had no choice but to acquiesce, and the division of labor continued until it was eliminated by the appointment of a general manager in 1936 as the link between a policy-making board and the program offices. The board members then gave up specific administrative responsibilities.

The H. A. Morgan–Lilienthal majority of two on the board and the separation of administrative responsibilities meant that agriculture and planning would follow H.A.'s ideas and that A.E. would be able to continue the programs of dam construction, navigation, and worker education and training. The major unresolved question was what TVA would do about the distribution of the electric power that would be generated by its dams. This was the most important question that TVA faced in its first years. Lilienthal was fearful that A. E. Morgan would give the private utility companies an opportunity to permanently stunt TVA's growth by his advocacy of a limited TVA service area. The young director distrusted utility holding companies on the basis of his Wisconsin experience, and he was skeptical that any good would emerge from a TVA effort to cooperate with the southern utilities.[30] H. A. Morgan supported Lilienthal on these matters, but the issue was important enough to require presidential decisions, and therefore Lilienthal could not automatically have his way through a vote of the board. He had to fight against A. E. Morgan at the same time that Wendell Willkie, the president of Commonwealth and Southern (C&S), the largest utility holding company in the Valley region, was gearing up to fight TVA. The "power fight" was thus on two fronts. Its eventual resolution, in Lilienthal's favor, had important consequences for the character of TVA beyond the power program itself. A. E. Morgan was to leave his position in defeat at the request of the president in 1937. Lilienthal was from then on the dominant figure in the authority, and it was his conceptions of TVA, derived in part from the ideas of H. A. Morgan, that prevailed. Therefore, the story of the "power fight" was both a struggle over a particular issue and a fight for the identity of TVA.

The Power Fight

The TVA Act defined the general aims of the power program. TVA was to distribute power to customers "within transmission distance," a vague phrase that theoretically would permit service to a wide region beyond the Tennessee Valley if enough dams were built in the Valley. Preference in service was to be given to nonprofit municipal and rural cooperative customers, with maximum encouragement being given for the use of electricity on farms. There was a caution against duplication of power facilities with private utilities.[31]

This language left the relative roles of TVA and the private companies open to interpretation and negotiation. A. E. Morgan did not want a fight with the power companies, fearing that such conflict might endanger other TVA missions, which he saw as just as important as the power program. Lilienthal did not trust the private companies because, on the basis of his experience, he thought them unalterably opposed to the existence of public power and feared that they would act to destroy TVA if they could. He thought it important that the TVA power program have a presence in several areas in the Valley as a competitive spur to the private companies and as bases of political support for TVA.

Lilienthal saw the competition with the utilities in terms of who would win public support in the Valley and the nation. TVA must get credit with the public for lower rates. He thought that the authority should first work out its own program of power distribution and wholesale and retail rates as a basis for public appeals before it began to negotiate with the utilities. Morgan and Lilienthal were unable to agree on the issue of territorial scope and took the question to Roosevelt. The president brokered a compromise according to which TVA was to operate its power program in a number of subregions of the Valley, adjacent to dams to be constructed, but would not reach beyond the Tennessee River watershed. Efforts would be made to avoid duplication.[32]

There were only a few publicly owned power systems near the Wilson Dam at Muscle Shoals, and Lilienthal hoped to buy some properties in the immediate region from C&S in order to develop a TVA service area. TVA had begun to build its own transmission lines from Muscle Shoals to the Norris Dam, which was under construction further up the Tennessee River, and was thereby creating the possibility of direct competition with private utilities in their Tennessee service areas.

But Lilienthal needed Willkie's cooperation if TVA was to acquire properties. At their first meeting, in Washington on 4 October 1933, Willkie proposed that his companies purchase all of TVA's electricity. In his view, there was no need to expand the energy market. He told Lilienthal that TVA might not survive the New Deal unless it found an outlet for its power. Lilienthal made no commitment, but after the meeting, he and his assistants negotiated an agreement with the publicly owned power company of Tupelo, Mississippi, for TVA to sell power to Tupelo beginning in February 1934. Lilienthal was putting pressure on Willkie by showing that TVA could get into business without C&S cooperation. Construction on the power transmission line from Muscle Shoals to Norris Dam also continued against Willkie's opposition. Lilienthal began to encourage municipalities to apply for funds from the Public Works Administration (PWA) to build their own plants and distribution systems. In the face of these bargaining chips, Willkie agreed to sell TVA properties in northeastern Mississippi, northern Alabama, and eastern Tennessee. As a concession, TVA would promise not to seek further territorial expansion. This agreement, of January 1934, was to last five years or until Norris Dam was completed.[33]

But except for the exchange of a few properties in Mississippi, the deal fell through. The Tennessee and Alabama companies placed too high a price on their properties for local public power distributors to buy them. When Lilienthal arranged with Willkie for TVA to buy the properties at a lower cost and then sell them to the communities, a New York bank that held the mortgages set impossibly difficult terms for the sale. A group of preferred stockholders then filed suit in federal court against the North Alabama Power Company and TVA, and the litigation delayed the sale of the Alabama properties.[34] When Willkie wrote President Roosevelt to complain that Lilienthal was encouraging communities to file for PWA funds to build their own systems, Lilienthal advised the president to reply to Willkie through Marvin McIntyre, his secretary, that Willkie should honor the original agreement of January 1934 to sell the properties, which McIntyre did.[35]

The TVA power program was stalled, and there was little forward movement in the acquisition of new properties until 1936, when the stockholders lost their suit. But in 1934 Lilienthal acted quickly to make the most of the few footholds in Mississippi. He turned the fight with the power companies into a public drama. In his public rhetoric Lilienthal combined H. A. Morgan's ideas about the necessity for TVA to work with local institutions with his own hostility to utility holding companies derived from his Wisconsin years. Lilienthal's lieutenants of the period describe him as engaging in a concerted strategy to stimulate public interest in wider electric service, cheaper rates, and increased usage, all through the development of new publicly owned companies that would buy electricity from TVA and extend its distribution to wider service areas, especially farmers, at lower rates than the private utilities had ever imagined possible.[36]

In 1934 Lilienthal and his assistants developed a rate structure for the purchase of electric power that was less than half as high as that offered by private utilities. The figure was really a guess and was based on the assumption that increased usage would follow the lowering of prices.[37] Lilienthal had expert help from able young lawyers and engineers in the process of developing the first contracts with local governments. One of them tells the story of Lilienthal and staff assistants working out the legal terms of the Tupelo contract in the car on the drive down to Mississippi for the announcement and ceremony. Lilienthal's injunction was that the contract should require the rates to be as low for consumers as could be justified.[38] Rural electric cooperatives were started in Mississippi during the same period by members of Lilienthal's staff. They were based on the concept of amortization so that in time the system would be debt-free.[39] The contracts with municipalities did not hold rates to costs. Excess revenues could be used for reinvestment in plant, to pay off bonds, or to build up cash reserves.[40]

Lilienthal also conceived the idea of a consumer credit affiliate called the Electric Home and Farm Authority, which gave low-interest loans for the purchase of appliances and worked with manufacturers to bring cheap appliances onto the market. He went to New York City to talk with the manufacturers of electric appliances about manufacturing simpler and cheaper products.[41] In 1934 he wrote Eleanor Roosevelt a letter describing his success:

> The first company to respond to our appeal for totally new design is The General Electric Company. They have designed and will soon have in production a combination electric refrigerator and electric range, which they have agreed that they will sell in the Tennessee Valley area for $125 for the two units. . . . The equipment is extremely ingenious in design and the price, while substantially lower than prices heretofore prevailing for equivalent service, will afford a small but reasonable margin for the manufacturer and the dealer.[42]

He invited Mrs. Roosevelt to visit the Valley to inspect the new product at the time of its delivery and told her that one would also be on display in the Bureau of Home Economics of the Department of Agriculture in Washington.

Lilienthal's boldness produced good results. The combination of low rates and increased opportunities caused the usage of electricity to soar. In Tupelo average consumption went from 49 kilowatt-hours to 178, and the price dropped from 7.40¢ to 1.58¢. In the Alcorn, Mississippi, cooperative, usage increased in three years from 49 kilowatt-hours to 139, and price dropped from 5.37¢ per kilowatt-hour to 1.82¢.[43]

The young director made sure that TVA, the president, and the New Deal got the maximum political mileage out of these achievements. Regular memos went from Lilienthal to Roosevelt about TVA achievements, not only as reports but as suggested raw material for presidential speeches around the country about public power. Before Roosevelt visited Tupelo in November 1934, Lilienthal supplied him with memoranda containing "Facts about Tupelo" and describing how usage had risen, rates had dropped, and the use of appliances had increased. FDR cited these facts in this Tupelo speech but also talked about what TVA meant for the Tennessee Valley in terms of hope for the future: "The great outstanding thing to me for these past three days has been the change in the looks on people's faces . . . today I see not only hope but I see determination—knowledge that all is well with the country and that we are coming back."[44]

In 1935 and 1936, TVA found itself with an increasing supply of electric power coming from newly constructed dams without market outlets for that power because of the stalemate with the utilities. Lilienthal embarked on a two-pronged strategy: TVA would seek to win its fights in the courts so that the legal and constitutional arguments used by the utilities against selling their properties would be demolished. In the meantime, the hopes of Valley publics about the possibilities of electric power use had to be sustained for the day when a greater market outlet for TVA power could be created. To that end, Lilienthal and his assistants embarked on a sustained campaign of public persuasion up and down the Valley. Governors and state legislatures were lobbied for changes in state law that would facilitate the creation of municipal and cooperative distributors. The few such newly established organizations were carefully nurtured by TVA.[45]

The strongest weapon in the fight was Lilienthal himself. A few pictures survive of the young Lilienthal speaking from the courthouse steps of Corinth, Mississippi, and other communities to attentive audiences of farm families about the wonders of electricity.[46] He drew on his experience and talents as a debater. One of his close associates remembered that he was not a particularly good speaker; substance and sincerity were the key to his success with audiences.[47] He himself felt that his small-town midwestern background helped him to understand the local leadership in the Tennessee Valley and to meet them on their own terms.[48] The assistant to Lilienthal who wrote many of the first power contracts remembered: "He had enormous gifts of leadership. He was a carpetbagger who was adopted very warmly by the people of the Valley. I don't know of anyone else who could have brought the people of the Valley to accept TVA. . . . He had a good feeling for what they were interested in and knew how to combine economic aspirations with expression of idealism so that following their economic interests would seem comfortable to them."[49]

Lilienthal drew strength from the experience, as an October 1935 entry in his diary about a series of speeches in Alabama reveals: "The most gratifying thing about the whole trip is to see how meeting directly with people out in the field revitalizes you and makes you feel that the program is worth carrying on." He knew that he was striking home. "There is somehow a magic about TVA kilowatts. We have really stirred public imagination about electricity" (53–54).

His speeches were not made in a political vacuum. The New Deal produced the Utility Company Holding Act in 1935, in Roosevelt's first term, and the Rural Electrification Administration was established in 1935 and strengthened in 1936. Lilienthal astutely linked the future of TVA with the New Deal and, implicitly, with Roosevelt's reelection campaign of 1936. The supposedly nonpolitical government corporation was depicted by Lilienthal as an ornament of the New Deal, and he, in turn, invoked the New Deal and Roosevelt as support for TVA. In a Memphis speech he said,

> We are proud to count among our leading enemies the whole Tory crowd concentrated in New York City and Chicago that always fights every move toward giving the average man and woman a better chance. The interests of this crew of reactionaries and your interests are diametrically opposed. There is a conflict here that cannot be reconciled. Either TVA has to be for you or it has to be for this other crowd. When that crowd begins to sing the praises of TVA it is time for you to throw us out.[50]

The Fight in the Courts

In 1934 fourteen preferred stockholders of the Alabama Power Company filed suit in *Ashwander* v. *TVA* challenging TVA's authority to engage in power generation and distribution at Wilson Dam at Muscle Shoals, Alabama. TVA received a blow when a federal judge decreed that TVA not be permitted to complete parts of the 4 January 1934 agreement with C&S for the sale of utility installations to TVA. This was the first of many lawsuits against TVA and the beginning of a four-year struggle in the courts for TVA survival. Lilienthal admitted later that at the time he was terribly worried about whether TVA could survive the onslaught. His response was to build up a strong legal department at TVA and to recruit nationally prominent lawyers to represent TVA in the courts.[51] Over the mild protest of the attorney general, and with the president's support, TVA chose to conduct its own legal work rather than to rely on Justice Department lawyers. Lilienthal wished to control the litigation and used the special statutory character of TVA as a government corporation as a justification—not the first or last time that the argument would be used by TVA to protect its autonomy from other parts of the federal government.[52]

In February 1936 the Supreme Court delivered an opinion in the *Ashwander* case that granted the federal government the right to generate and sell power at Wilson Dam.[53] TVA would be able to move ahead to find outlets for its power. However, the 1934 agreement with C&S was going to expire in November 1936, and a dispute developed between A. E. Morgan and his fellow directors about whether a new agreement should set limits on the TVA power service area. Morgan favored such limits, and the other two were opposed. The three board members took the question to Roosevelt in August, but pleading the press of the election, he would not decide, and he suggested that the existing contract be extended briefly.[54]

At this time the idea of a "power pool" emerged and captured Roosevelt's imagination. Lilienthal had spoken to him about it in mid-1936, but other advisers and friends of the president had also suggested such a plan. The idea was that TVA and C&S companies would sell power to a neutral pool organization, which would then sell to distributors, whether public or private. The yardstick principle whereby public power might demonstrate its greater efficiency and lesser cost could be exhibited through pooling, because the pool would buy power from the plants with the lowest production costs, whether public or private.[55]

FDR thought of the plan as a model for the nation. It also promised the possibility of peace between public and private power in an election year. Lilienthal was more skeptical. He had suggested the idea to the president as a short-run expedient to permit TVA to find power outlets, particularly in case of an adverse decision in *Ashwander*. But in the long run he opposed any territorial restriction, and he worried that a pooling arrangement might have that effect. When Willkie offered to sell the entire Tennessee Electric Power Company to TVA on the condition that the authority would expand no further, Lilienthal refused. Lilienthal entered the power pool discussions with the belief that the private utilities would not be cooperative and that this would be revealed in negotiations. A. E. Morgan had the opposite view and prepared a memorandum that sided with the utilities on most questions. The paper was circulated before the September 1936 White House meeting of TVA and utility executives convened by Roosevelt and served no purpose except to reveal TVA disunity. Lilienthal was furious and pressed Senator Norris and others to point out to FDR the great danger of yielding too much to Willkie and his allies.[56]

As a result of the White House meeting on the power pool, Lilienthal was required to agree to a three-month extension of the 1934 agreement with Willkie. At the time, he was pressing for an agreement with the city of Chattanooga by which that city would purchase C&S properties and buy power from TVA. The extension of the 1934 agreement delayed such action. But Lilienthal and Secretary of the Interior Harold Ickes pushed ahead with PWA loans to communities for the building of transmission lines for public municipal and rural cooperative distributors, never suggesting that such actions were included in any truce about TVA territorial limits. Lilienthal was determined to press every advantage.[57]

In May 1936, nineteen power companies had initiated a suit against TVA charging that its power program was unconstitutional. In December 1936, in the middle of the truce period, a federal district judge, John J. Gore, enjoined TVA not to expand its power program.[58] Willkie appeared to have gained a victory. Lilienthal immediately wrote the president and urged him to dissolve the power pool negotiations on the grounds that the utilities were not negotiating in good faith because they hoped to win in the courts. The president took the advice.[59]

Willkie and his allies had won a Pyrrhic victory. Five months later a federal court of appeals denied the Gore injunction, and the Supreme Court let the decision stand. Moreover, Roosevelt, fresh from a big election victory, was angry at the utilities and ready to side with public power advocates, including Senator Norris and Lilienthal, against A. E. Morgan, who still had not given up hope of cooperation.[60]

It was apparent that Willkie would have to sell C&S properties, particularly after the Supreme Court upheld the right of the PWA to finance transmission lines for publicly owned distributors. After many months of negotiations, the transfers were made on 15 August 1939. TVA purchased the entire Tennessee Electric Power Company and portions of the Alabama and Mississippi companies. The issue of territorial limits to the TVA service area was implicit in the sense that the authority now had a market for all the electricity it was producing.[61]

A. E. Morgan Departs

This narrative has only touched on the several reasons for the deep discord between A. E. Morgan and Lilienthal. Morgan wished for co-operation and abhorred conflict in both social and personal life. Lilienthal was a fighter on the public stage and within the board. Morgan believed that Lilienthal was diverting TVA from its mission to be an experimental organization by directing energy toward the power fight. Lilienthal saw Morgan as naive about the utilities. Morgan favored small-scale demonstrations such as handicraft industries, and Lilienthal recalled that at TVA "I voted for large-scale industry."[62] The beliefs and personalities of the two men were incompatible. Their political styles were also incompatible. A. E. Morgan believed that reasonable men would agree on correct answers, and he was bewildered when this did not happen. Lilienthal was an ambitious young man who, as he later put it, was "not as moderate" as he might have been, adding, "I liked to fight."[63] He did not hesitate to challenge A. E. Morgan, and according to witnesses, many of the board meetings were shouting matches in which Lilienthal baited the chairman while H. A. Morgan maintained a dignified silence that was totally supportive of his younger colleague.[64] In later years Lilienthal said that the contest with A. E. Morgan over the character of TVA was more important than the fight with the utilities. It was over the issue of whether TVA would plan for people or put tools in their hands and permit them to plan for themselves. He saw Morgan as a paternalistic planner.[65]

It finally became apparent to Roosevelt that the Morgan-Lilienthal conflict was doing great harm to TVA. In 1937, A. E. Morgan began to criticize his two colleagues in magazine articles, making vague charges about improprieties in regard to the use of political patronage in TVA employment and the granting of other favors for political reasons. When Lilienthal and H. A. Morgan complained to Roosevelt, he called all three to a White House meeting and asked the chairman to state specific charges. Upon his refusal to do so and his request for a congressional hearing, Roosevelt dismissed him from the board. A subsequent congressional investigation and report denied Morgan's allegations.[66] H. A. Morgan became chairman, but Lilienthal was in charge. The older man left all public activities to Lilienthal, including congressional testimony and lobbying. He was primarily interested in agriculture and was happy to give his younger colleague full scope to be the leader of TVA. Former senator James Pope took A. E. Morgan's place on the board, but he was not a strong factor in policy issues.[67] Lilienthal increasingly became identified in the public mind with TVA, and his accession to the chairmanship in 1941 was virtually a formality.

Lilienthal's Contribution to the Power Fight

Did Lilienthal make a difference in the power fight and thus in the character of TVA? The federal courts would probably have affirmed the authority's right to distribute power whether Lilienthal had been there or not. The actual development of TVA-sponsored distributors by 1937 was perhaps not much greater than what A. E. Morgan originally envisioned for model demonstration areas. It would have been possible to institute rate reductions and increases in usage in one demonstration area. This model might have impressed the utilities with the increase in electricity use and encouraged them to lower their own rates and extend services in response to the TVA example, as they in fact did.[68] Lilienthal made no technical contribution to the equation: his lieutenants supplied the technical expertise for the contracts written between TVA and electricity distributors. Nor did he invent the idea of low rates and increased usage: Canadian hydroelectric companies had been the pioneers in North America on that score.

Lilienthal's unique contribution was to provide the political leadership that TVA needed to survive. A small TVA demonstration area for the distribution of electric power might not have been able to survive politically even if the fight had been won in the courts. This would have been even more the case if A. E. Morgan had inaugurated some of his social experiments and treated TVA as an experimental and demonstration organization. There would have been too little popular support for TVA in the Tennessee Valley and much opposition to such experiments. A. E. Morgan lacked any sense of the need for TVA programs to have popular and political support. Lilienthal saw such support as a necessity for survival. His achievement was to mobilize widespread public support for TVA programs. He made sure that TVA was supplying electricity to distributors throughout the Valley, so that potential supporters were widespread. He then mobilized public opinion behind TVA and against the private utilities. Rhetoric was his chief instrument, but he could point to low rates and increased use of electricity. Rural people had little conception of the uses of electric power beyond the light bulb before the 1930s.[69] Lilienthal understood that fact, and the invention of the Electric Home and Farm Authority was a means to dramatize the many uses of electricity to farmers.[70] He described his hawking of electricity in a 1939 letter:

> I used to make speeches before county crowds with a lot of farm
> machinery gadgets (grinders for feed, brooders, etc.) set up on a big
> table in front of me, and would work these into the talk, indicating
> how some particular farmer somewhere had added to his net income

when he had these machines (most of which we designed ourselves to meet the problems of these poor farmers). . . .

Well, it was undignified as hell . . . but those farmers listened to every darn word, and came up afterwards and handled the gadgets. . . . And then a cooperative would be formed and the power lines would reach them; but they got more than power; they got a lift to their dragging morale, they got a bit of economic education the only way they could, by a demonstration. (80–81)

It was not all just education; he knew how to identify the enemy:

We kept talking about how money is drained out of the community by those remote-control power setups, and as the figures for community-owned distribution agencies (either public or cooperative) came in, those figures about people and towns that everyone knew about, came alive. (80–81)

He knew the value of a good fight. Writing in 1939, he asked himself why TVA water and agricultural programs had failed to capture the public imagination in the same way as electricity, and answered:

Isn't the answer that all the eloquence about land and water omits two factors almost essential to wide public interest of a lively kind, to wit, emphasis upon human beings and a fight? In my activities 'crusading' on the power issue, when we were surrounded by a 'ring of steel' and the getting of a market presented a problem, indeed, I sensed the crucial importance of stressing the human factors, the concrete picture of men and women, benefiting from low electricity rates, etc. . . . And, of course, the utility companies furnished the 'fight' element. (106–7)

Many years later he recalled: "I'm a fighter. I enjoyed the controversy. I happen to think that conflict is about the only thing that really produces creativity."[71]

David Lilienthal was prepared for the challenge furnished by the TVA situation in 1933. His ambitions and talent were well matched for his task as he understood it. His experience as a lawyer and a public service commissioner in Wisconsin had taught him the need to decentralize control of utility holding companies; and H. A. Morgan's grassroots ideas filled out the picture for TVA and gave Lilienthal a fighting ideology with which to defend both power and agriculture programs. His capacity for rhetoric pushed him to become a missionary for TVA in the Valley and permitted him to establish bonds of confidence with citizens. His aggressiveness and determination to press every advantage, joined to his longstanding ability to create and cultivate alliances with important people, such as senators and presidents, gave him political support that A. E. Morgan could not understand, much less imitate. The man and the historical opportunity came together.

Without the political leadership that he provided, TVA might never have gotten off the ground. Popular demand for cheap electricity would have been limited. Community leaders and businessmen would not have fallen in line behind TVA as they did. Congress might have been less disposed to finance the construction of TVA dams in the second Roosevelt administration without demonstrations of popular support. Lilienthal's skills at mobilizing opinion, joined to the invention of programs that people could see and experience, enabled TVA to take advantage of legal victories in the power fight.

The Creation of an Organizational Myth

In 1944 Lilienthal published *TVA, Democracy on the March*, in which he presented the TVA idea as an innovative principle of public administration.[72] The book expressed two complementary ideas. The first was that a government corporation for regional development would be most effective if it operated at the regional level in close contact with the people and resources with which it worked. Efficiency was enhanced by the union of diverse functions in one organization, and the fragmentation of programs across federal agencies was thus avoided. The second idea was that of grass-roots democracy. Lilienthal contended that TVA functions were based upon the principles of grass-roots participation in program implementation. He cited the agricultural demonstration programs for farmers, the decentralized ownership of municipal and rural cooperative power distribution systems, and TVA agreements with other federal agencies and state and local governments for collaboration on a host of problems, such as malaria eradication, forest improvement, and the development of public libraries.

The 1944 book is important as the chief expression of the organizational myth of TVA. A myth is not a fiction but a set of missions and aspirations that guide a bureaucracy and give it legitimacy. Political support for bureaucratic programs cannot rest on achievement alone; too few agencies would meet the test. There must be some accomplishments for there to be support at all, and the myth expresses the hope that the achievements will grow. Organizations are in particular need of myths at their creation and in times of change and adaptation. Myths bind the members of the organization together, give them direction, and foster external support.[73] The TVA of the 1930s and 1940s had one of the strongest and most distinctive myths of any American public agency. Lilienthal had more to do with its development and articulation than anyone else. The myth became a political resource for TVA and expressed the beliefs about bureaucracy that were to guide Lilienthal for the rest of his career.

The Fight with Ickes

In 1939 Lilienthal spent much time in Washington trying to persuade Congress to authorize the TVA purchase of the Tennessee properties of C&S. Hostility to the authority in Congress meant that considerable lobbying on his part was required. He was engaged in the annual request for appropriations at the same time. His summer journal entries reflect restlessness and impatience. He asked himself whether he should resign because he was in a rut; perhaps he had exhausted his usefulness to TVA? He had hoped that he would not have to continue the endless negotiations involved in the transfer of utility properties. He worried about the vitality of TVA as an organization. H. A. Morgan was passive, and "there is a slowing down of new ideas for the very reason that we are catching our breath. . . . It is important that I somehow find time to do the thing I am best at—to stimulate and prod and drive ahead. And that takes time—time to talk things over, time to visit the job and people in the Valley" (116).

Lilienthal found the opportunity he was seeking, but in the form of a fight. Combat was again to stimulate creativity. The Reorganization Act of 1939 authorized the president to issue executive orders placing independent agencies under the authority of departments. A legal opinion prepared for Lilienthal by TVA's chief counsel in September 1939 suggested that TVA could be reorganized out of existence if the president chose.[74]

A clue to the eventual TVA response can be seen in a memorandum written by Earl S. Draper, director of TVA regional planning, in August 1939, in anticipation of the visit to the authority by a number of congressional leaders. The task of persuasion, he told John Blandford, TVA's general manager, was not to present evidence of good work but to go further and

> convince them that other agencies to whom such work has previously been entrusted in the national programs could not be as effective as we are. I refer, of course, to the practical results of the regional approach in coordination of programs. If we can convince them that a better job of dam building can be accomplished by a regional agency than could be done by the same engineers employed by a national agency, then I would say we have presented an unanswerable argument for continuation of the regional approach to continuing problems. . . .

If we are successful in putting this viewpoint over, it would have to be by (1) convincing the parties that our relations with other federal, state and local agencies are most effective through our regional approach and (2) that through a regional understanding of all the factors involved we are able to consider aspects of every program that would ordinarily be overlooked in the normal approach to these problems.[75]

H. A. Morgan expressed these ideas in a letter to FDR in September 1939. Morgan wrote in response to a message from the Bureau of the Budget that Secretary of the Interior Harold Ickes was trying to persuade Roosevelt to place TVA and future regional bodies under the authority of the Interior Department. Morgan's letter stated flatly that "if the Authority is to be required to report to the head of one agency having comparable interests, it may with equal justice be directed to review its decisions with several. Then the Tennessee Valley Authority as an independent corporate agency will be destroyed. The experiment will be ended."

Morgan listed TVA's accomplishments under its existing form of administration: the building of dams with its own labor force, the purchase of land and relocation of populations, the promotion of land conservation and crop experimentation, pioneering in the construction of farm machinery, navigation and flood control, the generation of electric power. Such achievements, Morgan wrote, were testimony to the soundness of "a unified, decentralized approach."[76]

Morgan concluded that there was no middle ground. Either TVA must continue as a decentralized regional agency, with the special privileges inherent in its form, or it would vanish. If the authority were placed under one federal agency, it would no longer be possible to make decisions at the grass roots. TVA would be one federal agency among several in the Valley, and its coordinating role would disappear.

By this time Lilienthal had joined the fight. He enlisted the support of Senator Norris, who wrote FDR of his opposition to Ickes's plan. The TVA board members met with Harold Smith, director of the Bureau of the Budget, and won his support. Lilienthal met with Ickes to express his views.[77] Roosevelt, who had been listening to Ickes, backed off.[78] Ickes's reach for control had been prompted by his belief that the creation of additional regional authorities in the Pacific Northwest, the Missouri Valley, and other regions would require coordination of national policy from Washington. He continued to press this claim, joining it to attacks on TVA.[79]

The dispute's chief effect on Lilienthal was to revive his interest in leading TVA. He had found a role for himself as the articulator of the gospel of TVA working at the "grass roots." On 12 November 1939 he recorded his feelings in his journal:

> I am all excited these days, excited about TVA and the way it is working out, and by the fascinating place I have in it, the function of keeping it on its toes, eager and on the qui vive.
>
> This is quite in contrast with my feeling of a few months ago. The change has been due to the wholly unexpected effort to put us into the Department of Interior. . . . That aroused my fighting impulses, and made it necessary for me to do some intensive thinking about a particular issue. . . .
>
> All of this has been exhilarating. It has been great to touch off other people, to argue and match ideas, especially if it involved a field of thinking which is relatively fresh, not only to me but to anyone. (142)

He described in his journal the warm reception accorded to a speech given on 10 November to the Southern Political Science Association in Knoxville on the topic "The TVA: An Experiment in the 'Grass Roots' Administration of Federal Functions." The speech was the product of the thinking that he had been doing in the efforts to defeat Ickes and justify TVA autonomy. He added that the talk had stimulated internal morale and that he hoped that it would stir up controversy in Washington.[80]

Lilienthal regarded the conflict with Ickes as having stimulated him to think through the idea of grass-roots democracy. It was part of Lilienthal's uniqueness that he sought to derive ideas from conflict. He could realize his youthful ambition to be a man of action and a writer. He saw the speech to the Southern Political Science Association as an act of creativity. It was the basis for his 1944 book. But what did Lilienthal add to the stock of ideas in TVA about a decentralized, autonomous regional corporation? Had not Draper and H. A. Morgan expressed a commonly held TVA ideology? The answer is surely yes. Government corporations can lay claim to the appeal of professional, nonpolitical, decentralized, and comprehensive decision making.[81] But Lilienthal added the ideal of grass-roots democracy. The grass-roots gospel was drawn from concrete TVA operational experience, as Lilienthal understood it, mediated by the tutelage of Harcourt Morgan. The older man never tried to articulate the grass-roots idea. Lilienthal drew on Morgan's belief in self-help in agricultural development and joined it to the TVA experience with decentralized agriculture, power, forestry, and community development programs to express the ideal of grass-roots democracy as a principle of administration. A journal entry in 1935 makes clear that he was thinking in these terms in the early years:

I am constantly impressed with the difficulties of administration as we go along in this job. The difficulties seem to be inherent in any large-scale undertaking and are probably accentuated in any enterprise that has elements of novelty and elements of pioneering. This problem of whether we can organize community activities or even industrial activities so as to make them work is a central problem of the TVA job. In fact, it may be that when we are further along we will conclude that the chief problem we are attacking is whether the people can so organize themselves as to perform some of the functions which we are trying to perform. (49–50)

Lilienthal told a friend that the agricultural test demonstration program "brought H.A. and me together in a relationship which is the best thing I have gotten out of this job" (81). He believed that H. A. Morgan's preaching of the relation between human and natural resources was the key to TVA effectiveness. The central idea, as discerned by Lilienthal, was that TVA would make natural resources available for use by providing water, electricity, and fertilizer, but only the people of the Valley could develop those uses; TVA could not do it for them. Many years later he recalled visiting the small town of Decatur, Alabama, located on the Tennessee River near Muscle Shoals and Wilson Dam. Decatur was suffering terribly from the Depression. A group of businessmen asked Lilienthal what TVA would do for Decatur. He answered that TVA would do nothing for them; they must do it for themselves. And, indeed, the businessmen of Decatur did develop new enterprises based on their location on the river, in concert with TVA navigation programs.[82]

Lilienthal was a realist about grass-roots democracy. He knew that there were few such traditions in the American South. In February 1939 he wrote a friend about the need for TVA to show tangible results early in its fight for existence so that local leaders would support it no matter what happened in Washington: "The support of as many middle-class small business and professional men as possible was essential, for organized labor in the South was at that time almost a negligible factor, and of course farm organization, while it has made great headway in the past five years, was almost nil" (80). One close associate of Lilienthal's remembered that by "grass roots" H. A. Morgan meant "the power structure, not ten farmers."[83] Morgan's reliance on successful farmers for the test demonstration program was akin to Lilienthal's belief that the boards of municipal electric companies should consist of prominent local businessmen.

Lilienthal's rhetoric about the grass roots, in the 1939 speech and even more so in his 1944 book, as well as in countless public speeches

across the nation, described and idealized TVA grass-roots practices as
the embodiment of altogether new precepts of democratic public administration. Lilienthal presented this case in the Knoxville speech to the
Southern Political Science Association. He drew the distinction between
centralized government, with the authority to make policy, and decentralized administration. A strong central government was necessary
because of the need for policy decisions about national problems, but if
the problems of a region were to be addressed systematically, government administration in that region must be integrated. The TVA as a
multipurpose authority for regional development illustrated the thesis.
The grass-roots principle provided the method of operation within this
decentralized framework.

Lilienthal presented TVA's use of the agricultural extension service
county agents to stage test demonstrations for the use of fertilizer and
new techniques of cultivation and soil conservation as the prime grass-
roots model. The test demonstration farms were chosen by the farmers
themselves in meetings, and the eventual dissemination of results to
the farmers in a region came from their observation. Lilienthal emphasized that TVA lacked the power to compel farmers to adopt new
strategies. He also described TVA's work with state engineering schools
to develop an experimental plan to quick-freeze strawberries as an illustration of the TVA role in introducing new crops to the Valley; again,
the final decisions rested with farmers. Another example of the grass-
roots principle was the decentralized system of power distribution, in
which TVA sold electric power to rural and municipal distributors. TVA
controlled the generation and transmission of power and insisted on
uniformity of contracts in regard to rates, but ownership and management were local, as were possibilities for high efficiency and service.
Finally, he described agreements between TVA and federal and state
agencies for cooperation in fish and game development around TVA
lakes and cooperation with the Public Health Service and local health
agencies for malaria control in areas behind dams.[84]

These ideas form the framework of the TVA myth. They state organizational missions and modes of operating that are part reality and
part aspirations to be achieved. Lilienthal's rhetoric did not draw sharp
distinctions between ideal and reality, but that is the nature of myth.

Uses of the Myth

Lilienthal used the grass-roots speech in the fight against Ickes. He
sent a copy to Harold Smith, director of the Bureau of the Budget, who,
according to Marguerite Owen, head of TVA's Washington office, was
so impressed that he made it required reading for his staff.[85] The grass-

roots ideal became the standard TVA defensive argument against the encroachments of federal agencies on TVA missions.

Another use of the myth was as propaganda. TVA had a strong public relations program from the beginning, A. E. Morgan and Lilienthal made frequent talks around the country and regularly wrote articles for magazines. The annual reports were often written by professional journalists. Movies were made about taming the river and reclaiming the land. TVA photographers built an impressive archive of pictures about the grass roots that were featured in magazines and culminated in a TVA show at the Museum of Modern Art in 1941. There were TVA exhibits at world fairs and for high schools throughout the nation. Thousands of foreign visitors to Knoxville were given well-staged tours.[86] Visiting writers received special treatment. For example, Lilienthal cultivated Scripps-Howard writer Raymond Clapper, inviting him to tour TVA facilities on a visit to the Valley. A series of Clapper columns followed that were favorable to TVA and the grass-roots ideal.[87]

Such activities were perhaps inherent in a new enterprise of experimental character. But Lilienthal gave special attention to the grass-roots theme in his public rhetoric. In a 1938 letter to Dr. Alvin Johnson, of the New School for Social Research, he responded to an invitation to speak at the New School about the grass-roots idea more than a year before his speech to the political scientists: "There is a very important chapter in the work of the TVA, particularly as a demonstration in democratic method, that has never been told in any unified way, and that I am very keen to do, with the collaboration of some of our technical people."[88]

After the Knoxville grass-roots speech, he began a national campaign to spread the TVA idea across the nation. He recorded in his journal in late December that "I have become excited over the prospect of thinking through the meaning of TVA . . . and of trying to set it out so clearly and simply that everyone in the country can understand it, what the results we now have to point to mean to the average man and woman" (149). This campaign, which continued until he left TVA in 1946, was carried on through speeches before all kinds of audiences, from universities to Rotary Clubs. He engaged in extensive correspondence with scholars and professional people. His journal notes the enthusiasm of John Gaus, of the University of Wisconsin, and other "students of regionalism" for the grass-roots speech (146). After a speech at Columbia University in 1940 he talked with the historian Charles Beard about the grass-roots idea for three hours.[89]

Lilienthal explicitly sought to influence public thinking about the organization of new regional authorities. For example, in 1941 he asked the National Planning Association to revise a study of TVA that avoided the issue of how such authorities should be organized. TVA should be the model, he argued.[90]

The two parts of the myth were firmly united in Lilienthal's mind. The autonomy of a decentralized corporation also implied grass-roots participation. There is no necessary logical connection between the two ideas. To what degree was Lilienthal expressing aspirations about popular participation rather than reality?

The Myth Examined

Philip Selznick's *TVA and the Grass Roots* challenged the accuracy of Lilienthal's descriptions of popular participation in TVA programs.[91] Selznick's primary focus was on the program of test demonstration farms which TVA delegated to the land grant college–agricultural extension service system. In Selznick's view, this was an organized constituency that, by virtue of its delegated authority, strengthened TVA and influenced its programmatic direction. The authority was strengthened because through delegation it acquired the support, in the Valley and in Washington, of an administratively and politically strong constituency. But TVA thereby handed significant control over the development of the agricultural program to the agricultural "establishment." Large, productive farmers were helped more than small, marginal farmers. The black agricultural colleges and black farmers were helped very little. TVA and the land grant colleges waged a struggle to keep the Soil Conservation Service and its programs out of the Valley because it was seen as a competitive force.[92] Lilienthal had described the selection of the test demonstration farms as being made by the farmers themselves through democratic processes overseen by the county agent.[93] Selznick thought this description overdid the democracy part and underplayed the degree to which county agents selected the test farmers and managed the process.[94]

A subordinate analysis in Selznick's study describes TVA domination of municipal and rural distributors of electricity. Lilienthal had characterized the relationship as democratic in the sense that the distributors were governed by locally appointed boards and were responsive to the rate payers for efficient service. TVA supplied the power within a necessarily uniform rate structure. Selznick saw domination rather than democracy. There was no element of cooptation of TVA by private groups, as in agriculture. TVA set the rates through contracts, resisted state regulation of rates or the creation of state regulatory bodies, and insisted that the distributor boards consist of nonpolitical appointees. TVA strongly opposed the presence of elected politicians on these boards because of its own nonpolitical character. This had the effect of denying the distributor boards political roots and constituencies, at least in their first generation.[95]

Victor Hobday's careful analysis of the relation of the boards to TVA in the postwar years supports Selznick's analysis. The distributors were individually weak in relation to TVA as an organization. They were cut off from local governments. Citizen participation was non-existent. The real feat of public administration was TVA's achievement in welding together 160 diverse distributorships as a unified system through standardized power service contracts. In Hobday's view, the rhetoric about partnership was overblown. He concluded that the TVA power program was not run by the TVA board but by the authority's engineers, backed by TVA lawyers. The goals of cheap rates and increasing production of power were thus firmly institutionalized.[96]

Hobday reported that TVA engineers originally wanted to create an organization to carry electricity, but the board refused because Lilienthal believed that the public lack of confidence in the utility industry was due to its bigness and remoteness of control. Hobday concluded that despite its limitations, the partnership idea was sound because of TVA's need for local support for its programs, as seen in the popular support Lilienthal mobilized in the Valley during the power fight. TVA might not have survived politically if it had assumed the distribution function and had not managed the creation of local institutions.[97]

Selznick and Hobday saw institutional reality as more complex than Lilienthal depicted. Whatever Lilienthal's private view, he romanticized the facts of participation and local control in his public words. But an analytic and critical focus on participation and cooptation also missed a reality that Lilienthal perhaps understood from his experience. There had been a genuine popular mobilization of opinion in the Tennessee Valley in which Lilienthal's preaching had been matched by the creation of new programs in agriculture, power, and natural resource and community development. The Decatur, Alabama, story was the real one for him. He had told the city leaders that TVA would give them opportunities but that they would have to make the most of them. Formal notions of cooptation, in either form, were academic when set next to the reality of increased mobilization of grass-roots activity in the region in response to TVA programs.

Lilienthal also recognized that TVA could not be effective if it lacked popular support. His rhetoric helped create that support. For example, when TVA wanted to build the Douglas Dam in 1941, against the opposition of Tennessee senator McKellar, delegations of farmers and townspeople favoring the dam visited Washington to plead for it.[98] Of course, this was an instance of TVA's manipulating public opinion against politicians on its own behalf. It was difficult to tell popular mobilization of opinion from organizational propaganda in practice, a distinction about which Lilienthal was not concerned.

Lilienthal's strenuous and enthusiastic appeals to the people of the Valley during the power fight appear to have persuaded him that the grass roots was a reality. He was, in fact, mobilizing the public behind TVA in ways that he could see. At the same time, new municipal power companies and rural electric cooperatives were being created, and he could also see the public excitement about cheap electricity and what it could do for them. The core of the grass-roots ideology may have been forming in his mind for a long time, long before he articulated it as an ideology. In 1947 he wrote: "It is a basic notion of mine that it is only when one deliberately puts himself out on a limb that he gets anything done. Thus, in TVA I took a public position on decentralization . . . before I knew at all fully what this meant or how we would come through. By being on the spot, by my own voluntary and deliberate action, I had to come through—and pretty well did, both in act and in further statements of the philosophy."[99]

The Institutionalization of Myth

Rhetorical leaders, who create the myths by which organizations live, are succeeded by maintaining leaders, who institutionalize those myths.[100] Lilienthal himself contributed to the creation of TVA's organizational culture by his continuous preaching to TVA employees and to the public at large about the virtues of the TVA organizational ideal as embodied in a regional authority. He was succeeded in the leadership of TVA by expert public administrators who maintained the twin myths of technological autonomy and grass-roots participation as guides to action and for defense against efforts at external control. After World War II, TVA used its technological autonomy to become the power company for the Valley, with first steam and then nuclear power installation. The original grass-roots missions of agricultural development and technical assistance to states and communities for natural resource and economic development, once achieved, were succeeded by new recreation and economic development projects in efforts to fulfill the grass-roots ideal. Somewhere along the way, however, the myth became confused with reality within TVA, and the canons of the myth were invoked to defend TVA against criticism of the people whom it was supposed to serve.[101]

In the 1970s and 1980s, TVA lost the support of publics in the Valley. The authority foundered in response to the challenges of environmentalists and rate payers. The organizational autonomy of the first half of the myth seemed to be at odds with the grass-roots ideal as citizens complained about the high cost of electricity, juggling of cost-benefit estimates to justify water projects, and the pollution of the environment by TVA smokestacks. S. David Freeman, the board chairman from 1977 to 1981, deliberately sought to develop new grass-roots missions and participation as an antidote, thereby confirming Lilienthal's belief that TVA's effectiveness depended upon popular support.[102] Both the creativity of articulating the TVA myth and the necessary institutionalization of myth and later organizational rigidity were Lilienthal's legacies to TVA.

TVA's Influence on Lilienthal

Just as Lilienthal shaped the organization, so that experience shaped him. He carried two legacies for the rest of his career: mature skills of rhetorical leadership were forged in the power fight and in the popularization of the myth, and a belief in the necessity of democratic roots for bureaucracy guided his rhetorical style of leadership. For the rest of his life, he preached that the public had to understand, accept, and participate in bureaucratic programs if they were to work.

Lilienthal brought these skills and beliefs to the leadership of the newly created Atomic Energy Commission (AEC) in 1946. But his four years there were frustrating. The mission of the AEC was to oversee the military and peaceful applications of atomic energy through research and development. The military, which had administered the Manhattan Project for the development of the atomic bomb in World War II, was the AEC's chief consumer but was uneasy with the principle of civilian control. Lilienthal sought to apply the lessons learned at TVA but was disappointed. He thought it important that the American people understand the uses and dangers of atomic energy and continually emphasized that without public understanding, intelligent policy could not be developed. He therefore devoted much time and energy to giving talks about atomic energy around the country. But it was difficult to dramatize or hold out much hope for peacetime applications with such a meager base of research and development. And pressures for secrecy on behalf of military security caused much congressional criticism of his candor. He encouraged decentralization of the operations of the AEC and sought to delegate administrative discretion to the heads of regional laboratories. But again, concerns about secrecy and national security made it difficult to operate a decentralized bureaucracy. Perhaps most important, Lilienthal was increasingly uncomfortable with the AEC mission to manufacture atomic weapons. His TVA experience had caused him to conceive of technology in the service of humanity. As hopes for arms control agreements between the United States and the Soviet Union faded, Lilienthal found himself at odds with national policy. His last major action as a public official was to oppose the development of the hydrogen bomb in 1950. By then he was tired and dispirited and wanted only to leave government service.[103]

Five years in private business as an investment banker, from 1950 to 1955, did not give Lilienthal the personal satisfactions he had derived from public service. His journal entries for those years reveal a fascination with the workings of the world of business but frustration at the limiting nature of the work.[104] He wrote a book celebrating the virtues of "big business" in much the same way that he had praised TVA.[105] But he later recalled, "I was quite lost at Lazard Freres, one of the unhappiest, dullest periods of my life."[106]

In 1955 Lilienthal invented a nonbureaucratic organization that would permit him to express his skills and beliefs. The Development and Resources Corporation was an overseas development firm directed by a small staff in New York, with major operations decentralized around the world, in Latin America, Africa, and Iran.[107] It was a perfect vehicle for Lilienthal's skills and beliefs. He was able to preach the virtues of economic development at the grass roots to client governments. It was not a public arena, but he used his rhetorical skills in his work and continued to speak to and write for American audiences until his death in 1981.

There is a final irony, however. The corporation was forced to liquidate its assets after the 1979 revolution in Iran. Most of its overseas work in the preceding years had been in Iran; Lilienthal had preached the grass-roots ideology to the Shah and other Iranian leaders. But the technology of dam building could be transmitted across cultures more easily than the ideologies of American democracy. His wife recalled the impact of the Iranian revolution on Lilienthal: "His [journal] entries in this period, 1978–79, do not adequately reflect the bitterness he felt; so depressed was he by the events in Iran that for weeks at a time he would say nothing to me on the subject."[108]

David Lilienthal was a rhetorical administrative leader. The characteristics of such leadership are rhetoric, the use of organizational myths as the basis for action, and the development of mechanisms of popular control to temper bureaucracy. The strength of such leadership is in its rhetorical power and organizational inventiveness. The weakness is a danger of confusing rhetoric and myths with reality.

Notes

1. *The Journals of David E. Lilienthal*, 7 vols. (New York: Harper & Row, 1964–84).

2. *The Journals of David E. Lilienthal*, vol. 7, *Unfinished Business, 1968–1981* (New York: Harper & Row, 1984), 782.

3. *The Journals of David E. Lilienthal*, vol. 1, *The TVA Years, 1939–1945* (New York: Harper & Row, 1964), 7; page numbers for subsequent quotations from *The TVA Years* are cited parenthetically in the text.

4. John Brooks, "A Second Sort of Life," *Business Adventures* (New York: Weybright & Talley, 1969), 273. Tennessee Senator Kenneth McKellar often opposed Lilienthal and TVA in later years. Lilienthal's mention of "Minerals and Chemicals" refers to the firm that he put on sound financial footing for Lazard Freres, the investment banking firm for which he worked from 1950 to 1955. "D. and R." was the Development and Resources Corporation, which he founded in 1955 and headed until it was dissolved in 1979.

5. Henry Steele Commager, Introduction to Lilienthal, *The TVA Years*, xvi.

6. Lilienthal, *The TVA Years*, 13.

7. Joseph C. Swidler, interview with author, Washington, D.C., 4 July 1981. Swidler wrote the early power contracts with municipalities and was later TVA general counsel.

8. Lilienthal, *The TVA Years*, 14.

9. Ibid., 14–15, 16–17.

10. Ibid., 16–17.

11. Eli W. Clemens, "Public Utility Regulation in Wisconsin since the Reorganization of the Commission in 1931" (Ph.D. diss., University of Wisconsin, 1940), 11.

12. Lilienthal, *The TVA Years*, 16–17.

13. Paul K. Conkin, "Intellectual and Political Roots," in *TVA: Fifty Years of Grass Roots Bureaucracy*, ed. Erwin C. Hargrove and Paul K. Conkin (Urbana: University of Illinois Press, 1983), 22–23.

14. Lilienthal, *The TVA Years*, 102; Thomas K. McCraw, *TVA and the Power Fight, 1933–1939* (Philadelphia: J. B. Lippincott, 1971), 44.

15. Erwin C. Hargrove, "The Task of Leadership: The Board Chairmen," in Hargrove and Conkin, *TVA*, 90–95.

16. Ed Falck, interview with author, Washington, D.C., 21 July 1981. Falck was a young engineer who worked with Joseph Swidler to develop the first power contracts.

17. Hargrove, "The Task of Leadership," 90–95.

18. McCraw, *The Power Fight*, 54–55.

19. Hargrove, "The Task of Leadership," 90–95.

20. Vernon W. Ruttan, "The TVA and Regional Development," in Hargrove and Conkin, *TVA*, 153.

21. Hargrove, "The Task of Leadership," 95.

22. Lilienthal, interview with Charles Crawford, 6 February 1970, Princeton, N.J., TVA Oral History Project, Memphis State University, Memphis, Tenn.

23. Memo, Harcourt A. Morgan to Arthur E. Morgan and David E. Lilienthal, "Proposed Statement of Policy in the Planning Activities of the Tennessee Valley Authority," 3 October 1933, Administrative Files, TVA Technical Library, Knoxville, Tenn., vol. 49, file D54.

24. Hargrove, "The Task of Leadership," 95–98.

25. Harry Wiersma, interview with author, Knoxville, Tenn., 28 May 1981; and Neal Bass, interview with author, Nashville, Tenn., 20 May 1981. Wiersma was an assistant to A. E. Morgan in the early TVA years, and Bass was an assistant to H. A. Morgan and the first TVA chief conservation engineer.

26. Harcourt A. Morgan, Oral History Transcripts, spool 5, Harcourt A. Morgan Papers, University of Tennessee Library, Knoxville, Tenn.

27. Thomas K. McCraw, *Morgan vs. Lilienthal: The Feud within TVA* (Chicago: Loyola University Press, 1970), 63–64.

28. Ibid.

29. David E. Lilienthal and Harcourt A. Morgan, "Memorandum on Organization," 3 August 1933, Curtis-Morgan-Morgan Files, TVA Technical Library.

30. McCraw, *Morgan vs. Lilienthal*, 22.

31. McCraw, *The Power Fight*, 53.

32. Ibid., 54–58; Swidler interview, 4 July 1981.

33. McCraw, *The Power Fight*, 63–66.

34. Ibid., 67–70.

35. Wendell Willkie to President Roosevelt, 14 December 1934 (two letters); Marvin McIntyre to Lilienthal, 19 December 1934; memo, Lilienthal to McIntyre, 1 January 1935; McIntyre to Willkie, n.d., all in David E. Lilienthal Papers, TVA Technical Library.

36. Swidler interview, 4 July 1981; Falck interview, 21 July 1981.

37. McCraw, *The Power Fight*, 61; Lilienthal, interview with Ross Spears (for the film "The Electric Valley"), Princeton, N.J., May 1980.

38. Swidler interview, 4 July 1981.

39. Falck interview, 21 July 1981.

40. Swidler interview, 4 July 1981.

41. Lilienthal, interview with Spears, May 1980.

42. Lilienthal to Eleanor Roosevelt, 2 June 1934, Lilienthal Papers.

43. McCraw, *The Power Fight*, 74.

44. Memo, Lilienthal to President Roosevelt, "Facts about Tupelo," 16 November 1934; Roosevelt speech in Tupelo, Miss., 10 November 1934, both in Lilienthal Papers.

45. McCraw, *The Power Fight*, 122–23.

46. Lilienthal, *The TVA Years*, following 286.

47. Former TVA official, interview with author, Washington, D.C., 21 July 1981.

48. Lilienthal, interview with Crawford, 6 February 1970.

49. Swidler interview, 4 July 1981.

50. McCraw, *The Power Fight*, 124.

51. Lilienthal, interview with Spears, May 1980.

52. U.S. Attorney General Homer Cummings to President Roosevelt, 28 February 1935, Lilienthal Papers.

53. Ashwander v. TVA, 297 U.S. 288 (1936).

54. President Roosevelt to TVA board members, 25 August 1936, Lilienthal Papers; McCraw, *Morgan vs. Lilienthal*, 65–66.

55. McCraw, *Morgan vs. Lilienthal*, 68–71.

56. McCraw, *The Power Fight*, 95, 98–99.

57. Ibid., 101–83.

58. Richard Lowitt, "The TVA: 1933–45," in Hargrove and Conkin, *TVA*, 42.

59. Memo, Lilienthal to President Roosevelt, 12 January 1937, "Power Transmission Pool Negotiation"; and President Roosevelt to Lilienthal and other participants in the power transmission pool negotiations, 25 January 1937, both in Lilienthal Papers.

60. McCraw, *The Power Fight*, 133–38.

61. Lilienthal, *The TVA Years*, 119–20.

62. Brooks, "A Second Sort of Life," 268.

63. Lilienthal, interview with Spears, May 1980.

64. Bass interview, 20 May 1981; Mrs. Ruth Falck, interview with author, Washington, D.C., 22 July 1981. Mrs. Falck was A. E. Morgan's secretary.

65. Lilienthal, interview with Spears, May 1980.

66. McCraw, *The Power Fight*, 131–32.

67. Hargrove, "The Task of Leadership," 95–98.

68. McCraw, *The Power Fight*, 65, 74.

69. Robert A. Caro, *The Years of Lyndon Johnson: The Paths to Power* (New York: Knopf, 1982), chaps. 27, 28.

70. Lilienthal, interview with Spears, May 1980.

71. Ibid.

72. David E. Lilienthal, *TVA, Democracy on the March* (New York: Harper & Brothers, 1944).

73. Philip Selznick, *Leadership in Administration: A Sociological Interpretation* (New York: Harper & Row, 1957), 17–19, 138–40, 150–52.

74. Memo, William C. Fitts, Jr., to Lilienthal, 7 September 1939, Lilienthal Papers.

75. Memo, Earl S. Draper to John B. Blandford, Jr., August 1939, ibid.

76. Memo, Harcourt A. Morgan to President Roosevelt, 23 September 1939, ibid.

77. Lilienthal, *The TVA Years*, 123, 125, 136–38; Memo for record by Gordon Clapp, 3 November 1939, Administrative Files, TVA Technical Library.

78. McCraw, *The Power Fight*, 158.

79. Lilienthal, *The TVA Years*, 667.

80. Ibid., 142.

81. The Port of New York Authority has historically claimed to be a nonpolitical, decentralized government corporation (communication to the author from Jameson Doig).

82. Lilienthal, interview with Spears, May 1980.

83. Swidler interview, 4 July 1981.

84. David E. Lilienthal, "The TVA: An Experiment in the Grass-Roots Administration of Federal Functions" (Address delivered to the Southern Political Science Association, Knoxville, Tenn., 10 November 1939), Lilienthal Papers.

85. Lilienthal, *The TVA Years*, 146.

86. McCraw, *The Power Fight*, 146–48.

87. Lilienthal to Raymond Clapper, 19, 21 September, 4, 9 October 1940, Lilienthal Papers.

88. Lilienthal to Dr. Alvin Johnson, 29 October 1938, ibid.

89. Lilienthal, *The TVA Years*, 155.

90. Lilienthal to E. J. Coil, 13 July 1942; Coil to Lilienthal, 17, 27 July, and 1 August 1942; Alvin Hansen to Lilienthal, 3 July 1942; Lilienthal to Hansen, 15 July 1942, all in Lilienthal Papers.

91. Philip Selznick, *TVA and the Grass Roots: A Study in the Sociology of Formal Organization* (Berkeley: University of California Press, 1949; New York: Harper & Row, 1966), 47–59.

92. Ibid., 3, 4, and 5.

93. Lilienthal, *TVA, Democracy on the March*, 80–81.

94. Selznick, *TVA and the Grass Roots*, chap. 4.

95. Ibid., 238–42.

96. Victor C. Hobday, *Sparks at the Grass Roots: Municipal Distribution of TVA Electricity in Tennessee* (Knoxville: University of Tennessee Press, 1969), 38–50, 60, 71, 233, 240.

97. Ibid., 32–33, 236.

98. Lilienthal, *The TVA Years*, 392.

99. *The Journals of David E. Lilienthal*, vol. 2, *The Atomic Energy Years, 1945–1950* (New York: Harper & Row, 1964), 187.

100. James G. March and Herbert A. Simon, *Organizations* (New York: John Wiley & Son, 1958), 187.

101. Ibid., 37–40; Hargrove, "The Task of Leadership," 101–18.

102. Hargrove, "The Task of Leadership," 113–17; William Bruce Wheeler and Michael J. McDonald, "The 'New Mission' and the Tellico Project, 1945–70," in Hargrove and Conkin, *TVA*, 167–93; Richard A. Couto, "New Seeds at the Grass Roots: The Politics of the TVA Power Program since World War II," ibid., 230–60.

103. Lilienthal, *The Atomic Energy Years*; Richard G. Hewlett and Francis Duncan, *A History of the United States Atomic Energy Commission*, vol. 2, *Atomic Shield, 1947–1952* (University Park and London: Pennsylvania State University Press, 1969), chaps. 11 and 12.

104. *The Journals of David E. Lilienthal*, vol. 3, *Venturesome Years, 1950–1955* (New York: Harper & Row, 1966); Brooks, "A Second Sort of Life," 266–67.

105. David E. Lilienthal, *Big Business: A New Era* (New York: Harper & Row, 1953).

106. Lilienthal, *Unfinished Business*, 790.

107. Lilienthal, *Venturesome Years*.

108. Helen M. Lilienthal, "Editors' Note," in Lilienthal, *Unfinished Business*, xiii; see the excellent paper by Steven M. Neuse, of the University of Arkansas political science department, on the tension between Lilienthal's ideals and reality: "David E. Lilienthal and Public Purpose: A Critical Perspective" (1985).

3

Gifford Pinchot Creates a Forest Service

John Milton Cooper, Jr.

An institution is the lengthened shadow of one man." That celebrated epigram of Ralph Waldo Emerson applies with special force to the United States Forest Service and Gifford Pinchot. As its founding director and guiding spirit, Pinchot cast an extraordinarily long and sharply defined shadow over the Forest Service. Even now, more than eighty years since it began, more than seventy-five years since Pinchot ceased to have any official connection with it, and just over forty years after his death, he continues to exert an influence over it that is unmatched by any other person, living or dead. The attachment of the Forest Service to the Department of Agriculture, despite attempts to relocate it under the Department of Interior, stands as the principal government monument to Pinchot's views and efforts. The agency's major facility, the United States Forest Products Laboratory, owes its inception and location in Madison, Wisconsin, to Pinchot's negotiating skills. What is most important, the peculiar style and spirit of the Forest Service, especially of its central figure, the forest ranger, derive largely from Pinchot's ideas and personal example. Taken together, these and other accomplishments and influences rank him among the most successful institutional innovators in American government.

Yet Gifford Pinchot also illuminates different aspects of the role of the "policy entrepreneur." Pinchot was the first professionally trained American forester, and he spent his young manhood as the country's foremost promoter of "scientific" forestry. As such, he personified knowledge and concern about a particular field translated into institutional practice. But his accomplishments as a forester soon ceased to satisfy him. He expanded his policy horizons to encompass first the whole range of natural resource problems, then the functioning of the federal government, and finally the leading political issues of his time. Although he was in charge of government forestry operations at the federal level for nearly twelve years, he served as chief forester—the title he coined for the head of the Forest Service—for less than five years. This remains the briefest tenure of any chief in the service's history, and Pinchot was the only one to be fired from the job. Likewise, although he served under three presidents, Pinchot wrought nearly all his main feats of institution building and expansion under just one of them, while his dismissal sprang from his inability and unwillingness to adjust to the ways of a new presidential administration. Moreover, during his entire time in the federal government, he served under only one cabinet superior, a secretary of agriculture who was obliging to the point of abdication. Pinchot's career as the father of forestry in the federal government illustrates, therefore, both rewards and pitfalls in policy entrepreneurship.

First American Forester

Perhaps more than most builders of public institutions, Gifford Pinchot gained much of the viewpoint, advantages, and approach of his mature career from his birth and upbringing. He was born on 11 August 1865. His father, James Pinchot, was a well-to-do businessman of French descent, and his maternal grandfather, Amos Eno, was one of the richest men in the United States. Although Pinchot later served as a governor of Pennsylvania and repeatedly ran for office there, he was born in Connecticut, grew up in New York City, with lengthy family sojourns in Europe, and received his education at Phillips Exeter Academy and Yale University, graduating in 1889. His family's wealth ensured that Pinchot never had to earn his own living and allowed him to finance his careers out of his own pocket and their endowments. The family's social prominence and cosmopolitan connections opened doors of opportunity and influence from the outset of his education and work as a forester.[1]

Privileged youth hardly made him a wastrel or idler. Instead, like his intimate friend and patron of his adult years, Theodore Roosevelt, he felt a burning need to prove that his advantages had not unfitted him for social usefulness and demanding activity. Gifford apparently was always a serious and intense boy, and family influences probably played a big part in instilling in him the desire to be useful. His father first pointed him toward forestry. Pinchot remembered being asked shortly before his departure for Yale, "How would you like to be a forester?" The elder Pinchot, who had retired from business soon after Gifford's birth to travel and follow amateur scientific interests, had come to admire European forestry practices and had helped start a private forestry society in the United States. Besides the original suggestion, which Gifford evidently accepted rather docilely, his father also provided the main direction of his training, through books, science courses at Yale, and finally professional study, which had to be pursued in Europe because no forestry schools existed in America. Pinchot studied for part of a year as the first American to attend the French National School of Forestry at Nancy, and through his father's introductions, he met and received advice from the leading European foresters. Back home after a year of schooling and visits to German and Swiss forests, the young man immediately availed himself of paternal contacts to launch himself as the first professional American forester.[2]

Other family influences reinforced his choice of a career, while some conflicted with it. His mother, Mary Jane Pinchot, appears to have instilled a strong sense of religious obligation and social service in her children, and she later abetted the bent toward political insurgency and reform that affected both Gifford and, even more deeply, his younger brother Amos. Those family inclinations meshed neatly with Gifford's professional calling. Ever the potential zealot, as the years passed he viewed forestry increasingly as a defense of the public trust against selfish interests, while he waxed still more enthusiastic over the larger cause of conservation of natural resources. In another way, however, influences from the maternal side clashed with his pursuit of forestry. As Pinchot recalled long afterward, his multimillionaire grandfather Eno "thought highly of business, but very little of Forestry." At least twice his grandfather tried to tempt him away from forestry, finally in 1894 by offering to set him up as his right-hand man in the family enterprises. Although Pinchot declined the offer "with my Father's strong approval," the allegation of impracticality stung him. At the time of his grandfather's offer, Pinchot also recalled, "I was making Forestry pay." More important, subsequently, both as a government forester and as an advocate of conservation, he continually went out of his way to eschew aesthetic considerations and reject wilderness preservation for its own sake, as he preached well-planned, profitable exploitation of natural resources.[3]

Another youthful trait, for which he perhaps owed something to fear of impracticality and which shaped Pinchot's adult careers, was his incorrigible activism. By his own admission, he was no intellectual and read mostly for entertainment. Pinchot rarely sat still for long, and he always preferred being out in the "field" to office work. His claim to the accolade of first professionally trained American forester, though valid, rested on the slender foundation of that single year in France, Germany, and Switzerland which included scant hours in the classroom and laboratory. Spurning his European mentors' urging to remain longer and earn an advanced degree, Pinchot insisted on an early return home to begin practicing what he had learned. In fact, Pinchot never did learn much botany, horticulture, ecology, geology, or meteorology—the scientific bases of forestry. His training left him a generalist rather than a specialist in forestry, and breadth rather than depth of his acquaintance with the field fitted nicely with his activism and insistence on practicality. This combination of personality traits and approach to forestry underlay many of his greatest successes and perhaps some of his subsequent failures as a policy entrepreneur.[4]

One other legacy of his youth marked Pinchot more deeply still and had perhaps the strongest effect on his institutional innovations. His compulsion to compensate for a privileged upbringing included not just a vent for social service and economic utility but also a zest for elemental physical challenge. A college athlete with a tough, lanky build, Pinchot differed from Roosevelt, who had been a sickly child, but he displayed a similar yearning to show that he could hold his own against people of rougher origins in trials of strength, daring, endurance, and prowess. In 1897 the naturalist John Muir noted that on a wilderness expedition in Oregon the only member of the party who slept outside during the rainstorms was Pinchot. In his forties, as chief forester, he delighted in outdoing younger colleagues on the trail. "He could outride and outshoot any ranger on the force," recalled one of them. "If a camp was within a mile of a stream of any size, he invariably had his morning plunge; and if the stream came from a snowbank a few miles up-canyon all the better." Pinchot's insatiable appetite for proving himself physically probably played the largest role of any of his youthful inclinations in putting his personal stamp on the Forest Service.[5]

Shaping public institutions did not immediately appeal to the newly minted forester when he returned to America in 1890. Pinchot relied once more on his father's contacts to confer with prominent people about how to get started. His advisers included Bernhard Fernow, head of the Forestry Division of the Department of Agriculture, who offered the young man a position as his assistant. Pinchot declined. He recognized that the fledgling Forestry Division, which had previously limped along as a one-man operation on meager, nonpermanent budget allocations, did not provide a promising launching pad for his career. He also sensed that his personality and approach to forestry would not wear well with Fernow, a painstaking German-born and educated forester who stressed silviculture—the technical study of tree growing—and highly detailed surveys of forests. Pinchot decided instead to set up an office in New York as a free-lance private forester, operating in effect as a forestry consultant. His private income and connections greatly facilitated his choice. His first major client was a family acquaintance, George Vanderbilt, who hired him to develop plans for the maintenance and use of the forests of Vanderbilt's estate in the North Carolina mountains, Biltmore. There Pinchot was able to apply the knowledge of selective thinning and logging, reforestation, and watershed protection that he had trained for in Europe and to try to prove that forest management could be at least self-supporting if not highly profitable. The young man also wrote about forestry for magazines, spoke extensively to various organizations, and prepared an exhibit advertising his work at Biltmore for the 1893 Columbian Exposition in Chicago.[6]

Pinchot spent a little over seven years in the private practice of forestry, and he regarded the time as indispensable preparation for public service. Paid assignments and self-financed travels sent him throughout the country to visit forests, gauge potential support and opposition to forestry practices, learn the ways of business and government, and get to know people. When he returned from Europe in 1890, Pinchot recalled, not a single acre in the United States was under forest management. "The American people had no understanding either of what Forestry was or of the bitter need for it." His first task, therefore, was to create a demand for his services. He did that in two main ways. One was through the contacts he made not only in Washington but also among leaders in the lumber and cattle businesses and advocates of agricultural irrigation, all of whom were already beginning to grasp the value of careful management of forests to their enterprises. The other, even more important way Pinchot strove to stimulate demand for forestry was through publicity. He cultivated editors of metropolitan newspapers and national magazines, as well as local and regional journalists, particularly in the West. He not only spoke and wrote incessantly about forestry but never missed a chance to hammer away at his message that forestry meant profitable, practical use of timber resources, not beautification or preservation for their own sake. "Forestry has nothing whatever to do with planting of roadside trees," he asserted in 1894, adding that "scenery is altogether outside its province, and that it is no more possible to learn Forestry in an arboretum than to learn surgery in a drug store."[7]

At no time, however, did private forestry banish thoughts of government work from Pinchot's mind. In 1894 he told a friend that he regarded his consulting practice as "training for Head Forester of the United States." Years later he recalled that the federal government exerted an "enormous attraction for a forester." The public domain, largely in the West, contained so much of the forested lands of the United States, and—still more alluring to a man of Pinchot's activist temperament—"they were under one and only one ownership and control."

Pinchot did not shun public work during his years of private practice. He once accompanied Fernow as an unpaid volunteer on a forest survey, and he prepared a plan for state forest lands in New York. Most important, he wangled a place on the Forest Commission, the expert group appointed by President Grover Cleveland in 1896 to study and recommend procedures for managing federal forest lands. The other members of the Forest Commission, headed by a Harvard University botanist, angered and frustrated Pinchot by their insistence on working in secret, their refusal to employ foresters in their investigations, and their stress on preservation rather than use of forests. A storm of protest blew up in the West in February 1897 when Cleveland adopted the commission majority's recommendation to sequester 21 million acres of new forest reserves. Pinchot publicly dissented from that recommendation. The ensuing controversy confirmed him in his conviction that he knew a better way to run government forestry, particularly through publicity and outreach to groups concerned about use of forests.[8]

Pinchot did not have to wait long for a chance to show the way. Early in 1898, Fernow resigned his post as head of the Forestry Division of the Department of Agriculture to become director of the first American school of forestry, at Cornell University. William McKinley had replaced Cleveland in the White House the year before, and his new secretary of agriculture, James Wilson, promptly offered Fernow's job to Pinchot. A meeting with Wilson produced assurances, Pinchot recorded in his diary, that "if I would take the Forestry Division I could run it to suit myself. I could appoint my own assistants, do what kind of work I chose, and not fear any interference from him." Wilson meant what he said. The secretary told Pinchot that he had been about to fire Fernow, who had aroused congressional criticism for his plodding ways and ill-fated experiments with rainmaking, when the Cornell post had materialized. Wilson knew what he was getting in Pinchot. During the next twelve years, as the two men served under three administrations, the cabinet superior gave his hyperactive forester almost totally free rein. Pinchot hesitated briefly before accepting, and he had to go through the formality of taking a civil service examination, which he drew up himself. On 1 July 1898 the thirty-two-year-old Pinchot became head of the Forestry Division. "I was highly enthusiastic and deeply pleased," he recalled. "Yet the prospect was something less than brilliant."[9]

Those mixed feelings suited his situation and his prospects. Much had improved since Pinchot's return from Europe in 1890. Federal government science had grown in scope and prestige, thanks to the work, and even more to the promotional efforts, of such men as John Wesley Powell and W. J. McGee of the Geological Survey and F. H. Newell of the Reclamation Bureau, whose agencies were under the Interior Department. These men, particularly Powell and McGee, resembled Pinchot in that their formal training in their scientific disciplines was slight and that they functioned primarily as organizers, enthusiasts, and evangelists for the study and management of natural resources. Secretary Wilson, formerly a professor at the Iowa State Agricultural College, likewise intended to expand scientific work under his department. Pinchot's eight years of publicizing and practicing forestry on the outside also were a help. An embryonic constituency for forest preservation and management had formed among naturalists, sportsmen, and some lumbermen and cattle ranchers. An alliance was also starting to coalesce between them and farmers concerned about water resources for irrigation in semiarid regions of the West.[10]

The more strictly bureaucratic aspect of Pinchot's new position was less heartening. Despite recent growth, the Forestry Division remained a tiny, struggling outfit. All ten employees worked in one large room; only the head had a (cramped) private office. The staff included a single stenographer and one messenger, and its physical assets comprised scanty furnishings and a grab bag of outdated field equipment. The division's entire appropriation totaled only $28,250, of which $3,500 was Pinchot's salary. At once Pinchot began lobbying Congress for increased funds for staff and equipment. He testified persuasively and privately cultivated senators and congressmen, and he profited from the contacts and efforts of Secretary Wilson, a former congressman from Iowa. As a result, Pinchot got the appropriation raised to $48,520 during his first year; the next year he secured a further rise to $88,250. In July 1901, thanks mainly to his own lobbying on Capitol Hill and his extensive cultivation among various constituencies, Pinchot brought off the twin coups of more than doubling the appropriation—to $185,440—and getting the agency elevated in status, with the new title Bureau of Forestry. Meanwhile, the staff grew from what Pinchot dubbed the "original 11" to 179. Pinchot was acquiring the tools to implement his policy designs.[11]

The opposing influences of outside support and organizational constraint shaped much of Pinchot's work during his first seven years as the top government forester. Outreach to sympathetic people and groups and the defusing of opposition became two of his most insistent tasks. Publicity and speechmaking remained high priorities, as his staff cranked out reams of press releases about forestry and their own activities. Pinchot made the acquaintance of editors and reporters, whom he frequently invited to dinner and social gatherings at the mansion he and his mother built in 1900 on Scott Circle, in Washington's most fashionable neighborhood. Because he remained a bachelor until he was nearly fifty and after he had left the government, Pinchot had few distractions from his public career. He spent much of the year traveling, partly on agency business but more often to speak to just about any group that invited him. Particularly high on his wooing list were lumbermen, cattle and sheep grazers, timber-consuming mine owners, and their various organizations. In part, Pinchot was sharpening commitments to forest protection and management among groups that were already concerned over the depletion of timber resources and the assurance of water supplies for agriculture and town growth. But he was also building a clientele for the activist, expensive practice of forestry that he wanted to conduct. From early in Pinchot's tenure, his agency conducted surveys of woodlands for timber owners, and it later calculated and published yardstick prices for the lumber industry. The forester also reached outside to gain further allies. He quickly sided with western stockmen in their fight to open more public lands to cattle and sheep grazing, which was hampered by restrictive policies of the Interior Department and opposition from sportsmen and wilderness preservationists. These controversies prefigured the split in the conservation movement that would array Pinchot against leading naturalists, most notably John Muir.[12]

At the same time, even as he expanded and upgraded his agency, Pinchot made creative use of limits set by congressional jealousy and parsimony. He admitted that his wealth allowed him to forgo ever asking for an increase in his own salary, thereby gaining, he believed, a psychological advantage in pressing House and Senate committees for raises for subordinates. Pinchot's frugality and drive for practicality promoted efficiency in the Forestry Division and the Bureau of Forestry. In 1900 his agency became the first arm of the federal government to adopt the then novel system of vertical filing. Informality, speed, and hard work flowed from both Pinchot's directives and his example. He immediately abandoned his title, head of the Forestry Division, preferring to be called simply "the Forester." The staff referred to him as "G.P.," and after the founding of the Forest Service and his new title, as "the chief." All correspondence had to be acknowledged within twenty-four hours of receipt, and if special attention was required, a date for a full response was supplied in forty-eight hours. Pinchot's distaste for sitting behind a desk did not prevent him from putting in at least ten-hour days when he was in the office. The staff knew they were expected to emulate him.[13]

To stretch appropriation dollars, Pinchot drew upon ingenuity and personal and family funds. He served the dual purpose of expanding the agency's workforce and providing training for would-be foresters by hiring male college students to work as summer assistants, in the field and at headquarters. Some of the student assistants and new staff members received loans from Pinchot to tide them over until their first paycheck, while several lived for various periods in his house. Frequent invitations to the Pinchot home for what came to be called "baked-apple parties" also served several purposes. Copious quantities of milk, gingerbread, and baked apples furnished free meals for scantily paid assistants and junior staff members. Their chief's hospitality blended with his enthusiasm and sense of mission to inspire these fresh recruits to the cause of forestry. The founding of the Society of American Foresters, which also met for such occasions, allowed the agency staff to mix with sympathizers from other parts of the government and private life.[14]

In addition to supporting their elder son with relatively modest benefactions, the Pinchot family subsidized his profession in a major way. Even before he entered the government, Pinchot recognized that the dearth of trained foresters stood as a major obstacle in the path of his policy goals. Few Americans had the money or the command of languages to follow in his footsteps to Europe. The new forestry school at Cornell did not offer a promising alternative in Pinchot's eyes because of what he regarded as Fernow's shortcomings, as well as insufficient financial support, which caused it to close down in 1903. To fill the breach, Pinchot persuaded his parents to found a school of forestry at Yale, which began operations in 1900. The initial endowment from the family was $150,000, subsequently raised to $300,000. The Pinchots also set up a summer session for the Yale students at their country estate in Milford, Pennsylvania. The school's first dean was Pinchot's second in command in the Forestry Division, Henry S. Graves, who later succeeded him as chief forester. The availability of forestry training allowed Pinchot to make a forestry degree the unwritten requirement for a career in his agency. No official ties existed with the Yale forestry school, but as one early staff member recalled, "relations could not be other than intimate." Those relationships, together with Pinchot's penchant for hiring classmates and college friends, earned the Forestry Division and Bureau and the early Forest Service the nickname "the Yale Club."[15]

These activities set precedents for Pinchot's later accomplishments with the Forest Service. Building and maintaining constituencies among private interests would remain a hallmark of the agency's policies, while frugality and efficiency would continue to characterize its operations. Significant as those matters were, however, they did not represent Pinchot's major policy aim. From the beginning of his government service, he was not content to run an agency whose chief work was to serve private owners of forest lands and to persuade them to practice scientific forestry of their own volition. Rather, what he called his "chief object in life" as a government forester was always to gain control of the vast forested tracts of the public lands in the West. Virtually everything he did during his first seven years in government served that goal. Publicity, outreach, and internal efficiency made his agency more visible, more popular, and more capable not just to aid and promote private forestry but, more important, to advance its bid to manage the government's own forests. Busy as he was in the office, in the field, and on the speaking circuit, Pinchot devoted his greatest energies and shrewdest thought to getting jurisdiction over the forest reserves on the public lands transferred from the Interior Department to his agency. The transfer, which took place in 1905, was Pinchot's first great triumph as a policy entrepreneur.[16]

Bringing off that feat required not only lobbying skill of a high order but also a stroke of luck that bordered on the miraculous. Pinchot's quest arose from the muddled history of both his own agency and the forest reserves. Government forestry had found a home in the Department of Agriculture mainly because the lone-handed botanists who had preceded Fernow had likewise emphasized close study of trees and silviculture; evidently, no one had thought about relocating the miniscule Forestry Division. Meanwhile, public concern had arisen around the mid-1890s over the danger of a "timber famine" raised by the massive consumption of wood for building construction, agricultural fencing, mine tunneling, and especially railroad ties and trestles. President Cleveland's acceptance of the Forest Commission's recommendation to remove huge expanses of government-owned forest land in the West from all use had placed these reserves under the Interior Department, thereby creating the anomalous situation that greeted Pinchot when he entered the government in 1898. The forester—soon to be joined by other foresters—was under one department, while the forests were under another department.

The simplest solution might have been to move the foresters to the Interior Department, or so it appeared to a number of people then and later. From Pinchot's standpoint, the opposite solution had far more appeal, and he seized upon the outcry against Cleveland's action as an argument for transferring the forests to his agency. Most of the protests against the new reserves had come from westerners, who feared that land and resources essential to their region's developments were being locked away forever. In his cultivation of westerners, lumbermen, and stock raisers, Pinchot made his pitch for forestry on grounds of exploitation, albeit responsible exploitation, of these reserves. It was ironic, in view of the Interior Department's later reputation for excessive friendliness to developers, that officials there tended to side with wilderness preservationists and to favor creation of parks and recreation areas in the forest reserves. The irony would deepen after 1905 when Pinchot's Forest Service policies and conservation advocacy stirred up the wrath of development-minded westerners, but their support played a critical part in his getting control of the forest reserves.[17]

Pinchot's assiduous cultivation of influential interests and his patient lobbying among powerful senators and congressmen, together with Secretary Wilson's indispensable support, might have paid off sooner or later, but a fortuitous event in September 1901 hastened the transfer of the reserves and the birth of the Forest Service. When President McKinley's assassination catapulted Theodore Roosevelt into the White House, Pinchot's public career took a fantastic turn upward. Roosevelt shared Pinchot's developing views on conservation, the one area in which the new president, whose dynamic personality and blustery manner masked cautious political methods, was ready to get out in front of public opinion and take bold action. Even more important to Pinchot were the social and temperamental likenesses that forged a bond between himself and Roosevelt. Coming as they did from the same upper-class New York circles and sharing an ardor for the outdoors, the pair had already formed a close friendship, which soon made Pinchot a presidential confidant. During the next seven and a half years he usually called at the White House twice a day when he was in Washington, and he frequently accompanied Roosevelt on hikes, horseback rides, and camping and hunting trips, on which the two men constantly vied with each other in demonstrating their physical hardihood.[18]

The boon of the new president's backing soon became apparent. Roosevelt's first annual message to Congress, in December 1901, included a strong plea, written by Pinchot, for new governmental initiatives in the management of natural resources, particularly the transfer of the forest reserves to the Bureau of Forestry. When Congress failed to act on the request during the next three years, Roosevelt issued an even stronger call in his December 1904 message, which came just a month after his smashing election victory. This time Congress responded swiftly, and the Transfer Act, which turned over the reserves and created the Forest Service, was signed into law on 1 February 1905. Actually, it took a lot more than public pronouncements from the White House to break the legislative logjam. Besides lobbying senators and congressmen, Roosevelt augmented Pinchot's publicity efforts by cultivating editors and reporters on behalf of natural resource concerns in general and the Forestry Bureau in particular. More important, the president eased out of office a commissioner of public lands who was the chief opponent of the transfer within the government, and he appointed Pinchot to presidential commissions on public lands and government scientific work, which the forester used as particularly effective platforms for gaining support for transfer of the forest service.[19]

Yet, despite the obvious benefits, Roosevelt's patronage proved a mixed blessing. Passage of the Transfer Act fulfilled Pinchot's aims as a forester. At last he had both the means and the scope to implement the plans that had led him to enter public service. But Pinchot's changed status carried a price. Roosevelt's succession transformed him from an ambitious bureau chief with clearly focused interests into an intimate adviser and favored agent of the president over the entire sweep of natural resource issues and beyond. The first two years of Roosevelt's second term, 1905 and 1906, marked the apex of both men's careers. Pinchot wrought prodigious feats of institutional innovation as he shaped the Forest Service, and he made himself a national figure as a champion of conservation second only to Roosevelt. Yet already he was overreaching the bounds of forestry and even of concern for natural resources. By the last two years of Roosevelt's presidency, he would embroil himself thoroughly in the conflict between reformers and conservatives that was starting to tear the Republican party apart. The stage was set for the spectacular collapse of his official career.

The Birth of the Forest Service

The founding of the Forest Service brought Gifford Pinchot's finest hour. Although he believed that the transfer of the reserves "meant a revolutionary change" for his agency, much continued as before, only on a bigger scale. Like the Forestry Division and Bureau before it, the Forest Service operated frugally and efficiently and relied on publicity and outreach. Pinchot had already delegated much of the responsibility for internal administration and publicity to his second in command, Overton Price, while he concentrated more than ever on larger questions of policy and strategy and on public speaking. An expanded force and more extensive facilities brought no diminution in the promptness and clarity with which the agency executed its tasks. One of Pinchot's proudest moments came in 1908 when he commissioned a firm of private business consultants to evaluate the three-year-old Forest Service. Besides finding an extraordinarily high level of intelligence and dedication among the staff, the consultants concluded, "The volume of business transacted, in our opinion, compares most favorably with that in commercial practice, and is worthy of the highest commendation."[20]

The forest reserves also provided Pinchot with a new way to prove his practicality. Previously, the Interior Department had permitted limited logging operations on a fixed-fee basis, with the proceeds going into general revenues. Pinchot thought he saw an opportunity to make the reserves self-sufficient or perhaps even to make them return a surplus which might free the Forest Service from annual congressional appropriations. Accordingly, he saw to it that the Transfer Act included a provision reserving revenues from leasing timber, mineral, and grazing rights to the Forest Service. Once he took over the reserves, Pinchot expanded logging and opened it to competitive bidding. The average price per thousand board feet rose from $1.15 to $7, and Forest Service revenues nearly doubled, from $767,219 in 1905/6 to $1,300,000 in 1906/7. While the practice was economically attractive though competitive, it had political drawbacks. Only the largest lumber companies could pay the new prices, and smaller operators quickly grew to resent Forest Service restrictions. With grazing rights Pinchot was more cautious: he set fees low enough, he hoped, not to shut out less affluent cattle and sheep ranchers. Not only did the effort fail but, ironically, the political fallout from Pinchot's attempt to make Forest Service management of the reserves a paying proposition set off a train of events that contributed to his downfall.[21]

The chief forester gave his most impressive demonstration of overcoming financial restraints when he set up his agency's major installation, the Forest Products Laboratory. Roosevelt's succession had placed the greatest patron of science since Thomas Jefferson in the White House, and he had accelerated the growth of government scientific work that was already under way. Determined to rationalize the Forest Service's research activities and to carry out Roosevelt's mandate, in 1906 Pinchot called a conference of wood products manufacturers and users to publicize the need for a national wood-testing laboratory. When Congress predictably balked at financing the project, the chief forester hatched a plan to establish the laboratory in conjunction with a major university, which would supply land, furnish utilities, and share in research. The state universities of Michigan and Wisconsin emerged as the leading contenders. Pinchot privately favored Wisconsin from the outset, but he played the university administrations and politicians of both states off against each other and invited in a third competitor, Minnesota, to drive down the cost to the Forest Service. Wisconsin finally prevailed, and the new facility opened its doors at a site in Madison on the edge of the university campus in June 1910. Although Pinchot had left the government by then, the Forest Products Laboratory would stand as the greatest physical legacy of his tenure as chief forester.[22]

Despite his exaggeration of the novelty of his situation, Pinchot believed correctly that his work changed radically after 1905. Management of government forest lands, which were already extensive and grew vaster still thanks to Roosevelt's actions, necessarily altered the primary focus of Pinchot's agency. Whereas the Forestry Division and Bureau had concentrated on promoting voluntary adoption of forestry practices by private owners, the Forest Service devoted the bulk of its attention to enforcing such practices in places where it exercised virtually unlimited authority. The Forest Service not only put less time and effort than its predecessor agencies into private forestry but also slanted the well-established outreach and publicity programs increasingly toward the cultivation of support for its management and further expansion of the government reserves. Many years later, Pinchot admitted that concentration on the public forest lands had led him to neglect the more important area of privately owned woodlands. It remained a keen source of regret to the end of his life that the United States never adopted regulations to govern private forests like those in most European countries. He ruefully conceded that his own concentration on public forests had contributed to that failure.[23]

The shift in focus away from private forestry likewise contributed to the erosion of political support that subsequently undermined Pinchot's position. But before that happened, he made his most significant and lasting accomplishment. The extent and location of the forest reserves and the need for enforcement required a fundamental change in both the size of his agency's staff and the kind of work it did. The extent of the forest reserves—nearly 200 million acres by the time Pinchot left office—and their location—mostly in remote areas of the West—presented formidable administrative obstacles. Nearly all the officers managing those reserves would have to work alone, most of the time out of touch with headquarters. Moreover, although they would be working in attractive outdoor settings during fair weather, the West's long, severe winters would increase their isolation. Finally, the officers would have to enforce fairly complicated technical regulations over people who neither understood nor liked the whole idea of forest management. As Herbert Kaufman pointed out in his classic study *The Forest Ranger*, carrying out that potentially daunting assignment has been the signal accomplishment of the Forest Service.[24]

The credit for establishing the practices and norms that have permitted that accomplishment belongs at Pinchot's door. He met the challenge both by expanding his staff and further streamlining his agency and, more significantly, by spawning a new breed of government servant—the forest ranger. The Forest Service staff grew from 821 in 1905 to 2,536 when Pinchot left in 1910. The largest increase occurred in the newly created ranger force, which numbered 384 in 1905 and included 1,293 at Pinchot's departure. Expenditures also rose, from $508,886 in 1904/5 to $979,519 in 1905/6 and $1,830,000 in 1906/7. Pinchot's practices of expanding logging and competitive bidding on the reserves reduced but did not eliminate deficits, and he sought new ways to make the agency self-sufficient. To manage the expanded, far-flung force, the Forest Service established three district offices, soon increased to six. Pinchot's watchwords in organizing his new service were decentralization, informality, and communication. He insisted that the man in the field must be presumed the best judge of the situation, and he encouraged rangers to go outside channels to raise new ideas. Pinchot himself continued to delight in sharing the hardships of the trail with his men, and other supervisors were expected to do likewise.[25]

Pinchot's best efforts went into recruiting and training the men who would manage the forests—the Forest Rangers. In much of what he did with them he simply carried on the largely instinctive methods he had used earlier with new staff members, student assistants, and Yale forestry students. The "baked-apple parties" remained a fixture of agency life, but now new rangers sometimes found themselves rubbing elbows with the president of the United States. By all accounts, Pinchot excelled at inculcating dedication in his recruits. In 1909 a western newspaper observed that the young men of the Forest Service acted "as if they had been inoculated with the Roosevelt-Pinchot virus" and that, even more striking, Pinchot's own enthusiasm was his ability to "spread the contagion." Inspirational as he might be at home or on the speaker's platform, Pinchot acquired added powers in the field. William Greeley, a young ranger who later rose to be chief forester himself, recounted that on the trail "my admiration for the boss grew with every mile." Besides being "very much a man's man" and showing off his prowess as an outdoorsman, "G.P." shared his plans and visions around the campfire. "He made us all—rangers and fire guards and Mexican boys building trail—feel like soldiers in a patriotic cause. He was an outstanding evangelist and a great leader of men."[26]

Parties at a palatial home with the high and mighty, zestful treks in woods and mountains, inspirational gatherings under the stars by firelight—each represented an aspect of Pinchot's personality that he impressed on the rangers. Though democratic and informal in manner, he could not have hidden his upper-class origins if he had wanted to. Instead, like Roosevelt, he lent an aura of social glamour to his enterprises, while the Yale connection reinforced the sense of selection to an exclusive club. Physical challenge loomed largest in the example Pinchot set. Far from mitigating the notion of social desirability, his feats of horsemanship, gunplay, and woodcraft heightened the imagery of gentlemanly sport. Pinchot's evangelism likewise drew upon both elements. The cause to which he called his rangers was at once socially elevated, since it disdained material reward, and physically exciting, since it involved hardship and danger. Even Pinchot's appearance—the lean, sinewy physique, the burning brown eyes, the long, desperado-style moustache, the broad-brimmed hat worn at a rakish angle—helped him cut a romantic figure. Withal, he furnished a legend of heroic beginnings for the Forest Service.[27]

Important as that legend was, it did not go to the heart of Pinchot's achievement with the Forest Service and the Forest Rangers. His lasting innovations sprang from how he institutionalized his approach and example. The chief worked in large and small ways to make his agency distinctive. In place of the regular signs that most government offices used, Pinchot had a wooden plaque designed with the silhouette of a tree to identify all Forest Service facilities. As part of his stress on the man in the field, he had the service's regulations printed in readable form and in a binding small enough to fit into a ranger's breast pocket. The title he chose was the *Use Book*, which both stated the chief's expectation for the regulations and implied his whole philosophy of forestry. Staff members, unlike most civil servants, soon fell into the practice of saying that they worked for the Forest Service, rather than the government or their department. At the same time, Pinchot increasingly cherished the service's location under the Department of Agriculture because that set it apart from the other natural resource bureaus, under the Interior Department. He also grew to appreciate the utility of the Agriculture Department connection as a defense against what he regarded as less responsible development interests, which exerted so much influence over the Interior Department and its congressional oversight committees.[28]

Pinchot's greatest institutional accomplishment was the creation of the Forest Rangers. From the outset, he set them apart from a humdrum lot of forest managers, not only by personal inspiration but also by introducing special forms of identification, testing, and training. The name *ranger* itself lent distinction and appeal to the new force. The term had been in use in America since colonial times to denote mounted soldiers and had more recently been associated with a famous frontier police force, the Texas Rangers. Because of the rangers' law-enforcement duties, Pinchot sponsored a contest among agency employees to design a badge, which rangers were required to wear. Impressed in part by the practice of the Geological Survey, Pinchot also decided early on that forest rangers needed a uniform. Even before the Forest Service was formally installed, the chief-to-be appointed a committee to select the uniform, which came into use in 1906. Over succeeding decades, as the rangers' work in the office or in the field entailed law enforcement less and less, both the badge and the uniform would strike some inside and outside the Forest Service as superfluous accoutrements for officers of a civilian agency. Yet repeated surveys have found that the great majority of forest rangers favor retention of the badge and the uniform, even though on most assignments they are no longer required.[29]

By creating the Forest Ranger force as a special and self-conscious body within the government service, Pinchot created the bureaucratic mechanism for overcoming the administrative obstacles entailed by his agency's new assignment. As Kaufman argued, the rangers socialize their members to a set of values and a way of life, so that by internalizing those norms, they maintain high professional standards despite their decentralized organization and largely isolated conditions. Pinchot's model for the rangers was not hard to see. Their name's earliest connotation, the wearing of uniforms, and Greeley's observation that the chief likened them to "soldiers in a holy cause" all betrayed military motifs. What Pinchot created with the Forest Rangers was the closest equivalent in civilian government to an elite military force. The military analogy went beyond symbolism. The Forest Ranger ranks originally were open only to men. The force would remain all-male until the first woman was appointed in 1979. Tests for appointment included not only a written forestry examination but also physical trials at riding, shooting, axe handling, and camping. Although rangers differed from soldiers in working mostly alone, their early training inculcated institutional pride and identification, while frequent, unannounced inspections ensured that each ranger's station came up to rigorous standards of design and cleanliness.[30]

The highest utility of Pinchot's military model lay in allowing him to institutionalize his personal example. Like Roosevelt, he sought to apply the aristocratic virtues of devotion to duty, physical hardihood and courage, and nonmaterial aspirations in a democratic, commercialized, industrial society. The Forest Service and especially the Forest Rangers supplied the practical means to apply those virtues. For all their rough-hewn woodsiness, the rangers partook of the same social glamour as such specially exalted military officers as cavalrymen earlier and pilots and commandos later. Their dedication and their physicality spared them much of the stigma usually attached to government employees. The same western newspaper that marveled at Pinchot's contagious enthusiasm found the rangers "free from the taint of bureaucracy," having instead "the 'tang' of the woods about most of them as if they were fit to do their century [course of calisthenics] on a moment's notice or climb a Colorado peak for the love of the thing." Above all, the rangers' consecration to "service" carried the same connotations of patriotism, comradeship, and scorn for material comfort as military service. Fittingly, the Forest Rangers carried on Pinchot's romantic image to become the only civilian arm of government to have adventure novels and stories for children written about it.[31]

For the chief and his men, the first three years of the Forest Service constituted what Roosevelt liked to call their "crowded hour." It was a time of exhausting labors, fierce concentration and commitment, tension and excitement, and glowing convictions of doing great deeds that would last for generations. Looking back over nearly half a century, William Greeley remembered those days as "the Golden Age," when he and his comrades "were privileged to become G.P.'s ranger inspectors and supervisors in the thrilling job of setting up national forests on a hundred million acres of the raw West. It was a job packed with strange experiences and high adventure." Pinchot drove the rangers the way he drove himself. "The chief expected us to be supermen," Greeley recalled. "He wanted everything done at once." Even under calmer conditions and a less demanding boss, the Forest Service would have had its hands full establishing facilities, blazing trails, and surveying the trees, terrain, and water resources on the millions of acres that came under its control in 1905. Pinchot's opening the reserves faster to logging and grazing and introducing competitive bidding for timber operations added to the workload.[32]

What strained and excited the Forest Service most, however, was the rapid expansion of the reserves during its first two years. Ever since Roosevelt's succession to the presidency, more millions of acres of the public lands in the West had gone into the reserves. These additions had gradually aroused opponents in the West, who echoed the earlier outcries against Cleveland's removals. The most dramatic episode in the Forest Service's new life occurred in February 1907 when Congress attached a rider to the agricultural appropriation bill that took away the president's power to create further reserves in six western states. Roosevelt responded with his most arrogant display of presidential power. He flouted the spirit of the congressional mandate by authorizing the establishment of twenty-one new reserves, a total of sixteen million acres, in ten days before he signed the bill. "We knew precisely what we wanted," Pinchot recounted. The Forest Service had already geared up to assist. The chief assigned the entire Washington staff to the project. They worked around the clock. Telegraph lines hummed with information from field men in the affected region. Pinchot practically lived at the White House. He and Roosevelt spread maps all over the floor of the president's study and crawled on their hands and knees to draw up the boundaries of the new reserves.[33]

Such heady experiences were more thrilling than constructive. By 1907, as the congressional move showed, opposition to Pinchot's policies had grown to formidable proportions, and Roosevelt's response enraged opponents even more. Criticism of the chief forester sprang from diverse quarters and took different grounds. As earlier, development-minded westerners supplied the most vocal and politically potent resistance. Much of their opposition continued to reflect fears of being shut out of land and resources, particularly on the part of smaller farmers, ranchers, and loggers. Although Pinchot and Roosevelt liked to depict themselves as champions of the common people, they drew much of the western support for their forestry and conservation policies from bigger lumber and grazing interests, who could afford to take a longer view of the resources they were consuming. Water use on the reserves emerged as a singularly divisive issue because it pitted proponents of watershed protection for forest and grassland maintenance against advocates of diversion for agriculture, mining, and manufacturing. More generally, both the sequestering of lands and the introduction of regulations ran afoul of what Pinchot derisively dubbed the "pioneer attitude" of individualistic westerners who resented being told what to do and what not to do.[34]

To the extent that the chief's activism and impatience aggravated western opposition, blame for the Forest Service's troubles also belonged at his door. Some within the service and the Agriculture Department developed doubts about Pinchot's methods. A couple of years of managing a forest in California and working with local lumbermen tempered Greeley's idolization. "I became convinced that we were trying to accomplish too many changes all at once," he concluded. The massive creation of new reserves in 1907 bred disquiet in the normally complaisant Secretary Wilson. When he had to sign the orders that actually set up the reserves, Wilson questioned Pinchot about whether the action might not be regarded as breaking faith with Congress. "Have you thought this over carefully?" the Secretary asked. When Pinchot assured him that everything was all right, he replied, "Then let the matter go." Officials in the Interior Department, particularly in the Bureau of Public Lands, understandably resented the chief forester's bureaucratic encroachments at their expense.[35]

Much of the anti-Pinchot sentiment within the government, both in the Interior Department and on Capitol Hill, reflected sympathy with western desires for development. But some of his severest critics parted company with him for opposite reasons. The wilderness preservationists, sportsmen, and naturalists, dismissed in Pinchot's circle as "nature lovers," had long disagreed with his emphasis on exploitation of the reserves, while his policies of opening them to logging and grazing, especially sheep grazing, had drawn open denunciations, most notably from Muir and his cohorts. The rift between Pinchot and the preservationists was ironic because the forester had more than a bit of the "nature lover" in him. On the trail, he reveled in sheer delight at the sights and sounds of the wilderness, and his religious faith had a strain resembling the mystical pantheism that inspired a number of preservationists.

Pinchot's need to prove his practicality usually overrode any leanings that might have reconciled him to the Muir group, particularly when local western support was at stake. Not all westerners opposed him, and in one state he stood high in public esteem; that was, again ironically, Muir's home state of California. Much of the chief forester's support came from fast-growing cities, towns, and irrigated farm areas anxious to assure future supplies of water. The forest reserves enjoyed great popularity because they protected watersheds needed for reservoirs, and the California congressional delegation got their state exempted from the 1907 ban on further presidentially created reserves. Pinchot gladly repaid the Californians by favoring the damming of the Hetch Hetchy Valley for an additional reservoir for San Francisco. Because Hetch Hetchy adjoined and resembled his beloved Yosemite, Muir took to the warpath against the project and all its advocates, and he heaped special scorn on Pinchot as a false prophet of conservation. As before, the preservationists found their main allies in government in the Interior Department, which favored park and recreational use of Hetch Hetchy. The chief forester, in turn, waffled between continued disdain for parks and an attempt to wrest them away from the Interior Department, to be added to the Forest Service's domain.[36]

Curiously, the tide started to turn against Pinchot not because of his bureaucratic empire building but because of his frugality. In 1906, in continued pursuit of financial self-sufficiency for the Forest Service, he made a request to Congress for a ten-year, $5 million loan, with the forest reserves as collateral and for the purpose of making the agency pay its own way completely. The proposal proved to be a strategic blunder. The amount raised eyebrows on Capitol Hill, while the prospect of total financial independence caused predictable congressional qualms. The affair quickly turned into a rout for Pinchot. Congress not only turned down the request but took the earnings from the reserves away from the Forest Service and put them back into general revenues. Worse still, the incident gave western opponents their opening to insert the provision rescinding presidential authority to create forest reserves. Nor had Congress finished with efforts to clip the wings of the chief forester and his service. In 1908 the agricultural appropriation bill contained one clause that forbade the preparation of newspaper and magazine articles in the department and another clause that disallowed reimbursement for travel expenses except on strictly defined departmental business. The provisions' authors admitted that their targets were extensive publicity operations and public speaking by the Forest Service, especially its chief.[37]

Pinchot met the rising opposition with aplomb. Basking in Roosevelt's patronage, he told a friend in August 1908, "Undoubtedly, my time will come in the end, but just now the President's prestige is keeping us on the top of the wave." He was wrong. The Democrats were already making "Pinchotism" a leading campaign issue in the West against Roosevelt's hand-picked successor, William Howard Taft. Roosevelt's removal from the White House could not fail to change Pinchot's situation, and the signs of his unpopularity could not be ignored. It is interesting to speculate about what might have happened if he had devoted himself single-mindedly to a defense of the Forest Service and his forestry policies. The same skills as a promoter and lobbyist that had gotten him where he was might have allowed him to consolidate his own and his agency's position for years to come. Matters turned out differently, however, in part because Pinchot's special relationship with the president ended but more because his own interests and efforts had long since spread beyond forestry and the Forest Service. Less than a year after Roosevelt's departure, Pinchot would be gone too, publicly fired from his post as chief forester. One of the most spectacular bureaucratic careers in American government would end in a blaze of controversy.[38]

Conservation, Conflict, and Departure

A vision came to a lone man on horseback on a raw day in February 1907. That was how Gifford Pinchot described his awakening to the cause of conservation. "Suddenly the idea flashed through my head that there was a unity in this complication [of problems of forests, water, minerals, and game]—that the relation of one resource to another was not the end of the story." Dusk was falling as Pinchot rode in Rock Creek Park, but he felt as if he were "coming out of a dark tunnel. I had been seeing one spot of light ahead. Here, all of a sudden, was a whole landscape." After sharing his vision with his closest associates at the Forest Service, he presented it to Roosevelt, who "as I expected, understood, accepted, and adopted it without the smallest hesitation. . . . It became the heart of his Administration." Thus, according to Pinchot the "world movement" for conservation was born. It had come to him as a prophetic revelation.[39]

For all its drama, Pinchot's account did him the disservice of making him appear a late convert to conservation. This larger vision entailed no change in his advocacy of planned responsible exploitation of natural resources, and he had been involved for several years, even before becoming chief forester, with larger problems of government management and with other resources besides forest lands. As early as 1903, Roosevelt had appointed him chairman of a special commission to study and recommend reorganization of government scientific work. That commission and another on departmental methods in 1905, on which Pinchot also served, encouraged him to look beyond his own agency and grapple with questions of administrative coordination in the whole federal government. Still more important in expanding his policy horizons was membership on the Public Lands Commission in 1904 and 1905. Although Pinchot used that commission and the government science commission primarily as additional forums for lobbying for the transfer of the forest reserves, he did gain considerable acquaintance with other aspects of natural resource problems. As a result, Pinchot was transcending his original policy designs just when he was getting the chance to implement them.[40]

Whether his new interests helped or hurt his initial work with the Forest Service remains open to question. Pinchot's achievements in establishing the service and ranger force did not suffer from distraction by his broader aims. His larger vision may have helped by making him even more persuasive than he had been earlier. Forestry was a noble calling, but conservation was a "patriotic cause," as Greeley said. Forestry offered exciting man's work by day, but conservation held out ideals by firelight at night. Offsetting those advantages, however, was a standing temptation to exceed sensible limits and neglect necessary cultivation of support. By making Pinchot even more of a zealot than he already was, his conservationist ideas impelled him still faster down the path of expanding the forest reserves, thereby heightening western opposition. He continued to favor careful use of resources and opposed outright preservationists, as dramatized by the Hetch Hetchy controversy, but the reach and grasp of his expansion of the forest reserves blended with his superheated rhetoric about conserving resources for future generations to arouse legitimate concern on the part of people who were striving for more rapid agricultural and industrial development and population growth in those sparsely settled areas. Congressional critics succeeded in restricting publicity and speechmaking by Forest Service officers in part because those activities had become increasingly devoted to conservationist propaganda rather than promotion of forestry.[41]

The biggest impact of Pinchot's championship of conservation came in his relationships with other government officials. The chief forester was correct in saying that conservation "became the heart of his [Roosevelt's] Administration," but he was mistaken in seeing this as a departure after 1907. From his first days in the White House, Roosevelt had agitated and taken bold stands on natural resource issues. He had introduced legislation, appointed a series of presidential commissions to investigate resource problems, and expanded the forest reserves, culminating in the final grab of February 1907. The difference that Pinchot's new vision of a unified conservation movement made lay in its drawing him into even closer collaboration with Roosevelt. That collaboration raised Pinchot's standing within the government still further; at the same time, it plunged him into the midst of the hottest political conflict of the day. The new situation brought the greatest exhilaration of his public career, but it also set the stage for his swift downfall.

Roosevelt aptly described their final collaboration when he told Pinchot just before he left the White House, "There has been a peculiar intimacy between you and Jim [Garfield] and me, because all three of us have worked for the same causes, dreamed the same dreams, have felt a substantial identity of purpose as regards many of what we three deemed the most vital problems of today." Roosevelt and Pinchot's intimacy amounted to a symbiosis in which each man fed the other's sense of the vital importance of their policies and actions. From 1907 onward, Pinchot envisioned conservation as a catholic concern embracing not only expert management and wise use of natural resources but also the structure of the government for such management and basic allocations of public and private responsibility. Thereby, he included within his purview almost as grand a sweep of public policy as did the president himself. In effect, Pinchot promoted himself from confidant to prime minister.[42]

A less self-assured leader might have resented the forester's usurpation, and at other times Roosevelt did find his friend impractical and overzealous. But during the trying last two years of his presidency, Roosevelt welcomed Pinchot's intimacy and egged him on in his new role. Roosevelt had long viewed American politics from a viewpoint much like Pinchot's new vision. He was struggling to maintain his fundamentally conservative, centrist reform approach against what he regarded as irresponsible radicalism on one side and ignorant, selfish reaction on the other, and he found himself stalemated by Old Guard Republican bosses. Pinchot's embracing conservationist vision augmented his social and temperamental ties to Roosevelt with ideological sympathy and reassurance in the deepening intraparty conflict. He and Roosevelt also thought that Pinchot served as a lightning rod, drawing fire away from the popular president, especially in the West.[43]

But Pinchot got more than he gave in the final collaboration with Roosevelt. When the president celebrated their "peculiar intimacy" by including a third partner, "Jim" Garfield, he testified to an increase in Pinchot's power, not a dilution. From 1907 to 1909 the chief forester became the federal government's natural resources czar. Pinchot had license to direct the entire field of government resource management and scientific work. He enjoyed virtually unlimited latitude in proposing reorganizations within departments and among bureaus, drafting legislation, suggesting and serving on presidential commissions, and organizing presidential inspection tours and White House conferences. But James R. Garfield's inclusion in their inner circle was Pinchot's greatest boon. In 1907 Roosevelt appointed Garfield, who was a close friend of both, secretary of the interior. Garfield proved even more accommodating than Secretary Wilson. He and Pinchot walked to work together every morning and normally met again later in the day, when they played tennis or went walking or riding with Roosevelt. Garfield, who had little prior knowledge of natural resources, gladly followed Pinchot's tutelage. He even adopted a plan drawn up by the chief forester to reorganize the Interior Department and cede further responsibilities on public lands to the Forest Service.[44]

Gratifying as it might be to Pinchot, the situation was unsound and could not last. Although the forester understandably blamed his subsequent troubles on the shortcomings of the next administration, he misread his basic problem. By allowing Pinchot to act as he did after 1907, Roosevelt had created an administrative monster. Their collaboration was not a precursor to Col. Edward M. House's relationship with Woodrow Wilson or Harry Hopkins's with Franklin D. Roosevelt. Pinchot was no self-effacing figure without formal position who ostensibly sought only to serve in whatever ways his chief directed. He was a civil servant, an agency head, and a policy entrepreneur with passionately held views and sharply defined aims. Yet he was exercising responsibilities and setting policies that in a representative government should emanate from elected officials and their politically appointed subordinates. The line between an aggressive, broad-ranging policy entrepreneur and a politician frequently becomes unclear, and Pinchot had probably transgressed it more than once before 1907. With his conservationist vision, however, he had crossed a rubicon into the politician's realm.

If Roosevelt had run again and won in 1908, his collaboration with Pinchot and Garfield almost certainly would not have continued. Rather, if he had chosen to stay on, their collaboration probably would not have arisen in the first place. Roosevelt owed much of his difficulty with Republican conservatives, particularly the deadlock with the Old Guardsmen in Congress, to the pledge he had made in 1904 not to run again in 1908. Once it had become clear midway through his second term that Roosevelt meant to honor that pledge, Republican leaders on Capitol Hill, who disagreed with him on substantive issues and resented his enlargement and flaunting of presidential powers, began to defy the president on most domestic matters. Their defiance, in turn, goaded Roosevelt into far less cautious political behavior than he had allowed himself earlier. Final creation of the forest reserves and other unilateral executive initiatives, greater resort to presidential commissions in the face of congressional refusals to fund them, and public agitation about conservation and reform to curb bossism and the influence of big business in politics—these sprang from Roosevelt's anger and frustration during his last two years in the White House. In short, Pinchot's favored position rested on a temporary, unhealthy, and, for Roosevelt, hitherto uncharacteristic political stance.[45]

A new presidential administration inevitably brought changes in the chief forester's circumstances, but his downfall was largely his own doing. Pinchot and Taft had enjoyed friendly relations for several years, and they had a personal tie as fellow Yale alumni. For his part, Taft did not forget that he owed his succession entirely to Roosevelt, and he meant to do his best to carry on his predecessor's policies in all areas. In November 1908, right after the election, Taft spent an evening at the White House with Roosevelt and Pinchot to discuss natural resources. "Then and there Taft pledged himself to T.R., and incidentally to me," Pinchot recalled, "to stand by and carry on the Conservation fight." The president-elect repeated his pledges publicly in a speech later in the month. Privately he promised Roosevelt in December 1908, "You can count on my continuing the [conservation] movement as far as I can, and especially under the influence of Gifford Pinchot, whom I shall continue to regard as a kind of conscience in certain directions, to be followed when possible and to be ignored only with a sense of wrong done to the best interests of the country."[46]

Neither Taft's friendship nor his assurances satisfied Pinchot. When Roosevelt left in March 1909, Pinchot noted, "We who were to remain behind were anxious and uneasy." He had reason to be. Pinchot's earlier forays into other agencies' domains were coming back to haunt him. In 1908 his imposition of more restrictive standards for waterpower development had bothered Taft. It had encroached on Taft's own jurisdiction as secretary of war, and he had questioned its legal justification. As soon as Taft entered the White House, he and his newly appointed secretary of the interior, Richard A. Ballinger, rescinded the further, extensive withdrawals of waterpower sites on the public lands that had been made at Pinchot and Garfield's urgent behest in the last days of the Roosevelt administration. When Pinchot protested, Taft reversed himself and restored the withdrawals, but the incident got the chief forester off on the wrong foot with the new president.[47]

Actually, their chances of getting off to a good start were almost nonexistent. Even before Taft's inauguration, Pinchot regarded him as a traitor to the cause of conservation because he replaced Garfield with Ballinger as secretary of the interior. Although the chief forester unfairly suspected Ballinger of plotting to open the public lands to indiscriminate development, he rightly sensed difficulty for himself in the appointment. The root of the conflict between Pinchot and Ballinger lay not in differences of conservationist views, although those did exist, but rather in assertions of bureaucratic authority. Ballinger had clashed with Pinchot earlier when he had served as commissioner of public lands in 1907 and 1908. He had left after a little over a year, partly out of anger at Pinchot's empire building and disgust with Garfield's weakness in defending departmental turf. Not only did the chief forester lose a secretary of the interior who bordered on being his stooge but he gained an old foe with a combative temperament who was certain to resist his encroachments.[48]

The Ballinger-Pinchot fight began and ended quickly, although its reverberations lasted for decades. During the spring and summer of 1909, Pinchot repeatedly made thinly veiled public charges that Ballinger was undermining Roosevelt's conservation policies. Then, during the summer he learned of allegations that Ballinger had acted corruptly earlier as land commissioner in leasing coal reserves in Alaska. Apprised of the allegations and embarrassed by the public feud, Taft investigated the matter. Once he had satisfied himself that Ballinger had done nothing wrong, the president ordered Pinchot to desist from his attacks. The chief forester did not desist. Although Pinchot believed that the charges against Ballinger might be true, he cared less about his adversary's earlier conduct than about his own opportunity to hobble the secretary's policies and destroy his effectiveness, if not cause his departure. Pinchot made more speeches in the fall of 1909, arraigning Interior Department attitudes and actions. Also, he at least passively permitted Overton Price, his right-hand man in the Forest Service, to leak information to the press about the allegations of corruption against Ballinger. Especially damaging was an article that Price helped write for the *Collier's Weekly*. The leaks further embarrassed the administration, particularly Secretary Wilson, who grew even more distressed at Pinchot's administering the gentlest possible reprimand to Price. The climax came early in January 1910 when Pinchot wrote a letter to a sympathetic senator in which he reiterated the charges against Ballinger. The senator immediately made the letter public. An infuriated Wilson turned on Pinchot and insisted that he be fired. Taft took the responsibility instead. On the evening of 7 January 1910, the day Pinchot's letter was released, he received his dismissal from the president.[49]

Pinchot was delighted at the turn of events. "I'm all right. I'm just as happy as a clam," he remarked when he got the notification of his firing. Freed from the constraints of office, he fought resourcefully to press his case in several forums. Congressional hearings into the controversy turned into a public relations triumph for him, although the victory owed more to the Taft administration's ineptitude in presenting its side and to the skill of the counsel for *Collier's*, Louis D. Brandeis.

Pinchot also prevailed with Roosevelt, persuading the ex-president of the righteousness of his actions and of Taft's perfidy. The dispute with Ballinger played a big part in Roosevelt's estrangement from Taft, which eventually led him to run against his successor in 1912, first for the Republican nomination and then as the candidate of the new Progressive party. Pinchot and his brother Amos stood in the front ranks in those political battles, as financial angels, advisers on issues, organizers, speech writers, and speakers for successive anti-Taft drives and for the Progressives.[50]

Pinchot's greatest joy after 1910 came from no longer having to mask his political ambitions. His experiences as a public speaker and lobbyist had given him a taste of politics, which he privately admitted he relished. Assisting Roosevelt's presidential bid kept him from running for office in 1912, but two years later he became the Progressive candidate for senator from Pennsylvania. Pinchot finished a respectable second, well behind the strongly entrenched Republican incumbent but just ahead of a well-known Democratic challenger. His appetite whetted, Pinchot fished for other opportunities. Returning to the Republicans after the Progressives disbanded, he tried unsuccessfully for the Pennsylvania gubernatorial nomination in 1918. Four years later, he exploited factional rivalries to win the nomination and the governorship, and barred from succeeding himself, he made a comeback in 1930. During both his gubernatorial terms Pinchot attracted attention as a potential Republican nominee for president, but nothing came of it. In the 1930s he twice ran unsuccessfully for Republican senatorial nominations, and in 1940 he gained some notoriety for supporting the Democratic candidate for a third term as president, his old patron's distant cousin Franklin D. Roosevelt, mainly on foreign policy and conservation issues. By then, Pinchot was in his mid-seventies and was enjoying the status of elder statesman, which lasted until his death in 1946.[51]

Conservation remained his fondest cause for the rest of his long life. Aside from Progressive party politics, lobbying on natural resource issues occupied most of Pinchot's time during the first decade after he left the government. As the dominant force in the American Forestry Association and organizer of two broader groups, the Conservation League of America and the National Conservation Association, Pinchot exerted greater influence on forest, waterpower, irrigation, and rangeland issues than any other individual, even Roosevelt. Many fellow conservationists grew to dislike his prominence for a variety of reasons. Some suspected him of using conservation to advance his political ambitions, while his continuing conflict with wilderness preservationists rankled others. Hetch Hetchy finally did become a reservoir, but control of the national parks stayed under the Interior Department and was institutionalized with the establishment of the National Park Service in 1916. While Pinchot was still in government, a number of foresters and conservationists had begun to resent his preoccupation with federal legislation and policy. His continued neglect of local and state efforts after 1910 helped fragment conservationist groups into separate, unconnected bodies rather than an embracing, coordinated movement. On the federal level, Pinchot remained vigilant against moves to reverse his policies or undo his handiwork, especially with the Forest Service. Twice, in the early 1920s and late 1930s, he engaged in public combat with secretaries of the interior who sought to curtail the service's authority over the reserves and to transfer it to the Interior Department. Elder statesman or not, Pinchot still had plenty of the fire that he had unleashed against Ballinger and Taft three decades before.[52]

For all his activity and fame after 1910, however, he never again matched the feats he had wrought as the head forester of the federal government. The Forest Service survived in part because his successors selectively repudiated his example. When Henry Graves returned from Yale to take Pinchot's place as chief forester, he found the service muzzled and reined in by Secretary Wilson, who was smarting from the Ballinger-Pinchot fight. Only by combining his insistence on autonomy with efforts to lower the service's profile, Graves recalled, was he able to preserve his bureaucratic inheritance intact. Graves and his successors, especially Greeley in the 1920s, put renewed emphasis on private forestry, relaxed the enforcement of regulations, and, except in special cases, abandoned further expansion of the reserves. Later chief foresters also took care not to abuse their relationship with the secretary of agriculture. When Greeley faced onslaughts from the Interior Department in the early 1920s, he had "the fresh example of the Pinchot-Ballinger controversy" as a reminder not to embarrass or weaken the hand of his secretary.[53]

Despite Pinchot's watchful concern, he gradually drifted away from his old agency and profession. In 1933 a young forester assigned to help him draft a policy statement on forestry for President Roosevelt found him astonishingly ignorant on substantive matters. Even before Pinchot's death, the preponderance of influence among conservationists had shifted to wilderness preservationists, who increasingly rejected human use of resources as their central aim. Their viewpoint eventually infected professional foresters. A director of the American Forestry Association who was also head forester of Pennsylvania declared in 1965, "Nobody has a higher regard for Gifford Pinchot than I, but I think it is time we realized that there was something deficient in his view." How the mighty had fallen.[54]

Yet, in a deeper sense the decline in Pinchot's influence was more apparent than real. When later chief foresters preferred persuasion to compulsion, got back to grassroots activity, and paid more attention to private forestry, they were returning to the approach that Pinchot had originally used to build the agency. When they applied the brakes to his expansionism, they were fulfilling a necessary function in the organization's development. Pinchot had played the role of the entrepreneur in the classic sense. He had dreamed dreams, drummed up support, and identified worlds to conquer, thereby performing the functions of the innovator and initial organizer. Those who came after consolidated his accomplishments and introduced order and system into his inspirations. They played the equally classic role of the routineer, replacing the entrepreneur when the next stage is reached in the life of the organization. It was a shame for Pinchot that he did not stay on to preside over his creation, but he was not the first or the last such entrepreneur—whether in business, military service, civilian government, universities, churches, newspapers, or magazines—who had to be superseded.[55]

Neither successive chiefs nor passing years have really dimmed his memory. In the late 1950s a survey of rangers found that nearly all of them identified strongly with "the tradition of Gifford Pinchot." In 1981 the staff of the Forest Products Laboratory followed his old practice of holding a contest, this time to pick a name for the short street on which the building is located. The winner was Gifford Pinchot Drive. The first chief's shadow still stretches long and clear over the Forest Service.[56]

Notes

1. On Pinchot's family background see his own account in Gifford Pinchot, *Breaking New Ground* (New York: Harcourt, Brace & Co., 1947), 2–10; and the fullest of the several biographies of him, M. Nelson McGeary, *Gifford Pinchot: Forester-Politician* (Princeton, N.J.: Princeton University Press, 1960), 3–7, 11.

2. Pinchot, *Breaking New Ground*, 1; on his training see 5–9 and 11–14.

3. Ibid., 70.

4. On his activism and the sparseness of his training see McGeary, *Pinchot*, 20–21, 39. Pinchot himself later regretted that he had not learned more forestry, confessing to his chief European mentor, "The time has come, as you foretold it would, when I begin to feel the scantiness of my preparation" (ibid., 23). In contrast, for observations on the value of Pinchot's lack of specialization to his later work see James Penick, Jr., *Progressive Politics and Conservation: The Ballinger-Pinchot Affair* (Chicago: University of Chicago Press, 1970), 2–3; and George W. S. Trow, "Annals of Discourse (Forestry)," *New Yorker*, 11 June 1984, 44.

5. William B. Greeley, *Forests and Men* (Garden City, N.Y.: Doubleday & Co., 1951), 81. Muir's recollection is cited in Harold K. Steen, *The U.S. Forest Service: A History* (Seattle: University of Washington Press, 1976), 49.

6. On the work at Biltmore and the forestry exhibit see Pinchot, *Breaking New*

Ground, 47–57. On Fernow see Andrew Denny Rodgers III, *Bernhard Eduard Fernow: A Story of North American Forestry* (Princeton, N.J.: Princeton University Press, 1951).

7. Pinchot, *Breaking New Ground*, 27, 71.

8. Pinchot to James B. Reynolds, 13 August 1894, quoted in Harold T. Pinkett, *Gifford Pinchot: Private and Public Forester* (Urbana: University of Illinois Press, 1970), 35; Pinchot, *Breaking New Ground*, 79. On his work with the Forest Commission see ibid., 95–109; and McGeary, *Pinchot*, 42–43.

9. Pinchot diary, 11 May 1898, quoted in Pinchot, *Breaking New Ground*, 135–36; ibid., 136.

10. On Powell, McGee, and earlier government science see Wallace Stegner, *Beyond the Hundredth Meridian: John Wesley Powell and the Second Opening of the West* (Boston: Houghton, Mifflin & Co., 1954); and Curtis M. Hinsley, Jr., *Savages and Scientists: The Smithsonian and the Development of American Anthropology, 1846–1910* (Washington, D.C.: Smithsonian Institution Press, 1981). On Wilson see *Dictionary of American Biography*, s.v. "Wilson, James"; Pinchot, *Breaking New Ground*, 137; and Greeley, *Forests and Men*, 85. On the alliance with the irrigationists see Samuel P. Hays, *Conservation and the Gospel of Efficiency: The Progressive Conservation Movement, 1890–1920* (Cambridge: Harvard University Press, 1958), 22–24.

11. Pinchot, *Breaking New Ground*, 137–39, 153–54, 157–59. For a description of the offices and staff see also Ralph S. Hosmer, "Some Recollections of Gifford Pinchot, 1898–1904," *Journal of Forestry* 43 (July 1945): 558.

12. On Pinchot's constituency building see Steen, *U.S. Forest Service*, 55; Penick, *Progressive Politics and Conservation*, 2–5; Pinkett, *Pinchot*, 50–51; and Hays, *Conservation and the Gospel of Efficiency*, 33–35.

13. See Pinchot, *Breaking New Ground*, 279; Steen, *U.S. Forest Service*, 64–65; and Hosmer, "Recollections of Pinchot," 558, 561.

14. See Hosmer, "Recollections of Pinchot," 560–61; and idem, "The Society of American Foresters: An Historical Summary," *Journal of Forestry* 38 (October 1940): 839.

15. On the founding of the Yale forestry school see Pinchot, *Breaking New Ground*, 151–53; and Henry S. Graves, "Early Days with Gifford Pinchot," *Journal of Forestry* 43 (July 1945): 552.

16. Pinchot, *Breaking New Ground*, 244. For the "Yale Club" remarks see McGeary, *Pinchot*, 49.

17. On the origins of the forest reserves and Pinchot's cultivation of western support, see McGeary, *Pinchot*, 84–86, 173, 254–62; and Hays, *Conservation and the Gospel of Efficiency*, 33–42.

18. On Pinchot's relationship with Roosevelt see Pinchot, *Breaking New Ground*, 144–45, 190, 305–17; *The Works of Theodore Roosevelt*, ed. Hermann Hagedorn (New York: Charles Scribner's Sons, 1926), vol. 20, *An Autobiography*, 385; McGeary, *Pinchot*, 56, 65–67; and William H. Harbaugh, *Power and Responsibility: The Life and Times of Theodore Roosevelt* (New York: Farrar, Straus & Giroux, 1961), 319–20, 371–72.

19. See Roosevelt messages to Congress, 3, 6 December 1904, in *Roosevelt Works*, vol. 11, 102–4, 235–38. On the lobbying for the transfer see Pinchot, *Breaking New Ground*, 188–94, 240–46.

20. Pinchot, *Breaking New Ground*, 258, 298–99.

21. On the revenues from the reserves see Hays, *Conservation and the Gospel of Efficiency*, 45–46; and Steen, *U.S. Forest Service*, 60–61.

22. On the founding and location of the laboratory see Charles A. Nelson, "Born and Raised in Madison: The Forest Products Laboratory," *Forest History* 11 (July 1967): 6–14.

23. Pinchot, *Breaking New Ground*, 293–95.

24. See Herbert Kaufman, *The Forest Ranger: A Study in Administrative Behavior* (Baltimore: Johns Hopkins Press, 1960), esp. 64–65, 86–87.

25. On the expenditures see Steen, *U.S. Forest Service*, 77–78, 90–91.

26. *Denver Republican*, 29 April 1909, quoted in Pinkett, *Pinchot*, 70; Greeley, *Forests and Men*, 81–82.

27. For some comment on the upper-class atmosphere surrounding Roosevelt see John Milton Cooper, Jr., *The Warrior and the Priest: Woodrow Wilson and Theodore Roosevelt* (Cambridge: Harvard University Press, 1983), esp. 87–88, 241. For descriptions of Pinchot see Penick, *Progressive Politics and Conservation*, 1–2; and Owen Wister, *Roosevelt: The Story of a Friendship* (New York: Charles Scribner's Sons, 1930), 174–76.

28. On the plaques, identification with the service, and the utility of the Agriculture Department connection see Kaufman, *Forest Ranger*, 185, 196–98, 226; on the *Use Book* see Steen, *U.S. Forest Service*, 77–78.

29. On the term *ranger* see Mitford M. Mathews, ed., *A Dictionary of Americanisms on Historical Principles* (Chicago: University of Chicago Press, 1951), 1357; on the retaining of the badge and uniform see Frank J. Harmon, "What Should Foresters Wear? The Forest Service's Seventy-Five-Year Search for a Uniform," *Journal of Forest History* 24 (October 1980): 188–90; and on the later preference for selecting the badge and uniform see Kaufman, *Forest Ranger*, 184–85.

30. On female forest rangers see Michael Frome, *The Forest Service*, 2d ed. (Boulder: University of Colorado Press, 1983), 66–67.

31. *Denver Republican*, 29 April 1909. Curiously, the military analogy has not been drawn by analysts of the Forest Service nor by Kaufman. The military analogy can be carried still further. When the rangers fight a forest fire, they mount an effort that strongly resembles a military campaign. They have also had an airborne arm, the parachuting firefighters, called the "smoke jumpers," who were the elite of the elite among rangers. In both world wars the United States Army had forestry units, whose officers were drawn from the Forest Rangers. Greeley, who served as chief forester from 1920 to 1928, headed the forestry troops in World War I and was afterward known by his military rank of colonel.

32. Greeley, *Forests and Men*, 73.

33. Pinchot, *Breaking New Ground*, 300. For other descriptions by participants see Roosevelt, *Autobiography*, 395–96; and Greeley, *Forests and Men*, 65. In retrospect, Pinchot took the crisis in stride, devoting only three paragraphs to it in his autobiography and concluding matter-of-factly, "As usual our people were superb" (*Breaking New Ground*, 300).

34. On western opposition to Pinchot's policies see Penick, *Progressive Politics and Conservation*, 186; Hays, *Conservation and the Gospel of Efficiency*, 54–55, 64–65; and Elmo R. Richardson, *The Politics of Conservation: Crusades and Controversies, 1897–1913* (Berkeley and Los Angeles: University of California Press, 1962), 28–29, 34.

35. Greeley, *Forests and Men*, 75; Wilson, quoted in McGeary, *Pinchot*, 80.

36. On the split between Pinchot and the preservationists see Hays, *Conservation and the Gospel of Efficiency*, 141–46, 189–97. On his conflicts with Muir see Linnie Marsh Wolfe, *Son of the Wilderness: The Life of John Muir* (New York: Alfred A. Knopf, 1945), 275–76, 316–17, 322–26, 329; and Stephen Fox, *John Muir and His*

Legacy: The American Conservation Movement (Boston: Little, Brown & Co., 1981), 111, 115, 130, 139–46.

37. On the congressional attacks see Hays, *Conservation and the Gospel of Efficiency*, 45–46, 137–38; and Pinkett, *Pinchot*, 84, 86.

38. Pinchot to Sir Horace Plunkett, 23 July 1908, quoted in McGeary, *Pinchot*, 107. On Pinchot as a campaign issue in 1908 see ibid., 82; and Richardson, *Politics of Conservation*, 86–88.

39. Pinchot, *Breaking New Ground*, 322, 326. The quasi-biblical overtones of this account, particularly its implicit comparison to St. Paul on the road to Damascus, might raise questions about its authenticity. Pinchot probably did experience a flash of insight of some sort in February 1907. That would have suited both his mystical tendency and his agitated state of mind as he girded for the congressional attack on the forest reserves. Further, the tactic of attacking on a broad public front when faced with institutional barrier to his forestry policies fitted his combative personality.

40. On the earlier influences toward a broader view of conservation see Pinkett, *Pinchot*, 105–6.

41. On the broadening of the speaking and publicity efforts see McGeary, *Pinchot*, 88–89.

42. Roosevelt to Pinchot, 24 February 1909, in *The Letters of Theodore Roosevelt*, ed. Elting E. Morison et al., vol. 6 (Cambridge: Harvard University Press, 1952), 1535. For a similar view of Pinchot's role see Penick, *Progressive Politics and Conservation*, 10.

43. In fact, Pinchot did not serve as an effective lightning rod for Roosevelt in the West. Besides costing the Republicans votes in 1908, his policies hurt the Progressives in 1912, and Roosevelt did surprisingly poorly everywhere in the West except on the Pacific Coast (see Richardson, *Politics of Conservation*, 139–40).

44. On Garfield see *Dictionary of American Biography*, s.v. "Garfield, James Rudolph."

45. On Roosevelt's last two years as president see Cooper, *Warrior and Priest*, 108–18.

46. Pinchot, *Breaking New Ground*, 375; Taft to Roosevelt, 24 December 1908, Theodore Roosevelt Papers, Library of Congress (microfilm ed., reel 87).

47. Pinchot, *Breaking New Ground*, 382. On his earlier clashes and differences in approach with Taft see Hays, *Conservation and the Gospel of Efficiency*, 116–18.

48. As a resident of the state of Washington and former mayor of Seattle, Ballinger did sympathize with westerners' resentment of the massiveness and apparent high-handedness of the forest reserve and waterpower site withdrawals. He favored more local consultation and gentler application of regulations in resource management. By his own lights, Ballinger was as much a conservationist as Pinchot, and he was far more receptive to wilderness preservation and park development. For example, he sided with Muir and the opponents of the damming of Hetch Hetchy. On Ballinger's views see Penick *Progressive Politics and Conservation*, 19–23, 185–87.

49. The best account of their quarrel is in ibid., chaps. 3–5.

50. Pinchot, quoted in Steen, *U.S. Forest Service*, 102. On his activity with the Progressives see Martin L. Fausold, *Gifford Pinchot: Bull Moose Progressive* (Syracuse, N.Y.: Syracuse University Press, 1961).

51. On his later political career see McGeary, *Pinchot*, pt. 2.

52. In his last great fight over the Forest Service, Pinchot crossed swords with his old Progressive comrade in arms Harold L. Ickes, who was Franklin Roosevelt's

secretary of the interior. A much abler antagonist than Ballinger, Ickes matched Pinchot in self-righteousness and vituperation, even to the point of charging that Ballinger had been unfairly maligned (see ibid., 409–13).

53. Greeley, *Forests and Men*, 99. On Graves's policies see Henry Clepper, *Professional Forestry in the United States* (Baltimore: Johns Hopkins Press, 1971), 55–56.

54. Maurice K. Goddard, "A Conservationist Critique," *American Forests* 71 (April 1965): 9. On Pinchot's ignorance of forestry and waning influence among conservationists see Fox, *Muir and His Legacy*, 207, 289.

55. For a recent discussion of the concepts of the entrepreneur and the routineer see Sidney M. Greenfield et al., "Studies in Entrepreneurial Behavior: A Review and an Introduction," and Sidney M. Greenfield and Arnold Strickon, "Entrepreneurship and Social Change: Toward a Populational, Decision-Making Approach," both in *Entrepreneurs in Cultural Context*, ed. Sidney M. Greenfield, Arnold Strickon, and Robert T. Aubey (Albuquerque: University of New Mexico Press, 1979), 3–18, 329–50.

56. On the identification of rangers with Pinchot see Kaufman, *Forest Ranger*, 224. On the street naming see *Chips: Forest Products Laboratory Employees' Association (Official Newsletter)*, June and October 1981.

4

Admiral Hyman Rickover: Technological Entrepreneurship in the U.S. Navy

Eugene Lewis

Hyman George Rickover was probably the most unlikely four-star admiral in the history of the U.S. Navy. He is known as the "father of the nuclear submarine" and the "father of the nuclear Navy." He was also thoroughly disliked by very large numbers of his colleagues and superiors. He was one of a handful of military officers who were both extremely controversial *and* effective. Rickover was the engineer who brought the possibility of nuclear propulsion at sea into reality and thus altered the course of military power in vital ways. Had he accomplished only this, he would be worthy of careful consideration. But he did much more, and the meaning and consequences of his entrepreneurial deviation from standard operating procedures (SOPs) and the conventions of Navy life and career make him one of the more intriguing public figures of the late twentieth century.

Rickover entered the Naval Academy in 1918 and left active duty in 1981, long after his contemporaries and many junior to him had retired. He died in 1986. His career ought to have ended in 1953 when he was passed over for promotion to rear admiral for the second time; indeed, in every administration from Truman's to Reagan's, high-ranking military and civilian officials tried to have him retired. It was not until he reached the age of eighty-one (or eighty-three, depending on which account of his year of birth one accepts) that he was finally retired from active duty. Despite his long career, he never commanded a navy bureau, yet he controlled the design, construction, staffing, and maintenance of all nuclear vessels in the U.S. Navy.

On the other hand, Rickover commanded the respect and devotion of thousands of officers and men who served under his exacting command. Many of the most powerful men in Congress during the period

1950–80 considered him an ideal military officer, and he probably gave more testimony on more subjects than any other officer in history. He built a near-autonomous organization within the Navy and the Atomic Energy Commission (AEC). Rickover's operational span crossed many boundaries, including those separating politics and administration, public and private spheres, and civilian and military roles.

This analysis seeks to discover how and why this man became so very powerful, and therefore it must consider the person, the historical circumstances in which his entrepreneurial development occurred, and finally, the consequences of his entrepreneurship.[1] At this introductory point we can lay out the following tentative claims. First, Rickover, among others, saw the immense potential of nuclear energy to power submarines underwater indefinitely, but he was the only one to seize upon nuclear energy as an organizational resource. Second, Rickover perceived and acted upon an untenable relationship between the military and the AEC in a manner guaranteed to make him autonomous in relation to each and responsible to neither. Third, he realized that his long-term viability depended not so much on his civilian and military superiors as on Congress and private-sector contractors, both of which he alternately courted and castigated with consummate skill. Fourth, Rickover used his knowledge and control of the technology to successfully garner resources and power that otherwise would not have been his. Fifth, he created an "apolitical" shield and maintained it with careful public relations techniques in order to distance himself from partisan, Pentagon, and bureaucratic politics, all of which he manipulated.

Before we can take up these claims, we must briefly outline one of the longest careers in American military history.

A Biographical Sketch

According to his elementary school records, Rickover was born in Poland in 1898, but his Naval Academy records have him born in Poland in 1900.[2] Whichever was the case, Rickover arrived in America with his mother and his sister in 1904. In 1908 the family moved to Chicago, where Rickover was brought up. He graduated from high school in 1918 and entered the Naval Academy that same year. Not much is known about Rickover's childhood. He was physically small and known for his quick mind, diligence, and tenacity. He was not athletic, and one must surmise that he suffered from the usual difficulties encountered by children of immigrants. His parents were far from wealthy, but Abraham Rickover, a tailor, made a reasonable living after years of struggle. How much and in what ways his parents' experience affected Rickover's formative years is not known, but it is reasonable to speculate about Rickover's early life given what is generally known about the problems of ethnic assimilation during the first decades of the present century.[3]

Part of the appeal of America lies in its claim that hard work will bring reward no matter what the race, ethnicity, or religion of the worker may be. This element of the promise of America was particularly important to those first children of immigrants to whom English was the native tongue. Rickover was one of those children, and he, like many others, strove mightily to be American in all things, especially in school, *the* key to the upward social mobility and acceptance universally sought by immigrants. Young Rickover became a paragon of Yankee schoolboy diligence, working after school to help the family and saving money for college while doing so. Rickover's reports of his youth sound like something out of *Poor Richard's Almanac*, that parable of the Protestant work ethic. With a grain of salt or two, we can probably accept that view.

We must also consider the darker side of the Jewish immigrant experience if we are to gain insight into the formative years of this very complex man. The grains of salt with which we must take Rickover's account have as much to do with America as they do with the little admiral himself. While America remains the land of opportunity for all, it is still, even in the 1980s, a nation that does not fully live up to its promise. In the first two decades of this century overt and covert anti-Semitism was ubiquitous. The social distinctions between the wealthy few and the many poor were not yet blunted by a majority middle class. The psychological problems of youngsters caught between the conflicting values of immigrant parents and those of the new culture were exacerbated by the dual messages coming from that new culture: American is open to everybody, yet the likelihood of gaining full acceptance turns as much on accidents of birth as on hard work.

Within this complex and conflicted setting the young Rickover developed a strong, indeed willful, personality which was to be evident all the days of his life. Absolutely nothing was ever given to Hyman Rickover: he earned it all. He had to have known early on that the children of Yiddish tailors had to work as hard or harder than others to accomplish the same things. He also had to have learned that even among immigrant children with whom he grew up, "popularity" based on personality or athletic prowess or sociability often counted as much as earned accomplishment. The theme of his early life was constant toil in search of legitimated social status. His scholastic efforts were considerable, his accomplishments many, but his post-high-school chances were few. There were few scholarships and little money at home to send Rickover to college. It is important to recall in this present age of increasingly common bachelor degrees that going to college was once a statistically rare thing, especially in the early decades of this century among children of immigrants. Rarer still was attendance at one of the two military academies.

Rickover's congressman got him the appointment to the Naval Academy, and Rickover passed the entrance exams after some serious cramming. He entered the Academy in June 1918. It was at Annapolis that Rickover met the full force of the contradictions in American society. Judging by his subsequent thoughts on the subject, he never recovered from the encounter. The differences between the ostensible institution and the real one must have been painful indeed in 1918. On one side lay the academy of courses, grades, examinations, parades, and the like, while on the other were to be found the social system of hazing, esprit de corps, wardroom sociability, and old military families. Few minorities had ever become part of the American military establishment, and Rickover and the few other minority members of his class were excluded from much social contact as a matter of course. Rickover became a classic "grind" and avoided as many potentially humiliating encounters with his classmates as he could. He lived a life of study, disdaining athletics and parties as much as possible. He undoubtedly knew that his chances of ever commanding a ship, becoming a flag rank officer, or making a name for himself through the normal routes of ascension to the top were very slight. But Rickover was a persistent young man: like many children of immigrants, he had something to prove to himself and to the world.

The U.S. Navy of 1922 hardly seems a likely spot for a lonely, antisocial young Jew to "make it." The nation was in the throes of one of its periodic postwar disarmament episodes, and the prospects for rapid promotion were accordingly diminished. Rickover's interests lay in two areas: command of a ship and engineering. During the ten years following his graduation from the Academy, he moved from ship to ship, managed to get an M.S. in electrical engineering at Columbia University, attended submarine school at New London, Connecticut, and qualified for submarine command. In 1932 he married Ruth Dorothy Masters, to whom he stayed happily married until her death in 1972. She was a non-Jew, and his marriage to her involved a formal disavowal of faith, causing a break in his relations with his parents that took many years to heal.

Rickover was assigned to several tours in the Pacific, including sole command of a ship, the minesweeper *Finch*, based in Tsingtao, China. He and his highly educated wife traveled widely in Asia, a trip she later chronicled in one of her several books. Rickover was relieved of command of the *Finch* and was assigned to the Cavite Navy Yard in the Philippines in 1937. Two years later he was assigned to the Bureau of

Engineering (which later became the Bureau of Ships, or BuShips) in Washington. As World War II began, Rickover found himself heading the Electrical Section of BuShips, the part of the Navy responsible for supervising the design and production of warships. In this capacity he performed in the manner that was to become part of his legendary persona, in the Navy and out.

During the wartime emergency, the Electrical Section of BuShips had to expedite the production of systems that were likely to be put into immediate combat use. All sorts of ships were being built—at a rate unparalleled before or since. At the same time, the cost of haste could mean not only lost dollars but also lost lives. A circuit breaker that popped because of a proximate explosion could turn a warship into a blind, deaf victim very quickly indeed. Rickover, through ceaseless effort and attention to detail, made certain that his section quickly approved reliable systems. He drove himself and his staff in the office and ship- yards as though nothing else mattered. In the process, he began to develop a management style reminiscent of his shipboard performances, which were characterized by an utter indifference to anything other than the task at hand, a perfectionism and zeal that bordered on the fanatic, and a disregard for rank and status. Weekends, holidays, va- cations, personal problems, marriages, children—all of these were sec- ondary to duty.

During the war, the Electrical Section was a large enterprise that was part of a still larger enterprise.[4] The Navy and the civilian con- tractors involved were designing and producing ships in numbers pre- viously thought to be impossible. The vast scale of human and material resources to be organized and coordinated was outside of Rickover's (or anyone's) experience, but he learned very rapidly how things got done, and he took the lessons learned in the Electrical Section with him to what was to be his "second career." At this point it is useful to pause briefly and consider what those lessons might have been so that we may return to speculate on their effect on Rickover's subsequent behavior.

The most obvious fact about the wartime military establishment was that it was composed mainly of civilians who were there to win the war. Few civilians, in uniform or out, had ambitions in the postwar military. Rickover, for the first time in his adult life, dealt with civilian engineers, managers, and technical people who had little or no military background. Typically, they were uninterested in status differentiation based on rank, but they tended to value competence in and of itself. Second, BuShips was the prime mover of the doctrine that holds that one brings to the project the skills and resources needed at the moment and then moves on to the next step and the next set of resources and skills required. Such a doctrine required extraordinarily detailed and careful planning, scheduling, and management of unforeseen but somewhat predictable contingencies. Thus, one set of actors was required and employed on a project (say, a destroyer) for a given period and then was replaced by another set, and so on. The division of labor was used episodically *as the task demanded.* This "project management" technique later became famous at NASA and elsewhere, but it was the order of the day in the Navy and among its shipbuilding contractors during World War II, and Rickover found it quite congenial to his personality and his view of the world.

Project management tends to undermine fixed hierarchies of control, because the important actors are determined by the task at hand, which in turn is determined by planning and not by precedent. In any ultrastable organization, such a procedure can be tolerated only for short periods of time, or it must be segregated from the regular missions and chain of command. For Rickover the project-management idea must have been very appealing from the point of view of developing new technologies, for it called for expert knowledge irrespective of rank, status, or even formal affiliation. Private-sector actors were thus indistinguishable from those in the public sector as the task was being performed. During the war years, Rickover got to know many people who worked for the great electrical contractors, General Electric and Westinghouse. The friendships and acquaintances that he made during this period were to be very important to his "second career."

Given that Rickover did not retire from the Navy until 1981, it might well be asked what this "second career" was. By 1945 Rickover was a captain with twenty-three years service since leaving Annapolis. Officers in similar circumstances were retiring as a matter of course, and with the decreased need for military personnel after the war, it seemed likely that Rickover's career would end. He was not the most popular officer in the Navy. He had not served in combat, despite his requests to do so. His manner continued to be brusque, even unfriendly, and he was utterly alienated from wardroom good fellowship and country club sociability, so important to career advancement.

After brief service in the Pacific at the end of and shortly after the war, Rickover returned to Washington a captain with little future. He was saved by a set of events that began to unfold following the successful creation and detonation of the atomic bomb. After much heated debate, Congress passed the Atomic Energy Act in 1946 and gave the newly created Atomic Energy Commission a monopoly on all nuclear materials. The AEC became the recipient of the Manhattan Engineering District, the code name for the huge organization responsible for the development and production of the first fission weapons. This left the military services in the curious position of having to go to a civilian body to obtain the most formidable weapon and power source known to man. In the late 1940s, confusion as to who was to do what in this situation of split responsibility played into Rickover's hands.

The Navy, and in particular Adm. Earl Mills, chief of the Bureau of Ships, wanted a nuclear submarine very much. Mills had the complete support of submariners and of virtually all the Navy brass. He allowed Rickover to go to Oak Ridge along with some other officers to learn about nuclear technology but prevented him from starting a new office for nuclear propulsion. Mills wanted to see first whether the new AEC structure could be made to work. Also, Mills was thoroughly aware of Rickover's single-minded, no-nonsense, no-diplomacy attitude which had engendered such hostility among many in the Navy.

Mills finally unleashed Rickover when Mills became convinced (with some help behind the scenes from Rickover) that the AEC was not likely to get organized effectively soon enough to begin work on naval reactors. By 1947 Rickover had begun to make speeches to anyone he encountered to the effect that the nuclear submarine was "merely" an engineering problem, not an esoteric scientific matter for academics to ponder. In the end, Rickover got to command the new Nuclear Power Branch in BuShips (1948) and in the following year was appointed to the Division of Reactor Development in the AEC.

By 1951 Rickover had gotten the Navy and the AEC to approve the order for the first atomic submarine, the USS *Nautilus*, from the Electric Boat Company. That same summer, he was passed over for promotion to rear admiral. The following year President Truman laid the keel of the submarine. In March 1953 the reactor prototype for the *Nautilus* "went critical" on its test site at Arco, Idaho (that is, it achieved a controlled nuclear chain reaction), but Rickover had again been passed over for promotion the year before, which meant automatic retirement. Following an extraordinary battle (discussed below), the Navy was in effect compelled by Congress to promote Rickover or else risk having *all* of its recommendations for promotions to flag rank rejected. Rickover's "second career" had begun.

Rickover and his program had become a cause célèbre, and he would remain such for the nearly three decades he continued on active duty. From the moment in 1954 when he appeared on the cover of *Time*, Rickover was a public figure known to thousands beyond the confines of Washington as the little man who stood up to the entrenched forces and built the atomic submarine.[5] The creation of what only can be described as a mythic persona and the talent and energy that went into that public relations coup represent an extraordinary shift from the pattern of Rickover's life during his previous three decades in the Navy.

It is a watershed, and one vital to an understanding of his entrepreneurship. We return to it in the pages that follow.

It should be noted that when Congress insisted on Rickover's retention and promotion long past normal retirement age, it in effect guaranteed that Rickover would no longer be personally vulnerable to his opponents. The same could not be said for his programs. His intention, once the research, development, and operational testing phase of the *Nautilus* concluded, was to build a fleet of ever more sophisticated nuclear submarines and eventually to create an entire surface navy powered by nuclear energy. Concomitant with this vision was Rickover's desire to increase his influence and power over aspects of nuclear power that went well beyond typical research and development exercises. He sought and won control over the training of all officers and men who dealt with propulsion in nuclear ships and submarines, and this included captains and executive officers. He retained exclusive control over all aspects of safety—as *he* defined the term.

Through his lobbying efforts and often over the objections of his superiors and many members of Congress, Rickover managed to have nuclear power plants installed in most supercarriers, cruisers, and many other vessels constructed by the Navy during the period 1956–81. When the Eisenhower administration rejected plans for a large ship reactor in the early 1950s, Rickover managed to use the design to help out the AEC by building the first nuclear power plant to generate electricity in the United States. Triumph after triumph followed the Shippingport reactor in 1957.[6] The next year, the *Nautilus* reached the North Pole, and the *Triton* submarine, the first with multiple reactors, was launched.

The Rickover myth was further polished when Rickover's obvious engineering successes were contrasted with those of his peers at the time of the Sputnik launch. Rickover became something of a sage thereafter. He wrote books, made speeches, and gave endless reams of testimony to congressional committees on the failure of the American educational system to educate youngsters in technical and scientific fields. Predictably, he assaulted the Naval Academy in detail and with great passion.

Over the long span of his career, Rickover built what came to be called by his critics the "Rickover Navy." By this his critics meant that Rickover demanded total loyalty from those he commanded and expected it even after people left his direct command. His "nucs," as they were known to friend and foe, remained loyal to Rickover in many ways and in many situations, thus spreading the span of his influence well beyond his Nuclear Power Branch. When he finally retired after his eightieth birthday, he was a somewhat sad figure who had outlived virtually all of his contemporaries in the Navy and Congress, not to mention the hordes of executives in the shipyards and defense industries. In 1985 he was officially censured by the Secretary of the Navy for having accepted over sixty thousand dollars' worth of gifts of various kinds over a ten-year period. Virtually all of these gifts seem to have been trivial, and many were simply given away to subordinates. None was of a magnitude sufficient to lead one to believe Rickover's decisions were influenced improperly by contractors. Yet the episode is a sorry footnote to a career characterized by open, honest, and uncompromising devotion to duty.

Leadership Style

Nothing about Rickover is more subject to legendary treatment than his uncompromising style of leadership. His views appear to have been consistent over the course of his long career. Indeed, he publicized certain traits. In his biography of *Rickover*, constructed during the retirement crisis of 1953, Clay Blair relates the story (which could only have come from and been approved by Rickover) that the child Rickover had his front teeth chipped by his father as the man tried to get medicine down the obstinate child's throat! What is one to understand from this tale supplied by a middle-age captain to an approved biographer?

Utter tenacity of character and determination to have one's will done are heroic messages to a world beset by managerial psychologies, virtually all of which Rickover detested. Rickover's style was spartan in virtually all respects. He always insisted on devotion to duty above all else, including family, social life, and even career. Detail was his forte, and no one did his homework better than Rickover himself. He was one of the first task-oriented managers in military history. Normal hierarchical relationships, patterns of deference and rank, and even the division of labor tended in his view to be impediments to completing a task.

We have indirect statements from Rickover via the Blair biography (written, incidentally, in Rickover's office and edited by Captain and Mrs. Rickover) to back these as his views. Blair tells the story of Rickover serving on the battleship *Nevada* as electrical officer in 1925. He had spent hours whipping his unit into shape for an inspection by the highest ranking officer in the Pacific Fleet only to have the Admiral require the men to strip down to their undershirts so that he might inspect those. Rickover recounts his anger in a remark to a friend at the time: "What the hell kind of Navy is this if the Commander-in-Chief of the Pacific Fleet has nothing better to do than to go around inspecting sailors' undershirts!"[7]

This tale epitomizes virtually everything Rickover had to say about the Navy way of leadership and the Rickover way during his lengthy career. He always believed that the task or mission was everything, and he conducted himself with that in mind in every detail of his life. Saturdays and Sundays were workdays for Rickover and for his people as well. Holidays, family illnesses, and other mission-detracting aspects of life such as girlfriends were subjects of Rickover tirades time and time again.

Perhaps the most eloquent summary of his style comes from the literate submariner hero of World War II, Captain Edward L. Beach, author of the wonderful *Run Silent, Run Deep*, who wrote in the *Washington Post* in 1977:

> Rickover: a compulsive, driven, fiercely competitive person, one of a kind, who relishes that role and will never give it up. A genius at managing people, who has discovered the singular ability to establish perfection as commonplace among those working for him, or with him, so that the smallest hint of either pleasure or displeasure from him carries 50 times the weight coming from anyone else. A man who fully realizes his strength comes from self-effacement (which is more apparent than real), his willingness to knuckle down with anyone, high or low, on a technical matter provided only that the other party is expert on the thing at issue (this is both apparent and completely true). A man adept at flattering the Congress or the press, yet unusually susceptible to the most elementary flattery himself. A man self-serving to an unbelievable degree, devoid of appreciation of or sympathy for the differences in people, intent only on getting his job done as he and he alone conceives it should be done.[8]

This singleness of purpose, this relentless pursuit of perfection in men and machines, engenders the sort of fear and respect that few leaders enjoy. Much of this has to be mythic once one reaches the scale of organization Rickover had to oversee when the NRB was created. One simply could not oversee six different sites staffed by hundreds of managers and engineers, all engaged in specialized activities about which no single person could know everything. And yet Rickover did an excellent job of seeming to be able to do just that.

He maintained this myth of ubiquity in several ways. First, he placed his civilian and military personnel in the manufacturing plants, engineering buildings, shipyards, nuclear training facilities, and the like, so that he could have direct and timely information about any ongoing operation. He repeatedly and vehemently insisted that his people report to him by telephone and memorandum what they observed. He guarded against the predictable tendency for people in decentralized organizations to "go native" with the threat of humiliating reprimand, poor performance evaluation, and/or outright dismissal, and he made loud public examples of those who strayed. Rickover made it well known that he did not mind questions from anyone, but he would get furious at those who failed to ask questions. His phone was always available for questions and reports from the field, and when *he* had questions, he would call anyone at virtually any time of the day or night, including company presidents and other corporate moguls.

Rickover's second major contribution to the ubiquity myth lay in his obsessive reading of "pinks," the carbon copies of all memoranda and letters emanating from anywhere in his command. Such carbons would often come back to their originators with spelling errors noted and with savage attacks on grammatical mistakes, not to mention comments and commands on matters of substance. It seemed that nothing happening under his command escaped his watchful eye.

A third aspect of the heroic and ubiquitous myth was noted by Beach in the article quoted above. Rickover was a man who did his homework on every technical issue his command had to face. It is important to recall that Rickover was an engineer as much as he was a naval officer and public entrepreneur. He realized that in order to succeed in the push to *Nautilus,* he would have to train himself and others in an engineering discipline that did not yet exist, nuclear engineering. He went to Oak Ridge in his late forties with absolutely no sophisticated understanding of nuclear physics and trained himself and his small cadre of engineers in this discipline. He wrote manuals and other materials that remained in use for years. The key point here is that Rickover's leadership style included as part of its mythic content the notion that engineering in the Navy was a process of continual education, and the paragon of self-education was none other than H.G. Rickover.

A fourth element in his leadership style is nicely symbolized by the matter of uniforms. Without commenting on the personal psychological aspects of Rickover's longstanding disdain for uniforms, it is possible to consider the effects of uniforms on leadership style in the context of the sort of organizations Rickover managed. Uniforms do at least two things: they identify rank and therefore deference patterns, and they indicate specialization of task, person, and experience. Thus one "reads" from the uniform how one is to deal with the other, what is to be expected about his fields of knowledge and experience, and especially, whether one is subordinate, what not to say, and how not to say it. Rickover avoided wearing uniforms to a degree others might find obsessional. In their lengthy biography of Rickover, Polmar and Allen have a picture of Rickover that they claim is the only known photograph of him in the uniform of a full admiral. They say that he had to be ordered by the secretary of the Navy to appear in it for, of all things, the dedication of Rickover Hall at the Naval Academy![9]

Was this merely a peculiar foible, or did it have to do with a particular style of leadership? While many naval officers would argue that it was merely an instance of Rickover's hostility or disrespect for the Navy, some consideration ought to be given to the effects uniforms have as semiotic devices in complex technical organizations. It should be noted that the best thinking on technical matters is as likely to come from the young, recently graduated as it is from the gray-haired senior member, simply because technical and scientific training and curricula become dated with increasing rapidity. Nowhere was this more apparent than in the race to solve the many technical problems entailed in the design and construction of the world's first shipboard nuclear propulsion system. In addition, the Navy had to rely on civilian brains to accomplish such tasks. Rickover—and this is true of all technical entrepreneurs like him in the public and private sectors—sought to solve problems that were new and different, not to maintain extant systems.

To solve a problem, especially one that can wreck a project if left unsolved, one needs the best brains, not the highest rank. If there was ever a military officer who realized this, it was Rickover. His discouragement of uniforms (and virtually no military officer in his command wore one) had the effect of limiting the normal "self-censorship" that lesser rank implies. Moreover, his project-management way of proceeding with the many aspects of the *Nautilus* and her successors elevated the status of one man or group of men, regardless of rank, while their problem area was being attended to. When the problem was solved or gotten around, the people involved either were reassigned to a new group or left the project entirely. Saluting uniforms and deferring to rank simply detracts from accomplishing the mission effectively and efficiently in such circumstances.

Finally, one must ask of a leader whether he had the demonstrated ability to inspire others to follow his example. On this score Rickover succeeded quite well, not only because he built a nuclear navy but because officers and men who served under him continue to believe in him as someone worthy of emulation. His striving for excellence, for perfection in all things, served as a model for the conduct of lesser men, which includes most of humanity. The most famous survivor of his infamous screening interviews is, of course, former President Carter, whose career was most deeply influenced by Rickover and his ideas.[10]

Perhaps the measure of Rickover's sense of his mission and purpose was best revealed in these well-known, highly mythologized interviews he used to conduct with every volunteer for the nuclear program. In these exercises, Rickover would misdirect, confuse, humiliate, and interrogate like the Grand Inquisitor with a sense of dark humor. The putative point of the interview was to select only the best officers for the nuclear Navy, and perhaps the interviews did serve some purpose in that regard. The latent function, however, was to perpetuate an idea of Rickover, of his standards, his expectations, and above all of his zealous commitment to excellence, in every aspect of a person's duty.

Another aspect of the Rickover leadership style had to do with the ways and means whereby Rickover did the essential thing that entrepreneurs do: obtain new mandates, missions, or organizational domains and the resources to support them. Rickover employed several strategies and a wide variety of tactics during his long career in the Navy, and it is to some of these that we now turn.

New Missions, Mandates, and Domains

The single greatest triumph of Rickover's career was the creation of a nuclear submarine. The bare facts of the story deserve repeating today, given what is more usually the case with research and development of weapons systems employing untested or unprecedented technologies. The *Nautilus* was ordered in August 1951; the reactor prototype went critical in March 1953; and the submarine was under way on nuclear power on 15 January 1955. It must be recalled that no one on earth had ever built a reactor for propulsion. No one had tried to actually build an operating system that would convert nuclear power to steam power to drive a vessel or vehicle, and no one had actually put such a system to the test of day-to-day operation.

Rickover had persuaded Admiral Mills to take a chance on him after Mills had become alarmed and then annoyed at what he viewed as the footdragging of the AEC. This involved the usual rounds of maneuvering and memo drafting that subordinates normally do when trying to gain a particular goal and want to overcome, not opposition, but the normal inertia of bureaucracy. There is no evidence to support later claims by Rickover that important actors in the Navy opposed the idea of the nuclear submarine. Indeed, the idea was a relatively old one, and no one familiar with the diesel submarine's need to surface frequently to recharge batteries could fail to support any idea that would rid the boats of this dangerous dependency. Submariners, many engineers, and others in BuShips supported the nuclear concept, but there were concerns about Rickover's involvement, and many individuals within the AEC scientific and engineering community had practical as well as political doubts.

The latter concerns had to do with the Navy's (or, for that matter, any of the armed forces') "getting ahead" of the AEC and thereby absorbing potential resources that otherwise might be available for basic scientific research. Rickover, of course, in situation after situation, kept repeating that the nuclear submarine required *no basic scientific research*. It needed only engineering, according to him, and he inveighed against the scientists who disagreed with him. He managed to convince first Mills and then the AEC commissioners that the labs and directors left over from the Manhattan District were simply not structured to deal with a problem like the nuclear submarine.

Who was?

Rickover had developed fairly good relations with Westinghouse and General Electric during his days in the Electrical Section. These he nurtured carefully, and by the mid–1950s he had essential control over a Westinghouse plant that worked solely under contracts from his NRB. General Electric was not about to lose control over any of its elements, but it still received and worked on contracts from Rickover. Thus the major elements for Rickover's new domain fell into place.

Once the NRB was created in BuShips and the Division of Reactor Development was secured in the AEC, Rickover began to wear whichever hat suited him when he was confronted with opposition or difficulty from either of his superiors or from external clients. These clients fell into two groups: those marginally dependent on Rickover and those fully invested. General Electric fell into the former category, Westinghouse and Electric Boat (builder of submarines for the Navy) in the latter. Rickover realized early on that the inertia in the Navy and the confusion in the new AEC constituted a resource of great potential.

This was a brilliant insight and marks the public entrepreneur. Where others saw chaos, Rickover saw an opportunity to accomplish that which informed opinion believed highly desirable but unlikely to happen in the foreseeable future. Rickover, with the zeal born of the impassioned, marginal naval officer and engineer, saw the nuclear submarine as the dream of his lifetime.

The years leading up to that moment in 1955 when the *Nautilus* went to sea under nuclear power are among the best of Rickover's life and among the most fascinating in the history of modern technology. What Rickover did was to bring the people and resources together to face the unknown and known contingencies involved in turning theoretical knowledge into practical application. Technical problems of wholly unprecedented sorts were scheduled to be solved along the path of development before anyone knew how (or if) they were to be solved. Today this is called "technology forcing"; then it was simply crazy. Yet Rickover, eschewing rank, formal lines of authority, the public/private distinction, and a host of lesser constraints, put together teams of people to solve these very serious problems. He and his teams of exhausted men and women managed to pull it off. The Rickover legend began to spread with the success of the *Nautilus*.

By the mid-1950s Rickover had secured a place for himself and his two organizations by virtue of holding a monopoly over reactor development for military purposes. This was, strictly speaking, an R&D role that in the normal course of events required that the finished product be produced in factories, installed in ships, and given over to operational commanders of the fleet. Rickover had larger ambitions, and these began to be apparent following the retirement crisis of 1952–53. He had failed to convince the Eisenhower administration and the AEC to further fund a large ship reactor (LSR) that he had begun work on in hopes of building the first nuclear supercarrier. This project was the first public signal of Rickover's next great mandate, or at least his hoped-for mandate: the construction of a nuclear surface fleet. But the setback did not deter Rickover, and the ineffectiveness of the AEC played into his hand, fortuitously once again.

To make a long story short, the AEC had been created to develop both the military and the civilian aspects of nuclear power, one of the more obvious of the latter aspects being the generation of electrical power.[11] The means for doing so were to involve venture capital *from the private sector* under the watchful and benevolent eye of the AEC. Regrettably for the AEC, no private-sector actors were very interested in putting money into such a potentially costly and risky enterprise when so many cost-plus contracts were available already from the Defense Department (DOD). Public utilities, already indemnified by state and local government, tended not to take risks on new technologies. So the AEC never did develop a civilian reactor. It should come as no shock that the AEC found someone who did indeed have a reactor design and prototype ready for adaptation to their needs. The revamped LSR became the first nuclear reactor to generate steam to turn turbines to light the homes of those folks in western Pennsylvania serviced by the Duquesne Light Company. And this was courtesy of Admiral Rickover.

Rickover's dream for the Navy, though, was far from realized. Following the path of the nuclear submarine, one finds Rickover repeatedly insisting that the system was so extraordinary that new structures and procedures had to be created to avoid grave danger and ensure success. This single line of reasoning was the sole justification for entrepreneurial leaps into the most traditional preserves of the Navy: staffing and operations at sea.

What began as the quite reasonable claim that the officers and men of the *Nautilus* should be trained in the operation and maintenance of the nuclear power plant ended up with the creation of the "Rickover Navy." As the number of nuclear submarines increased, so too did Rickover's influence over the naming of officers and men. And as the number of nuclear-powered surface ships increased, again Rickover increased his influence over who got to command (or to have the hope of one day commanding) ships. Rickover always felt that engineering officers had suffered unfairly throughout the history of the Navy and believed it a fatal flaw for line officers not to be thoroughly knowledgeable about the propulsion system upon which their ships depended.[12] The transition from sail to steam had been characterized by the stigmatization of the engineer by the above-deck officers. Indeed, in the early years, engineers were not even naval officers, and it was not until 1916 that the Navy finally created a special class of officers, Engineering Duty Only (EDO). Rickover was an EDO, and although EDOs were not to command ships, they did have a route to upward mobility within the Navy, though few made it to admiral before the modern era. With his efforts to create a totally nuclear navy, Rickover could ensure through his training schools that virtually everyone would be one of his "nucs" eventually.

The operations of ships at sea, once they have been accepted by the Navy from the builder, traditionally follow regular Navy procedure: fleet commanders issue orders. Period. Except in the case of a nuclear ship: on a nuclear ship, a line of communication was kept open to the NRB so that safety and maintenance problems and routines could be constantly monitored. In other words, Rickover kept his finger in the pie long after the ship or sub became operational. Indeed, one of the things that the NRB did was to call inspections at any time, and when he had the chance, Rickover himself would appear and terrorize the ship's company as he put it through its paces.

The justification for all of this was always the same: the safety of the nuclear ship and its crew. In testimony before Congress, Rickover always argued that there was no danger to the operation of onboard ship reactors, but he held at the same time that eternal vigilance was required. (Rickover forbade the entry of nuclear-powered ships into crowded American harbors for years.) It is impossible to find anyone whose influential reach compares to Rickover's within the Navy. His span of influence and power is all the more remarkable given the ostensible role of the NRB within the Navy. How this unique status was gained is a question we now address.

External Constituencies: Boundary Spanning for Survival and Expansion

The retirement crisis is easily marked as the moment when Rickover became something more than just another naval officer. It will be recalled that even with the rapid and very successful progress of the

nuclear submarine project, the Navy had passed Rickover over for promotion once in 1951 and a second time in 1952. This meant that he was
to retire automatically in 1953. According to several interviews with
his peers, Rickover's way of looking at the world changed in 1951, when
he was first passed over. The point is made that until he was passed
over, Rickover had contemplated a normal promotion to rear admiral,
then perhaps a regular tour as BuShips chief, followed by retirement
in his late fifties or early sixties.

Apparently, Rickover never discussed this point with anyone, so
the above must remain speculative. Whatever might have been the case,
a "new" Rickover became evident in two new areas of entrepreneurial
concern, and these were to drive him for a generation. The first of these
involved the direct lobbying of Congress, and the second, a major investment in public relations. The nurturing of Congress as an external
constituency had begun quietly and predictably in the course of the
struggle to gain a beachhead in the Navy and the AEC in order to build
the nuclear submarine.

Nearly all contacts had been programmatic and according to Hoyle
prior to 1951. Rickover had met his share of influential people before
1951, but when the *Nautilus* was ordered, a whole new period began.
Rickover's advocacy of the nuclear submarine before formal and informal groups of politicians was both Messianic and extraordinarily well
prepared. He made a very strong and quite favorable impression with
his insistence on meeting deadlines and his concern for cost and safety.
By the time he was passed over for promotion in 1951, those who knew
him in Congress were already very impressed. When Sidney Yates, who
represented Rickover's old district in Chicago, learned of the passing
over, he and some allies went on the warpath. By the time of the second
promotion rebuff, both houses of Congress were energized, including a
newcomer to the Senate, Henry ("Scoop") Jackson of Washington, who
had met Rickover and spent many hours with him on a long plane ride
to a nuclear test site in the Pacific in the late forties.

The general familiarity of Congress with Captain Rickover came
about as much from his investment in public relations as from his direct
association with politicians. Clay Blair, a long-time Luce publications
reporter and World War II submarine veteran, published stories in *Life*
and *Time* that established Rickover's legend as a tough, no-nonsense,
honest officer trying to save the Navy from its own bureaucratic obesity.
In 1952 Truman laid the keel of the *Nautilus*, and Rickover got more
publicity. Yet, within a month, the selection board met and Rickover
was effectively retired. Blair, kept informed by Rickover's staff, fired
the first guns of what was to be the beginning of a public entrepreneurial
assault on traditional boundaries.

In the 4 August 1952 issue of *Time* there appeared an article on the passing over of Rickover for promotion. Headed "Brazen Prejudice," the article took the selection board to task for failing to acknowledge the role of EDOs in the complex technological Navy of the future. Many interpreted the title as referring to the fact that Rickover was a Jew (or at least that he had been born a Jew, for by this time he had become an Episcopalian). It is impossible to know what was in the minds of the men who made up the selection board, since no records are ever kept of the board's deliberations and members swear to keep discussions secret. There is no direct evidence that Rickover was discriminated against, but many of those who disliked him also mentioned his Jewish birth.

Rickover himself stayed far behind the scenes during this period. Blair and Rickover's top staff worked on the campaign to save Rickover, and soon a Blair draft, submitted to the Navy for security clearance but actually intended to stir up the opposition to see what it was up to, put the fat in the fire. The Navy was on the defensive, and trying to counterattack, it lost the battle. The Navy found itself defending its promotion procedures in general and attacking Rickover as, in effect, a sore loser. Never was there a more willing Goliath to Rickover's David. Blair moved into offices near Rickover's and began writing Rickover's biography. Ray Dick, one of Rickover's staff from the early days at Oak Ridge, quietly but effectively began to lobby Congress. Yates and Jackson soon had allies, and by early 1953 the Navy retreated in the face of the humiliation that a rejection of its entire promotion list would have meant.

The Navy created a new selection board with a precept that one of the EDOs chosen was to have the substantial nuclear power experience that happened to be possessed only by Rickover. Rickover was thus guaranteed promotion. He had also developed along the way a new constituency and a public persona which became a marvelous resource. He managed to run (or approve) a publicity campaign and a lobbying strategy while simultaneously appearing to do neither. He remained the reluctant informant, the no-nonsense guy just trying to do his job despite the sluggish bureaucracy, presumed social bigotry, and a host of other impediments. No matter how powerful he became, he continued to convey this image.

The retirement crisis left Rickover with some permanent lessons. The first was to curry favor with Congress directly rather than to rely on the Navy hierarchy. His status following the retirement issue required such a posture, for it was obvious that without that crucial external constituency, there was no career left for Hyman Rickover in the Navy. No lobbyist ever exercised such thorough care and feeding of congressmen. Rickover held meetings of subcommittees on submerged nuclear submarines; he had subs named after the more powerful committee members and had their wives do the ceremonial launching. For years he would write personal notes to relevant politicians on ship's stationery headed "On the maiden cruise of the U.S.S. _____ ."

He was both adored and feared by the naval and private-sector shipyards, since any vessel constructed with a nuclear power plant entailed Rickover and his ubiquitous staff's monitoring everything. Westinghouse, General Electric, General Dynamics, and hundreds of smaller firms did huge amounts of business with Rickover, and despite attempts to keep him out of contracting and procurement, nothing related to the nuclear Navy escaped his comment, and often his interference. Rickover's proclaimed point of view could be nothing but pleasing to most contractors and congressmen. On the one hand, he could expedite contracting and payment schedules, including lots of change orders, in a manner that pleased contractors and vendors; on the other hand, he could excoriate those contractors and vendors whom he thought were giving the Navy less than it had contracted for. Such a balance was very much like the one he had maintained during his public relations exercises: he was a powerful naval officer *and* a David fighting Goliath. He was a thrifty, letter-of-the-law contractee *and* a man who spent billions on programs that might well have cost more than they were worth.

Rickover's boundary spanning began for purposes of his own survival. As a consequence of becoming a lobbyist and publicist who never failed to identify himself with his program (as though the two could never be pulled apart), he created a power base in Congress and in the press that was to endure for nearly thirty years. On that base he built an empire, the nuclear Navy.

Once Rickover had built a nuclear navy, the functions of the NRB, his internal constituencies and his external support network had to change. This was so because Rickover had managed to add to the NRB new areas of responsibility that took it far beyond research and development. By the years of Carter's presidency (1977–81), Rickover's schools had trained thousands of men, many of whom had moved up in the hierarchy of the nonnuclear Navy. They were known as "nucs," and their devotion to Rickover remained strong in most cases, well after they had left his command.

Rickover's claims about nuclear propulsion's potential for naval warfare were shared by several generations of naval officers by the mid-1970s. His commitment to duty continued to inspire many, including those who could not live up to it. The net result of his years of recruitment and training led naturally to a large, loyal internal constituency that looked after Rickover's interests throughout the Navy. Indeed, they did so well that Rickover was accused of creating, not a nuclear navy, but rather a "Rickover Navy." Thus, sympathetic naval officers plus Rickover's great sway in Congress provided conditions for maintaining the operational and personnel authority Rickover possessed well beyond the R&D and shipbuilding phases.

His friends on Capitol Hill, in the press, in the AEC, in the Pentagon, and in the Navy kept a watchful eye out for Rickover, warning him, when necessary, of sharks in the water. But such warnings were seldom needed, for Rickover's "sharks" had always been the regular Navy and civilian political appointees who believed they were to direct and control the future of the Navy. Going back to Lewis Strauss, the chairman of the old AEC under Eisenhower, one civilian after another had tried to limit Rickover's demands for a totally nuclear navy. Robert McNamara and Paul Nitze, among many civilian political appointees, opposed either his programs or Rickover himself.

The objections to Rickover personally derived from two sources. The first was the familiar complaints from the regular Navy, and the second had to do with his tendency to undercut DOD budget and program submissions before Congress when they did not, in his view, sufficiently support the nuclear Navy. He opposed any proposal that showed an increase in the number of conventionally powered ships. Thus, a proposal to build two small carriers powered by oil rather than one nuclear supercarrier was, according to Rickover, simply wrong logistically, strategically, and certainly tactically, even if the proposal came from the secretary of defense and the president. In the latter case, Rickover did not overtly assault the administration: he simply attacked instead the bad advice from what he termed "idiots" or worse in the Pentagon. Rickover's sources of vulnerability in the environment were well known to him and to his "nucs."

Technical Expertise: The Legitimation of Entrepreneurship in the Navy

The building of the first nuclear-powered propulsion system was one of the great engineering feats of the past fifty years. The creation of a nuclear-powered fleet of submarines *and* surface ships was one of the great organizational and political triumphs of public entrepreneurship in the modern era. But the piecemeal restructuring of large parts of the U.S. Navy by an obscure naval engineer is almost beyond rational explanation if one believes that peacetime military services are not highly plastic organizations. To a large extent, this chapter has offered explanations in brief detail as to how these changes took place. These explanations and descriptions have dealt with institutions, situations, and personalities and little with the larger questions of culture, both the culture of the West in general and the culture of the Navy specifically. Our concern with technical expertise in the case of the nuclear Navy turns us now to the idea of technical culture.

Rickover once wrote a speech entitled "The Role of Engineering in the Navy." In it he chronicled the development of new engineering marvels like the steam engine, but what was more significant, he spoke of engineers as the unsung heroes of the Navy, long neglected and despised by their glorious peers at the helms and guns. A very deep, long-lasting concern is clearly spelled out in this 1974 speech. Following an outline of what he required of every modern nuclear ship line officer, Rickover said:

> These requirements produce line officers who are familiar with the operating details of their propulsion plants and are not afraid to get their hands dirty. When reports from subordinates conflict, or where they doubt the accuracy, they know enough to look for themselves and to put the weight of their own experience behind the decision. They also know how to train their officers and men and inspect their plant. They possess that essential requisite of leadership—to educate and to train. I would much rather have officers with this kind of experience than those with postgraduate degrees in systems analysis, computer science, management, or business administration—as many of the Navy's line officers now have. The machinery does not respect these irrelevant capabilities.[13]

Indeed, it is to machinery that one must turn to understand much about Rickover's success. "Man/machine systems" is a short but adequate definition of technology that points us in Rickover's direction, for he was a military officer far ahead of his time in comprehending the new relations between fighting men and their machines.[14] A ship is both a social system and a weapon. As the years go by, the effectiveness and safety of the ship depend more and more upon machines, complex machines that see, hear, move, and communicate. The ships on which Rickover served in the 1920s bear little but a cosmetic relationship to the modern edition. The basics remain the same: men (and now women) afloat on a vessel whose purpose is to frighten or destroy potential or actual enemies.

The similarities begin to disappear with a closer inspection. They need not be elaborated in detail here. We note that the ship is propelled by the action of a nuclear reactor, that it sees and hears its environment with machines of various types to navigate and to target weapons. Each one is a substitute for an earlier machine and an earlier weapon. We must note the passing of the gun and the introduction of the guided missile and of course the presence of nuclear weapons for both tactical and strategic purposes. This web of machines and people at sea is the modern ship, and the modern ship mirrors and is reflected by the modern Navy.

With respect to the headlong introduction of new technology, Rickover was a prophet *with* honor in his own land. There is little question that the *Nautilus* would have been built by the Navy sooner or later, but the point remains that Rickover did build it and defined many of the conditions for the human web that came to surround it. The organization adapted itself to the new technology, and Rickover was the agent of adaptation in this case. While there were fights over turf and over Rickover's high-handed methods, there is no evidence that others suggested a different way for the Navy to adapt to the new technology. Above all, the technology *seemed* to require new methods of training, safety precautions, and the like.[15]

To its internal and external constituencies the nuclear Navy appeared both necessary and desirable once it was possible. For others it appeared inevitable, and if this "march of progress" seemed overdetermined, there was always the Soviet Union to cap the argument. The litany is most familiar to the modern reader: if we do not build it, the Russians will, and then they will have an advantage, and so on, and so on. Whatever variation of such claims one prefers matters little: the results are identical. Rickover perceived such technological inevitability and acted on the fact that virtually everyone else believed in the argument in some form. He thus had a legitimating vehicle for his entrepreneurship, the theme of technological innovation. Rickover's emphasis on technical accomplishment and expertise had added historical force during his career, one unavailable to private entrepreneurs who typically must please someone involved in market transactions.

The intense and dangerous rivalry between the two superpowers formed the historical context for Rickover's entrepreneurship. A continuing aspect of this rivalry has been an unparalleled arms race of which the nuclear Navy is certainly a part. The job of selling external and internal constitutencies on the idea of a nuclear submarine may have been impeded by competitors' demands upon the same resources Rickover sought, but no one argued against the desirability of the submarine itself. Where Rickover differed from others selling one military technology or another lay in his attempt to restructure the Navy itself to become a more technologically sophisticated military force. This he succeeded in doing to a remarkable degree because he was converting the already nearly converted.

World War II was the watershed for the shift to a technological

Navy from one that had been at best reluctant to accept major change. The role of airpower in the destruction of the fleet at Pearl Harbor and the decisive role of carriers in the pivotal battle of the Pacific theater at Midway altered thinking about technology and strategy. Radar won the Battle of Britain as surely as those brave young men in their Spitfires. The toll taken by enemy submarines on Allied shipping was a lesson of World War I finally given full recognition only after another world war. The list of potentially war-winning technologies was, of course, headed by the atomic bomb, which many professional military men thought would end warfare as they knew it forever.

Rickover's fight with those whose status (or hoped-for status) depended on an evidently dead technology like the battleship was far from over, but the forces of retrograde traditionalism were on the run. Rickover wanted them to disappear, and in creating "his" Navy, he accomplished much on this agenda. He did so in part because of his clever use of the "technology determines my actions" argument discussed above. The experience of World War II converted or almost converted many in the Navy to the view that to fail to introduce new technologies was to risk falling behind the Soviets and, worse still, the U.S. Air Force, that new creation of 1946 fabricated out of a rib of the Army. The Air Force's interest in strategic missile development and air power seemed to threaten the Navy's future as the longest arm of American military power.

The forces that tended to act as stimuli to technological change were positive and powerful. Rickover was determined to use those forces to build a navy of technowarriors filled with a sense of duty and the technical expertise to accomplish the mission of the Navy. Although he did not win his war against the systems analysts, Rickover did manage to elevate technical expertise to a core position among "nucs" and thereby in large chunks of the Navy. Whether the Navy could have or would have continued to be the conservative, socially limited, old-boy network Rickover criticized so vigorously is unknowable.

It is reasonable to suggest that the technical expertise and sophistication of those who have served in the nuclear Navy is probably greater than it would have been had Rickover not had total control over nuclear matters. His dogged insistence on technical training and the many years during which he was able to enforce his will made his influence on the general level of technical expertise in the U.S. nuclear enterprise great indeed. It must be remembered that his influence goes far beyond the Navy. The personnel of the civilian nuclear industry are, according to one estimate, graduates of the nuclear Navy to a majority extent. As a diffuser of nuclear engineering technology, Rickover had few rivals, inside the military or out.

Conclusions

The long-term impact of Rickover's entrepreneurship can be only partially assessed, since it is only a few years since his retirement from active duty, but some evaluation is possible. The most visible and least debatable impact on the United States and the world is, of course, the nuclear submarine. Combined with the Polaris missile, the nuclear submarine became the least vulnerable and therefore the most potent weapon yet devised by mankind. The successors to the Polaris boats, the mighty Trident types, are now at sea, and their numbers grow yearly. The hidden nuclear submarine, capable of delivering an enormous megatonnage at tremendous range with great accuracy, owes much to the work of H. G. Rickover.

Rickover's impact on the way the Navy trains its nuclear crews is evident because his program of training remains after his departure. Perhaps more important is his impact on the men who now run the Navy and its nuclear ships at sea. He inspired people to work harder and better than they thought they could, and in this he followed his own dictum that good leaders are good educators and trainers. He inspired people during the great adventure of building the first nuclear submarine. Once his triumph had become institutionalized, however, his leadership changed, and there is some reason to argue that in his later years he became rigid and temperamental.

A central question in the idea of entrepreneurial behavior in the public sector has to do with the problem of comparability. Was Rickover simply so unusual, so talented, and so lucky that there is little in general to learn from his career? Or are the circumstances of his "luck" likely to be repeated in this age of policy analysis and collective decision making? Perhaps a brief return to the questions posed at the beginning of this chapter will help to arrive at some conclusions, if not answers.

It was claimed above that Rickover "saw the immense potential of nuclear energy . . . but was the only one to seize upon nuclear energy as an organizational resource." Rickover, we may guess, is not likely to be the last nor certainly the only person to seize upon a technology and ride it as far and as fast as he or she is able. Certainly, this is a parable of the private-sector ideology of the 1980s. Absent the profit motive, the NRB and the little four-star admiral who created it might be the envy of the "high-tech" firm so loudly applauded today. New technologies with the potential for greatly altering the extant pattern of resource allocation in either the public or the private sector are a vital resource for growth. But technologies tend to be self-augmenting only if they have the fuel of human ambition to drive and nurture them.

There are few better examples of this than the nuclear Navy.

Earlier I also argued that Rickover exploited the structural confusion created by the Atomic Energy Act which, it will be recalled, established a civilian monopoly over all nuclear technology and materials. It is an old idea to exploit overlap and contradiction to obtain a whole that is greater than the sum of its parts. The most famous example of this was Alfred Sloan's decision to restructure General Motors as if it were five competing companies. Unfortunately, the U.S. government in its wisdom attempted to do precisely the opposite: that is, to totally separate military from civilian control over the atom. Rickover played the GM game: he pretended that the two entities were separate when it suited him. Much as Chevrolet "competed" with Pontiac, the head of the Naval Reactors Branch of the AEC could rule a Navy request out of line, thereby forbidding the assistant chief of BuShips from doing this or that. One wonders whether Rickover ever forgot which hat he was wearing! Entrepreneurs tend to see opportunity in structural confusion, while managers tend to want to rationalize things so that contradiction and overlap are disposed of by organizational design.

Rickover realized after the retirement crisis that his future depended more on mobilizing external constituencies than on pleasing the hierarchy above him. Again this is entrepreneurial behavior, not so different from that of modern private-sector entrepreneurs. It is a cliché today to note the young engineers who seek venture capital outside the organization that employs them so that they can break away and start a rival organization. Public-sector types seek the same autonomy and power, either by creating new organizations or by restructuring old ones. Eventually, the new creation must come into conflict with the parent or other competitors. At that point the spanning of boundaries in order to buffer the core that is the new baby becomes paramount. Thus Rickover began to court Congress lovingly when he became a major competitor for the resources likely to be allocated to the Navy as a whole. Our claim that Rickover, like other public enterpreneurs, sought support outside the Navy in order to ensure the long-term viability of his organization seems sustained by the analysis so far.

One of the curious and important elements of American political ideology has to do with the term *political*. Another aspect of political ideology centers on the word *bureaucracy*. As a nation we must surely stand out as among the truly gifted in hypocrisy, and this is no small accomplishment, for the field is crowded. We hate anything that is "political" or "playing politics," yet our system of government, about which we are justly proud, was intended to be run by politicians engaging in politics. The stigma of "politics" is removed only after death, it seems. Lincoln is remembered today as a hero, a secular saint, certainly not a politician. While he lived, he was a politician if ever there was one.

A *bureaucracy* comprises hierarchically structured offices and roles characterized by professionalization, rules, and specialization of task. In popular parlance, IBM is a *corporation*, not a *bureaucracy*. Few polite terms rank with *bureaucracy* for odiousness. No politician who runs against bureaucracy can be making a mistake. Modern presidential candidates all run on cleaning up the mess in Washington by getting rid of all that bureaucracy and those unnecessary rules. No one cheers bureaucracy. The fact is, however, that no public purpose of any significance or duration was ever produced or sustained without politics and without bureaucracy.

Rickover realized that the two terms needed special handling if his entrepreneurial activities were to be seen in the proper light. He was always and everywhere "above politics" while being a consummate politician. He regaled Congress and the press with anti-Pentagon, anti-bureaucratic rhetoric while building a remarkable bureaucracy of his own. Rickover was a "public servant," not a politician; an engineer, not a bureaucrat. His recognition of the language games of American political hypocrisy was an important asset for a bureaucratic politician bent on building and maintaining his organization.

It would be wrong to conclude that Rickover merely wanted to build an empire for his own personal benefit. Rickover was a complex zealot, a man who, like all men, was moved by multiple, sometimes contradictory forces of psyche and circumstance. His dreams and his fears for America and for the Navy arose as much from reason as from the insecurities of an immigrant child trying to make it in that most American of places, the U.S. Navy. In the end his ego became so removed from events that it was possible for him to have General Dynamics executives do him small favors that would eventually result in a letter of censure from the Navy. What is so remarkable about this is that Rickover, of all people, should have ignored even the appearance of a conflict of interest.

Rickover represents a combination of traits, both unique and general, that typify the public entrepreneur. His energy, ambition, and tenacity were truly remarkable. Every account of the man remarks on his tireless energy, his virtually constant work schedule, his studious attention to detail, especially technical detail. Public entrepreneurs typically work longer and harder than other people.

The linkage of his career with the growth and development of a new technology within the context of the cold war and in a social era enamored with technical fixes is crucial. The manager-engineer-entrepreneur has approximated a cultural hero since the Civil War and rivals the Jeffersonian yeoman of the ante-bellum era. Men like Edison, Herbert Hoover, Thomas Watson, and David Packard combined technical and organizational skills of various degrees with a zeal for making something new and lasting. Rickover belongs in such company, for he fulfilled so many elements of the American dream: a poor, lonely boy fighting against bureaucracy and prejudice makes it to the top through dedicated hard work and devotion to a dream greater than his own glory.

If there is utility in the notion of public entrepreneurship, then Rickover surely demonstrated it. Theories of American politics do not account for the person who arises from public bureaucracy to create something new and significant without benefit of election or political appointment. Our heroes and villains arise out of large, complex organizations in the late twentieth century, and it is likely that they will do the same in the twenty-first century. The life and times of Hyman G. Rickover provide an interesting moment in the past to learn something about the future.

Notes

1. The analytical structure of this essay follows the general outlines of the discussion of Rickover in Eugene Lewis, *Public Entrepreneurship: Toward a Theory of Bureaucratic Political Power* (Bloomington: Indiana University Press, 1980).

2. Biographical material dealing with Rickover's early years through his years in the Electrical Section of the Bureau of Ships comes from Norman Polmar and Thomas Allen's lengthy biography, *Rickover* (New York: Simon & Schuster, 1982). This excellent narrative is a useful antidote to Clay Blair, Jr., *The Atomic Submarine and Admiral Rickover* (New York: Henry Holt & Co., 1954), which is interesting because it represents what Rickover and his wife wanted in the public press during the retirement crisis.

3. The relevant sociological and anthropological literature is vast, as are the popular accounts, both fictional and nonfictional. The works of Glazer and Moynihan, Gans, and Roth, among others, testify to the structural conditions Rickover encountered in his formative years (see Nathan Glazer and Daniel P. Moynihan, *Beyond the Melting Pot* [Cambridge: MIT Press, 1970]; Herbert J. Gans, *The Urban Villagers* [New York: Free Press of Glencoe, 1962]; and Henry Roth, *Call It Sleep* [New York: Cooper Square Publishing, 1976]).

4. Most of the factual elements covering the period from World War II through the early years of the Kennedy administration come from Richard G. Hewlett and Francis Duncan, *Nuclear Navy, 1946–1962* (Chicago: University of Chicago Press, 1974). The Nuclear Reactors Branch (NRB) was established in 1948 in the Bureau of Ships and in the Atomic Energy Commission. Thereafter, it was split between the Naval Reactors Branch of the AEC and the Nuclear Power Division of the Bureau of Ships.

5. There is a penetrating cameo of Rickover in David E. Lilienthal, *The Journals of David E. Lilienthal*, vol. 3, *The Venturesome Years, 1950–1955* (New York: Harper & Row, 1966). Lilienthal, who met Rickover on a train in July 1954, one year after

the retirement crisis, described him thus: "There is something exceptional about his face. It is a small face, almost as if one were looking at him through the wrong end of a telescope . . . that kind of smallness. There is a kind of Chinese, or in any case an Oriental, repose or immobility in his expression which is strange, considering that what he says is usually severely condemnatory of others and extreme" (531).

6. Richard Pfau, *No Sacrifice Too Great: The Life of Lewis L. Strauss* (Charlottesville: University of Virginia Press, 1984), 139, 186.

7. Blair, *Admiral Rickover*, 47.

8. E. L. Beach, "Life under Rickover," *Washington Post*, 27 May 1977.

9. Polmar and Allen, *Rickover*, following 286.

10. Jimmy Carter, *Why Not the Best?* (Nashville: Broadman Press, 1975), 55–60.

11. Richard G. Hewlett and Francis Duncan, *History of the United States Atomic Energy Commission*, vol. 2, *Atomic Shield, 1947–1952* (University Park and London: Pennsylvania State University Press, 1969). David Lilienthal, in his train meeting with Rickover in 1954 (see n. 5 above), told Rickover that he thought the idea of civilian nuclear power to generate electricity was economically unsound. He expected strong disagreement from the admiral but instead got a sad, philosophical agreement.

12. Hyman G. Rickover, "The Role of Engineering in the Navy" (Speech delivered to the National Society of Former Special Agents of the FBI, Seattle, Wash., 30 August 1974, Mimeo).

13. Ibid., 17.

14. Elting E. Morison deals with this theme in several chapters of his excellent collection of essays *Men, Machines and Modern Times* (Cambridge: MIT Press, 1966).

15. William H. McNeill, *The Pursuit of Power* (Chicago: University of Chicago Press, 1982), explores this interrelationship between military men and their technologies in a brilliant history of the subject.

5

To Claim the Seas and the Skies: Austin Tobin and the Port of New York Authority

Jameson W. Doig

The first months of 1961 were more eventful than usual for Austin J. Tobin, executive director of the Port of New York Authority. In January he set forth a detailed proposal that would expand Port Authority operations into the rail transit field; in March he urged that his agency construct a seventy-two-story world trade center near the Brooklyn Bridge; in May he submitted a report on the need for a great new airport in northern New Jersey; in June he was found guilty of criminal contempt of Congress and sentenced to thirty days in jail.

If these months were unusual, however, they differed only in degree from other months and years of Tobin's adult life—stretching back to the early days of World War II, when he assumed command of the nation's largest port authority, and still further back, to his battles in the 1930s to preserve tax-exempt bonds from the onslaughts of Franklin Roosevelt and Henry Morgenthau.

During all of these years and many more, Austin Tobin had been a member of the career staff at the Port Authority. He joined the agency in 1927, when Calvin Coolidge was in the White House and the Port Authority had no bridges or tunnels or, indeed, any operating facilities at all. As a member of the law department, Tobin worked on real estate acquisitions needed as the Authority went forward with plans to construct a freight terminal, several bridges, and the Lincoln Tunnel. Fifteen years later, in 1942, he was chosen as executive director, and his days and nights thereafter were occupied almost entirely with the programs and the needs of the Port agency. He was, from this perspective, an exemplar of the career civil service tradition.

However, if that tradition implies neutral competence in the service of goals and policies decided elsewhere (by elected leaders and by the electorate), then perhaps he was not the ideal civil servant. For Austin Tobin enjoyed the exercise of power too much, looked forward too eagerly to the challenge of battling vigorous opponents, and had too clear a vision of how his agency could shape the future of the New York metropolis to sit in careerist harness, awaiting orders. He was, in brief, too entrepreneurial to be neutral.

Between 1942 and the summer of 1961, when he faced the judge's bench, Tobin led the Port of New York Authority into new fields of endeavor—wresting three major airports from Fiorello LaGuardia, Robert Moses, and the city fathers of Newark; adding marine terminals in his home community of Brooklyn and at Hoboken, Newark, and Elizabeth on the New Jersey shore; and constructing two of the biggest truck terminals in the world and an immense bus terminal. In support of these goals and other values he believed were important, Tobin and his aides also established new training and affirmative-action programs, reorganized the Port Authority staff so that the concept of responsibility centers (and profit centers) could be applied in program leadership and evaluation, and created a new type of revenue bond which would increase the Authority's flexibility in reaching out for new program areas. Moreover, his interests were not limited to the New York region; throughout his career, Tobin took on wider challenges—orchestrating the national battle against Treasury Secretary Henry Morgenthau's 1938 plan to eliminate tax exemption on municipal bonds, organizing the airport operators in the 1940s to resist the airlines' pressures for municipal subsidies, and working with other port authorities in order to strengthen maritime commerce in his own country and to improve port facilities in developing nations.

Although Austin Tobin appeared in these ways to reach beyond the tradition of "neutral" career official, it would be incorrect to view Tobin and his Port Authority simply as freewheeling entrepreneurs, indifferent to the shackles of legislative control and the sentiments of the general public, going their own way much as did the railroad barons of the nineteenth century. No major program initiatives could be undertaken by the Port Authority without legislative support; indeed, the legislatures of two states, New Jersey and New York, had to vote their approval. And the influence of the two governors was potentially overwhelming: they could block any new program by failing to sign legislative bills; moreover, every month they received the minutes of actions taken by the Port Authority's commissioners, and each governor held the power to veto any and all items in those monthly minutes. There were other reins of accountability too, as we shall see below.

Mindful of the central lines of gubernatorial and legislative control, we might conclude that Tobin's initiatives were closely reviewed and guided—that despite evidence of great entrepreneurial activity, he actually did operate within the appropriate range for an energetic yet "neutrally competent" career government official. This is essentially the view expressed by Tobin himself. As he explained to a group of elected officials in 1960, the legislatures of New Jersey and New York State "carefully delineated the functions the Authority was to perform and the manner in which it was to perform them." On another occasion, reviewing the web of legislative and gubernatorial controls, he called attention particularly to the governor's power to veto all policy actions of the agency's leaders:

> Very few authorities are so completely subject to review by the elected representatives of the people. This is a complete answer to the alleged autonomy of the Port Authority, and yet it is cavalierly dismissed by critics simply because the Governors have rarely had occasion to exercise the veto.[1]

Within the domain of the Port Authority, too, Tobin operated under substantial constraints, for Authority policies were formally determined not by the executive director but by the board of commissioners—twelve individuals appointed by the governors, six from each state—who relied upon Tobin and his staff for "day-to-day management of the organization."[2]

None of these factual characterizations is erroneous, but the reality is more interesting and more complex. For years on end, the legislatures of both states and the two governors carefully delineated functions and policies for the Port Authority—but they did so, with few exceptions, in response to the Authority's own carefully developed proposals. During the 1940s and 1950s Tobin and his staff devised impressive plans for improving transportation and terminal facilities in the New York region and took them to business leaders, local officials, and the press for discussion and quite often for applause. The Port Authority's own commissioners were also informed, at an early stage; a few made suggestions which modified the proposals in modest ways, and many of them used their own enthusiasm and persuasive energy to convince their colleagues in the business world to support these plans. Governors and other key officials in Trenton and Albany were consulted too.

And then these plans, crafted with imagination and skill, honed and modified in negotiations with influential leaders and groups, were laid upon the legislative desks—with a promise that the Port Authority would cover all costs. For the traffic across Austin Tobin's bridges and through his tunnels, later joined by the revenue from airports and marine terminals, generated enough income that the Port of New York Authority could pay out of its own pocket for every new project its officials proposed. Perhaps it was not surprising, then, that through these years state officials were generally willing to approve the Port Authority's plans, which arrived with wide public and press support, would not cost a penny in state taxes, and might, if approved and carried out, reflect credit on governors and legislators too. Even if some of these officials might prefer that these funds be employed in other ways—for other transportation programs or even for hospitals or education—those choices were not presented and essentially were not available. And so the projects favored by Tobin and his aides went forward. Not all of them, but many, large and small.[3]

By 1960, however, Tobin's entrepreneurial reach seemed to have exceeded his grasp, as plans for a massive new jetport tumbled out of the sky and a congressional committee attacked the integrity of the agency's works and the independence of its style. In 1960 and 1961, Tobin was involved in sharp conflict over the Port Authority's activities in several program areas—in rail transit, air transport, and its proposal to build a world trade center. Then, in the summer of 1961, a federal judge meted out a jail term to Tobin because he refused to permit the House Judiciary committee to examine all his agency's internal records; this was, perhaps, the nadir of a very difficult two-year period.

But Austin Tobin did not go to prison; the sentence handed down by the district court in *United States* v. *Tobin* was overturned on appeal the next year. Instead he held the executive reins for ten more years, as the Port Authority moved the world trade center plan across to the west side of Manhattan and sent it skyward 110 stories above the Hudson River, constructed a transportation center in Jersey City, took over and rehabilitated the decrepit Hudson and Manhattan Railroad, expanded the nation's largest containerport at Elizabeth/Port Newark, introduced bus-only lanes on the approaches to the Lincoln Tunnel, and devised plans to enlarge the bus terminal by 50 percent. To his disappointment, however, Tobin never was able to construct that vast new airport, which would have extended across more than ten thousand acres in the Great Swamp area of North Jersey.

Then in 1971, as the Port Authority passed its fiftieth birthday and Tobin began his forty-fifth year with the agency, the tension and the division in the region and within the Port Authority itself began to take their toll. The two governors—Nelson Rockefeller in New York and William Cahill of New Jersey—were pressing Tobin to throw his agency into rail transit projects that he thought were dubious and risky; and the unanimous support that he had enjoyed from his commissioners for a quarter-century was replaced by dissension and sometimes by carping criticism in board meetings. As fall slipped into winter, the joy and challenge that had kept this career official bent to the executive wheel for nearly thirty years slowly slipped away. The job was "not fun any-more," he confided to a close friend; and in December 1971, Austin Tobin resigned.

And when he did, the *New York Times* and other observers of the passing scene acclaimed his entrepreneurial skills. Headlines called him "Master Builder," the "Quiet Giant," and "Mr. Port Authority," and the *Times* praised the "sweeping nature of his achievements."[4] To some he was a "man of mystery" whose leadership entailed "stubborn, firm per-sonal control" over the agency, while others emphasized "the breadth of his vision and the courage to stand by his convictions."[5]

This chapter, drawn from a longer study of Tobin and the Port Authority, first outlines the origins and early activities of the Authority and then traces the evolution of the man from his Brooklyn origins in the early years of the twentieth century to the heights of his powers at mid-century and then to his resignation and death in the 1970s. Here we see his early break with institutions that nurtured Tobin and his family—the Catholic Church and Democratic clubhouse politics; his energy and his optimism, and his interest in expanding his range of activities and influence; his extraordinary dedication to the Port Au-thority ("The Port Authority was his life," colleagues and family agreed); his capacity to attract and develop a staff of high quality; and his great charismatic ability within the agency. "It wasn't just charm," a long-time associate explained. "Austin was able to inspire an almost fanatical desire at all levels to do what they thought he wanted done. Churchill and FDR perhaps had this quality; so did Tobin, within the organiza-tion."[6]

In examining Tobin's values and behavior, we will explore the strat-egies that he and his associates used to identify new missions for the agency, to gather support and neutralize opposition, and to maintain high levels of technical skill and motivation within the Authority. In the course of this exploration, I note some disagreement with Robert Caro's discussion in *The Power Broker* of the influence of Robert Moses and the relationships between Moses and Tobin's Port Authority.[7]

Finally, I comment briefly on the activities, successes, and failures of the Port Authority during these years in terms of the question, What difference, if any, did the efforts of Austin Tobin and his colleagues make? In view of the many political and economic forces that impinge upon an organization, can the efforts of particular leaders modify the organization's goals and behavior in significant ways? Or, as Herbert Kaufman and others have suggested, do the values and strategies of individual leaders have little influence on their organization's direc-tion?[8]

Years of Preparation

Creating a Regional Fabric

> Keen instruments, strung to a vast precision
> Bind town to town and dream to ticking dream
> > —Hart Crane, *The Bridge*

When Hart Crane began his epic poem on the Brooklyn Bridge, in the 1920s, the New York area had just taken its third major step in four decades to challenge localism in outlook and politics under the banner of regionalism. Historically, the cities and towns clustered about Manhattan had been deeply divided, torn into parts first by wide rivers and bays and then by the state line separating the densely populated New York communities and their eastern suburbs from New Jersey's wary and often jealous clusters of smaller towns—Hoboken, Jersey City, Bayonne, Newark, and dozens more. The first of the three major steps to join what God and early politics had put asunder was the Brooklyn Bridge. Completed in 1883, it leaped over the wide East River and brought the growing population centers of Brooklyn and Long Island into easy congress with Manhattan's thriving employment districts.

The second step was a matter of political rather than engineering design. In the 1890s a campaign to combine the independent city of Brooklyn, then the fourth largest in the nation, with old New York City (Manhattan and some portions of The Bronx) was carried forward in earnest. And though many Brooklynites opposed the merger and some Manhattan politicos were uncertain too, the state legislature finally adopted a new charter in 1897 which consolidated Brooklyn, Manhattan, The Bronx, and rural Queens and Staten Island into a "Greater" New York on the first day of January 1898.

The third step, also political but more tentative in the joining of regional forces, was the creation of the Port of New York Authority. In the early twentieth century, commercial activity in the bi-state New York region expanded rapidly, and each state sought to increase its share. For some political and business leaders in northern Jersey, economic growth and vitality seemed much more likely if marine and rail traffic could be attracted from Manhattan and Brooklyn to their own shores, and both public criticism and legal action were directed toward that end. New York interests challenged the New Jersey effort and sought to maintain the competitive position of the eastern side of the harbor. But some of its spokesmen also emphasized the need for cooperative bi-state action to reduce acute congestion in the harbor and at major terminal points, and to enhance the economic vitality of the entire region in meeting challenges from other East Coast ports.[9]

The intellectual leader in developing the case for bi-state cooperation was Julius Henry Cohen, an imaginative lawyer who was familiar with the Port of London Authority (created in 1908) and who urged that a bi-state port authority be created to undertake the necessary regional effort. This proposal, first put forward in 1918, generated extensive opposition, particularly from local politicians in New York City and Jersey City, who feared a loss of local sovereignty and who were unhappy that a new agency might be created that would not be easily controlled for patronage and partisan purposes. As a result of the opponents' efforts, the strong regulatory and planning powers envisioned by commissions studying the bi-state issue were omitted from the final proposal. However, with wide support from business and civic groups on both sides of the Hudson River, bills creating the Port of New York Authority as the joint agency of the two states to ensure "faithful cooperation in the future planning and development of the port of New York" were passed in Trenton and Albany early in 1921, and the compact was then approved by Congress.

On 30 April 1921, the Port Authority came into being with Julius Henry Cohen as counsel and a governing board of commissioners, half appointed by the governor of each state for six-year overlapping terms. The agency at once embarked on the specific tasks its founders had envisioned—to develop a plan that would reduce the congestion and cost involved in handling rail and waterborne freight on both sides of the harbor; and to negotiate with the railroads and other interests in order to achieve improved efficiency and vitality for the port and its region. It was an effort that would soon meet with failure, but in failing would open new possibilities for Cohen and his small band of regional entrepreneurs.

A Son of Brooklyn

Politics and the harbor were part of the heritage of the Tobin family, growing up near the Brooklyn Bridge, close to Prospect Park in Brooklyn.[10] Austin's grandfather, who had emigrated from Ireland, had worked on and near the Brooklyn waterfront while the great bridge was under construction. Killed in a dock accident at the age of thirty, he left a son, Clarence, and one sister. To help support his family, young Clarence became a messenger boy, but he soon caught the eye of a leader of the Brooklyn Democratic organization, who urged him to "go to school; become a stenographer." And so he did; and through his political connections Clarence gained appointment, beginning in 1901, as stenographer to local officials. In 1907 he was appointed to the staff of the state trial court, where he served for forty-two years, until his retirement in 1949.

Meanwhile, in 1902 Clarence married Katherine Moran, and they had four sons. Austin Joseph was the first. Born on 25 May 1903, Austin received an education that was in a formal sense thoroughly Catholic but also—when mixed with Tobin's personal chemistry—thoroughly emancipating. Austin attended parochial school and graduated from St. John's Catholic preparatory school in 1921. His next four years were spent at Holy Cross College, in Worcester, Massachusetts, from which he graduated near the top of his class in 1925. Later that year he began the study of law at Fordham.

Holy Cross was, a college classmate of Tobin's recalls, a "very rigid Catholic school." Austin liked parties, and he was not averse to a little drinking and gambling, so he sometimes broke college rules, and he accumulated a large number of demerits in his four years at school. But his challenge to authority was more intellectual than social. Tobin loved reading, and he was a highly rational being ("as his Jesuit teachers had taught him to be," one friend commented). And he was stubborn; once Austin had thoroughly explored a question and reached a clear position, he was unyielding. When he discovered that some of his class assignments were excerpts and that he was forbidden by the Catholic *Index* to read other portions of great works, he argued with his teachers, and the arguments were sometimes heated. And when he pursued the assumptions of his religion with teachers and fellow students, and introspectively, he found that he could no longer make the needed leap of faith. Austin broke with the Church during his college years, and he was steadfast in refusing to take part in Catholic services during the next forty years.

Although he broke with the Church, Tobin's intellectual development showed clear marks of his Jesuit training. Not only was he highly rational but he loved classical literature and the rhythm of language, and these loves were encouraged by his teachers and his fellow students. At St. John's Prep he won awards for oratory, and high-school classmates still recall the subjects on which he spoke. At college he walked with friends on the campus hills, reciting Virgil and Horace and debating the great and small issues of the day. And he could write; this talent too was encouraged by Holy Cross, where Austin penned essays and poems for the literary magazine. Like Hart Crane, Tobin was touched by the romance of the harbor and the sometimes destructive intensity of the growing cities.[11]

In these early years, great personal energy, commitment to a cause, and "a terrific desire to win" were perhaps Austin's most distinctive qualities. During his first two years at Holy Cross, Tobin developed great loyalty to the institution and was a fervent supporter of the football team and other athletic endeavors. Later, as a senior, he agreed to take the lead in organizing a college dance; to ensure a large turnout, he buttonholed dozens of his classmates and persuaded them to attend. His yearbook entry captured some of the distinctive elements of Tobin's personality:

> In these artificial days, there are only a few compelling people who become so sincerely bound up in every task to which they are assigned, that they positively fill the atmosphere with their determination. Austin is of that rare and valued type. No half-way measures for him; do it well, or don't do it at all—with a vengeance. In fact, we would be inclined to smile at his earnestness, if he had not a wealth of genuine talent to justify his actions.[12]

These sentences capture not only the Tobin of four years at Holy Cross but important elements of his next four decades as well.

After graduation in 1925, Austin returned to Brooklyn and married Geraldine T. Farley, a graduate of Adelphi College whom he had known since high school. And he enrolled at Fordham Law School, attending classes in the evening, while working as a clerk at a Manhattan law firm and casting about for what he should do next. Although Austin's father was active in Brooklyn politics, Austin had little taste for working in that field. He visited the local Democratic club with his father once or twice, but he felt uncomfortable in that society—of party members who kept their hats on and chewed cigars while they exchanged news about local political issues and devised strategies for the next campaign.

Although Tobin was reluctant to throw his energies into local party work, his view of government was strongly positive. Like his father, Austin held Woodrow Wilson in high regard, and in the tradition of Wilson and Theodore Roosevelt, he viewed government as an appropriate instrument to meet broad social goals.

One of the newest experiments in "positive government" was the bi-state Port of New York Authority. In the early 1920s the Port Authority had attempted without success to gain the railroads' support for a regional rail plan. Then it had turned to studies of vehicular bridges which might aid freight and passenger movement in the region, and by 1925 the Authority had approval from both states to construct three bridges between New Jersey and Staten Island, as well as a vast span across the Hudson River. Groundbreaking ceremonies for the first of these projects took place in September 1926 with much publicity, and the future of this fledgling bi-state enterprise looked promising. Moreover, its general counsel, Julius Henry Cohen, had a national reputation for his innovative approach to important legal and substantive problems.[13]

Here was a natural place for an aspiring lawyer interested in the harbor and the region, especially for a young man eager for opportunities to use his considerable energy. In 1926 a friend of Tobin's was hired by the Port Authority as a real estate lawyer, and he soon urged his compatriot to apply too. Austin did, and on 14 February 1927, Tobin joined the Port Authority's small staff as a law clerk. A year later he had his law degree and was promoted to assistant attorney in Cohen's office.

As symbols of America at the end of the 1920s, one could do worse than Hart Crane and Austin Tobin. The first a poet of tortured contemplation, who lived in a time of cultural chaos and whose life was in emotional disarray, who sought meaning and order in a city of clanging machines and "lonely and herded men" and found that order in the massive stability and "choiring strings" of Brooklyn Bridge. Who found that respite only temporary and jumped into the sea and drowned in 1932, at the age of thirty-one.[14] The second a man who saw in the uncertainties and disturbances of the new era not severed humanity but opportunity and who could, therefore, direct his considerable physical energies toward the challenge of finding new strategies for progress. Yet Tobin was, in these years, sensitive to the destruction that might accompany "progress," and he could write of the new age in mocking tones. Indeed, his romantic sensitivities resonated well with Crane's. But Austin Tobin would rather conquer the sea than be conquered by it.[15]

The Rise of a Real Estate Lawyer

> If it wasn't nailed down, he would grab it.
> —A colleague, reflecting on Tobin's activities in the law department

Although there is some risk of oversimplification, it would not be far wrong to say that in the 1930s the Port Authority and Austin Tobin were on divergent trajectories, the Authority slipping slowly downward, Tobin spreading his wings, moving up. For the Port Authority, the decade opened with great achievement and much promise. By 1931 the agency had completed three bridges between New Jersey and Staten Island, and the great George Washington Bridge, the longest suspension bridge in the world, now spanned the Hudson River. In 1930–32 the Authority also took control of the Holland Tunnel, with its lucrative toll revenues, built an inland freight terminal in Manhattan, and obtained legislative approval to construct a new vehicular tunnel under the Hudson River.

However, under the impact of the Depression, automotive traffic declined drastically, yielding barely enough revenue in the mid-1930s to pay debt service on outstanding bonds. A mood of caution soon permeated the board and the senior staff. Led by chairman Frank Ferguson, a conservative banker from Jersey City, the Authority sought no new duties and behaved as though its main goal was "to retire debt in all haste."[16]

In the Port Authority's law department, however, the atmosphere was not one of prudent investment and caution but one of lively challenge and legal inventiveness. The Authority was the first agency in the United States constructed as a semi-independent "authority," and its staff was continually confronted with complex problems of legal drafting. Also, many of its actions generated court suits by those who argued that the agency was exceeding its appropriate—but not yet clearly defined—powers.

In 1928 the agency identified a site in lower Manhattan for an inland freight terminal. Condemnation procedures were required to obtain portions of the site, and in 1930 Cohen turned that task over to Tobin, who was named to the new post of real estate attorney. When the Authority announced that it planned to erect an office building on top of the freight terminal in order to generate revenue on the terminal site, private interests sued, arguing that such a building would exceed the Authority's statutory powers and that any such facility should pay full real estate taxes. Tobin met with Cohen and suggested that "since this case is related to our real estate concerns, I assume you want me to take it." Cohen agreed. Tobin took the lead in preparing the brief, and Cohen then argued the case, which the Port Authority won in the lower court in 1934.[17]

While this case was in the courts, the Internal Revenue Service initiated a series of actions, arguing that salaries paid to employees of the Port Authority (and similar agencies) were subject to federal income taxes. Since Tobin was already involved in (real estate) tax litigation, he had no difficulty in again approaching Cohen with the suggestion that since this was "another tax case," he should take it on too. Again Cohen assented.

Now Tobin was extremely busy. He worked long days and evenings, and he worked on weekends. "He was always very wrapped up in his job," a family member commented. Often Sidney Goldstein, a member of Tobin's staff, would come home with him, and they would "talk through dinner and after dinner, for hours." But to Tobin the long hours were no burden. "I'm the luckiest guy in the world," he would tell his friends. "I love my work!"

To some who knew of his sharp break with the Church, a connection seemed apparent. As one commented, "Austin adopted the Port Authority as a religion; it was his whole life." However, the Port Authority was not quite his whole life, though it was a substantial chunk. He enjoyed parties, he would take long walks with Geraldine and his two children, and he and Gerry went on several trips, which were planned with the same energy and completeness that marked his other efforts. In all these activities, Austin demonstrated not so much the impact of a break with the Church as the impact of lessons, learned at home and in school, on the value of hard work. And he demonstrated too the perspicacity of the anonymous writer who drafted his biographical sketch for the Holy Cross yearbook.

By 1935 Tobin was in charge of all tax litigation for the Port Authority and was anxious to shed the "backwater" image of a "real estate lawyer." Cohen accepted his argument that a change of title was appropriate, and Tobin was promoted to assistant general counsel. Meanwhile, because the issue of tax exemption for salaries affected many municipal and state agencies, Tobin and one of his aides, Daniel Goldberg, contacted attorneys general in several states, as well as other public authorities, and obtained supporting briefs; indeed, Tobin and Goldberg drafted the briefs submitted by New York State and by the American Association of Port Authorities.

The Port Authority and its allies won the initial court round but finally lost the salary cases in the U.S. Supreme Court.[18] FDR and Treasury Secretary Morgenthau then took the next step, as expected: they challenged the tax-exempt status of bonds issued by state and local governments and their agencies. In 1938 Roosevelt's allies in Congress created a special Senate committee to consider legislation that would strip tax exemption from these securities; a detailed Department of Justice study supporting the Morgenthau position was provided to the committee; and hearings were scheduled for early 1939. FDR and his advisers were known to be strongly in favor of such legislation; they argued that tax exemption of income from these bonds gave undue benefits to investors, many of whom were wealthy individuals. A "short and simple statute," as Roosevelt put it, would end the problem.[19]

Tobin then went to Cohen and to General Manager John Ramsey with the suggestion that the Port Authority, building on the alliance developed in the salary fight, take the lead in opposing the proposal. That proposal, he argued, was particularly threatening to the Port Authority's ability to sell bonds and carry forward its program. He urged that the Authority use its own greater flexibility in allocating staff and funds in order to underwrite and direct the campaign.[20]

Cohen, Ramsey, and the commissioners accepted Tobin's analysis, and Tobin and Goldberg then turned to the attorneys general of New

Jersey and New York State, who agreed to send telegrams, calling for a meeting on the tax-exemption issue, to their colleagues across the country. At that meeting, Tobin and Goldberg spoke, arguing that federal taxation of state and municipal bonds would increase financing costs by 25 percent or more and that this would require higher state and local taxes and might drive some cities into bankruptcy. The assembled officials agreed to join together in a Conference on State Defense in order to resist the "inevitable onslaught" from the federal government. Tobin was named secretary and was asked to develop a plan of action.

During the winter of 1938/39, Tobin and his aides, especially Goldberg and Mortimer Edelstein, devised a strategy and, with the endorsement of the titular leaders of the conference, carried it out. They traveled across the country, visiting state capitals and city finance offices, urging that letters and telegrams opposing the Treasury plan be sent to members of Congress. They located experts who were willing to testify against the proposal, and they helped prepare the needed testimony. They sent out frequent reports to their allies, discussing substantive issues and political developments. "It was Tobin's idea and a great tool—to keep all the people around the country informed and to unify their efforts," recalls one member of the team. Tobin was the editor, and "he made sure Cohen, Ramsey, and the commissioners saw copies," noted another person active in the campaign.

Tobin had tremendous energy, and his enthusiasm infected the staff in New York and their allies across the country. "We put in hundred-hour weeks," an associate recalls. "He worked as hard as anyone, and he gave us opportunities to try out our own ideas; and he gave credit when one of us made a useful contribution," another remarked. "Austin inspired great loyalty. We loved to work for him."[21]

Until this fight, Tobin had had almost no contact with people in the financial world. But now Tobin and his aides met with top bankers in New York and other leaders in finance; and they in turn got to know Austin Tobin and his remarkable organizing ability.

At the hearings of the Special Senate Committee in early 1939, Tobin orchestrated the opposition to the Treasury plan; and he and his associates helped prepare the testimony presented by state and local officials, investment bankers, scholars, and civic associations. Then they turned to the House Committee, which was scheduled to hold hearings that summer. They believed that the ten Republicans on the House Committee were opposed to the proposal, but there were fifteen Democrats who might be expected to support FDR. So they identified the congressional districts of these fifteen, divided them into two groups, and Tobin and Goldberg took off on their own campaign swings. With them they carried information on the tax rate and debt of each city and town in each district; they met with the mayor and city council ("or the city manager, or whoever would talk with us"), and they explained the impact that Roosevelt's bill would have on the town's debt. And they got results: resolutions from towns across the country landed on the doorsteps of the Democratic committee members. By the fall of 1939 neither the House nor the Senate had much appetite for the proposal, and though the Special Senate Committee voted for the bill by a bare majority, the Conference on State Defense lobbying continued, and when the bill reached the Senate floor in 1940, it was defeated. This was a "bitter defeat for the administration," one participant recalls.

But Morgenthau and Treasury were only temporarily subdued; having lost in Congress, they soon turned to the courts. In March 1941 the Internal Revenue Service targeted several individuals who held tax-exempt bonds issued by public authorities and began proceedings to collect income taxes on the bond interest; one of the individuals was Alexander Shamberg, a long-time commissioner of the Port of New York Authority. So Tobin and his colleagues went back to work, devoting much of 1941 to preparing the briefs and organizing the effort to counter the IRS position in the courts.

This was an exciting time in the law department, especially in Austin Tobin's division. Julius Henry Cohen, nearly seventy, suffered from health problems and was not very active, but he gave plenty of leeway to his colleagues. Tobin and his aides were fully engaged in these years, handling real estate issues arising from the Manhattan freight terminal and the Lincoln Tunnel project while battling the Roosevelt administration on the tax issue. The main problem facing Tobin and his associates was that they were joined to a large organization that seemed to be going nowhere.[22]

The "Unanimous Choice" of a Divided Board

By early 1942 the Port Authority had been operating under tight financial constraints for ten years, and with World War II now under way, gasoline rationing would soon be in force. Traffic would probably decline again, and more Authority staff members might have to be laid off. John Ramsey, the agency's top staff member, was reluctant to "tackle a whole new round of problems"; he was eligible to retire, and he decided it was time to leave.

But who should replace him? One group of commissioners, led by chairman Frank Ferguson, favored Billings Wilson, then assistant general manager, who could be counted on to exert strong managerial control, reducing expenses while maintaining the bridges and tunnels in good repair. Overall policy would be set by banker Ferguson and his colleagues, with excess revenues being used to pay off the bonds.

To another group of commissioners, Ramsey's departure offered an opportunity to break free from the cautious approach of the previous decade. What was needed was an executive team that would look ahead a few years to the economic opportunities facing the New York region once the war was over, and that could identify projects the Port Authority might undertake to aid the region's economic growth and devise strategies to gain public support for the Authority's plans. This faction was led by Howard Cullman and Joseph Byrne. Cullman, whose family was wealthy, had decided on public service rather than a business career, had worked closely with Al Smith when Smith was governor of New York State, and had welcomed appointment to the Port Authority board in 1927 as a way to help keep the New York region a vital commercial center. Cullman was energetic and a risk-taker, and he found the cautious approach of Ferguson and his allies uncongenial.[23] Byrne, a New Jersey commissioner since 1934, had served as a city commissioner in Newark, and he was alert to the possible benefits that a reinvigorated Port Authority might bring to his own city's commercial vitality. As Tobin had taken on the legal issues confronting the Port Authority, Cullman and Byrne had gotten to know him, and they liked the young man's style, his enthusiasm and his capacity to develop a dedicated and able staff, and his ability to devise and carry out complex strategies in the political arena.

The lines of battle were sharply drawn during meetings in the early spring. It was, as a staff member reflected later, "a fight for the soul of the Port Authority." At one point, when Tobin emerged as the choice of a majority of the board, Ferguson threw his own hat into the ring, offering to resign his bank presidency and take on the full-time executive job at the Authority. But the majority held firm for Tobin, and Ferguson retreated to his bank, nursing his wounds and waiting for the time—soon to come—when he might use the power of the chairman's post, which he retained, to shackle this upstart or force him out.

On 4 June 1942 the Port Authority announced that Austin Tobin had been chosen as Ramsey's successor, the title now being executive director of the agency. The announcement was hardly a ringing endorsement of the Cullman-Byrne position, however, for it emphasized the need for "retrenchment" and "managerial caution" in the "troublous days ahead." So the entrepreneurs conceded the initial public relations victory to the conservative cause. In return, the conservative members agreed to announce that Tobin was the "unanimous choice" of the board. Moreover, the board approved one other step of importance: the Bureau of Commerce was set free from Billings Wilson's tight operating control and established as an independent Department of Port Development, reporting directly to Tobin; and the Authority's best economic analyst and planner, Walter Hedden, was appointed to head the new department.

While the import of these changes seemed lost on a sleepy metropolitan press, which wrote not a word of the conflict in philosophies or the battle that had preceded the change in regime, their meaning was clear to shrewd members of the Authority staff. As David McKay, a senior official at the agency, commented to a colleague on hearing the news, "Now we're going to see things zing!"

Years of Expansion

Austin Tobin was thirty-nine when he assumed the top staff position at the Port Authority. He had already served a long apprenticeship—fifteen years—at the agency. In some ways it was a specialized apprenticeship, focused on legal challenges. Yet there were broadening aspects, of a kind somewhat unusual for a civil servant, for much of Tobin's energy during the previous four years had been devoted to organizing constituencies nationally in support of a controversial policy position and then directing his allies' efforts in order to provide sustained political pressure on elected officials in Washington.

In the next fifteen years, Tobin applied what he had learned during the apprenticeship, and he learned still more—on the substantive issues of economic planning and project development, on the relationships of ethical principles to political power (as he fought chairman Ferguson and then Robert Moses), on the managerial principles needed to lead not the dozen associates who had been under his command in the law department but several thousand in the Port Authority as a whole.

During these years, 1942–57, the Port Authority expanded from a bridge-and-tunnel outfit to embrace a wide range of new goals and projects, including a vast and innovative marine facility at Newark/ Elizabeth, three major airports, a large bus terminal in midtown Manhattan, and a pair of extensive truck terminals. Moreover, working with state highway officials and with Robert Moses—in an alliance that ended years of conflict—the Authority's leaders developed a plan to construct new bridges across the Narrows in New York Bay and across the western end of Long Island Sound, add a second deck to the George Washington Bridge, and build a network of circumferential highways in the larger region.

The primary task of this section is to describe Tobin's approach in identifying new goals for his agency and his strategies, successes, and failures in this first decade and a half as chief executive officer of the Port Authority.

Reviving the Entrepreneurial Spirit

Until he was chosen to be executive director in the spring of 1942, Tobin had been absorbed in matters of law and politics. He had devoted little attention to the transportation and economic-development problems facing the New York region or to the possible role of the Port Authority in meeting those challenges. During the summer and fall of 1942, Tobin spent long hours reading about these issues and opportunities, and he gathered around him staff members who could help him devise strategies to meet the region's needs. Walter Hedden, the agency's top planner, was especially crucial; now promoted to head the new Department of Port Development, Hedden worked closely with Tobin in developing plans for the postwar era.

By June 1943, Tobin and Hedden had completed a confidential study of regional problems and identified a number of activities the Port Authority might undertake to help maintain the region's position as "the gateway for world commerce." Included on the list were several projects that had been proposed by Hedden and others in earlier staff reports: truck terminals, produce centers, and a Manhattan bus terminal. Tobin and Hedden also suggested other and larger tasks: the Port Authority might take over the dilapidated piers in New York City and along the New Jersey waterfront, reconstruct them, and operate a series of marine terminals; and perhaps it should take on a central role in the development of air transport in the bi-state region.[24]

Tobin then went to the board to obtain funds for detailed studies in each project area. Chairman Ferguson and his allies objected to financing any new initiatives in this era of reduced revenues; and only after a month's delay did the board majority agree to go forward with the surveys. It was clear to Tobin that his hopes for revitalizing the agency could be realized only if the dominant sentiment on the board shifted from a concern with protecting current income to a lively interest in finding new challenges and using the Authority's influence to shape economic growth in the bi-state region. Tobin and his aides used several strategies to encourage this change.

Throughout the rest of 1943 and 1944, Tobin and his staff held a series of meetings with business and civic groups, and they met with federal officials as well, in order to identify postwar needs in the marine and air terminal fields. Their activities were followed in the press and endorsed by leaders of New York's business community. Meanwhile, in frequent meetings with the board and in his "Weekly Reports," sent to all board members and the senior staff, Tobin reminded the commissioners—perhaps *educated* is a better word—as to the importance of thinking optimistically and aggressively about the future role of the port and its Port Authority.[25] By the end of 1944, Ferguson could count on only two or three commissioners to support his conservative banker's orientation.

Then, at the close of 1944, one of Ferguson's supporters on the board died, and the term of another expired, and their successors turned away from the chairman. At the February 1945 board meeting the commissioners replaced Ferguson with Howard Cullman as chairman and named Joseph Byrne as vice chairman. Both were enthusiastic advocates of vigorous Port Authority efforts to reach out in new directions, and both were strong supporters of Austin Tobin. At last the board was essentially unified behind Tobin's leadership and ready to support an aggressive Port Authority role in grappling with the region's problems. It was a state of harmony that would last for more than two decades, until the battles of Tobin's final years.

Airports and Marine Terminals: Strategies for Action

Even before the board had ousted Ferguson from the chairmanship, Tobin and his aides had begun the analytical and public relations efforts that would bring within their orbit the region's major airports and a large chunk of its marine facilities as well. These strategies, begun in 1943 and extended into the 1950s, were pursued with the following guidelines as central.

1. *The "self-supporting" criterion.* The Port Authority would undertake construction projects, rehabilitation programs, and other activities only if the new facilities would, in the long run, generate sufficient revenue to meet their total costs. Having no direct access to tax revenues and very limited access to federal and state grants, the Authority's leaders were unwilling to commit their funds and energies to any project that seemed likely to become a permanent drain on the agency's revenues. Therefore, careful studies of consumer demand and other market factors and of construction methods and costs were essential. The possibility of federal aid or other outside funding that could reduce the total to be funded through the Authority's bridge-and-tunnel revenues should also be actively explored.

2. *The need for "regional balance."* The creation of the Port Authority in 1921 had been possible because business and political leaders had tentatively agreed to replace conflict with cooperation in seeking economic growth for the New York region. But suspicion between officials of the two states had not been abolished by waving the Port Authority wand. Tobin and his associates realized that proposals to aid commercial vitality in New York must be balanced with projects to

assist the cities of New Jersey, whose elected officials were always ready to denounce the agency for charging Newark and Jersey City citizens fifty cents a car to journey to Manhattan.

3. *The passive stance of the Port Authority.* The agency's leaders believed that its political and public relations position would be weakened if they took the initiative by announcing a range of programs that the agency was ready to undertake, for that initiative would encourage the fears of those who viewed the Port Authority as a sort of octopus, reaching out to claim new domains and to squeeze the life from municipal government. Therefore, Tobin and his aides preferred to have suggestions for Authority action emanate from others—from business associations, civic and planning groups, mayors and governors—permitting the Authority to respond to such requests. If a project involved action to take over an existing municipal activity, it was especially crucial that the initiative come from other groups in the region. The Port Authority would then gather the best experts, study the proposal, and report the experts' conclusions. Deciding whether any action should then be taken to require the Port agency to go forward with a project would be the responsibility of the elected officials at the two state capitals.

4. *The need to deflect political pressure for reducing bridge-and-tunnel tolls.* Before the war, there had been recurrent demands that the Port Authority reduce the fifty-cent charge on its bridges and tunnels.[26] With the probable increase in postwar traffic, the Authority's toll revenue would rise, and pressure to drop the fifty-cent rate might become intolerable. However, such action would siphon off the surplus funds needed if the agency was to venture into new fields. Therefore, it was important to develop a portfolio of major projects and to ensure that influential business and civic groups were willing to press for action to carry out such plans. Then any campaign for toll reduction could be challenged, and perhaps defeated, because of the trade-offs involved: if the tolls were reduced, less money would be available to carry out projects that were "urgently needed" to enhance the economic vitality of the region.

These four guidelines represented a complex mix of real constraints and public relations strategies. They tended to be ingrained in all Authority staff members whose activities in the 1930s involved both analytical studies and political negotiations; thus the previous experience of Tobin and some of his assistants was invaluable. But many of the Authority's projects in the postwar world would require learning how to operate in new terrain—where technological uncertainty was greater and where a tradition of municipal control made Port Authority initiatives more difficult politically.

Using the confidential 1943 report as a basic inventory of possible Port Authority initiatives, Tobin marshaled and deployed the agency's resources for action. A complex array of analytical studies, behind-the-scenes negotiations, and public battles then followed, as the Port Authority moved to build two large truck terminals and (over the opposition of Robert Moses) the Manhattan bus terminal; to take over the marine terminals at Newark and Hoboken (with a solid try for New York City's piers, but that effort failed); and to wrest the most glamorous transportation projects of the postwar era—the airports—from Newark's political legions, from New York City's mayors, and from Moses's own competing agency. The effort to extend the Port Authority's reach in these several directions occupied the first ten years of Tobin's thirty-year reign in office, and those years are particularly interesting in terms of the concept of entrepreneurial leadership. To illustrate these entrepreneurial patterns, I focus below on the Tobin initiatives that involved the most complex strategies—those that brought the Newark and New York City airports and Newark's seaport into the Port Authority's fond embrace.

During the fall and winter of 1943–44, Tobin and Hedden created a small staff to analyze the prospects for air transport growth in the postwar era, the costs of developing major airport facilities across the bi-state region, and the income that could be expected from airline leases and terminal concessions to offset these costs. They also met with federal officials to urge that federal aid be provided for airport development. Similar studies and negotiations were carried out by Tobin's staff in the seaport area. By early 1945 it seemed clear that if given the opportunity, the Authority could modernize and operate major airports and selected marine terminals in the New York region on a break-even basis.

A second element of Tobin's approach was to ensure that the Port Authority attracted favorable press attention as it studied ways to improve air and marine facilities. Here Tobin turned to Lee K. Jaffe, who was hired in 1944 to help reverse the agency's negative press image. Tobin and Jaffe "hit it off immediately," as a close observer recalled, and she was soon included in policy meetings with Tobin, Hedden, and the agency's airport planner, James Buckley. Building on a decade of experience as a reporter and government press officer in Washington and New York, Jaffe established close working relationships with editorial writers and reporters on all the region's daily newspapers, kept them constantly informed of new studies and human-interest stories in the Port Authority's domain, and suggested ways of making a story newsworthy.[27] By late 1944 and 1945, stories and editorials on the Authority's activities in air and marine transport were appearing with increasing frequency, providing the groundwork for editorial and public support for the Authority to take a central role in postwar air and seaport operations.

In addition to a careful economic analysis and a skillful public relations program, Tobin's strategy involved a crucial third element— developing close relationships with experts engaged in surveys of airport and seaport issues and broader development needs in the New York region. By 1944–45, Hedden and his aides were working with the Regional Plan Association and with the U.S. Department of Commerce and other federal agencies to develop a plan for airports in the region. Most important, with the assistance of Joseph Byrne, his board's vice chairman and a prominent citizen of Newark, Tobin had made contact with planner Harland Bartholomew, who had been engaged in 1943 by Newark's business leaders to study that aging city's development needs. Early in their studies, Bartholomew and his associates concluded that expansion of Newark's airport and revitalization of its decaying marine terminal were crucial steps in aiding the city's postwar economy but that the city government lacked the managerial talent and the political capacity to convert these two havens of patronage into engines of economic growth. Confidential meetings between these planners and Authority staff members led to an informal understanding: that the Port Authority stood ready to study a possible takeover of the Newark airport and seaport *if* Bartholomew took the lead in recommending Port Authority operation as desirable.

And so he did. In October 1945 the Bartholomew report was made public, and its conclusions were spread prominently across page 1 of the region's newspapers: in view of the Port Authority's large staff with "long experience in all forms of transportation" and its tradition of using "good business practices," the Authority should be asked to lease and operate Newark's airport and marine terminal. In addition, Bartholomew set forth an argument that would frame the airport issue in a way consistent with Tobin's long-range goals: seaport and marine terminal development throughout the New York region should be part of an "integrated" system, and the "greatest usefulness" of Newark and other air and sea terminals would only be attained when they were all combined in a coordinated regional system.

"Our Statutory Duty": The Reluctant Dragon Stretches Her Wings

The Newark planning board, composed of civic and business leaders in the city, soon endorsed the Bartholomew proposal and urged the Port Authority to meet with Newark's elected officials to explore the possible takeover of the airport and marine facilities. Tobin moved cautiously, however, for he knew that interstate rivalry was ingrained in the hearts and minds of some Newark officials.[28] Only in response to an official city request, Tobin said, could the Port Authority properly allocate the staff time and funds needed for a definitive survey. The city fathers then reluctantly asked for a study, and the Port agency quickly agreed to go forward with one.

Now the Port Authority could turn to larger game—New York City's two airports and those who guarded their gates, New York's mayor and its other major-domo, Robert Moses.[29] During Fiorello LaGuardia's twelve years as mayor, he had fought successfully to displace Newark as the region's primary air traffic center, and in 1944 and 1945 he had pressed for large city appropriations to improve LaGuardia Airport and to develop Idlewild, later renamed Kennedy Airport, as the Northeast's largest air terminal. In January 1946, however, the Little Flower was succeeded by William O'Dwyer. The new mayor preferred to husband New York's capital funds for schools, streets, and other urgent needs, and he endorsed an alternative suggested by Moses—creation of a new city airport authority to develop and run the two air terminals.

In order to counter the Moses-O'Dwyer plan, the issue would have to be redefined for the business and political leaders of the region. Prompted by the Port Authority, the major daily newspapers began to carry stories that framed the issue of air transport in a larger perspective—as a long-term investment program, requiring millions of dollars before the air terminals could be self-supporting; as a complex package of engineering and administrative challenges, which could best be carried out by an organization with a highly qualified technical staff and a proven track record; and as a regional problem, best resolved through coordinated planning and action, not through narrow competitive actions by individual cities. The Port Authority's commissioners took the lead in preaching the regional gospel, and their speeches against the "barriers of provincialism" were picked up and amplified by friendly reporters and editors.[30]

These energetic efforts did not halt Robert Moses, who, with O'Dwyer's support in hand, strode to Albany to urge that state legislation creating his city airport authority be enacted forthwith. By early April 1946 both houses of the legislature had voted for his bill, Governor Dewey had signed it, and three commissioners selected by Moses and the mayor had been sworn in and stood poised to take control of LaGuardia and Idlewild airports.

To block the Moses strategy, Tobin would now need to devise alliances with several crucial groups—the airline executives; the investment banking community, whose members would have to purchase the new authority's bonds before the Moses enterprise could sign contracts and move ahead with expansion plans; and influential business and political leaders, whose support for Port Authority action might permit the bi-state agency to gain control of the two New York fields before the City Authority could develop its own plans.

The airlines were readily brought into the Port Authority camp. Their leaders were already wary of the City Authority, for they knew that agency could turn LaGuardia and Idlewild into first-rank postwar airports only if it could tap a large pool of funds. O'Dwyer had already made it clear that local tax revenues could not be counted upon; and the other readily available source—so Moses had argued publicly—was sharply increased fees levied by the City Authority on the airlines themselves. In contrast, the Port Authority could draw on growing bridge and tunnel revenues to build the airfields and terminals the major airlines would need as traffic increased. The airline executives supported the Port Authority cause through informal contacts with business and government leaders and by commenting publicly on that agency's abilities and vision. Invited to view the Port Authority's developing plans at Newark, for example, airline officials expressed "great surprise and gratification" at the Port Authority's ideas for that airport.[31]

Members of the investment community also had their doubts about the City Airport Authority's ability to repay any bonds it attempted to float. In the spring of 1946, Moses urged the City Authority's commissioners to issue $60 million in bonds to finance development of Idlewild Airport, but financial experts friendly to the Port Authority informally contacted O'Dwyer to warn him that sale of these bonds would be difficult or impossible and that the City Authority solution to the airport problem probably would not work.

Meanwhile, Tobin and Hedden pressed ahead toward completion of the Newark studies. Stories linking the Port Authority plans to "25,000 new jobs" in the Newark area soon reached the press, and on 30 July Tobin announced a $55 million program for Newark Airport which would "provide one of the greatest airports in the world."[32] In New York, sentiment began to turn away from the Moses-O'Dwyer City Authority, and among the city's business leaders, pressure for O'Dwyer to ask the Port Authority to study New York's airport needs intensified.

Moses denounced the idea, but he was soon outmaneuvered. Cullman and Tobin had already begun holding informal meetings with Harry F. Guggenheim, who chaired the City Authority, and in late July he resigned, urging the mayor to "get the airports out of politics" and turn them over to the Port Authority. Then a leading investment banker who had worked closely with Tobin on the tax-exempt-bond fight called O'Dwyer and paved the way for the mayor to confer with Tobin and Cullman on the airport issue. On 2 August 1946, O'Dwyer abandoned the Moses plan and asked the Port Authority to study the takeover of New York's airports in order to "relieve the city of a tremendous burden of future airport financing."[33]

Tobin and his aides quickly responded, and in December the Port Authority announced a $191 million proposal to rehabilitate and expand New York's two airports. Moses's creation, still alive though headless, said it could do the job for less than half that total. For the financial analysts and editorial writers in the region, the choice was easy: the Port Authority had outlined a far more ambitious program, which seemed more likely to meet the needs (or at least the hopes) of the city's business community; and the Port Authority had great financial resources and staff expertise, especially compared with those of the untried, unfunded City Authority. Moreover, the Port Authority's extensive efforts to persuade the region's opinion leaders to think in regional rather than narrower terms now paid dividends, as commentators noted that airports were "a regional business" and therefore desirable meat for the Port agency's bi-state jaws.[34]

Moses then abandoned his City Airport Authority, but he did not abandon all hope. In early March he persuaded O'Dwyer that the city government should keep the airports and run them with a "bare-bones" investment strategy. Again, the Port Authority legions swung into action: Tobin and Jaffe explained the options in meetings with the editorial writers and commentators, who then attacked O'Dwyer for relying on a "makeshift, patch-and-ragtag program" and urged that the Port Authority do the job.[35] A close friend of Tobin's in the banking community met with O'Dwyer to emphasize the dangers of adding the airport burden to existing city debt obligations. And Tobin agreed to modify the original Port Authority proposal, providing the city with three-quarters of any net profits at the airports (rather than the fifty-fifty split proposed initially). On 17 April 1947 the Port Authority and the city agreed that the bi-state agency would develop the city's airports under a fifty-year lease.

In Newark, meanwhile, the Port Authority's July 1946 plan had met with enthusiastic support among local business leaders and New Jersey editorial writers, but the proposal was vigorously attacked by Newark's elected officials. Several months of negotiations with city officials led nowhere, and in early 1947 Tobin and his allies began to tighten the noose around the necks of the reluctant Newark leaders. Tobin and his New Jersey commissioners met with Alfred Driscoll, who had been elected governor of the state in November 1946, and in January Driscoll announced his support for Port Authority operation of the airport and marine terminal. Working in harmony, the *Newark News* and Port Authority leaders then urged Newark's city fathers to act, warning them that the Port Authority's large plans for Idlewild and LaGuardia airports would soon outstrip other air terminals, which would then be little more than "whistle stops on a suburban line."[36]

Still the city's elected officials hesitated, and early in the fall Tobin and the New Jersey board members again asked Governor Driscoll to lend a helping hand. Driscoll then reminded the Newark commissioners that they would need his support for state programs to help Newark and other older cities; and in four days of intensive discussions with local leaders, he pressed them to accept the Port Authority offer.

At last the combined forces of local, regional, and state pressures overcame the attractions of municipal independence and patronage, and the city fathers succumbed. On 22 October 1947, Newark and the bi-state agency signed an agreement leasing the city's airport and marine facilities to the Port Authority for fifty years. Now air transport service in New York and New Jersey could be planned and developed on a "truly regional basis," Tobin commented to his board. Moreover, Tobin noted, in adding Port Newark, the Authority had also taken an important step toward "unification of pier and waterfront activities" across the region.[37]

Larger Dreams, Imperial Years

Even before agreements were achieved on these air and sea projects, Tobin and Hedden had marshaled their energies for action in other fields identified in their 1943 report. It was clear by 1945–46 that the Port Authority would have growing financial resources to support such initiatives, and Tobin's restless energy impelled him to press forward in several directions at once—lest an opportunity be delayed, or missed.

One central factor in any plans to extend the Authority's domain would be the attitude of the board of commissioners. During the spring of 1947, Tobin reflected on the change in the board's perspective since the Ferguson years and took the occasion to compliment his commissioners—and to prepare them for new battles ahead. Since early 1945, he noted, they had been unanimous in rejecting a "static role as a collection agency" for the Port Authority and in accepting "the dynamic challenge" of reaching out for new projects. "The bridges and tunnels are to be looked to not as an end in themselves," Tobin wrote, "but rather as the credit basis of a vital and expanding program . . . throughout the greatest metropolitan area in the world."[38]

Another crucial factor would be the entrepreneurial skills gathered in and about the executive office. Earlier, Tobin's work on the bond fight had provided him with a valuable opportunity to develop his talents for selecting and using staff members, gathering and organizing information, and orchestrating action to achieve important goals. The airport and seaport battles refined and added to these skills. The main dimensions of Tobin's entrepreneurial perspective were now established, and in the next ten years Tobin and his aides would employ these strategies with great skill and considerable success.

Basic to Tobin's approach was the identification of long-range goals, and here the confidential 1943 Tobin-Hedden report provided a valuable quiver, filled with attractive arrows that could be sent winging as the political climate permitted. However, it was essential that someone from outside the Port Authority agree to send the arrows aloft: civic organizations, newspaper columnists, business leaders, or government officials must take the lead in urging the Authority to reach out for new tasks. And those arrows should be lofted in a balanced way, to land on both shores of the Hudson, so the Authority would not be vulnerable to charges of favoritism to one state. A bi-state strategy also had the valuable attribute, as the airport controversy illustrated, of providing additional leverage for Authority action; neither state would want to lag behind while millions of dollars flowed from the Authority's coffers into development across the River.

The requirement that Port Authority projects be self-supporting was an important element in Tobin's negotiations with city officials on the airport issue, and it continued to be a valued protection, helping to fend off demands during the coming decade that the Authority take on deficit operations in the rail or other fields or that it lower its bridge-and-tunnel tolls. The guideline of financial self-support also served as a strong motivating force within the Authority's own staff, encouraging Tobin and his aides to search continuously for ways to add revenues and control costs at the airports and at other facilities so that in time they could pay their own way.

As detailed studies and behind-the-scenes negotiations went forward, Tobin sought expert guidance in each new area, using consultants in economic analysis, airport management, and other fields and adding specialists to the Authority's permanent staff as well. Moreover, he and Jaffe and Hedden, and their aides, maintained active contact with business leaders, editors, the Regional Plan Association, and others in order to enlist their support and keep them informed—about new projects, about intransigent local officials who might adopt a broader view if counseled privately or subjected to the glare of publicity, and about the economic and other benefits that would flow from proposed improvements. Active liaison was maintained at the state capitals too, with Tobin, Assistant General Counsel Rosaleen Skehan, and two or three other aides in continuing contact with the two governors and their top staff members.

Building staff strength and external alliances as he went forward,

Tobin could often gain consent for new Port Authority initiatives without conflict. But when opposition arose and critics tried to block the path of progress, Tobin was ready to fight. Indeed, he loved a good fight, and there were many during these postwar years; and he loved to win, and in the late 1940s and 1950s he usually did.[39]

The story of Port Authority proposals, projects, and battles during these years is rich and complex. In this essay, a brief summary of major initiatives, successes, and failures must suffice.[40]

Marine terminals almost everywhere. Even before the agreement leasing Newark's marine facilities to the Port Authority was signed, Tobin and his aides were in touch with New York City's mayor in order to explore the possibility of adding New York's two hundred docks and piers to the Port Authority ledger. In October 1947, Mayor O'Dwyer formally asked the bi-state agency to study the problems of pier modernization, and a few months later, Tobin submitted a proposal for rehabilitating and operating the vast city waterfront, at a cost of $114 million. Under considerable pressure from the longshoremen's union and from those who viewed the waterfront as a priceless city resource that should not be yielded to "outsiders," the city's Board of Estimate rejected the proposal in the fall of 1948. At O'Dwyer's urging, Tobin and his aides tried again, outlining a $91 million plan in April 1949; but that proposal too was turned down by the board, which opted instead for a more modest program, to be carried out by city agencies—which would use funds to be squeezed from the city's hard-pressed capital budget.

Meanwhile, officials from Hoboken, a small New Jersey community directly across the Hudson from Manhattan, had asked the Port Authority whether it could take on the job of revitalizing that city's decaying piers. While negotiations with Newark dragged on in the summer of 1947, Tobin set his staff to developing a program for its sister community, and in September he laid before the Hoboken commissioners a $17 million proposal entailing rehabilitation of three piers and construction of a large, new double-deck pier that would be the "finest marine terminal on the Atlantic Coast." Seeking higher payments from the Port Authority in exchange for turning over its waterfront area, Hoboken's elected officials rejected the offer in 1948 and again in 1949. The Port Authority enlisted Hoboken's business leaders and Governor Driscoll to help press Hoboken to agree, and when their combined efforts failed, Driscoll threatened to bypass city officials and to have the Hoboken waterfront rehabilitated by the Port Authority under a direct agreement with the state. The much beleaguered city fathers finally acquiesced, signing an agreement with the Port Authority in September 1952. The city would receive seventy-five thousand dollars a year for four years and 75 percent of net revenues during a fifty-year lease. The first two new piers were completed at the end of 1956, several years ahead of schedule, and by 1957 tonnage at the Hoboken–Port Authority piers had nearly tripled compared with the 1953 total.

While construction was under way at Hoboken, Tobin and his chief marine-terminal aide, Lyle King, concluded that cargo through the Port of New York might be further expanded if additional facilities could be developed. Looking again for a foothold on the New York side of the harbor, they circumvented the city's reluctance to turn its own piers over to the bi-state agency by purchasing two miles of Brooklyn's waterfront from a private dock company. Then, in mid-1955, the Port Authority announced an $85 million "self-supporting harbor redevelopment program" which would replace two dozen aged piers along this area just south of the Brooklyn Bridge. A few months later, in December, New Jersey's governor (now Robert Meyner) shared the spotlight with Port Authority officials as he convened a press conference to announce that the Authority would construct a vast new marine facility in Elizabeth, just south of Port Newark, turning an "unused marshland into one of the most important port areas in the world." The plans were based on a Port Authority study "which had been requested by Governor Meyner."[41] Thus was born the Elizabeth project which in a few years would become the largest containerport in the United States.

A success and two failures—large terminals for buses and trucks. In the cautious years before the war, the Port Authority had explored the possibility of constructing a bus terminal in Manhattan, to serve all the interstate buses entering the city from the west and thus reduce the heavy traffic congestion caused by street-level bus stations and waiting passengers across mid-Manhattan. In 1945 Tobin revived the project, outlining plans for a multistory bus terminal at Eighth Avenue and 40th Street. The plan crossed the desk of city construction coordinator and city planning board member Robert Moses, who was at the same time fighting to keep the city's airports out of the Port Authority's clutches. In 1946 Moses blocked the city approvals needed before Tobin could go forward; and once again the Port Authority appealed to its friends in the news media and business community. By the fall of 1947, Moses had lost the fight, and demolition of the old buildings on the bus terminal site had begun. During the next three years, Moses continued a relentless effort to overturn the city ruling endorsing the Port Authority project, but he fought without avail.[42] On 15 December 1950 the largest bus terminal in the world was opened for business, and hundreds of buses a day were thereafter kept off Manhattan's streets.

The Port Authority's initiatives in the trucking field proceeded more quickly but less successfully. Before the war, initial studies had been

carried out to evaluate the potential impact of two large truck terminals—one in Newark, the other in Manhattan—in reducing traffic
congestion and the cost of freight handling in the New York region.
These terminals were included in the 1943 Tobin-Hedden report, and
in 1945 the Port Authority board and the two cities quickly approved
them, with construction beginning in 1947. The Manhattan terminal
was opened in 1949, but labor and scheduling problems abounded. Meanwhile, the Newark truck terminal was "completed and ready for use"
in July 1950, which is another way of saying that it remained vacant
and unused from July 1950 onward because of opposition from the local
teamsters' union. Unfortunately, these two immense buildings were
planned and built without close study of the willingness of truck companies and teamsters to use a joint terminal and engage in "more efficient" loading practices. The vacant Newark terminal was leased to
the U.S. military during the years 1951–55, while the New York terminal limped along, generating traffic and income far below what had
been anticipated. Since the mid-1950s both terminals have been leased
to private truck operators.

   The flexible use of money and staff. In another era or another
public agency, the red ink generated by the truck terminals, and by the
air terminals and other projects before they became self-supporting,
might have crippled the organization. But behind these projects, and
the other possibilities that Tobin and Hedden and their associates sketched
out in their heads and on paper, stood an immense and growing stream
of revenues. Fueled mainly by automobile, bus, and truck traffic across
the George Washington Bridge and through the Lincoln and Holland
tunnels, the Authority's revenues responded to the growing rush of
postwar travel. In 1941, the last peacetime year, 30 million vehicles
had crossed Port Authority facilities, and after the wartime doldrums
that number had been duplicated in 1945. But the 1946 figure was
41,200,000, an all-time high, and in 1947 another record was set:
44,500,000 vehicles. That year operating revenues broke all records,
with a total of $28.6 million. And since operating expenses absorbed $8
million, and interest and related payments took $7 million, more than
$13 million remained—from 1947 revenues alone—to provide backing
for existing bonds and for new bond issues and support of new Authority
initiatives. Operating revenues and net earnings continued to rise steadily, with revenues reaching $42 million in 1950 and $54 million in 1954,
in a steady climb that extended throughout the 1950s and beyond.

   As the Port Authority began to enter new fields in the 1940s, construction was financed out of bond issues tied to particular projects, with
Air Terminal Bonds and Marine Terminal Bonds linked in a complex
way to bondholder guarantees which ultimately relied on the big money-

makers, the Holland, Lincoln, and George Washington crossings. Investors sometimes needed detailed explanations before they would put their money into new issues of such specialized bonds. As Tobin and his aides looked forward in 1950/51 to new projects and plans, it seemed likely that more than $500 million in new bonds would be needed during the next ten years, perhaps extending into fields not covered by existing securities. In order to increase the Authority's flexibility and speed in raising money, Tobin's chief legal researcher, Daniel Goldberg, proposed in 1952 that the Port Authority create a new financial device, to be called Consolidated Bonds, which could be issued for any new project or other purpose. Tobin agreed, the plan was quickly accepted by the board, and the bi-state agency now had easier access to the bond market for any new projects approved by the commissioners.

By 1950/51 it was also clear to Tobin and several of his top associates that a major change was needed in the internal organization of the agency. Traditionally, planning and development of new facilities had been undertaken by specialists—for air, marine, bus, and truck terminals, as well as other areas—located in the port-development department. However, actual operations at these facilities (aircraft landing, police protection, field maintenance, and so on) were controlled by the operations department, which had its own director. This system of divided responsibility had worked reasonably well in bridges and tunnels, but in new and expanding facilities, especially at the airports and marine terminals, conflict between the operations department and other specialists frequently occurred. When costs exceeded agreed-upon limits, it was especially difficult for Tobin and his financial control unit to fix responsibility.

In 1951, Tobin's chief management aide, Matthias Lukens, explored ways of overcoming the weaknesses in the traditional system, and an outside consultant was called in to study the problem. After much internal debate, the management structure at the Port Authority was fundamentally altered: four major operating departments were created (aviation, marine terminals, tunnels and bridges, and terminals), and the director of each department was given responsibility for planning, development, operations, and cost containment within his unit. This 1952 reorganization was one of the earliest uses of the concept of "responsibility centers" in government, and it provided Tobin and his aides with an effective route to identifying managerial strengths and weaknesses, and financial problems, as each department head attempted to shape his programs to achieve the long-term goal of financial self-sufficiency.[43]

Friends who become enemies—Tobin and the airlines. As it turned out, the conflicts leading to Port Authority responsibility for the New

York region's major air terminals were only the first of several battles that would occupy Tobin and his aides in this new field. During the initial Port Authority studies in 1946–47, Tobin had been assured by his staff and outside experts that LaGuardia and Idlewild airports could in time become self-supporting operations, under the leases the airlines had signed with Mayor LaGuardia. Tobin's assurance that those contracts need not be renegotiated was welcome news to the airline presidents, who knew that Robert Moses wanted to tear up the leases and squeeze more money out of their metallic hides. As a result, the airlines actively supported Tobin's campaign against the Moses stratagems and aided Tobin in the Newark battle as well.

By early 1948, Tobin realized he had received bad advice. The New York air terminals could not become self-supporting unless the LaGuardia leases were sharply revised to produce more revenue. The airlines objected to any changes, and a long battle ensued, punctuated by Governor Dewey's active intervention to achieve a tentative agreement in 1949; final negotiations were not completed until 1953. Meanwhile, indignant at the intransigence of Juan Trippe, Eddie Rickenbacker, and the other airline executives, Tobin launched a campaign built on his experience in the bond fight of the 1930s: he and his air transport aide, James Buckley, made contact with municipal-airport operators throughout the United States, urging them to develop common negotiating strategies in pressing the airlines for higher landing fees and to exchange information on other ways to meet airport costs. Under Tobin's leadership, a national Airport Operators Council was established in 1948; and collaborative action was taken in the next several years that brought higher fees from the unhappy airlines and increased revenues from restaurants and stores, turning many of the local airports—which had operated in the red, requiring subsidies from local taxpayers—into profitable municipal enterprises.

Antagonists who become friends—Robert Moses and regional highway planning. The image conveyed by Caro's volume is a Moses nearly invincible in the 1940s and 1950s; the reality is somewhat different. He wanted control of those glamorous enterprises of the postwar world, the air transport centers, and he lost out to the Port Authority. He wanted to block Tobin and his associates from creating a massive bus terminal too, and again he was defeated. There was, however, an area of potential cooperation—the planning and construction of arterial highways across the region, including, perhaps, new additions to the magnificent string of bridges across the Hudson and other major waterways. As traffic continued to expand in the early 1950s, congestion built up on the roadways and crossings on both sides of the Hudson. Neither the Port Authority, whose bridges and tunnels were restricted to interstate waterways, nor Moses, whose agencies had to operate entirely within New York State, could readily encroach on the other's jurisdiction as highway expansion went forward. But they might cooperate and enhance the opportunities available to both.

A joint program did evolve. But how? In Caro's interpretation, it was Moses who saw the possibility of a circumferential scheme that would permit him to build the great Narrows Bridge, the Throgs Neck Bridge, and new arterial highways across the region; who laid the plan before a surprised Austin Tobin and his commissioners; and who got their agreement to go forward with a joint program that would also include a second deck on the George Washington Bridge and highways extending into New Jersey.[44]

Based on evidence available at the Port Authority, in Moses's files, and through interviews, an alternative story seems closer to the mark. By 1953, traffic congestion at the Lincoln and Holland tunnels and the George Washington Bridge had become severe, especially during rush hours, and business leaders and others urged the bi-state agency to construct additional tunnels or bridges across the Hudson. A second tube at the Lincoln Tunnel had been opened in the late 1940s, and a third tube would be completed in 1957; it seemed likely to the Authority that any additional crossings into the Manhattan business district would be useful only in rush hours and would not generate enough traffic to pay for construction and operation. Moreover, when Roger Gilman, who replaced Hedden as the agency's chief planner in 1953, and his staff analyzed the traffic patterns of automobile travelers, it became clear that many of them wanted to travel between New Jersey and points outside Manhattan—into Westchester County to the north, or east to Brooklyn and Long Island.

In 1953 Gilman and his aides sketched out a set of highway routes that would respond to these growing circumferential patterns and discussed them with Tobin. Rough engineering and financial projections were obtained from other staff departments, Tobin agreed that the general plan made sense and obtained board approval, and in late 1953 Tobin visited his old enemy at his office on Randall's Island and outlined a plan for a joint study. ("I left the door open behind me when I went in," Tobin later recalled, "in case I had to make a fast exit.") But Tobin was welcomed with something close to open arms, for his proposal offered the possibility that Moses could at last construct the jewel of the region's arterial system—a great bridge, the longest single span in the world, across the Narrows between Staten Island and Brooklyn. Moses's own agency, the Triborough Bridge and Tunnel Authority, did not yet have the funds available to finance such a project; but if detailed planning bore out initial studies, the Port Authority might, Tobin suggested, be able to advance the funds to Moses so that the Narrows Bridge could be started very soon.

A year-long joint study was soon agreed to, and in January 1955 the Port Authority and Moses announced that they were prepared to construct bridges across the Narrows and at Throgs Neck, to add a second deck to the George Washington Bridge, and with state and federal funds to go forward with a range of related highway projects, at a total cost of $600 million. (The Throgs Neck Bridge would be in "Moses territory"—joining Queens and the Bronx—but the Authority staff, not Moses, conceived the idea for that new link in the regional highway system.) With operating revenues still rising—to more than $68 million in 1955—the Port Authority prepared to press ahead with the arterial program. During the next several years the three major bridge projects were carried forward to completion.

The Dynamics of "Administrative Competence"

In summarizing these plans and projects, it is easy to lose sight of the crucial role played by the Port Authority's career staff.[45] Certainly the availability of large amounts of funds was essential to Tobin's ability to add new projects; and the support of Cullman, Byrne, and the other commissioners was crucial too. But equally important were the dozens of staff members whose skills in planning, engineering, traffic analysis, law, public relations, and other fields gave the Authority a strong reputation in all its fields of operation and also permitted Tobin to obtain careful studies of new projects. (Not always faultless studies, as the truck terminal and airline-lease cases illustrate, but generally better studies than could be obtained by other government agencies or many private firms.) The Port Authority staff had numbered 1,030 when Tobin assumed the helm in 1942, it had grown to 1,500 in 1946, and in the late 1940s the number of positions had surged to more than 2,000 as the Authority began to meet the engineering and operating tasks at three airports and the Newark seaport. More important than the numbers and their quality (which was judged strong by outside observers) was their energy, dedication, and morale. And those characteristics appeared to be connected closely with Tobin's style of leadership.

He worked extremely hard—night and day, it seemed—and he reached out and tried to understand the complexities of finance, engineering, planning, and operation that confronted his staff; and usually he could stay on top of the details as well as the broad issues. Tobin called upon his associates to work as hard as he did, and he was impatient with staff delays in completing assignments; but he applauded their efforts and successes, and he told the commissioners and the press of their work. He learned the names of traffic officers, secretaries, and other staff members at positions high and low throughout the organization, and he spoke with them—not just *to* them—as he visited offices, bridge crossings, and construction sites.

In 1944, Tobin and the commissioners had established Port Authority service emblems, to be worn by employees who had been with the Authority for five years or longer; a medal of honor, to be awarded to employees who had carried out meritorious acts at personal risk; and a distinguished service medal, "to recognize exceptional service of employees on the job." The commissioners awarded these medals at large staff gatherings, and Tobin often spoke too. There he would avoid the somewhat stiff set speech that was becoming his hallmark in public ceremonies. He spoke informally and personally of the medal winners, of the importance of the staff, and of his aspirations for the Port Authority and the New York region, and those who listened could hear the energy and enthusiasm that had made him a leading orator in high school three decades before. And his voice and hopes were infectious. "Morale was very high," recalls one of Tobin's close associates in these years. "People at the Port Authority were not only very respectful of Austin Tobin; they loved him dearly."

Those outside the Authority who worked with Tobin's staff members on planning, legislative, or engineering tasks also came to recognize the attitude that seemed to pervade the Authority, and their perceptions helped to clear the way for Tobin and his aides as they sought cooperation and support within the region and in Albany and Trenton. As a top aide to Governor Dewey recalled, "I did not have much direct involvement with Austin Tobin then. But I worked closely with a few staff members and I talked occasionally with others. I could see that they had tremendous esprit, and that Tobin was the spirit that moved them. He was deeply revered." "So I became biased toward the Port Authority," he remembers. "With that kind of leadership and dedication their great powers didn't worry me. Their independence seemed to me better than permitting political control and political inroads."

Years of Travail

In February 1957, Austin Tobin completed thirty years of service at the Port Authority, and a few months later, in July, he celebrated fifteen years at the agency's helm. Like many of the years that had gone before, 1957 was a time of great accomplishment and wide-ranging activity. At Port Newark two new terminals were completed and an additional $6 million facility was under construction. Next door, the Authority began plans for the new seaport in Elizabeth, and across the bay the Brooklyn marine-terminal program was getting under way. In 1957 the

Manhattan bus terminal set new passenger records, aided by the third tube of the Lincoln Tunnel, which opened on 25 May, Tobin's fifty-fourth birthday. Seven miles north, Port Authority staff members completed detailed plans to double the capacity of the George Washington Bridge by constructing a $183 million lower deck, and they won city approval to build a new bus station at the Manhattan terminus of the Bridge. Major expansion projects also went forward at all three commercial airports, as air traffic continued to increase dramatically: in 1949, 4 million passengers had used the Port Authority's terminals, and that total had risen year by year until in 1957 more than 13 million travelers passed through the airport gates.

The Port Authority's many activities brought acclaim to the agency and its leaders from business associations, editorial writers, and elected officials across the region. New York City's Mayor Wagner, once wary of the Authority's eagerness to take control of city-owned terminals, spoke at dedication ceremonies for the new arrival building at Idlewild (later renamed Kennedy) and congratulated the agency for its "superlative airport." New Jersey's Governor Robert Meyner, who had attacked the Port Authority during his campaign for office in 1953, now praised the agency's wide-ranging efforts: "It has transformed destructive competition into constructive cooperation, completely free of provincial influence."[46] At a special ceremony in July 1957 the board of commissioners announced the creation of the Howard S. Cullman Distinguished Service Medal and awarded it to Austin Tobin, in recognition of "his human spirit, his wisdom, his great courage, his tireless efforts and his rugged integrity, and for the conspicuous inspiration and leadership he has brought to the staff of the Port Authority."[47]

However, if the Ghost of Christmas Future had appeared to the leader of this marvelously successful bi-state agency at the end of 1957, he might have spoken of other and gloomier things:

> In the next few years, Austin Tobin, you will see air traffic in the New York region expand rapidly, and you and your colleagues will become convinced that a massive new jetport is needed for the safety and economic well-being of the region's citizens. You will fight long and hard for that airport, but it will never be constructed.
>
> You and your aides will also make plans for a world trade complex on the east side of Manhattan, and after an exhausting battle, the center will finally rise, the largest collection of office buildings in the world, on the west side. But before that effort is finished, you will have resigned, and you will refuse to attend the dedication ceremonies for the World Trade Center.
>
> Moreover, as hard as you have ever fought *for* anything, you

will fight *against* Port Authority involvement in one major field—
rail transit. There you will lose, and you will finally embrace, even
with modest enthusiasm, the iron maiden you have long shunned.

In the course of these battles, the editorial boards of the region's
newspapers, formerly your friends, will turn away from you, your
close ties with elected leaders at Albany and Trenton will be sorely
tested and nearly broken, and the winds of low politics and vindic-
tiveness will blow from Washington, leading to your indictment for
contempt of Congress, to your vigorous defense of your agency's independence, and to antagonisms that will return to block your efforts
and stifle your creative leadership years later.

None of those conflicts and results were predicted by the Authority's
leaders or close observers in the golden days of 1957. Yet within two
years all of these battles had been set in motion, and during the next
decade and more all of these predictions would come to pass.

To describe and analyze the leadership strategies, successes, and
failures of these years is a complex task, much of which must be reserved
for another place.[48] In the following pages, the major developments of
Tobin's final years in office (1957–72) are briefly summarized in relation
to the themes set forth in chapter 1.

New Initiatives

During the late 1950s and early 1960s, Tobin pursued most of the same
entrepreneurial strategies that had characterized his work since the
1930s. He and his aides continued to identify new missions for the Port
Authority; they maintained a skilled and dedicated staff to analyze new
possibilities and to carry out complex tasks; and they reached out to
build support for their old and new programs from governors and other
elected officials, as well as from business leaders and other constituencies in the region. In 1957–58, for example, aviation department director John Wiley and his staff concluded that burgeoning air travel
would soon overwhelm the capacity of the New York region's existing
airports, and a task force was created and charged with exploring possible solutions. By early 1959 the best solution in terms of passenger
convenience and safety had been identified and endorsed by Tobin and
the commissioners: a gigantic new airport should be constructed in the
sparsely settled Great Swamp area of northern New Jersey. Discussions
were then held with Governor Meyner, who agreed with the plan, and
Tobin and his aides turned to the problem of obtaining support from
the region's business leaders and major newspapers, in order to neutralize the opposition that could be expected from local residents in the
Great Swamp area.

Meanwhile, in 1958–59, Port Authority planners learned that David Rockefeller and other business leaders in lower Manhattan were interested in finding ways to revitalize the downtown area; and in a series of meetings representatives from the two groups concluded that a "world trade center," an idea that some Authority officials had long favored, would help meet both the revitalization problem and an important Port Authority aim—enhancing the efficiency and competitive strength of the New York region in international trade. Consistent with the Authority's traditional strategy, it was agreed that the agency would conduct a detailed study of such a project if the business leaders (through their Downtown–Lower Manhattan Association) would first recommend such a study. The association did so in a report released in January 1960; and the Port Authority immediately began consultation with elected officials and a detailed analysis of a possible trade mart at the proposed site—on the East Side, below the Brooklyn Bridge. A year later, in March 1961, the Authority announced that a trade center, to be built at a cost of $355 million, would be financially self-supporting and that it was ready to build and operate the center if state officials passed authorizing legislation.

During 1960 and 1961, opposition to both projects arose, but that was hardly surprising. Tobin and his associates were used to battling critics of new programs and expanding Authority jurisdiction, and sometimes they even welcomed opposition, as a way of clarifying for the region and its publics the importance of sustained efforts to maintain the vitality of commerce in the New York metropolis. What was surprising in the early 1960s, perhaps, was that Tobin and his aides failed to comprehend the range and depth of resistance to their plans and that—as they took steps to "neutralize the opposition"—they misplayed some of their hands.

In previous decades, major Port Authority projects had been compatible with widely held public values—for example, that better airports and more highway facilities were needed to reduce congestion and improve efficiency for commerce and individual travel; or that large investments in marine terminals were desirable not only because of the direct jobs created but also because of their impact in aiding the regional economy more broadly. The pockets of opposition that arose could be viewed as narrowly self-interested and parochial, and they usually were defined in those terms by the region's newspapers and civic leaders.[49] The Port Authority's projects, in contrast, would garner support from those who took a "broader" view of the region—prominent business and civic leaders, the *New York Times* and other major newspapers, most state legislative leaders, and, most important, the two governors.

Now, in the early 1960s, some of the opposition was different. Many of those who objected to a ten thousand-acre jetport in the Great Swamp area were local residents, and no doubt they were as parochial as the residents in the path of the Lincoln Tunnel expansion. But some of them were wealthy and unusually influential politically; prominent among the jetport opponents was Congressman Peter Frelinghuysen, whose estate would be graced with a jetport runway. And they were soon joined by others, who were part of the new wave of environmentalism and objected to driving wildflowers and wildlife out of the swamp. Moreover, the Port Authority was more exposed as it began the battle of the Great Swamp than it generally was, because it had not followed its traditional rule. Rather than letting civic leaders or elected officials take the initiative, the Authority itself had cast the first stone, beginning the public debate by proclaiming that a gigantic new airport was needed and that it should be built in the Great Swamp.[50]

Frelinghuysen and his fellow North Jersey congressmen also opened another, broader line of attack, urging Congressman Emanuel Celler of Brooklyn, the powerful chairman of the House Judiciary Committee, to undertake a general investigation of the Port Authority. Celler, who had previously sought assistance for his law-firm clients from the Authority and had been rebuffed, responded with alacrity. In the spring of 1960 he launched an inquiry into the Authority's policies and integrity and demanded that Tobin open all the agency's files to his investigators. When Tobin protested that the Port Authority was a state agency, whose internal files should not be subject to a general federal probe, and (with the support of the governors of both states) refused Celler's demands, Celler asked the House to cite Tobin for contempt. Tobin was indicted in August 1960, and in June 1961 a federal judge found him guilty of criminal contempt of Congress.[51]

Although that verdict was overturned on appeal in 1962,[52] vindicating Tobin in his refusal to let Celler roam through the Port Authority's files, the effort to grapple with the House investigation absorbed a vast amount of Tobin's time and energy—and the sustained attention of some of his best staff people—in 1960, 1961, and 1962. As a result, less attention and creative energy were available in the executive offices to monitor and assess the impact of new values beginning to sweep across the American scene—the environmental movement; the increasing resistance to highway expansion and its traumatic impact on local communities; and the effort to develop "community control" as a central political value in suburban towns and larger cities.[53]

But the Celler probe also had other, more direct effects. Celler's investigators identified and publicized several cases in which Tobin and his aides appeared to have used bank-deposit accounts and insurance contracts in order to curry favor with state legislators, and they exposed

one staff member who had obtained payoffs in awarding Authority contracts. So the Port Authority's nonpolitical image was challenged in an
effective if limited way. Moreover, the Celler hearings conveyed—to
some members of his committee and to others in the hearing room and
in the New York region—the impression that the Port Authority was
efficient, immensely knowledgeable on issues of law and project development, and arrogant.

The Problems of Arrogance and Large Projects

Arrogance was always—is always—a danger for the Port Authority.
The Authority could offer more in salary to the best college graduates
than could New York City or the best state agencies in the East and
the West, and it "got things done"; and so for those interested in public
service in the United States, the Port Authority had long been a premier
employer. In planning and carrying out large projects, this large and
able staff had long seemed to some observers too insulated, too unwilling
to respond to the concerns of those who questioned its programs and
policies. And now Austin Tobin, unyielding and combative, had stood
before the Judiciary Committee and said he had no regrets and would
reconsider nothing that he and his loyal staff had done.

In that forum, ultimately, he won, pursuing the righteous cause
through the courts. But in these years of the early 1960s, Tobin's stub-
bornness, and the Port Authority's desire to make "no little plans,"
reinforced the theme of arrogance. The jetport issue was one major
source of concern, not only as a specific project but also for what it
seemed to say about the Authority generally. Despite widespread local
opposition throughout 1960, and despite a 20–1 vote in the New Jersey
State Senate that year against the Great Swamp site, the agency's
officials continued to defend that location as the only one that was
acceptable; and its next detailed report, in May 1961, reaffirmed that
position and concluded that all other possible sites in the New York
region (sixteen were studied) were unacceptable. Frelinghuysen and his
fellow residents then sought to block the Authority permanently by
appealing for federal action; their political strength was underscored
as federal officials declared the Great Swamp a national wildlife refuge
in 1964 and a national landmark in May 1966. Still the Port Authority
stood firm, issuing another report in December 1966 which stated again
its view that the Great Swamp was the best, indeed the only, place for
a gigantic jetport. To residents of North Jersey and other observers, the
entire episode suggested that Tobin and his aides were strikingly insensitive to local concerns and legislative opinion.

In its initial steps toward creating a world trade center, the Port
agency had followed a more cautious course. The first public suggestion

that the agency undertake the project had come from business leaders, who had suggested a cluster of buildings of moderate size near the Brooklyn Bridge; and the Port Authority's initial proposal in 1961 sketched out a similar plan, centered on a seventy-two-story building and a thirty-story structure, at a total cost of $355 million. As a result of negotiations with officials of both states (described below), the trade center site was then moved across Manhattan to a Hudson River location. Now Tobin and his trade-center planners struck off on their own, devising an entirely new plan which featured "twin towers of gleaming metal, soaring 110 stories" and displacing the Empire State Building as the world's tallest building.[54] When the new proposal was unveiled by the Port Authority in 1964, it was supported by both state governors, and the *New York Times* thought that "no project has ever been more promising for New York." As the cost of the project escalated to $575 million in 1966, however, the *Times* joined other critics in wondering whether the project was so costly that it would divert the energies of the Authority from other important concerns such as mass transit. A year later the *Times* referred to the project as "enormously expensive and grandiose" and argued that it should be cut down to "realistic and efficient size"; otherwise a trade center would be only a monument "to the city's former glories as a port and to the Authority's audacious ability to get its own way."[55] Tobin and his aides resisted any change, however, and the World Trade Center went forward, its costs rising year by year until they exceeded $1 billion.

By the late 1960s, then, Tobin and his associates had entered into several battles over a decade that had generated vigorous opposition and left a legacy of wariness and ill feeling in parts of the bi-state region. That ill feeling was directed not only toward particular projects but toward the Port Authority and its leaders more generally, for they seemed intent on building gigantic, expensive projects even when those in the way, and some neutral observers, doubted that projects of such size were needed; and they seemed insensitive to new values (regarding the environment and local community participation) that were gaining strength across the country. And while the critics may at times have been unfair in their allegations, perhaps they touched on a basic problem. Traditionally, Austin Tobin preferred to meet complex challenges by seeking large-scale, dramatic solutions, solutions that reached beyond the immediate problem and would meet the needs of the next decade and longer. In seeking to "make no little plans," Tobin had gathered around him planners and specialists in all fields who shared this general perspective, and together they had created the largest bus and truck terminals in the world, developed the busiest airport system in the world, and reached out with massive investments to expand the region's highway system and to lead the "containership revolution." And with few exceptions, this approach was strikingly successful. By the early 1960s it was difficult for men and women reared on this rich diet to look skeptically at great new plans and to gather and understand evidence that sometimes signaled that smaller might be better, in political, in social, and even in economic terms.[56] As Machiavelli argued, "One who has prospered by following one kind of policy will not be persuaded to abandon it."[57]

There was, however, another side of the ledger. In 1960 the Port Authority had reversed its longstanding reluctance to undertake commuter rail operations. At a dramatic legislative hearing in Trenton, Tobin had announced that his agency would be willing to purchase, rehabilitate, and operate the bankrupt bi-state Hudson and Manhattan Railroad, using the Authority's own revenues from other sources to meet all deficits. In order to protect Authority bondholders, the two states would have to agree to a firm limitation on future rail burdens that might be undertaken by the agency; even so, as the plan evolved in 1961–62, it seemed likely that in addition to meeting the H&M deficits, the Port Authority might be able to allocate several million dollars each year to help revitalize other rail facilities in the region. In the course of negotiations with New York officials, the H&M purchase was combined with the trade center project (which was shifted to a site directly over the Lower Manhattan terminal of the H&M), and both states approved the two projects in 1962. For their imaginative approach, Tobin and his agency were widely praised by commuter groups and others concerned about the commuter rail problems in North Jersey.[58]

Final Conflicts

For a while, the good will garnered by the rail plan seemed to balance the pockets of opposition to the Port Authority in New Jersey and New York. Moreover, Tobin had managed to retain a staff of real ability and to maintain high morale during the difficult years of the Celler investigation and the Great Swamp foray. Quite possibly he and the Authority could have gone forward together to new initiatives and new accomplishments in the 1970s had it not been for two happenings.

The first was the growing cost of rehabilitating and operating the decrepit H&M. The annual burden on other Port Authority revenues increased rapidly, and by 1968 the deficit from that operation reached $11 million, which essentially wiped out the funds that might have been available, according to early estimates, to meet other rail needs. Once again, commuter groups and suburban officials in northern New Jersey began to criticize the Authority for its "inaction."

The second event was the election of William Cahill as governor of

New Jersey in November 1969. A member of Congress from South Jersey, Cahill needed support in the more populous northern counties, and as he campaigned in Morris, Essex, and Bergen counties in the summer and fall of 1969, he found that crowds responded enthusiastically when he attacked the Port Authority—for its jetport plans (which Tobin had not yet abandoned), for its limited efforts to meet the commuter rail problem, and for its alleged insulation and arrogance.

Cahill's gubernatorial victory brought together several major strands of conflict that Tobin and his allies had faced during the previous ten years. Cahill entered office firmly opposed to a jetport anywhere in North Jersey; and he was equally certain that Tobin and his agency must throw their energies and their funds much more vigorously into the rail commutation field. Moreover, Cahill's views on the world trade center differed sharply from those of previous governors in either state. He was highly skeptical that vast sums should be alloted from the Authority's coffers to construct a complex of buildings in Manhattan, particularly when the North Jersey rail problem needed active attention and much money. And finally, William Cahill was not only a congressman from South Jersey; he had also been a member of the House Judiciary Committee, and in 1960 he had been a member of the subcommittee through which Emanuel Celler had investigated the Port Authority. One of the votes to cite Tobin for contempt of Congress had been cast by Cahill, and neither he nor Tobin could forget that division. So when Cahill took office in January 1970, two stubborn Irishmen, with a history of conflict both substantive and personal, squared off.

In his first months in office, Cahill pressed Tobin to undertake further rail studies and to find a way to devote more Authority funds to rehabilitating and extending the region's rail system; but Tobin, though agreeing to permit staff studies, refused to consider any plans for additional Port Authority rail operations, since, he argued, that would violate the agency's obligations to its bondholders. Then Tobin, meeting with the governor and his aides to review the Port Authority's other activities, mentioned that the agency was planning to add a hotel to its trade-center complex. Cahill was outraged at Tobin's readiness to throw more funds into a dubious "commercial" enterprise while resisting action to meet the commuter rail problem. Thereafter, Cahill barred Tobin from meetings on rail issues, though he called in Tobin's subordinates, and the governor also pressed the New Jersey members of the Port Authority board to urge their New York counterparts to help in reversing Tobin's policies in the rail field.

Meanwhile, New York's Governor Rockefeller appointed his chief transit aide, William Ronan, to the Port Authority board in 1967, and in 1970 Ronan joined some of the New Jersey commissioners in challenging Tobin's policies and plans during and between board meetings. By early 1971 the sense of mutual regard and unified support from the commissioners which Tobin had experienced since Ferguson's departure in 1945 had broken down. Tobin and his views still commanded a majority on the board, but there seemed to be continual, often carping, criticism. Moreover, he could no longer expect active support from the two governors for new programs and other innovations. By the fall of 1971 the job was more a burden than a range of new and stimulating challenges.

In December, Tobin telephoned his top aides and then announced publicly that he was leaving, immediately turning the reins of office over to his deputy and formally retiring in March 1972. So a career that had spanned more than four decades, with nearly thirty years in the top executive post, came to an abrupt end.

Following Austin Tobin's departure, the Port Authority would spend five years in divided and uncertain leadership, would be touched traumatically by charges of misuse of funds, and then would rise again— under new leadership but with many of Tobin's associates in key positions.[59] And Austin Tobin, now nearly sixty-nine years of age, would leave the Port Authority without much turning back and would join the International Executive Service Corps, where he spent portions of the next several years traveling to Israel and other lands, advising their governments on port development issues and port management strategies. He also had the satisfaction of seeing his position on the need to protect the Port Authority's bondholders from large transit deficits upheld by the United States Supreme Court in an opinion that essentially rejected the positions taken by Cahill and Rockefeller during the early 1970s.[60] In the mid-1970s he declined an invitation to attend the dedication ceremonies for the World Trade Center, but in 1977, ill from cancer, he went by taxi from his Manhattan apartment to the Trade Center, stepped out onto the plaza, and looked up admiringly at the twin towers, now completed, rising far above and symbolizing the aggressiveness and the dominance of the New York region in worldly matters, an attitude and a position for which Tobin had fought through thirty years of struggle. Now, perhaps, he could rest.

On 8 February 1978, Austin Tobin died in his Manhattan apartment, of cancer. In 1982 the plaza area, a summer place for noontime crowds and playful concerts, was named the Austin J. Tobin Plaza.

"The Unsheltered Battle"

Unlike some of the entrepreneurial leaders whose strategies, successes, and failures are analyzed in this volume, Austin Tobin is not a prominent public figure. Compared with Robert McNamara, for example, or Hyman Rickover, he does not command national recognition. And in the New York region, he is far less known than Robert Moses or Fiorello LaGuardia.

In part, no doubt, this relative lack of visibility is the result of his being a contemporary of Moses, who even without Robert Caro's persuasive biography seems larger than life in shaping the physical development of the metropolis. And in part it is the result of Tobin's own style and strategy. Governors and Port Authority commissioners announced the new projects and gave the ceremonial speeches. And at the staff level, many others shared the spotlight, for Tobin gave creative scope and public credit to those who worked with him; and so he was able to attract and nourish a staff that could identify dramatic initiatives which would then shape the choices available to his commissioners, governors, and legislators, that would permit the Port Authority to enter the battle to shape regional priorities unusually well prepared, and that would usually permit it to emerge victorious—against local political leaders, against corporate opponents like the airlines, and against Robert Moses.

It may well be, as Herbert Kaufman has argued, that some public officials who hurl themselves "into the fray" and fight "to influence the course of events" have little impact, making their mark "in inches, not miles."[61] But the story of Austin Tobin and the Port of New York Authority does not fit these generalizations. A few months after taking office in 1942, Tobin had begun to employ the range of entrepreneurial strategies set forth in chapter 1 of this volume and to redirect the agency; and within a few years, he had added large new programs to what had become a rather humdrum toll-collection agency. Moreover, he had taken steps to stamp out patronage and favoritism at the Port Authority and to attract men and women with the skills and energy needed to meet the challenges of the postwar era.

Tobin's efforts made a significant difference, but that difference would have been measured only in feet and yards if he had not had Walter Hedden, Roger Gilman, and their aides at work on regional planning; Daniel Goldberg, Rosaleen Skehan, and others engaged in complex legal and political strategies; Lyle King, James Buckley, Fred Glass, John Wiley, and other experts in marine and air transport; and Lee Jaffe with her careful orchestration of media events. And many more. It is to Austin Tobin's credit that people of this caliber and energy came to the Port Authority, found the atmosphere and the opportunities to their liking, and stayed; but it is they who deserve credit for suggesting and developing ideas—for creating containerports, for joining the trade center to the H&M rail project, and others—that crucially shaped the Authority's activities, and for carrying out the technical studies and complex programs that were essential to the reality and the reputation of the Port Authority's success. It was almost entirely Austin Tobin's team from 1945 until 1971. But the team made a difference. As it did with David Lilienthal and James Webb and some of the other entrepreneurs who populate this volume.

Indeed, Tobin's influence must be measured in part by his legacy, not only of completed projects with their impact on the region's economy but of skilled staff members who remained beyond his tenure—and who in the 1970s and 1980s had central roles in shaping the Port Authority's further evolution.[62]

In emphasizing the impact of Tobin and his associates, it would be wrong to neglect the importance of external forces. Exceptional leaders everywhere depend on opportunities provided by external factors, and they find themselves constrained by traditions, economic trends, and technological forces that they can affect only marginally. Thus Tobin's ability to marshal human and financial resources and to take vigorous action was shaped powerfully by other factors: the unusual flexibility given to leaders of any public agency that obtains most of its revenues from user fees rather than from taxes; the particular financial advantage that the Port of New York Authority gave to its leaders, especially as Tobin assumed the executive reins—a revenue flow based on vehicular tolls, which surged in the postwar world; and the tradition of high quality in staff and projects that the Port Authority had gained in its first two decades.[63] Even with these advantages, Tobin probably could not have wrested the airports and marine terminals from Newark, Hoboken, and New York if their city governments had not suffered from great weaknesses: a tradition of poor management and patronage at their seaports, and legal limitations on municipal debt which constrained their ability to float bonds for capital improvements. Had these factors been otherwise, the first decade of the Tobin era might have been highlighted only by a bus terminal and two misbegotten truck terminals, achievements to be measured in inches, or at best in feet.

In the final pages of his book on federal executives, Kaufman argued that leaders "should not overestimate" what they can achieve; people may perform better "if they recognize how little they can do" in the face of the complex reality of social and technical forces.[64] That view seems unappealing, for it would, if it were accepted by the Austin Tobins and David Lilienthals of the world, dampen their creative energies and turn them from active and influential public service to other endeavors, where they might hope to accomplish more. Even if such men and women do not always achieve their goals, we might want to encourage them to try—to be public leaders who, like Schumpeter's private entrepreneurs, "delight in ventures" and are motivated by the "joy of creating, of getting things done."[65]

That "delight in ventures" is not an attitude that most men and women can sustain for many years; as Schumpeter notes, it is "rare for anyone always to remain an entrepreneur throughout the decades of his active life."[66] During his forty-five years with the Port Authority, Austin Tobin did maintain that rare condition, the same high level of energy that he had expressed to his college classmates at his commencement address in 1925, when he urged them to join him in the plunge into "the unsheltered battle of the competitive world." It was a battle Tobin and his colleagues carried forward with optimism and enthusiasm from the halcyon days of the 1920s through the harsher years of the 1960s and early 1970s. It was a band that dealt not in obstacles that would block action but in possibilities that with energy and craft might be brought into being.

Notes

This chapter is drawn from a study of leadership strategies, innovation, and accountability at the Port of New York Authority during the years 1932–72, with financial support from the Lavanburg, Sloan, and Daniel and Florence Guggenheim foundations. Interviews referred to in this chapter were conducted by the author during the years 1980–86.

The author acknowledges with thanks the assistance and comments of Donald Bagger, Harland Bartholomew, Charles Breitel, Joseph Byrne, Jr., Stacy Tobin Carmichael, Mortimer Edelstein, Edna Goelz Falconer, John Fitzgerald, Louis Gambaccini, Roger Gilman, Fred Glass, Daniel Goldberg, Peter Goldmark, Sidney Goldstein, Lee Jaffe, John Kohl, Edward Kresky, Daniel Kurshan, Thomas Lamb, Doris Landre, Francis Mulhern, Edward Olcott, Harvey Sherman, Richard Sullivan, Austin Tobin, Jr., Rosaleen Skehan Tobin, Robert Tuttle, Robert Wagner, Sr., and John Wiley. Helpful comments on draft papers were also provided by Charles Adrian, Erwin Bard, John Cooper, Fred Greenstein, Erwin Hargrove, Pendleton Herring, Herbert Kaufman, Duane Lockard, Alpheus Mason, Richard Neustadt, Philip Selznick, Clarence Stone, Robert Tucker, Annmarie Walsh, Martha Weinberg, and Margaret Wyszomirski, The assistance of Bevin Carmichael and Julianne Bauer in gathering and organizing the materials is gratefully acknowledged.

Portions of the first half of this chapter are also included in an essay by the author, "Coalition-Building by a Regional Agency," which will appear as a chapter in *The Politics of Urban Development*, ed. Clarence N. Stone and Heywood T. Sanders, to be published by the University Press of Kansas.

1. Austin J. Tobin, address to the New Jersey freeholders, June 1960; statement at joint public hearing of the New York State Assembly Committee and the New Jersey Legislative Commission, 5 March 1971, 36.

2. Austin J. Tobin, "Management Structure and Operating Policies in Public Authorities—The Port of New York Authority," Occasional Paper, September 1963, 3.

3. To use an analogy suggested by one close observer of Port Authority activities

at the state capitals, the Port Authority chef appears before an assembled throng of hungry legislators, one of whom calls out, "What is on the menu today?"

"Excellent bluefish, sir!" responds chef Tobin.

"OK, but I think I'd like beef today," the legislator replies.

"Ah, but the bluefish is excellent, and it's free. And there isn't anything else on the menu today," the chef explains.

"We'll take bluefish!" the legislators cry in unison.

4. The headlines in the text are from, respectively, the *New York Times* 15 December 1971 (editorial); *Airport News*, 28 January 1972; and the *Newark Star-Ledger*, 19 December 1971. The quotation is from the editorial in the 15 December *New York Times*.

5. John Fletcher, "The Dream of the Quiet Giant," *Airport News*, 28 January 1972; *New York Daily News*, 14 December 1971 (editorial).

6. Interview 44, December 1983. *Charisma* is meant here in the way it is used by Max Weber and Peter Blau. As Blau notes, "Devotion to the leader and the conviction that his pronouncements embody the spirit and ideals of the movement are the source of the group's willing obedience to his commands" (*On the Nature of Organizations* [New York: Wiley, 1974], 43).

7. Robert Caro, *The Power Broker: Robert Moses and the Fall of New York* (New York: Random House, 1974).

8. See Herbert Kaufman, *The Administrative Behavior of Federal Bureau Chiefs* (Washington, D.C.: Brookings Institution, 1981), 135, 196–97.

9. The political and legal conflicts during these years are described in Erwin W. Bard, *The Port of New York Authority* (New York: Columbia University Press, 1942), chap. 1.

10. Information in this section comes mainly from interviews in 1983–86 with Austin Tobin's high-school and college friends and with family members.

11. See, for example, Tobin's essay "Lost—Between Camelot and New York," published in the college literary magazine, *Holy Cross Purple*, December 1922.

12. Holy Cross yearbook, 1925, 228.

13. In addition to devising the interstate compact strategy that led to the creation of the Port of New York Authority, Cohen had done pathbreaking work on the arbitration of commercial disputes.

14. Hart Crane's life is sketched in Waldo Frank's Introduction to *The Collected Poems of Hart Crane*, ed. W. Frank (New York: Liveright, 1933), vii–xxix. The first quotation in the text is from Frank's essay, p. x; the second is from the opening section of Crane's *The Bridge*.

15. These themes are seen in Tobin's salutatory address at the Holy Cross commencement in 1925 and in his several essays and poems in the college literary magazine during the years 1922–25.

16. Bard, *Port of New York Authority*, 266.

17. *Bush Terminal Co.* v. *City of New York and Port of New York Authority*, 152 N.Y. Misc. 144 (1934). The discussion of Tobin's attitudes and actions in the 1930s is based on interviews with those who worked closely with him in the law department during these years.

18. *Helvering* v. *Gerhardt*, 304 U.S. 405 (1938); *Graves* v. *N.Y.* ex rel. *O'Keefe*, 306 U.S. 466 (1939).

19. "President Seeks Tax Immunity End . . . ," *New York Times*, 18 January 1939.

20. Because of budgetary restrictions set by legislative committees and central budget offices, it was difficult for state agencies and local officials to shift funds and

personnel in the middle of a budgetary year. The Port Authority could reallocate funds and shift duties readily, as long as the general manager and the board of commissioners approved.

21. Interviews 62 and 201. Compare the "special inspiration" with which Woodrow Wilson could infuse his personal relationships (John Milton Cooper, Jr., *The Warrior and the Priest: Woodrow Wilson and Theodore Roosevelt* [Cambridge: Harvard University Press, 1983], 94).

22. As Erwin Bard concluded in his definitive study of the Authority's first two decades, "Its policy has become totally receptive rather than aggressive." The agency sat passively, Bard concluded, "on dead center" (Bard, *Port of New York Authority*, 320, 327).

23. "Howard liked new things," an associate recalls, "and he loved to bring new things into being." See also the extended review of his activities in the obituary headed "Howard S. Cullman, 90, of Port Authority, Dies," *New York Times*, 30 June 1972.

24. The quotation and other information in this paragraph are taken from the confidential Tobin-Hedden report on the "port planning program," dated June 1943. I am indebted to Edward S. Olcott, who held Hedden's post in recent years, for locating the document.

25. In Tobin's "Weekly Reports," modeled after his reports in the 1930s on the tax-exempt-bond fight, he pointed out, for example, that the Port of London Authority was planning to develop a large airport; that members of his own staff were meeting with Newark officials to discuss important marine and airport needs in that city; and that the federal government was considering financial aid for airport planning and developments. The "Weekly Reports" provided a steady drumfire of news to the commissioners about postwar needs and opportunities.

26. These included the George Washington Bridge and the Lincoln and Holland tunnels between New Jersey and Manhattan, plus three bridges between New Jersey and Staten Island (Bayonne, Goethals, and Outerbridge).

27. "She always had the facts," recalled one of the region's best veteran reporters, "and if you needed more, she would get them and call you right back. . . . She was head and shoulders above anyone else in the public relations field."

28. Tobin had received a forceful reminder of Newark's concerns only a few months earlier, when the possibility of Port Authority operation of its airport and seaport had been suggested publicly by Vice Chairman Byrne. Newark commissioner John A. Brady had attacked the proposal as "municipal suicide," which would cause Newark's destiny as a great air and marine terminal center to "vanish into the stratosphere." He had also criticized the Authority's "powerful, arrogant administrative staff" for its tendency to treat Newark as a "service station for Manhattan" (see "Brady Attacks Port Proposal," *Newark News*, 30 April 1945).

29. The discussion below draws upon Herbert Kaufman's detailed case study "Gotham in the Air Age" (in *Public Administration and Policy Development*, ed. Harold Stein [New York: Harcourt, Brace, 1952], 143–97) and Port Authority documents. Caro's massive study of Moses includes only a few lines on this important Moses venture and defeat (see Caro, *The Power Broker*, 763, 766–67).

30. See, for example, "Regional Air Plan to Solve New York–Newark Issue?" *Christian Science Monitor*, 3 January 1946; "Area Airport Authorities Seen Needed in U.S.," *New York Herald Tribune*, 13 January 1946; and "City Airports and State Lines," ibid., 13 May 1946.

31. See "Airlines Fear Moses Authority," *New York Post*, 6 February 1946; and "Air Lanes," *Newark News*, 18 March 1946.

32. See, for example, "25,000 in Port Jobs Predicted," *Newark News*, 27 July 1946; and "Newark Airport Projected to Rival Idlewild," *New York Herald Tribune*, 25 July 1946. Tobin announced at the same time an $11 million plan for Port Newark (See Port of New York Authority, *Development of Newark Airport and Seaport* [New York, July 1946]).

33. See "Airport Proposal Derided by Moses," *New York Times*, 25 July 1946; "O'Dwyer Invites Port Authority to Run City Airports," *New York Herald Tribune*, 3 August 1946; and Kaufman, "Gotham in the Air Age," 171ff.

34. Leslie Gould, "Port Authority Offers Better Airport Deal," *New York Journal American*, 14 February 1947.

35. See, for example, Allan Keller, "City Air Leadership Periled," *New York World-Telegram*, 20 March 1947.

36. The comment is from a speech by Cullman, Port Authority chairman, quoted in "Time for Decision," an editorial in the *Newark News*, 19 May 1947. See also editorials in the *Newark News* on 23 January and 28 March 1947.

37. For a description of Driscoll's role, and Tobin's observations, see Tobin's "Weekly Report," 18 and 25 October 1947.

38. "Weekly Report," 18 April 1947.

39. So Tobin seems to fit Schumpeter's suggested personality profile for the entrepreneur, whose actions are shaped by "the impulse to fight . . . the will to conquer" and by the "joy of creating, of getting things done" and "the dream and the will to found a private kingdom" (Joseph Schumpeter, *The Theory of Economic Development* [Cambridge: Harvard University Press, 1934], 93–94).

40. These are discussed at greater length in Jameson W. Doig, "The Quiet Entrepreneur" (draft manuscript), 1986.

41. The quotations are from the Port Authority's *1955 Annual Report* (New York, 1956), 2, 8.

42. Reflecting on Moses's antagonism to the Port Authority's projects, one civic leader commented in 1950, "He hates the Port Authority, because it does, and does well, all the things he would like to do himself—builds bridges, tunnels, bus terminals [and airports]" (confidential interview #7).

43. The development of responsibility centers at the Port Authority (and more generally) and the relationship of these centers to staff departments are discussed in Harvey Sherman, *It All Depends: A Pragmatic Approach to Organization* (University: University of Alabama Press, 1966), 31–34, 66–74, 114–15; and John R. Wiley, *Airport Administration* (Westport, Conn.: Eno Foundation, 1981), 105–9. Both men served for many years as top staff aides to Tobin.

44. See Caro, *The Power Broker*, chaps. 33ff.

45. This section is intended to illustrate our argument in chapter 1 regarding the "density of administrative competence" (James March's term) and its relationship to executive leadership.

46. The quotations from Wagner and Meyner are taken from their speeches at the arrival-building dedication, 5 December 1957, as reprinted in the Port Authority's *1957 Annual Report* (1958), 4–5.

47. Quoted in part in ibid., 52.

48. See Jameson W. Doig "In Treacherous Waters" (draft manuscript), 1986. A summary of events, with less attention to issues of leadership, is in Michael N. Danielson and Jameson W. Doig, *New York: The Politics of Urban Regional Development* (Berkeley and Los Angeles: University of California Press, 1982), 123–33, 222–26, 244–47, 316ff.

49. This was the fate, for instance, of local residents who objected to expansion

of the Lincoln Tunnel and associated highways or who wanted to close the major airports to large planes because of noise; of the Newark city fathers who were viewed as more concerned with patronage than economic growth when they tried to keep their seaport out of the Port Authority's clutches; and of the Greyhound officials, who resisted the Manhattan bus terminal. As illustrated earlier, the Port Authority's skilled staff often helped to shape these critical assessments.

50. See Port of New York Authority, *A New Major Airport for the New Jersey–New York Metropolitan Area* (New York, 14 December 1959); and newspaper articles in early December.

51. *United States* v. *Tobin*, 195 F. Supp. 588 (D.C. 1961).

52. *Tobin* v. *United States*, 306 F.2d 270 (D.C. Cir. 1962), *cert. den.*, 371 U.S. 902 (1962).

53. See, for example, Jane Jacobs, *The Death and Life of Great American Cities* (New York: Random House, 1961).

54. The quotation is from the Port Authority's *1963 Annual Report* (1964), 41.

55. The quotations are from editorials in the *New York Times*, 20 January 1964, 24 December 1966, and 12 April 1967.

56. This point is discussed with reference to the jetport in the author's paper, "In Treacherous Waters," 13–33.

57. Niccolo Machiavelli, *The Prince* (1513), trans. T. Bergin (New York: Appleton-Century-Crofts, 1947), chap. 25.

58. The H&M, which connected Newark, Jersey City, and Hoboken to several stations in Manhattan, was then renamed the Port Authority Trans-Hudson Corporation (PATH). For detailed discussion of these developments see Jameson W. Doig, *Metropolitan Transportation Politics and the New York Region* (New York: Columbia University Press, 1966), chap. 9.

59. On these years see Danielson and Doig, *New York*, 244–50, 343–44.

60. *U.S. Trust Company* v. *State of New Jersey*, 431 U.S. 1 (1977). The two governors had led a successful fight for state legislation overturning the 1962 statutory provision protecting Port Authority bondholders. The Supreme Court decision rejected that legislation as undermining bondholder security, in violation of the contract clause of the U.S. Constitution.

61. Kaufman, *Administrative Behavior of Federal Bureau Chiefs*, 135, 174.

62. As Peter F. Drucker commented, "Tobin's Port Authority still stands, and I don't mean as a legal construct but as a living institution—whereas none of the other great public servants of that period in New York City have left any institutional traces. Neither Bob Moses, nor LaGuardia. ... [The difference is] Tobin's building people as well as bridges. Whereas Moses only built bridges and LaGuardia made headlines" (letter to the author, 12 November 1985). In 1972 the agency was retitled the Port Authority of New York and New Jersey.

63. On these general and specific advantages see Annmarie Walsh, *The Public's Business: The Politics and Practices of Government Corporations* (Cambridge: MIT Press, 1978); and Jameson W. Doig, " 'If I See a Murderous Fellow Sharpening a Knife Cleverly . . . ': The Wilsonian Dichotomy and the Public Authority Tradition," *Public Administration Review* 43 (1983): 292–304.

64. Kaufman, *Administrative Behavior of Federal Bureau Chiefs*, 196–97.

65. Schumpeter, *Theory of Economic Development*, 93–94.

66. Ibid., 78.

6

James Webb and the Uses of Administrative Power

W. Henry Lambright

Without a doubt, James E. Webb is one of the giants of American public administration. He served as Truman's budget director and undersecretary of state. But it was as administrator of the National Aeronautics and Space Administration under presidents Kennedy and Johnson that he established his reputation firmly and indelibly. While not particularly well known by the general public, among professionals in government he is today a "Washington legend."[1] For those who wish to know how to accomplish great deeds through public policy, bureaucratic veterans cite Webb's example. He managed America to the moon and, in so doing, left a legacy of actions and memories that have caused him to be the focus of innumerable awards and testimonials. For example, in 1982 the Smithsonian Institution created the James E. Webb Fellowships to provide training for young persons interested in the administrative aspects of institutions like the Smithsonian, devoted to the increase and diffusion of culture and knowledge; and in 1983 a special fund and lectureship for Excellence in Public Administration was established in his name by the National Academy of Public Administration.

Webb was a forceful man who used his administrative power to the fullest. At the height of the space program, the system he headed utilized thirty-five thousand civil service employees and four hundred thousand contract workers in twenty thousand separate companies. He fought hard for the resources to accomplish the tasks assigned to NASA in the National Aeronautics and Space Act, NASA's basic legislative foundation. He was responsible for billions of dollars, yet he eschewed personal publicity and many of the perquisites of office. He turned down the limousine he could have had and made a black checker cab his symbol during his seven-year tenure at NASA.[2]

Webb was indeed good at his job. But he was not without blemishes. During his tenure at NASA, the Apollo capsule fire occurred that took the lives of three astronauts. Under the Webb system of management, such a tragedy was not to have happened, but it did. Moreover, the way he dealt with the congressional inquiry that followed made him appear secretive and overly protective of his contractors, and possibly himself. NASA's political support in Congress diminished. Also, Webb failed in a major effort to redirect universities known as the Sustaining University Program (SUP). His aim was that out of a large number of universities in the SUP, at least a few would mount an effort to better understand, teach, and use high technology and systems engineering in a multidisciplinary framework to help government and industry accomplish broader social goals. Millions were spent to widen the vision of universities, and very little that was asked by Webb of universities bore fruit while Webb was at NASA. Finally, Webb was not able to garner a firm post-Apollo mission as a legacy to pass on to his successor. He left a NASA still searching for a public and political base that would support a new manned mission, an agency experiencing cutbacks and layoffs.

Yet he succeeded where it counted most. Not long after he left, Apollo landed on the moon, and world history changed. Perhaps better than anyone before or since, Webb married science, technology, management, education, and politics in pursuit of a monumental goal. President Kennedy made the Apollo decision, but Webb was the single most important shaper of that decision.[3] After the decision, he was the dominant individual in making sure that decision was implemented.

Moreover, while his university effort failed in the 1960s, much of what was being undertaken in the 1980s through industrial contracts in support of university research was inherent in the SUP. And while he could not obtain his goal for a new manned space flight for NASA, he did leave his institution moving forward in a range of areas of aeronautics and space. Even in this painful transition, the management policies Webb inherited from NASA's first administrator, T. Keith Glennan—use of contracts and grants to industry and universities—and upon which he built, enabled NASA to phase down without losing its basic organizational capability. Large strides continued to be made in the area of space science and applications. NASA adapted and survived the cutbacks and was able to proceed with new manned missions such as Skylab and Shuttle when support could be obtained in the 1970s.

For what he did he has been justly honored. Because he achieved much, and also fell short because he tried to do so much, Webb's capacity as an entrepreneurial administrator is exceptionally worth attempting to describe and analyze. A great deal can be learned about leadership in the public sector, especially leadership of large-scale organizations with a high scientific and technological content.

The Making of a Public Manager

James E. Webb was born on 7 October 1906 in rural Granville County, North Carolina. He got an early appreciation of administration in a political environment from his father, who was the county superintendent of schools for twenty-six years. This was an elected position, and the senior Webb was ultimately defeated for his efforts in consolidating local one-room schools.[4]

Webb's family did not have much income. He had to work while in high school, and he had to leave the University of North Carolina (UNC) after his first year to go back to work in order to get funds for college. By this time he had acquired a number of business skills, and when he returned, he secured a position with the Bureau of Educational Research in the university's School of Education. Working with the bureau while pursuing a degree in education, Webb became acquainted with a number of the leading professors in this field at UNC. He also gained an appreciation of how universities could achieve academic distinction while also providing practical services. Intelligent, hard-working, and persistent, Webb graduated Phi Beta Kappa in 1928.

Webb's capacity to "get things done" was evident to the university, and upon graduation, he was retained by the bureau as its full-time secretary and de facto business manager. At age twenty-two, with the bureau, Webb wrote his first check for one thousand dollars.

Webb was restless and ambitious. R. G. Lassiter, president of a construction company and for whom Webb had worked as a personal aide prior to attending UNC, believed Webb had the makings of a lawyer, and he arranged for him to study law while running the office of his brother's law firm in Oxford, North Carolina. Webb worked all day and studied at night with Ben Parham, a partner in the firm and a graduate of Harvard Law School. Webb's capacity to impress those for whom he worked was notable. His attitude was to do "whatever was necessary to advance the business of the law."

But again Webb grew restless and ambitious to move on, frustrated by the absence of opportunity in Oxford, hard-hit by the depression. He read that the Marine Corps was going to train eighteen Marine Corps aviators as part of a reserve of men skilled in the still new technology of flight. Webb perceived this as a way out of Oxford and to New York, where he understood the training was to be. In New York he would seek new opportunity, preferably in banking.

Webb's experience with the marine aviation school proved significant. Just as he had excelled academically at UNC, he excelled at the aviation school. He later recalled: "With only 18 chosen from the whole United States going into this aviation reserve program, there were lots from Princeton, Harvard, very outstanding young men who had been to the best institutions and had every advantage of family and money, and I guess this was where I learned that I could compete with them."

Webb wound up being stationed not in New York but at Quantico, Virginia. When he left the Marine Corps in 1932, he became secretary to Congressman Edward W. Pou of North Carolina, powerful chairman of the House Rules Committee. The job was arranged by Lassiter, the same benefactor who had helped Webb get a job with his brother's law firm.

Through Pou, the twenty-six-year-old Webb began learning a great deal about the inside workings of Congress. Also through Pou, he met O. Max Gardner, former governor of North Carolina, who came to Washington in 1934 to set up a law office. Webb wanted to finish his law degree, and an arrangement was made whereby Webb left Pou to work as Gardner's assistant, with time provided for him to pursue his legal studies at the George Washington University Law School. Webb worked for Gardner for two years and was admitted to the Washington, D.C. bar by examination in 1936. During this time, Webb learned still more about the ways of Washington from a different perspective.

Gardner was close to President Franklin Roosevelt. In Gardner's office, Webb learned legal administration and also specialized in certain key policy areas of concern to Gardner, particularly aviation. Gardner was general counsel for the Aeronautical Chamber of Commerce of America, and Webb helped Gardner in his lobbying activities on behalf of the aviation industry. During this period, not only did Webb get to know legislators and high-ranking administration people but he also became known to industry officials.

In 1936, Webb moved to New York City to be personnel director and assistant to the president of the Sperry Gyroscope Company. Webb was now thirty years old. He had a good knowledge of Washington, and now he was engaged as part of management of a major technology-based corporation. Webb's responsibilities grew as the company expanded. Webb was with Sperry from 1936 to 1943, during which time the number of people employed by the company grew from eight hundred to thirty-three thousand. The volume of business increased from $5.2 million to $500 million. Webb advanced to secretary-treasurer and then vice president of Sperry. The man who had once written thousand-dollar checks at UNC now was signing checks for millions as a Sperry executive. Throughout this period, Webb stayed close to government, averaging one day in Washington a week.

In 1944–45, Webb left Sperry for a brief tour of duty as a major with the first Marine Air Warning Group. He was involved with the planning of Pacific operations and was scheduled to participate in the Japanese invasion when the war came to an end.

In 1945, Webb returned to work half-time for O. Max Gardner, who was involved with the Office of War Mobilization and Reconversion (OWMR), reserving the rest of his time for other interests. In 1946, when Gardner became undersecretary of the treasury, Webb moved to the Treasury Department as Gardner's executive assistant. Gardner told Webb he needed him because the Treasury Department had 106,000 employees, and Webb was the only one he could put his hands on who had experience with a very large organization. He asked Webb to come aboard to help him for just six months, and then Webb would be free to do as he pleased. At this point, Webb was not intending to stay in government. Nor, however, did he wish to go back to Sperry.

What he got instead, after going to the Treasury Department, was a request from President Truman that he become director of the Bureau of the Budget (BOB). Truman did not know Webb well. Apparently, it was John Snyder, secretary of the treasury, who suggested Webb to Truman as someone with whom the Treasury Department could work. Thus, in 1946, at age forty, Webb was appointed director of BOB, reporting directly to the president.

It was as director of BOB that Webb revealed fully the degree to which his entrepreneurial leadership skills had developed. At this time, BOB was ripe for change. Under Harold Smith, it had developed fully its "institutional" role. A professional public administrator, Smith had taken the idea, implicit in the Brownlow Report, that BOB was a presidential budget staff resource and turned it into a reality. He had established it as the institutional heart of the Executive Office of the President.[5] Neustadt has observed that Smith "equipped himself to be an institutional chief-of-staff for the President, receiving separate inputs that incorporated different viewpoints, so his focus and his tasks of recommendations would be somewhat like the President, except in respect of the purely personal and the party political, these Smith regarded as domains for 'personal' staff."

BOB had problems, however. OWMR emerged from World War II an apparent rival for BOB responsibilities for administrative coordination and legislative clearance. Whether BOB would remain the anchor within the Executive Office was not clear, and there was also much concern among BOB senior staff when James Webb, an unknown, was named. Would this mean BOB subordination to the Treasury Department?

Webb turned what many saw as a problem into an opportunity. The situation was fluid, and one in which BOB could have an enhanced rather than a diminished role. Webb was definitely not close to Truman when he took the BOB job; indeed, Truman had trouble remembering his name in a press conference at which he announced the appointment. At the conclusion of his tour with BOB in 1949, however, he was definitely a Truman insider. For reasons apparently independent of Webb, OWMR was abolished. Webb, meanwhile, showed that he was no emissary from the Treasury Department. He was his own man, the president's man, and BOB's man. Webb saw BOB as dependent on the president, but the president could be made more effective as a policy manager through better services from BOB.

The White House staff was still small in this period, and under Smith, extremely competent individuals had been recruited to government in BOB. Smith had tried to keep his staff at arm's length from the White House staff, for fear of mixing administration with politics. But Webb "saw immediately the need to make himself and his organization indispensable to the President and he proceeded to do so with great dispatch, great vigor, and tremendous intelligence. He made the Bureau staff available to the White House staff to work with them. He volunteered to take some of the difficult problems the President faced back to the Bureau for further analysis." "These problems," Larry Berman noted, "included drafting legislation on Taft-Hartley, the Employment Act of 1946, the problems of the Fair Employment Practices Commission, Medicare, unification of the Armed Services, the National Defense Act, and harnessing atomic energy for peaceful purposes."

Webb turned what had been a negative tool—legislative clearance—into a "prime means of focusing staff efforts to help meet the President's needs." He led BOB staff in a "watchdog" role, tracking legislation of interest to the president, providing analysis and, where warranted, veto messages. He revealed an important trait of administrative style: he was willing to share the spotlight. Thus, unlike Smith, Webb brought staff members with him when he went to the White House, even holding dry runs in preparation so as to maximize the ability of his group to be helpful. He helped not only the president but those on whom Truman relied. Webb felt that Smith was overprotective of BOB. Webb believed that BOB was strong enough to maintain its integrity in the political turbulence closest to the president. Moreover, Webb expanded BOB's role in congressional relations so that the president's views on pending bills could better be known on the Hill.

What Webb did was take the BOB he inherited from Smith and

redirect it into "the program development process." This enhanced staff morale. Their skills were being used to the fullest. They felt useful for presidential policy, but not in an overtly partisan/political manner. Somehow Webb built a relationship among BOB, the White House staff, and the president in which all gained. There are "many observers [who] view the Webb period as the golden age of the Bureau of the Budget."

Energetic and dynamic, talking quickly and with great enthusiasm, Webb displayed to all who cared to look a remarkable administrative entrepreneurship as director of BOB. Truman was one who was impressed. In 1949, however, he decided he needed Webb more in the State Department than in BOB.

Truman asked Dean Acheson to be secretary of state, and he asked Acheson whether it would be all right with him to appoint Webb as his under secretary. Exactly why Truman wanted Webb there is unclear. Acheson has indicated that Truman, like other presidents, was unsure about the State Department and no doubt wanted someone he knew and trusted to be in charge when Acheson had to be away.[6] Also, he may have wanted a more smoothly run, more responsive institution, one that would better stand up to the military agencies in questions of national security policy. In the postwar/cold war years, with military unification taking place, the lead role of the State Department was not necessarily secure. Webb was undoubtedly seen as an individual who could strengthen State as an organization. Acheson thought well of Webb, although he regarded him as more proficient in administration than in foreign policy. He recalls that Webb was "never, I think, altogether happy in the Department." Nevertheless, "he served faithfully and well for three years, accomplishing what both the President and I hoped for from him."[7]

Webb must have found his role in the State Department much more confining than that of BOB director. While he continued to deal with Truman, it was Acheson who played the lead role on the largest issues. Webb was number two. Also, Webb and the foreign service, which dominated the career State Department, were quite different in style. Webb pushed hard to "get things done," and sometimes this corresponded to what State's bureaucrats wanted. But they wanted to do it their way. Webb's health deteriorated in his three years at State. Working long hours in the era of the Korean War and Soviet expansionism, out most nights for one diplomatic gathering or another, Webb suffered increasingly from severe migraines. These migraines forced him to resign.[8]

Hence, while Webb's ebullient personality was somewhat contained (and perhaps stifled) during his years at State, in his own sphere of administration he did achieve some major accomplishments. He expanded the role of the executive secretariat as a vehicle for bringing information upward from country desks and other sources of expertise in the State Department to a level where senior officials could act on it. Although Acheson himself gave some time to the "care and feeding" of State, it was Webb who made sure that the organization was tending to the vast bulk of the foreign-policy work that did not reach the level of presidential decision making. He established science attachés in embassies in recognition of the interplay of science, technology, and foreign policy. For what he did, Acheson states of Webb: "I remain deeply grateful to him."[9] But as noted, the match between Webb and State was not as felicitous as that between Webb and BOB.

In 1952, Webb, now forty-six, went westward toward private enterprise. He served as president of the Republic Supply Company, director of the McDonnell Aircraft Company of St. Louis, Missouri, and director and assistant to the president of Kerr-McGee Oil Industries, in Oklahoma City. Within a few years he had made enough money to begin reducing his corporate activities so as to devote himself more to public-service interests. He was active on a succession of government advisory committees during the Eisenhower administration, commuting to and from Washington frequently. He became involved in matters ranging from urban affairs, to civil defense, to the reform of science education. By 1961 he was devoting two-thirds of his time to public service and only one-third to business. Then, in February 1961, at age fifty-five, he was asked by President John Kennedy to lead the National Aeronautics and Space Administration.

Webb at first said no, pointing out his lack of scientific and engineering expertise. Kennedy said, however, that he wanted a man with broad policy experience, and Webb was the man he wanted. Kennedy did not know Webb very well at the time and was largely taking the advice of Vice President Lyndon Johnson. As Senate majority leader, Johnson had led the fight for the creation of NASA. Kennedy had made Johnson chairman of the National Aeronautics and Space Council (NASC), an Executive Office body to coordinate military and civil space affairs, and thus his principal adviser on space. Johnson had become aware of Webb when Johnson was in Congress and Webb was serving Truman. He thought well of Webb. Johnson's high regard was shared by Senator Robert Kerr, chairman of the Senate Aeronautical and Space Sciences Committee (and co-owner of the oil company for which Webb worked in Oklahoma). Kennedy pressed, and Webb agreed.

NASA in February 1961

When Webb joined NASA, it was still in its formative years. NASA had been created in 1958 as a response to Sputnik, launched by the Soviet Union in 1957, and subsequent Soviet "firsts." There was consensus that the United States needed a strong space program. The major decision of the Space Act of 1958 was that the program was to be run by a civilian agency. This was a decision made primarily by President Dwight Eisenhower.

There was also a sense that this had to be a vigorous agency. It was to be independent, not part of another organization, and run by a single administrator rather than a commission (as was true of the Atomic Energy Commission). The basic building block upon which it was formed was the National Advisory Committee for Aeronautics (NACA), created in 1915. This was an assemblage of large national laboratories devoted to basic and applied research in aeronautics, a nucleus of approximately eight thousand scientists and engineers. Transferred from the Army to NASA during the Eisenhower years were the Army Ballistics Missile Agency team, headed by Wernher von Braun (forty-three hundred employees), and the Jet Propulsion Laboratory, managed by the California Institute of Technology (twenty-four hundred employees).[10]

The first administrator of NASA, T. Keith Glennan, an engineer and previous president of the Case Institute of Technology, had as his deputy (and only other political appointee in NASA) Hugh Dryden, formerly head of NACA. They hired Robert Seamans, an engineer and former Massachusetts Institute of Technology professor, as associate administrator and de facto general manager.

The NASA administrator had a legislative mandate that was remarkably broad and simple: to "plan, direct, and conduct aeronautical and space activities"; to involve the scientific community in these activities; and to widely disseminate knowledge and information concerning aeronautical and space activities. He also had the authority to hire hundreds of new employees at salaries above civil service levels, without regard to the usual personnel classification restrictions.[11]

While significantly building up the employment base of NASA, Glennan established as basic policy that NASA would accomplish most of its work via industry and universities. Large contract and grant programs were initiated under Glennan. He also presided over the initial successes of NASA in space, namely, the development and application of communications satellites.

However, because President Eisenhower was determined not to engage in an all-out space race with the Soviets, he refused to approve what he regarded as exceedingly expensive manned space efforts. NASA was able to launch Project Mercury, a program to orbit a man around the earth and bring him back, but more grandiose goals were held in check. NASA's technical planners, for example, devised a program to send a man to the moon and return him safely to earth, but this program—called Apollo—did not get very far with the Eisenhower administration.

Continuity

Webb's first decision was to ask the president to retain Dryden as the number-two man at NASA. He then asked Seamans to stay as associate administrator. This made for maximum continuity in the agency's senior management. Under Glennan, the three had served as a de facto senior management triumvirate. Webb made explicit what had been implicit: NASA would be run by a team, and Webb said so.

The three men would make the major decisions together. No one of the three would act to do violence to the strongly held views of either of the other two. Webb would later say: "This was a policy which intentionally put us in chains. We bound ourselves in these hoops of iron."[12] The idea was cooperation at the top in the processes of analyzing a problem or opportunity and also in the decisions concerning projects, patterns of organization, and personnel assignments. This method wedded different kinds of expertise and made sure that those below knew that top management had examined in depth and was together on a particular issue, so that no one could make end runs or play one off against the other. Below these senior officials were very able, ambitious, hard-driving men. They fell into two categories. One included the headquarters program managers (e.g., of manned space flight, space science, space applications), and the other included the directors of the various large laboratories, or as NASA called them, centers. One of these individuals, von Braun, was better known by far, nationally and internationally, than Webb, Dryden, or Seamans.

In terms of emphasis, the division of labor was obvious. Seamans handled most of the day-to-day management matters; Dryden dealt with the engineering and scientific communities; and Webb focused on the overall organizational and larger administrative and political problems. Webb understood his special role in relating NASA to its political environment. As he wrote later: "The environment is not something apart from the [large-scale] endeavor; it is not just something in which the endeavor operates and which it needs to adjust; it is an integral part of the endeavor itself. . . . The total job (managerial job) encompasses external as well as internal elements, and success is as dependent on effectiveness in the one as in the other."[13]

Webb's emphasis on a "triad" leadership may have been especially important in a science and technology agency. Webb, a man untrained technically, gained legitimacy in decision making within NASA (and probably outside) to the degree that he cloaked his own policy preferences in the mantle of senior associates who were technically trained. Certainly, Webb guided the triad in directions he regarded as wise for the agency as a whole.

Change: Launching Apollo

Webb inherited an agency that knew what it wanted to do. The issue for Webb was not what *could* be done but what *should* be done. He knew that this was a decision only President Kennedy and Congress could make. He knew that Kennedy was already getting advice on space from two other sources: Vice President Johnson, who wanted the United States first in space as soon as possible, and Kennedy's science adviser, Jerome Wiesner, who represented the scientific community's view. This view opposed manned flight programs because they cut into the budgets for unmanned, science-oriented programs.

Webb assumed virtually from the outset that there would be a boost in space funding from Kennedy. What he did not know was whether Kennedy would favor a major project like Apollo. Webb was himself somewhat ambivalent initially, since he knew that NASA would be responsible for carrying out the decision, should one be made. He feared that there might not be the long-term political support necessary to sustain such an objective.

By early March, Webb, Dryden, and Seamans had decided that NASA should accelerate its planning relative to the long lead-time elements of Apollo and that the goal should be to accomplish the mission in the period 1969–70, rather than after 1970, as was presently being planned by NASA.[14] He spent considerable time with Vice President Johnson and other members of the NASC. Both Johnson and Webb felt that not only should Apollo be pushed but it should be pushed at maximum speed.

Now the problem was to sell the mission to Kennedy. On 17 March, NASA submitted a request to BOB for supplemental funding over the fiscal-year 1962 Eisenhower budget. This included sizable funds for developing a range of technologies (such as large engines for the Saturn rocket) necessary for Apollo. BOB denied most of what NASA had requested, saying that the president had yet to become involved in space affairs sufficiently to consider policy changes. On 22 March, NASA appealed to the president for a reversal of BOB.

In meeting with Kennedy, Webb stressed the importance of making an early decision to speed up the development and coupling of a new rocket (Saturn) and a new space vehicle (Apollo). This would make possible "flights about the earth with multiple crews or trips to the vicinity of the moon." Kennedy listened and asked questions but made no decisions. The next day he met with Johnson, Wiesner, David Bell, director of BOB, and Edward Welsh, staff director of the NASC. Following this meeting, Kennedy essentially "split the difference" between BOB and NASA, giving NASA funds to speed up development of Saturn but no funds for the vehicle atop Saturn, Apollo.

Webb regarded the decision as less one *against* Apollo and more the president's way to preserve his working relationship with Bell, Johnson, and Webb. Bell later said that this "was deliberately intended as a partial decision which would leave him (the President) free, within a considerable range, to decide later how much of a commitment to make." Kennedy's intent, it was generally believed, was to consider anything of the magnitude of an Apollo moon decision in the context of discussions about the fiscal-year 1963 budget, in fall 1961.

On 12 April, however, the Soviet Union launched Yuri Gagarin as the first man in space, and Chairman Nikita Khrushchev boasted: "Let the capitalist countries catch up with our country!" The U.S. reaction was one of complete chagrin and frustration, especially in Congress. Kennedy defended the U.S. program, as did Webb, but the propaganda advantage gained by the Soviets was huge. Then on 19 April it became known that the Bay of Pigs invasion of Cuba was a disaster. America's spirits—and Kennedy's—sank to a new low. On that date the president turned to Johnson and asked him to make recommendations for a U.S. space program that would make the U.S. first in space.

Johnson talked with many in industry, Congress, and the executive branch, but the man on whom he relied most was Webb. In discussions with Johnson, Webb realized that it was possible to recommend a program beyond anything NASA had thus far proposed to an administration. New technology programs involving an Apollo spaceship had been recommended to Eisenhower and Kennedy in March; however, the goal of a moon landing and return had not been made explicit. In this respect, Webb was more cautious than Dryden and some other senior NASA managers. Webb was not about to propose a scheme that went "beyond what I thought Kennedy was willing to approve."

Now the opportunity was there, and Webb made the most of it. He told Johnson that placing a man on the moon was something the Soviet Union could not do with the technology it now had. With enough money, NASA could develop the technology to surpass the Soviets. It could be done within the decade. Johnson spoke with Senator Kerr, head of the Aeronautical and Space Sciences Committee. Kerr told him "that if Jim Webb says we can land a man on the moon and bring him safely home, then it can be done."[15] At Johnson's direction, Webb and Secretary of Defense McNamara prepared a memorandum the centerpiece of which was the option of a manned lunar decision. Johnson passed this on (with his endorsement) to Kennedy on 29 April.

Webb now spoke with Johnson, Wiesner, and leaders in the administration and Congress about the requirements for carrying out such a decision. With Johnson, who was fully in favor of the decision, Webb emphasized the need for political support over the long haul, once the mood of crisis had faded. In talks with Wiesner, representing a community unenthusiastic about manned programs in general, he emphasized that he would make certain that there would be more to the program than space spectaculars; there would be a program of genuine scientific and technological value. Webb and Johnson both spent many hours with key legislators in Congress emphasizing the need for support.

On 5 May, the first U.S. manned space flight, with Alan Shephard, proved successful. Kennedy announced at a press conference that day that he planned to undertake "a substantially larger effort in space."

There followed another round of discussions led by Johnson concerning what the president might actually put in a formal program submission to Congress, as well as in an address to the public. Agreements involved the Pentagon as well as NASA. Again a memorandum was prepared and signed by Webb and McNamara. This went to Johnson, who in turn sent it, endorsed and unchanged, to Kennedy on 8 May.

While no target landing date was mentioned in the Webb-McNamara memo, budget planning was proceeding on what NASA and Department of Defense (DOD) technologists were saying was possible: 1967. Webb, however, using what he called an "administrator's discount," urged two years for flexibility on the assumption of technical or political problems along the way. This was accepted by the president as part of the decision he was about to announce. On 25 May, 1961, Kennedy spoke before Congress and declared: "I believe that this nation should commit itself to achieving the goal, before this decade is out, of landing a man on the moon and returning him safety to earth."

Expanding the Mission

Kennedy asked for more than $500 million in addition to the earlier supplement requested to augment the Eisenhower space budget. Congress gave him all he asked for, with little debate. There was no reason to believe that this mood would not continue for at least another budget year. On the other hand, Webb was not sanguine about support lasting forever. After the Kennedy decision, Webb wrote Johnson that unless there was a long-term commitment from the White House, McNamara and he would be "like two foxes running in front of two packs of hounds.

We will be pulled down." He wanted the administration to be conscious of this fact. By "hounds" he meant the press and Congress. Like any new president who uses his post-election honeymoon period to the utmost, so Webb used the Apollo decision for an administrator's honeymoon. The program he sent Kennedy, and which the president and Congress backed, was much more than a lunar landing and return. It was a broad and far-reaching program to carry out the objectives in the National Aeronautics and Space Act of 1958. It aimed at advancing space research and development along a wide front with a new family of large boosters, communications and meteorological satellites, scientific satellites, and exploration of the planets.[16] Most of these efforts had been started by Webb's predecessor, T. K. Glennan. Webb was in a position to expand on them.

NASA had to move quickly. Industry would be the key performer, and NASA's centers would provide technical management as well as research and development. Similarly, NASA would work closely with universities through grants and contracts. Webb spoke of an R&D partnership, through which NASA would get the job done. Its partners would be also a constituency from around the country, one that could help bolster political support for the agency.[17]

By the end of 1961, Webb's first year as administrator, NASA had negotiated many of the key Apollo contracts. These included the award of the largest of all peacetime contracts, for the Apollo command and service modules, to the North American Aviation Corporation. The man who at the University of North Carolina had signed thousand-dollar checks, and at Sperry, million-dollar checks, now was responsible for contracts costing billions. An elaborate structure was established to weigh the merits of these contract awards, but ultimately, the big decisions were made by Webb, Dryden, and Seamans.

In addition to letting major contracts for developmental work, Webb spent the months following the Kennedy decision augmenting the capacity of his own organization. In one thirty-day period, from 24 August to 23 September, NASA selected Cape Canaveral, Florida, as the site for a new center and "space port"; picked a government-owned ordnance plant in New Orleans for fabrication of launching vehicles; hired new managers at various levels; and reorganized the agency to strengthen top management's leadership and control over program offices and centers.[18] Perhaps the biggest decision in this period was to create a new manned-spacecraft center to undergird and help manage Apollo. This center happened to be located outside Houston, Texas, in the district of the congressman who oversaw NASA's budget.

At the headquarters level, Webb approved Seamans's recommendation to appoint D. Brainard Holmes to head the key Office of Manned

Space Flight (OMSF). Holmes was a hard-driving RCA engineer who had been project manager for the Ballistic Missile Early Warning System.[19] In appointing Holmes, Webb made it clear that Holmes (and Apollo) were under the leadership triad of Webb, Dryden, and Seamans. There was to be no Apollo "czar." Webb had not let von Braun move into this role, and he was not going to let Holmes do so either. The creation of a manned center at Houston created a measure of competition for leadership in space science and technology utilizing very large engines and spacecraft with von Braun's Marshall Space Flight Center, in Huntsville, Alabama.

One reason Webb was emphatic about control was that he felt that while Apollo was a major mission and focal point, it was not NASA's only goal. The point was to strengthen the nation's capability to understand and operate in space to meet any need that emerged. Capability required new space scientists and engineers, as well as spin-offs from space technology to uses in the commercial and educational sectors. The moon, for Webb, was a goal that required a total capability. There was more to NASA than Apollo.

Webb was acutely conscious that important sectors in the scientific community were not fully behind Apollo or him. He was also aware that there was a concern that America was not graduating enough scientists and engineers to meet its needs. It was clear to Webb that NASA should do its part in the educational expansion taking place. It would support university research in the space field through interdisciplinary institutional grants. It would help universities to better help NASA by providing facilities (buildings) without the usual matching requirements. This effort—the Sustaining University Program—was launched in the name of Apollo. It reflected Webb's desire to use his honeymoon to do what had to be done to make the United States preeminent not only in space but in science and technology generally. Also, Webb hoped that the university program would prove to the scientific community that Apollo was going to be an asset to space science, not a draw of resources.[20]

When Webb took charge of NASA, he said he hoped to be as innovative in management as NASA would be in science and technology. For some critics, he was too innovative. But, with budget soaring, he responded to the call to get America moving in space. The SUP and technology utilization efforts were small relative to Apollo. In Webb's view, however, they were important in broadening the understanding of space and enabling NASA to play a greater role for social and economic development on earth.

Securing Control

In 1962, the Apollo program continued to expand, and a most important decision was made. The decision was a technical one, but it was also political, in the sense of testing NASA's autonomy. The question initially was whether NASA should go directly to the moon, in which case, it would be necessary to develop a rocket even more powerful than Saturn, called Nova, or rendezvous outside the earth's gravity and send a detachable spaceship to the moon. Saturn would be adequate for the rendezvous approach. Once rendezvous was selected, a dispute erupted between the president's science adviser and Webb. NASA favored lunar orbit, while Wiesner favored an earth-orbit rendezvous. The debate went all the way to Kennedy. The president decided that Webb was responsible for the success of Apollo, and he gave him his support.[21]

The question of who was in charge of Apollo came up again in 1962. This time the threat to Webb's leadership came from within. The head of the Office of Manned Space Flight, Holmes, came to Webb and demanded an additional $400 million beyond what the president was requesting in the budget. Webb did not believe it politically wise to go beyond what was already being asked, and he refused to take the money from space science, aeronautics, or some other "lower-priority" NASA program. Three-quarters of NASA's budget was already in manned space, and there was a limit beyond which Webb would not go, lest Apollo overwhelm everything else. Holmes and Webb were both adamant, and this issue also went to Kennedy. Again, the president backed Webb, and Holmes soon was back in industry, replaced by an administrator more willing to recognize Webb's authority and work with the Webb, Dryden, and Seamans team.

Defending Distinctive Competence

The principal threat to NASA came from the Air Force, which had worked hard with both Eisenhower and Kennedy to be assigned the space mission and had its own ideas about how to run a manned space program. In 1961, Webb reached an understanding with the civilian management of DOD that neither agency would initiate the development of a new launch vehicle without first seeking the other's consent. The Air Force, however, never was satisfied with this understanding and was unremitting in its effort to gain autonomy from NASA. At one important stage the conflict centered on Gemini, a program NASA established in 1961 as a follow-on to Mercury (which placed one man in orbit) and prelude to Apollo, which would launch three men to the moon and bring them back.

Mercury was proving a great success, with each flight improving upon the predecessor. Alan Shephard made a suborbital flight on 5 May 1961; John Glenn made a three-orbit flight on 20 February 1962; and Gordon Cooper's twenty-two-orbit flight culminated the program on 15–16 May 1963. Now came Gemini. This two-man series had as its purpose "demonstration of ability to rendezvous and dock with target vehicle; demonstration of value of manned spacecraft for scientific and technological experimentation; performance of work by astronauts in space; use of powered, fueled satellite to provide primary and secondary propulsion for docked spacecraft; long-duration space flights without ill effect on astronauts; and precision landing of spacecraft.

In late 1962, Secretary of Defense McNamara proposed a division of labor between DOD and NASA. DOD (i.e., the Air Force) would be in charge of space programs near earth, whereas NASA would be the principal agency in deep space (e.g., the moon). Webb rejected that general principle, as well as the notion that Gemini should be placed under DOD management. Webb also opposed the idea of a jointly run program. Finally, in January 1963, Webb and DOD formally agreed that NASA would be the program manager of Gemini and that the Air Force would participate. This was not good enough for the Air Force, which pressed McNamara and sought allies in Congress. In July 1963, Vice President Johnson telephoned Webb to ask how much of "our present peaceful space program can be militarily useful." Webb replied that "all of it can be directly or indirectly militarily useful."

In December 1963 a proposed Air Force "spaceplane" called Dynasoar was canceled by McNamara. Approved in its place was a new program, Manned Orbital Laboratory (MOL), a small space station using Gemini concepts. NASA was not happy about this. However, there was strong support in Congress for a military manned space program of some sort. Throughout 1964 the pressure built up. By this time Lyndon Johnson was president. Johnson remained a strong supporter of Webb and NASA, but now he had broader responsibilities, and he wanted to show support for military space. Aware of Johnson's attitude, Webb officially endorsed MOL in January 1965. Johnson gave presidential sanction in August 1965.

Gemini, meanwhile, was a great success. Its flights, initiated in 1965, continued in 1966, fulfilling all the goals NASA had set for it. NASA coordinated with DOD, arranging for several military experiments to be flown. However, NASA knew that the Air Force was a serious and powerful rival for the lead role in manned space and that there would be a protracted struggle between the two agencies over roles and missions. NASA had to be on guard to defend its place in the development of space technology, lest it became subordinate to the Air Force.

Crisis Management

By 1966, with the visible successes of Mercury and Gemini, NASA had gained enormous good will in Congress and the White House. It was now an agency with over thirty thousand civil servants and manager of an industry-university team that had grown to over four-hundred thousand. Webb's own considerable reputation as a government manager had benefited. But as Webb was later to write, "A large-scale endeavor is so complex that its chief executive and senior associates cannot have detailed knowledge and expertise for every facet of its operation. They must delegate important responsibilities to lower echelons and then find ways to make sure the delegations accomplish their purposes without harmful compartmentalization."[22]

Ninety percent of NASA's work was being performed by industry. As Webb saw it, the traditional way government managed industry was to write a contract such that if performance and cost goals were not met, the company would suffer financially. NASA could not accept anything less than the very best performance from its contractors. Delays in any part could delay all. Hence, NASA used a number of devices to assure rapid feedback from industry when problems arose. This feedback was based on a sense of partnership and trust between NASA and its contractors. NASA would be involved deeply in overseeing companies' actual management of technical projects. When problems arose, NASA and the contractors would tackle them together, and solve them. The emphasis was on fast action in a problem-solving partnership, management through interdependency.[23]

Then, on 27 January 1967, three astronauts—Virgil Grissom, Edward White, and Roger Chaffee—were killed when a fire ignited in the Apollo command module as it sat on a launch pad at Cape Canaveral, Florida. For a program that had been going so exceptionally well, this event was a total shock. There obviously had to be an investigation. Webb told President Johnson that as far as he was concerned, any form of investigation the president wanted made would be satisfactory to him, and Webb would cooperate completely. But the problem was to find out what had happened, deal with the problem, and fly again. And NASA, Webb argued, could do that better than any group of outsiders. Johnson agreed that NASA should conduct the investigation.[24]

Webb later said that this tragedy "didn't shake my faith in the fact that the management structure we [had] created could do the job. It did raise serious questions in my mind about why some of our best people had not seen the early signs of difficulty. . . . the effect of the fire on me was that we had to find out what happened and fix it and move ahead, that we had to do that expeditiously and we had to maintain our support while we had to be very careful not to destroy the system that gave us success."[25]

There were critics as well as supporters of NASA in Congress, and some of them were vocal. NASA initiated its investigation in the early months of 1967. Committees in both the House and the Senate, meanwhile, conducted hearings on the fire. It was found that the cause of the fire was hard to pinpoint. North American Aviation, the prime contractor, had not done all that was necessary to assure safety. Neither had NASA. It was made known during the hearings that NASA had selected North American originally in spite of the fact that it had not been rated first by NASA's own technical source review board. Also, NASA had been aware of certain technical and managerial deficiencies on the part of North American, since these had been documented in a report written by the NASA manager, Gen. Sam Phillips, after he had conducted an investigation in 1965.[26]

Webb explained that he, Dryden, and Seamans had indeed made the decision to use North American as the Apollo spacecraft contractor, because they considered North American to be as competent as the company rated higher by the review board. In addition, they recognized the wish of the astronauts for a company that had experience with high-performance manned aircraft, such as the X-15, rather than only missiles. North American had such experience, and its major competitor did not. This explanation may have been acceptable to most legislators, but some senators saw the choice influenced by certain Washington power brokers, particularly one Bobby Baker, an aide to Lyndon Johnson when he was in the Senate and a lobbyist for North American.

With the insinuations about Baker in the background, Webb found himself under great pressure when Congress demanded to see the so-called Phillips Report. For Webb, making public this document (which was more a collection of notes than a formal report) would undermine the elements of trust he had tried to instill in the government-industry management system NASA had constructed. With such advanced state-of-the-art equipment being developed on a fast-paced timetable, there were always problems with many contractors. NASA found contractors far more likely to report these problems and to work with government to solve them if they felt such information would be kept "in the family." There were technical difficulties in practically every NASA development contract. This one, obviously, had worse problems than others, and design errors and faults in testing procedures may have led directly or indirectly to the loss of three lives. But to reveal the details of the Phillips Report, Webb said, would undermine all confidential dealings between NASA and industry. It would seriously injure a basic relationship that was responsible for much of the success NASA had had up to this point.

Webb did let a few senior legislators see the report, and he trusted them not to leak it. To deal with Congress generally, he asked for (and received) an opportunity to answer his critics in executive session before the Senate Space Committee. When asked why he did this, he said: "I decided a long time ago never to answer criticism in public. You can follow this policy if you have nothing to hide, if you've been honest. After the fire, when I was being criticized, particularly by one or two Senators, I demanded a closed session of the Senate Committee. That was, of course, the last thing my detractors wanted—a private session. But we sat down, with the doors closed." Webb indicated that various individuals made their concerns known, and "I corrected them where they were wrong."[27] Senator Brooke, a committee member and Webb critic, indicated at this time that he had followed Webb's approach in answering criticism when he had been attorney general of Massachusetts.

Webb had inundated the relevant committees with information about the administration of NASA. Usually he had given them more knowledge about the program than they could digest. He knew a number of legislators well, personally. There was a basic sense of trust between Webb and most individual legislators with whom he dealt. That Webb was able to satisfy the Senate (and House) reflected the general good will he had amassed over the years with Congress. It reflected a genuine skill in dealing with legislators. His relations with Congress were a strength at this time of trial.

After a great deal of examination of the NASA, North American, and Phillips Report situations, Congress essentially left it to Webb to make whatever changes were necessary to make certain that such an event would not reoccur. On the basis of NASA's own investigation, Webb and his associates decided that it would be essential to have stronger topside review within NASA of decisions made below. A reorganization followed. Webb also decided that a stronger check was required on some of North American's detailed, day-to-day technical work.

Webb asked the Boeing Company, manufacturer of a large section of the Saturn rocket, to take over the job of monitoring the Apollo equipment on top of the rocket. Boeing was to integrate and certify the entire rocket/space capsule machine for flight. Said Webb: "This was a broadside use of a very large company with great capability to help us do the total job, to have a second look, so that NASA and Boeing had to be satisfied that the equipment was ready to fly." North American did not like this and declined to cooperate. To enforce its decision, NASA began negotiations with other contractors for the Apollo task being performed by North American. Realizing that NASA was indeed serious, North American accepted fifty Boeing inspectors on its production line.[28]

The manned-flight schedule was delayed eighteen months because of the fire. A sweeping redesign of the command module to reduce fire and other hazards was accomplished. When Webb and Seamans (Dryden died in 1965) were satisfied that NASA had done all that it could do to assure the safety of the crew, NASA gave the go-ahead to resume the program. It is noteworthy that while Webb had not foreseen the Apollo fire, he had anticipated some kinds of problems along the way. That was why he had originally taken an "administrator's discount" on NASA's technical projection of a 1967 landing. He wanted two years extra, just in case. It turned out that he had the additional time when it was needed.

Throughout the ordeal, NASA had support from most of the principals on the space committees. Moreover, President Johnson said to Webb essentially what Kennedy had said to him earlier: "Fly when you're ready and don't go until you are ready. Don't let the political pressures force you to go too soon, and don't hold back if the time is right."[29]

Selling Post-Apollo

There comes a point when an organization and its leader must look beyond its present mission to new missions, especially if the existing mission has a finite lifetime. Webb had the problem of advising the president and Congress as to not only what NASA would do for post-Apollo but when and how to sell the program. The selling of Apollo in 1961 was expedited by a political environment that was ripe, made ripe by the competition of a series of Soviet firsts. There was a growing national consensus that the United States had to "do something." NASA careerists planned Apollo as the "natural" technical goal for the agency. Webb contributed mightily to translating the technologists' goal into a presidential objective of restoring national pride and power. Congress was fully ready to go along, as the absence of debate on Kennedy's decision made clear. But in the latter 1960s, when Webb was trying to define and promote a post-Apollo program, the political environment had changed.

First, NASA's own success made a difference. During the 1960s, America began to do quite well in space, while the Soviet Union seemed to lose much of its early momentum. Second, the nation and President

Johnson were increasingly distracted from space by two other even larger national efforts: the Great Society and the Vietnam War. Third, at a time when gaining support for post-Apollo was most critical, Apollo was yet to be completed. Fourth, the overall space budget was suffering cutbacks in a period of general financial stringency, and the NASA priority had to be to spend its diminishing resources to maintain Apollo rather than to establish post-Apollo efforts.

The process of defining and selling post-Apollo began early, at a time not of Webb's choosing. In January 1964 the President, at the urging of his science adviser and BOB director, asked Webb to begin specifying NASA's future goals. Of particular concern to the science adviser and BOB was NERVA, a nuclear rocket NASA was seeking to fund as a long-term development project. The objectives for NERVA were not clear.

The president had set September 1964 as the deadline for a report on future plans. It was not until January 1965 that Webb responded to Johnson's request. He did so by providing a compendium of possible options based on NASA's growing competence: short-range, intermediate, and long-term.There were no priorities. Webb explained that the priorities would emerge from a process of national consensus building. Donald Hornig, Johnson's science adviser, disagreed. He called it a "shopping list." Webb later explained his rationale:

> First, the announcement by NASA in the mid-1960s of a long-term goal would make the agency vulnerable. It would provide ammunition to critics, who would be able to shoot down the proposed program as being too expensive or impractical, thereby raising the possibility that long-range technology developments tied to the announced goal would be cut out. . . .
>
> Second, should NASA announce a long-term, post-Apollo goal, critics would claim that the lunar landing was simply an interim goal, subordinate to the new effort. . . .
>
> Third, the major effort required for planning, proposing, and defending a new long-range goal would tie up the energies of top NASA leadership and key scientists and engineers, diverting them from concentrating on making Apollo a success.[30]

So Webb held back. Meanwhile he pressed for start-up funds for new programs, such as NERVA. What could NERVA be for? It was to be more powerful than Saturn, providing for much longer flights. It would be ideal for a manned flight to Mars or for carrying large supplies for possible colonies on the moon. But this was speculation—for Webb was careful not to speak in terms of explicit goals. He wanted to make sure that there was support for such goals before committing to them.

Meanwhile, he sought funding for the long lead-time technologies that would make them possible to realize. The 1965 Air Force MOL decision, however, made it clear that NASA could not delay its own decisions indefinitely. It was not the only space agency in town.

By 1966, NASA had settled on a new program called Apollo Applications, which would serve as a short-term effort that would keep NASA going at a high momentum, without substantial lay-offs, after the lunar landing. It was for a "mini-space station" using Apollo hardware that would possibly provide a demonstration for what a permanent civilian space station could do. Within NASA, there were those who regarded such a program as unwise, even unfeasible. But Webb decided to give Apollo Applications the go-ahead. This effort and NERVA constituted two of the key post-Apollo programs for which NASA sought commitments. The president, however, was anxious to avoid new starts in space and deferred decision in 1966. Johnson told Webb he had to hold the line on NASA's budget.

Publicly, Webb defended the president's "no new starts" space budget before Congress. Privately, he argued the opposite case vociferously. On 26 August 1966 Webb wrote Johnson that unless matters changed, NASA would have "no choice but to accelerate the rate at which we are carrying on the liquidation of some of the capabilities which we have built up. Important options which we have been holding open will be foreclosed. . . . Struggle as I have to try to put myself in your place and see this from your point of view, I cannot avoid a strong feeling that this is not in the best interest of the country."[31] Webb pointed out that the NASA budget should go up to $6 billion. BOB was seeking to keep NASA at $5 billion. The BOB director agreed that Apollo Applications had to be started, but at a lower level of funding than Webb wanted. As for NERVA, BOB favored phasing down the program rather than stepping it up, as Webb desired. BOB wanted research, not development.

Webb told the president that he believed that it would be "extremely important for you to be able to point to a continuing nuclear rocket program when the USSR unveils a launch vehicle larger than our Saturn V, which may be soon and may involve a nuclear stage."[32] The President's Science Advisory Committee, however, told Johnson that it "did not see any urgency in proceeding to the development of a nuclear rocket stage at this time."[33]

During the budget deliberations, Johnson decided to go with Apollo Applications at the lower level recommended by BOB. He postponed deciding on NERVA, but after the Apollo fire of January 1967, he gave his approval, possibly as a gesture of support for Webb. The legislative environment for post-Apollo was set by Johnson's 1967 request for a 10 percent tax increase to help pay for debts arising mainly from the Vietnam War. The House Ways and Means Committee told Johnson it would not support the tax unless Johnson cut his budget.

With Apollo continuing to be protected, Congress took its toll of NASA's future. In questioning Webb, the Senate Appropriations Committee tried to make him state his priorities on post-Apollo, but Webb replied, "I don't want to give any aid and comfort to anyone to cut out a program."[34] If Webb would not set priorities for cutting, Congress would cut on its own. Thus, both Apollo Applications and NERVA were curtailed.

Webb was cross-pressured. He wanted the $6 billion budget. At the same time, as he told the House Appropriations Subcommittee:

> The President has reviewed with me personally the "blackboard exercise" and his concern about the deficit that is indicated at $29 or $30 billion, his concern about the borrowing capacity of the nation, his concern about the necessity to reduce expenditures at the same time he is making an urgent request for tax increases, and he is asking me to do everything in my power to help him with these programs.[35]

On 21 August 1967, Johnson signed a congressional bill that drastically reduced the post-Apollo programs. Johnson stated that ordinarily he would have opposed such cuts, but circumstances had changed, and "we must moderate our efforts in certain space projects."[36]

Five hundred million dollars was excised from the NASA budget, with much of this removed from Apollo Applications and NERVA. The next year, it was more of the same. NASA's total final appropriation for fiscal-year 1969 was $3.9 billion, another cut, and far below the $6 billion that Webb had said the agency had to have to prevent the "liquidation" of the NASA capabilities built up to go to the moon.

On 16 September 1968, Webb spoke with the president and then announced his decision to retire from NASA, effective 7 October 1968. In his announcement, Webb said that the retrenchment meant that the United States would be in second place for years to come.

The situation for NASA did not improve for fiscal-year 1970. Johnson left, and Richard Nixon became president. Apollo Applications devolved into the short-lived Skylab; NERVA was canceled altogether. Only the shuttle program, a space initiative of Nixon's, saved manned space from virtual extinction. NASA survived in the 1970s, with a program about half the size of what it had been in the 1960s.[37]

Conclusion

In 1969, NASA did send men to the moon and return them safely to earth. As the administrator in charge of NASA during the 1960s, Webb's place in history is assured. The goal that mattered most was achieved. Achieving that goal was an extraordinary administrative as well as scientific and technological success. It was also a political success, for necessary funds had to be obtained from the White House and Congress every year.

Webb significantly influenced the original presidential decision, thus providing for his agency the long-term mission it needed. He also made certain he controlled the agency as it implemented the mission, establishing an executive secretariat to provide him with a constant flow of information concerning the pattern of decision making as it developed throughout NASA. He made certain that he and his senior associates were in charge. This meant that no one got between him and the president. It also meant that the strong-minded center directors and program managers had to work within the approved lines of endeavor. There was to be no czar, not even for Apollo. Every few years there was a reorganization that affected power relationships, preventing NASA's becoming too "settled." From Webb's point of view, a certain amount of disequilibrium was good. Nor, really, did Webb make himself a czar. He was an "organization man," if ever there was one.

While he was clearly the man at the top, Webb also gave credit and glory to others. This was evidenced by his willingness to share authority with Dryden and Seamans, who formed with him a "collective leadership." It could also be seen in his willingness to let astronauts, managers such as Mueller, Gilruth, Pickering, Newell, Siverstein, Debus, and von Braun, and many others throughout the organization participate in decision making and enjoy public recognition. As NASA succeeded in the 1960s, it did so as an organization. Indeed, it did so as an organizational system. Webb spoke of a research partnership, a government-industry-university team. When he discussed the NASA workforce, he included the contractors and grantees in his numbers. When he spoke of liquidating capability, he meant capability outside NASA, as well as scientists and engineers in the NASA centers.

Webb had various tensions with the presidency and Congress over the years, but he always retained a reservoir of trust and support. He needed it during the Apollo fire controversy—the principal threat to his management system and his own reputation.

Virtually everything NASA did was highly visible. Webb knew the media would be watching, and he made the media an asset rather than a liability through his policy of attentiveness and accommodation. When launches were not going well, failures were reported. But as the program began succeeding, achievement was also reported. NASA gained many prominent friends in the media, among them the nation's principal evening-news anchor man, Walter Cronkite.

Webb was a great success at NASA, but not in every area. Aside from Apollo, the program that was more identified with Webb personally than any other was the SUP. This program had many purposes, including the political purpose of providing funds to universities in congressional districts that mattered. However, the more significant Webb purpose that evolved over the decade (aside from student fellowships and faculty interdisciplinary research) was to bring the universities into a new mode of interaction with industry. He sought the kind of regional development that he had seen along route 128 in Massachusetts, that he had attempted to encourage in Oklahoma prior to joining NASA, and that in the 1980s developed in many areas.

This program really mattered to Webb. He provided new space science buildings to universities and signed memorandums of understanding with their presidents. The presidents promised to work energetically with regional industry to accelerate the transfer of space technology to civilian technology. Few presidents did this. Nor, in Webb's view, did his own Office of University Affairs do all it could to implement the Webb perspective. The SUP ended not long after Webb left. Today, it is generally regarded as not having achieved its broader objectives.

There were other problems. Webb could not prevent Air Force incursions into NASA's territory via MOL, for example. But perhaps the most serious was Webb's handling of the post-Apollo program. Webb said that the post-Apollo program would come from a new national consensus. But such a consensus did not come—at least not the kind Webb wanted. No one led a consensus-building process. Webb tried to do so within government, but President Johnson wanted to put off decisions and asked Webb to let the post-Apollo decision wait. Webb felt that he could not be explicit about goals, since there was no consensus, so he spoke in terms of capabilities, such as Apollo Applications and the nuclear rocket. It was not enough to promote space R&D as a mission. Thanks to Apollo, the nation expected goals. But the political climate was not ripe for choosing among goals.

By the time Johnson was willing to back Webb's capability-oriented goals, he had Congress demanding spending cuts as the price of new taxes. Space was a lower priority for the president, Congress, and the nation in an era of Vietnam War and domestic unrest. Moreover, NASA's very successes (and Russia's lack of visible evidence of being ahead) made for complacency among many policy makers. Webb labored, mostly inside government, to alert leaders to what he perceived as the risks of falling behind again, and frustration was his reward.

So the record is not perfect. Webb was the right man in the right organization at the right time for getting to the moon. But his reach was greater than his grasp where the SUP was concerned, and he could not define or get the nation's strong commitment to new post-Apollo goals before he left. Another administrator, however, probably would not have even thought of SUP, and it is doubtful that anyone could have sold a post-Apollo program in the environment of the late 1960s. Webb, therefore, deserves credit for what he did and tried to do, and his accomplishments in leading Apollo were of historic proportion. To this day, in terms of philosophy and management practices, NASA bears Webb's stamp. NASA administrators are measured by how they compare with Webb. Webb accomplished a great mission and was the prime builder of a successful government agency.[38]

What makes an exceptional administrator? Most people who worked for Webb (or observed him) point to a man with an extraordinary ability to enthuse large groups of people and get them moving in a common direction. This is leadership. And it may require certain settings. The evidence is that Webb was successful in BOB in the postwar years and in NASA in the 1960s. He was less successful in the State Department. One reason was that he was "on top" in BOB and NASA, and thus was less constrained. Another is that these were organizations that "fit" Webb's skills as an administrator. The State Department, with its foreign service officer base, thinks policy, not administration, and even looks down its nose at administrators. Foreign service officers perform as individuals rather than as a team. Individuals are harder to lead in common directions than groups. Webb did much at State, but it was not as congenial a home for his skills as BOB or NASA. NASA was really the ideal setting for Webb as an organizational leader. There was a common goal, and engineers are accustomed to project approaches involving large-scale management.

What is important about Webb's administrative style is that he combined a sense of control (what it took to be in charge) with a sensitivity to "organizational nurturing." He consciously thought about how to strengthen the capacities of his organization to do its job. Participation in decisions was one method. Reorganization that kept NASA alert, responsive, and adaptive was another. What was needed at one time was not necessarily what was needed at another. In 1961, Webb reorganized to bring power to top management; in 1963 he reorganized to let it slip back to the program offices and centers. Later, there were other reorganizations as part of administrative strategy.

Teaching was a third administrative mechanism. By *teaching* I mean a constant effort to improve other administrators in the practice of management and political action in Washington. He would take the time to talk with his staff and managers about managerial-political activities. He showed them how they could turn problems (e.g., congressional inquiries) into opportunities (ways to win friends in Congress). He read books about administration and brought outside scholars inside to study the NASA organization and techniques. He wanted his organization to be as open and innovative as possible. He felt that his managers could learn from being studied, just as those doing the studying could learn from NASA.

Nothing Webb achieved would have been possible without great personal energy, stamina, determination, intelligence, and optimism. Where do great administrative leaders come from? Are they born or made? The physical and mental energy have to be in the genes. The optimism and enthusiasm, as well as political and administrative skills, obviously are acquired along the way. Webb had a series of experiences in government and business from which he learned and grew as a public administrator. He understood the inseparability of his inside and outside roles. When the 1960s came, and the United States looked for leadership in space, it needed an uncommon man to chart a course and see it through. Webb was ready.

Notes

1. Christian Williams, "James Webb and NASA's Reach for the Moon," *Washington Post*, 24 September 1981.

2. Ibid.

3. James Beggs, "James E. Webb: A Force for Excellence" (Inaugural lecture of Fund for Excellence in Public Administration, National Academy of Public Administration, Washington, D.C., 18 November 1983).

4. James E. Webb, interview by Robert Sherrod, 28 April 1971, transcript, NASA Historical Files, Washington, D.C. The information in the next several paragraphs is from this interview.

5. This information and that in the next several paragraphs is from Larry Berman, *The Office of Management and Budget and the Presidency, 1921–1979* (Princeton, N.J.: Princeton University Press, 1979), 36, 40, 42.

6. Dean Acheson, *Present at the Creation* (New York: Norton, 1969), 250.

7. Ibid.

8. The headaches were chronic with Webb and later were diagnosed as due to allergies connected with smoking and drinking, two "vices" he found virtually unavoidable in his years at State (Sherrod interview).

9. Acheson, *Present at the Creation*, 250.

10. John D. Young, "Organizing the Nation's Civilian Space Capabilities: Selected Reflections," in *Federal Public Policy*, ed. Theodore Taylor (Mt. Airy, Md.: Lomond, 1984), 47.

11. Ibid., 48.

12. Williams, "James Webb."

13. James E. Webb, *Space Age Management: The Large-Scale Approach* (New York: Columbia University Press, 1969), 73–74.

14. John Logsdon, *The Decision to Go to the Moon* (Cambridge: MIT Press, 1970), 90. Unless otherwise indicated, the information in the balance of this section is from ibid., 91–129.

15. Beggs, "James E. Webb," 6.

16. Young, "Organizing the Nation's Civilian Space Capabilities," 50.

17. Arnold Levine, *Managing NASA in the Apollo Era* (Washington, D.C.: NASA, 1982), 3.

18. Daniel S. Greenberg, "The Space Administration: It Was Once Criticized for Slowness But Is Now Criticized for Speed," *Science* 134 (September 1961): 930–32.

19. Levine, *Managing NASA*, 19.

20. For a detailed analysis of the NASA university effort see W. Henry Lambright and Laurin L. Henry, "Using Universities: The NASA Experience," *Public Policy* 20 (Winter 1972).

21. Levine, *Managing NASA*, 20–21. The information in the next several paragraphs is from ibid., 23–232 passim.

22. Cited in Beggs, "James E. Webb," 11.

23. James E. Webb, interview by James Burke, 23 May 1979, transcript, NASA Historical Files, Washington, D.C.

24. Transcript, James E. Webb, Oral History File, LBJ Library, Austin, Texas; see also Burke interview.

25. Burke interview.

26. Levine, *Managing NASA*, 25.

27. Williams, "James Webb."

28. Burke interview.

29. Ibid.

30. Cited in Arthur Levine, *Future of the U.S. Space Program* (New York: Praeger, 1975), 119.

31. James Webb to President Johnson, 26 August 1966, "Outer Space" Files (7/21/66–11/15/66), Ex OS (1/29/66), White House Central Files, LBJ Library.

32. Memo, Webb to Johnson, 14 December 1966, Files of the Director of the BOB, National Archives, Washington, D.C.

33. Memo, Donald Hornig to Johnson, 22 December 1966, Papers of Donald Hornig, LBJ Library.

34. U.S. Congress, Senate, *NASA Appropriations: Hearings on H.R. 12474*, 90th Cong., 1st sess., 1967.

35. U.S. Congress, House, Committee on Appropriations, Subcommittee on Independent Offices, *Hearings: NASA Appropriations for 1968*, 90th Cong., 1st sess., 1967.

36. Emmette S. Redford and Orion F. White, *What Manned Space Program after Reaching the Moon? Government Attempts to Decide: 1962–1968* (Syracuse, N.Y.: Inter-university Case Program, 1971), 207.

37. The Air Force MOL program was killed by the Nixon administration.

38. NASA had virtually unparalleled success until the Challenger disaster of 1986. For an analysis arguing that NASA gradually "ran down" as an organization after Webb, see Joseph Trento, *Prescription for Disaster* (New York: Crown, 1987). Also, there is an interesting and not particularly flattering depiction of Webb in

Walter A. McDougall, . . . *the Heavens and the Earth: A Political History of the Space Age* (New York: Basic Books, 1985). McDougall's assessment is limited, however, by his incomplete appreciation of the political constraints under which Webb, and executive-agency leaders generally, must operate.

Administrative Entrepreneurs

7

The Politics of Art: Nancy Hanks and the National Endowment for the Arts

Margaret Jane Wyszomirski

The history of federal involvement with the arts can be characterized as sporadic, mostly indirect, frequently controversial, and seldom pursued as a matter of arts policy. Throughout much of the nation's history, both government officials and artists regarded each other from a wary distance. Despite such mutual distrust, Lyndon Johnson's Great Society embarked upon a radically different course. With the establishment of the National Endowment for the Arts (NEA) in 1965, the federal government took an important, albeit tenuous, step toward developing a federal policy of continuing, direct support for the arts. In doing so, it also opened the door for potentially fruitful and congenial partnerships between government and artists, between the public and nonprofit sectors, and between the federal and state governments in the quest for an improved quality of life for the citizens of an enlightened civilization.

Although the seeds of change were sown during the late 1960s, they were cultivated to full bloom during the succeeding Nixon administration under the leadership of Nancy Hanks, who served as chairman of the NEA from 1969 to 1977. The flowering of federal arts policy could be seen in the endowment itself, in the thriving proliferation of the arts, in the expansion of the American arts audience both numerically and geographically, and in the transformation of official and public attitudes about the arts as well as of the opinion of artists about government patronage.

When Hanks took office in early October 1969, the NEA was a small, young agency teetering on the brink of its "initial survival threshold."[1] By the time she resigned in October 1977, the NEA had become a mature, institutionalized, successful federal agency. During her eight-year tenure Hanks increased the agency's budget by 1,200 percent and its staff by nearly 600 percent. This, in turn, had sustained a vast increase both in administrative workload and in federal arts patronage. The number of applications coming into the NEA multiplied by over 900 percent, from about 2,000 to nearly 20,000, while the grants it awarded rose by nearly 600 percent, from 584 in 1969 to over 4,000 in 1977. The agency fostered and contributed to state programs in all fifty states and six territories and engaged in cooperative efforts with other federal entities. Finally, the scope of activities that its programs supported grew to embrace virtually every type of grantee, creative style, and form of art.

Equal to these significant administrative accomplishments was the NEA's record in nurturing an arts "boom" and in dispersing it across the nation. With the agency's support, the number of artists and art institutions in America grew tremendously during the 1960s and 1970s. The number of artists in the labor force nearly doubled, to over 1 million individuals.[2] The number of professional orchestras and opera companies each increased by 400 percent, while dance companies proliferated by 1,100 percent.[3] Additionally, geographic dispersion increased as artistic institutions were established in communities across the nation, most especially outside the old urban centers of the Northeast. Indeed, by the late 1970s the United States had "for the first time moved to the first rank in world terms in almost every major art form."[4]

Concomitantly, the public constituency reached by artists and arts institutions also "boomed." Theater audiences grew from 4 million to 13 million, opera attendance increased from 2.5 million to 11 million, and the dance audience exploded from 1.5 million to 16 million.[5] Public support grew in other ways as well. Between 1970 and 1978, state appropriations for the arts rose by over 900 percent. Corporate contributions quintupled, from $40 million to $210 million, and foundation support doubled, from $114 million to $289 million.[6] By 1980 a nationwide Harris poll discovered that 81 percent of the public wanted "more and better arts facilities" and that 65 percent of those surveyed would be willing to pay ten dollars more in taxes to help support arts activities.[7]

Finally, the wariness with which artists and politicians historically had regarded one another was largely dispelled. Assessing the situation in early 1969, the first NEA chairman, Roger Stevens, announced that "we've killed the bugaboo of government control of the arts."[8] In fact, only the first steps had been taken toward assuaging the artist's mistrust of government support. By 1974 this change had progressed to the point where Deputy NEA Chairman Michael Straight could report that artists "no longer seem threatened" by "the danger that government interference could lead to the stifling of creativity or to political control." Indeed, artists and arts administrators had come to regard the NEA as a source of "hope and encouragement" and credited government funding with having "greatly raised the self-appreciation and self-understanding of artists throughout the country."[9]

Among politicians, attitudes had changed and support had grown. A core group of strategically positioned, bipartisan congressional supporters had been cultivated, and advocates at the state level had been mobilized around the establishment and annual legislative funding of state arts councils. In 1977, House majority whip John Brademas declared the arts to be "politically saleable."[10] Thus, within a decade, congressional opinion had changed from viewing federal support for the arts as a risky political venture to seeing it as a legitimate and effective method of fostering the arts in America.

The improvement in the stature, vitality, and popularity of art in America in the two decades since the establishment of the NEA is incontrovertible. Equally obvious is the fact that the NEA played an important part in promoting and sustaining this development. Crucial to this performance was the leadership of Nancy Hanks. A brief listing of her most significant achievements would include the following:

1. The legitimization of the "principle of public funding of the arts in Congress and with the artists, themselves."[11] Furthermore, she gave concrete shape to this abstract principle in the form of a partnership composed of the government and private sectors; of federal, state, and local agencies; of individuals and institutions—all joined in collaborative support of the arts.

2. The establishment of the endowment as a leader of the arts constituency. Indeed, Hanks helped to coalesce the diverse arts interests into a genuine artistic community and then to mobilize it into an influential political constituency.

3. The institutionalization of the agency and the routinization of its procedures and programs instead of continuing the "rather improvised personal arbitrary decisions of the (former) Chairman and of the then program directors."[12]

To appreciate how Nancy Hanks achieved these results requires an understanding of the political and bureaucratic resources and constraints with which she had to work; of her personality, style, and experience; and of the environmental context in which she operated. In other words, one must analyze and assess the entrepreneurial leadership of the woman who took a small agency commissioned to implement a politically risky and ambiguous federal arts policy and transformed it into a bureaucratic and political success presiding over a legitimate policy of catalyzing an effective public-private partnership of support for the arts.

The Context and Legacy: Hanks Takes Office

When she was confirmed in October 1969 as the second chairman of the NEA, Nancy Hanks assumed the leadership of a nascent organization that was riding a tide of political, economic, social, and aesthetic change. That wave carried both opportunities and risks, just as the legacy of the young agency presented both resources and constraints.

Throughout the 1960s the vitality and quality of the arts in America were starting to surge, while the financial and institutional stability of arts institutions remained precarious. The postwar period had given rise to an American citizenry that was increasingly better educated, prosperous, and leisured—and therefore more likely to become arts consumers. Concurrently, international conflict between East and West had extended beyond the military, diplomatic, and economic dimensions to include a competition between ideologies, ideas, and cultures.[13] In the cold-war struggle for the minds and souls of the world's people, the arts had come to be a key component of public diplomacy. Excellence in the arts was held to be an indication of the virtues of democratic civilization as well as a refutation of the charge that the United States had an excessively materialistic culture devoid of an appreciation of things intellectual and aesthetic.

These conditions provided millions of Americans with both a desire and an opportunity to join the arts audience. Furthermore, President John Kennedy's interest in the arts (as seen in the inclusion of artists in his inaugural ceremonies and in White House soirees, which featured the performance of artists such as Pablo Casals) seemed to galvanize many to explore this new frontier. Museums and performing arts institutions of all types began to attract such large audiences that they often needed to expand seasons or extend hours to accommodate the crowds. Such popularity was, however, a mixed blessing, since the costs of expansion for such labor-intensive, expensive activities were great, while financial resources were limited and unpredictable.

Indeed, the financial state of the arts in America was undergoing a dramatic change. Many of the most prestigious arts institutions had outgrown the patronage capabilities of individual supporters. While foundation funds were available—and crucial—in support of both artistic growth and artistic proliferation, they too would soon be inadequate. Corporate philanthropy, so plentiful in the 1980s, was meager, and only a miniscule amount went to the arts and humanities. In 1969, government support was also miserly: the federal government contributed $8.5 million thru the NEA, all state governments combined added another $4–6 million, and municipal governments (when they did anything) generally helped to support only the local museum.

Thus, some sources of support were insufficient to meet a growing need, while others held only a promise of providing greater assistance in the future. Meanwhile, arts organizations also confronted limits upon the amount of additional income they might earn from raising prices for fear that they might discourage actual as well as potential arts consumers if tickets became too costly.

Throughout the 1960s, evidence was mounting that the arts were in financial trouble. The unprecedented 1961 musicians' strike of the Metropolitan Opera was perhaps the first harbinger of these impending problems. The second half of the decade saw the release of a number of prestigious foundation reports that sought to examine the issue and to raise the level of public concern. In 1965 a Rockefeller Brothers Fund report, *The Performing Arts: Problems and Prospects*, identified a host of problems facing the live, professional, performing arts; discussed the shifting patterns of their financial support; and made recommendations for possible improvements, including a call for stronger support from the state, local, and federal governments. The following year, a Twentieth Century Fund report documented the economic dilemma of the performing arts, calling it a virtually inescapable "income-earnings gap."[14] Finally, in 1968 the Belmont Report outlined similar problems facing museums. Indeed, 1969 found American art in the paradoxical position of being internationally acclaimed and domestically popular yet faced with an "economic crisis."[15]

In the fall of 1969 the NEA was a small, threatened, drifting agency. The National Foundation on the Arts and Humanities Act of 1965 had called for the establishment of an independent executive agency that would have two operating endowments—the National Endowment for the Arts and the National Endowment for the Humanities (NEH). Each endowment was to be directed by a chairman, appointed by the president for a four-year term, subject to confirmation by the Senate. The chairman was, in turn, to consult with and be advised by a twenty-six-member National Council on the Arts (NCA), to be composed of private citizens prominently engaged in or knowledgeable about their respective disciplines. Council members were to be appointed for staggered six-year terms. Furthermore, the chairmen of the two endowments were to be members of and consult with a Federal Council on the Arts and Humanities, which was to include seven federal officials from other government agencies that administered projects in the arts and humanities.[16]

Hanks's predecessor, Roger Stevens (who had chaired the NEA since its inception), had a flamboyant, personalistic, and partisan leadership style. During the 1940s and 1950s he had pursued a career as a successful real estate developer and had also become one of Broadway's busiest producers, backing hit plays such as *Cat on a Hot Tin Roof, The Four-Poster*, and *The Bad Seed*. Stylistically, Stevens was a man of great personal presence who possessed a gambler's willingness to take risks but the successful speculator's knack for carefully assessing potential gambles.[17] Politically, he had first become active as a volunteer for Adlai Stevenson in 1952; four years later he served as finance committee chairman for the Democratic National Committee during Stevenson's second run against the Eisenhower-Nixon ticket. In September 1961, President Kennedy appointed Stevens to the board of trustees for the development of a national cultural center. In 1964, Congress named the proposed center the John F. Kennedy Center for the Performing Arts and appropriated $15.5 million toward its completion; Stevens became chairman of the board, a position he still occupies. With such combined partisan and artistic credentials, it was perhaps natural that LBJ should turn to Stevens to pilot the administration's efforts to establish, first, a national advisory council on the arts and, eventually, the NEA. Thus, in 1964 Stevens also became special assistant to the president on the arts. When a National Council on the Arts was created as a preliminary step toward an arts funding agency, Stevens was tapped, in February 1965, to become its first chairman. Six months later this carried him into the chairmanship of the newly created NEA, where, for a while, he continued to wear all three hats.

As head of the agency, Stevens had a philosophy of "not believing in democracy—that is, giving everybody a little money. Instead he tried to create an impact where a small sum could make a difference." He also worked closely with the NCA, which during the earliest years functioned virtually as NEA staff, originating project ideas and carefully reviewing individual grants. For both philosophical and practical reasons, the initial emphases of the agency were grants to individuals, rescue grants to a few arts institutions, experimental/developmental projects, and demonstration programs in arts education.[18]

For example, the very first award given by the NEA was an emergency grant of $100,000 to the American Ballet Theatre, for which the agency was applauded as having "saved a national treasure."[19] Another $250,000 was added to help sponsor a national tour by the company. Individual grants were given to choreographers, as fellowships to arts school graduates, as sabbaticals for teaching artists, and as distinguished service awards to poets, critics, and composers. The first matching grant for a public sculpture went to Grand Rapids, Michigan, to help commission Alexander Calder's *La Grande Vitesse*. Experimental "laboratory theatres" were started as pilot projects in New Orleans and Providence. A 1967 grant of $1.3 million was the first of many awarded toward the development of an American Film Institute for the preservation and cultivation of the nation's cultural resources in film. An artists-in-the-schools program was begun and collaborative funding for its expansion secured. Grants in support of arts programming on educational television and radio were also made. Finally, an emergency program directed at minority groups was carried out in sixteen cities as the Inner City Arts Program, one small part of a larger administration effort to "cool down" the inner cities that had flared into riots during the summers of the late 1960s.

Yet, throughout most of Stevens's tenure the agency seemed stalled at an appropriations level too low to allow it to do much more than sponsor demonstrations or make an occasional rescue grant. After a 1966 start-up appropriation of $2.5 million, the budget averaged approximately $8 million for each of the next three years. For FY 1970, an incremental increase of 7 percent raised the budget slightly, to $9 million. Clearly, such resources were quite insufficient if the NEA was to have any discernible national impact upon the arts. Nor could the agency do much to alleviate the growing economic crisis in the arts with a mere $9 million, when the 1968/69 gross deficit for professional nonprofit theatre, opera, dance, and symphony orchestras was expected to be nearly $100 million.[20]

Politically, congressional support for the arts was uncertain and not fully bipartisan. During reauthorization hearings in 1968, considerable criticism had focused on grants made to individual artists. Indeed, the House voted to revoke the agency's authority to award such grants; this was, however, amended in conference to allow for grants to persons of "exceptional talent." Furthermore, suggested authorization figures varied widely throughout congressional debate that year, indicating that little legislative consensus existed concerning the agency.[21]

In general, liberal Democrats were more likely to support the NEA than were Republicans, with notable exceptions such as Senator Jacob Javits (R-N.Y.). Similarly, the Democratic party had gone on record in its 1964 platform as supporting the agency and the principle of federal support for the arts, while the Republican platform had made no mention of the subject.[22]

Thus, the future of the agency under the Republican administration that would take office in January 1969 seemed questionable. The fate of Roger Stevens, however, was clear. President Nixon certainly did not want to reappoint a prominent Democrat, particularly one who had raised funds for Democratic candidates who had campaigned against Nixon himself. Presidential assistant Leonard Garment was given the task of finding a suitable replacement—a task that subsequently stretched over many months.

Stevens's term at the NEA expired in March 1969, at which time his deputy of less than a year, Douglas MacAgy, assumed acting command. During the next six months the agency drifted. A number of staff members resigned, as did three members of the NCA. Congress was reluctant to appropriate funds for an agency without a chairman. Many possible appointees were considered, but each proved to be either unavailable or unacceptable to key congressmen or senators. Indeed, one observer noted that the position seemed to require "a political virgin who can produce political results."[23] Nancy Hanks proved to be just the person who could meet those specifications.

Formative Experiences and an Emergent Administrative Style

In naming Nancy Hanks to become the second chairman of the NEA, President Nixon chose neither an artist nor a politician. While Hanks was "almost . . . a lifelong Republican,"[24] she had not been involved in partisan electoral politics. Although she was not a stranger to Washington when she assumed direction of the endowment, neither was she a member of the Washington establishment or even an "in-and-outer." Although she had a long association with the Rockefeller brothers (especially Nelson), they were not her mentors, nor was she their protege. Born in Florida to Texan parents, she attended high school in New Jersey, earned a bachelor's degree in political science at Duke University in North Carolina (1949), and spent a summer in Colorado and another at Oxford. A single, attractive, middle-aged woman who combined femininity with a sense of traditional propriety, Hanks became one of only a handful of female federal executives, but she was no feminist.

Hanks had been a philanthropic administrator concerned with the arts, but she was neither an artist, an arts patron, nor even an arts administrator. Aesthetically eclectic, she was an aficionado of no specific art form or style, but rather was "open to sampling and enjoying everything."[25] Her only personal artistic endeavor was the making of needlepoint typewriter covers. In a field filled with imposing, dramatic, public personae, she was a charming, down-to-earth, and very private person. A workaholic who paid meticulous attention to detail, Hanks was neither an artful writer nor a captivating formal speaker. In describing her own particular talent, she once said: "My one art is budgeting. I'm an administrator and a good listener . . . I'm creative in putting a program into a political context."[26] Thus, pre-NEA, Nancy Hanks was on the margins—politically, artistically, and even socially—just as the agency itself was. In moving the endowment to the center of the arts world and establishing its social and political support, she also found her particular niche. Thus Hanks's personal journey from marginality to leadership paralleled the developmental transformation she wrought for the NEA.

In the early 1950s, Hanks had come to work for Nelson Rockefeller in Washington, and from the mid-1950s through most of the 1960s the Rockefeller connection had carried her to the fringes of the art world.[27] At the Rockefeller Brothers Fund she coordinated the pathbreaking and influential study *The Performing Arts: Problems and Prospects*, which helped to build support for the creation of the NEA. This project accorded Hanks a broad overview of the major issues and personalities in the worlds of the theatre, dance, opera, and symphonic music. Later, she served as a member of the search committee for a new director for the Museum of Modern Art, in the process becoming acquainted with virtually every important figure in American museums. Then, in 1968, as a member of the Belmont Committee, she became familiar with the conditions, needs, and possible solutions to the critical problems then confronting museums.

Finally, in 1969 she was named president of the Associated Councils of the Arts (ACA), a diverse, nonprofit membership association dedicated to the support and development of the arts in the United States and Canada. This organization included individuals involved in state and regional arts activities, as philanthropic and corporate patrons of the arts, as artists and arts administrators as well as representatives of unions, public arts officials, and public-opinion pollster Louis Harris.[28]

The cumulative effect of this record was to make Hanks a generalist who was also an "authority on the arts"; "politically skillful" but not a politician; and familiar with most of the leading artistic individuals and institutions but taking no side or holding no strong opinions in the wars of taste, style, and school that sweep the arts.[29] While many individuals might have been more expert in a particular art form, few of these would have had as wide a range of artistic experience or so catholic tastes. While others might have been more partisanly worthy, they would also have been likely to be partisanly suspect. Thus, Hanks had the advantage of many relevant assets for the job but few distinct liabilities or opponents.

She had also acquired various working habits and operational skills that proved to be useful in piloting the agency into favorable straits. First, she had been thoroughly schooled in the consultative, networking style of foundation work. Her work as the coordinator of special projects for the Rockefeller Brothers Fund had involved the forming of expert panels, coordinating advisory committee decisions, integrating diverse viewpoints, and distilling bountiful information and opinion into an acceptable and practical product. Furthermore, in working for the Rockefellers, she had worked with individuals who had the means, methods, and procedures to implement their projects. Hence, much of Hanks's administrative perspective was dominated by a sense of the possible rather than a concern with obstacles. She "believed that there wasn't anything that couldn't be done." Indeed, one of her favorite statements to staff members was, "I'm sure you'll find a way."[30] These experiences and the skills they sharpened were directly transferred to her performance at the NEA.

As a matter of law, the NEA chairman has to consult with an advisory committee (the NCA), just as the Rockefeller Brothers Fund special projects coordinator had had to. Hanks herself maintained that "I never attempt to make statements that are not based on Council thinking."[31] Under her direction, the NEA came to rely increasingly upon panels of experts to review applications and to maintain close contact with the artistic community. Hanks would frequently sit in on panels meetings and just listen. She would even occasionally have her deputy chair the quarterly NCA meetings so that she could pay closer attention to the views being discussed. Throughout, as Lawrence Reger, her former director of planning and management, observed, she showed "an uncanny ability to take into account incredible amounts [and] variety of opinion and really react to them in what ultimately works out to be the best way. She synthesizes and she sympathizes." In fact, Janet Gracey, one of her former assistants, thought that part of Hanks's charm stemmed from her ability to make others feel "that when she listened to you, you had absolutely her full attention."[32]

As an administrative assistant to the Rockefellers, Hanks had been accustomed to working behind the scenes and leaving the spotlight to others. When this apparent modesty was combined with her equally apparent ambition to do the best job possible at the NEA rather than to treat it as merely a stepping stone to other opportunities, she quite readily and genuinely gave others much of the public credit for designing and furthering federal arts policy.

No doubt Hanks's tendency to be a very private person had been reinforced during her years as an unacclaimed staff assistant. Because she did not crave the limelight, she was perhaps more than willing to share credit and praise for accomplishments with others. Such generosity not only helped her to win political friends and bureaucratic loyalists but, in the long run, may have accorded her some insulation from the inevitable criticism that occurs in any policy arena.

First and foremost among those whom Hanks applauded was the president himself. For example, she praised President Nixon's announcement that "one of the important goals of my Administration is the further advance in the cultural development of our nation."[33] Persistently, she gave the president credit for being the originator and motivator of expanding federal support for the arts and for seeking to make the arts more available to more Americans, particularly youths and minorities. When asked by reporters how she had gotten the president to "go along" with the first proposal for a major increase in the agency's budget, she had replied: "He was not dragged. . . . On the contrary he couldn't have been more enthusiastic . . . he asked me to develop an effective program and he agrees that we can be effective if we can get this money." The next year's request for another funding increase found Miss Hanks " 'ecstatic' at the President's decision."[34]

Furthermore, by crediting the president as the pacesetter of federal arts policy, Hanks helped President Nixon get some of the best press of his administration. For example, a 1971 *New York Times* article praised Nixon for making "the most solid contribution to the arts of any President since FDR"; and the *Washington Post* speculated in 1972 that Nixon might "go down in history as the nation's most enlightened presidential patron of governmental architecture and design as well as a great patron of the arts." Or as political columnist David Broder remarked, one welcome relief from "the wretched Watergate business" was the administration's record on the NEA—an area where President Nixon had "been superb . . . making first class appointments and strongly backing increased funds for the program."[35]

Hanks was also willing to share the role of agency spokesman with her deputy chairman, Michael Straight. This too generated a number of advantages. As a member of the Whitney family as well as former editor and owner of *The New Republic*, Straight was obviously well-connected and had virtually inherited an interest in the arts. Indeed, Straight himself had been a possible candidate for the NEA chairmanship, but as a liberal Democrat, he was not wholly acceptable as a replacement for that other liberal Democrat, Roger Stevens. It was, however, agreeable to Hanks, Straight, and Garment (speaking for President Nixon) that Straight assume the second place at the NEA, a position he held until Hanks's successor was confirmed in November of 1977. In accepting Straight as her deputy, Hanks made an unmistakable statement about the nonpartisan character of federal arts support and at the same time improved her ability to cultivate bipartisan support for the agency. Straight was also a charming and proficient public speaker, always ready with an illustrative tale or a notable quotation citing anyone from Aeschylus to Thomas Wolfe. In contrast, Hanks was uncomfortable as a public speaker, being at her best in small or informal settings instead. Therefore, Hanks could and did delegate many of the public address tasks to Straight. As a result, the agency gained not one but two artful and persuasive spokesmen, each skilled at a different type of communication.

A final significant factor in setting Hanks's administrative style can be found in the relatively small, intimate, and highly personalistic settings in which she had gained her pre-NEA experience. Such environments prevailed when she was with Nelson Rockefeller at the President's Advisory Committee on Government Organization or at the White House staff, as well as in the philanthropic world and in the arts. Everyone knew everyone else in these circles. Influence was as likely to flow from personality, access, and information as from formal position and tangible power. Such environments both required and responded to extensive networking, proficiency in consensus management and coalition building, social and informal as well as authoritative consultation and follow through, and personalized management. All these habits were appropriate to the administration of federal arts policy in the 1970s and, indeed, characterized Nancy Hanks's style as chairman of the NEA.

Among other qualities, one can clearly see her reliance on a personal touch at both the most powerful and the most clerical of levels. In dealing with the administration, Hanks had impressive and direct personal access to key actors: to presidential assistant Leonard Garment and, through him, to the president and to the directors of the Office of Management and Budget (OMB).[36] She would also reinforce these ties through personal service, such as helping Tricia Nixon host a White House pumpkin-carving contest or getting a monumental modern sculpture that the president disliked moved from the lawn of the Corcoran Gallery.[37] Similarly, Straight bought a box at Kennedy Center and each Tuesday night invited two congressmen and their wives to dinner and a concert.[38]

At the bureaucratic level, Hanks would go out of her way to visit even the secretarial pool and to get to know all of the staff at the NEA. This very personal networking underpinned Hanks's ability to get things done individually and also contributed to her organization's competence and cohesion. The fact that "she never lost contact with anybody" fostered a returned loyalty from her associates and enhanced her ability to call upon many people for assistance when she needed it. Furthermore, she gave her staff "a lot of authority," expected them to be "generalists" with a shared "approach to problem solving," and kept them well informed about what was happening and what was pending. As earlier at the Rockefeller Brothers Fund, she expected every person on her staff to "know exactly what was going on and be able to pick up the phone and speak intelligently about anything."[39] Such a staff system not only gave the impression of her organization's competence but fostered both internal and external communication by minimizing the bureaucratic red tape anyone encountered. Finally, such a staff, since it was also loyal, was likely to be able to head off, if not anticipate and avoid, problems at an early stage.

Hanks also paid attention to detail, including the apparently trivial and the superficially symbolic. For example, she concerned herself with the appearance of the staff coffee room and the design and use of a new logo for the agency.[40] Her command of specifics derived, in part, from meticulous preparation. One former associate recalled that Hanks "never went into a meeting without knowing the outcome that she wanted" or "without being aware of everyone's view on the subject" and having taken steps to try to defuse "troublemakers" "so that things didn't get out of hand at (the) meeting." Such a personalized and detailed administrative style was time-consuming—so much so that "much of her social side was business," and she was "inclined to work herself into exhaustion."[41] But it also paid off in the long run. It allowed her to assemble and cultivate a capable, stable, loyal staff—the core of which remains close-knit and protective of Hanks to this day. It also contributed to the development of a distinct and positive image for the young agency.

Entrepreneurial Strategies

Some elements of Nancy Hanks's style have begun to emerge from the preceding section. A full discussion of her administrative strategies and record could be expanded into a virtual history of the endowment and of arts policy during the 1970s. Such comprehensive treatment is, however, inappropriate for this essay. Instead, I have chosen to highlight some of the major tactics she employed in her general strategy of bureaucratic entrepreneurship. As used here, *strategy* is regarded as the art of using various types of resources to afford the maximum support and the most advantageous conditions for the pursuit of articulated policy ends. *Tactics* are means used to achieve strategic ends.

It is not unusual to find explications of strategy in the annals of battlefield conflict or of athletic team competition. On the other hand, the statement of a strategy for public policy, complete with an articulation of general goals, methods for securing adequate resources, project programs for implementation, and an assessment of political feasibility, is quite rare. Yet, just such a master plan for federal arts policy was drafted by Nancy Hanks and endorsed by President Nixon at the very beginning of her tenure as chairman of the NEA.[42] Indeed, Hanks had made basic agreement upon the general outlines of the plan a precondition for her acceptance of the appointment.[43]

The overall strategy, laid out in the October 1969 memo, entailed presidential support for the reauthorization of the NEA, a commitment to propose substantial budget increases for the next three to four years, and a promise to work for the congressional appropriation of such increases. This long-term financial growth strategy would allow the agency to develop a three-pronged artistic policy aimed at

1. *cultural resources development*—designed to assist primarily the "major nonprofit institutions of the traditional arts (theatre, dance, opera, orchestras, museums)";
2. *availability of artistic resources*—designed to encourage the "wider distribution of artistic resources throughout the nation"; and
3. *advancement of our cultural legacy*—intended to "encourage new opportunities for audience and artist alike."[44]

The pursuit of this strategy would require clear and sustained White House support, the strengthening of congressional and arts constituency support, and the successful implementation of a number of new NEA grant-awarding programs. To obtain and retain these strategic objectives, Hanks employed a repertoire of tactics. Four of the most important were:

1. Establishing momentum quickly
2. Building a capable, committed, stable administrative staff
3. Securing substantial increases in agency resources, both financially and politically, through
   a. the sequential advancement of new rationales for obtaining "synoptic" budget increases;[45] and
   b. extensive efforts to mobilize constituency support and to cultivate bureaucratic and political coalition allies.
4. Adopting pretested program initiatives

Each of these tactics is described briefly in the succeeding subsections.

Establishing Momentum Quickly

Hanks was confirmed as chairman of the NEA on 2 October 1969. By the end of 1969—a mere three months after assuming office—Hanks had already begun to move federal support for the arts into a new and more ambitious phase. Not only had she taken command of the agency but she had arranged to move it into new and larger quarters.[46] Furthermore, she had established a firm working alliance with presidential assistant Leonard Garment, who would serve as an arts advocate within the White House as well as a communications link to the president and to OMB. Together, she and Garment had provided the president with extensive arts policy proposals that called for an immediate doubling of the budget for the arts and humanities endowments.[47] These proposals argued that this would be an extremely cost-effective way for the administration to demonstrate dramatically "its commitment to 'reordering national priorities,' " that the proposed increase was adequate to achieve a discernible impact upon the financial problems of arts institutions, that this initiative would "be a high impact move among opinion leaders," and that a strong constituency was "waiting in the wings" and ready to "enthusiastically endorse" such a policy. Furthermore, Hanks and her NEA staff had informally ascertained that key bipartisan congressional actors were ready to back such a budget proposal without seeking any major revisions.[48] In other words, a full "game plan" was presented to President Nixon for his approval and was ready to be put into action. The low budgetary cost but high political yield of the plan was undeniably appealing to Nixon. He not only acquiesced but gave the initiative a full presidential send-off—complete with a December Special Message to Congress on the arts and humanities and the inclusion of a proposal to nearly double the endowments' fund in the budget that he was sending to Congress the following January.[49]

Meanwhile, Hanks was helping to organize a campaign among the arts community in support of the president's proposal. First, she enlisted the assistance of the American Symphony Orchestra League in getting a letter and telegram wave started.[50] Throughout the spring, as appropriations hearings proceeded, persistent efforts to raise public and official consciousness regarding the imperiled state of U.S. cultural institutions, especially orchestras, continued. Major metropolitan newspapers ran stories about the problems of orchestras. The National Symphony Orchestra (NSO), in Washington, seemed to epitomize the plight of orchestras nationwide, as it teetered on the brink of insolvency and President Nixon himself appealed to corporate representatives to support the NSO's fund-raising drive.[51] Congressional testimony by orchestra representatives argued that they were "starving" for funds. Endowment grants announced in March tried to assist those orchestras in the most acute crises but primarily served to illustrate the inadequacy of current governmental support.[52]

In the end, this orchestrated lobbying campaign was effective. On 20 May 1970 the Senate approved a combined NEA/NEH appropriation of $40 million, or double their current budgets. The House followed suit on 30 June with a strong, bipartisan vote of 262 to 78, thus "offering strong endorsement of the validity and continuity of Federal support on the arts and humanities."[53] Soon thereafter, orchestras began to reap the rewards for their political support, as the agency announced the award of more than twice as much money to nearly three times as many orchestras as had been possible under the previous budget.[54]

This first "battle of the budget" illustrates a number of ingredients that would be used repeatedly by Hanks to leverage major increases in the budget for her agency. These were to

1. focus on one or two distinct issues to justify a large-scale funding increase;
2. link these primary issues to particular segments of the arts constituency capable of mobilizing effective lobbying effort with Congress;
3. offer suggestions of other possible benefits and new programs that more funding might also support;
4. follow a distributive policy strategy of offering more benefits to all arts constituents in reward for lobbying efforts and their consequent increase in appropriations (avoiding a redistributive strategy that would reward some constituents only at a cost to others);
5. secure a firm OMB commitment to, and publicly involve the president in, support of budget increases;
6. build a bipartisan congressional coalition in support of the proposed budget increase; and
7. deliver immediate "rewards" to the arts constituency in the form of more and bigger grants once increased appropriations have been obtained.

Building a Capable, Committed, Stable Administrative Staff

To sustain the initial momentum for rapid programmatic and budgetary expansion, as well as to preside over the artistic diversification of the NEA, it was necessary for Hanks to both expand and stabilize agency staff.[55] Furthermore, since she had inherited some agency personnel from her predecessor, she needed to cultivate the loyalty of the staff and to instill it with an esprit de corps. These personnel matters involved two interrelated functions: recruiting "good" staff and promoting staff cohesion.

Hanks brought to these tasks an acquaintance with a large pool of prospective appointees as well as experience in putting together specialized staffs and advisory boards gained at the Rockefeller Brothers Fund. Hanks's very broad network of acquaintances was further extended at the NEA by consultation with NCA members and through the agency's peer-review panels. Locating prospective appointees who were capable and committed thus posed few problems for Hanks. Furthermore, such networking was an administrative habit she had honed to a fine art in the foundation world. As a result, "relations between staff, panel, and council were extremely warm . . . [characterized by] a sense of camaraderie and respect."[56]

In other ways, Hanks's task was facilitated by the character of the agency and staff she inherited as well as by the opportunities she had to hire new personnel. Indeed, the staff she inherited presented less of a problem than might have been expected. Stevens had employed a total staff of no more than three dozen people. By the end of Hanks's first term as chairman (1973) agency personnel had nearly quadrupled, to about 120. By the end of her tenure the staff numbered over 215. Thus, Hanks had so much opportunity to increase personnel that "her" employees naturally outnumbered any that she had inherited. Since she made a point of getting to know "everybody on the staff" and of paying "particular attention to the people in positions least likely to get attention from top management,"[57] she cultivated the loyalty of staff at all levels, among both the new and the inherited staff.

Furthermore, during the six-month interregnum between the expiration of Stevens's term and the confirmation of Hanks, a number of program directors had resigned and were replaced by the then acting chairman. Thus, a number of the key staff Hanks inherited had not actually worked with her predecessor. By keeping these individuals on, at least for a reasonable transition period, Hanks avoided the disruption and inefficiency entailed in a wholesale restaffing and earned for herself the good will of most of the incumbent staff. In many cases she fully integrated continuing program directors into her administration. For example, the directors of the education, state, music, theatre, and visual arts programs, although appointed before Hanks took office, retained their positions for most of her tenure.

Hanks also had many opportunities to make new appointments, both programmatic and administrative. In some instances, as the agency initiated new programs, more and new personnel were required. Thus, as new programs for museums and expansion arts were established, new directors for these programs were appointed. In other cases, as the activities of the programs in architecture and design, literature, and public media diversified, their directors were replaced by new appointees. Thus by 1971/72, Hanks had put her stamp on all of the program directors.

Program directors were not only dependable but artistically informed and, in a number of cases, either journalistically or politically experienced as well. For example, Brian O'Doherty was editor of *Art in America* for three years concurrently with his service as head of the NEA Visual Arts Program, and Chloe Aaron, head of the Public Media Program, was also a senior editor of *Videorecord World*. Such links to cultural publications no doubt helped to build the endowment's image both among the general public and in the art world. Others, such as Leonard Randolph of the Literature Program, had had prior experience as congressional administrative assistants. Still others, such as Vantile

Whitfield (Expansion Arts), from the Performing Arts Society of Los Angeles, or Ralph Rizzolo (assistant music director), from the American Symphony Orchestra League, represented links to major arts institutions and constituency groups.

Administrative personnel followed a similar pattern. There were a few key carry-overs (such as Ana Steele, who became director of budget and research) and call-backs (for example, Fannie Taylor, who had been music director in the late 1960s and was recalled in 1972 to head the new public information office, and Livingston Biddle, who had been Stevens's deputy chairman and returned in 1975 to serve as congressional liaison). Meanwhile, many of the newcomers had valuable contacts or experiences; for example, press assistant Florence Lowe had been a news service correspondent, and executive assistant John Clark and evaluation director Charles Kirk had both been policy analysts at OMB.

Thus, Hanks's personnel selections were generally respected, loyal, and multitalented. It should be noted, however, that in relative terms, the proliferation of directoral staff was greater on the administrative side than on the programmatic. In other words, as the size and complexity of the agency grew, the need for more numerous and more functionally specialized administrative staff became obvious. New positions were created or split off from existing ones. For example, both the offices of budget and research and of planning and management were split into four separate offices, with the former director of budget and research taking over planning and the directorship of management being upgraded to the level of assistant chairman. New offices for evaluation, program information, and employee orientation were also created.

Despite these many changes, staff, once appointed, tended to remain fairly stable even though titles and responsibilities were likely to vary with periodic programmatic evolution and administrative restructurings. Indeed, during Hanks's chairmanship the NEA underwent a classic phase of bureaucratization—that is, it became increasingly specialized in its division of labor and progressively routinized. Clearly, the recruitment and molding of such a capable and committed staff not only enhanced the agency's operational capabilities but extended and complimented Hanks's political and programmatic capacities.

Securing Substantial Increases in Agency Resources, Both Financially and Politically

Hanks's initial experience in establishing momentum for the agency and her leadership of the agency contained many of the tactical elements that she would use repeatedly to support and accomplish the growth of the NEA. Fundamental to this expansion was the need to obtain greater budgetary resources, which in turn would underwrite programmatic and staff expansion. Simultaneously, increased funds would become both an instrument of constituency service and an incentive for the mobilization of political support and the attraction of coalition allies. A key to the successful pursuit of additional resources was the advancement of a series of rationales that would justify the need for such increases while also attracting sufficient political support to secure them.

During the congressional hearings in 1970, alleviating the financial crisis of American artistic institutions, particularly orchestras, was the primary rationale Hanks put forward for increasing the NEA budget from $9 million to $16 million.[58] With this 81 percent increase, the endowment could begin to pursue the "president's" tripartite arts policy and could offer some assistance to the most hard-pressed of the major cultural institutions.

Similarly, in 1971, the economic crisis of the arts was the key justification in seeking to boost the budget from $16 million to $31 million, although the list of those explicitly identified as endangered was expanded. If agency funds were doubled (as proposed), Hanks argued, the NEA could assist more orchestras in more states. Also, other musical organizations—opera companies and choral groups—would receive "substantial assistance for the first time."[59] Furthermore, the $1 million pilot program for the support of museums could be expanded to $4 million. Since orchestras and museums had the most numerous, most widely distributed, and best organized constituencies in the arts, they could mount an extensive lobbying effort in support of these potential benefits. Opera companies, while less numerous, could nonetheless call upon prestigious and influential board members to carry their case to federal legislators.

While these major institutional arts communities carried the brunt of the persuasive effort, other interests were also wooed with promises of new or expanded arts programs. For example, minorities were courted through the announced intention to broaden support for jazz projects and to make a special effort to aid the artistic development of inner-city-, neighborhood-, and minority-based cultural groups. In addition, the states—most of which had, by then, established state arts councils and were therefore receiving annual grants-in-aid from the NEA—were enticed by the prospect of increasing their annual grants from $75,000 to $100,000 each, for a total of $5.5 million, if the proposed budget increases were approved by Congress. Meanwhile, programs in support of dance, theatre, literature, film, architecture, and folk arts would all continue and, in many cases, be expanded. Thus, the entire arts community stood to benefit if the NEA's proposed budget was approved. Because of this prospective general benefit, the arts pulled together as never before.[60] Indeed, it was said that "few requests for money for a Government agency have been endorsed by so many constituents in letters, telegrams, telephone calls, and personal visits."[61]

Once again, the president was active in spearheading the campaign for an expanded federal arts policy. Not only did President Nixon again submit a request for greatly increased funds to Congress but he made his support clear both externally and internally. Publicly, he addressed a meeting of over five hundred representatives of state and territorial arts councils gathered in Washington for the annual conference of the Associated Councils of the Arts. He was warmly received, and, in turn, he treated the delegates to a White House tour and a reception hosted by Mrs. Nixon. The delegates then dispersed to visit their individual congressmen to urge them to support the president's proposed budget. Internally, the president issued a memorandum to all federal agency heads requesting that they assess both how their agencies "can most vigorously assist the arts and artists" and "how the arts and artists can be of help to your agency and to its programs."[62] Hanks, as chairman of the NEA, was to coordinate responses to this call and present a report and recommendations to the president.

Following congressional approval, more and/or bigger grants were soon going out from the NEA to its deserving constituency. In August, sixteen museums in fourteen states were awarded $10,000 each for the purchase of contemporary American art works. The following month, thirty-nine nonprofit theatres across the nation were granted a total of $1.6 million.[63] By December the NEA had reached ninety-three orchestras with assistance totaling $5 million.[64] Thus, all the ingredients of a successful budget-increasing strategy, as identified in 1970, were recombined in 1971.

In subsequent years Hanks would continue to follow this same recipe, although not always with the same degree of success. For example, in 1972 an increase from $31 million to $40 million for FY 1973 was propelled by a planned increase in the Expansion (minority) Arts Program and the establishment of a governmentwide Federal Design Improvement Program. Indeed, two later observers would comment that this design effort "was a good example of Nancy Hanks' success in public office based on her ability to take existing programs, activities and assignments and, by bringing them together, create new alignments and new impetus."[65]

Planning and maneuvering for FY 1974 were well under way by June 1972. Hanks and her ally in the White House, Leonard Garment, launched another memo campaign to persuade the president and OMB to support a second sequence of substantial budget authorizations. The timing was affected by many elements: the pending need in 1973 to reauthorize the agency and to set projected three-year funding levels, the ongoing 1972 presidential reelection campaign, and long-range planning for the Bicentennial. In a 6 June 1972 memorandum to OMB Director Caspar Weinberger, Garment laid out a proposal and rational for bringing NEA's authorization up to $200 million by FY 1976. He pointed out that "the President's program of financial support for the arts has been one of the domestic success stories of this Administration." Further, he noted that this policy was "popular not only with Republican elite types, but with people in both political parties and generally with the public, including all economic and racial groups." Garment also argued that strategically, the Bicentennial provided an excellent occasion to put forth a "new Presidential arts initiative" and that the announcement of such an intention should be made so "as to permit its inclusion in the Republican Platform."[66]

Similarly, while suggesting that "we all lie low until after the election" and "most assuredly not let . . . the Arts Endowment get into politics," Hanks was working behind the scenes with Weinberger and Garment as well as the arts community to use the Bicentennial as the necessary leverage for a new three-year series of major funding increases. As in 1969, she provided evidence of waiting-in-the-wings lobbying support, suggested tactics to avoid criticism on possibly sensitive issues, and even suggested language the president might want to use in official or press statements.[67]

This campaign was successful again—but not completely so. President Nixon did recommend doubling the NEA's funds for FY 1974, proposing a budget of $80 million and approving three-year authorization levels that would bring the agency up to $200 million by 1976. The arts community rallied behind the president, praising the proposal as "wonderful" and the president for moving "Federal aid for the arts toward levels that will be truly effective." Three months later, the Senate approved a bill authorizing a total of $160 million for the NEA and NEH combined for FY 1974, $280 for FY 1975, and $400 million for FY 1976. Although the vote was a solid 76 to 14, it was nonetheless accompanied by strenuous objections to such increases when other domestic programs were being severely cut. Senator John McClellan, chairman of the Senate Appropriations Committee, called the increase "clearly out of line," and Senator William Proxmire called it "unconscionable."[68]

In the next few months, the House voted to authorize the full budget sought by the president, but then its Appropriations Committee cut back the two endowments to a combined total of $106 (rather than $160) million, while shifting money to other programs covered by the Interior Affairs appropriations bill. Chairman Julia Butler Hansen called the reduction in the proposed budget for the arts and humanities "one of the most difficult decisions" her subcommittee had had to make and pointed out that the agency budgets would still receive a healthy increase.[69] Certainly, this 37 percent raise to $64.5 million for the NEA was substantial, but it also marked a slowing of the dramatic growth pace of the previous three years and was an indication of a changing attitude in congressional support for the agency.[70]

As the FY 1975 budget was being formulated and debated, the general strategy unraveled for reasons largely beyond Hanks's control. The expanding Watergate investigations and impeachment proceedings preoccupied the president and his counselors; hence, Hanks's friends in the White House had little time or concern to spare for the fate of the arts endowment. In August 1974, Nixon resigned from office and was succeeded by Gerald Ford. In addition, Hanks suffered the loss of her father, to whom she had been quite close. Soon thereafter, in the spring of 1974, Hanks fell seriously ill and was hospitalized with pleurisy aggravated by near exhaustion. Indeed, this episode probably marked the recurrence of an old health problem that would eventually lead to her death from cancer. Despite these disruptions, the agency managed to secure an additional $15 million, but that only brought the total up to about half the level that had been optimistically projected in its 1973 reauthorization bill. Clearly, the agency's momentum had begun to slow, and Hanks's previously successful budget tactics had begun to encounter obstacles. Indeed, growth might have virtually ceased had Hanks not "invented" justifications for increases during her final years.

For FY 1976, Hanks used the change in the federal budget year to secure a windfall in extra funds for the NEA. Pursuant to the Budget and Impoundment Control Act of 1974, the start of the federal fiscal year was shifted from 1 July to 1 October, with the change taking effect at the end of the 1976 "old" fiscal year. This change produced a "fifth" quarter which bridged the period from 1 July through 30 September 1976, thus serving as a transition into the "new" fiscal calendar. Hanks argued that because of the grant-award cycle at the NEA, a number of expensive programs were scheduled for this transition period, thus justifying larger than simply proportional expenditures in this quarter. With this rationale and a judicious allocation of the quarter's prospective funds to major arts interests, Hanks obtained $33.9 million for the quarter, or $10–13 million more than might otherwise have been forthcoming. As per the established pattern, the bulk of these funds went to those large and politically influential constituencies that had helped to lobby for the additional monies: over $12 million was divided among the state councils; $6 million went to orchestras; $3 million to theatres; another $3 million to opera companies; $2 million to museums; $1 million to dance companies; and another $1 million to the American Film Institute.[71]

For FY 1977, the allocation for general program funds grew only incrementally, from $74.5 million to $77.5 million. A new grant category was initiated—challenge grants, which required an extraordinary three-to-one match of private money for every federal dollar—designed to appeal to the major arts institutions in all disciplines. New challenge grant funds accounted for $9 million of the overall $12 million increase that Congress gave the agency for FY 1977. Finally, the NEA secured an additional $29.8 million in FY 1978 by doubling challenge grant funds and by winning congressional approval for the separation of the administrative staff previously shared by the two endowments. Since this reorganization necessitated an increase in the administrative funds accorded each agency, the NEA gained an added $3.4 million for administrative support expenses.

Obviously, the sequence of budget-increasing rationales had been a key tactic of Hanks's entrepreneurial leadership. Equally clear, however, was the implicit limitation of this tactic: premising the agency's growth upon its financial ability to reach an increasingly inclusive constituency ran the eventual risk of running out of new and organized interests that could be coopted and would pay the "initiation fee" with lobbying support. By the late 1970s, Hanks found that there were few artistic interests that she had not already engaged in her political support coalition. Furthermore, she found the very principle of cumulative budget and program expansion challenged by the zero-based budgeting philosophy of the new Carter administration.[72]

The foregoing rationales were necessary to justify increases in financial resources for the NEA. Equally necessary, and related to these programmatic and policy proposals, was the effort to mobilize political support for these initiatives in both government and the arts community. The importance of successful coalition building within the corridors of governmental power (particularly with the Executive Office of the President) and among congressman on both sides of the aisle (especially Congresswoman Julia Butler Hansen, Congressmen John Brademas and Frank Thompson, and Senators Claiborne Pell and Jacob Javits) has already been illustrated. Another element of Hanks's coalition building involved the establishment of alliances with various bureaucratic agencies. Thus, the NEA became a partner with the Department of Education in arts education programs, as well as an adviser to the U.S. Information Agency on its artistic exchange programs and to the General Services Administration on its program of commissioning works by contemporary American artists for inclusion in new federal buildings.[73] While considerable evidence has been presented pertaining to the effectiveness of Hanks's efforts to organize and mobilize the arts community into a potent political interest group, the methods she used to achieve this end still require some examination.

The organization of a diverse and diffuse arts community into a coordinated political interest group was accomplished largely through the building and/or strengthening of arts service organizations. When Congress was considering the establishment of the arts and humanities endowments in the mid-1960s, most of the public support for these measures came from the humanities constituency composed of higher-education interests, including "nearly 5 million students, several hundred thousand faculty members and colleges, universities or junior colleges in many congressional districts in the country."[74] Few elements of the artistic community were sufficiently organized at that time to be a useful lobbying force. Moreover, some of the few organized groups were unsure of the merits of a federal arts agency. For example, while representatives of artist unions such as Actors Equity and the American Federation of Musicians testified in favor of the creation of an arts agency, ASOL did not (largely because its membership was divided about the advisability of such governmental involvement in artistic matters). Similarly, many of the most prestigious arts institutions "were suspicious of politicians and felt they had more to lose than to gain from the political process."[75]

Such a weak and divided constituency was insufficient to support the policy and budgetary potential of the NEA. Under Hanks's leadership, the agency became a "patron of political action," attempting to politically mobilize a constituency from the top down by encouraging groups that could "promote new legislative agendas and social values." These groups were arts service organizations—nonprofit associations that provided services (whether artistic, technical, managerial, or informational) to their respective fields and engaged in political advocacy.[76]

Since 1970, the NEA has annually awarded between 5 percent and 9 percent of its combined program and treasury funds to the support of such organizations and their activities. Furthermore, the agency often accorded these organizations special treatment by exempting them from the general eligibility requirement that all applicant organizations had to have a two-year record of independent existence before they could qualify for federal assistance. Instead, the NEA not only supported relatively untried groups but also promoted the establishment of completely new organizations, including the National Opera Institute, Opera America, and the National Assembly of State Arts Agencies.[77] Thus, in a spiraling pattern of cause and effect, the NEA patronized the political action of a constituency which, in turn, supported the agency's quest for more resources that could be channeled back into the very constituency the agency had helped to expand and organize.

Adopting Pretested Program Initiatives

Hanks had a reputation for emphasizing "programs that could demonstrate results."[78] A significant contributing factor to this record of programmatic effectiveness was her practice of adapting ideas that had already been piloted elsewhere. Knowledge about such experiments was constantly flowing into the agency via the program staff and NCA members, who were closely connected to the arts community and its private and state government patrons. Meanwhile, information about projects undertaken by other federal agencies or by prior administrators came to Hanks through her political communications network, as well as through many of the administrative staff who had had work experience elsewhere in the government bureaucracy.

In some cases, worthwhile projects had originally been undertaken on a large scale by foundations at a time when the endowment was relatively new and had very limited funds. For example, in 1966, when the NEA's total budget was a mere $2.5 million, a single private source— the Ford Foundation—had committed $82 million to a five-year orchestra program. Indeed, between 1957 (when it started funding the arts) and early 1969, the Ford Foundation had awarded $184.6 million to the arts.[79] In comparison, federal support for all the arts (as granted by the NEA) did not cumulatively surpass this figure until FY 1976.

Indeed, foundation patronage had sustained many of the institutional art forms (orchestras, theatre, dance, museums) during the late 1960s and early 1970s, when public support was either nonexistent or only miniscule. But later, as foundation funding for specific arts projects began to be phased out or redirected, the NEA had usually had the time to float a "pilot" program and secure additional federal funds that could be used to expand public support for such organizations and activities. Thus, it was not mere coincidence that the NEA undertook to launch and quickly increase an orchestra program during 1970 and 1971, just as the Ford five-year orchestra program was expiring.

In other cases, foundation projects on the arts often amounted to policy experiments from which the NEA could discover what worked, or worked best. In this way, private philanthropic endeavors absorbed the costs of experimentation and thus helped to minimize the uncertainties the endowment faced in trying to design programs that would be artistically effective as well as politically acceptable and administratively feasible. For instance, two of the endowment's most successful multidisciplinary programs—challenge grants and artists-in-the-schools—had been pretested by private patrons and had had trial runs as NEA pilot projects before being implemented as bona fide public policy programs.[80]

In yet other instances, programs had their origins in governmental actions. The Expansion Arts Program, designed to meet the cultural needs of minority, inner-city, and regional groups, had its prototype in the 1968 New York State Arts Council Ghetto Arts Program. The idea had been picked up by Roger Stevens at the NEA and tested as an Inner-City Arts Program. Therefore, Hanks, seeking a means of addressing the "vital artistic expression from diverse groups" as well as President Nixon's goal of making "the arts available to all the people," simply nurtured the seeds of an expansion arts program that had already been sown.[81] Similarly, the governmentwide Federal Design Improvement Program, spearheaded by the NEA during the mid-1970s, was a revival of President Kennedy's effort to improve federal design and an extension of some of the ideas put forth in his administration's "Guiding Principles for Federal Architecture."[82] In a number of cases, exploratory programs were sponsored under the agency's catch-all special projects division until they could become independent programs. Both the Folk Arts Program and the Fellowships in Arts Management Program followed this route to institutionalization.

Thus, in arts policy, as in many other domestic policy areas, innovative ideas were seldom totally new. Rather, they were often "old" ideas that had incubated for years, slowly amassing public interest and political support. In a sense, therefore, Hanks was fortunate to serve when the times and sentiments were ripe for arts policy initiatives. Conversely, the times were also fortunate that a policy entrepreneur of Hanks's caliber was appointed to a key position from which she could act on the opportunities that she recognized.

The Problems of Success: The Limits of Entrepreneurship

The key to Hanks's entrepreneurial leadership at the NEA was being "the right person, at the right place, at the right time." In prior sections of this analysis, I have sought to identify personal, contextual, and organizational factors and to demonstrate how these seemed to converge and interact as Hanks assumed the chairmanship and carried forward her plans to expand the NEA's resources and influence. The resultant blend supported and sustained a period of growth, innovation, and accomplishment—in other words, successful entrepreneurship.

Such complex chemistry, when it occurs, produces dramatic effects. But it is a delicate compound, susceptible to change from many different quarters. If any of the major elements begins to move out of synchronization with the others, what was an ingredient of success could become a retardant, perhaps even a liability. Indeed, such centrifugal tendencies can be seen during the last three years of Hanks's tenure. Her case thus becomes illustrative of both successful and declining entrepreneurship.

Hanks had been nominated by a new administration to assume direction of a small, virtually invisible agency, presiding over a policy area that was still highly suspect in Congress. She was selected because she was a "political virgin," a competent administrator, and an informed generalist on the arts. In 1969, art activity was booming, but the financial condition of artists and of arts institutions was precarious. Five years later much had changed.

President Nixon's August 1974 resignation had numerous ramifications for Hanks and the NEA. Hanks had taken pains to portray arts policy as a presidential priority. In the wake of President Nixon's disgrace, that linkage ceased to be an asset. While this policy association may not have become a liability under his successor, it was nonetheless clear that the arts did not enjoy the same importance with President Ford.

Similarly, the executive alliances Hanks had cultivated within the Nixon executive office were also lost in the change of administrations. As Laurence Leamer put it, "With Leonard Garment gone, the agency no longer had a special friend in the White House."[83] Garment had no counterpart on the Ford White House staff. Despite Hanks's earlier association with the Rockefellers, it quickly became apparent that given internal White House politics, an alliance with Vice President Rockefeller was likely to be counterproductive.[84] Similarly, the faces at OMB were new, as were many in the other departments and agencies with which the NEA had collaborated. Hence, the network of relationships that had been so carefully cultivated and productive during the Nixon years had to be recast and reconstructed with the advent of the Ford administration.

While there was little outright opposition or hostility to Hanks or the endowment, neither was there great interest or support. The pattern of the Nixon administration alliances could not be replicated as effectively under President Ford. Having to start over at the expanded level of the 1974–75 NEA was a different and more difficult undertaking than the task in 1969. Such problems were repeated and intensified in Hanks's last year in office, as she confronted the task of starting over yet a third time with the Carter administration, which professed different partisan loyalties, other aesthetic preferences, and a new administrative style and philosophy.

Positive support on Capitol Hill had also begun to erode by 1974. Congresswoman Julia Butler Hansen, chairman of the Interior Appropriations Subcommittee, which funded the NEA, retired at the end of her term that year. Thus a new working relationship would have to be established with her successor, Congressman Sidney Yates—a task likely to be influenced by the newly resurgent and reformist mood of a Congress that sought to reassert its power vis-à-vis the executive and that was, among other things, redesigning the federal budget calendar and process. Congressman John Brademas, another key NEA supporter, had sponsored hearings and a bill to establish a special program providing general operating support for the nation's museums. Hanks could not support this idea. She argued that it might fragment the arts constituency and eventually lead other major interests—dance, music, theatre—to seek direct congressional funding; in addition, such a move would undermine the NEA's authority and flexibility.[85]

The effort to "line item" support for museums dragged on for the next three years, before an Institute of Museum Services was finally established. In the meantime, as Hanks had feared, another special interest supported by Brademas—the American Film Institute—attempted to split off from the endowment but failed to secure separate funding from Congress.[86] Although relations between Hanks and Brademas remained cordial, the museum-support debate marked a turning point in the attitudes of key congressional supporters.

Brademas, for one, had begun to fear that Hanks was building herself "a bureaucratic fiefdom immune from Congress and the rest of government." Thus, instead of regarding the NEA as "a proud offspring," he was coming to see it as a "runaway agency he could do very little to control." Another friend of the arts, Congressman Frank Thompson (D-N.J.), began to worry that "the federal government shouldn't dominate the field," and a number of senators—notably Javits (R-N.Y.), Stevens (R-Ala.), and Pell (D-R.I.)—voiced increasing concern about the fair and national distribution of agency grants.[87] Ironically, Hanks's political acumen now became a liability. She had been so successful in winning congressional supporters and in mobilizing constituency influence upon public officials that she and her agency now seemed impregnable and therefore politically unaccountable.

Similar problems stemming from success also affected the relations between Hanks and the arts community. The state arts councils, which the NEA had done so much to nurture, had matured, formed their own service organization, and begun to demand a bigger and more equal role in policy formation.[88] Indeed, they wanted a partnership with the federal government rather than simply patronage from it.

Likewise, the agency had supported (and even sponsored) service organizations in each of the various artistic fields and had been an important factor in the proliferation of artists and arts institutions throughout the nation. By FY 1975, however, the NEA's spectacular budgetary expansion had slowed; indeed, if adjusted for the effects of inflation, its financial base was virtually static. As a result of these combined factors, the agency now found itself contending with more and more applicants, who were increasingly better organized into special-interest associations, competing more strenuously for a share of a shrinking common pie. Furthermore, as Hanks ran out of new and persuasive rationales to justify synoptic increases in appropriations, the competition and the intraconstituency tension intensified.

Once again, previous success had created later problems, particularly as it seemed to spark unfulfillable expectations among the agency's clientele. Paradoxically, Hanks began to find that the very constituency she had helped to expand, mobilize, and organize could be as effective a critic as a supporter.[89]

Finally, within the agency itself, signs of restiveness became evident. Relations with the NCA began to sour. Some members had come to feel that the chairman "wasn't listening to them or that they were being expected to rubber-stamp her."[90] This was significant not merely in itself but because the members of the NCA reflected changes occurring in other elements of the agency's political environment, such as Congress, the White House, and the arts constituency at large. Perhaps a telling indication of the magnitude of the transformation can be seen in the "capture" of the master-memo tactic that had served Hanks so well upon her assumption of the chairmanship. No longer was such articulated strategy a "brainchild" of the chairman, adopted by White House friends and given presidential confirmation. By 1976–77, long-range planning was a complex, cumbersome effort carried on at the NCA's instigation and by congressional request. In 1969 the Hanks plan had been a seven-page memo that sped from composition through approval to public declaration in a matter of weeks. By 1977 it had taken nearly six months merely to produce a three hundred-page draft report on "Future Directions."[91]

Indeed, this last example might be regarded as emblematic of the more general administrative burden of success. Agency growth had been rapid and substantial. By 1974 the agency had outgrown the organizational size and complexity that Hanks found comfortable or consistent with her administrative experience and style. Hanks was accustomed to being involved in all aspects of agency operations, but the scope of those operations now exceeded her grasp. Staff, as well as outside critics, contended that she did not delegate enough and that bureaucratization had gone too far.[92]

In part, these contradictory views coincided with the emergence of two staff generations. On the one hand, the "old" staff, who had signed on early, were generally highly committed, energetic, and creative individuals who viewed themselves as part of the art world rather than as government bureaucrats. Many continued to pursue private artistic activities. Some even lived in New York City and commuted to work in the capital. They were accustomed to a rather freewheeling style. As one remarked, "You weren't accountable in dress or time . . . you could really accomplish something. I used to work from seven in the morning 'til late at night. I broke rules to organize programs."[93] As the NEA grew and began to routinize, some of these people began to feel shackled by rules, requirements, and schedules and thought the agency was becoming depersonalized. During 1976 and 1977, such discontent became manifest as the programmatic team Hanks had assembled began to break up. The directors of state, architecture, and media programs resigned, and the dance program changed directors four times in as many years.

In contrast, "new" staff was concentrated in the administrative ranks of the agency and was comprised of bureaucrats rather than artists. These individuals sometimes complained that Hanks would not delegate and that she was "in effect sitting on absolutely everybody's shoulder all the time.[94] Others felt that the staff was too static and that it was judged on the basis of loyalty rather than competence. Critics outside the agency maintained that there were problems of "waste, ossification, sluggish-ness and self-perpetuation," as well as " 'misdirected energy' expended on duplicate chores, unworthy research, and public relations."[95] Staff were accused of enjoying an inflated, extravagant lifestyle, of being overly concerned with the agency's image rather than its mission, and (if anyone left the agency) of providing for each other through the awarding of grants and contract awards.

Hanks, too, found her time increasingly occupied with administrative concerns rather than policy or politics. These included tasks such as engineering the division of the staff shared with the NEH and the consequent reorganization in 1978 of a separate administrative staff for the NEA; debating staff classifications and promotions with the Civil Service Commission, as well as personnel ceilings with OMB; and of recasting and justifying budgeting submissions in elaborate detail for the zero-based budget system of the new Carter administration. Thus, Hanks found her own creativity stifled by the changing political and bureaucratic environment.

Finally, even personally things began to go wrong for Hanks. Following the 1973 death of the father she loved dearly, Hanks, as the only surviving child, was called upon to support her mother emotionally, so she decided to move her to Washington, where she could be of more comfort and assistance. The strain of this, coupled with her unremitting work pace, led to a serious illness and hospitalization in the spring of 1974. Thus, Hanks's own energy and exuberance were beginning to flag.

On 29 August 1977, Hanks announced her intention to leave the endowment at the close of her term, on 2 October. She took pride in having spurred a growing public and official awareness of the cultural, sociological, and economic importance of the arts and of promoting a collaboration among public, private, and corporate support for the arts.[96] She had the wisdom to act on the realization—increasingly evident through her last two to three years as chairman—that she was no longer the right person for the time and place. The agency now seemed to require a consolidator and reformer, with closer links to Congress than to the president. Her successor would have to manage with little growth and the strong prospect of having to redistribute benefits within the arts community. These were not her talents, and after eight years, Hanks saw the necessity of retiring and had the grace to do so.

She returned to a quiet private life on the fringes of the art world and began to cultivate an interest in environmental issues. The entrepreneurial phase of her career was over. When she died of cancer in early 1983, she was mourned by hundreds at memorial services held both in Washington and New York. In an extraordinarily prompt and uncontested move, Congress enacted a law that designated the revived and reconverted Old Post Office Building, which now houses the NEA, as the Nancy Hanks Center in tribute to her memory.[97]

Except for her chairmanship of the NEA, Hanks would have led an unexceptional life, leaving little visible impact upon public affairs. Her leadership of the endowment marks the most significant phase of that agency's history to date. As Leonard Garment remarked, "She (was) an impossible act to follow."[98] Yet, like all institutional leaders, Hanks had to be succeeded. It is, therefore, the final measure of her impact that Hanks has become, whether appropriately or not, the standard against whom her successors have been measured.

Notes

I would like to thank Professors Erwin Hargrove and Jameson Doig for their comments on earlier drafts. I am also grateful to Arch Dotson, Judith H. Balfe, and Harry Balfe for their editorial and substantive suggestions and to Kathryn Olson and Laurel Anderson for their invaluable assistance in preliminary research and manuscript preparation. Finally, I am indebted to Marianna Dunn, of the NEA, for making various agency documents available for my use and to those individuals who gave of their time and memory in interviews for this research.

1. The notion of "initial survival threshold" is that of Anthony Downs; see his *Inside Bureaucracy* (Boston: Little, Brown, 1967), 9. For a related discussion of the stages of bureaucratic development at the NEA see Lawrence Mankin, "The National

Government and the Arts: Recent Experiences—the Biddle Years" (Paper presented at the annual meeting of the American Political Science Association, Chicago, 1–4 September 1983).

2. For a review of U.S. Census data on American artists see John C. Beresford and Diana Ellis, "Using Census Data to Study Characteristics of American Artists," in *Research in the Arts: Proceedings of the Conference on Policy Related Studies of the National Endowment for the Arts*, ed. David Cwi (Baltimore: Walters Art Gallery, 1978), 90–96. For an overview of information on the population, earnings, and employment of American artists see National Endowment for the Arts, *Five-Year Planning Document, 1986–1990* (Washington, D.C., 1984), 83–89.

3. According to figures in *The New York Times*, 26 May 1985, sec. 2, there were 42 professional orchestras in the United States in 1960 and 166 by 1984. Thus, orchestras increased by 400 percent. Similarly, there were 17 U.S. opera companies in 1970 and 81 in 1984, representing a 470 percent increase. (See Opera America, *Profile: 1984* [Washington, D.C., n.d.], 6). Finally, while there were only 35 dance companies in 1965 (most in the New York City area), in 1983 there were four hundred dance groups located in over one hundred communities nationwide (see U.S. Congress, House, Appropriations Subcommittee on Interior and Related Agencies, "Testimony of Dance/USA," 99th Cong., 1st sess., 28 April 1983, 3).

4. Waldemar Nielsen, *The Endangered Sector* (New York: Columbia University Press, 1979), 139.

5. Comparisons are based on early figures found in Rockefeller Brothers Fund, "The State of the Arts," A Special Studies Project (New York, 13 October 1969, Mimeographed); more recent figures are drawn from National Endowment for the Arts, *Five-Year Planning Document, 1986–1990*, 116.

6. Kenneth Goody, "Arts Funding: Growth and Change between 1963 and 1983," *Annals* 471 (January 1984): 144–57.

7. American Council for the Arts, *Americans and the Arts, 1980* (New York: ACA Publications, 1980). It should, however, be noted that this Harris poll uses a very inclusive definition of the arts which includes, among other activities, film attendance. Therefore, its figures are likely to exaggerate the extent of public support for the range of arts activities supported by the NEA.

8. *New York Times*, 11 January 1969.

9. Michael Straight, "A New Artistic Era (If the Money Lasts)," ibid., 20 October 1974, sec. 2; Malcolm N. Carter, "The National Endowment for the Arts: Will Success Spoil Our Biggest Patron?" *ARTnews*, May 1977, 47.

10. *New York Times*, 4 September 1977, 18.

11. Excerpt from an interview with Michael Straight by Rodney Campbell as quoted in "President Nixon Did More for the Arts Than Any Other President in Our History," chap. 16 in "Ten Years for Tomorrow," ed. Rodney Campbell (Mimeographed draft manuscript), 32.

12. Ibid., 36.

13. Jacques Barzun, "Art-by-Act-of-Congress," *The Public Interest* 1 (Fall 1965): 64.

14. Rockefeller Brothers Fund, *The Performing Arts: Problems and Prospects* (New York: McGraw Hill, 1965); William J. Baumol and William G. Bowen, *Performing Arts: The Economic Dilemma* (Cambridge: MIT Press, 1966).

15. The Ford Foundation released its report on "The Economic Crisis in the Arts" in March 1969 (see *The New York Times*, 2 March 1969). At its 1969 annual meeting, the American Council for the Arts declared that it would focus its attention on the economic crisis in the arts (see ibid., 3 February 1969).

16. In addition to the chairmen of the NEA and NEH, the other federal members were to be the U.S. commissioner of education, the secretary of the Smithsonian Institution, the director of the National Science Foundation, the Librarian of Congress, the director of the National Gallery of Art, the chairman of the Commission on Fine Arts, and a member designated by the secretary of state.

17. Fannie Taylor and Anthony L. Barresi, *The Arts at a New Frontier: The National Endowment for the Arts* (New York: Plenum Press, 1984); on Stevens's background see 55–59.

18. Ibid., 77; derived from chap. 3, "The Roger Stevens Years," ibid., 55–126; Michael Straight, *Twigs for an Eagle's Nest* (New York: Devon Press, 1979), 14–16; NEA, *Annual Reports*, 1964–65 thru 1969 (Washington, D.C.: GPO, 1965–69).

19. *New York Herald Tribune*, 13 February 1966.

20. Rockefeller Brothers Fund Report, "The State of the Arts," 7.

21. The House oversight committee (Education and Labor) had originally suggested a two-year authorization total of $135 million for the NEA and NEH combined. The House eventually approved a one-year authorization of only $11.2 million for both endowments. The Senate supported a two-year appropriation at a figure between the high and low variously suggested by the House. The figure finally approved after conference called for a combined two-year total of $47.5 million for both endowments (see Taylor and Barresi, *The Arts at a New Frontier*, 116–17).

22. See Terri Lynn Cornwell, "Party Platforms and the Arts," in *Art, Ideology, and Politics*, ed. Judith H. Balfe and Margaret Jane Wyszomirski (New York: Praeger, 1985), 243–63.

23. R. L. Coe, "The Politics of Art on Capitol Hill," *Washington Post*, 17 July 1969, as quoted in Taylor and Barresi, *The Arts at a New Frontier*, 126.

24. *Chicago Daily News,* 15–16 November, 1969, 6.

25. Ana Steele, interview by the author, Washington, D.C., 30 November 1984; *Chicago Daily News*, 15–16 November 1969, 6.

26. Quoted by Sophy Burnham in "Nancy Hanks, Santa Claus to the Arts," *Town and Country*, December 1975, 125.

27. Laurence Leamer, "The Gifted and Endowed," *Playing for Keeps in Washington* (New York: Dial Press, 1977), 315–47.

28. Background material on Hanks is derived from a biographical sketch from NEA files, dated 28 August 1969, and from the author's interviews with Janet Gracey, New York City, 18 December 1984, and Ana Steele, Washington, D.C., 30 November 1984. Information on the ACA is from Joan Simpson Burns, *The Awkward Embrace* (New York: Alfred A. Knopf, 1975), 292–99, and from ACA membership and publication materials.

29. *New York Times*, 6 September 1969; Lincoln Kirstein, of the New York City Ballet, as quoted in Burns, *The Awkward Embrace*, 383; ibid., 384.

30. Gracey interview, 18 December 1984.

31. Excerpt from an interview with Nancy Hanks by Rodney Campbell as quoted in chap. 16 in Campbell, "Ten Years for Tomorrow," 7.

32. Steele interview, 30 November 1984; excerpt from an interview with Lawrence Reger by Rodney Campbell as quoted in chap. 16 in Campbell, "Ten Years for Tomorrow," 44; Gracey interview, 18 December 1984.

33. Press release, "Statement by the President on the Appointment of Nancy Hanks as Chairman of the National Endowment for the Arts," 3 September 1969, Nancy Hanks Papers, National Archives, Washington, D.C.

34. *New York Times*, 11 December 1969; 16 January 1970.

35. Frank Getlein, "The man who's made the most solid contribution to the arts

of any President since F.D.R.," *New York Times Magazine*, 14 February 1971; *Washington Post* critic Wolf Von Eckardt, comments of 3 May 1972 and 16 September 1972, as quoted in an advertisement supporting President Nixon's reelection (see *New York Times*, 29 October 1972); *Washington Post*, 22 July 1973.

36. The pattern of communication that emerges from the personal papers of Hanks (as well as those of Leonard Garment) clearly point to close, supportive, and frequent contact. Similarly, the frequency with which one encounters personal correspondence between Hanks and OMB directors and deputy directors, particularly Caspar Weinberger, indicates that the linkage there was also direct and friendly. Indeed, many of the exchanges are on a first-name basis between "Cap" and Nancy. Apparently Weinberger, who would acquire the nickname Cap the Knife and a reputation as an intrepid budget cutter, was won over as a supporter by Hanks and Garment quite early; see, for example, the memorandum from Caspar Weinberger, deputy director of OMB, to Leonard Garment, dated 2 November 1970, where Weinberger remarks that

> certainly a most persuasive case is made. As you know, we are trying to reduce expenditures for most agencies in order to meet the ceilings desired by the President and this kind of process usually precludes doubling the budget of any agency, but we will certainly do our best to recommend an adequate amount for these important subjects.
>
> I might say that personally I would infinitely rather allocate Federal resources for activities such as these than for highways or some of the other things we are required by continuing formulas to finance.

In the Papers of Leonard Garment, Library of Congress.

37. For an account of the sculpture incident see Straight, *Twigs for an Eagle's Nest*, 31–33. This incident was also recounted by Bradley Patterson, who was then working as a White House assistant to Leonard Garment, in a conversation with the author, Washington, D.C., 3 May 1985.

38. Straight, *Twigs for an Eagle's Nest*, 22.

39. Steele interview, 30 November 1984; Gracey interview, 18 December 1984.

40. Internal memo, Hanks to Mr. Berman (on the subject of purchasing a folding screen), 29 December 1969. Found among the uncataloged papers of Nancy Hanks stored by the NEA. As part of a federal design initiative spearheaded by the NEA in the mid-1970s, considerable attention was paid to the design of a suitable symbol for the agency and establishing its consistent use as the official logo for the NEA (see Taylor and Barresi, *The Arts at a New Frontier*, 155).

41. Gracey interview, 18 December 1984.

42. Nancy Hanks, "Memorandum for the President," 17 October 1969 (draft 3), in Hanks Papers.

43. For an account of her appointment as chairman and of the consultations with President Nixon and presidential assistant Leonard Garment on the administration's intended arts policy goals see Hanks interview, in Campbell, "Ten Years to Tomorrow," chap. 16, 2–8.

44. For each of the three major goals of the arts policy Hanks proposed, she quoted President Nixon's own words as the basis for these new directions. For example, both goals 1 and 2 were part of the president's statement to the press in September 1969 when he announced Hanks's nomination as NEA chairman.

45. *Synoptic* is used as the antithesis of *incremental*, the presumedly more frequent form of policy making, particularly of making changes in budgetary allocations. See, for instance, M. A. H. Dempster and Aaron Wildavsky, "On Change: Or There

Is No Magic Size for an Increment," *Policy Studies*, June 1980, 371–89; and discussion in B. Guy Peters, *American Public Policy* (New York: Franklin Watts, 1982), 132–35.

46. Taylor and Barresi, *The Arts at a New Frontier*, 133.

47. Since both the NEA and the NEH were established as part of the National Foundation for the Arts and Humanities, they are generally paired for legislative authorization and appropriation. Indeed, until 1977 they shared administrative services and personnel. Also, between 1966 and 1973 the appropriations for the two agencies were maintained at parity. Beginning in 1974, however, the total funds approved for each agency began to differ, with the NEA generally receiving between $1 million and $3 million more each year. In 1974 the NEA received nearly $10 million more than the NEH, and for the 1976 transition quarter, the NEA received $33.9 million, compared with the NEH's $21.2 million. The gap between the two agencies has continued to grow during the 1980s: for FY 1985 the NEA appropriation stood at $163.6 million, while the NEH's was $139.4 million.

48. For the Hanks memorandum to President Nixon of 17 October 1969 see n. 42. Leonard Garment summarized her memo and forwarded it with his own cover letter to the president on 23 October 1969. He then followed, on 26 November 1969, with a detailed assessment of the proposed arts policy initiative (see Leonard Garment, "Memorandum for the President" on "The Quality of Life in America: Presidential Leadership for the Arts and Humanities," 26 November 1969, Garment Papers, National Archives).

49. Richard M. Nixon, "Special Message to the Congress About Funding and Authorization of the National Foundation on the Arts and the Humanities," 10 December 1969, in *Public Papers of the Presidents: Richard M. Nixon, 1969* (Washington, D.C.: GPO, 1970), 1018–20. For press coverage on the message see *New York Times*, 11 December 1969.

50. The American Symphony Orchestra League (ASOL), one of the oldest and largest of arts service organizations, had sent out a contact letter to almost five thousand board members of symphony orchestras throughout the country encouraging them to contact their political representatives on the proposed arts budget. In a 28 December 1969 note from Hanks to Richard Wangerin, president of ASOL, she reported that "responses are pouring in and The President couldn't be more pleased with wires, not to mention editorials, and the letters are starting. This will give us a lot of good sales talk when we approach Congress" (NEA storage files, Shoreham Building, Washington, D.C.).

51. See *New York Times*, 10 March 1970.

52. According to the *New York Times*, 11 March 1970, the NEA announced the award to grants to twelve symphony orchestras, totaling $706,000. Both the meager total and the small number of orchestras funded underlined dramatically the limitations of current government funds and therefore helped to demonstrate the need for increasing appropriations for the NEA. In 1970 there were twenty-six major symphony orchestras and at least twice as many professional orchestras of smaller sizes.

53. *New York Times*, 8 July 1970.

54. On 6 August 1970 *New York Times* reported that the NEA had just awarded $1.68 million to thirty-four orchestras. This was a marked increase from the previous year's grants of $706,000 to only twelve orchestras. For a list of the awardees see *New York Times*, 25 August 1970.

55. This discussion of staff draws on personnel and position listings found in NEA annual reports for the years 1968–77; on internally circulated biographical

sketches compiled by the agency; and on press releases announcing the appointment of program directors and administrative personnel. Also useful was Taylor and Barresi, *The Arts at a New Frontier.*

56. Steele interview, 30 November 1984.

57. Ibid.

58. Budget figures through FY 1977 include program, treasury, and challenge funds as well as half of the administrative funds allocated for the combined National Foundation for the Arts and Humanities.

59. *New York Times,* 16 January 1971.

60. See the comment of Amyas Ames, head of Lincoln Center, as quoted in ibid., 17 January 1971. Ames organized and headed a citizen support group called Partnership for the Arts which in 1971 called for government funding for the arts to increase to $200 million. On the launching of this group see ibid., 6 January 1971.

61. *New York Times,* 29 July 1971.

62. *New York Times,* 26, 27 May 1971; Richard M. Nixon, "Memorandum about the Federal Government and the Arts, 26 May 1971," in *Public Papers of the Presidents: Richard M. Nixon, 1971* (Washington, D.C.: GPO, 1972), 681–82.

63. *New York Times,* 5 August, 15 September 1971.

64. This was an increase from the previous year's record of $3.7 million in grants awarded to seventy-three orchestras (see *New York Times,* 5 December 1971).

65. Richard M. Nixon, "Statement about Increased Attention to the Arts and Design in Enhancing Federal Buildings and Publications, 16 May 1972," *Public Papers of the Presidents: Richard M. Nixon, 1972* (Washington, D.C.: GPO, 1973), 601–2. For a description and discussion of the Federal Design Improvement Program see Taylor and Barresi, *The Arts at a New Frontier,* 154–57; the quotation is from ibid., 156.

66. Leonard Garment, "Memorandum for Caspar Weinberger: Some Thoughts on the Arts, the Bicentennial, and the Campaign, 6 June 1972," in Papers of Leonard Garment, Library of Congress, Washington, D.C.

67. See informal memo, Nancy Hanks to Leonard Garment, 8 August 1972, Hanks Papers. In this memo, Hanks pointed out that the administration would have a "built-in" lobby with the Ames group (Partnership for the Arts) that would mobilize the large artistic institutions as well as "heavy state council" support. Further, she suggested that a "strong expansion arts program and artists-in-the-schools" program would protect the agency and the president from getting "attacked as 'establishment.' " In addition, by commissioning new works to help commemorate the Bicentennial, the individual artists would "become enthusiastic."

68. *New York Times,* 31 January 1973; and for the comments of Senators McClellan and Proxmire see ibid., 3 May 1973.

69. Ibid., 20 June 1973.

70. The 1971 budget represented an 81 percent increase over the previous year; in 1972 the agency budget increased by another 92 percent; and in 1973, by 58 percent. After 1974, budget increases were much more modest. In addition to the Bicentennial, the continuing problems of museums were another "cause" argued as part of the 1974 budget campaign. A survey of museums by the NEA, *Museums: USA* (Washington, D.C.: GPO, 1974), documented many of the financial problems this constituency continued to confront despite large increases in federal and state funding (see *New York Times,* 9 December 1973). While museums continued to support increases for the NEA for FY 1974—and were rewarded by an increase in the agency's museums program grants, which jumped from $4.6 million in 1973 to $9 million in 1974— they also sought congressional support for the creation of a separate institute for the

improvement of museums services (see ibid., 20 July 1973). Hanks, for reasons to be discussed later, did not support this initiative—a stand that put her at odds with prime congressional arts supporters such as Senator Claiborne Pell and Congressman John Brademas.

71. Program figures derived from NEA, *1976 Annual Report* (Washington, D.C.: GPO, 1977).

72. One encounters a sense of the new assumptions and philosophy implicit in the zero-based budgeting approach from internal memoranda during 1977; see, for example, "Memorandum," P. D. Searles (assistant chairman) to Nancy Hanks, 7 September 1977 (found in miscellaneous Hanks correspondence stored by the NEA).

73. On the history of the GSA's Art-in-Architecture Program see Don W. Thalacker, *The Place of Art in the World of Architecture* (New York: Chelsea House, 1980).

74. See Milton C. Cummings, "To Change a Nation's Cultural Policy: The Kennedy Administration and the Arts in the United States, 1961–63," in *Public Policy and the Arts*, ed. Kevin V. Mulcahy and C. Richard Swaim (Boulder, Colo.: Westview Press, 1982), 161. On the legislative history of the establishment of the NEA and the NEH see Taylor and Barresi, *The Arts at a New Frontier*, 17–54.

75. Joseph Wesley Zeigler, "Passionate Citizenship," *American Arts*, May 1983, 23–24.

76. The phenomenon of federal sponsorship of interest group formation is discussed by Jack L. Walker in his "The Origins and Maintenance of Interest Groups in America," *American Political Science Review* 77, no. 2 (June 1983): 390–405. For a discussion of NEA policy toward arts service organizations see Margaret Jane Wyszomirski, "Arts Service Organizations: Aide, Ally, or Competitor?" (Paper presented at the Conference on Social Theory, Politics, and the Arts, College Park, Md., October 1984).

77. National Endowment for the Arts, "National Council on the Arts: Policy and Planning Committee Report on Service Organization Support" (Washington, D.C., 1980, Mimeographed), 50, 68.

78. Gracey interview, 18 December 1984.

79. *New York Times*, 2 March 1969.

80. The Ford Foundation had established a $10 million cash reserve grant program in late 1971 designed to help financially troubled arts organizations retire their accumulated deficits and to create a more viable cash-flow system (see *New York Times*, 18 October 1971). Similarly, challenge grants were to help major arts institutions become more financially stable, build new sources of revenue, and engage in long-range planning. Various kinds of artist-in-residence programs had a long history dating back to 1936. Thus, in creating its artists-in-the-schools program, the NEA had prototypes and a substantial performance record from which to draw lessons. Furthermore, Roger Stevens had experimented with a poets-in-the-schools program in cooperation with the U.S. Office of Education beginning in 1966 and had a broader-based version in process by 1969, when Hanks became chairman. Between 1969 and 1976 the artists-in-the-schools program had grown from one that placed six artists in secondary schools to a $4 million program that brought more than two thousand artists into seven thousand five hundred schools in all fifty states and five special jurisdictions, reaching nearly one million students. For an account of the AIS program and its roots see Taylor and Barresi, *The Arts at a New Frontier*, 209–24.

81. Taylor and Barresi, *The Arts at a New Frontier*, 157–59; NEA press release, "Expansion Arts Program Announced," 16 December 1971.

82. Taylor and Barresi, *The Arts at a New Frontier*, 154–57.

83. Leamer, *Playing for Keeps in Washington*, 339.

84. It seems that Vice President Rockefeller was pushed out of President Ford's inner councils virtually before he was even confirmed. On the Rockefeller vice presidency, particularly on his role in domestic affairs, see Michael Turner, *The Vice-President as Policy-Maker* (Westport, Conn.: Greenwood Press, 1984). Ana Steele, who worked closely with Hanks throughout her tenure, could not remember Hanks's trying to engage a Rockefeller connection during his term as vice president (Steele interview, 30 November 1984).

85. For Hanks's official position on the prospect of establishing an institute for museum services, see U.S. Congress, Senate, Committee on Labor and Public Welfare and Committee on Rules and Administration, Joint Hearing of Special Subcommittee on Arts and Humanities and Subcommittee on the Smithsonian Institution, "Museum Services, 1973: Oral Testimony of Nancy Hanks, Chairman of the National Endowment for the Arts," 93d Cong., 1st sess., 18 July 1973, 44–221. See also U.S. Congress, Senate, Committee on Labor and Public Welfare, 94th Cong., 2d sess., 1976, 1–29; U.S. Congress, House, Committee on Education and Labor, Select Subcommittee on Education, 93d Cong., 2d sess., 1974; and U.S. Congress, Joint Hearings before the House Subcommittee on Select Education and the Senate Labor and Public Welfare Committee, Special Subcommittee on Arts and Humanities (on the Arts, Humanities and Cultural Affairs Act of 1975), 94th Cong., 1st sess., 12–14 November 1975. For internal correspondence discussing the NEA's position and concerns about a museum services act, as well as an assessment of congressional reaction, see "Memorandum from Livingston Biddle to Nancy Hanks, 9 September 1975," and "Memorandum and Supporting Materials from Fred Lazarus, 11 November 1975," in uncataloged NEA documents.

86. On the effort to establish direct funding for museums and for the American Film Institute see *New York Times*, 4 September 1977, sec. 2.

87. Leamer, *Playing for Keeps in Washington*, 345–46; Carter, "The National Endowment for the Arts," 46–47.

88. For an account of "the strong undercurrent of unrest and dis-satisfaction" among state and local arts agencies that began surfacing in mid-1973 see Taylor and Barresi, *The Arts at a New Frontier*, 179–88.

89. As an example of the range of criticism coming from the various components of the arts constituency see Carter, "The National Endowment for the Arts."

90. Steele interview, 30 November 1984.

91. Earlier NCA discussions had prompted the chairman and her staff to prepare a preliminary list of questions on future directions for the agency and to present these at the November 1976 NCA meeting. The following February, the NCA was presented with the draft volume "Future Directions," numbering some three hundred pages.

92. For a critical discussion of Hanks's management of the NEA see Gael M. O'Brien, "The Arts Endowment's Hanks: Good Politician, Poor Manager?" *Chronicle of Higher Education*, 7 March 1977, 9.

93. Leamer, *Playing for Keeps in Washington*, 339.

94. Steele interview, 30 November 1984; Leamer, *Playing for Keeps in Washington*, 337–39.

95. Carter, "The National Endowment for the Arts," 39–40; Michael Newton, director of the ACA, as quoted in ibid., 40; ibid., 42.

96. NEA press release, 29 August 1977.

97. In renaming the Old Post Office Building for Hanks, Congress took only half

an hour to act unanimously. Leonard Garment noted that "no American president has been memorialized so quickly and with so little partisan commotion" (see Garment's memorial article, "Nancy Hanks [1927–1983]," *ARTnews*, April 1983, 106).

98. Ibid.

8

Entrepreneurship in Public Management: Wilbur Cohen and Robert Ball

Theodore R. Marmor
with the assistance of Philip Fellman

The challenges of American public management in the twentieth century are daunting. Americans are suspicious of public authority while holding moralistically high-minded standards for their leaders. The Constitution expresses this suspicion in its determined fragmentation of power and responsibility, and the informal norms of American politics typically sanction the visible amassing of the trappings of high office. For most of America's history the job of government has been quite limited, the constraints of liberal politics taken for granted in fears of both socialism and traditional authoritarianism. In the twentieth century, however, American government has come to take on the full range of tasks common to Western industrial democracies.[1]

Despite these broader tasks, America's ethos of limited government remains the accepted rhetoric. The nation has a very large civil service but a mixture of disdain for and suspicion of its civil servants. Rarely is the American higher civil service respected as an elite corps, as it is in Britain, France, Sweden, or Japan. Yet the tasks of government—from huge pension and public medical insurance programs to global defense and macroeconomic planning—are immensely difficult. Modern government calls for gifted managers to negotiate program complexities, and American public life has distinguished examples of such managers.[2] Our leading civil servants, however, are without the benefits of great formal authority and wide public respect. It is no wonder, then, that we can regard determined, effective public leadership as worthy of exceptional note.

The subjects of this essay on public entrepreneurship—Wilbur Cohen and Robert Ball—are two noteworthy examples of unusual enterprise in American public administration. Hardly household words in the national community, they are well known in the world of social welfare. Called "high priests" by some of their detractors, they are more admiringly known as Mr. Social Security and Mr. Social Welfare. But both their detractors and their admirers agree that the careers of Cohen and Ball illustrate successful entrepreneurialism in American public management. Noted for managerial skills and famous among experts for their dedication to social insurance, Cohen and Ball have been heroes to some and threats to others.

As we explore the careers of these two remarkable men, it is important to keep in mind both the nature of their activities and the terms of complaint and admiration they have prompted.[3] Critics blame Ball and Cohen for incremental and surreptitious expansion of social programs and accuse them of unresponsiveness to congressional and administrative wishes to rein in this growth sector of American government.[4] Praised or blamed, Cohen and Ball are regarded as central to this expansion of government. And as we shall see, it is their firm commitment to an activist conception of government in social welfare that distinguishes Ball and Cohen from those public managers who move rather easily from one sphere of government to another.[5]

Wilbur Cohen and Bob Ball both entered public service as young men, but at very different levels. In 1934, at the age of twenty-one, Cohen graduated from the University of Wisconsin and immediately began work as a research assistant to Edwin Witte, then the executive director of the Committee on Economic Security. In this way Cohen began near the top. For nearly fifty years thereafter he remained close to the central decision-making authorities not only in social security but in education, public welfare, and poverty policy as well, ending his formal government career in 1968 as Lyndon Johnson's secretary of Health, Education and Welfare (HEW). Ball, on the other hand, began public life as an entry-level field assistant in the Newark, New Jersey, district Social Security office in 1939, where he came to the attention of his superiors and began to rise rather rapidly through the levels of the Social Security Administration (SSA).[6] During the 1950s Ball, a deputy commissioner, was the SSA's most central bureaucrat. He formally became commissioner of social security in 1962 and remained so until 1973.

This essay is an exercise in public biography, not a history of two leaders. We first discuss four contrasting styles of public management, setting out the differences between the program entrepreneur; the generalist manager, who moves across different sectors; the loyal zealot, who fails to manage; and those with neither program commitment nor managerial gifts. In that context, we next look at the backgrounds and careers of Cohen and Ball. Then we turn to more detailed consideration of the roles of Ball and Cohen in three periods of twentieth-century social policy: implementation of the new social security programs (1935–50); expansion in programs and administrative scale (1950–72); and financial crisis amid stagflation (1973–present). The essay closes with an appraisal of the effect of these two figures on the policies, programs, and institutions they sought to shape.

Political Executives as Entrepreneurs

The conception of entrepreneurship that focuses on turning new ideas into successful business ventures is not well suited to understanding the management challenges of large-scale public enterprise. There is, to be sure, the recognizable account of the experimenter in public administration, the initiator of the new program who starts from scratch—the analogue to the Silicon Valley hero in the 1970s or the Xerox and IBM of an earlier period.[7] There is much to be learned about the organizational circumstances of birth in public, private, and nonprofit settings. But the interest of this chapter—and the book of which it is a part—is in what differences individual leaders make in the evolution of substantial public programs over decades, not months.

To understand those matters better, distinctions that sort out types of public administrators are helpful. Consider, for instance, the simple figure below that characterizes program administrators by their commitments to policy and their degree of managerial skill. The two axes

Figure 8.1

		Managerial Skills	
		Low	High
		ADMINISTRATIVE SURVIVORS	GENERALIST MANAGERS
Commitment to Program Goals	Low	Non-Leaders	Mandarins and In-and-Outers (Spiral Career Movement)
	High	PROGRAM ZEALOTS (Unsuccessful Managers and Administrators)	PROGRAM LOYALISTS (Vertical Career Movement)

proceed from low to high and produce four combinations for analysis. We shall term them, for purposes of discussion, survivors, generalist managers, zealots, and program loyalists. Our subjects—Cohen and Ball—combined great managerial skill and deep program commitment. They exemplify the lower right-hand cell and can be illuminatingly compared with other types, particularly their skilled managerial colleagues who ascend in spiral fashion, shifting from program to program, subject matter to subject matter.

Managerial skill and program commitment both represent, of course, a continuum, with individuals arrayed in more complex positions than a simple typology suggests.[8] Stereotypes, however, for all their dangers, are of analytical utility; they provide the sharp contrasts that make rather than mask a point.

At one extreme there are *survivors*. With both modest managerial skills and equally modest managerial gifts, this group exemplifies the bureaucratic inertia with which every senior administrator must contend. To characterize them as survivors is to describe them, not to malign their motivation. Many such persons no doubt perform their assigned tasks conscientiously, and no large organization operates without those who do their job without special zeal or special gifts.

There is a second group of unskilled managers we call *zealots*. Zealots are those whose program enthusiasm exceeds their expertise at getting things done in complex organizations. Such figures may have awesome technical competence. But neither knowledge nor formal intellectual skills are substitutes for the mundane but necessary managerial capacities required to get tasks accomplished.[9] Those capacities include the ability to articulate a program's mission, to lead subordinates and warrant confidence from superiors, and to combine the resources available, the mandate of the organization, and the political constraints into a workable, long-term program operation.

At the other extreme are the skilled *generalist managers*, a group that is in fact quite heterogeneous and includes both mandarins and in-and-outers. The highly skilled generalists we call mandarins closely resemble the civil service elites in France, Britain, and many other industrial democracies.[10] Their operating conventions rule out zealous program commitment. As promising leaders, they commonly start their careers in the budget and finance ministries and then are shifted around the departments of government, two years here, three years there.

The American mandarins, while not nearly so celebrated or so easily identified as their European counterparts, exhibit many of the same characteristics. These American versions are marked as able to get things done, to manage in diverse settings, and to follow the policy directions of legitimate, elected public authorities. They are not marked by devotion to a particular set of programs (social insurance, for instance) or commitment to a given set of policy goals. What they share is practical knowledge of government and managerial skill in making things work. Jim Webb started in the Bureau of the Budget (BOB) but came to public attention most vividly through the National Aeronautics and Space Administration (NASA). Elmer Staats, the recently retired comptroller general, had a long career in government, reaching back to the immediate postwar period and including service in BOB. Likewise, Rufus Miles, who as a Princeton academic coined the expression "where you stand depends on where you sit," moved with ease among BOB, the Department of Labor, and HEW before moving to academic life.

The other version of what we have called the gifted generalist manager is the widely cited "in-and-outer." Unlike both the program loyalist and the career mandarin, such figures go in and out of government work, typically occupying positions of high responsibility in law firms, investment banks, or corporations when not "in politics." In their careers as lawyer-advisers during the New Deal and afterwards, Jim Rowe and Tommy Corcoran exemplified this sort of manager. Chester Bowles and Douglas Dillon illustrated the business-government type in the forties, fifties, and sixties. More recently, the distinguished, wide-ranging careers—both in and out of government—of Caspar Weinberger, Robert McNamara, Joseph Califano, and Elliot Richardson come to mind.

Both types of generalists are, by definition, less programmatic in their concerns than are loyalists. They tend to follow career paths that move more horizontally between different departments and programs than vertically up the rungs of a single administrative hierarchy. Such movement means that generalists sacrifice substantive program expertise for breadth of application. This very mobility gives rise to their reputation for broad competence; having handled one set of problems satisfactorily, they may then move on to a new position in a different area and try to impose "manageability" there as well. In this respect the generalists resemble the ideal of the private-sector generalist, the problem solver trained in the case method for "general management."

All generalists can speak for the administration they serve. But partisan in-and-outers, more willing to pursue an administration's objectives than to protect the traditional mission of their agency, can be controversial when the administration is hostile to a popular program's goals. Anne Gorsuch, as head of President Reagan's Environmental Protection Agency, James Watt, as secretary of the interior, and David Stockman, as director of the Office of Management and Budget (OMB), have demonstrated the problems that can arise when partisan loyalty conflicts with goals of popular programs.

Program generalists must be concerned with the vagaries of career advancement through lateral moves. They may frequently focus on issues and program options that highlight personal performance, particularly in a polity that does not empower an elite civil service to reward its generalist highfliers. As a result, program generalists are less likely to focus their efforts on producing unglamorous, incremental program changes, even if they are needed.

Program loyalists, by contrast, are public administrators with a long time horizon in particular parts of government. They treat their programs as if they were their own business enterprise. Wealth and fame are not the driving objectives, though many such public entrepreneurs could earn both in other settings. There are no stock options in public management to reward success in launching and bringing to maturity an important organization.

Another aspect of the public entrepreneur's character is that as with the private-sector entrepreneur, his "business" (in the case of Ball and Cohen, American social insurance) comes first. That is, the successful achievement of program goals dominates the life of the public entrepreneur whether in or out of office. Thus, what might have been for others a few years' temporary involvement (as in the case of generalist Caspar Weinberger as secretary of HEW) has been, for Cohen and Ball, a lifelong dedication to social insurance, or, as some would say, an obsession with it. This fifty-year commitment to the creation of a comprehensive program of American social insurance is the essence of the chronicle that follows.

Backgrounds and Careers—A Sketch

Wilbur Cohen, the son of a variety store owner, grew up in Milwaukee, Wisconsin, and after public high school graduated from the University of Wisconsin. Robert Ball, the son of a Methodist minister, grew up on the East Coast and received his B.A. from Wesleyan, the small liberal arts college in Middletown, Connecticut, where he studied English and economics. Both men began their government service with a common dedication to the principles of social insurance and rose during the subsequent decades to become team champions of this version of social welfare policy.

Comparably gifted and regularly working as a team for over forty years, Ball and Cohen could hardly be more different physically. Ball, six feet one inch, is a white-haired, broad-shouldered man whose gravity is lightened by a readily available twinkle and chuckle. He wears black-rimmed, prominent glasses that he takes on and off when shifting from speaking to reading. His expression is frequently softened by his easy smile and firm but unaggressive manner. At meetings he leans forward intently in his seat and, with a formalism that seems now a little old-fashioned, begins to speak in a manner instilled by years of testifying before Congress: "Mr. Chairman, let me begin by stating that I am in full agreement with the general thrust of Mr. X's remarks. But I would like, if I may, to bring up three somewhat technical points about social security. . . ." Ball could have posed for pictures of executive presence in *Fortune* during the 1950s and 1960s. But in Bob Ball's case, the imagery captures much of the man, not a myth. Ball did indeed come to stand for the SSA and its reputation for honest, competent, reliable service to Americans, who were regarded as clients, not supplicants.

Nearly half a century of partnership between Cohen and Ball has done little to erase the marked differences between the two. If Ball was the tight end of the SSA—steady, determined, a pillar of strength but working within a clear, circumscribed field of action—Cohen was the energetic quarterback of social security in the wider world of social policy. He ranged over issues of poverty and welfare, education and social services, policy making and legislation. Never the line administrator of a large operational unit in government, Cohen nonetheless respected the difficulties and importance of detail, determination, and clear purpose in public administration. He is a product of Wisconsin's progressive flagship, the University of Wisconsin at Madison. A nimble badger of a man, Cohen is short, with a small nose that holds the unobtrusive glasses he uses for reading. His lively face is round, with wisps of grey hair now astride a balding top. Cohen is both elflike and elusive. He scans his immediate environment with the attentiveness of the top student he was in high school and college, a bit like the scholarship kid who knows he will have to please. A merchant's son, Cohen has all the willingness to attend to customers we associate with the best of that livelihood.

Ball, the minister's son, has just the slightest hint of deep reserve, while Cohen's bearing suggests a negotiator's sensitivity behind the smile, the readiness to bargain, and the ready, well-thought-out answers he has to offer. Social security has had both men for decades of advocacy. If someone was needed to speak before the American Bankers Association, Ball would have been the right choice to win the bankers' confidence, if not their agreement with his policies. If a deal had to be struck between the White House and HEW, Cohen would have been the first choice. And if the House Ways and Means Committee wanted to know what was going on in social security, both would be called, with easy exchange between the two.[11]

Dual guardians of social security, the two symbolized the ethnic diversity of American life. Ball, the WASP of the social gospel, loves badminton and the quiet of his island summer retreat in New Hampshire. Cohen, the son of Milwaukee's Jewish community, likes the library more than the playing courts. And when he moves about in the countryside in white tennis shoes and black socks, the observer knows he reads the *Washington Post* much more often than *Field and Stream*.

Beginning in 1934, when he took his first job with the Committee on Economic Security, Cohen was for two decades the major policy aide to the leading administrative figures in social security.[12] As the titles for the social security program changed over time, Cohen never left the inner circle.[13] His memoranda informed much of Arthur Altmeyer's thinking in the first twenty years of social security's operation. His ideas on how to incorporate health insurance in American social policy, in collaboration with I. S. Falk among others, shaped the early proposals for national health insurance. He crucially redirected what came to be known as "the Medicare strategy" of health insurance expansion.[14]

As assistant secretary for HEW legislation under President Kennedy, Cohen was a major figure in the department, arguably overshadowing the succession of political appointees who served as secretary.[15] Informally the quasi secretary of HEW, he became secretary in fact during the last year of the Johnson administration and then again "retired" from public service to academic life. He found no refuge from the wars of social policy, however, and over the succeeding years has continued his relentless efforts to bolster the institutions of the New Deal, to sustain the creations of the Great Society, and to forge new policy options for the mature American welfare state of the 1970s and 1980s.

No history of American social policy since the New Deal can be written without a major role for Cohen. How he is best understood as a participant in larger ideological and administrative forces during that period is a question this essay seeks to answer. But as spokesman, facilitator, or cause, Cohen is an ever-present figure in that history.

If Cohen spread his influence widely across American social policies, Ball concentrated his energies more on the administration of social insurance. He spent much of the 1940s preparing himself and the nation for the eventually much larger social insurance system.[16] Social security, after all, was a small program in the 1940s, covering very few Americans and paying out modest amounts to those already retired (see table 1). Ball learned the intricacies of policy, politics, and administration well, turned his considerable energies to training the staffs in the ethos of social insurance, and early on came to understand how important it was to transmit that ethos to a variety of American publics.

By the mid-fifties, Ball was social security's Mr. Administrator to Cohen's Mr. Policy. Ball's nominal titles did not fully convey his effective influence within the agency. By 1952 he had become the deputy director of the Bureau of Old-Age and Survivors Insurance (BOASI) and the de facto deputy director of the SSA. He administratively directed the BOASI under the benevolent commissionerships of Tramburg, Schottland, and Mitchell. By this time he had already become a crucial player among a group of insiders—"program executives," to use Martha Derthick's phrase—who planned the politics, legislation, administration, and bargaining over the current shape and future prospects for social security. Like Cohen, he was central in the deliberations over disability insurance and the structuring of the medicare options in the late 1950s. In the early Kennedy administration his title—commissioner of social security—brought reality and formal designation together. His tenure as commissioner extended through the Kennedy and Johnson years and the first term of the Nixon administration.[17]

Less wide-ranging in policy scope than Cohen, Ball was the quintessential program entreprenuer, tending to social security's administrative burdens while scanning the environment for dangers and opportunities. Ball revealed himself as the tireless advocate in his writings, the patient negotiator in his dealings with Congress, the fount of information about current operations for his presidents (six in all) and HEW secretaries, and the personal embodiment of the argument that humane societies require stable institutions of social insurance to soften the blows of capitalism's harshest features.

Leaving the Nixon administration in 1973, Ball joined Cohen in

Table 8.1.   Social Security (OASI) Tax Contributions and Benefit Payments Selected Years (in millions of dollars)

	Employer/Employee Contributions	Benefit Payments
1940	325	35
1941	789	88
1942	1,012	131
1943	1,239	166
1944	1,316	209
1945	1,285	274
1950	2,667	961
1955	5,713	4,968
1960	10,866	10,677
1965	16,017	16,737

Source: Social Security Bulletin, April 1970, table M-5, p. 52.

trying to sustain the social policy legacy of the New Deal and the Great Society.[18] Like Cohen, Ball became a crucial player in the complicated political games of the 1970s and 1980s that shaped the fate of social security amid the pressures of stagflation.[19]

Over seventy now, Cohen and Ball continue as nominal retirees, working daily in their self-directed tasks.[20] As many have noted, both are public leaders of a sort we may not see again. The character of their leadership—and their legacy—is the topic to which we now turn.

Social Security, 1935–1985: The Impact of Ball and Cohen

We have already sketched the roles both men played in the first fifty years of social security's history. The following section addresses the question of whether their unquestionable prominence reflected substantial impact on the policies and institutional character of the organizations they sought to foster and expand. In the simplest formulation, did they have a major effect on America's institutions of social insurance and public welfare? or did they become the most highly touted exemplars of policy ideas and institutional developments whose causes they could neither deflect nor markedly speed up? Since the maturing of social security and welfare policy coincided with the careers of these two figures, no easy test is possible. Covariance is a problem in biography as well as in survey research. There are grounds for arguing that Ball and Cohen both were and were not crucial to the development of social security, understood in the narrow social-insurance and the broader welfare-state sense of that expression.

The Start-Up of Federal Social Insurance: 1935–1950

Were the careers of Ball and Cohen crucial to the start-up and shape of America's social security program? As young men working for the Social Security Board (SSB), even well-placed young men, neither Cohen nor Ball especially was in a position to alter the course of events significantly. Cohen, it is true, personally assisted the major figures—first Witte, then Altmeyer—and was central *in*, though not perhaps *to*, the deliberations. Ball, by contrast, began at the periphery and eventually came to the central office to conduct training sessions for new employees. Yet both, in different ways, laid the foundation for their future influence in these early years.

Cohen and Ball each played supportive roles in the early years of social security. Not high priests, they became altar boys to the first generation of leaders, with Cohen clearly the more influential at that time. So if the question is whether they—even taken together with Altmeyer, Frances Perkins, Harry Hopkins, J. Douglas Brown, and others—gave a distinctive cast to social security's *original* form, the answer is that most probably they did not. The birth of social security was occasioned by the Depression, conditioned by thirty years of American thinking about social insurance, constrained by the experience of Wisconsin and other states with unemployment insurance and workman's compensation, and produced through a complex bargaining process involving Congress, the Committee on Economic Security, and President Franklin Roosevelt.[21]

The crossnational evidence supports neither a "conspiratorial cabal" nor a "great leader" account of America's broad development of social security. All the industrial nations of the world have the same elements of social insurance; surely not all of them had the particular features of a cabal.[22] And to the extent that each had leaders who embodied the ideas of social insurance, the crucial explanatory factor is the common cause of the common leadership response—the combination of the harshness of industrial capitalism and the responsiveness of mass democracies to widely felt troubles. Only scholarly provincialism could lead one to attribute the origins and scope of American social security to the characteristics and resolve of its social insurance leaders.

The subsequent evolution of social security—and even more important, the securing of wide public support for its mission and expansion—is quite another story. At its outset and for some fifteen years, social security was a very small program. The amendments of 1939, although they made other important adjustments, moved further away from the model of a partially funded system and hastened the earlier payment of benefits.[23] During World War II and immediately thereafter, social security was in one sense an insurance company's ideal, with many contributors and few recipients of monthly checks. But the program was small, overshadowed financially by old-age assistance, and unstable politically. Ball realized this well and, as noted earlier, left the old-age and survivors program in order to advance his and the program's cause. What he did with his time out is instructive. Ball was staff director of the citizens' advisory council on social security of the Senate Finance Committee, reviewing the program and charting its future;[24] he also conducted special seminars for elites inside and outside of social insurance and there gave voice to his lifelong interest in securing a wide, national constituency for the mission of social security.

The first fifteen years of federal social insurance are properly understood in developmental terms: birth, infancy, childhood, and adolescence. A healthy start was the first priority of the founders. But the issue for the early years was whether the habits, training, and disposition of the young organization were appropriate for solid growth and performance later on. Social security is a firmly rooted American institution in the 1980s, but its fate was terribly uncertain in the late 1930s and early 1940s.[25] Did the early careers of Ball and Cohen have much influence on the subsequent evolution?

To assert that Cohen was "responsible" for the early amendments to the Social Security Act—or that Ball later "ran" the SSA—is to describe visible activity, not necessarily leadership or institutional influence. Pay-as-you-go financing of social insurance, encouraged by a key amendment in 1939, is a common feature internationally. Disability insurance is found in every major industrial country.[26] Cohen and Ball— or anyone else—are no more responsible for the American presence of pay-as-you-go financing or disability insurance than the obstetrician is responsible for the birth of a child. Only if a birth is unusually difficult does one concentrate on the obstetrician. The question is whether these admittedly well-placed players shaped the early history of the organization on whose behalf they have been active for half a century.

During social security's early period, Ball and Cohen are best understood as participants in a much broader process of creating social insurance as an acceptable American institution. For that to happen, three developments were crucial. One was the popularization of social insurance theory, or "principles," as the founders would say. The second was inculcating among the personnel of social insurance both the mission and the mandate to deliver benefits to the right person at the right address at the right time and in the right amount. The third was creating a political formula for adjusting benefit levels to social security financing so that changes were routinized and not the occasions for fundamental clashes of principle.[27] Cohen and Ball energetically participated in these institutional accomplishments, but neither as architects of their form nor as idiosyncratic managers of their pace. Rather, they were part of a cadre of committed social insurance advocates who learned well the lessons of public administration and social insurance that Altmeyer, Brown, and others had taught. Willing and able students, Ball and Cohen were testimony to the successful transmission of the social insurance ethos by the first generation of leaders to the second.[28]

These early years of social security were marked by the remarkably high quality of the initial recruits. The first administrators not only were obsessed with careful selection and serious training but were mentors as well.[29] Altmeyer nurtured Cohen's development and no doubt helped to soften the aggressive edge of the sharp young social scientist from Wisconsin. Altmeyer and Cohen, in turn, recognized Ball's talents and potential relatively early on and, with John Corson's help, made it reasonably easy for Ball to absorb the leadership's philosophy. Cohen and Ball had good coaches, but for the first years it was the whole team that counted more than the young runners.[30]

The Growth of Social Security: 1950–1972

The growth of social security in the two decades after 1950 is striking. During this period social insurance programs expanded sharply in the scope of their benefits, the number of beneficiaries, and the scale of administration. They exhibited the features of adolescent change—sudden growth spurts, intermittent conflicts, and the gradual taking shape of what would become the mature structure. The scale of change is concretely suggested by the tax increases in social security between 1950 and 1970. In 1950 combined employer-employee contributions to OASI amounted to 3 percent of the first $3,000 of income; two decades later the figure was 8.4 percent of a taxable base of $7,800. By 1950, ten years after social security's first payments were made, only 16 percent of Americans over sixty-five were eligible for benefits. In 1960 this figure had climbed to 70 percent, and by 1970 it was over 90 percent.[31] Similarly dramatic changes are evident in the size of the SSA. In 1950 some twelve thousand persons worked for the SSA, split between the central office in Baltimore and the extended network of field offices. By 1970 this number had grown to slightly over fifty thousand.[32]

It was during these two decades that Ball and Cohen assumed their central, more visible roles in the expansion and administration of social insurance. Part of the change became more evident when Altmeyer retired in 1953, permitting the new Eisenhower administration to choose another commissioner. Cohen, no longer Altmeyer's able young aide, became the head of research and statistics at that time, taking a pay cut as a result. He devoted himself to a broad set of policy concerns— the planning for disability insurance, the consideration of how hospital insurance could be grafted onto social security, and the extension of pension coverage to many more Americans. Leaving the government in 1956, Cohen taught social welfare subjects at the University of Michigan and, as I have suggested, participated prominently in shaping the medicare proposals. Returning to HEW in 1961, Cohen played a broad policy and legislative role, concentrating on medicare in the early 1960s but extending his reach as the politics of social policy required.

Allies throughout, Ball and Cohen diverged during this period with respect to where they placed their energies. Ball continued the process of internal ascent within what we now call the Social Security Administration. By 1952 his official title was deputy commissioner of the BOASI, but in reality he was the major administrative figure of the entire SSA. What that meant in practice is best revealed by the roles Ball and Cohen played in the enactment and administration of disability insurance in the mid-1950s and medicare in the mid-1960s.

Once united as full-time government employees, they occupied, in the mid-1950s, very different positions. Ball, on the inside, was the chief policy and administrative figure in social security, while Cohen, the academic on the outside, was able to advocate without restraint. Ball and Cohen divided their tasks in a manner that was to shape their pattern of cooperation for the next thirty years. In the legislative push for disability coverage, Ball was the central player within the SSA. It was he who dealt extensively with Roswell Perkins, HEW's generalist assistant secretary, who was the Republican appointee most opposed to disability insurance. It was not that Cohen was unconcerned—or un-consulted; rather, the detailed negotiation within the Republican administration required continued discussions with those responsible for administering social security and planning to implement new pro-grams. In part, then, the division of labor was between the policy gen-eralist of social welfare (Cohen) and the administrative leader of social insurance (Ball).[33]

This cooperative division of turf was also reflected in the way Cohen and Ball approached medicare politics. Medicare was Cohen's major concern, the unfinished item of health insurance from the heyday of the New Deal. This continuity was maintained even after Cohen left for Michigan in 1956. There he had his students examine health insurance issues affecting the elderly. In Washington Cohen remained a central participant in the informal group who were nurturing, in the late 1950s, the idea of adding hospital insurance for the aged to the scope of social insurance.[34]

The broad political message was that health insurance was a logical complement to the old age, survivors, and disability program of Amer-ican social insurance. However popular national health insurance had been among American liberals in the Truman period, it faced stalemate during the Eisenhower years. Cohen, along with Oscar Ewing, I. S. Falk, and others, had again seized upon medicare in the early 1950s as a first step toward national health insurance.[35] By 1959–60 Congress had rejected the social insurance approach and had adopted a trial period of means-tested health coverage for the elderly poor, the Kerr-Mills bill of 1960. It is symptomatic of the influence Cohen and Ball had with social insurance conservatives, both Democratic and Republican, that Cohen helped Senator Kerr of Oklahoma and Congressman Mills of Arkansas draft the Kerr-Mills plan.[36]

Cohen continued to play the leading legislative role when the Ken-nedy administration started the drive for medicare in 1961. For the next four years, the SSA supplied the facts, figures, and briefing books that Cohen annually took to Congress for testimony. Accompanied regularly by Ball, Cohen, as assistant secretary for legislation, was the chief HEW spokesman on medicare.

Once medicare was enacted in 1965, the assumed division of administrative responsibility reasserted itself. Cohen took seriously Ball's administrative experience and, even more, the notion—which Ball shared—that responsibility for "running" a program, once enacted, had to be clearly given to a line administrator. So it was that the SSA took over implementation, Arthur Hess was made the head of the Bureau of Health Insurance within the SSA, and the principles learned in the early years under Altmeyer were put into practice.[37]

In addition to their adherence to models of administrative clarity, another important point about these program entrepreneurs emerged with the enactment of medicare. By clearly ceding medicare administrative authority to Ball and his lieutenants, Cohen reinforced the idea that the SSA was administratively expert, that years of training its cadre of middle managers had paid off in ample capacity, and that only those left free to handle management problems can develop the confidence and public reputation for autonomous competence that the early generation had sought.

The effort required to start medicare was prodigious and is easily forgotten after twenty years of operation. The special voluntary feature of physician insurance (technically known as Part B) meant that millions of older Americans had to be contacted. In that task, Ball and his colleagues used all the instruments of public authority, getting the Forest Service to assist them in outlying areas, called upon the Post Office to make sure hard-to-reach persons were contacted, not to mention mobilizing a large new bureau to negotiate with the fiscal intermediaries Congress placed between hospitals, doctors, and the medicare methods of reimbursement.[38] Within a year, the formidable tasks of preparation were complete, and on 1 July 1966 the program began with hardly a hitch.[39]

It was during the Kennedy and Johnson administrations that Cohen and Ball solidified their hold on American social policy. For the public who attend to social security matters, the evidence of their prominence was unmistakable. First, Ball became commissioner in 1962, with Cohen already assistant secretary for legislation in HEW. By 1968 Cohen was not only undersecretary but Johnson's choice for secretary of HEW. Thirty-three years after the start of social security, two of its brightest stars were firmly in positions of leadership. The swearing in of Cohen as secretary of HEW, with Ball a fellow dignitary, was like a roll call of the New Deal's contribution to social insurance and public welfare reform. Equally important for our purposes, this was the formal consolidation of the authority both men had had before they took the top jobs. For this pair, the 1960s were the heyday of their administrative influence, whatever their official position. But for the admirers of social security, it must have been gratifying, indeed moving, to see their own at the top of the heap.

The Altmeyer theory of public administration stressed energetic recruitment, intense training, and politically sophisticated nonpartisanship for social security. By the 1960s the young generation of the New Deal were in their fifties. Already recruited to a career with social security, long-since trained in its ethos and practices, this cohort was like an elite spreading itself across SSA operations. Alvin David, one of the promising stars of the early 1940s, was head of policy planning. Ida Merriam brought scholarly industriousness to the division of research and statistics. Alanson Willcox was HEW's general counsel, with Irwin Wolkstein one of the SSA's most experienced policy and congressional experts. In medicare, Arthur Hess (who had administered the disability program) headed this large, new, important bureau. Finally, as actuary there was Robert Myers, the organization's key Republican, who combined nonpartisan technical expertise with a reputation for unquestioned integrity in the delivery of actuarial data.

These were the publicly visible social security executives. But supporting them, with long experience dating back to the very earliest days of the SSB, was another cadre—the general administrators. Hugh McKenna, for instance, was in at the beginning and moved from heading the district offices to directing the payment centers across the country. Joseph L. Fay was another example, the head of accounting whose career reached back into the 1930s, as was Jack Futterman, the expert in budgeting and financial management who was Bob Ball's executive assistant during these years. Oscar Pogge, the long-time bureau chief of OASI who had taken over when John Corson left that job, was a capable administrator. Ewell Bartlett, a lawyer who headed the claims policy unit, was, according to Ball, "very influential" inside the bureau. Continuity, cohesion of purpose, and proven experience made this team of the 1960s a public entrepreneur's dream. With its support, Cohen and Ball could negotiate the legislative, executive, and media environments with the assurance that internal administrative tasks would be reliably performed.[40] Within a very few years that reputation (and reality) was to change somewhat. But that takes us ahead of our story.

The 1960s closed with this organizational pattern intact. Only Cohen left the team, returning to the University of Michigan, this time as dean of education. But Cohen's departure caused hardly a ripple in the already well-established policy and administrative processes. The Vietnam War had defeated Johnson, and Nixon had brought a Republican team to HEW, but the SSA continued on its well-worn path.

The first Nixon administration constituted, for social security loyalists, a vindication of their organizational design for American social insurance. There was continuity at the top—with Ball the commissioner, the officially nonpartisan careerist leader who, with obvious Democratic affiliations, carried on the leadership of a largely mature organization. Incremental expansion had brought all the elements of the original social insurance design to the federal government: retirement protection, pensions for survivors, disability insurance, health insurance (albeit for the elderly alone under the SSA). Coverage was nearly universal; benefits were regularly adjusted to changing price and wage levels (and indexing was only to be the ratification of the recent patterns of adjustment). The bureaus were led by experienced managers trained within the agency supervising competent workers imbued with the confidence that they were doing well a job worth doing, if not with the clarity about the philosophy of social insurance that the policy experts and the top managers could recite as catechism. After twenty years of expansion, the major tasks were managerial, not policy transformation. The stage appeared set for adjustment and fine tuning, not major reconsiderations. As we know, this happy scenario did not transpire.[41] But its prospect in the 1968–72 period provides the context in which we can assess the impact of Ball and Cohen on the period of programmatic growth.

Both were central figures in the 1950s, when controversial new programs were devised, promoted, and, in the case of disability coverage, enacted and implemented. In both the disability and medicare cases, it was less that new ideas were introduced than that older visions were reintroduced in more amenable times. In his external role, Cohen was central to the nourishing of congressional allies and the accommodation of critics through cordial visits, respectful attention, and bipartisan offering of expertise on social policy initiatives. The instance of Kerr-Mills offers a good example of this support-building role, with Cohen the legislative author of a federal-state health program for the elderly poor that was far short of the medicare program he and others were energetically promoting. Ball remained throughout the explicator of social insurance, addressing Congress regularly, successfully, and confidently and making sure that the message of social security's mission was widely disseminated among the larger public. Both carried on the Altmeyer tradition of muted partisanship within the agency itself, nourishing particularly the Actuary Office's deserved reputation for unbiased technical competence.

What is more important, Cohen and Ball attended to the concern—an issue in all large organizations—of maintaining and enhancing the capacity of long-term employees to do their jobs efficiently, competently, and with an esprit de corps. Not only had they learned the lessons of

Altmeyer's administrative philosophy but they put them into practice. Altmeyer had emphasized attention to congressional constituencies, sensitivity to constitutional issues, and nurturing a workforce completely disassociated from congressional patronage. Training, research and information, an ethos of service toward entitled claimants—all were central to the technical competence and motivation of social security employees. It was the expectation that employees would extend themselves beyond the acceptable—to dispense, efficiently and courteously, the right social security check to the right person at the right time and in the right amount—that defined the administrative ideal. And to a considerable extent that ideal constituted the reputation, if not the full reality, of the organization Ball headed in 1968, as the Nixon administration took office. He had filled amply the shoes of the formative leader, Arthur Altmeyer. He enjoyed a cadre of competent, committed employees. He had, with the help of many others, continued the tradition of intensive training, identifying promising middle managers and encouraging their development. And he had found ways to nourish external constituencies during the very periods when large new administrative burdens—such as initiating medicare in 1966—faced the agency. For most of that period, Ball had concentrated on social security's administration but had cooperated with Cohen on the legislative tactics and strategy that brought disability and medicare to enactment. And during the 1960s, Cohen attended to the broader policy and political world, scanning the environment for threats and responding with the alertness of a family businessman. Ball was given wide discretion to scan the internal world of the SSA for vulnerability and remedial action, joining with Cohen as the twin spokesman for the flowered development of the New Deal's social policy initiatives.

The history of the period 1950–72 is one of substantial growth for the SSA and stable institutionalization of its organizational philosophy and operations. That history supports the assessment that both Ball and Cohen did their tasks well. But did they actually affect history? Would social security's growth and development have been notably different had other likely administrators filled their roles? That question we shall try to answer in the conclusion of this chapter. For now it is simply worth noting that the stresses at the end of this period were derisory compared with those that were to come. Welfare reform embroiled HEW in bitter wrangling during the first Nixon administration, and the enactment of the Supplemental Security Income (SSI) program in 1972 was to produce strains within the SSA, many of whose managers were not enthusiastic about implementing a means-tested program with an agency whose ethos subordinated such practices to its central mission of social insurance. But changes in the wider economic environment were to prove even more important to social security and the challenges its leaders faced through the 1970s.

Stagflation, Social Security, and Fiscal Strain: 1973 to the Present

The ten years from 1973 to 1983 were more difficult ones for the SSA than the preceding decade. Rapid inflation during the Vietnam War brought pressure to increase benefits, and amendments in 1972 both increased benefits by 20 percent across the board and automatically indexed future payments to inflation. Two developments brought unexpected controversy to this further improvement of social insurance benefits. Stagflation, which produced revenue losses simultaneously with benefit increases, ignited fears of financial insolvency and gave evidence of trust fund shortfalls by the mid-1970s. And a technical feature in the formula for indexation unexpectedly exacerbated the pressures by producing higher benefits than planned. By 1977, Congress had remedied the technical problem, but only after four years of persistent criticism that social security would, without change, "go broke." These twin developments, coming so soon after Ball and Cohen's heyday in office, caught the social security experts by surprise. Accustomed to negotiating quietly with their congressional overseers, both Ball and Cohen found themselves defending social security against the broadest of public criticisms.[42]

The pressure of stagflation—highlighted and worsened by the oil shocks of 1973 and 1974—brought increased media attention to social security, hitherto generally ignored by the nation's political reporters. The potential bankruptcy of the system became a major news story.[43] And at the same time, unexpected tasks were assigned to the SSA, which further damaged its previously untarnished reputation. The start-up in 1974 of SSI, the new federal welfare program for the aged, blind, and disabled, came precisely at the time that Ball and HEW Secretary Richardson were emerging from a social security struggle with the Republican White House. Ball had threatened to resign as commissioner so as to thwart President Nixon's plan to advertise the 20 percent benefit increase in notices sent to pensioners just before the 1972 election.

An additional problem emerged as well. The cadre of experienced administrators within social security was being rapidly depleted. Retirement held out nearly irresistible advantages for the Hesses, Wolksteins, Davids, and others of the Ball-Cohen generation. Civil service pay was frozen for much of the period from 1969–74, but retirement income was not. As inflation persisted, these officials lost considerable income each year they received frozen salaries rather than indexed civil service pensions. And the struggle within HEW made the sacrifice of income all the more galling. With Ball's departure, an additional incentive to stay on the job disappeared. Finally, the criticisms of the SSA's implementation of SSI—itself a program at odds with the social insurance tradition—brought unexpected denunciations of the SSA's administrative competence to a generation unused to such broadsides.[44]

The reactions of Ball and Cohen to this new context illustrate both their passion for social security institutions and their characteristic way of defending them. Ball took up residence as a senior scholar at the National Academy of Sciences Institute of Medicine and, after more than three decades "inside," spent part of his time defending social security from the outside. He began writing a book that would explain social security's principles and defend them against the now widely disseminated charges. His magnum opus, *Social Security: Today and Tomorrow*, published by Columbia University Press in 1978, is a four-hundred-page compendium of historical fact and social insurance theory organized around hundreds of questions for which Ball supplies reasoned answers. The book closes with thirty-one propositions to guide the less informed in their thinking about the future of American social security.

Ball also worked energetically with social security's allies in Congress. Based in Washington, Ball was somewhat more accessible to Congress than Cohen, in Michigan. Free to lobby openly, Ball found himself now in the position Cohen had occupied during the late 1950s. And lobby he did, in print and in person. The rhetorical flavor of his efforts is evident in the peroration to his 1978 book. Social security, Ball concludes, "is America's most successful program of social reform. Built on the conservative principles of self-help, with the protection growing out of the work that people perform, it has nevertheless created a revolution, transforming life for millions of our people from poverty and insecurity to relative economic well-being. An America without social security is almost unimaginable today" (487).

But Ball went on to question how much social security was wanted. He urged American workers to ask themselves how much they would "reduce a current level of living while at work in order to build protection against the loss of earnings because of old age, disability, and death." Unselfconsciously, Ball cast the question in the rhetoric of high purpose, the terms in which social insurance and the social gospel met. "Since the decision is so determining of the quality of our civilization," Ball concluded, "it cannot be made by each individual alone; it must be a collective decision," one, following Lincoln, that treats the government obligation to the community as doing "whatever they need to have done but cannot do at all or cannot do so well for themselves in their separate and individual capacities" (487).

Cohen was no less alarmed by this new round of fundamental assaults on social security in the 1970s. But he was now in a position to rally pressure groups as well as to consult with congressional offices. Both Ball and Cohen undoubtedly viewed the debacle of Watergate as the likely prelude to another Democratic administration in 1977. But neither could have predicted that the Carter victory of 1976 would embroil them in fights with prominent Democrats whose political reverence for social security they largely assumed. How Cohen and Ball responded to the struggle over social security between 1977 and 1983 will be our focus here. This choice means that much of the period will be left out. But our concern is not with the detailed history of social security in these years; it is with assessing the role Ball and Cohen played in that history.

The Carter administration was warmly welcomed by both Ball and Cohen. The new team at HEW—Joseph Califano and Hale Champion especially—knew them both and understood their revered reputation with the career staff of the department. And during the 1976 election, Ball had come to the attention of both Carter and Stuart Eisenstadt, later the White House policy chief. Since their joint service in the first Nixon administration, Ball had known Tom Joe, the experienced welfare expert who had done work in Georgia when Carter was governor. Ball was consulted regularly during the transition about how to solve the technical problem with indexation and what posture the HEW administration should take toward social security in the light of continued budget pressures. And Cohen, who had worked closely with Califano during the Johnson administration, had every reason to expect that he would be listened to. Champion, the broad-ranging undersecretary of HEW, as California's director of finance in the 1960s administration of Governor Pat Brown, had dealt regularly with Cohen on a variety of fiscally important matters in social welfare and had worked with Ball on the important 1977 amendments to social security.

The social policy strategy of the Carter administration centered first on welfare reform and second on national health insurance. Stalemated on reforming welfare, the Califano team, after studying national health insurance, opted to push hospital cost containment as a necessary first step toward any major expansion of America's welfare-state programs. By 1978 they realized that margins for adjustment of other HEW programs were severely restrained by rising inflation, serious unemployment, and budget pressures that partly resulted from both. To the surprise of Ball and Cohen, the HEW team then contemplated modest cutbacks in social security, if only to increase their room for maneuvering elsewhere. The members of the HEW team were neither enemies nor champions of social security. Califano was a generalist in-and-outer, ready to take each topic, problem, and assignment in turn. If the budget required trimming a valuable program, he reasoned, surely the gifted manager would administer the painful prescription. Champion, the versatile budget officer from the 1960s, was chastened by what he regarded as too many programs, too much spending, and all too little attention to disciplining the products of the New Deal and the Great Society. Simple arithmetic told him that no one could get a managerial hold on HEW without bringing social security's growth down. And Stan Ross, the new commissioner, was a Califano intimate who had practiced tax law and saw social security as another tax-transfer program that generalist managers could sensibly adjust if they turned their attention to it. Mandarins faced off against program loyalists, and the battle was at times fierce.

The struggle over social security during the later Carter administration is unintelligible at the level of budget and programmatic detail alone. The 1977 amendments shored up the social security trust funds and in their character revealed the influence of Ball, with administration and HEW backing, on the congressional deliberations. The hope was that those changes—increasing the percentage of worker incomes subject to the social security tax and increasing the tax level (in 1981, 1985, and 1990)—would leave the social security system "financially sound until the end of the century."[45] But by 1978–79 there were some doubts within the administration as to whether social security had been properly fixed for the long term. And within the Department of Health and Human Services (HHS) there were some controversial plans to cut benefits for short-term budget reasons.[46]

It was on that symbolic level—the proposed cutting of benefits during a Democratic administration—that HHS's managerial generalists and the social security entrepreneurs warred in 1978. Cohen, Ball, and Nelson Cruikshank, the long-term labor expert on social security who was also advising Carter within the White House, were aghast at what seemed to them HHS's apostasy.[47] They had a meeting with Califano and, in a much celebrated tiff, argued heatedly. In the end, very minor changes emerged from the Carter administration and its Congress. But rancor was there, and the struggle continued.

The Ball/Cohen struggle with Califano's generalist team had been bitter, instructive, and largely successful. The suggestions by Democratic officials of even small benefit cuts (burial benefits and college scholarships for survivors, to name the most prominent symbols) had broken a convention and would later ease the rhetorical way, after 1980, for the budget warriors within the Reagan administration. But Ball and Cohen saw the Califano team swept away in 1978–79; they greatly influenced, through Ball's White House connections, the selection of

William Driver as Stan Ross's successor as head of the SSA. What is most important, they helped arouse congressional and public opposition to treating social security cutbacks as just one of many ways to balance the federal budget. By the time of the election of 1980, Ball and Cohen were like a mobile government department, consulted by policy makers, preparing testimony, writing opinion pieces, appearing on television, and trying to persuade journalists to see the rightness of the social security cause.

This clash of generalist and program loyalists illustrates the distinctions we made earlier. Generalists move on; public entrepreneurs stick to their program. Since the Carter years, none of the Califano team has been central to deliberations over social security. Califano wrote a book about his cabinet experience, but social security figured as only one of many chapters; he now practices law in Washington and writes, as a member of Chrysler's board of directors, about the wonders wrought by business leadership in containing health costs. Champion returned to Harvard but devotes himself to broad public management issues, not the fate of social security in particular. And Stan Ross, the short-term commissioner, returned to tax law and occasionally testifies on social security issues.

Ball and Cohen, by contrast, have been tireless advocates during the Reagan period, seeking every opportunity to protect social security against budget cuts. The tax cuts of 1981, coupled with the rapid build-up of defense expenditures, put OASI (and Medicare) in a squeeze. The looming $200 billion budget deficit gave social security critics the occasion to criticize; the Reagan recession of 1982 brought renewed pressures to stave off bankruptcy, as OASI trust funds teetered on the brink of inadequacy. The congressional elections of 1982 made social security electorally relevent, and millions of elderly Americans, angered by Reagan's proposed benefit cuts after promising in 1980 to "leave social security alone," disproportionately changed from Republican to Democrat in their congressional choices. The program executives had survived a serious challenge, and although change was now necessary, they were well placed again to shape it.

On the outside, Cohen publicly led the forces of SOS ("Save Our Security"), calling upon former HEW secretaries such as Arthur Fleming, Elliot Richardson, and Robert Finch to criticize publicly the new assault on social security. Also on the outside, Ball, with the confidence of Speaker of the House Tip O'Neill and majority leader Jim Wright, was appointed to the bipartisan Social Security Commission of 1982–83. There he took the lead in negotiating the Democratic terms that Alan Greenspan (President Reagan's chairman) faced in extended bargaining sessions. In the end, the commission fashioned a bargain that raised social security taxes faster, trimmed some benefits slightly, and moved through Congress in 1983 largely unamended.[48]

The election year of 1972 marked, with the benefit of hindsight, the last period in which social security incrementally expanded without bruising conflict. Since then there has been serious dispute in Congress, dissension within several administrations, and, after the election of 1984, relative quiescence, but without even the hint of program expansion. During these recent years, Ball and Cohen, nominal retirees, were exceedingly active. The story we have told reveals the program loyalists hard at work, shoring up supportive constituencies and in a great variety of ways seeking to block any substantial revision of the program they both, in different ways, helped to expand. The efforts are obvious and the results clear.

By the mid-1980s, social security was again largely immune from annual retrenchment. So much was evident in the presidential election of 1984, when Ronald Reagan finally embraced social security with a clarity previously reserved to legatees of the New Deal. For all the uproar, the social security loyalists could rest content that the most fearful scenarios of disruption had been averted. But did our subjects make a substantial difference? Did they, with the forces at work precariously balanced, tilt the result toward program autonomy, stability, and continuity?

This question, like our earlier observations, takes us into the world of counterfactuals. What would developments have been, absent Ball and Cohen? There are good grounds for believing that the program entrepreneurs made a large difference during this period. It is well to begin with the differences they surely did not make. No one was attempting seriously to terminate a major social security program, though in 1981 Stockman's OMB sought substantial pension reductions. It is therefore foolish, given the absence of wholesale reversals in any industrial democracy during the period of stagflation, to attribute outright program "salvation" to our subjects. But if one asks what would have happened if they had retired from social security deliberations in American politics, the plausible answer includes some of the following.

The storm over SSI's implementation and the threatened deficits in social security would have been greater. Ball and Cohen were, as retirees, far more prominent in countering criticisms of social security than their formal replacements in the SSA and HEW. What is more important, it is likely that the congressional changes of 1977 would have made further inroads on benefits than they did. Later, Ball and Cohen checked the program-cutting enthusiasm of Califano's team in that period, using a variety of methods to constrain the choices of the HHS secretary and his appointees. They brought together the supporters of social security and, in the later deliberations of the 1983 commission, directly and indirectly led the way toward adjustments well within acceptable policies.

In the absence of Ball and Cohen, could other program loyalists— Arthur Fleming and Robert Myers, to name but two—have conducted the public and congressional battle that so constrained the Reagan administration in its 1981–83 handling of social security? There is no doubt that a popular program like social security had numerous public advocates—eloquent ones like Senator Moynihan, zealous ones like House Speaker O'Neill, experienced insiders like Myers. But could any of those have combined the program expertise, public prominence, and loyalist following in the way these two retirees did? It is doubtful.

The irony, to which we shall return shortly, is that these program entrepreneurs seemed most powerful when their cause was threatened. The analogy is to the firm in distress, calling upon its older executives to lead the way out of trouble. The ability of Ball and Cohen to combine political acumen, commitment, and competence was unrivaled. In the earlier period there was a cohort committed to the expansion of social insurance; had Ball and Cohen disappeared, the broad shape of the 1960s would have been little different. It may be that they managed the expansion better than others—got a bit more, enlisted additional support, administered with a healthier contribution to agency morale. But it is less clear that the SSA would have been radically different in 1970 without them.

The special challenge of macroeconomic misery is quite another story. In 1970, social security was an exceedingly popular program. Nearly two decades later, it is a stable program, little changed in its fundamentals. Its popularity explains much of the hesitancy of those politicians who would otherwise have liked to see the program substantially transformed. But it is in the extended fight over decrements that these seasoned loyalists had their greatest effect. The public today is worried about social security's future. Polls show a degree of uncertainty about future benefits among current workers that actuarial experts would deem foolish.[49] Even if social security is not in equilibrium in the larger polity, its legislative position is secure, the period of immediate crisis is over, and few Democrats or Republicans think there is any advantage to be gained in attacking the program frontally. That was not obvious in the worst of the stagflation period and, particularly, in the early days of the Reagan administration. Take Ball and Cohen out of the picture from 1974 to 1983 and it is hard to imagine, from the standpoint of social security's admirers, a less benign counterfactual.

Conclusion

By 1985 the politics of social security had moved almost full circle. Begun as a separate Social Security Board in 1935, the administration of social insurance had been from the outset in the hands of experienced managers devoted to a cause. Over the next fifty years each cohort replaced itself with like-minded managers and policy makers. Altmeyer and Brown begat Cohen, Ball, David, and others, while Cohen and Ball begat Hess and Wolkstein among others. The organization moved in the 1950s from board status, separately financed and separately administered, to an agency position, separately budgeted and within HEW. By the late 1960s the SSA was firmly enough established that its leaders, while admittedly uncertain that they could prevail, did not vigorously resist its inclusion within a unified federal budget. Now, after a decade of bruising conflict, the loyalists have opted again for a separate organizational form, a Social Security Board, bipartisan at the top, separate from HHS, staffed by a career service in the mold of Altmeyer's formative vision.[50] All of this has ingredients of a cabal, a dedicated band of enthusiasts trying to protect social security from the discipline of both congressional mandates and executive control by the temporary incumbents of the White House.

There is much truth in the description of a dedicated group of social security advocates pressing for expansion and fighting off retrenchment.[51] The principal figures of this essay indeed devoted their careers to the social security system, as I have argued. But their principal scholarly critic, Martha Derthick, while accepting this portrait of their efforts, suggests that Ball and Cohen and their allies were excessively influential, designing "social security to be uncontrollable." For Derthick it would have been better to have policy formulated in a more open, democratic forum.[52]

This argument is, according to one interpretation, simply untenable. Since Derthick disapproves of the explosive growth of social security in the 1960s and 1970s, she thinks a more open debate might have forestalled that expansion. What we know in the 1980s is that the more open the debate the more unlikely are cuts in social security. The roles Cohen and Ball played in the 1970s and 1980s are inconceivable in the absence of broad public support for social insurance. The reason Jimmy Carter turned to Ball for advice is that Ball spoke on behalf of an enormously popular institution. The fact that Cohen could quickly organize SOS—and enlist the cooperation of former HEW secretaries both Democratic and Republican—depended less on conspiracy than on reflected influence. What influence Ball and Cohen had on the big questions of social security rested not only on secret deals but on congressional appreciation of the electoral consequences of tinkering with social security. The influence of Ball and Cohen is less that of secret negotiators than that of gifted articulators of a popular mission.

Indeed, the impact of these two figures lies as much in their public articulateness as in their quiet bargaining. From the mid-1940s to the publication of his massive book on social security in the late 1970s, Ball was faithful to the conception of the public administrator as educator (or "marketer," in the jargon of business schools). His enunciation of the doctrine of entitlement—in testimony, on radio and television, in books and articles—became its standard expression. In this sense Ball was not only the inside administrator, steeped in the details of social security's operations, but the exemplar of an important "external" ingredient in the search for managerial excellence. The capacity to articulate a mission and the ability to ensure that an organization delivers on its promises are crucial to the institutionalization of an organization operating across a country as large as the United States. Personal ties, charismatic flourishes, and bargaining across tables cannot explain the transformation of a fledgling organization—SSB—into the large, efficient, and reliable SSA of the 1960s. To a considerable degree, Ball was the public emblem of social security, the negotiator in the environment of America's tumultuous politics. And for this, he, more than Cohen, helped to turn social security into an institution that even the Republican rule of the past fifteen years has been unable to turn back.

The combination of internal attention to performance and external attention to support typifies Ball's efforts to shape social security. When Herbert Kaufman, in his interesting account of the lives of federal bureau chiefs, regards these officials as severely limited in shaping institutional direction, he omits the Robert Balls of the administrative world. He finds short tenure and busy fire fighting the standard story.[53] But Ball had long tenure and fought fires in connection with a long-term objective; and the effect he had is found in part in the internal adaptability of the managers and operators he helped to train and the supportive public he helped to create. The impact of a leader like Ball is shown as much by the resiliency of an organization under siege as it is by the dramatic contests of television and Washington gossip.

Cohen's influence has been as great as Ball's but slightly different in character. Ball took care of social security's operations from the early 1950s through 1973. Cohen took charge of the process of coordinating congressional mandates, background research, and support within the executive branch and the labor unions. He played this role while holding a number of official positions whose formal titles tell us little about what he did. He was confidant to the early leaders and managed the search for, and the distillation of, policy ideas until he left government in 1956.

Once outside government, Cohen continued to play the same role, keeping his house in Washington while living in Ann Arbor, Michigan. And when he returned to government in the Kennedy administration, he was arguably the most important official within HEW. Both President Kennedy and President Johnson placed a great deal of trust in Cohen, allowing him a high degree of autonomy, and he was relied upon by Ribicoff, Celebrezze, and Gardner to guide the course of health insurance legislation. Cohen's commitment to his program's goals extended beyond the temporal boundaries of formal office: both in and out of official roles, he used the expertise of many others to serve a set of related ends.

Were these men giants in their own time? Did they attend to all the tasks of great public entrepreneurship? Here a number of observations arise from the narrative of the preceding pages. The formative years of social security were not reflections of our program loyalists. As we have argued, both Ball and Cohen learned crucial lessons during the reign of Arthur Altmeyer, but as young, promising team members, not entrepreneurs in their own right. They were, as noted earlier, crucial members, not leaders, of the early team.

The period of social security's great expansion emerged from the vision of the founders. During the 1950s and 1960s Ball and Cohen did not embark on any new programs unnoticed by the first generation of leaders. Indeed, what they did was to nourish program expansion with their legislative skill and administrative expertise. What they represented during expansion was continuity of the central presumptions of the founders. Not everyone within social security had felt deeply the teaching of Altmeyer, Brown, and the others for whom the history, philosophy, and administrative style of social insurance constituted a secular creed. To continue its expansion required some measure of what we identify as entrepreneurial qualities. Ball and Cohen nourished external constituencies as they sought program expansion along lines widely accepted by insiders. They worried about both the competence of routine administration and the training of recruits to the service philosophy of social insurance. They were attentive to scandal and maintained, during expansion, an organization with a remarkable record of prudent behavior. They took seriously the gathering of information about program operation and not only motivated many to extend themselves but supported training for each level of the organization. And, importantly, they remained attentive to threats within and without the organization, Ball responsible for internal matters and Cohen attentive to any vulnerability in the wider environment. Above all, they stayed with the program long enough to put their own stamp on its operations. Their own stamp, however, was a close facsimile of what their mentor Altmeyer would have done in those years. Impact they had, but along lines that one could imagine others, albeit with fewer gifts, having had as well.

The clear answer is that Ball and Cohen were giants, but with a crucial failing. What they were unable to do was ensure the supply of similarly gifted and wide-ranging leaders to follow them. Ball tells an interesting story about how Altmeyer, once retired, left social security alone. He told Ball that it was time for another generation to take over and that they did not need the meddling of the founders.[54] Neither Ball nor Cohen could afford to take this luxurious course; Altmeyer had them, as well as the Davids, Hesses, Merriams, and Wolksteins who supported Cohen and Ball. Ball and Cohen did not have comparable successors. And so for the 1970s and 1980s these two men in their sixties and seventies came to personify the current leadership of social security.

But why was that so? Only partly was it a matter of presidents' wanting to choose their own people from a pool uncontaminated by deep program commitment. It was also that mandarins appealed comparatively because the supply of social security entrepreneurs was so thin. This is not to suggest that the SSA lacked figures of distinction. Rather, it is that they fell into two groups neither of which had the requisite gifts and training to play the roles Cohen and Ball had performed. They were either specialists in policy and congressional relations—Merriam, Fullerton, and Wolkstein, to name just three—or specialists in program operations. Ball and Cohen, as mentors, did not give enough attention to the formative experiences they themselves had had at the side of the Altmeyers, Corsons, and others of the early period. They did not make sure that promising administrators were rotated through the policy-making, research, and congressional relations worlds so as to acquire, firsthand, different understandings of the threats and opportunities facing social insurance. Nor did they turn policy experts into field managers on loan, thus copying the pattern of almost every successful large corporation in American life.

The key point of this essay—that managerial skill and program zeal must be fused for long-term institutional impact—becomes the criterion by which the stewardship of Ball and Cohen is to be criticized. However gifted they were and however influential they were in negotiating social security's path to a secure place in American government, they did not produce their own institutional children.[55] And in the end, their retirement was much busier than Altmeyer's, testimony to their devotion, their continued gifts, and their major disappointment.

Notes

Philip Fellman, a Yale graduate student in management, ably assisted in initial research and drafted early versions of parts of this chapter. Others were extraordinarily helpful in their comments, taking time to read drafts carefully and to make detailed suggestions for revisions. I particularly want to thank my colleagues Jim Fesler and Robert Lane for such assistance during what was supposed to be their retirement from political science. This volume's editors, Jim Doig and Erwin Hargrove, were stimulating critics and sympathetic editors, and I am exceedingly grateful for that. Students in a seminar I taught with Professor Jerry Mashaw on America's welfare state made constructive suggestions at a later stage. But four persons require special note. My colleague and friend Jerry Mashaw was instrumental beyond his knowledge in stimulating my thinking about America's social insurance. Elizabeth Auld, my assistant, provided the typing, editing and balanced good sense that is so necessary in an extended essay of this sort. Lastly, I want to thank my subjects— Bob Ball and Wilbur Cohen—for their cooperation in this enterprise and others. They generously provided detailed comments on a draft of this chapter and answered innumerable telephone inquiries. I am very grateful for such help, as I was twenty years ago when Wilbur Cohen took me in as his assistant in the first months of medicare's administration.

1. For a recent, thoughtful treatment of the gap between American political beliefs and practice see Samuel P. Huntington, *American Politics: The Promise of Disharmony* (Cambridge: Harvard University Press, Belknap Press, 1981), 39–41, 167–73.

2. It may well be the case that the American form of politics requires entrepreneurial gifts—especially dedicated effort over very long periods of time—to produce lasting policy and organizational changes. This, at least, is the presumption of this chapter. The illustrations from the careers of Ball and Cohen make the presumption more plausible but do not, of course, make the case for its truth. This point emerged in useful conversations between the author and one of the book's editors, Erwin Hargrove, 11 September 1985.

3. The attribution to Ball and Cohen of influence in matters large and small is quite commonplace. Some analysts, skeptical of the commitment to expanding social insurance that Ball, Cohen, and others represented, stress the collaboration of these "program" executives, congressional Democrats, and organized labor. In Martha Derthick's reading, all of these program executives made most of America's social insurance policy. That "relatively constricted and autonomous set of actors with a strong sense of proprietorship in the program" operated so that "decisions about social security were generally made in isolation from decisions about other governmental activities, both structurally and financially," with the result that the "dominant mode [of policy] was maintenance and enlargement of the program." (*Policymaking for Social Security* [Washington, D.C.: Brookings Institution, 1979], 76).

Historical analysts less critical of social security's growth unselfconsciously report the "clout" of both Ball and Cohen (see Paul Light's *Artful Work: The Politics of Social Security Reform* [New York: Random House, 1985], 180; and W. Andrew Achenbaum, *Social Security: Visions and Revisions* [New York: Cambridge University Press, 1986], 39).

4. Namely, the old-age and survivors insurance (pension) program of 1939 (OASI), the disability program of 1956 (DI), the "welfare" programs of Aid to Families with Dependent Children (AFDC), Older Americans Act (OAA), and, since 1972, Supple-

mental Security Income (SSI), the medicare and medicaid programs of 1965, and the wider net of educational, public health, and child service programs that have developed since 1935. Derthick presumes that the social security system would have been very different if the program executives, especially Cohen and Ball, had encouraged the consideration of major alternatives (*Policymaking,* 7).

5. Gaylord Nelson, foreword to Robert M. Ball, *Social Security: Today and Tomorrow* (New York: Columbia University Press, 1978), vii–x; Frank D. Campion, *The AMA and U.S. Health Policy since 1940* (Chicago: Chicago Review Press, 1984), 117–18; Derthick, *Policymaking,* 64, 391.

6. Ball's later prominence in the SSA is well known; his initial start is not. In 1942 Ball was promoted to the central office as chief of an editorial unit in the analysis division of OASI. This was followed by a posting in August 1942 to the training office at the BOASI, where he remained until 1945.

7. Entrepreneurial enterprise in public management is not a well-charted field of inquiry. Studies of entrepreneurial personalities are common, but they concentrate almost exclusively on private firms. Moreover, the studies are usually short-term in perspective, focused on how ideas turn into businesses that grow rapidly and make their founders economic tycoons. And just as surely has come the problem of adapting the bright upstart to new competitors and the managerial tasks of large corporate enterprise. If Steve Jobs, the founder of Apple Computer, is an emblem of the free-spirited, inventive entrepreneur, then John Scully, Jobs's replacement as head of Apple, stands for the disciplined skills of trained managers who have to put entrepreneurial houses in order. A dichotomy has emerged—entrepreneur versus manager—that even in the field of private management casts a partial shadow over the heroic image of the individualistic entrepreneur of the small, struggling firm.

There are, however, some studies of long-term organizational leadership of the sort Ball and Cohen represent. Annmarie Walsh has charted the careers of leaders in public authorities in *The Public's Business: The Politics and Practices of Government Corporations* (Cambridge: MIT Press, 1978). Interesting private analogies include the development of McDonald's, charted by Thomas J. Peters and Robert H. Waterman, Jr., *In Search of Excellence: Lessons from America's Best-Run Companies* (New York: Harper & Row, 1982), and of Hewlett-Packard, described by Bro Uttal in "Mettle-Test Time for John Young," *Fortune,* 29 April 1985, 242.

8. Ball points out, for instance, that we miss the important category of the dedicated career administrator at the second, third, and fourth levels—the district office managers as well as mid-level managers in the central office, a category we call "competent loyalists." These individuals are comparable to career people in the military, the foreign service, or the public health service. In their loyalty to one program and their quite capable managing of their part of that program, they fall between the administrative zealots and the high-level program loyalists; they are, in short, competent program managers.

9. Wilbur Cohen is fond of recalling instances of gifted theoreticians in economics and social analysis who wanted to "tinker" with a social security system whose organizational mission, internal structure, and operating history they did not understand. The clash of bright zealots is all the more difficult to manage when their expertise leads to conflicting claims, a development likely to arise as large units like the SSA or the Department of Defense require annual budgetary review, enabling legislation, or legislative amendment.

10. The top of the British civil service is in fact so labeled in popular discourse. For a useful portrait of higher civil servants in Europe see James Fesler, "The Higher Public Service in Western Europe," in *A Centennial History of the American Ad-*

ministrative State, ed. Ralph Clark Chandler (New York: John Wiley & Sons, in press).

11. Derthick, *Policymaking*, 34–55, 58–59, 329.

12. First with Witte from 1934 to 1935, he worked from 1935 to 1953 directly for Arthur Altmeyer, the first career head of the Social Security Board (SSB). John Wynant, of New Hampshire, was the first short-term head of the SSB. Altmeyer was an original member of the board and became chairman in 1937 (ibid., 18–19).

13. From 1935 to 1946 the SSB was responsible for administering old age insurance and the other programs authorized by the Social Security Act. The bureau within the SSB in charge of old age insurance was called first the Bureau of Federal Old Age Benefits, then the Bureau of Old Age Insurance, and then, after the 1939 amendments, the Bureau of Old Age Survivors Insurance (BOASI). In 1946 the SSB was replaced by the SSA, but it continued to oversee the BOASI and the bureaus responsible for the other programs. In 1963, following a reorganization of HEW, the SSA became responsible only for old age, survivors, and disability insurance; the other programs were moved to other units of HEW (ibid., 18).

14. Ibid., 320, 323, 329; Theodore R. Marmor, *The Politics of Medicare* (Chicago: Aldine, 1973), 60–61, esp. 64. See also Richard Harris, *New Yorker*, 9 July 1966, 35; and Campion, *The AMA and U.S. Health Policy*, 254–56, 268.

15. It is worth noting that in Derthick's landmark history of social security policy making there are no citations in the index to John Gardner and Anthony Celebrezze and only two to Abraham Ribicoff, all secretaries of HEW during the period 1961–68.

16. Ball moved in and out of the executive branch during this crucial decade. In February 1946, Ball reports, he left the government to form, with Karl de Schwinitz at the American Council on Education, a university government center devoted to training upper-level employees in OASI, unemployment insurance, and public welfare, as well as university and college teachers who covered social security in their courses. In November 1947 he was named staff director to a citizens' advisory committee on social security to the U.S. Senate Finance Committee. Ball returned to the government in late 1949 as an assistant director of the BOASI in charge of research and statistics (Ball, comments to the author, November 1985).

17. Derthick, *Policymaking*, 19. See also Gaylord Nelson, foreword to Ball, *Social Security*, vii–viii.

18. The exact circumstances of Ball's leaving SSA and the proper interpretation of it are subject to some disagreement. Some interpret the change as Nixon's "firing" of Ball. As Ball himself acknowledges, the Nixon administration "had decided that the small number of Democratic holdovers in high office would go" and that he could "not have stayed in the second Nixon term." But others, including Ball, suggest that "firing" wrongly suggests a personal rejection of Ball. "Had Richardson stayed at HEW," Ball comments, "he might have prevented my departure, but Cap Weinberger became Secretary of HEW, had had little association with me, and had no reason to fight for my continuation in office."

Ball emphasizes his willingness to leave, but reveals the program loyalist in his qualifications. He reports making "no attempt to use any outside groups or Hill influence to try to stay on." Though Ball did not "fancy staying on under Weinberger in a second Nixon administration in any event," he does say that he would have felt some obligation to try to put the SSI program into effect along with the other 1972 amendments had they wanted him to stay. What is clear is the respect Ball earned from the Nixon cabinet and widely enjoyed within the department. He left in the wake of a series of receptions and farewells, culminating in a reception at the State

Department that had Jack Veneman, undersecretary of HEW, as master of ceremonies, with several cabinet officers attending, including Weinberger, George Schultz,
and Elliot Richardson. Departure though it was, Ball's leaving the government could
hardly be called a typical firing of the other party's social security official. (Ball,
comments to the author, November 1985).

19. Achenbaum, *Social Security*, chap. 3.

20. Ball, comments to the author, November 1985; Derthick, *Policymaking*, 64,
n. 2; Edward D. Berkowitz, "The First Social Security Crisis," *Prologue: The Journal
of the National Archives* 15, no. 3 (Fall 1983): 133, n. 2.

Since leaving the cabinet in 1968, Cohen has remained active in the social welfare
field. He served on the National Commission on Social Security from 1978–81, was
from 1978–80 chairman of the National Commission on Unemployment Compensation, and won a variety of public-service awards, including the Jane Addams–Hull
House Award, the International Association for Social Security Award, the Merrill-
Palmer Award, and the Foran Award of the National Council of Senior Citizens.
Cohen continues to be active as a teacher and social welfare consultant; he is currently
professor of public affairs at the Lyndon Baines Johnson School of Public Policy at
the University of Texas at Austin.

Following his retirement from the SSA, Ball remained active as a consultant
and policy advocate on social security matters. Specifically, he has been a senior
scholar at the Institute of Medicine (National Academy of Sciences), as well as visiting
scholar at the Center for the Study of Social Policy. He provided continued advice
on social security to those who would listen and was a member of the 1978–79
Advisory Council on Social Security and of the 1982–83 National Committee on
Social Security Reform (1982). Like Cohen, Ball has received a bevy of awards for
public service, including the HEW Distinguished Service Award (1954), the National
Civil Service League's Career Service Award (1958), the Rockefeller Public Service
Award (1961), and the Clarence A. Kulp Award (1980).

Both Ball and Cohen became founding members of the National Academy of
Social Insurance in 1986.

21. This history is admirably told by Arthur Altmeyer in *The Formative Years
of Social Security* (Madison: University of Wisconsin Press, 1966), esp. chaps. 1–4.

22. Ball is fond of pointing this out in response to Martha Derthick's penchant
for seeing Cohen and Ball as leaders of a social security cabal (Ball, comments to
the author, November 1985).

23. Robert M. Ball, "The 1939 Amendments to the Social Security Act and What
Followed," in *The Report of the Committee on Economic Security of 1935*, Fiftieth
Anniversary Edition (Washington, D.C.: National Conference on Social Welfare, 1985),
161–72.

24. It is difficult, some thirty years later, to recall the precariousness of social
security's retirement program in the late 1940s, but the threats to its survival were
vivid to its administrators at the time. A decade had passed, with only reduced
coverage to show. Benefits had increased by only 10 percent, to an average monthly
level of twenty-five dollars, while both inflation and wage levels had increased much
faster. Even more important, old-age assistance—the "welfare" payment to destitute
retirees—had twice as many beneficiaries in 1949 as OASI. In addition, OAA monthly
benefits had doubled since 1939, to an average level of forty-two dollars. It was in
this context—one that Arthur Altmeyer characterized as "decisive as to whether the
OASI system would survive as a contributory wage-related" program (Altmeyer,
Formative Years, 169)—that Ball worked with the Senate advisory committee. That
committee's role in Ball's career, and in fashioning knowledgeable and sympathetic

senators and staff, was more than the lateral movement of what we have called the government mandarin. It was social security work "on the outside."

25. Cf. n. 24; and Altmeyer, *Formative Years*, chap. 7, "The Crucial Years, 1948– 52," 169–208.

26. See Deborah Stone, *The Disabled State* (Philadelphia: Temple University Press, 1983).

27. How successful they were at these tasks is illustrated in Robert M. Ball, "Assignment of the Commissioner of Social Security" (Mimeograph, 1972), 1–5. The formulation of this aim of routinized benefit/tax adjustments is clear in Altmeyer, *Formative Years*, 231.

28. Altmeyer, *Formative Years*, 48, 52–53, and esp. 239.

29. The public administration theories of social security's founders are less widely known than their conception of social insurance. Altmeyer's institutional history, *Social Security: The Formative Years*, pays explicit attention to what was needed to get the program properly started and expertly maintained. He was particularly concerned with questions of "constitutionality, administrative feasibility, and congressional relations," noting that those executive officials who ignore the latter are "apt to find their appropriations and legislative programs (suffering) accordingly." He was preoccupied with the importance of ridding social security of the legacy of welfare office patronage in the states and localities; he was equally concerned with the pressure from Congress for patronage appointments in the midst of the Great Depression. His faith was in the appointment of dedicated and highly qualified individuals, on a "nonpolitical basis," who would set the tone for social security's administration and, with the freedom to "select equally dedicated and qualified staff," assure that administrative compliance with the spirit of social insurance would be regularly expected. The model was one of nonpartisan merit appointment, extensive training, continuing research, and a posture of expert advice on social insurance matters to all those in Congress who requested it. Above all, he argued, "the success of any organization, governmental or private, is largely dependent upon having officials who are completely committed to carrying out the purpose of the organization." He warned explicitly about drawing social insurance's top leaders from the pool of able generalists, arguing that "if leaders owe their appointment to someone outside of the organization, there is always the danger of conflict of loyalties affecting their actions" (ibid., 15, 51, 48).

30. See ibid., 52–53, for concurrence with this view.

31. Joseph A. Pechman, Henry J. Aaron, and Michael K. Taussig, *Social Security: Perspectives for Reform* (Washington, D.C.: Brookings Institution, 1968), table B-8; Peter J. Ferrara, *Social Security: The Inherent Contradiction* (San Francisco: Cato Institute, 1980), tables 1 and 2; Ball, *Social Security*, 107.

32. Of the twelve thousand employees in 1950, just over five thousand worked in Baltimore; of the fifty thousand working for the SSA in 1970, almost two-fifths were in the central office (SSA, personal communication, June 1986).

33. Derthick, *Policymaking*, 300–314; interviews with Ball, August 1985, and Roswell Perkins, 1983.

34. This story has been told elsewhere. See Marmor, *The Politics of Medicare*; Richard Harris, *A Sacred Trust* (New York: New American Library, 1966); and Altmeyer, *Formative Years*, 193–94, 262–69.

35. Altmeyer, *Formative Years*, 193.

36. Cf. Marmor, *The Politics of Medicare*, 36; and Derthick, *Policymaking*, 323– 24.

37. See n. 29.

38. Marmor, *The Politics of Medicare*, 88–90.

39. For a discussion of how policy decisions made in the course of implementation rendered the job of containing costs more difficult over the next twenty years see Theodore R. Marmor, "Medicare at Twenty," in *Social Security in Contemporary American Politics*, ed. T. R. Marmor and J. L. Mashaw, in preparation; and Lawrence D. Brown, "Technocratic Corporatism and Administrative Reform in Medicare," *Journal of Health Politics, Policy and Law* 10, no. 3 (Fall 1985).

Ball's account of this period stresses the gap between the issues of 1965–66, the early 1970s, and the very different 1980s. He explains that "the general concern [when medicare was passed in 1965] was that the new program not make basic changes in the health care system. . . . The majority opinion [in 1972] clearly supports the use of any large-scale paying mechanism like medicare not merely to relieve an economic risk, but to help provide the leverage to bring about constructive change in the delivery of health care. Today the operation of [medicare] is more apt to be criticized for interfering too little, rather than not interfering enough" ("Assignment" 48–49).

40. Ball and Cohen, interview by the author, September 1985; and Ball's comments, November 1985).

41. Ball's presumptions about the future were written down in his 1972 sketch of the commissioner's job. The "current state of the social security cash benefit program," he wrote, "appears to be one of considerable stability." He regarded the changes made in 1972 as having "settled many important questions about the future of the program, and major change is not to be expected for a considerable period of time." Where Ball erred as a futurist was in imagining the indexing of benefits and future tax requirements as essentially stable. Had the stability Ball predicted come to pass, Cohen and he would have been far less busy in retirement than they, in fact, have been.

42. Ball, *Social Security*, 44–45.

43. Publications ranging from *Time Magazine* to the *New York Review of Books* treated the impending crisis in social security with such headlines as "What the Nation Can Afford: A Debt-threatened Dream" (*Time*, 24 May 1982) and "Social Security: The Coming Crash" (Peter G. Peterson, *New York Review of Books*, 2 December 1982). Ferrara, in *Social Security: The Inherent Contradiction*, devotes one full chapter to the topic of social security and bankruptcy.

44. Beryl Radin, "Can We Learn from Experience? The Case of SSI," *Policy Analysis*, Fall 1976, 615–21.

45. Ben W. Heineman, Jr., and Curtis A. Hessler, *Memorandum for the President: A Strategic Approach to Domestic Affairs in the 1980s* (New York: Random House, 1980), 354.

46. In 1978, with the creation of a separate Department of Education, the Department of Health, Education, and Welfare became known as the Department of Health and Human Services.

47. Cohen, in comments to the author, 25 October 1985, illustrated this view of the mandarins' strategy: "The fundamental error made by Califano-Carter, Champion, and Ross was their belief they could tinker with details of the social security program to make it more 'efficient' and cost-beneficial without undermining the statutory commitment embodied in the contributory entitlement system. They thought they could make the girl just a little bit pregnant without involving any moral question. They did not comprehend the implications of reducing benefits on the confidence of the contributors to the system. They justified their meager and minimal changes by calling Ball, Cohen, and Cruikshank the 'high priests' who believed the

system was 'sacrosanct.' What they did not appreciate was that a Democratic administration tinkering at the margins gave others a basis for justifying radical changes at the center, as was the case of President Reagan on May 12, 1981."

48. The story of how this bargain was struck is to be found in Light, *Artful Work.*

49. James Tobin, "The Future of Social Security: One Economist's Assessment," in Marmor and Mashaw, *Social Security in Contemporary American Society.*

50. In 1986 such a proposal passed in the House of Representatives, but its future in the Senate in 1986 is doubtful.

51. Derthick, *Policymaking,* 416–17.

52. Ibid., 417–21; the quotation is on 417.

53. Herbert Kaufman, *The Administrative Behavior of Federal Bureau Chiefs* (Washington, D.C.: Brookings Institution, 1981), 135, 174.

54. Ball, interview with the author, June 1986.

55. The subjects of this chapter are, understandably, reluctant to accept this characterization. As Ball writes, "We tried pretty hard to produce institutional children." Indeed they did, sponsoring the ordinary training and middle-management courses that any responsible administrator of a large agency would embrace. There are still those "developed during the Ball-Cohen years," as Cohen reminds the author, "who are active and influential in key places in the Social Security Administration." And, indeed, there are such persons, as I have suggested. But the problem is indirectly suggested by Ball's wondering "whether there is any way to develop clones or something close to clones." It is the special, wide-ranging nature of the Ball-Cohen leadership that I am addressing, not the continued presence of capable, competent program managers.

The irony is that twin forces, largely outside the control of Ball and Cohen, may well have made their efforts to perpetuate their leadership more difficult. One was the effect of an early cohort, a set of managers brought into an organization young and trained by the founding leaders to assume high responsibility. Ball and Cohen took on this role skillfully, but it was difficult, given their extended period of leadership, to keep others ready, waiting to take on the preeminent position. Moreover, social security, once established, had a harder time attracting to it the most vigorous new civil service recruits. Other causes, particularly civil rights in the 1960s and environmental protection in the 1970s, were bound to attract those who in the 1930s would have gravitated to new programs like social security. The first of these factors was a necessary consequence of the enduring role of our subjects; the second presented constraints for which one is hard pressed to imagine remedies. But it is interesting to note that both Ball and Cohen took the lead in establishing a National Academy of Social Insurance in 1986. Their purpose, as Cohen noted explicitly, is to "extend into the future the role of those who support, as experts, the principles of social insurance." This move in the 1980s is testimony that despite great effort, the leadership transition of the 1970s was incomplete. (comments to the author: Ball, November 1985, and Cohen 25 October 1984).

9

Elmer Staats and Strategic Leadership in the Legislative Branch

Wallace Earl Walker

O rganizational leadership is an arcane endeavor. It sounds simple when described. Essentially it entails diagnosis, formulation, and implementation. That is, leaders must define the situation facing the organization, formulate a course of action to address the situation, and implement that course of action by mobilizing support.[1]

But like any organizational activity, the simplest things are very difficult in practice. Difficulties accumulate such that organizational leadership is like movement at night in an unfamiliar and fast-flowing river. In such circumstances, every motion is surprisingly slow and subject to careful calculation. The resistance encountered is beyond the ken of most observers, who masquerade as knowledgeable critics but are essentially weak swimmers. Strong and experienced swimmers know to move downstream, working with and not against the current. And yet, even the experienced continually encounter unexpected obstacles. Varying winds and other obstacles endow the sport with unique episodes which must be anticipated but not feared.[2] As this metaphor is meant to suggest, organizational leadership is the most talked about, but least studied and understood, phenomenon in organizational life. This chapter seeks to develop propositions about organizational leadership and to apply these propositions to the comptroller general of the United States.

The obstacles to organizational leadership may be classified into two categories: environmental and institutional. The environmental obstacles include the agendas and demands of the organization's overseers, such as superordinate departments; presidential agencies, such

The views contained herein do not necessarily reflect those of the Department of Defense, the Department of the Army, or the U.S. Military Academy.

as the Office of Management and Budget; members of Congress, their subcommittees, and staffs; and congressional support agencies, such as the Office of Technology Assessment. Also included are the organization's constituencies inside and outside the government, as well as stagnant technologies that continue to be accepted in spite of their lack of suitability for public needs.

Institutional obstacles also constrain leaders. Executive and career elites may resist change, as might professionals who design and implement organizational policy. Hierarchical arrangements, institutional planning, and review procedures also can impede new organizational designs. Finally, institutional regulations, precedents, routines, and operating procedures also are constraints on leaders.[3] To borrow from Herbert Kaufman, organizational leaders are "almost sure to encounter vigorous obstacles in the form of organized resistance from individuals and groups both inside and outside [the organization]."[4]

At times these obstacles may present opportunities. Elements in the environment or the institution may demand or be amenable to change, thereby permitting creative leaders to redesign the enterprise. Where such demands exist both in the environment and in the institution, strategic leadership is possible. Such leadership is the entrepreneurial spirit applied to public organization. The mission is realignment of organizational culture. It entails three tasks: a new or transformed vision for the organization, a new structure for the enterprise, and new policies to implement both the vision and the structure. This new vision initially provides a "potent mechanism for directing and influencing others."[5] As it is adopted and internalized, it becomes the new organizational ideology.

Strategic leaders must also fundamentally alter the structure or form of the organization. Such fundamental shifts restructure internal relationships, patterns of behavior, and professional outlooks. Also required in such shifts are policy changes to accommodate such a restructuring. Structural change may modify the institution's hierarchy, planning system, or administrative processes. It may also modify the personnel system, which entails the procedures for managing executive and career elites and for recruiting, socializing, training, and promoting new professionals.[6]

Strategic leaders must be creative. Creativity demands gifts of both intellect and temperament. The intellectual gifts required are not those of brilliance, but rather the capacity of a strong mind disposed to inquiry, skepticism, and a comprehensive approach to problems. Such a mind possesses the trait described as *coup d'oeil*—the ability to see the truth simply, quickly, and clearly.

The second gift demanded of creative leaders is a sound temperament. Such a temperament is composed of determination, nerve, and character. Determination is the courage to face unexpected obstacles without fear or hesitation and the persistence to follow a course of action wherever it might lead. Steady nerves are needed to deal with the unexpected, to respond to external assaults on a course of action, and to resist for prolonged periods the friction implicit in organizational leadership. Finally, a strong character is needed to repel obstacles. As Clausewitz put it, such character can "summon the titanic strength it takes to clear away the enormous burdens that obstruct activity."[7]

Thus, leadership is a seasonal and contingent endeavor. The season is dictated by the environmental and institutional circumstances. To be sure, imaginative leaders can manipulate their external and internal environments, but usually only in marginal ways. Effective organizational leadership is contingent upon creativity. Therefore, the first task of a creative leader is to recognize the objective circumstances or season facing the organization. The task then is to design a course of action to align the organization with these circumstances, a course that demands neither too little from the institution nor too much from the environment. His task is then to implement that course of action with determination, nerve, and enthusiasm.

This article examines strategic leadership and creative leaders in a government bureaucracy. The principal focus is on Elmer Staats, who was appointed comptroller general of the General Accounting Office (GAO) in March 1966 and served out his full fifteen-year term, retiring in 1981. I begin with a discussion of the GAO and Staats as they were in 1966 and then turn to the environmental conditions that the GAO encountered during Staats's term. Next I examine the changes Staats and his lieutenants made and the impact these changes had on the GAO, the government, and the society at large. Thereafter I seek to assess Staats's leadership, and close with some tentative conclusions about organizational leadership gleaned from the GAO case.[8]

Preconditions for Leadership

When Elmer Staats arrived in 1966, the GAO was in turmoil. It had been rebuked by Congress, some of the career elite had resigned, the morale of the professional auditors was low, and one of its principal repertoires—the defense contract audit—had been curtailed. It was perceived as an institution that had not kept pace with societal and government changes.

The proximate cause of the turmoil was the Holifield Hearings, which were highly critical of the defense contract audit. By 1965 that audit routine was considered out of control. When the auditors determined that a contract was inconsistent with the best interests of the government, they would name defense contractors and their senior executives deemed guilty of "overcharges" and "excessive pricing," as well as government officials considered responsible for waste or mismanagement. The reports also recommended that contractors voluntarily refund "extraordinary profits" derived from negotiated contracts.[9]

In the end, the auditors became too aggressive in the eyes of some within Congress, particularly those dependent upon political support from defense contractors. These congressmen pressured Chester Holifield (D-Calif.), chairman of the Government Operations Committee, to investigate and modify GAO audit procedures. The Holifield Hearings were conducted in 1965, and a report was released in 1966.

Institutional Conditions

The underlying institutional arrangements, however, were the real cause of the GAO's difficulties. To understand this, we must first understand some of the GAO's administrative history, as well as the leadership exercised by Staats's predecessors.

The GAO was established in 1921 by the Budget and Accounting Act. That act was passed out of congressional frustration with the archaic government accounting procedures, which had impeded the nation's efforts in World War I, and with the assertiveness of such presidents as Theodore Roosevelt and Woodrow Wilson. It also reflected the nation's preoccupation with businesslike norms of economy and efficiency and with scientific management techniques.[10]

Congressional expectations for the GAO and the comptroller were ably reflected in the words of the act's principal sponsor, Congressman James Good. As he noted, "By creating this department [the GAO], Congress will have applied *practical business policy* to the administration of the Government's fiscal affairs. . . . This *independent* department will necessarily serve as a check against extravagance in the preparation of the budget." The comptroller general was to become "the real guardian of the treasury" by promoting "real economy and efficiency" in government. The comptroller was "to discover the very facts that Congress ought to be in possession of and . . . fearlessly and without fear of removal present these facts to Congress and its committees."[11] Thus a powerful GAO was created to (1) guard the treasury and check the president and (2) inform Congress.

The first comptroller general, John McCarl, sought to concentrate on the first of these functions. His strategy for the new institution was to exert maximum control over government expenditures so as to ensure that the value of economy was properly celebrated. He reserved virtually all organizational decisions to himself. Finally, his strategy also included correct but distant relations with Congress and a pugnacious and somewhat overbearing attitude toward executive agencies.[12]

Although McCarl sought to exercise strategic leadership during this period, he was not a creative leader. He was preoccupied with a rigid adherence to the norm of economy, or what some might call penny-pinching, and oblivious to the changes in government wrought by the New Deal. Many of the GAO's decisions during this period disallowed executive expenditures for social and welfare programs.

Smarting under the GAO disallowances, President Franklin Roosevelt appointed the Brownlow Committee, with a mandate to review government procedures to include the auditing process, and proposed that the GAO be transformed into the General Auditing Office, with responsibilities to perform the second of two functions detailed in the 1921 act, namely, to inform Congress about executive expenditures. The accounting control and disallowance powers, the first of the functions in the 1921 act, were to be shifted to the Treasury Department.[13] When Congress defeated these proposals in 1938, Roosevelt sought to alter the GAO through careful selection of the next comptroller general. He appointed Lindsay Warren, a respected congressman from North Carolina and a New Deal supporter.[14]

Thus, when Lindsay Warren entered office in 1940, both the institution and the task environment were ripe for a change. Unlike McCarl, Warren proved to be a creative leader whose exercise of strategic leadership was masterful. Recognizing that the New Deal and World War II had transformed government, Warren both built new elites into the office and generated a new strategy. The new executive or appointed elite were GAO veterans with progressive ideas, while the career or professional elite were newcomers with credentials as certified public accountants and experience in both industry and government. The strategy was for the GAO to study government operations and report deficiencies in management and programs to Congress. Thereafter, it was to be the responsibility of Congress to see that these deficiencies were corrected.[15]

To implement this strategy, Warren and his elite developed five principles to design the new structure: responsiveness, cognizance, professionalization, precision, and evaluation. *Responsiveness* meant that the GAO on its own initiative or at the behest of Congress was to provide experts to testify as they were needed. *Cognizance* required the GAO to keep auditors in the field reviewing the activities of federal agencies across the spectrum of their operations.

To *professionalize* the GAO, Warren and his elites turned to experienced accountants or younger, college-educated accounting majors who could be properly reared in GAO training programs. *Precision* meant accuracy and balance in reporting observations to Congress. Finally, the GAO was to *evaluate* agency financial systems and management by comparing performance with the standards promulgated in the laws, orders, and regulations of the government.[16]

These principles were enshrined in law and thereby legitimized. The 1950 Budget and Accounting Improvement Act was the most important of the ten laws affecting the GAO during Warren's tenure from 1940 to 1954. It not only established reporting as the GAO's preeminent function but also mentioned each of Warren's five principles.[17]

Although Warren was not able to institutionalize all of his principles into the GAO's new structure, his actions proved to be the embodiment of congressional needs in the postwar era. His concern for economy and efficiency in government was consistent with congressional concerns for reasserting legislative power and redesigning the government's financial mechanisms. His artful leadership blunted the managerial, executive-oriented proposals for accounting reform proposed by both the Brownlow Committee and the Hoover Commission and yet created a compromise that was satisfactory to the agencies, Congress, and the GAO. In the end, Warren and his elites had not only fended off calls for reform without sacrificing organizational integrity but also fashioned a new strategy that expanded the GAO's mandate and responsibilities.

Faced with this new strategy and an incomplete structure, Warren's successor should have focused his efforts initially on structural change. Clearly, the environment no longer demanded change, but the institution needed structural modifications to ensure institutionalization of Warren's vision. Unfortunately, Comptroller Joseph Campbell, like his predecessor John McCarl, was not a creative leader. That is, he sought to modify institutional routines by directing his efforts toward the personnel system and routinizing the audit repertoire. He was preoccupied with these matters and had a personal distaste for associating with the GAO's "clients," that is, members of Congress. This disposition meant that Campbell was oblivious to the developments near the end of his term in both Congress and the government at large that required strategic leadership, that is, reformulating Warren's strategy and principles to new conditions.[18]

The Holifield Hearings prompted Campbell's departure. By 1965 his health was failing, and the strain of the hearings proved to be too much. He was forced to seek a disability retirement. Thus, as in 1940, the GAO as an institution was ripe for change.

Environmental Conditions

Two environmental transformations also promoted change during Staats's tenure as comptroller general. First the crafts of auditing and evaluation changed. New technologies developed in the nation's leading business administration schools were retailed to the government during World War II and then adopted wholesale in the 1960s. Operations research was used in that war for a variety of tasks. In the 1960s, Robert McNamara institutionalized both operations research and systems analysis in the Pentagon. By the 1970s these techniques, along with the planning, programming, and budgeting system, cost-benefit analysis, zero-based budgeting, and management by objective, were widely used in the executive branch. Members of Congress also began to call for their use by GAO auditors.[19]

Private-sector auditing changed too. To more effectively service corporate clients, the large, private-sector accounting firms began to go beyond the function of attesting to financial statements toward providing management consultant services. As public disenchantment with government grew, accounting firms were also called upon initially to assess the managerial efficiency of local and state government agencies and later to evaluate agency effectiveness. Given the close relation between GAO and the accounting profession, these developments spurred the GAO to broaden its accounting repertoire.[20]

The second transformation was a reassertiveness by Congress to a presidency grown more powerful as a result of the New Deal, World War II, the cold war, and the Great Society. This reassertiveness transformed government policy making. It took the form of new control and oversight mechanisms used predominantly, not by committees, which had dominated congressional policy making during the first half of the twentieth century, but by subcommittees and individual legislators.[21] Among these new mechanisms were a growth in both member staff support and support staffs. The growth of individual staff support from 4,489 in 1957 to 13,969 in 1979 meant that legislators could influence legislation on their own and had the assets to more effectively oversee executive implementation.[22] New support staffs to provide analytical support were created in the Office of Technology Assessment in 1972 and the Congressional Budget Office in 1974. The Legislative Reference Service became the Congressional Research Service in 1970, with new responsibilities to provide policy analysis.

During this period, Congress did not neglect the GAO. With the active involvement and support of Elmer Staats, during his comptrollership Congress enacted seven principal pieces of legislation and over eighty subsidiary ones that expanded or reasserted GAO audit authority in virtually every endeavor of the federal government. At the end of his period, the following previously sacrosanct agencies were subjected to the legislative audit: the Federal Bureau of Investigation, the Internal Revenue Service, the Federal Reserve System, the Comptroller of the Currency, and the Bureau of Alcohol, Tobacco and Firearms. For a brief period Congress even required the GAO to monitor presidential campaign contributions.[23]

These environmental transformations confronted the GAO with both risks and opportunities. The failure to accommodate to these transformations would have spelled doom for the GAO. Almost certainly, GAO resistance to change would have seen the GAO swallowed whole or in part by other organizations or condemned to a tidepool existence, with its clients fleeing to other, more responsive agencies.

Simple accommodation would also have been insufficient. Such a response would not have satisfied congressional demands, nor would it have been consistent with the institution's character. Throughout the period, congressional demands changed as the legislature confronted social unrest in the cities, calls for the equality of blacks and women, the travails of the Vietnam War, and the intransigence of both the Johnson and Nixon administrations. Each of these challenges prompted new legislative adjustments. Responding serially would have been insufficient, because GAO actions never would have caught up with the congressional demands. Furthermore, simple responses would have required constant shifts in the GAO's structure, thereby creating turmoil and uncertainty among GAO elites and professionals. Finally, serial responses would also have fundamentally changed the GAO's distinctive character. That is, serial changes, such as adding technology-review responsibilities in 1972 and budget-scorekeeping tasks in 1974, would have been inconsistent with the GAO's historical development, the technologies it had fostered, and the clientele it traditionally had served. These accommodations eventually would have required replacing many of the auditors with new professions as many new internal structures were created to respond to new functions.

Opportunities were also apparent. Clearly, Congress was intent upon expanding its control over public policy and administration, a task the GAO was uniquely equipped to support. By fulfilling congressional needs for oversight information, the GAO could draw closer to its patron and be assured of more established and more enduring support for its activities. A new relationship could also preclude a reoccurrence of the Holifield Hearings as Congress became more reliant upon the GAO and perhaps could go as far as establishing the GAO as the principal legislative device for oversight of the executive branch.

To realize these opportunities, the comptroller general and his agents needed to be actively involved in congressional demands for change. Creative and strategic leadership were essential to harness environmental turmoil to serve institutional purposes. Such leadership required active involvement in congressional designs for changing both the GAO and other congressional support agencies. This involvement would ensure that the fundamental character of the GAO remained intact, unsullied by the shifting external demands. Furthermore, strategic leadership was essential to designing a new vision, a new structure, and new implementation policies for the GAO.

The New Comptroller

To these challenges came Elmer Staats, nominated to be comptroller general by President Lyndon Johnson. At first glance, Staats did not appear to be the man for the job. A subdued, controlled man, Staats seemed to have almost no fire in him. In fact, journalists frequently complained that they could find no "angles" upon which to hang a human-interest story. His life seemed to be his work, and his work was always done both meticulously and without much apparent flair. Furthermore, as deputy director of the Bureau of the Budget (BOB), Staats had been passed over by President Lyndon Johnson for the director's job in 1965 in favor of Assistant Director Charles Schultze.

Yet these appearances were deceptive. As one old BOB hand observed, "I thought at first Elmer was rather slow, but I soon learned that he was terribly sensitive to the Hill—he knew what they wanted." Another observed that Staats was committed to government service, a man with a strong sense of duty to BOB and the president. In fact, he tended to see himself as a carrier for the ideals and values of the bureau.[24] President Johnson also liked and admired Staats. As he remarked during the swearing-in ceremony on 8 March 1966, Staats was appointed for his faithful service and wise counsel to four administrations. "Elmer Staats has always been a builder, a believer—not a doubter."[25]

Staats's professional background consisted of almost continuous service in the Executive Office of the President from 1939 to 1966. Over this period, he had been deputy director of BOB under Presidents Truman, Eisenhower, Kennedy, and Johnson and executive officer of the Operations Coordinating Board of the National Security Council (NSC) under President Eisenhower.[26]

Staats possessed a keen sense of congressional and bureaucratic politics. It was widely believed that "Elmer always sat on a three-cornered cushion"—one side for the Democrats, one for the Republicans, and one for vague situations.[27] In spite of this reputation, he had amassed a wide circle of friends and admirers in the executive branch and on

Capitol Hill. His work in the Executive Office had given him an unusually broad overview of the operations of the federal government and had acquainted him with virtually all the administrators and their principal deputies in four administrations. His nose for Congress was sensitized by his marriage in 1940 to the daughter of Congressman Robert F. Rich (R-Pa.), an avowed fiscal conservative. President Truman found Staats particularly useful as a congressional liaison because of this family connection with the Republicans. Staats's confirmation hearing before the Senate Committee on Government Operations provided further evidence for the strong relationships he had developed on Capitol Hill. After listening to oral testimonials from seven senators and written support from six others, the committee unanimously reported his nomination to the floor in open session. Two days later the Senate quickly confirmed him.

Staats had also studied government and public administration. A Phi Beta Kappa graduate of McPherson College, he earned a master's degree in political science and economics from the University of Kansas in 1936 and a doctoral degree from the University of Minnesota in public administration in 1939. From 1940 to 1946 he served as a lecturer in government and public administration at American and George Washington universities. He was active in the American Society for Public Administration, serving as president of the Washington, D.C., chapter in 1948–49 and national president in 1960–61.[28] In 1960 he published a paper calling for the evaluation of program effectiveness in government.[29]

Staats's personality was shaped by his experiences in BOB. In BOB, neutral competence and political sensitivity were dominant norms.[30] To survive the political shoals there, one had to be circumspect and had to work to a consensus. To deal with executive agencies and with Congress, one developed a collegial, participative style. Hugh Heclo has described this participative style as due-process leadership, in which the views of all are given a fair hearing prior to the announcement of a decision.[31] Such a style was particularly well suited to the legislative branch, with its many committees and assertive personalities.

Thus, the institutional and environmental circumstances in 1966 made the GAO ripe for change. To this task came an experienced bureaucratic operator in Elmer Staats, a man who had worked behind the scenes for decades in the Executive Office. His vision for the GAO and his managerial style were central to the GAO's regeneration.

Elmer Staats and Strategic Leadership

Staats's vision for the GAO was essentially a refinement of Lindsay Warren's strategy and principles. That is, Staats sought to adapt Warren's vision of reporting to Congress to the new circumstances facing the GAO. In Staats's view, GAO reporting was to enhance both congressional oversight and governmental accountability to the public. Accountability could be achieved by publicizing the faults of government and its programs. Staats was convinced that such publicity would pressure agencies and Congress to improve management and program effectiveness and thus enhance the reputation of government.[32] Therefore, finding fault in all aspects of agency performance became virtuous, because it enhanced accountability and in the end would make the GAO more central to congressional decision making.

Staats's philosophy was important to this vision. At root, Staats was a subscriber to the underlying values of the field of public administration. That is, he believed that government could be efficient and effective, that rationality could be introduced into policy making, and that administrative processes could be refined by using businesslike methods. He was fascinated with the workings of the government and could easily recall mountains of detail about various programs, administrators, and congressmen. He believed in better government. This concern was not limited to waste and mismanagement—the traditional preoccupation of previous comptrollers general—but also included an interest in improving personnel management, internal auditing and budgeting, and program performance.[33]

Each of Warren's five principles were redesigned. The principle of responsiveness became more than issuing reports and occasional testimony before Congress by the comptroller and a few career elites. It came to mean energetic oversight of established programs, frequent testimony and coordination with members of Congress and their staffs, and forecasting the legislature's agenda. Energetic oversight was "getting our money's worth from old and established programs. From our vantage point, it appears that both the executive and legislative branches have been more concerned with starting new programs than with making certain that those we already have are working satisfactorily or could be improved."[34] The frequency of testimony grew from an average of two times a month in the mid-1960s to an average of fifteen times a month by the end of the 1970s.[35] Furthermore, auditors had to establish congressional interest in an area before they began an audit. Finally, the comptroller sought to lead Congress into new areas of oversight, rather than follow. As Staats said in 1977, "We try to focus on issues which we think are coming up or that we think Congress should get interested in. There are many issues we identify where there doesn't seem to be much interest in the Congress. We try to get their attention to get something done."[36]

Staats also broadened the principle of cognizance beyond site auditing. The chill that Campbell had imposed on relations with executive agencies was lifted, with Staats and his auditors candidly discussing management and program issues with agency appointees and senior bureaucrats. Staats also opened up new relations with a broad array of federal and nonfederal agencies by campaigning for an inspector general to be installed in all federal departments and publishing pamphlets detailing GAO auditing practices. Finally, the GAO became an active force in the International Organization of Supreme Audit Institutions, with one of Staats's assistant comptrollers serving as editor of the organization's journal.[37]

Precision was to be achieved by new mechanisms for overseeing the auditors and the audit process. That is, a large headquarters staff was designed that consolidated the functions of personnel management, budgeting, and program planning. An information system was imposed to calculate the resources assigned to various lines of audit, and a program planning system was put in place to design and coordinate the audit effort.

Evaluations came to mean more than review of agency financial systems and management. The new star was program auditing, which was to assess the effectiveness of federal programs in achieving the objectives contained within the law. Thus, a new and challenging repertoire was added to the audit. In many ways, program auditing was the essence of Staats's contribution to the GAO, for it was intended to draw the GAO closer to Congress by responding to actual legislative needs, thereby enhancing congressional oversight and government accountability.

Temperament

The leadership style of Elmer Staats was important in implementing this new vision. Due-process leadership, incremental change, and looking out for GAO's interests characterized Staats's management of the GAO. In line with his experience in BOB and the NSC, Staats would hold lengthy conferences, often lasting two or three hours, to consider legislative strategy or internal matters. Division and office directors would present their budgets and their plans for future audit work in forums similar to the agency budget hearings held by BOB.

Where groups did not exist to advise him, he would create them. To deal with the concerns of minorities and young auditors, Staats constituted the Women's Advisory Committee, the Equal Employment

Opportunity Advisory Council, and the Youth Advisory Council. Sessions held with these committees and groups were meant not only to encourage those involved to feel a sense of participation in the final decision; they also kept Staats informed on developments within the GAO and the government as a whole. When a decision or policy had to be made, he would decide in private and then announce his decisions in writing. By a determined effort to manifest a certain collegiality, Staats both reduced tensions and enhanced accountant identification with the shift in the GAO's function.

He favored both incremental change and delegating daily management to his directors. As Staats noted in 1972, the transition to new auditing techniques "must start modestly and expand slowly. There must be gradual development built on expertise gained—the auditor must walk before attempting to run. . . . It behooves the auditor who is expanding his efforts beyond financial and accounting matters to develop his competence gradually, but surely."[38] Indeed, Staats was a patient and calm man who seemed never to be agitated, no matter what the circumstances. By slowly building up auditor skills and patiently working with Congress, such that each year it passed a new piece of legislation enhancing GAO power, Staats was able to achieve a great deal. His statutory fifteen-year term gave him the luxury of moving slowly on organizational change, and he took full advantage of it.

Content to leave most of the day-to-day management to his immediate subordinates, Staats was primarily interested in the broad directions of the GAO. When he felt it necessary to intervene in such matters as organizational policies or new audit directions, he would suggest rather than order. As one particularly knowledgeable Staats-watcher pointed out, "His technique is that he just keeps leaning into matters. He never gets mad, and he never gets tired." An order from Elmer Staats was usually phrased "We should think about that" or "This is a matter we should consider" or, when the suggestions needed to be more definitive, "I think we should do something about this."

Much of his workday was spent "looking out" for GAO interests.[39] Staats "listens and watches for the undercurrents . . . he knows and meets lots of people." Staats prided himself on being "politically aware." Others observed that Staats was "on the lookout" or was "personally involved in a wide range of issues with congressmen and people outside of government." For instance, in fiscal years 1968 and 1969 he spoke before forty-eight business and professional organizations and testified before Congress on twenty-nine occasions. During the first ten years of his comptrollership, he testified before Congress a total of 187 times.[40] Not only did he willingly appear before congressional committees but he was always ready to meet with congressmen or to discuss matters on the telephone.[41] His speeches were published widely in professional journals.[42] Thus, Staats was a man of steady nerves and solid character.

Elite Redesign

To institutionalize his vision, Staats was forced to reconstitute the GAO elite, which had been badly battered by the Holifield Hearings. First Staats slowly eliminated the old career elite from operational control by promoting them out of their line positions to serve as his assistants; as expected, they soon retired. In their place he created three new classes: an executive elite, a novitiate career elite, and a counterelite.

The executive elite initially was composed of the deputy comptroller general and the general counsel, both of whom Staats selected himself.[43] To further expand this group, Staats persuaded Congress to provide five assistant comptroller-general positions and the authority to appoint them as he saw fit. To fill these executive-level-IV positions, Staats chose outsiders who had extensive management experience in the executive branch. Later he turned to bright and energetic GAO auditors who shared his agenda for changing the organization.[44]

The novitiate career elite was expanded dramatically as Staats created new divisions and staff offices. Chosen to fill these positions were positive and enthusiastic auditors who had risen quickly in the GAO. Certified public accountants (CPAs) all, they embraced the values traditionally linked to the accounting profession. When queried about the values they associated with the GAO, they named accounting valuables: independence, objectivity, impartiality, integrity, authoritativeness, and accuracy. Although the CPAs were initially inclined to avoid audits of top-level policy issues, Staats worked hard to broaden their horizons. Frequent conferences were held to discuss new audit directions so that their views would be included in projected organizational changes. They were called upon to chair GAO-wide committees on issues facing the GAO and to prepare memoranda for meetings of division directors. Training programs were begun in order to expose them to new analytical tools as well as broader issues facing all of government.[45]

Finally, a counterelite was installed to set the pattern for the new form of evaluation and to force existing auditors to follow it. Two outside policy analysts comfortable with social-science evaluative techniques were brought in at the highest civil service grade, quickly elevated to the august position of division director, and provided line auditing divisions. As an insider from one of these divisions observed, "Our reason for being is institutional change."

Other outsiders were chosen to fill newly created staff positions in areas that Staats thought needed particular attention. A journalist was hired to be an information officer, a systems analyst was employed to create an internal management information system, and personnel management experts were recruited to manage the GAO's equal employment opportunity program. The counterelite was further bolstered by a staff of auditing heretics who were to implement the new program planning and personnel management systems. These accountant auditors served to erode the dominance of the career elite by implementing systems for resource allocation and personnel management that provided the executive elite access to the auditors' professional sanctuaries.

Structural Change

Once the vision was designed, Staats and his new elite sought to institutionalize it by redesigning organizational mechanisms to ensure its acceptance. Structural redesign meant both reorganization and alterations to the personnel system designed to enhance auditor service to Congress through the new program audit.

Reorganization. In addition to the creation of a staff to coax the auditors into a new audit repertoire, Staats functionalized the audit divisions and rationalized the GAO field structure. New audit divisions were created to oversee broad policy areas in government such as human resources, community and economic development, acquisition, and energy and minerals. Each division was conceived to lead in its given functional area; that is, it was expected to plan and organize audits relying on its resources as well as those of other divisions that had overlapping mandates in various issue areas such as food, productivity, and military preparedness.

In addition to enhancing functional expertise, this reorganization had two additional purposes. It opened the organization up for inspection by Staats and his executive leadership. Furthermore, it flattened the organizational hierarchy to provide more senior, career elites able to respond to a fragmented Congress that was requesting more program audits.[46]

Ever since Lindsay Warren had decentralized the audit, the GAO field structure had constituted about one-half of the professional audit staff. By the late 1960s this staff was structured into regional offices dominated by older auditors resistant to the new program audit. To redirect these office, the GAO began to send out promising middle-grade auditors from headquarters to assume the role of regional manager. Furthermore, the headquarters division responsible for overseeing these offices began to impose administrative policies approved by the GAO elite.[47]

Personnel system alterations. To overcome career auditor opposition to the program audit—and there was a great deal of opposition— the GAO sought to install a personnel management system that would promote the new repertoire. When Staats arrived, the professional staff comprised two thousand one hundred auditors educated as accountants and one hundred lawyers.[48] Socialized by CPAs in the office, the accountants were committed to the norms of auditing. The program audit threatened these norms, which consisted of carefully defined audit standards and numerical comparisons. For the auditors, criteria to measure programs seemed mired in fuzzy legislation, and program evaluation audits seemed resistant to accounting techniques.

Given this resistance to program evaluation, the GAO leadership sought young recruits with other college backgrounds and upper-level hires with specific expertise in policy or program evaluation.[49] There were also numerous efforts to broaden the perspectives of older and newly hired auditors. GAO training courses were provided to recruits as well as to junior- and middle-grade auditors. The GAO also used its magazine, the *GAO Review*, to acquaint auditors with the techniques of program evaluation.[50] Auditors deemed to have considerable promise were sent to short, university training courses and encouraged to seek advanced degrees through various night schools.[51]

The professional staff itself grew dramatically during Staats's tenure. The last vestiges of older auditing routines were eliminated. Thus, many new positions opened up, and the professional staff grew from two thousand two hundred to four thousand one hundred by 1981. The GAO reclassified most of the professionals as "evaluators," describing this position as a "series unique to the GAO" that "accurately describes the role of our auditing staff."[52]

Also during the Staats era the GAO grade structure spurted upwards. Whereas in 1966 the GAO had only 36 supergrade (GS-16 to GS-18) auditors, by 1979 it had 87 such positions. In the senior auditor grades of GS-13 to GS-15, the numbers swelled from 743 to 1922. Thus, by 1979 the median grade of all GAO employees was GS-12.[53] The GAO also made a number of administrative changes in the personnel system. Offices of Personnel Management and Staff Development were created to centralize recruiting, training, and promotion policies; this reorganization wrested personnel decisions away from the line audit divisions, where it had resided during the Campbell era. A competitive promotion system was also installed.[54]

Policy Changes

Vision and structural changes are not enough to guarantee that a new strategy is policed and implementation will occur. Policies must be changed as well. In the GAO, Staats did this through use of his new elite, through planning mechanisms, and by personal review of new audit and personnel initiatives.

In his first year as comptroller general, Staats created a program planning staff in his immediate office to consider new audit and organizational initiatives. After seven years of experimentation with alternative designs, the staff proposed, and Staats accepted, a system that embodied a lead division and issue area concept. Later this staff became the Office of Program Planning, entrusted with the custodianship of this new mechanism to coordinate organizational output.

Also proposed by the Office of Program Planning was a financial-management information system, which permitted Staats to oversee division audit efforts.[55] This and the program planning system permitted Staats to intervene and gain some control of GAO priorities. The system also permitted Staats to monitor and assess the operation of each division by comparing plans with actual auditing efforts, to judge younger auditors, who were frequently called upon to brief him at planning meetings, and to learn about new developments in each issue area.

The Impact of Strategic Leadership: Organizational Reaction

Assessing the impact of strategic leadership, that is, isolating leadership from the many variables that impinge on organizations, and then tracing the leadership variable through to the impact of the organization on its environment is a conjectural exercise.[56] Indeed, the web of interaction among leaders, elites, and professionals within organizations and among the overseers, clients, and technologies outside the organization appears seamless.

Standards also provide problems. For instance, how are we to measure the success of leadership? What standards are to be used for judging organizational success? Assuming that such standards can be collected, we must then agree on a time frame. Are we to judge success in the short term—say, one to five years—or the long term—five years or more? One way to proceed is to ascertain what changes have in fact taken place within the organization and then to seek to assess any changes in the impact of the organization on its environment. Then, through a series of suppositions, one can try to eliminate other variables that could have impinged on organizational change. If the leader can be isolated as the principal force in changing the organization, then we can plausibly argue that the differential impact of the organization on its environment can be primarily ascribed to leadership efforts.

In the next three sections, I seek to accomplish these tasks. In the first section, I look at the changes that took place in the behavior of

GAO auditors, now retitled evaluators. Then I consider what the differential impact of the organization has been. In the third section, I assess Staats's leadership.

A New Culture

From the conduct of GAO program evaluations, one could infer the presence of certain ideal types each of which played a role in the issuance of a report: line auditors, staff auditors, auditor managers, and auditor advocates. The line auditors and the auditor managers were present in the GAO before Staats arrived. During his tenure the auditor advocates and staff auditors were added.[57]

Line auditors were normally found at audit sites located adjacent to agency operations or contractors' plants around the country. They were in the entry or lower-middle civil service grade. They collected information for evaluations. Their work involved sifting agency data to discover deficiencies in agency operations and programs.

The role of the staff auditors was to promote organizational change espoused by the comptroller general and to ensure that reports did not damage the GAO's reputation. They also provided administrative support to the other three types of auditors and carried out maintenance tasks for the institution.

The auditor managers supervised the evaluation process. They not only supervised line auditors but were responsible for guiding surveys and reports through the GAO's internal review process. Like the auditor advocates and staff auditors, they were in the middle and upper grades and were located in the regional headquarters or the GAO headquarters.

The auditor advocates planned and marketed GAO evaluations. Unlike the auditor managers, they saw themselves as policy analysts. They reached across GAO division boundaries to plan and coordinate reviews to satisfy the demands of the new GAO planning process. As advocates, they marketed GAO reports to congressmen, congressional staffers, agency bureaucrats, and the press. They also maintained contacts outside the GAO with other policy analysts interested in their topical areas.

The auditor managers and the auditor advocates were the most interesting types at the GAO, because they were the organizers and movers behind each evaluation report. Despite this similarity, they had very different perspectives. The auditor managers and the line auditors were still very much accountants at heart. As accountants, GAO line auditors and auditor managers concentrated on figures and workpapers, employed accounting logic, and insisted that facts and figures be completely reliable. Such auditors "go out and try to find something quantifiable; they prefer that to making judgments which cannot be quantified." They thought in terms of "rules and regulations, dollars and cents." Auditors liked to count and "are very detail oriented." Workpapers were very important. "Auditors are always happy with a piece of paper."

Accounting logic was also important to such auditors. At the GAO "the technique and logic of accounting are applied to a different set of circumstances." Auditing required inquisitiveness. "Accountants fit into this pattern, [because they] can be trained" to "sort out facts from judgment" and to "avoid theoretical and normative assessments." "Accountants make good auditors because they think logically."

The auditor advocates were, for the most part, social scientists educated in public administration or economics and trained as policy specialists. The successful advocate was intimately acquainted with the multitude of government programs constituting his chosen field. In order to maintain relation with and market their products to Congress, the executive branch, the universities, and interest groups, the advocates had to reach out and maintain contacts with like-minded policy specialists.

A principal way for the advocates to reach out was through the use of consultants, who were now playing a large role in many GAO audits. Many of the audits most popular with Elmer Staats employed consultant panels. For instance, for the series of three reports on the service academies completed in 1975 and 1976, the GAO employed a panel of seventeen consultants made up of former service academy superintendents and educators from the civilian community.[58] Another report, the liquid metal fast breeder reactor audit, also employed a panel of experts, in this case drawn from power companies and the academic community.[59] Using consultants was an important technique in legitimating GAO audits, in forging alliances with policy specialists not formally affiliated with government agencies, and in gaining intelligence about agency operations.[60]

The managers and advocates thus differed not only in terms of their backgrounds but also in terms of their horizons. Conflict was exacerbated by the fact that accountants had traditionally been considered the "more elite" group. One auditor manager noted the tensions between the accountants and the economists. "It is hard for these two groups to communicate. When I worked with an economist, I found that we thought on different wavelengths."

Conflict was further aggravated by the fact that many auditor advocates originally joined the GAO as upper-level hires. That is, they were not socialized as were the accountant auditors. Auditor advocates were not seen as part of the team by the managers; they "act on their own thinking" or "don't understand working papers and documentation." This tension both complicated and advanced auditing. Both the advocates and the managers performed roles that were important in the evaluation repertoire. Reconciling the roles of each group and their relative status required considerable attention from Staats and the GAO elite. Yet the tension also advanced auditing by making the program audit possible. Without the auditor advocates to point the way, GAO audits would not have been as relevant to congressional needs. Their presence in the organization was directly tied to the new audit format envisioned by Staats, to his elite design and his hiring policies.

The New Audit Direction

In spite of the presence of staff auditors and auditor advocates, one cannot say that the audit repertoire had changed much by the end of Staats's term in 1981. The dominance of the line auditors and the auditor managers in the field, where the data was collected and the draft reports were written, ensured that the established audit repertoire in the search for "cause, criteria, and effect" was maintained. The audit repertoire consisted of three phases. The survey phase was a quick examination of a target area to discover any deficiencies that might exist. The review phase was an in-depth exploration of the target to gather the facts to substantiate a deficiency. Finally, the report phase recorded those deficiencies in an evaluation report to Congress.[61]

Cause, criteria, and *effect* were the terms used by the line auditors and auditor managers to conceptualize their craft. The cause of the deficiency was the reason why the financial system, the management, or the program failed to meet the standards required. The required standards for measuring performance were the criteria and could be found in audit standards established by CPAs, laws, agency regulations, or codes developed by private professional groups. Once the criteria were applied and the cause of a deficiency had been settled upon, the effect was sought. The effect was the impact a condition or deficiency had on government, the agency, or the public. Generally speaking, the impacts of deficiencies had to be adjudged serious or severe, or auditors would seek to close out the review and move on to more fertile ground.[62]

So all evaluations were like. Auditors applied simple, easily remembered formulas to their work. Armed with the skills of an accountant and investigator, line auditors used a host of unwritten rules, techniques, and procedures which constituted the evaluator's faultfinding repertoire. These shortcuts were developed over decades of auditing and passed on to new auditors as part of the socialization process.

Yet, even with this enduring repertoire, program audits were instituted during Staats's tenure. These audits assessed effectiveness. That is, they sought to determine whether the desired results or benefits of a program as established by Congress or by the body of professional opinion were being achieved. They also considered whether a program was being administered in an efficient way and whether its expenditures were being used in an economical manner.

Several examples illustrate these objectives. The first involves a computer system for the Veterans Administration (VA). Under pressure from veterans and the congressional Veterans Affairs Committees, the VA tried to update its outmoded payment system by purchasing a new computer system which it called Target. This new program was enthusiastically supported by VA Administrator Max Cleland soon after he was installed in the spring of 1977. Disposed to make many changes in the agency, Cleland felt that Target would reduce overhead, make it possible to maintain better records, and provide for more accurate benefit payments. Several members of Congress were not as enthusiastic about the program and so requested a GAO cost-benefit study. The GAO report of 20 July 1977 called Target a "risky venture" whose costs and benefits had not been thoroughly evaluated. Furthermore, the VA had not adequately considered alternative ways of meeting its need for processing veterans benefits.[63] So in the GAO's view, Target was not an economical use of resources.

Another GAO program evaluation involved the sale of a sophisticated radar plan called AWACS (Airborne Warning and Control System). In June 1977, President Carter notified Congress of his program to sell several AWACS to Iran to secure its borders from the Soviet Union. Alerted by press reports in May that such a sale would be proposed, six senators, including John Culver and Thomas Eagleton, requested that the GAO analyze the program in terms of the risk that it might compromise the secret equipment aboard each aircraft.

In July the GAO issued its report. Based on data provided by the Pentagon and intelligence assessments from the Central Intelligence Agency, the evaluators concluded that the sale of AWACS to Iran would indeed risk the U.S. lead over the Soviet Union in electronic warfare. Furthermore, the GAO found that the administration had not considered alternative radar systems that could meet Iran's security needs, nor had it accurately assessed the total cost to Iran of an AWACS-based defense.[64]

As is clear from these reports, evaluating effectiveness was to apply the same conceptual framework employed in the discovery of any finding—cause, criteria, and effect. The conceptual framework of a *system* dominated the thinking of program auditors. They found that only the president had the authority and recourse "required to establish a unified government telecommunications system." In another evaluation, the auditors recommended that the Interior Department develop a "systematic coal-drilling program."[65]

The criteria used in effectiveness audits were the program goals or cost-benefit calculations. In reviewing the development of oil and gas resources on the outer continental shelf, auditors found that the secretary of the interior should more "clearly define Shelf leasing goals and specify how these goals will be met and how they relate to overall national energy goals and plans." As illustrated in the Target evaluation, costs and benefits provided another favorite criterion. In reviewing the implications of deregulating the price of natural gas, the auditors felt that "the additional supplies of gas likely to result from deregulation must be weighed against the additional costs to consumers."[66]

The cause—that is, the reason why the condition and the criteria are not the same—in program evaluations was ascribed both to agency management and to Congress. Agency management was told to establish more consistent criteria in order to clarify vague laws; that is, the agencies were told to legislate. In the 1975 audit cited above, the secretary of the interior was advised to "clearly define shelf leasing goals." GAO program evaluators urged Congress to provide more resources to achieve the goals prescribed by existing laws. Reports contained sections that suggested "Matters for Consideration by the Congress" or "Issues for Consideration by the Committees on Appropriations." Such "matters" and "issues" called for more law and more money. For example, a 1974 audit of federal programs for educating the handicapped advised that "the Congress should consider amending pertinent legislation . . . and eliminating formula allocation factors."[67]

Thus, we can conclude that there were significant shifts in the GAO during Staats's comptrollership. The village life or culture had changed, with new types of auditors added to the organization. Also being pursued was a new audit form, one designed to assess program effectiveness and to be of more interest to Congress than the old contract audits that had predominated during the term of Staats's predecessor, Joseph Campbell.

The Impact of Strategic Leadership: The Environment

What impact did the GAO have in the late 1970s and how did that differ from its impact in the period before Staats assumed office? Clearly, in 1965 the GAO's principal audit form, the defense contract audit, had been repudiated by Congress in the Holifield Hearings. It was widely felt that the GAO's performance did not conform to congressional expectations. The organization was considered remote, unresponsive, and unnecessarily harsh in its audit reports.

Staats's vision for the GAO was to emphasize congressional service and governmental accountability. Translated into operational terms, this vision was to publicize in a constructive manner the deficiencies in executive agency management and programs through reports that would satisfy congressional needs and make government more efficient and effective. As might be expected, the GAO's impact on the government and the society at large did not wholly conform to the aspirations contained in this vision.

To be sure, GAO reports did publicize deficiencies. Each year the organization sent hundreds of audit reports to Congress, with copies provided to executive agencies, the press, academicians, and outside groups.[68] Occasionally these reports were printed in full by congressional committees or referred to in committees reports. The House and Senate Appropriations Committees received abstracts of all GAO reports for use in their hearings. Occasionally senators and congressmen would refer to a GAO report in their remarks on the floor. The reports were also mentioned in books, journals, the specialized press, and the elite press, such as the *New York Times* and the *Wall Street Journal*.[69]

Yet these reports were not used by Congress in the fashion intended. That is, GAO reports were seldom used by members of Congress to correct deficiencies in agency management or programs. Instead, their use tended to be highly episodic and generally as a result of a member's interest in a policy or bureaucratic area; GAO reports seldom, if ever, motivated a congressman to delve into a new issue. The interviews did suggest that GAO reports were read by congressional staffers but generally served as one of many sources of information about executive operations.

This lack of attention to GAO reports reflected congressional ambivalence about the function of oversight. Members viewed oversight as potentially hazardous politically—it could stir up otherwise quiescent groups—and as requiring large investments of time to learn the complexities of an issue. Thus for Congress, oversight was a latent function, exercised sporadically when members saw electoral or publicity advantages.[70]

From this discussion one must conclude that the GAO was not central to congressional affairs. Certainly, as illustrated in the Target and AWACS examples described above, the GAO could play a role. But that role was decidedly a subsidiary one in which the GAO supported congressional staffers who had become the barons of legislative oversight of existing policy and administration.[71]

The reasons for such a subsidiary GAO role were fourfold. First, congressmen and GAO evaluators valued different things. Congressmen valued reelection and influence, not efficiency and effectiveness in government. Second, with the growth of congressional staffs, members had to focus more and more of their time on their own enterprises;[72] little time was left to follow the findings developed by GAO evaluators. Third, the action in Congress had shifted from the appropriations process to the budget process.[73] The budget committees were principally served by the Congressional Budget Office, not the GAO. What the GAO found in its audits might potentially save the government millions of dollars, while the more pressing issues surrounded billions of dollars of deficit. Fourth and finally, congressmen and staffers did not find their preferred sources of information in the legislative branch. Outsiders could provide details and analyses more quickly than GAO evaluators, who were dominated by an arduous, faultfinding repertoire that required an average of eighteen months to produce a report.

This conclusion is further substantiated by the details of how Congress actually relied on the GAO. Office evaluations were at once a symbol of executive accountability, an occasional bludgeon to achieve programmatic ends, and sometimes a tool for electoral activities. The GAO served as a symbol to Congress that executive-branch decision making was accessible to legislative review. Enabled by its unique statutory access to and cognizance over agency personnel and programs, the auditors could provide congressional committees with details of organizational behavior and program performance. Clearly, much of the GAO-related legislation since World War II can be considered as a concerted effort to open up the executive branch to congressional scrutiny through the audit. Such a symbol was comforting, for it reassured members that certain functions were being discharged and thereby permitted them to pursue other, preferred activities.

When congressmen or staffers did wish to intervene, the GAO provided a convenient bludgeon for expressing displeasure or for stirring up interest groups attentive to agency programs. Where congressional staff members or congressmen were dissatisfied with agency management or program performance, the GAO, with its preoccupation for faultfinding, could be employed to dig up deficiencies to embarrass administrators. As Herb Roback, a recent staff director of the House Committee on Government Operations, observed, critical GAO reports "put agency heads and program managers on notice that improvements are expected if future authorizations and funding are to be allowed."[74]

The GAO could also help build support for new legislative initiatives. Just as policy evaluation shapes the climate of opinion surrounding an issue and serves to mobilize government action,[75] GAO evaluations could recognize the existence of a particular problem and thereby involve program and agency constituencies to support a legislative solution. As exemplified above in the Target example, such evaluations were usually employed in tandem with other techniques for coalition building such as hearings and press releases.

Finally, the GAO could be a useful tool for electoral activities. Any congressionally initiated GAO evaluation invariably occasioned at least two press releases—and perhaps a press conference. The request for an evaluation report permitted the congressman to claim credit for putting the GAO onto a serious problem faced by the government and to take a position on the evils of this or that program, the swollen nature of government, or the inefficiency of agency management. Once the GAO had provided the congressman with his report, it waited for forty-eight hours or so before releasing the report to the public in order to permit the legislator to issue another press release or hold a press conference, again claiming credit and taking a position. Local newspapers were usually attentive to press releases from their congressmen. Furthermore, such releases were grist for congressmen's newsletters to constituents.[76]

The impact of GAO reports on executive agencies reflected congressional involvement. When members, committees, or staffers showed interest, agency managers were likely to respond to a report and its recommendations. Since Congress was not generally interested in most GAO reports, they did not have much influence on agency management or public programs. Interviews with executive officials suggested a hostility and disdain for both the auditors and their recommendations. Managers felt that the reports simply parroted what they had told the auditors about the flaws in their operations. Futhermore, the managers felt that the auditors were unqualified to comment on operations because of their inexperience in the policy area. In most cases the managers were aware of and would have corrected the faults before they identified them to the auditors had they had the resources or bureaucratic support to do so.

Assessing Strategic Leadership

Without question, Elmer Staats made a significant difference in realigning the GAO. It was in shambles when he arrived. His vision for the organization provided a new direction for the auditors. He also reconstituted the elite by broadening it and committing it to this new vision. Together he and this new elite restructured the organization and established new policies to oversee organizational performance. Through these efforts, new auditor types were brought in. In turn, these auditor advocates created a new audit routine in the program-effectiveness review.

In spite of this internal transformation, however, it would seem that the new GAO could only be considered a limited success in environmental terms. It did produce and distribute reports on agency efficiency and program effectiveness, and it did promote more effective government audit organizations throughout the United States. Yet, using the standard of the impact of GAO reports on executive agencies and their use by Congress, Staats's efforts would not appear to have been successful. The reports were generally ignored by executive managers and played only a subsidiary role in the congressional function of oversight.

Yet, these standards as an indicator of the effectiveness of leadership miss a crucial point, namely, that criteria for success differ from observer to observer. By GAO criteria of promoting efficiency and effectiveness, the organization was not successful. But internal criteria are not necessarily relevant to external constituencies and taskmasters. External agents matter more, because they provide the resources. The key point is that Congress was satisfied. Furthermore, as suggested above, the GAO was more a symbol than an influential reporter. Its presence on the federal scene placed executive managers on notice that their actions would be reviewed. As long as Congress and agency managers considered it a viable force that *could* be called upon to reveal executive performance, it fulfilled its function of promoting businesslike government.

We must also measure Staats's and the GAO's performance in terms of the realities that faced the GAO. Its taskmaster and principal client was the U.S. Congress, a disaggregated and adversarial institution that itself underwent considerable ferment in the 1970s. During this period, subcommittees and members themselves came to play a more salient role in policy making. The struggle between Congress and the executive branch, established as it is by the U.S. Constitution, was further exacerbated during Staats's terms by the actions of the Johnson and Nixon administrations. Congressional response through a series of landmark laws beginning in 1970 and extending into the late 1970s further complicated the GAO's relationship with its taskmaster and client.[77]

Another reality facing the GAO during this period was the body of enabling legislation that committed it to promoting businesslike government. That legislation began with the 1921 Budget and Accounting Act and was sustained up to and throughout Staats's tenure. The norm of businesslike government that that legislation emphasized is irrelevant to the operations of government. Democratic governments operate through advocacy and bargaining. As Harold Seidman has pointed out, "Economy and efficiency are demonstrably not the prime purposes of public administration. . . . The basic issues of Federal organization and administration relate to power: who shall control it and to what ends?"[78]

Businesslike government is also inconsistent with democratic values. The political system that has evolved out of the U.S. Constitution is rife with redundancy: separated branches that share power; federalism in which local governments, states, and the federal government compete for influence and resources; overlapping terms of office; and a multitude of other arrangements that serve to check legislative and executive power.[79] The American system celebrates pluralism and consensus. In fact as Theodore Lowi has argued, the government seeks to create groups where none exist.[80] In turn, these groups strive to establish government bureaus and then agencies to defend their interests,[81] thereby ensuring an even less businesslike government. For a democratic government, good decisions gain consensus and ignore such external criteria as economy, efficiency, and effectiveness in government.[82] Thus, the GAO's dominant norm of promoting businesslike government saddles the organization with responsibilities that constrain leadership and organizational flexibility.

Given these realities, did Staats have any alternative courses of action that would have been preferable to those he chose? Some of those interviewed argued that Staats should have worked harder to block the creation of the Congressional Budget Office (CBO) and the Office of Technology Assessment (OTA). They suggested that those organizations had captured new responsibilities that rightfully belonged to the GAO. Yet this argument ignored the statutory realities discussed above and the organizational essence that had evolved around those realities. That essence was accounting, and the composition of the GAO was predominantly accountants. To assume the functions entrusted to the CBO or the OTA would have required hiring other kinds of professionals, thereby destabilizing the organization.

Other interviewees, especially the auditor advocates and staff auditors, argued that Staats should have been more forceful in moving the GAO into program auditing by firing accountants resistant to this new format and hiring more advocates to replace them. Such a course of action would have involved a number of problems. First, Staats was not comfortable with such behavior. Second, Joseph Campbell had used that style and had created considerable paranoia and hesitancy within the organization. Third, such a course of action would have met considerable resistance within the GAO and from Congress. This resistance might well have backfired by putting Staats on the defensive and thereby inhibiting his reforms.[83]

Still other interviewees quibbled with one or another of Staats's reforms—the planning system, the lead division concept, or the new personnel procedures. But these changes suited Staats's style and did end up expanding the perspectives of the accountants. Other reforms may indeed have been marginally better, but that marginal difference would not have altered GAO performance.

Thus, there would appear to have been no other suitable courses of action. That is, there were apparently no other courses of action that fit environmental demands, institutional needs, and the character of Staats himself. This conclusion does not, however, confirm that Staats was an effective or successful leader. We still lack a suitable standard against which to judge success.

Philip Selznick offers two criteria that are persuasive. First, successful leaders manage tensions among internal groups such that organizational output is enhanced. Second, such leaders also maintain an organization's distinctive character against external assault.[84] To put it another way, successful strategic or entrepreneurial leadership can best be measured by whether an organizational culture is created or transformed in a way that brings the organization into better alignment with its task environment.

Staats's performance as comptroller general satisfied all of these criteria. His introduction of the auditor advocates and the staff auditors while simultaneously retaining the services and enthusiasm of the line auditors and auditor managers ensured the establishment of the program audit and transformed the GAO's culture. He also protected the GAO's character from assault after the Holifield Hearings and during the tumultuous period of the 1970s. Furthermore, he instituted the program audit, which satisfied congressional needs.

No factors other than leadership are relevant in explaining the differential impact of the GAO on its environment. Within the organization, Staats was the primary force, for he created the new executive and professional elites. Without, Congress was preoccupied with reasserting its constitutional authority and seemed ready to support the GAO only if it was disposed to seek a new role in this enterprise. That is, Congress was willing to pass laws expanding the GAO's mandate if GAO leaders were so inclined. Beyond Congress, no other environmental force was potent enough to demand a GAO resurgence. In fact, Staats's accomplishments went beyond Selznick's criteria of management and protection by expanding the GAO's mandate and independence. By the end of his term, virtually no government agency was exempt from GAO audit, and Congress had legitimized much of Staats's vision in numerous pieces of legislation. Furthermore, the GAO not only was respected by Congress as the foremost symbol of accountability for the executive branch but also was endowed with a firm mandate to conduct program-effectiveness audits. Thus by Selznick's criteria and the criteria of cultural change, and through the process of elimination, Staats must be considered a successful leader.

He was also a creative leader. His creativity, of course, grew out of his experiences and his personality. Certainly, his vast experience in the executive branch had armed him with the skills necessary for the position of comptroller general. But of perhaps more importance was his belief in the gospel of public administration, which proclaimed the perfectability of government through the tenets of economy and efficiency in administration. This belief seemed to evoke an evangelical spirit within him and appears to have been the motivating force behind his initiatives for the GAO. This spirit animated his speeches, his writings, and many of his observations in meetings with both outsiders and GAO insiders. Clearly, his undergraduate and graduate education in this field, as well as his early years in the old BOB, formed and shaped his style and philosophy.

Conditions for Creative Leadership

As we have discussed it here, leadership demands creativity and insight. Creative leaders must possess first the intellect to uncover organizational commitments and frailties. They must also have the temperament to set and persist in a course of action. Such a temperament demands determination, nerve, and strength of character. Those leaders who possess creative abilities can discover the environmental conditions that promote or block change.[85]

In the case of the GAO, the comptroller general's term was unusually long by government standards. Fifteen years is an extended period for most government leaders, whose average tenure is twenty-two months.[86] Each of the four comptroller generals discussed here had the opportunity for strategic leadership. Two of them lacked the necessary creativity. In McCarl's case, the New Deal provided opportunities for change, and in Campbell's, congressional objections to the defense contract audit. Neither saw these opportunities; they preferred to preoccupy themselves with marginal modifications in institutional routines. In the end their leadership failed, because they were unable to protect the GAO's essence or character from congressional assault.

Both Warren and Staats were creative enough to recognize the opportunities missed by their predecessors. Warren regenerated the GAO in the face of assaults by President Roosevelt, the Brownlow Committee, and the Hoover Commission. Staats faced the condemnation of the Holifield Hearings and the unpredictable environment created by the congressional reassertion of power in the 1970s. Staats was able to both see and exploit the opportunities in that era in order to realign the GAO.

Thus, when both the environment and the institution are ripe for change, the creative leader can exercise strategic leadership. Strategic leaders can generate a new institutional vision, new structures to institutionalize that vision, and new policies to enshrine it. These opportunities are rare in the experience of most organizational leaders. Such a happy coincidence of environmental and institutional forces is probably present for less than 5 percent of all leaders.

Leadership, therefore, is an exhausting and dangerous endeavor. The metaphor of leadership as swimming at night in an unexplored, turbulent river thus takes on more meaning. Only those who have developed the requisite skills of intellect and temperament will survive the sport. For most survivors, success cannot be measured in unending accolades for their efforts; in fact, success is quickly forgotten. External and internal critics dwell on failures, missed opportunities, and improper decisions. Perhaps the only enduring satisfaction for leaders is a personal one: that during their plunge into the waters, their institutions advanced a few yards or perhaps, in unusual circumstances, a few miles.

Notes

Portions of this paper were taken from Wallace Earl Walker, *Changing Organizational Culture: Strategy, Structure and Professionalism in the U.S. General Accounting Office* (Knoxville: University of Tennessee Press, 1986).

1. Robert C. Tucker, *Politics As Leadership* (Columbia: University of Missouri Press, 1981), 18–19.

2. Carl von Clausewitz, *On War*, ed. and trans. Michael Howard and Peter Paret (Princeton: Princeton University Press, 1976), 119–20; Herbert Kaufman, *The Administrative Behavior of Federal Bureau Chiefs* (Washington, D.C.: Brookings Institution, 1981), 134.

3. Philip Selznick, *Leadership in Administration: A Sociological Interpretation* (New York: Harper & Row, 1957; paperback Berkeley: University of California Press, 1984), 66; Herbert Kaufman, *The Limits of Organizational Change* (University: University of Alabama Press, 1971), 10–11.

4. Kaufman, *Limits*, 10.

5. Andrew Pettigrew, "On Studying Organizational Cultures," *Administrative Science Quarterly* 24 (December 1979): 578.

Alexander Leighton writes about organizations under stress as being ripe for change; see his "Leadership in a Stress Situation," in *Studies in Leadership*, ed. Alvin Gouldner (New York: Harper & Brothers, 1950), 608. For uses of strategy and structure as concepts see Alfred D. Chandler, Jr., *Strategy and Structure* (Cambridge: MIT Press, 1962); and Samuel P. Huntington, *The Common Defense* (New York: Columbia University Press, 1961), esp. 123–35.

6. See Tom Cronin, "Thinking and Learning about Leadership" (Occasional Paper, Fall 1983), 13. On leadership as gamesmanship see Lawrence Lynn, *Managing the Public's Business* (New York: Basic Books, 1981), 145.

7. Clausewitz, *On War*, 104–5, 107. On temperament see also Richard E. Neustadt, *Presidential Power* (New York: John Wiley, 1960), 180–83.

8. My research on the GAO included extensive interviewing, documentary research, and observation of GAO meetings. During the period 1972–77, I interviewed 153 GAO employees at all levels of the organization, including the senior leadership, nearly all of the GAO division and office directors, audit managers in all GAO audit divisions, and auditors in four of the GAO's regional offices. Additionally, I discussed GAO activities with 34 executives and senior bureaucrats from six federal departments and agencies, with 17 congressmen and congressional staff members, and with 8 newsmen, all of whom were familiar with GAO audit activities. Finally, I was permitted to attend several GAO planning meetings chaired by the comptroller general or the deputy comptroller general. In all cases I promised interviewees anonymity.

I also reviewed all the comptroller general's annual reports from 1921 to the present, consulted numerous internal documents and congressional documents and statutes. Furthermore, I consulted scores of books, dissertations, and journal articles that discussed the GAO or its audit activities. Finally, I took a graduate-level course in financial management and accounting to better understand the accountant's discipline.

My conclusions about the GAO are contained in Wallace Earl Walker, "The Bureaucratic Politics of Fault Finding: The Cultures of Auditing in the General Accounting Office" (Ph.D. diss, MIT, 1980); and in idem, *Changing Organizational Culture: Strategy, Structure and Professionalism in the U.S. General Accounting Office* (Knoxville: University of Tennessee Press, 1986).

I am also grateful to Erwin Hargrove, Jim Doig, Dick Neustadt, and Fritz Mosher for their comments on drafts of this paper.

9. U.S. Congress, House, Committee on Government Operations, *Comptroller General Reports to Congress on Audits of Defense Contracts: Hearings before a Subcommittee*, 89th Cong., 1st sess., 1965, 646 (hereafter cited as *Holifield Hearings*); and U.S. Congress, House, Committee on Government Operations, *Defense Contract Audits: H. Rept. 1344*, 89th Cong., 2d sess., 1966, 4, 8, 9 (hereafter cited as *Holifield Report*). See also the following *Comptroller General's Annual Reports*: 1962, 250–54; 1963, 285–90; 1964, 376–84; and 1965, 66 (hereafter cited as *CGAR, 19——*).

10. Walker, "Bureaucratic Politics," 38–43.

11. U.S. Congress, House, Congressman James Good, Speech on the Budget and Accounting Act, 17 October 1919, 66th Cong., 1st sess., and 5 May 1921, 67th Cong., 1st sess., *Congressional Record*, 66, no. 7:7085–86 (emphasis added), and 67, no. 2:1090.

12. Walker, *Changing Organizational Culture*, 30.

13. President's Committee on Administrative Management, *Report of the President's Committee on Administrative Management in the Government of the United States* (Washington, D.C.: GPO, 1937). Hereafter I refer to this committee as the Brownlow Committee, so named for the chairman, Louis Brownlow.

14. Wellington Brink, "Lindsay Carter Warren: Whip over Public Spending," as contained in U.S. Congress, House, Extension of Remarks of Congressman Graham A. Barden, 9 May 1946, 79th Cong., 2d sess., *Congressional Record*, 17, no. 2, A2560–62; "Footnotes on the Headlines," *New York Times*, 4 August 1940.

15. Warren's strategy was inferred from a careful reading of the *CGAR*s from 1940 to 1954 (*CGAR, 1954* was most useful). This section is also reliant on articles about and by Warren in numerous newspapers and in the *Congressional Record*, some of which are cited in no. 11 and 14, above.

16. Walker, *Changing Organizational Culture*, 45–48.

17. Budget and Accounting Procedures Act, in U.S. Code, 1970, title 31, secs. 65, 66, 67 (1950).

18. Walker, "Bureaucratic Politics," 135–99.

19. Herbert Roback, "Program Evaluation By and For the Congress," *Bureaucrat* 5 (April 1976): 11–12; U.S. Congress, Senate, speech by Senator Roth, "Public Program Analysis and Evaluation for the Purposes of the Executive and the Congress," 8 June 1972, 92d Cong., 2d sess., *Congressional Record* 13, no. 16, 20179–80.

20. See Neil Churchill and William Cooper, "Auditing and Accounting—Past, Present and Future," in *Eric Louis Kohler: Accounting's Man of Principle*, ed. William Cooper and Yuji Ijiri (Reston, Va.: Reston Publishing, 1979), 226; William Cooper and Yuji Ijiri, "Accounting and Accountability Relations," ibid., 204–6; Roger Wilkins, "Mayors Are Taking a New Look at Problems of America's Cities," *New York Times*, 9 April 1979; and Jacob Birnberg and Natwar Gandi, "Toward Defining the Accountant's Role in the Evaluation of Social Programs," *Accounting, Organizations and Society*, 1976, 5–10.

21. Lawrence Dodd and Richard Schott, *Congress and the Administrative State* (New York: John Wiley & Sons, 1979); James Sundquist, *The Decline and Resurgence of Congress* (Washington, D.C.: Brookings Institution, 1981).

22. Harrison Fox, Jr., and Susan Hammond, *Congressional Staffs* (New York: Free Press, 1977), 171.

23. The campaign to bring these sacrosanct agencies to heel was extensive. Much of the work was done by the Senate Committee on Government Operations and by Congressman Wright Patman. For more details see Walker, "Bureaucratic Politics," 293, n. 17, and 300, n. 80. On GAO monitoring of campaign contributions see *CGAR, 1972*, 27–31; *CGAR, 1975*, 9–10, 295–96; and Linda Charlton, "Inquiry into Democratic Break-In Strips General Accounting Office of Some of Its Anonymity," *New York Times*, 3 September 1972.

24. As noted in n. 8, numerous not-for-attribution interviews were conducted for this study. Interview II48 provided me the details here. Hereafter I will use a similar shorthand notation.

25. Lyndon Johnson, "Remarks at the Swearing In of Elmer Staats as Comptroller General of the United States," 8 March 1966, *Public Papers of the Presidents: Lyndon Baines Johnson, 1965–1966* (Washington, D.C.: GPO, 1967), 287–88.

26. Unless otherwise noted, the material on Elmer Staats in this section is taken from the following sources: "Biography: Elmer B. Staats," supplied by the GAO, Washington, D.C.; U.S. Congress, Senate, Committee on Government Operations, *Nomination of Elmer B. Staats: Hearing*, 89th Cong., 2d sess., 1966; "Presidential Appointments," *Washington Post*, 13 February 1966; "Press Release of Senator John Kennedy," 19 December 1960, Palm Beach, Fla.; and Louis Brandt, "New Head of General Accounting Office Has Long Experience in Budget Bureau," *St. Louis Post Dispatch*, 20 February 1966.

27. Interview II34.

28. U.S. Congress, Senate, Senators Carlson, Stennis, and Dirksen on "Elmer B. Staats—New Comptroller General," 16 February 1966, 89th Cong., 2d sess., *Congressional Record*, 112, n. 3: 3022–32; U.S. Congress, Senate, Senator Mondale on "Careful Canvass," 17 February 1966, ibid., 3374; interviews II5, II30, III23.

29. Elmer Staats, "Evaluating Program Effectiveness," in *Program Formulation and Development: Selected Papers on Public Administration*, ed. David Bowen and Lynton Caldwell (Bloomington: Indiana University Press, 1960), 52–76.

30. Hugh Heclo, "OMB and the Presidency—The Problem of 'Neutral Competence,'" *The Public Interest* 38 (Winter 1975): 80–98.

31. Hugh Heclo, *A Government of Strangers* (Washington, D.C.: Brookings Institution, 1977), 164–66.

32. Elmer Staats, "Intergovernmental Relations: A Fiscal Perspective," *Annals*, 1974, 33–39. On Staats's strategy, thirty-five interviews were helpful, as well as the *CGAR*s.

33. Elmer Staats, "New Problems of Accountability" (Speech before the American Society of Public Administration, n.d.), 2; reprint provided by the Information Office of the GAO, Washington, D.C.

34. U.S. Congress, Senate, Committee on Government Operations, *Government Economy and Spending Reform Act of 1976: Hearings*, 94th Cong., 2d sess., 1976, 126.

35. *CGAR, 1966*, 22; *CGAR, 1981*, 89.

36. "Elmer Staats Defines GAO Role, Scope," *Washington Star*, 10 January 1977.

37. Interviews II64, III23, IV3. See also Roger Sperry et al., *GAO, 1966–1981: An Administrative History* (Washington, D.C.: GPO, 1981), 63, 65–67.

38. Elmer Staats, "Management or Operation Auditing," *GAO Review*, Winter 1972, 27.

39. Heclo, *Government of Strangers*, 166–70.

40. *CGAR, 1968*, 12; *CGAR, 1969*, 12; "Statements before Congressional Committees by the Honorable Elmer Staats," supplied by the Office of the Comptroller General, GAO, August 1976.

41. For a few of the many examples see the following: U.S., Congress, Senate, Committee on Government Operations, *Capability of the GAO to Analyze and Audit Defense Expenditures: Hearings*, 91st Cong., 1st sess., 1969, 170; Eric Redman, *The Dance of Legislation* (New York: Simon & Schuster, 1973), 204; and William Selover, "Congressional Watchdog—Protecting the Tax Dollar," *Christian Science Monitor*, 11 March 1968. For testimonials from three noted scholars (Alton Frye, Harvey Mansfield, Sr., and Roy Crawley) on the GAO's responsiveness to Congress see U.S. Congress, Joint Committee on Congressional Operations, *Congressional Research Support and Information Services: Hearings*, 93d Cong., 2d sess., 1974, 79, 103, 109.

42. See the following articles authored by Elmer Staats: "Future of the American City," *GAO Review*, Spring 1978, 1–5; "Acquisition Management Needs Realistic Forecasting to Close the Confidence Gap," *Defense Management Journal*, April 1974, 20–23; "The GAO—How Its Work Affects Local Government," *Government Finance* 2 (August 1973); "GAO Audit Standards: Development and Implementation," *Public Management*, February 1974, 2–7; and "The Nation's Stake in Congressional Budget Reform," *National Public Accountant*, December 1975, 3–7. See also Frederick Mosher, *The GAO* (Boulder, Colo.: Westview Press, 1979).

43. U.S. Congress, Senate, Committee on Government Operations, *Nomination of Robert F. Keller: Hearing*, 91st Cong., 1st sess., 1969.

44. *CGAR, 1977*, 2; U.S. Congress, Senate, "General Accounting Office Positions," 3 December 1971, 92d Cong., 1st sess., *Congressional Record* 117, no. 34: 44485; GAO memos, Elmer Staats to all employees, 25 January 1972, "Strengthening GAO's Organization to Meet the Demands of the 1970's," and 6 May 1976, "Organizational Changes."

45. *CGAR, 1971*, 8; *CGAR, 1972*, 2–3; *CGAR, 1978*, 1; *CGAR, 1966*, 16. GAO memos, Task Force on Treatment of Policy Issues to the assistant comptroller general and division and office directors, 13 December 1976, "Problem Solving Working Paper for the Williamsburg Meeting"; Directors of the Office of Program Planning and the Office of Policy to the comptroller general, 19 October 1976, "Communication"; and

Executive Secretary of the Conference Committee to the Director's Conference attendees, 24 November 1976, "December Director's Conference."

46. GAO memo, Chairman of the Organization Planning Committee to the comptroller general, 30 August 1971, "Proposals for Reorganization of the General Accounting Office"; numerous interviews; numerous *CGARs*, including *1971*, 9; *1972*, 2–3; *1974*, 39; and *1976*, 74, 85.

47. U.S. Congress, House, Select Committee on Congressional Operations, *General Accounting Office Services to Congress: An Assessment*, 95th Cong., 2d sess., 1978, H. Rept. 95–1317, 12; numerous interviews in field offices and at GAO headquarters.

48. *CGAR, 1966*, 5.

49. U.S. Congress, House, Committee on Post Office and Civil Service, *Separate Personnel System for the General Accounting Office: Hearing before the Subcommittee on Civil Service*, 95th Cong., 2d sess., 1978.

50. For example, the spring 1972 issue of the *GAO Review* contained articles on engineering applications to the program audit, use of Delphi techniques in program auditing, use of questionnaires in gaining information on federal programs, new GAO responsibilities in federal campaign reporting, and details on the new GAO reorganization. The winter 1978 issue contained articles on computer-assisted auditing, a program audit on needs of the aged, studying the impact of the regulatory agencies, and supplying information to Congress on federal programs.

51. *CGAR, 1966*, 119–21; *CGAR, 1972*, 154–56; GAO, Office of Personnel Management, *Training Newsletter*, 1 April–30 June 1976.

52. *CGAR, 1981*.

53. *CGAR, 1966*, 276; U.S. Congress, House, Appropriations Committee, *Legislative Branch Appropriations for 1980: Hearings*, 96th Cong., 1st sess., 1979.

54. Elmer Staats, "Career Planning and Development: Which Way Is Up? *GAO Review*, Fall 1976, 1–6.

55. GAO, Program Planning Staff, "Proposed Conceptual Design of an Integrated Management Information System for the U.S. General Accounting Office," September 1968; GAO, Comptroller General's Order Number 2.17, "Data Processing Center," 9 February 1970; numerous interviews and *CGARs, 1966–81*.

56. Jameson Doig, "Entrepreneurial Leadership in the 'Independent' Government Organization" (Paper prepared for the annual meeting of the American Political Science Association, Chicago, 1–4 September 1983).

57. Unless otherwise noted, this section is based principally upon interviews. The quoted material without attribution is from GAO evaluators themselves or close observers of the GAO in the bureaucracy, Congress, or the news media. Also useful in this paper, particularly in detailing the audit process were GAO, *Comprehensive Audit Manual, I* and *II* (Washington, D.C., 1972); ibid., *Report Manual* (Washington, D.C., 1976). For more details on these interviews see Walker, "Bureaucratic Politics," 347–53, 401–8.

The late Professor Jeffrey Pressman, of MIT, suggested that perhaps the best way to talk about the GAO auditor-evaluators was to let them talk for themselves. Since the auditors are doing the talking, their remarks are in the present tense.

58. See the following reports of the comptroller general: "Financial Operations of the Five Service Academies, FPCD-75-117," 6 February 1975; "Academic and Military Programs of the Five Service Academies, FPCD-76-8," 31 October 1975; and "Student Attrition at the Five Federal Service Academies, FPCD-76-12," 5 March 1976. Hereafter all references to audit reports will include their title, GAO number, (e.g., FPCD-76-12), and date.

59. The consultants for the liquid metal fast breeder reactor study included the following: Dean Abrahamson, environmentalist, School of Public Affairs, University of Minnesota; Manson Benedict, nuclear engineer, MIT; Hans Bethe, nuclear physicist and Nobel Prize winner; Ralph Lapp, nuclear physicist and author of books on science; John Taylor, general manager, Breeder Reactor Division, Westinghouse Corporation; and Charles Luce, chairman of the board, Consolidated Edison of New York (see U.S. Comptroller General, "The Liquid Metal Fast Breeder Reactor: Promises and Uncertainties, OSP-76-1," 31 July 1975).

60. The use of consultants is much like the use of contract arrangements employed by executive agencies. As Harold Seidman notes, "Contracting may broaden the base of public support by fostering alliances with politically influential organizations and groups in the private community" (see his *Politics, Position, and Power*, 2d ed. [New York: Oxford University Press, 1975], 292).

61. For more details on the audit repertoire see Walker, "Bureaucratic Politics," 354–400.

62. U.S. Comptroller General, *Standards for Audit of Government Organizations, Programs, Activities, and Functions* (Washington, D.C.: GAO, 1972); Darwin Casler, *The Evolution of CPA Ethics*, Michigan State University Graduate School of Business Administration Occasional Paper, no. 12 (East Lansing, 1964); Robert Rasor, "Operational Auditing: Training Booklet Number 1" (N.p.: R. Rasor for GAO, 1973).

63. "Veterans Administration Justification of Costs and Benefits of Proposed Computer System (Target), HRD-77-98," 20 July 1977. This example is based on the following interviews: IV26, IV31, IV38, IV43, IV44, and IV51. Also, numerous newspaper clippings were provided by the interviewees.

64. Pat Towell, "Case Study: Carter and Congress on AWACS," *Congressional Quarterly*, 3 September 1977, 1857–63.

65. "Review of Status of Development toward Establishment of a Unified National Communications System, B-166655," 19 July 1969; "Role of Federal Coal Resources in Meeting National Energy Goals Needs to be Determined and the Leasing Process Improved, RED-76-79," 1 April 1976.

66. "Outlook for Federal Goals to Accelerate Leasing of Oil and Gas Pressures on the Outer Continental Shelf, RED-75-343," 19 March 1975; "Implications of Deregulating the Price of Natural Gas, OSP-76-11," 14 January 1976.

67. "Federal Programs for Education of the Handicapped: Issues and Problems, B-164031(1)," 5 December 1974.

68. For example, the following numbers of reports were prepared: in 1968, 1,153; in 1971, 975; in 1974, 1,079; and in 1977, 1,082 (data from the *CGAR*s).

69. For some examples see the following: Senate Committee on Government Operations, *Capability of the GAO to Analyze and Audit Defense Expenditures, Hearings*; "Review of Economic Opportunity Programs," as reprinted in U.S. Congress, *Review of Economic Opportunity Programs*, 91st Cong., 1st sess., 1969, Joint Economic Committee Print; "Summary of Conclusions and Recommendations on the Operations of Civil Departments and Agencies, HRD-77-33," 17 January 1977; U.S. Congress, Senate, Senator Nelson on "A Unique and Unprecedented Audit of the OEO," 91st Cong., 1st sess., 20 March 1969, *Congressional Record* 65, no. 6: 7017–19; and Roback, "Program Evaluation."

70. Seymour Scher, "Conditions for Legislative Control," *Journal of Politics* 25 (1963): 531–33; Stephen Bailey, *Congress in the Seventies* (New York: St. Martin's Press, 1970), 84. See also Sundquist, *Decline and Resurgence of Congress*, 327.

71. James Thurber, "The Evolving Role and Effectiveness of the Congressional

Research Agencies," in *The House At Work*, ed. W. Cooper and G. C. Mackenzie (Austin: University of Texas Press, 1980), 300.

72. Robert Salisbury and Kenneth Shepsle, "Congressional Staff Turnover and the Ties-That-Bind," *American Political Science Review* 75 (1981): 381–96.

73. Among those who have discussed this development, perhaps the first was Allen Schick. See his "The Appropriations Committees in Congress" (Paper prepared for the annual meeting of the American Political Science Association, San Francisco, 2–5 September 1975).

74. Roback, "Program Evaluation," 29.

75. Martin Rein and Sheldon White, "Can Policy Research Help Policy?" *The Public Interest*, 1977, 126, 130–35.

76. Interviews I12, I147, IV39. See also, for example, Richard Madden, "Aspin Gets Leverage with Press Releases," *New York Times*, 3 February 1976; and Steven Roberts, "Proxmire Thrives in His Chosen Role as Senate Maverick," ibid., 19 September 1977.

77. Sundquist, *Decline and Resurgence of Congress*.

78. Seidman, *Politics, Position, and Power*, 27–28.

79. Martin Landau, "Redundancy, Rationality, and the Problem of Duplication and Overlap," in *Bureaucratic Power in National Politics*, ed. Francis Rourke, 4th ed. (Boston: Little, Brown, 1986), 478.

80. Theodore Lowi, *The End of Liberalism* (New York: W. W. Norton, 1969), 83.

81. Seidman, *Politics, Position, and Power*, 105–151, 224.

82. Charles Schultze, *The Politics and Economics of Public Spending* (Washington, D.C.: Brookings Institution, 1968), 52.

83. On the matter of changing organizations slowly see Leighton, "Leadership in a Stress Situation," 606. Donald Warwick notes that "decimation" engenders massive resistance (see his *A Theory of Public Bureaucracy* [Cambridge: Harvard University Press, 1978], 209–10). See also Lewis Anthony Dexter, "Some Strategic Considerations in Innovating Leadership," in Gouldner, *Studies in Leadership*, 598–600.

84. Selznick, *Leadership in Administration*, 62.

85. On the importance of correctly reading culture see Terrence Deal and Allan Kennedy, *Corporate Cultures: The Rites and Rituals of Corporate Life* (Reading, Pa.: Addison-Wesley, 1982), 17.

86. Heclo, *Government of Strangers*, 103–4.

10

Marriner Eccles and Leadership in the Federal Reserve System

Donald F. Kettl

In February 1933 a group of Utah businessmen gathered in Salt Lake City's elegant Hotel Utah. They had invited Stuart Chase, a Roosevelt administration insider and prominent economics writer, to speak to them, but a snowstorm delayed their guest. The meeting's chairman stalled for as long as he could, but finally, to keep the audience from growing too restless, he invited a prominent local banker, Marriner Eccles, to speak until Chase arrived. Eccles began delivering one of his usual orations. The Depression, he told the audience, was the result of a failure of leadership, both political and financial. The depth of suffering was the consequence of the nation's failure to marshall its strength to revitalize the economy. Contrary to what many businessmen were arguing, the problem was not excessive federal spending and an unbalanced budget but too little extravagance in federal spending. The federal government, he said, had the resources to put people back to work, and it ought to be doing so. Eccles was, in the early 1930s, a Rocky Mountain pioneer who preached the virtues of compensatory fiscal policy, a Keynesian who had never heard of Keynes.

Eccles had barely gotten warmed up when Chase finally arrived. By this time, however, there was little time left for a speech and no time left for lunch. Eccles joined a small group that took Chase out for a meal, and he missed no chance to ply Chase with questions about the Roosevelt "brain trusters." Finally, perhaps to get a bit of lunch himself, Chase asked Eccles, "All right, now, supposing you had a job in Washington, what would you do specifically to achieve recovery? You tell me while I'm eating." Eccles repeated his speech. Impressed with what he heard, Chase suggested to Eccles, "Why not get yourself a larger audience?" Eccles told Chase that he would have such an audience in a few weeks when he appeared with two hundred other financial leaders before congressional hearings in Washington. "Well, in that event," Chase told him, "why don't you go up to New York and see Rex Tugwell [Roosevelt's brain truster for economic policy] and have a talk with him about the things you've been telling me? I'll write him a letter saying you are coming to see him."[1]

Eccles had his meeting with Tugwell a few weeks later in a drug-store booth near Tugwell's Columbia University office. Eccles urged on Tugwell a program that the Utahan called "logical radicalism": large federal spending—and a large federal deficit—to begin putting people back to work. Eccles made a good impression, and in October Tugwell wrote Eccles asking him to visit Washington. Tugwell introduced him to Mordecai Ezekiel, a long-time employee of the Department of Agri-culture, and to Henry Wallace. They joined a few other guests at Eccles's hotel for a wide-ranging discussion of the economy, and Eccles repeated his familiar points.[2]

Eccles had just returned home when he received a telegram asking him to return to Washington. Treasury Secretary Will Woodin had resigned because of illness, and Roosevelt had made a recess appoint-ment of Henry Morgenthau, Jr., to succeed him. Morgenthau had found the Treasury "an empty shelf," and he wanted Eccles to serve as his assistant. Eccles turned the question over in his mind. On the one hand, he told himself, he had been "full of talk about what the government should and shouldn't do. You ought to put up or shut up." On the other hand, he had not worked for anyone since the age of twenty-two. "I've always been my own boss. I'm proud of that, I like to do things in my own way, and in my own time" (138–39). Finally, he decided that if he did not take the job, he would regret it for the rest of his life. He told Morgenthau he would come to Washington for a year and a half. That schedule would allow his children to return to school in Utah in the fall of 1936.

Eccles had barely had a chance to settle into the Treasury when Eugene Black, governor of the Federal Reserve Board (as the board's chairman was then called), resigned in June 1934. At a White House conference in August, Morgenthau leaned over to Eccles and whispered, "Marriner, I've been talking to the president about your filling Eugene Black's place"(165). A few weeks later Roosevelt asked him directly if he would accept the job. Eccles boldly replied that he would find the job appealing only if fundamental changes were made in the Federal Re-serve System. Roosevelt asked what changes in particular Eccles had in mind, and Eccles requested time to put them in shape.

He returned to Roosevelt with a three-page memo. "If the monetary mechanism is to be used as an instrument for the promotion of business stability," he wrote, "conscious control and management are essential." Such control, he argued, was then impossible because the system was dominated by the heads of the twelve regional Federal Reserve Banks, who "cannot help but be profoundly influenced by a narrow banking rather than a broad social point of view." The board should be reorganized, he said, to concentrate control of the system in the hands of the board instead of the Reserve Banks.[3] Eccles was proposing nothing less than the complete restructuring of the Federal Reserve System and a recasting of the compromise that in 1913 had created the Federal Reserve, a compromise in which the autonomy of the Reserve Banks had been a key element.

"Marriner," Roosevelt replied, "that is quite an action program you want. It will be a knock-down and drag-out fight to get it through. But we might as well undertake it now as any other time. It seems to be necessary." And he added, "Gossip has gotten around about my considering appointing you Governor. It is only fair you should know that formidable opposition has developed as a result. However, I don't give a damn. That opposition is coming from boys whom I am not following." Eccles told Roosevelt, "Well, Mr. President, if you don't give a damn, I don't see why I should" (175). A week later Roosevelt appointed Eccles governor. The man who came to Washington to serve for a few months stayed for seventeen years and became perhaps the most powerful chairman the Federal Reserve has ever had.

Early Days

Marriner's father, David, had moved from Scotland to America about the time of the Battle of Gettysburg to join Brigham Young in Salt Lake City. The family was very poor, and David worked digging potatoes and milling grain to feed them. David Eccles, however, soon escaped poverty by parlaying a series of lumber contracts into the prosperous Eccles Lumber Company. He then put some of his lumbering profits into the first sugar beet factory in the region. The two ventures made him a millionaire within a few years. Along the way, he also acquired two families. He first married Bertha Jensen, who bore him twelve children. Then, shortly before the Mormon Church forbade bigamy, he also married Ellen Stoddard. Marriner, born in 1890, was the oldest child of this second marriage and was named after the Mormon apostle who performed his parents' marriage.

As a young boy, Marriner worked for his father, at five cents an hour for a ten-hour day. If he saved his money, David Eccles told Marriner, he would be allowed to buy one share of his father's Oregon

Lumber Company stock, at par value, for one hundred dollars. "It's worth much more than that," Marriner's father told him, "and if you come to own a share you will be a capitalist." It took the boy three summers to earn enough money to buy his share, and then at the age of eleven Marriner finally became a capitalist. He proudly wrote in his memoirs, "I've never ceased being a capitalist since then" (27).

After graduation from high school in 1909, the last formal education of his life, Marriner went off to serve two years as a Mormon missionary in Glasgow, where, Eccles later confessed, "the number of converts I made could be counted on the fingers of one hand" (29). He then returned home for a different kind of mission: to keep down costs at a hydroelectric plant his father's company was building. He was working at the camp when he learned, on 5 December 1912, that his father had died.

David Eccles left behind an estate worth more than $7 million and no will. By Utah law, the first wife and her children inherited five-sevenths of the estate, leaving only two-sevenths to Marriner and his family. He soon became convinced that his half-brothers were ruining the family companies, and he determined either to change their practices or to divest his family from the estate. Marriner parlayed several investments into a large position in his father's construction and sugar businesses, and then he went to his half-brother David with a simple offer: he could buy out Marriner's side of the family, or Marriner would buy him out. David refused and threw Marriner out of the office.

Marriner then went to the directors representing the rest of the oustanding shares and arranged for a majority of shareholders to support him. A repeat meeting with David had a different tone and a new ultimatum: David would have to buy out Marriner and his colleagues, or David and his managers would have to resign immediately. David tried unsuccessfully to raise cash for the purchase, and Marriner finally bought him out for sixty cents on the dollar. "The aftermath in my personal relations with two older half-brothers," he remembered later, "was quite unhappy" (47).

By the age of thirty, Marriner had built a remarkable empire. He had skillfully and ruthlessly outflanked his brothers and established himself as unquestioned financial head of the families. He formed the First Security Corporation, one of the nation's first bank holding companies, to coordinate a chain of more than fifteen banks scattered throughout Idaho, Wyoming, and Utah. He was president of the Eccles Investment Company, the First Security Corporation, the First National Bank, and the First Savings Bank of Ogden. He managed hotel, lumber, and milk products companies. He was vice president of the sugar business and served as director for the construction, railroad, coal, lumber, and power companies. His was a land, as he titled his memoirs, of "beckoning frontiers," and by thirty years of age he had conquered the frontiers within his grasp.

In the coming years, he concentrated most of his energy on his banking empire, and the banking crises of the Depression severely tested his acumen. A competitor of one of Eccles's Ogden banks did not open one Monday morning, and that led to a run on his own bank. He asked his staff to come in an hour early, and he told them, "Go about your business as though nothing unusual were happening. Smile, be pleasant, talk about the weather, show no signs of panic." He instructed everyone to make any payments requested—but to do so slowly, using small bills, and checking signature cards. Eccles arranged for the bank to stay open as late as there were customers. The next morning, by prearranged signal, guards arrived from the Federal Reserve branch bank in Salt Lake City carrying bags of money. Eccles and an officer from the Federal Reserve Bank reassured the assembled crowd that there was plenty of money to meet everyone's needs. (Eccles did not tell them that the money belonged to the bank; it did not—it was borrowed from the Federal Reserve.) Eccles than changed his strategy and directed his staff to pay out the money quickly to avoid any lines. Customers who walked in saw no long lines and no sense of panic. They left their money in the bank, and the run ended. Twenty years later, in his memoirs, Eccles's relief was still palpable. "I thanked God," he wrote, "for the nerves I inherited from my father and mother" (62).

If the banking crises brought danger, they also brought great opportunity. Eccles picked from among threatened banks to enlarge his empire and even succeeded in acquiring the oldest national bank in the state, founded by Brigham Young and owned by the Mormon Church. When panics threatened his banks in other cities, he broke them with large banners outside reading "Your money is here for you. Come and get it" (70). His own success in weathering the banking crisis and the marked failure of others led him to believe that the Depression was a phenomenon that went beyond economic theory. At its roots, he concluded, was a crisis in confidence. The lack of confidence, however, was not itself a cause; rather, it was the very understandable product of economic circumstances. There was no reason for a businessman confidently to invest in new equipment because he could not sell the goods he had already produced. Glowing speeches bolstering the public's will, he concluded, would not do the job. Instead, he came to believe in a government program of a deliberately unbalanced federal budget, where the federal government's spending would stimulate private production and put idle men to work when the private sector was not up to the task. He did not recommend a perpetually unbalanced budget; a balanced budget, he believed, could help "offset the danger of a boom on the upswing, just as an unbalanced budget could help counteract a depression on a downswing" (79). He concluded, "The only way we could get out of the depression was through government action in placing purchasing power in the hands of people who were in need of it" (81).

Eccles had bettered harsh Western weather and stiff competition to build a remarkable empire. He had even managed to take advantage of the Depression's opportunities to expand his holdings. But he doubted the ability of free enterprise to pull the country out of its crisis. He was an entrepreneur who had built his fortune on free competition, but he had come to believe that the solution to the Depression lay outside the business world in aggressive action by the federal government.

Battles on Capitol Hill

The Federal Reserve challenge was one Eccles could not resist, but he did not win the job without a vigorous fight with Sen. Carter Glass. The Virginian had helped write the legislation for the Federal Reserve in 1913, and for more than twenty years he had felt a keen sense of proprietorship over the system. "Next to my own family," he told Comptroller of the Currency J. F. T. O'Connor, "the Federal Reserve System is nearest to my heart." Others were not so kind. An old Wilsonian, Josephus Daniels, wrote Roosevelt that Glass was "obsessed with the idea that the Federal Reserve Act, of which Carter thinks he is the sole author, makes no other legislation necessary." Daniels concluded that "Carter's mind is both closed and sealed to new ideas."[4] Roosevelt ruffled Glass by not consulting him on the Eccles nomination, so much so that Glass delayed his subcommittee's consideration of Eccles's nomination for three months and then the fight against him on the floor. The Senate finally confirmed Eccles with Glass standing alone in voting no.

In a short time Eccles once again ran afoul of Glass. Eccles tried to assuage Glass's hurt feelings by promising to discuss the banking bill reform with Glass before taking it up with anyone else. The bill arrived on Capitol Hill before Glass had seen it, however, and the senator was sure that once again Eccles and the administration were trying to maneuver around him. Eccles vainly tried to explain that advance consultation had become impossible because the interdepartmental committee reviewing the bill had worked until the last minute in making changes in the legislation. Eccles himself did not get a copy until after the bill had gone to Congress. But Glass ignored Eccles's apologies and intimated that the governor was lying to him. The error made Glass a fierce enemy of the banking bill and nearly cost Eccles the reform measure he had insisted on before taking the job. As a former banker who steered his own course, Eccles had developed little sense for Washington's political manners. "Had I any experience in these matters before that time," he wrote in his memoirs, "I would most certainly have worked much closer with Glass and seen to it that he was kept advised of all developments. But I was still a stranger in Egypt" (195–96). In the coming years, he developed a greater appreciation for the need for advance consultation with political powers, but he never came to enjoy it.

Eccles stirred deep dispute with his proposals. The passage of the original Federal Reserve Act had been a sharply contested battle. Just as populists worried about bankers' control, financiers worried that a government-controlled central bank would only fuel inflation. The Depression had only worsened the political conflict. Herbert Hoover struggled with the Federal Reserve and condemned it as a "weak reed for a nation to lean on in time of trouble."[5] The series of banking crises that rocked the country, furthermore, were the very catastrophes the Federal Reserve had been created to avoid. "If I had to depend on the Open Market Committee [run by the Federal Reserve Banks] to pull us out of this hole we would not be where we are to-day," Treasury Secretary Morgenthau complained to Eccles in 1935. "The Open Market Committee has done nothing in the interest of the government."[6] The Federal Reserve was gravely weakened and enjoyed little public support.

Eccles's bill proposed three fundamental changes in the Federal Reserve. First, working with Roosevelt economic adviser Laughlin Currie, he set more ambitious goals for the Federal Reserve's monetary policy. Congress had declared in 1913 that the system's policies "shall be fixed with a view of accommodating commerce and business." Currie, however, found the phrase "vague to the point of meaninglessness." Every critic saw in the phrase his own view of what the Federal Reserve ought to be doing, while during the Depression the Federal Reserve sat back on the phrase and did very little. Eccles and Currie worked together to propose a new mandate to Congress: "It shall be the duty of the Federal Reserve Board to exercise such power as it possesses in such manner as to promote conditions conducive to business stability and to mitigate by its influence unstabilizing fluctuations in the general level of production, trade, prices and employment, so far as may be possible within the scope of monetary action and credit administration."[7] The plan set a more aggressive role for the Federal Reserve and increased the chairman's (as its head was to be known) discretion to set the proper course.

Second, the bill proposed to remove most powers from the Federal Reserve Banks and concentrate them in the Federal Reserve Board. When Congress had passed the act in 1913, many populists had feared that Eastern bankers might quickly gain control of a central bank, so the Federal Reserve Act had created twelve reserve banks around the country to prevent any region from gaining control. Congress, furthermore, had decentralized most of the system's power to these banks, with the Washington-based board exercising only general oversight. That decentralization had made it almost impossible for the system to act during the Depression. "Decentralized control is almost a contradiction in terms," Currie wrote Eccles. "The more decentralization the less possibility there is of control." With the current Federal Reserve organizational structure, he concluded, "it is almost impossible to place definite responsibility anywhere."[8] Furthermore, the system's most valuable tool, open-market operations—the purchase and sale of securities to raise or lower the supply of money—was in uncertain hands. Eccles and Currie proposed to change that by shifting open-market powers from the Federal Reserve Banks to the Federal Reserve Board, which would be advised by representatives from five Federal Reserve Banks.

Finally, they argued that the Federal Reserve's monetary policies had to be far more closely tied to the administration's fiscal policies. The Federal Reserve's supporters had long championed the Supreme Court metaphor: the Federal Reserve, they said, ought to be just as autonomous as the U.S. Supreme Court in setting monetary policy. At this Currie took issue and argued, "There is no economic problem more important than achieving and maintaining prosperity, and since the actions of the monetary authority have a direct bearing upon the strength of business activity they must be subject to the control of the Administration."[9] Fiscal policy was to play the primary role in the New Deal, but monetary policy had an important supporting role: to create the conditions in which the recovery could flourish and to make sure it was not prematurely choked off. This in turn depended upon open-market operations under the firm control of a strong board, a board sensitive to the state of the economy and to the administration's needs. Eccles dealt with the old Supreme Court argument by saying that the Federal Reserve had to be "publicly controlled, rather than governmentally controlled."[10] The Federal Reserve was to act in the public interest but would not be the captive of any administration.

The bill won a vote of support from a special committee of the American Bankers Association, which agreed with nearly all of its provisions. Support from the financial community at large, however, quickly began to erode. Most bankers knew that legislation to strengthen the board was inevitable, but many of them feared that a stronger, centralized board with close ties to the administration would fail to take politically unpopular steps to rein in inflation when necessary. They joined with Glass to propose splitting the Federal Reserve reforms off from other parts of the banking bill. The administration, however, had carefully sweetened other titles of the bill with items of special interest to bankers. One title liberalized federal deposit insurance to the bankers' advantage, while another title removed a provision in existing law that would have forced banking officials holding loans from their own banks to resign. Roosevelt insisted that the bill remain intact, and his personal support led to victory in the House.

Glass, however, was waiting in the Senate. He charged that a more powerful Federal Reserve Board was antithetical to the basic principles of regional banking he had established twenty-two years before, and he argued that the bill was a personal power grab by Eccles. "This isn't an administration bill," he said. "It's Mr. Eccles's bill."[11] The senator stacked the hearings against Eccles by scheduling all of the opponents of the bill to testify before Eccles. Winthrop Aldrich, who earlier had signed the American Bankers Association report, switched his position and charged that the bill was "a concentration of authority as had not been known heretofore in the United States."[12] The U.S. Chamber of Commerce joined the opposition with a resolution arguing that "the centralized control of credit resulting from such a fundamental change would amount to little short of political dictatorship over the individual deposits and credit of our people."[13] The real fear was of political control of the banking system. "Politics necessarily involves doing the popular thing," one banker told the Senate committee, while "sound banking on the other hand frequently requires unpleasant and unpopular refusals."[14] A central bank under political control, he argued, would fear to rein in inflation when necessary. When Eccles finally did appear, Glass grilled him without mercy.

The Glass subcommittee finally reported out a substantially different bill, and the Senate passed it without a recorded vote. In a difficult conference, the two chambers worked out their differences. Eccles eventually got a much stronger board, with seven members and higher salaries. The board gained supervision over the appointment of Federal Reserve bank presidents, but Eccles's opponents insisted on compromises. The secretary of the treasury and the comptroller of the currency, who had been on the board since 1913, were removed to insulate the Federal Reserve from excessive administration influence. The act consolidated control over open-market operations in a new Federal Open Market Committee, where, for the first time, the seven Federal Reserve Board members could initiate and vote on open-market policy. Five of the twelve votes stayed with Federal Reserve Bank presidents, and Eccles was forced to share open-market policy making with the banks. The mandate was the same as the vague 1933 version: policy making was to proceed "with a view to accommodating commerce and business and with regard to their bearing upon the general credit situation of the country."

The changes, which Roosevelt signed into law on 23 August as the Banking Act of 1935, gave Eccles most of what he wanted. Congress refused to vest the Federal Reserve with broader responsibility for managing the economy, although nothing in the law prevented Eccles from working as closely as he wished with the administration. Eccles had boldly set banking reform as the condition for taking the chairmanship. The principles for the bill were largely his, and although he worked closely with Roosevelt's staff in refining them, it was his bill that the administration adopted.

He proved considerably better at drafting than at negotiating, however, and he so bungled his first efforts at congressional relations that he nearly lost his bill. Only Roosevelt's personal intervention saved it. "Marriner was naive politically, particularly when he first came and at the time of the Banking Act," recounted Sam Carpenter, a close friend and secretary to the Federal Reserve Board. "Without Roosevelt helping him and standing behind him," he said, "he'd never have gotten the Banking Act in a million years." He was a pragmatic manager and a grand strategist, but he had little patience for political maneuvering, building coalitions, or paying his respects to elder statesmen. "He thought if he came up with the right ideas, everybody would say, 'come on, let's do it.' "[15] Eccles had little hesitation in telling anyone—his staff, senators, even presidents—what ought to be done, and even his friends found him abrasive with both superiors and subordinates.[16]

Eccles proved through his ragged performance on the Banking Act of 1935 that he was no slick politician. He had little flair and almost no taste for bargaining and building coalitions. Furthermore, he had little interest in managing the Federal Reserve's day-to-day operations. Instead, he sought to increase the Federal Reserve's institutional power to help ensure the success of the New Deal. Recovery demanded renewed confidence in the banking system and a steady supply of money to fund large federal deficits. The success of the New Deal thus depended on a different kind of Federal Reserve—and a different kind of Federal Reserve Board chairman—than had previously existed. Herbert Hoover sometimes hesitated even to contact the Federal Reserve for fear of applying political pressure. Eccles, on the other hand, could never have been content in a Federal Reserve where board members studiously kept their distance from the White House. Neither could he have been content with a Federal Reserve System where most power lay scattered among the Federal Reserve Banks.

Eccles supported the administration's strategy for recovery, and he wanted to make sure it worked. He was an entrepreneur with a clear sense of how his institution should contribute to economic management. That role depended on his access to and influence upon the administration's policy-making councils. In Eccles's mind, therefore, both the Federal Reserve's institutional health and his own personal power depended on playing the game of bureaucratic politics. The Banking Act of 1935 was the base from which he played that game.

Rebuilding the Fed

Roosevelt had a personal stake in strengthening the Federal Reserve. As he dedicated the Federal Reserve's new Constitution Avenue building in 1937, he told his audience that if the Banking Act of 1935 had been passed earlier, the system "would have been in a far better position to moderate the forces that brought about the great depression." With the act, he said, the Federal Reserve's powers "have been concentrated to a greater degree than before in a single public body, so that they can be used properly and effectively in accordance with the changing needs of the country."[17] For an administration dependent on substantial deficit spending, an adequate supply of inexpensive credit was crucial. The Roosevelt administration would have been on dangerous ground with the old Federal Reserve, which in its disorganized and conservatively inclined state might, by design or accident, have weakened or derailed the New Deal.

Eccles, in turn, was a vigorous supporter of the New Deal both within and outside of the administration. He never achieved the influence on economic policy that Tugwell and Morgenthau enjoyed, but he did win a prominent voice. Roosevelt, for example, accepted his argument for a large public works campaign and a consciously unbalanced budget to be announced in the 1935 State of the Union Address: "The problem of recovery," Eccles wrote Roosevelt, "is primarily that of bringing about a large expansion of expenditures by corporation men, municipalities, and home builders."[18]

The Federal Reserve chairman and the New Deal president found themselves in mutually happy company. Eccles faced the task of rebuilding the Federal Reserve and restoring the banking system, Roosevelt of rejuvenating the economy. Eccles's own ambition and drive met a happy coincidence in Roosevelt's strategies. Neither man was an economic theorist, and both were pragmatists. Eccles had never attended college and until the late 1930s had never read Keynes. "We came out at about the same place in economic thought by very different roads," he wrote Sen. Harry F. Byrd later, "and we have had the common experience of being highly unpopular in orthodox circles."[19] For his part,

Roosevelt was more a tactician than a theoretician, and he made little use of the economic arguments available to him.[20] Eccles was therefore of great importance to Roosevelt, especially in the president's first term. Eccles's voice was one of the few inside the administration urging the conscious use of stimulative fiscal policy to bring about economic recovery, and his public speeches helped create an intellectual case for Roosevelt's tactics.

As the 1936 presidential election approached, Roosevelt wanted to do something to reduce the deficit, which threatened to grow further as more than $2 billion in World War I veterans' pensions came due. Eccles and Tugwell joined in framing a plan for an excess profits tax, and against Morgenthau's judgment, the president proposed the plan to Congress. It met stiff congressional opposition, however, and Congress eventually passed only a small excess profits tax coupled with a much larger increase in the corporate income tax. Morgenthau feared that continued government deficits would impair the federal government's credit and would increase inflation. What was just as important, he was furious over having been outmaneuvered in an area that was the Treasury Department's quintessential domain. He was jealous that his protege seemed to enjoy better access to and influence with the president on a matter about which he cared so deeply.[21] Eccles nevertheless continued to press for expansive federal spending. He argued for creation of the Federal Housing Administration, which helped provide money for home building, and he battled against cutting government spending until the economic recovery was assured.[22]

Morgenthau and Eccles continued to cross swords as the president's second term began. In 1937, fearful that the economy was overheating, Eccles urged a new program of restrained expenditures on Roosevelt. "The recovery is now assured," he wrote the president, "and requires no further positive stimulation by government." Without restraint, he feared, there was the danger of another slump brought on by the increase in prices. He argued, not for a cutback in federal programs, but for promoting shorter work weeks and reducing exports. "Notice could be served on industrialists," he said, "that the Administration did not approve of the extent of recent price advances."[23] A month later he told Morgenthau that he planned to visit Roosevelt and press on him the need to balance the fiscal 1938 budget. He asked the Treasury secretary to join him in the plea. Morgenthau, of course, had been urging that course on Roosevelt for years, and he was greatly amused by what he saw as Eccles's change of heart. He solemnly told Eccles that beyond a certain point one could not press the president. For Eccles, the recommendation was not so much a change of heart as a temporary change in tactics. The economy, by his estimate, was heating up too much, and it was time to switch to the restraint side of his quasi-Keynesian calculus.

A more serious dispute between the two arose soon afterward. The reserves held by banks were growing substantially, largely as a result of gold inflows from other nations. There was substantial pressure within the Federal Reserve System to sell government bonds so as to soak up the extra reserves to quell inflation. Morgenthau, however, feared that such action would weaken the prices for Treasury bonds, and he strongly opposed it. Eccles and the Federal Reserve Board nevertheless decided to act on their own. Morgenthau was enraged. He claimed that he had not been consulted in advance about the decision and had only learned about it by reading the newspaper. He called Eccles and complained furiously. Later he wrote in his diary, "I certainly put the fear of God into him and doubt if he will pull off another fast one. I can't make Eccles out unless he wants to be important."[24] He counterattacked by establishing a Treasury Department fund to counteract Federal Reserve actions and to blackmail the Federal Reserve into keeping the Treasury's borrowing costs low.

Further bickering between the two eventually led to a showdown with Roosevelt. Morgenthau insisted that the Federal Reserve be forced to keep an "orderly market," which was his way of saying stable bond prices. Roosevelt agreed, and to make sure the deal stuck, Roosevelt sent Morgenthau to the next meeting of the Federal Open Market Committee. He made a long statement, saying, "Now, I never threaten," but he added that he hoped that the committee would "use the machinery which you have and give us an orderly market." If the committee refused, "the Government will, and that's the whole story."[25] Faced with the simple choice—giving Morgenthau the policy he wanted or being rendered impotent when Morgenthau released his gold—Eccles and the committee had little choice, and they caved in. Federal Reserve officials had been concerned about inflation, Morgenthau about the price of Treasury bonds. With the president's support, Morgenthau won.

Despite these conflicts, Eccles kept the president's ear, especially because of his vigorous defense of the administration's fiscal program. Within the Federal Reserve, however, Eccles had continuing problems, especially when bankers became increasingly restive about growing and apparently unending budget deficits. Morgenthau complained to Eccles that the system had "lost caste" because of the dispute over the reserve requirements. Eccles countered that he was doing everything he could to support the administration, and he argued, "I've got a tough job here with a tough group of fellows." He told the secretary, "I can't get into a meeting of 12 people [the Federal Open Market Committee] and simply use a club, you know. After all, you wouldn't get cooperation."[26] There was little doubt that he believed Morgenthau's program was wrong and that he resented being blackmailed. But in any case, he faced uneasy bankers on the committee and board members who were becoming more concerned about the dangers of inflation from budget deficits. The pressures from inside the Federal Reserve gave him little maneuvering room in dealing with the Treasury.

Eccles, meanwhile, delivered vigorous public and private support for the administration's fiscal program. Within the administration, he wrote Roosevelt in 1939 urging him to call on cabinet members to publicly support the administration's "compensatory fiscal policy," as Eccles christened it. A week later Roosevelt did indeed ask his cabinet officials to promote the administration's "compensatory fiscal policy."[27] In public, Eccles received the greatest publicity as a result of his radio duel with conservative Sen. Harry F. Byrd (D-Va.), a vocal critic of the administration's deficits. In a December 1938 speech, Byrd complained about "loose talk and loose thinking of a new liberalism which will sweep away the clouds of depression." He suggested that "a modern liberal is tested and judged in proportion as to how liberal he is willing to be with other people's money." He especially attacked Eccles and the philosophy he attributed to the chairman: "The more you borrow and spend, the more prosperous you are." Byrd warned of economic disaster if the budget were not balanced. An exchange of letters led to radio addresses by each man in January 1939. Byrd argued about "the menace of continued deficit spending" and of government attempts to "purchase prosperity." Eccles countered, "I *do not* believe in government spending at any time for spending's sake. I *do* believe in government deficit-spending in depression periods as a supplement and stimulant to private spending, using only the man power, materials and money that otherwise would be idle, and using them only in a way that avoids competition with private enterprise."[28]

Roosevelt found in Eccles a skillful and vocal defender for expansionary fiscal programs. The chairman's attractiveness as a spokesman was no doubt enhanced by the fact he was not part of the president's official family and could make strong statements without their directly reflecting on Roosevelt. Eccles, in the meantime, had increased his support from key members of Congress, which added to his political standing in Washington. He enjoyed easy access to Roosevelt, although to Eccles's annoyance, he sometimes had to compete with the president's dog Fala for Roosevelt's time and attention.[29]

The relationship Eccles developed with members of the administration, and especially with the president, was far different from that of any previous Federal Reserve official. His imprint on the New Deal, both philosophical and practical, was unmistakable. He did not win all of his battles, but he did establish himself as a force with which to be reckoned in the inner circles of the Roosevelt administration. The accomplishment was all the more remarkable given the unsteady support he had within the Federal Reserve System. Eccles thus came to wear two hats, one as personal adviser to the president and one as institutional head of a powerful but still fragmented agency.

At this game he proved considerably more adept than at congressional relations. He had the self-assurance that came from clear views about what ought to be done, and he pressed those views on the president and on his colleagues in the Federal Reserve System. Often what he told the president conflicted with what his internal constituency wanted; the Federal Reserve Bank presidents certainly had no enthusiasm for "compensatory fiscal policy." But he maintained enough support within the system to maintain his effectiveness with the president, and his Roosevelt connection added greatly to his leverage within the system. By the time Roosevelt began his third term, Eccles had restored the Federal Reserve to a position of unquestioned prominence and had established himself as an intellectual force of great importance within the administration.

The Struggle over Wartime Finance

Over the years, Eccles was barely able to keep a lid on his continuing disputes with Morgenthau. It was a battle between two strong persons competing for the president's ear, a battle fought with continual skirmishes on substantive issues. For years Eccles had struggled to unify all banking supervision in the Federal Reserve, including review of national banks under the Treasury Department's comptroller of the currency. Morgenthau told Carter Glass that Eccles "wants to absorb every federal agency he can lay his hands on." The secretary continued, "He wants to be everything except President and he'd like to be that if he can."[30] Eccles thought he had an agreement with Roosevelt to consolidate banking supervision, but World War II intervened, and a new problem—financing American involvement in a major war of unknown proportions—took over. The old disputes remained, however. "I regret to say," Eccles wrote in his memoirs, "that each of us who served in Washington during 1940–45 fought a civil war within an international one" (337).

The crucial issue in financing the war was debt management. The country would have to borrow heavily to pay for armaments, and the Treasury Department wanted the Federal Reserve's assurance that it would be able to borrow the funds it needed at low and stable prices.

After Pearl Harbor, Eccles and the Federal Reserve immediately jumped to full support, pledging "to assure an ample supply of funds" to win the war.[31] But Federal Reserve officials were also concerned to avoid the mistake of World War I: financing the war through an expansion of bank credit, which had led to rising rates as the war progressed and a large inflation after the war. Instead, Federal Reserve officials wanted to defer as much nondefense spending as possible, to rely on taxes and individual savings to pay as much of the immediate costs as could be arranged, and to ensure a stable bond market with fixed prices.

In the first days after the outbreak of war, Eccles proposed a fixed pattern of rates, known as the "peg," which guaranteed that no Treasury offering would fail during the war. While the Federal Reserve's peg guaranteed the success of the Treasury's war financing, it left the system with little effective control of the money supply. As a result, the United States relied more heavily on borrowing to finance the war than did its major allies. Great Britain and Canada, for example, financed half of their war costs through taxation and half through borrowing. In the United States, on the other hand, taxes raised only 40 percent of wartime needs, while borrowing accounted for the other 60 percent. And of the amount borrowed, 40 percent came from the banking system. As a result, the money supply more than tripled, creating what the board of governors warned was "an inflationary potential."[32] *Fortune* echoed the system's fears. A long article in May 1945 blamed the Treasury for financing the war so heavily and so willingly on borrowing and complained, "The forces making for inflation are certainly boiling."[33]

Financing the war so heavily through bank borrowing ran directly against the principles the Federal Reserve had established at the beginning of the war. The results were large profits for banks and speculators and the imposition of inflation as a wartime tax. Eccles worried in November 1944 that inflation would pose "the main challenge to our postwar economy." A few months later he warned a congressional committee about inflation. "If left uncontrolled," he said, "the vast and rising tide of war-created liquid funds could overwhelm the markets for real estate, urban and rural, and for stocks and commodities generally." The results "would be calamitous for Government financing. It would wreck the stabilization program. It would make a mirage of the G.I. Bill of Rights."[34] Eccles followed his warnings with an anti-inflation plan, which he presented to the new president, Harry S. Truman, in July 1946. In accord with his Keynesian-style principles, he called for a large budget surplus derived from higher taxes and reduced expenditures.[35]

The Treasury, however, had far different worries. It faced a massive job of refinancing the federal government's debt, and Treasury officials wanted to keep the peg steady to minimize their costs. Federal Reserve officials, however, put a high priority on removing the peg as quickly as possible. Eccles kept up the pressure, and in December 1946 he again asked the Treasury to end the peg. The war was over and the Victory Loan campaign was a success, Eccles told Vinson. The peg, he warned, was "an element of weakness in our battle against inflation."[36] But the Treasury refused.

Eccles continued to pressure the Treasury for release from the peg, and finally, in early 1947, the Treasury gave in on the short end of the market. John Snyder, who had succeeded Vinson when he became chief justice, was more worried about maintaining the price of government obligations than about the rate on short-term issues, and the Federal Reserve agreed to maintain support of prices. Eccles continued to worry about inflation, and he issued a stream of warnings to Truman. He argued that "inflated prices must be reduced to levels at which the great mass of consumers will be able to purchase goods and services in sufficient volume to maintain a stable high level of production and employment."[37]

Eccles's third four-year term as chairman was to expire on 31 January 1948, and on 23 January Eccles was shocked to learn from John Steelman, Truman's special assistant, that he would not be redesignated as chairman. Truman did want him to remain on the board (his term as a member would continue until 1958), Steelman said, but he could not elaborate on the president's decision. Eccles asked for a meeting with Truman and pressed him for an explanation. When he had met with the president just a few weeks before, Truman had not indicated that there was any trouble. Furthermore, he challenged the president's strategy of waiting until only a few days before the end of the term to make his decision. Had Truman acted earlier, Eccles told him, he could have resigned and avoided embarrassment for everyone.

Truman replied that he had not thought about the question in December. The reasons for refusing to name Eccles as chairman again, he added, were best known to himself alone, a cryptic response that scarcely satisfied Eccles or salved his wounded pride.[38] They finally arranged an exchange of letters in which Truman explained that his decision not to redesignate Eccles as chairman "reflects no lack of complete confidence in you." Truman asked him to stay on the board as vice chairman, and Eccles agreed.[39] Three months passed, however, without Truman's keeping his end of the deal to designate Eccles as vice chairman, and Eccles, bitterly disappointed, finally withdrew his name from consideration to prevent further sniping in the press.[40]

Truman's decision sparked an enormous amount of press speculation. Eccles himself believed that the Federal Reserve's investigation into the Giannini family's Transamerica Corporation banking empire, in which it was suggested that the family was trying to monopolize banking in the West, cost him his job. The investigation, Eccles thought, might have jeopardized support in California for Truman in the upcoming election.[41] It was just as likely, however, that Snyder and Truman feared that Eccles was getting cold feet in supporting the rates and prices of Treasury bonds. With a huge amount of Treasury securities coming due for refinancing—$1 billion in short-term obligations alone per week—rising rates would increase the costs. Truman himself complained, "I didn't like the way Eccles first spoke in the Senate. He talked one way to them and another way to the President. I didn't want a chairman like that."[42]

Truman appointed Thomas B. McCabe, chairman of the board of the Philadelphia Federal Reserve Bank, to replace Eccles. He hoped for an improvement in Treasury–Federal Reserve relations, but Truman later protested that McCabe was "just as bad" as Eccles.[43] The pressures for increases in interest rates and a break from the peg continued to build within the system. Eccles, now freed from the need to be in the Treasury's good graces, led the fight from within the board. In a speech to the National Industrial Conference Board, he warned of a "surrender to inflation" and noted, "So long as you support the government bond market, you find it impossible to control either the banks or the insurance companies, or anyone else who wants to sell bonds."[44]

When Roosevelt died, Eccles lost a friend and protector within the administration. The president had mediated disputes between Morgenthau and Eccles and had always managed to keep the team working together. After Roosevelt's death, however, the coalition dissolved. Morgenthau left the administration, and Eccles's battles with the Treasury took on a new, more urgent, less compromising tone. Truman and Snyder were far more concerned with the reality of refinancing the debt than with the prospect of inflation. Where Roosevelt might have issued a friendly warning, given a deaf ear, or allowed his subordinates to scrap, based on a long history of mutual support, Truman simply fired a man who was becoming increasingly difficult to deal with.

That scarcely kept Eccles from continuing his warnings or from criticizing the Treasury's "chronic bias toward cheap money in all seasons" (422). Within weeks, McCabe was picking up the refrain, if singing it less loudly than his predecessor. Each time Federal Reserve officials requested an end to the peg, however, the Treasury's staff replied that at least in the short run such a move was impossible. Snyder's advisers worried about "soft spots appearing in the economy" and suggested postponing any decision about ending the Federal Reserve's support "until greater confidence has returned to the Government bond market."[45]

Eccles continued his own guerrilla campaign, and in 1949 he testified before Sen. Paul Douglas's committee: "So long as the Reserve System is expected to support the government bond market and to the extent that such support requires the system to purchase marketable issues, whether sold by banks or others, this means that the System is deprived of its only really effective instrument for curbing overexpansion of credit." Douglas joined the attack and argued, "The Treasury and the Federal Reserve have become Siamese twins."[46] In a subcommittee report a year later, Douglas wrote that "the freedom of the Federal Reserve to restrict credit and raise interest rates for general stabilization purposes should be restored even if the cost should be a significant increase in service charges on the Federal debt and a greater increase in inconvenience to the Treasury."[47]

The Treasury, backed by Truman, remained intransigent. At a dinner given by the chairman and directors of the Federal Reserve Banks, Truman said, "Now gentlemen, you represent the greatest financial institution in the history of the world, except the Treasury of the United States."[48] There was no doubt in his mind who was master, a feeling shaped in large measure by his experiences after World War I. As a returning veteran, he repeatedly said, he was able to sell his hundred-dollar government bonds for only eighty-two dollars. He argued that if a citizen paid a hundred dollars for a government bond, he ought always to be able to get a hundred dollars for it. Truman believed that the Federal Reserve's duty lay in supporting the price of bonds, and he was aghast at hints that the system might back away. It was of little importance to him that the bonds sold to citizens during World War II were a different type, with the yields guaranteed.[49]

The problem came to a head with the outbreak of war in Korea, which unloosed a fearful inflation. Wholesale prices rocketed up 16 percent from June 1950 to February 1951, and the nervous money markets worried about the "threat of a near-runaway inflation."[50] Months of double-digit inflation would quickly destroy the value of the government's 2.5 percent bonds. In January 1951, Treasury officials feared that the Federal Reserve was going to cut all support for the bonds, and their fears increased when the Federal Reserve allowed the price of Treasury bonds to slip slightly on 29 January. That led to a meeting at the White House between Truman and the Federal Open Market Committee. Afterwards, the White House released a "Dear Tom" letter Truman had written to McCabe thanking him for his "assurance that you will fully support the Treasury Defense financing program" and that the bond market would be "maintained at present levels."[51]

The members of the committee remembered the meeting entirely differently. The conversation had been cordial, but they had made no such promise, and Eccles leaked to the Washington newspapers a confidential copy of the committee's own minutes. Then, as Eccles said with tongue in cheek, "the fat was in the fire" (496). The story made front-page news, stirred up members of Congress like Senator Douglas in support of the Federal Reserve, and forced Truman to back down. In the coming weeks, the Treasury and the Federal Reserve negotiated an "accord": the Treasury agreed to allow the price and rate of government bonds to vary with market conditions, and the Federal Reserve promised to consult with the Treasury before making policy changes. Since coming to the Federal Reserve, Eccles had fought for independence from the Treasury: first from his mentor, Henry Morgenthau, and then from the Treasury Department's insistence on unwavering support of its obligations. His obstinacy had cost him the chairmanship and some of his stature within the system.[52] But in the end, from his subordinate seat on the board, he won the victory for which he had been struggling.

His continued presence on the board after McCabe became chairman made life very difficult for his successor. Eccles's friends recalled that he resented McCabe and relied on several allies on the board, who owed him their appointments, to continue to press his own opinions. He had never showed much talent for reconciliation, but once freed of the chairmanship, he spoke his mind with even less reservation than in the past.[53] All of this combined to weaken McCabe's support within the Federal Reserve and his leverage with the rest of the government. McCabe tried to serve as a bridge between the Federal Reserve and the Treasury, but Eccles's opposition undercut him on one side, and the Treasury's distrust of the system weakened him on the other. In the end, it was Eccles's alliance with members of Congress who agreed with the need to attack inflation and the vestiges of his power on the board that finally led to the resolution of the Treasury–Federal Reserve dispute. With the battle won, Eccles resigned from the board on 20 June 1951.

Leadership Forged through Crises

Over the course of his careers in business and government, Eccles was a master of making opportunity out of crisis. His world was one of "beckoning frontiers," and at several points in his memoirs he quoted from a favorite Mormon hymn: "Come, come ye saints, no toil nor labor fear; But with joy wend your way." In the family dispute following his father's death, in the banking crises of the Depression, in the Banking Act of 1935, and in the inflation that ignited after World War II, he seized on highly charged disputes with big risks to build new power for himself. What others might have seen as threats he saw as chances, and he seized on those chances by deciding what ought to be done and pushing doggedly ahead along that track.

Often, he was so single-minded of purpose that he created problems for himself. Even his most loyal staff members described him as abrasive and hard to get along with. His lack of tact with Glass almost cost him the banking bill, and his running feud with Morgenthau, which lasted ten years, was a constant thorn in Roosevelt's side. That abrasiveness and single-mindedness spilled over into his personal life. He married happily in 1913 at the age of twenty-three, but he confessed in his memoirs that "the demands of business and later of public affairs cast their shadows" between him and his wife. "I was doubly guilty of neglect," he wrote, "as a husband to her and as a father to our three children" (40). In fact, his family gets only a half-page mention, when he discusses the early stages of his life, in his five-hundred-page memoir. And of six pictures he selected for the book, one is of his mother, to whom he dedicated the volume; one is of his father; and the other four are of himself.

His life revolved around the challenges he faced, and his single-mindedness made intermediaries necessary to keep his manner in check. Roosevelt was adept at keeping Eccles and Morgenthau from destroying each other. He cleverly played each one off against the other, but he refused to allow either one to dominate. Roosevelt sometimes rode with his prestige into the breech to save one of Eccles's initiatives, as he did when the chairman almost fumbled the banking bill in 1935. And within the Federal Reserve, Eccles hired Elliot Thurston, a journalist, to help with press statements, correspondence, and congressional relations. Thurston served as Eccles's personal liaison with other groups, and according to one Federal Reserve official who knew them both, "He exercised a very tempering influence on Eccles."[54] These intermediaries helped to smooth the rough edges and to channel his unbridled energy.

Eccles combined that energy with remarkable inventiveness. He dreamed up schemes to keep his banks afloat when others around him were sinking, and he proudly reported later than no one ever lost a penny in any of his banks. He supplied fuel for the intellectual fires of the New Deal, anticipating Keynes's *General Theory* even though he had had only a high-school education and no formal training in economics. What is most important, he pulled the Federal Reserve back from the edge of catastrophe. The banking crises of the Depression were the very events the Federal Reserve had been created to avoid, and when the system proved unable or unwilling to act, many new plans emerged. Some suggested doing away with it, while others suggested altering it into an unrecognizable form. Eccles took this opportunity to centralize power from the Federal Reserve Banks and enhance the power of the Federal Reserve Board. Later, when the Treasury Department insisted on keeping the peg, he led the battle for independence first as chairman and later as a member of the board.

Thus, according to the criteria defined by Jameson Doig and Erwin Hargrove in chapter 1 of this volume, Eccles was a quintessential entrepreneur. First, in identifying new missions and programs, Eccles was one of the few persons in the early 1930s who had a clear idea of what role the Federal Reserve ought to play in the economy—and in the federal government's new management of it. He first impressed the New Dealers with clear and promising ideas that stood out clearly in an age of despair, and he pressed those ideas in reshaping the Federal Reserve: the system was to have an important but secondary role in making a stimulative fiscal policy work; when necessary, it would help put on the brakes to check a boom. Banking reform in the first years of the New Deal might well have taken a very different course had it not been for an entrepreneur who knew what he wanted to make of the Federal Reserve and who knew that the institution would serve as the base for his own power.

Second, he helped develop external constituencies, especially the president, for the Federal Reserve. Earlier, Federal Reserve officials had prided themselves on their insulation from political officials, but in economic crises that insulation immobilized them. Had it not been for the president, Eccles might well have lost his banking bill or been swallowed up in his struggle with Morgenthau and the Treasury. Eccles also worked to build a broader base of public support through his speeches in defense of the New Deal, and he gained the respect of bankers for his stand against inflation in the postwar economy. But of all sources of external support, the president's clearly was the most important. After Roosevelt's death, Eccles's effectiveness waned rapidly.

Third, he worked to develop internal constituencies in support of his policies, although he had less stomach for this task than for many others. He was a man of ideas who had ruled private institutions; he expected to be able to give orders, and he never quite got used to bargaining for support within his own institution. He naturally picked up some internal support for his stands against inflation, but he constantly found himself on uneasy ground: trying to support Roosevelt's programs, which usually meant providing easier money, while keeping the votes of his Federal Open Market Committee, where Federal Reserve Bank presidents typically favored tighter money to prevent inflation. The president's backing gave him the upper hand in many of these contests.

He was fortunate, furthermore, in leading a collegial institution without a large bureaucracy, where the chairman could transform his external role into internal support.

Fourth, in terms of technical expertise, he brought in a few senior staff members to deal more effectively with congressional and press liaison. It was for his effectiveness in strengthening external relations, rather than in building the expertise of the organization, however, that he has come to be revered within the Federal Reserve.

Fifth, he sought to motivate his coworkers within the Federal Reserve through the force of his ideas. He never faced a problem without a strategy. His ideology was pragmatic, his leadership gung-ho, his power built on ideas.

Finally, he proved especially adept at scanning the environment to identify points of vulnerability. He came to the Federal Reserve when its mission was in shambles, and he rebuilt it with the Banking Act of 1935. He pressed in negotiations over the peg to keep war borrowing at a minimum. He was less successful in this but could do little about it; to oppose the Treasury during the war would have been unthinkable. But at the first opportunity, he started sounding the alarm about postwar inflation. Without Roosevelt's support, he first lost his clout and then his chairmanship, but in the end the drumbeat of his criticism led to the final battle when the Treasury backed down.

Above all, he built a model of the chairmanship that survived for a generation after him. The chairman's job, after Eccles, was to keep institutional support within the system for its policies so as to enhance the chairman's personal relationships with other government officials, especially the president. That meant working carefully with the Federal Reserve Banks, keeping alert to their bias against inflation, and preserving the Federal Reserve's autonomy from the Treasury. He rebuilt the institution and cast the model in which William McChesney Martin, Arthur Burns, and Paul Volcker served. Few men cast such a long shadow across their institution.

Notes

1. Marriner S. Eccles, *Beckoning Frontiers: Public and Personal Recollections* (New York: Alfred A. Knopf, 1951), 85–87; subsequent quotations from *Beckoning Frontiers* are cited parenthetically in the text.

2. Ibid., 115, 129–31.

3. Eccles to Roosevelt, 3 November 1934, OF 90, box 1, Franklin D. Roosevelt Library, Hyde Park, N.Y.

4. Arthur M. Schlesinger, Jr., *The Age of Roosevelt*, vol. 3, *The Politics of Upheaval* (Boston: Houghton Mifflin, 1960), 296.

5. Herbert Hoover, *Memoirs*, vol. 3, *The Great Depression, 1929–1941* (New York: Macmillan, 1952), 212.

6. Henry Morgenthau, Jr., notes on telephone conversation with Eccles, 15 May 1935, Morgenthau Diaries, 90–91, Roosevelt Library.

7. Currie to Eccles, 1 April 1935, box 14, folder 3, Marriner S. Eccles Papers, Marriott Library, University of Utah, Salt Lake City, Utah.

8. Ibid.

9. Ibid.

10. U.S. Congress, House of Representatives, Committee on Banking and Currency, *Banking Act of 1935*, Hearings, 74th Cong., 1st sess., 1935, 273.

11. *New York Times*, 14 April 1935.

12. Quoted in Schlesinger, *Politics of Upheaval*, 298.

13. *New York Times*, 3 May 1935.

14. Statement of Elwyn Davis, Clearing House Banks, Wilmington, Del., U.S. Congress, Senate, Committee on Banking and Currency, *Banking Act of 1935*, Hearings, 74th Cong., 1st sess., 1935, 262–63.

15. Carpenter Oral History, 8, 10, Eccles Papers.

16. See, for example, Merritt Sherman Oral History, 22, Eccles Papers.

17. *Federal Reserve Bulletin* 23 (November 1937): 1062.

18. Eccles to Roosevelt, 6 March 1935, box 5, folder 5, Eccles Papers.

19. Eccles to Byrd, 11 June 1942, box 44, folder 1, ibid.

20. See James MacGregor Burns, *Roosevelt: The Lion and the Fox* (New York: Harcourt, Brace, 1956), 334; Schlesinger, *Politics of Upheaval*, 407–8.

21. Eccles, *Beckoning Frontiers*, 256–59; Schlesinger, *Politics of Upheaval*, 505–9; John Morton Blum, ed., *From the Morgenthau Diaries*, vol. 1, *Years of Crisis, 1928–1938* (Boston: Houghton Mifflin, 1959), 280.

22. Eccles, *Beckoning Frontiers*, 304; Herbert Stein, *The Fiscal Revolution in America* (Chicago: University of Chicago Press, 1969), 93.

23. Eccles to Roosevelt, 12 March 1937, Morgenthau Diaries, 376–86.

24. Entry of 15 July 1936, ibid., 98–99.

25. Minutes of meetings, 3 April 1937, ibid., 266–326.

26. Notes on telephone conversation, 3 April 1937, ibid., 242–50.

27. Eccles to Roosevelt, 11 January 1939; Roosevelt to cabinet, 21 January 1939, OF 962, box 2, Roosevelt Library.

28. Byrd speeches, 10 December 1938, box 40, folder 1, and 16 January 1939, box 40, folder 2; and Eccles speech, 23 January 1939, box 40, folder 2 (emphasis in the original), all in Eccles Papers.

29. Eccles, *Beckoning Frontiers*, 328–31.

30. Transcript of telephone conversation, 17 December 1936, Morgenthau Diaries, 255–57.

31. Board of governors, Federal Reserve System, *Twenty-Eighth Annual Report, 1941*, 1.

32. Board of governors, Federal Reserve System, *Thirty-Second Annual Report, 1945*, 1, 2.

33. "The American Dollar," *Fortune* 31 (May 1945): 118.

34. Eccles, speech to the National Industrial Conference Board, 16 November 1944, box 80, folder 16; and Eccles, statement to Vinson Committee, 8 February 1945, box 32, folder 1, both in Eccles Papers.

35. Eccles to Truman, 19 July 1946, President's Subject File, OF 229A (1945–47), Harry S. Truman Library, Independence, Mo.

36. Eccles to Vinson, 13 December 1945, box 11, folder 2, Eccles Papers.

37. Eccles to Truman, 24 April 1947, box 5, folder 13, ibid.

38. Eccles, *Beckoning Frontiers*, 436–39.

39. Truman to Eccles; and Eccles to Truman, both 27 January 1948, box 3, folder 7, Eccles Papers.

40. Eccles to Truman, 16 April 1948, ibid.

41. Eccles, *Beckoning Frontiers*, 443–56.

42. Truman's statement in Snyder's memoirs, 33, Truman Library. Cf. G. L. Bach, *Making Monetary and Fiscal Policy* (Washington, D.C.: Brookings Institution, 1971), 80; and Robert J. Donovan, "Truman's Perspective," in *Economics and the Truman Administration*, ed. Francis H. Heller (Lawrence: Regents Press of Kansas, 1981), 15.

43. Truman's statement in Snyder's memoirs, 33, Truman Library.

44. Eccles, Speech to the National Industrial Conference Board, 23 September 1948, box 81, folder 23, Eccles Papers.

45. Haas to Snyder, 27 October 1948, box 13, "Federal Reserve Bank—Interest, 1948," Snyder Papers, Truman Library.

46. U.S. Congress, Joint Committee on the Economic Report, *Monetary, Credit, and Fiscal Policies*, Hearings, 81st Cong., 1st sess., 1949, 216.

47. U.S. Congress, Joint Committee on the Economic Report, *Monetary, Credit, and Fiscal Policies*, Report, 81st Cong., 2d sess., 1950, Sen. Doc. 129, 2–3.

48. Quoted in Stein, *Fiscal Revolution in America*, 260.

49. Donovan, "Truman's Perspective," 14–15.

50. Milton Friedman and Anna Jacobson Schwartz, *A Monetary History of the United States, 1867–1960* (Princeton: Princeton University Press, 1963), 597–611.

51. Truman to McCabe, 1 February 1951, "Federal Reserve 1951," Snyder Papers.

52. It cost McCabe his job as well. He resigned shortly after the accord was announced.

53. Carpenter Oral History, 14, Eccles Papers; Sherman Oral History, 14, ibid.

54. Merritt Sherman, interview by the author, 11 June 1984, Washington, D.C.

11

The Private Sector Political Entrepreneur: Bernard O'Keefe at EG&G

Martha Wagner Weinberg

At first glance, Bernard J. O'Keefe, chairman of EG&G, Inc., might seem to have little in common with his counterparts in the tumultuous world of public organizations or, indeed, in heavily regulated or highly politicized private-sector firms. EG&G, a Fortune 500 company with approximately twenty thousand employees and over $1 billion in sales in 1984, could be characterized as a private-sector firm well insulated from many of the destabilizing forces we associate with politicization and fragmentation: it is diversified; it is not heavily regulated by government; it operates with tight financial and managerial controls according to well-known procedures; and, by all conventional measures, it has been consistently profitable and successful in the marketplace. O'Keefe has worked for the company since its founding and as the dominant figure in EG&G's management for more than three decades, he has enjoyed both the formal authority and the legitimacy to make important decisions. In short, one might expect EG&G to be a prime setting for what Joseph Bower has called "a technocratic managerial system"—characterized by organizational stability, clear goals, tight controls, and professional or technical dominance—and one might expect O'Keefe, as the chief executive, to personify technocratic management.[1]

But when closely scrutinized, O'Keefe seems to defy the widely shared stereotype of a top executive in a highly structured, rationalized private-sector firm. Although his company is not heavily regulated, O'Keefe spends at least one day a week working with government and civic organizations. He has written a book about the nuclear age. He talks freely and openly to representatives of the media and, indeed, frequently initiates media relationships by writing editorials and guest columns. And although his company is not involved in heavy industry, he has served as chairman of the National Association of Manufacturers.

Equally interesting are the tasks and responsibilities O'Keefe has chosen to shed or delegate to others as EG&G has grown and prospered. He has steered away from heavy involvement in the company's Business Development Committee, the group of top executives who review budgets and individual business plans with representatives of each of the company's more than 150 profit centers. During his tenure as chief executive officer (CEO) and chairman, he had no ongoing personnel selection process to fill top management positions. Most of the senior management of the company came into EG&G through the acquisitions process and rose through the company ranks: O'Keefe imposed no personally chosen outsiders to ensure that the business ran according to his own style and procedures. And despite his training as an engineer, throughout his career O'Keefe has demonstrated a preference for spending time on untidy, often uncontrollable aspects of the business rather than on new technology and its applications or the details of rationalizing business components and making them more profitable.

O'Keefe's conduct reflects an implicit recognition of a fact of organizational life that is seldom acknowledged in the discussion of leadership of private-sector firms; namely, that astute executives who face unstructured situations or who must plan for and manage the process of change must not only understand the technocratic work of their firms but also be able to function as political leaders. This is true for a simple reason: despite the fact that we often design the formal structure of firms as if they were strictly economic entities, all businesses are in fact political economies.[2] Economic incentives do not always carry the day, nor do hierarchical chains of command always work. Therefore, the true corporate leader must be as well versed in the art of "statecraft" as in the management of economic and technocratic systems. The management of the political side of the house involves negotiation, bargaining, and the accumulation of influence in order to build the coalition necessary to achieve corporate purpose. Because it is always directed at a moving target, the political leadership of the firm requires the flexibility and agility characteristic of the entrepreneur; therefore, it is appropriate to label one set of roles that the chief executive of even the most stable and successful company plays as those of the "political entrepreneur" and to attempt to differentiate those roles from the functions the chief executive performs as manager of the economic business of the firm.

All executives are faced with problems that involve uncertainty, defy systematic solutions, and therefore require flexible responses to changing situations. But while the technocratic manager's job is to match the capacity of the organization to a recognized task, and to manage that match through to completion, the job of the executive in his or her capacity as political entrepreneur centers on the definition and articulation of problems and on the mobilization of constituencies both inside and outside the organization into a stable coalition that agrees on goals and purpose. General managers who focus on the technocratic work of the firm worry about developing the procedures necessary both to turn the ongoing organization to new work and to mesh the performance of new tasks with ongoing routines and rules. In their role as political entrepreneur, on the other hand, executives concern themselves more with setting the terms of the contract and the parameters of the organization's belief system than with defining the procedures to achieve their purpose: in doing so, their task is to change values rather than to tinker with the rules of the game.

Indeed, in performing the political work of the firm, private-sector executives often resemble their public-sector counterparts in the obstacles they face and the skills they require. Political entrepreneurs must rely on influence and persuasion and must be comfortable with frequent renegotiations, even of basic premises. They must look beyond the formal hierarchy of their own organization for support; informal networks and associations often become significant and provide the leverage necessary to bypass formal relationships or to change the perspective of individuals accustomed to seeing problems in a sharply defined way. Because political problems involve conflicts over basic values, they are always characterized by constituency overload; therefore, as in the public sector, the private-sector political entrepreneur must be closely attuned to the demands and strongly held feelings of those outside the firm as well as those inside and must feel comfortable navigating between both worlds. Finally, unlike the executive in his technocratic role, the political entrepreneur cannot delegate the central tasks for which he or she is responsible. Political work must be done by individuals, not by systems. It is based on the values, skills, and proclivities of individuals and is fueled by an assumption that individual style and personality are important and can affect organizational outcomes.

To recognize the importance of political entrepreneurship does not dismiss the significance of technocratic systems. Indeed, the selective and successful application of technocratic systems is what allows many political entrepreneurs to focus on problems involving the resolution of uncertainty and gives them a significant advantage over executives who must operate organizations that lack stable systems with known rules. Further, one might argue that successful political management depends on understanding the value of technocratic systems in grounding any large organization and on avoiding unwarranted meddling with systems that support and maintain organizational purpose.

Perhaps the most useful way to bring this discussion out of the realm of the abstract is to look at individual executives through the lenses of the political analyst and to ask what aspects of their behavior and its impact upon the firm this approach helps explain. By focusing on O'Keefe and his career at EG&G, I do not mean to imply either that he is solely or directly responsible for EG&G's successes or failures or that his own form of political entrepreneurship is somehow typical of that of all skilled private-sector top managers; individual style is surely such an important variable in understanding leadership of organizations that we will never be able to arrive at a formula that defies context and personality. Rather, I suggest that it is only by examining individual executives like O'Keefe and by detailing their careers that we can begin to achieve some understanding of the significance of the exercise of "statecraft" and political skill in their own firms and build a base for eventual comparison with other executives in both private- and public-sector organizations.

The Setting: EG&G

EG&G, Inc., is a diversified firm that produces a variety of technical and scientific products and services for commercial, industrial, and government customers throughout the world. The company develops and manufactures sophisticated measuring instruments and components for electronics equipment and industrial applications. In addition, EG&G runs base support operations at NASA's Kennedy Space Center and provides technical, operational, and logistical support at two large Department of Energy test sites, the Idaho National Engineering Laboratory and the Nevada Test Site. In 1983 *Forbes* listed EG&G first of firms in the electronics industry in return on equity (29.4 percent), first in return on total capital (25.2 percent), and second in growth of earnings per share (26.8 percent).[3]

EG&G, Inc., was founded in 1947 by Harold Edgerton, Kenneth Germeshausen, and Herbert Grier, a trio of MIT scientists who had worked together since 1931 to develop the key components of stroboscopic equipment. (The initials of their last names form the firm's acronymic name.) During World War II stroboscopic techniques became essential in the design of atomic weapons' firing sets. After the war, as it became clear that the government would need increasingly sophisticated firing and measurement techniques for testing and developing weapons, officials at MIT suggested that the group form a corporation and move their government business off campus.

During the late 1940s and throughout the 1950s, EG&G revenues came primarily from government contracts. However, by the mid-1950s the company had begun to move into government and commercial programs involving peacetime uses of nuclear energy and sophisticated measuring equipment. The company began to shift from atomic testing to the development of commercial products during the 1958–61 moratorium on atomic testing, but this shift was temporarily disrupted when the United States responded to a Soviet break in the moratorium and continued testing until the limited test ban treaty was ratified in 1963.

In 1960 EG&G went public and was favorably received by the stock market. Throughout the early 1960s the company's sales and profits continued to grow. But by 1965, when O'Keefe was named president, the boom in the fortunes of many narrowly focused high-technology companies seemed to be slowing. In response to this apparent trend and under O'Keefe's direction, the company began to diversify. From 1965 until 1969 EG&G acquired more than twenty technically oriented companies, which more than doubled the number of business areas in which it was involved.[4] Diversification was halted briefly in 1969 when, as the result of a large cost overrun on a government contract, the company lost money for the first and only time in its history. This loss precipitated a reexamination by top management of the company's control procedures and, more broadly, its style of doing business.

The early 1970s were watershed years for EG&G. Until then, it had been run by innovative engineers whose primary experience was in developing state-of-the-art technology. But as the company entered the 1970s, it began to take on the trappings of the increasingly sophisticated business it was becoming. Dean Freed, a manager with experience in high-technology, fast-growth companies was recruited. While O'Keefe continued to focus on the financial management of the company, Freed worked with members of the existing planning department and with outside consultants to develop and put in place a rigorous planning process in which all units of the company participated. The process had two major parts: the five-year plan, aimed at strategic positioning over time, and the profit plan, designed to provide detailed performance information on a monthly basis.

These procedures provided management with detailed, consistent information and with a vehicle for articulating and controlling financial and strategic goals. Moreover, and perhaps even more significant, planning changed the company's whole vocabulary and style of doing business. The firm's steady growth throughout the 1970s—sales rose from more than $160 million in 1973 to more than $500 million in 1979—was far from haphazard; it represented a careful assessment of the strengths and weaknesses of EG&G's more than 100 business elements. Each business element was scrutinized in terms of its compatibility with the company's strategy of entering or remaining in relatively specialized market areas in which EG&G could be the market leader or performance competitor. The planning process forced management to focus on those parts of the organization that were not functioning as predicted. Business elements that deviated from the targets established for them became the objects of immediate and intensive examination and often were sold or phased out. In short, during the 1970s EG&G changed from a company whose culture and atmosphere were dictated by the sporadic high excitement of technological innovation to a business that was being managed to eliminate uncertainty and to smooth the processes of change and growth. The basis had been laid for a company whose day-to-day operations were regulated according to the dictates of systems with known rules, deadlines, and managerial incentives.

In the 1980s these carefully planned procedures and strategies have taken hold at EG&G. The company has more than 150 business elements, defined as "business systems which involve a single product line or a particular capability being supplied to satisfy the needs of a single market segment." Each business element reports to a division manager, who is responsible for profit and loss and return on investment as determined in the annual plan. Each division is part of one of five business areas headed by group vice presidents. Each group, in turn, reports to either the senior vice president who manages EG&G's commercial activities (with, in 1983, 5,600 employees and $200 million in sales) or the senior vice president who supervises Government Systems and Services (with 15,000 employees and $700 million in sales). In addition to these two executives, top management includes senior vice presidents for finance and for acquisitions and planning, the CEO, and the chairman. A corporate staff of approximately 100 handles personnel, audit, and legal matters. However, most day-to-day management is decentralized into the operating units, with the planning and budgetary mechanisms linking corporate staff to the other units.

O'Keefe and His Career at EG&G

Bernard J. O'Keefe, an engineer by training, has spent almost his entire business career at EG&G. He has hardly been a prototypical EG&G career employee, rising through the company ranks, however. Indeed, one might argue that his style and the significant autonomy he has enjoyed during his tenure at EG&G are more products of his reaction to experiences outside the firm—at Los Alamos and in civic and government work—than to particular job experiences or working relationships inside the company. A feisty man with a quick wit, at first meeting, O'Keefe could easily be mistaken for a gifted elected official. His self-professed eagerness to understand the political and social climate, coupled with his experience in an unusually broadening array of technical and scientific settings, has facilitated his exposure to the often mutually exclusive worlds of business, politics, and pure technology.

O'Keefe grew up in an Irish working-class neighborhood in Providence, Rhode Island.[5] His exposure to politics began early. His father was active in local politics and helped O'Keefe's older brother get a job as an elevator operator in the U.S. Senate. O'Keefe inherited the job from his brother, and from 1937 until 1941, while he was studying physics and electrical engineering at George Washington and Catholic universities, he observed New Deal Washington.

The politics of the time were turbulent and heady. Franklin Roosevelt had put many of his social reforms in place and was attempting to pack the Supreme Court. The Republican party was beginning to rejuvenate; in 1939 it regained control of the House of Representatives, putting an end to Democratic domination of national politics. Adolf Hitler invaded Poland, and debate about U.S. involvement in the war raged. Washington was the site of both technical and political discussions about the feasibility and utility of developing nuclear energy. O'Keefe observed closely and was fascinated; indeed, he has said that at the time he could as easily imagine making a career as an elected official as he could speculate about pursuing his interests in engineering and physics.[6]

After graduating from Catholic University in 1941, O'Keefe accepted a job at the General Electric Company, where he worked on its engineering test programs. Because his job was deemed critical to the war effort, O'Keefe was deferred from military service until he persuaded the Navy to accept his application for officers' candidate service. First detailed to work on radar at MIT, O'Keefe was later assigned as a jack-of-all-trades ensign to the top-secret Manhattan Project at Los Alamos, New Mexico. His assignment was fortuitous—he had no particular expertise that made the Los Alamos project a natural site for his work. But this experience was to reshape his career and give him a powerful informal network of friendships and associations on which he would rely throughout his professional life. In addition to some of the generation's greatest physicists, including Niels Bohr, Hans Bethe, and J. Robert Oppenheimer, the Los Alamos contingent with whom

O'Keefe worked included many of the scientific, technical, and military personnel who would go on to dominate both the management and the politics of the nuclear age.

After an initial assignment to the unit specializing in the design of the atomic bomb's arming radars, O'Keefe was transferred to work on the crucial firing units; he prepared for firing the weapon that was dropped on Nagasaki. With the Japanese surrender, O'Keefe was ordered to report to MIT for temporary duty assisting Herbert Grier in redesigning the firing sets; this proved to be part of an ongoing weapons development program. O'Keefe's assignment stretched into a job of many months, during which he also founded his own business, Radiation Instruments. The formation of EG&G coincided with the decision of O'Keefe and his partner, Donald Hornig, to sell their business, and in 1947 O'Keefe went to work for EG&G.

EG&G's Early Years

In its early days, EG&G was organized around two central cores, a fledgling commercial business based on Edgerton's work with the strobe and measuring devices and a continuation of the testing business, the dominant focus of the company. Each of the founders had his special interests which sprang from involvement in ongoing research. Edgerton was less interested in building a commercial enterprise than in extending his own work; he gradually retreated to MIT to continue his teaching and research. Grier's major interest was in testing; he focused on running the test site in Nevada. Germeshausen, an inventor by inclination, was particularly concerned about improving the company's technical capacity in selected areas; although he was president and CEO, his interests did not center on managing a growing commercial enterprise. This left O'Keefe, the executive vice president—also in charge of the biennial atmospheric tests on Bikini Atoll and Eniwetok—with the primary responsibility for converting a postwar organization of scientists and technicians into a competitive performer in the marketplace. O'Keefe was not unhappy to be ceded the responsibility for developing the administrative side of the business: it allowed him to continue his involvement with some of the most exciting technical issues of the day while broadening his exposure to the problems involved in running an organization. Essentially operating with the approval of the founders as a minister without portfolio, he initiated some of the systems that would begin to convert EG&G into a diversified business.

These systems were crude at best. As O'Keefe humorously describes it, all budgeting was done on a blackboard, with the hope that the figures would not be erased; it was real progress to adopt a system of taking Polaroid pictures of the blackboard.[7] Not until after the company went public for estate reasons in 1960 did O'Keefe have a mandate to work on stabilizing and diversifying the business; that mandate was cemented when he was named president and CEO in 1965.

O'Keefe's External Activities

Even during his early years at EG&G, O'Keefe did not abandon his interests in politics and external activities. In the early 1950s he made a commitment to himself to devote at least one day a week to external affairs; if anything, he has exceeded that pledge. As he explains it: "I had never had time to get advanced degrees. I decided early on that I needed to get outside what was an ingrown technological company for two reasons: I needed to find out how other businesses ran, and I needed to understand a broader spectrum of social activity. I relied on having an information base outside the company. And I liked it, enjoyed it. It allowed me to learn and grow."[8]

O'Keefe's first foray into civic activities involved the Boston Chamber of Commerce, of which he eventually became president. Although EG&G has never had a strong employee presence in Boston and although the chamber's focus is on regional and local commercial activity and economic development, O'Keefe did not consider this affiliation illogical:

> I had to start somewhere to work my way up the ladder. The chamber had an office downtown, which allowed me to get a look at the world.
>
> I volunteered for committees, the most time consuming of which was a committee whose purpose was to get the space center located in the Boston area. I knew that we didn't stand a chance of getting it. A space center is a place where people work outside. It has to be warm. But we certainly did get ourselves into the bargaining process, and eventually got the electronics center. I learned all about the Kennedy-Johnson axis, and some important lessons about how to work in the government, and I began to be known around the town.[9]

As a result of his involvement in the chamber of commerce and the contact it afforded him with local executives, O'Keefe was asked to join the boards of directors of several Massachusetts-based companies. In addition, he expanded his public-service activities to include work in state government, where he served as chairman of the Massachusetts Board of Higher Education and chairman of the Governor's Management Task Force.

In the late 1970s O'Keefe became active in the National Association of Manufacturers (NAM); he was named chairman in 1982. The NAM, like the chamber of commerce, would not at first seem to be a natural forum for O'Keefe: its membership consists predominantly of heavy manufacturing businesses, and it has a reputation for stodginess. But O'Keefe had reasons for investing energy in the NAM:

> First, I needed exposure to broad national issues of concern to business. I was initially drawn in by my concern about the energy crisis, and felt I had a real contribution to make. Second, as our company passes $1 billion a year in sales, we're going to have to understand how to manage in the product area, which is what the NAM guys do. Third, it's turned out to be an invaluable source of contacts and an extremely efficient way of getting information. If you get to know these guys and work with them, you can ask questions and get answers that you would never get even if you invested huge amounts of money in a major research or consulting project.[10]

In addition to his work with government and business organizations, O'Keefe has maintained a public presence and has been regularly covered in the media. He frequently testifies before Congress. He writes guest columns in newspapers and regularly contributes to trade publications. His widely reviewed book, *Nuclear Hostages*, is an impassioned plea for an end to the arms race—not what might be expected from the top official of a company whose base is in weapons testing. At first glance this activity might appear to be merely a personally gratifying exercise of O'Keefe's not inconsiderable ego. In fact, however, his role as a publicist is very much in keeping with O'Keefe's view of the relevant forums a responsible businessman should address. For O'Keefe, the linkage between the specialized world within the company and the broader environment has been a hallmark of a basic philosophy of management. The media and the government arena have provided him with a bully pulpit from which to speak to two audiences—the "outside" world and the EG&G organization—and, in so doing, to establish himself as the essential link between the company and its technical competences and the broader environment in which it is ultimately embedded.

Political Entrepreneurship and the Work of the Firm

Gordon Donaldson and Jay Lorsch have argued that top-level managers spend much of their time balancing the needs of three crucial "constituencies"—the capital market, the product market, and their organization—while making every effort to exercise their own discretion.[11] Why, then, does O'Keefe, a busy executive in a fast-growing company, spend so much time and energy on outside activities involving groups and individuals whose significance is not defined by the marketplace?

Certainly such activities are personally satisfying and provide a form of ego gratification often missing within the confines of a private-sector organization. Moreover, top management's participation in civic and government work, if carefully targeted, serves as a form of advertising and helps enhance the company's image. (This explanation of O'Keefe's activities is widely accepted at EG&G.) But if one examines O'Keefe's career at EG&G, it becomes clear that his forays into the world outside his company can also be read as a metaphor that describes a style of leadership heavily dependent on the existence of informal relationships, a willingness to negotiate with and learn from others outside the realm of a formalized hierarchy, and the flexibility to change direction in response to problems or climatic conditions beyond the capacity of the formal, technocratic systems of the organization to anticipate or to call.

Jameson Doig has described the work of entrepreneurial leaders as focused on six activities: (1) identification of new missions and programs for the organization; (2) development of external constituencies; (3) creation of internal constituencies; (4) enhancement of the organization's technical expertise; (5) motivation and training of members of the organization; and (6) identification of areas of organizational vulnerability followed by remedial action.[12] O'Keefe's entrepreneurial activities neatly correspond to at least two of these categories, and his ability to perform them has been enhanced by his experience and familiarity with dealing with non-market-defined constituencies. He has always maintained ties to both formally organized constituencies, such as government and business organizations, and a less formal, personal network of individuals with whom he has shared experiences or interests. He has relied on these external constituencies to give him advice and help and to provide him with leverage in bargaining and building up influence with members of his own firm whose range of contacts is narrower.

O'Keefe has also fostered the admiration of members of his own firm and actively worked at creating internal constituencies. He has done this, paradoxically, by cultivating a reputation as someone who is different from others in the firm. In interview after interview with members of EG&G's top management, one theme recurred consistently: "Barney's the spirit of the company, the guy who's willing to go on a hunch while the rest of us engineers are plodding along." Had he seemed to be exactly like the others, he would not have taken on the symbolic importance that he enjoys in the firm, nor would he have achieved the informal influence that, together with his formal authority, has been necessary to persuade employees that their routines and vision of their work had to be modified to accommodate such major changes as rapid growth and detailed control procedures.

The other activities identified by Doig can be collected into two more general categories that seem to be at the center of O'Keefe's particular brand of political entrepreneurship. First, O'Keefe has consistently scanned the external environment, identified changes that seemed significant, and incorporated his vision of these changes into his strategy for the organization. For example, he understood the politics of nuclear weapons well enough to recognize that during the 1960s the business of testing nuclear weapons was going to be anything but stable; accordingly, he moved to develop the commercial side of EG&G's business. At the same time, EG&G did not withdraw from weapons testing completely and did maintain a capacity to respond to urgent requests to gear up for another round of nuclear testing, a move that served the firm well in setting the tone for its relationship with the government for years to come.

O'Keefe's move toward diversification is another illustration of his willingness to incorporate changes in the environment into his definition of direction for the company. Responding to a go-go climate of support for growth of high-technology companies, O'Keefe sensed that EG&G faced the choice between remaining a small, single-product company and following a pattern that he thought would be the dominant one for growth in American business. O'Keefe himself has admitted that his acquisitions were not motivated by any particular product rationale and that the company's stated policy of diversification to achieve maximum flexibility was arrived at after the fact. As he put it, "When we saw it used in a couple of annual reports, we had to admit that it sounded good."[13]

O'Keefe's ability to survive and prosper in his role as a political entrepreneur has helped him as he has faced two of the central tasks of top management. His participation and active involvement in a world broader and less structured than that defined by the formal boundaries of his company has bolstered his authority and confidence to set direction for the company during periods when major strategic redirections were imperative. In addition, his establishment of his own brand of "statecraft" and of ties to constituencies and networks beyond the ken of many EG&G employees has given him leverage inside the company and has helped him accrue influence in the ongoing process of managing the informal relationships that in any organization defy the system of formal authority. Perhaps the most useful way of understanding how O'Keefe's ability to perform the role of the political entrepreneur has helped him both to change direction while retaining authority and to build influence is to examine briefly several examples of each.

The Political Entrepreneur and Strategic Redirection

In any setting, public or private, one of the central functions of the entrepreneur is to distinguish new opportunities for markets or products and to build into his or her organization the capacity to gain value from them. One might argue that for the political entrepreneur, this often takes the form of identifying and benefiting from groups or individuals who are not recognized as having formal significance for the organization. During his career at EG&G, O'Keefe has faced at least three situations in which the company required strategic repositioning: the period of diversification; the one-year period when the company took a financial loss; and the period after 1970, when the company underwent an organizational restructuring. In each case, O'Keefe's carefully cultivated alliances with individuals and groups outside his own firm and industry helped bolster his formal authority in at least two significant ways: they provided easy access to perspectives and experiences broader than those available inside the company, and they served as a source of informal but, during times of rapid change, extremely significant support.

Diversification. O'Keefe had begun to think about diversifying EG&G into broader-based commercial and government work even before he became president. After 1960, when the company went public, EG&G of necessity had taken on a broader range of external constituencies, the most significant of which was the financial community. The visible interest and attention of this constituency carried with it an implicit expectation of continued growth and demonstration of sophisticated managerial capability—previously not a key concern of EG&G's three founding professors. Upon assuming the company presidency, O'Keefe assigned himself the task of diversifying and buying new businesses.

O'Keefe's stints on boards of other companies stood him in good stead. His own description of the major challenges he faced illustrates the significance of his work in the world outside EG&G:

> I was certainly no expert on acquisitions. But here I was sitting in a company filled with technological people. At least I had had some experience on boards of companies like the John Hancock that had been investing in a variety of businesses for a long time.
>
> Several things were clear to me. First, we didn't want to be only in the testing business, nor did we want to be totally dependent on the government for our work. That meant that for the first time we had to have some sense of marketing. No longer could we expect to have customers show up on our doorstep. That meant we needed some people with management skills.

We weren't strapped for cash. Therefore I picked businesses to buy that, in addition to seeming to fit in a vague way with what we did already, had good managers in place. I thought about diversifying as a way of pushing EG&G. I thought about what businesses we wanted to get out of and about how I could seed the company with new kinds of people.

The groups that required most attention in this process were not the ones that the former executives of the company would have looked to for signals—that is, the employees and the stockholders. The employees accepted the acquisition process with dignified acquiescence: they just wanted to do their work. The stockholders loved us: we were a "hot rock" company, on the cutting edge of innovation. Instead, I devoted a substantial amount of my attention to the financial community and to building a board that would give us necessary expertise and with which I could work.[14]

A majority of EG&G's current top management was brought into the company during this period. In addition to expanding the scope and size of the business, the acquisition process generated new excitement in the firm. "It was clear that this was an innovative, moving company," one senior executive recalls. "And Barney personified that movement, although ironically enough, a lot of what he was trying to do was nail down loose ends."[15] O'Keefe was, indeed, also using expansion as an opportunity to build a board of directors whose members could not only advise him on how to diversify but also help him reposition EG&G as a market-driven business. The board was expanded to include a prominent investment banker and several outside directors, all of whom were to become crucial O'Keefe advisers and allies during the critical period ahead.

The nose-dive of 1969. Perhaps the most traumatic event in EG&G's history occurred in 1969, when the company overran a fixed-price government contract and took a $3 million loss. The company's stock price plummeted, and all of the top management suffered considerable financial losses.

O'Keefe had had premonitions that the company's lack of a strong control system might cause it major difficulty and had already taken several steps to address this problem. He had asked William Pounds, the dean of MIT's Sloan School of Management, to join EG&G's board, with the understanding that Pounds would work with top management on tightening controls and asset management. EG&G had also commissioned Arthur D. Little, Inc., a leading management consulting firm, to assess the company's strengths and weaknesses. Finally, O'Keefe had begun to think about recruiting into the company someone to manage the day-to-day operations of the commercial business and to focus on tightening up the company's balance sheet. However, none of these processes had progressed far enough to prevent the cost overrun; the crisis convinced most of EG&G's managers that the future success and even survival of the company depended on the institution of a smoothly functioning control system.

The period following the loss was difficult for the company and most particularly for O'Keefe. But his moves in response to the crisis were those of the political entrepreneur rather than the technocrat faced with an untidy situation. Within twenty-four hours of becoming aware of the problem, O'Keefe had telephoned both the officials of the Air Force responsible for administering the contract and all the financial analysts with whom he had dealt in Boston during his tenure as CEO. In addition, drawing on advice given him by a colleague on a board of directors, he took the $3 million loss in December, when it occurred; by January the company had moved back into the black.

During this period O'Keefe relied for counsel on several of the outside sources he had already begun to cultivate. He stayed in close contact with his board of directors and paid particular heed to the recommendations that they had already begun to develop on asset management. In addition, he acted on the recommendation of his outside consultants that he bring in someone to focus on the internal management of the company and hired a professional search firm to locate a suitable candidate. He hired the firm's recommended candidate, Dean Freed, and worked hard to integrate him into the company.

At first glance these measures would seem to have cost O'Keefe autonomy and authority inside the company. In fact, it was probably his abilities to deal with uncertainty and to identify and mobilize resources outside the company that allowed him to survive and EG&G to weather the crisis. He gradually surrendered almost all internal control of operations to an outsider whose style and predilections were entirely different from his own and by all reports worked diligently to move Freed into authority over every issue involving asset management. Although much of the considerable loyalty and admiration that O'Keefe enjoyed among employees was built on his reputation as a visionary enthusiast not tied down by life's red tape, he supported Freed's installation of the detailed planning and control system. As Freed describes it, "Barney was quite magnificent about moving me into *his* company. I'd say I wanted to do something and he'd say, "Fine, just keep me informed." He didn't meddle in my areas, and, in fact, would open doors that allowed me to get control. For example, he created the

Business Development Committee with me as chairman but with no fixed mandate. It became the focus of the internal management of our company."[16]

Changes in internal management. Freed's arrival marked a definite and permanent change in managerial responsibility and style at EG&G. He successfully instituted a detailed system of planning, budgeting, and information that became the central process by which the company did its business. In addition, during the 1970s, as chief operating officer he became the acknowledged manager of EG&G's ongoing commercial operations. O'Keefe continued to supervise the government contracts, which, although they provided 85 percent of the company's cash flow, were less in need of a new style of management than the market-driven commercial businesses. O'Keefe also retained control of relations with the financial community, investors, the press, and government and civic organizations, all of which frequently required personalized attention and "renegotiated agreements."

A superficial observer might suspect that O'Keefe's reservation of these activities to himself represented a desperate clinging to some vestige of power and a salvaging of insignificant "statesman" functions. But this is not the case. A significant amount of top management's work involves dealing with the uncertainties of nonstructured, uncontrollable environments; O'Keefe's involvement in the external world gave him a natural forum from which to affect the political business of the company. He gained credibility and visibility in the outside world, which in turn gave him leverage within the company at a time when there were few top managers with his broad set of contacts and eclectic mix of skills.

At one point in the mid-1970s, O'Keefe and Freed agreed that Freed should begin to manage a significant portion of EG&G's government work. O'Keefe's account of an event that followed illustrates both the contrast between the styles of the two principals and the very different requirements for managing political and technocratic situations:

> Our biggest government contract, responsible for 70 percent of our cash flow, was up for renewal. Unbeknownst to us, several government officials were dissatisfied with some part of our operation, dissatisfied enough that they decided to rebid the contract, and on an eighteen-month rather than a five-year basis. Freed was in charge at this point, and was sitting waiting to find out what the bidding procedures would be and what the government asked us for.
>
> When I later learned that they might have rebid the contract, I almost went through the roof. If it had been rebid, it would have been gone. What actually happened was this: I had an old connection that turned out to be very important. The assistant secretary who

had to sign off on the contract was an old associate from atomic testing days. He had continued to work in the government and in 1960
had been in charge of getting the United States back into the business of testing weapons. Even though at that time EG&G was working to expand our commercial businesses, we had turned the company inside out for him and the testing people so that we could get
up to speed with the Soviets.

Needless to say, he had never forgotten that. When he saw that
it was EG&G's contract that was about to be put up for bid, he suggested that we be given an eighteen-month extension to see if we
could straighten out the problem areas. He also called me and asked
me what the hell was going on. I knew right away that we were in
trouble, and we moved in to clean up the problem.

I did what you have to know how to do if you work in my business: understand what's significant information (even if it's not formally laid out) and move on it quickly. If we'd waited for the systems—ours and theirs—to grind out their paper, we'd still be
waiting.[17]

It was not simply the face that the government was involved that
made O'Keefe's style of management essential. (In fact, in recent years
government contracting procedures have become increasingly technocratic and less subject to any kind of informal influence.) Rather, there
are clearly situations involving either internal or external management
of business that cannot be handled according to fixed rules and procedures and that, because they involve uncertainty, require the use of
informal influence and ad hoc solutions. As O'Keefe puts it, "seventy
percent of what I do involves dealing with and trying to manage externalities."[18]

Political Entrepreneurship and Managerial Influence

To one conditioned to assume that the management of large-scale organizations is fraught with ebbs and flows of individual influence, one
of the most striking aspects of the story of O'Keefe's career at EG&G
as told by many observers inside and outside the organization is the
extent to which O'Keefe seems steadily to have built and consolidated
his influence within the organization. Certainly some of this relatively
smooth pattern of influence can be explained by fortuitous circumstances. He had been at the company from its beginning, and in the early
days he was one of the few persons interested in general administrative
work in a technical company; by the time EG&G acquired the commercial companies, with a group of managers who were interested in
running businesses, O'Keefe was well ensconced. As O'Keefe puts it, "I

was lucky: I was there and I wasn't making mistakes."[19]

However, it would be an oversimplification to assume that there were no challenges to O'Keefe's authority in the company. Perhaps O'Keefe's own assessment of the strongest challenge he faced inside the company can be taken as illustrative of the style in which he built influence in informal ways:

> One of the guys I eventually had to deal with on this issue of who would run the company was our outside legal counsel, who eventually joined the company. Mr. X was a pompous but prescient man who saw early on that the company had value. He thought he might like to run it.
>
> He had a few things going for him. He was close to Grier. But his real strength came from these mystiques he would build up. His base of power was the law. He had handled several important patent suits, and he liked to set up his negotiations with the AEC over boiler plate as something which only he could understand. Even though nobody in the scientific community paid any attention to the AEC because they were just contract administrators, he used them as his leverage. It was this mystique, but it was powerful. . . .
>
> Once I caught on to X and his use of the mystique, I had him. One example I remember of his attempts to use this to give him control was in the area of personnel. This was in the mid-1950s, when management science was all the rage. He went to some seminar given by Walter Clark in Florida on "activity vector analysis" and came back insisting that all employees be tested to see where on the four vectors they fell. He then interpreted their scores and, in so doing, actually began to control a chunk of personnel selection in the company. For a time the company was governed by this: you wouldn't have believed the number of forms floating through here.
>
> It took a while before the light dawned for me: it was the mystique business all over again. When I realized what was happening, I went to Florida and took the course, and, by the way, was bored stiff after two hours. But having done this, I realized we needed to shatter the mystique. So I sent *all* of our top managers to Florida so that *everybody* could analyze AVA scores. Mr. X lost control of an important mechanism of influence. . . .
>
> Poor X. . . . He was defeated in his attempt to run the place by two things. He never read a book: he didn't know anything beyond technical mumbo-jumbo. And he couldn't do what I could do: because of my background, I was popping in and out of every piece of the business. He wasn't familiar with our technology; in fact, his big problem was he could only speak one language.[20]

O'Keefe's analysis of the causes of his challenger's inability to control the company implicitly points up his own style of management, a style that relies as heavily on the use of political skills to build influence as on the constant assertion of formal authority. Four hallmarks of his style seem to be especially significant in his accumulation of influence inside EG&G. First, unlike Mr. X and several of his other rivals, he was able to build and sustain an aura of being able to do what no one else in the company could do. Much of this was derived from his highly visible forays into the outside world, which permitted him to interpret government, other businesses, and historically significant parts of the scientific community. This, in turn, gave him leverage within EG&G. As one of the other top managers of the company put it:

> Barney owns a piece of the company that nobody else can touch. He has a style all his own. He's sort of like the third eye. I can't tell you why I've always believed that he knows more about the world than I do. I guess, objectively speaking, there's no basis for it, but I *believe*, and so does everybody in this company.
>
> Sure, there are times when he's made us mad as hell. But he's decent about it. And he's been right so often about things we might not have caught wind of. . . . If he takes on an issue, it's probably because he sees something there that I can't.[21]

Second, the fact that he has traveled so broadly among a variety of groups both inside and outside his company has enhanced his reputation as a broad-based but flexible person who is both temperamentally suited and trained to handle the decisions on the basic strategic direction of the company. O'Keefe has managed to turn what might in other circumstances be construed as a dilettante's flirtation with a variety of situations not directly involving his company into a major source of strength both inside and outside his company. A high-ranking Massachusetts state government official describes it this way:

> The source of Bernie's effectiveness . . . that's a hard one. He's very smart, but not a dazzling, overpowering intellect. And it's certainly not his physical presence or charismatic demeanor: I mean, dealing with the guy is like dealing with Santa's most feisty elf.
>
> I guess he's so good at what he does because he's so flexible: he understands where other people are coming from. He's one of the least provincial people I've ever met. He's principled, but you always have the sense that he'll move and learn.[22]

Third, O'Keefe has built his influence in the company by focusing on understanding the many "languages" of the broad variety of groups with which he has dealt, thereby enabling himself to take on the central

organizational position of translator. Unlike many of the more technocratic managers at EG&G, O'Keefe has always regarded many of the
formally stated goals of the company as vehicles of communication rather
than sacrosanct, quantitatively "correct" targets. When asked to talk
about the origins of the company's long-held growth goal of 15 percent
each year, O'Keefe describes it as

> having come out of my head. Why 15 percent? Two easy reasons. It's
> a nice number, and I knew we could beat it.
>   But what you really have to understand about the significance
> of the growth goal is that it's a way of communicating commitment
> and reassurance to the various groups that care about the company.
> It's a nice, simple shorthand for the securities analysts. And in a
> highly diversified company where you can't set a product goal, you
> have to arrive at some mechanism for all the guys to understand
> what they're doing, to hit on something that keeps all of the repre-
> sentatives of our different groups from turning our meetings into a
> Tower of Babel. You can do a lot to set the direction of the company
> simply by understanding where the common ground lies, then com-
> municating it.[23]

Fourth, one of O'Keefe's most significant ways of gaining leverage
in the company has come from his work in establishing EG&G's "constitution," or set of governing rules, and then in playing by those rules.
Perhaps ironically, much of O'Keefe's influence seems to have been
enhanced by the manner in which he has given away authority over
parts of the company. Even as he ceded control over the planning and
control process, and eventually over the commercial operations of the
company, he was cementing his position. As one official of the company
puts it, "If Barney says he's giving you a job to do, he gives it to you
and then steps back. The only thing that will make him take it back is
if you totally screw it up. He knows that, and we know that."[24] Even
in the case of Freed, who in many respects posed the greatest challenge
to his authority at a time when he was most vulnerable, O'Keefe delegated a major part of the executive job, then stepped back. As he
explains it,

> I needed Freed. He was like the windshield wiper in a blinding
> snowstorm. Sure, he made a few passes at me. But the way to get
> him away from doing that was to agree with him about how to di-
> vide up the world, then act on it. I told him what I was going to do,
> and I did it.
>   This is a nonadversarial company. It's got to be to work well. It
> simply couldn't function with a sense of betrayal. Much of my legiti-

macy came from my setting the contract, then letting people work within known rules. If this hadn't been the norm, this company would have dissolved into battling fiefdoms long ago.[25]

Personal Style and the EG&G Context

Although I have emphasized the nonsystematic entrepreneurial aspects of O'Keefe's work as he helped change the strategic direction of the company and build a position of influence in the organization, I do not mean to suggest that he has focused only on "political" work or that all other executive functions pale in comparison with the tasks of the political entrepreneur. In fact, O'Keefe is an accomplished engineer who has logged in many hours wearing the hat of the technocratic manager and systematically solving both routine and challenging technical and managerial problems. Indeed, one of the lessons from an analysis of his career may be that the political entrepreneur cannot be successful in an institution that does highly specialized or technical work without an understanding of the most specialized technical functions of the organization.

O'Keefe's posture and style at EG&G were obviously not contrived to suit a temporary need of the organization or to respond to a request for a particular brand of leadership. In a company as successful and relatively stable as EG&G, one might be tempted to portray O'Keefe as a political entrepreneur by choice rather than by necessity. But it is clear that O'Keefe's own skills and style evolved over a long period and were as much a reflection of his own personality and view of the world as of organizational imperatives.

O'Keefe was able to translate his talent for political entrepreneurship into successful leadership of the company because of an apparently fortuitous mesh of circumstance and style. EG&G, begun as an enterprise of individuals whose primary interest was in solving technical problems, required a setting, coherence, and vision in order to become a functioning organization. With his comprehension of the technical issues and his relationship with the company since its beginning, O'Keefe had established his credentials and was not suspect as he followed his instinct to look beyond the boundaries of EG&G for cues on how to shape the company. This leadership style was not only compatible with the needs of the organization but also congruent with his own values, beliefs, and outlook on the world. He viewed his venture into the world of business as a chance for a personal education; where others might have been struck primarily by the uncertainty that this world presented, O'Keefe saw instead an opportunity. An unusual hybrid engineer-politician since at least his college days, he also appears to have learned how to define his own distinctive role in the organization; he has been comfortable and even relaxed about being different from both the founding partners and, later, the rest of the top management of EG&G. In this respect, he has consistently demonstrated that he has another trait typically associated with political entrepreneurs, the ability to work by himself in furthering the organization's interest.

A major feature of O'Keefe's brand of political entrepreneurship has been his continuing attention to balancing political and technical leadership in his organization. In his analysis of the job of the chairman of the Tennessee Valley Authority (TVA), Erwin Hargrove has written that "the crucial task of leadership for a TVA chairman is to combine technology and politics in the definition and creation of support for TVA missions." Like a business organization such as EG&G, the TVA presents itself as a "nonpolitical" organization; but as Hargrove suggests, the "myth of a nonpolitical organization has itself been a resource for those who know how to use it."[26] O'Keefe has left much of the technical work of the firm to Freed; the top management of the firm is convinced that the basic work of the firm is conducted according to fixed and well-accepted rules and procedures. It is this widespread belief that the "constitution" of the organization is known and will remain intact that has allowed O'Keefe leverage to suspend the rules during times of major change.

O'Keefe, like any skilled political entrepreneur, has understood the importance to the firm of the basic political work of recognizing and working with constituencies and of holding together a working coalition by use of influence as well as formal authority. At the same time, he has demonstrated respect for both the technical base of the firm and the technocratic systems that allow this work to proceed. In this respect, one might argue, his most significant work has involved an exercise of restraint rather than positive action. O'Keefe allowed Dean Freed to take over many of the central managerial functions of the company, such as the establishment of budget and control systems and commercial product development, and resisted the temptation to meddle, even though he thereby denied himself the luxuries of hearing some of the company's good news or of making managerial or technological breakthroughs himself. Instead, he focused on the central strategic functions of the political entrepreneur, spotting changes in the external environment that require a major change in organizational direction or pulling out of the ongoing organization issues or tasks that seem to have become politicized and that therefore threaten the ongoing mission of the enterprise.

It is impossible to pinpoint the exact effect that O'Keefe's form of leadership has had on EG&G. But there is significant evidence of O'Keefe's impact on the firm during his tenure as chief executive and chairman. First, by all traditional measures, EG&G has prospered as a business during O'Keefe's years at the helm: the commonly agreed-on measures of business success, such as profit and growth, would suggest that at EG&G someone is doing something right. Second, he has played a visible role in steering the company through such periods of uncertainty as the 1969 nose-dive and the ongoing process of diversification while maintaining for EG&G the confidence of the board, the stock market, and the technical and scientific community. Third, he has solidified his role within the company as a symbol of EG&G's ability to change, take risks, and accommodate itself to externalities. There is no more telling indicator of this role than the concern, expressed over and over again by employees at all levels, about where EG&G will get its spunk and capacity to take initiatives "after Barney leaves." Finally, the stability of the partnership between the more technocratic Freed and the more political O'Keefe is a testament to EG&G's ability to incorporate political and technocratic talent; indeed, at every critical juncture in EG&G's history, O'Keefe seems to have ensured the availability of the material, political, and institutional resources necessary to buffer excellent technical work from uncertainty.

Public- and Private-Sector Political Entrepreneurs Compared

In acting as political entrepreneurs, O'Keefe and other private-sector chief executives take on a function crucial to the success of *any* ongoing organization that requires management of unstructured situations. But while public- and private-sector political entrepreneurs necessarily perform some of the same activities, a private-sector political entrepreneur such as O'Keefe enjoys certain advantages. These advantages are primarily the product of different standards of accountability in public and private firms, rather than ownership structure itself. Public-sector political entrepreneurs must not only balance constituencies with the particular interests in a working coalition but at the same time demonstrate that they are serving a broad public interest. As a result, they can always be attacked for recognizing and taking into account the focused interests that make politics necessary in the first place. Thus, no public-sector political entrepreneurs, no matter how good they are at delegating and at defining technocratic functions, can ever assume that *any* parts of their organizations can be insulated from the charge of politicization; every aspect of the organization must be subject to continuing scrutiny in order to ensure that it does not become a political liability.

O'Keefe's career, on the other hand, suggests that while private-sector political entrepreneurs may also expend a great deal of energy tending to constituency balancing and negotiation of uncertainty, they enjoy a greater flexibility which comes from what is expected from them and the organizations they head. This is not to suggest that they have the license to live by the rules caricatured in the statement that "what's good for General Motors is good for the U.S.A." Certainly, the private-sector political entrepreneur can be held accountable for inappropriate behavior or poor performance by all of the constituencies with whom he or she has to work, including stockholders, the board, employees, regulatory bodies, and segments of the general public. But the accountability of private-sector executives is more likely to be defined by the imposition of a minimum level of success. If, like O'Keefe, they produce a profit, seem to be able to ensure continuity in their companies, and manage their relations with significant external constituents such as the government, their financial backers, and other relevant publics so that there are no flare-ups, they have broader license to do their political work without the charge of favoritism or politicization to which their public-sector counterparts are subject. As one of the members of EG&G's board, William Pounds, has said of O'Keefe and his work, "By all measures Barney has been superb. The company's profitable. He's in control of it. The operating systems are working. Sensible plans for succession are in place. The company seems to be prospering. That's all we as a board need to know. To be further involved in the details of managing the company would be inappropriate."[27]

This notion of accountability has allowed O'Keefe several advantages in directing and sustaining his organization. First, it has given him leeway to make some mistakes. As long as the company remained profitable—and even in 1969, when it did not—the tolerances for error were greater than they would have been in the public sector, where the *process* of dealing with uncertainty is at least as important as the outcome. For example, O'Keefe could readily admit to making mistakes on some of his acquisitions without risking his career. As long as the basic indicators of success—profitability and stability—seemed favorable, his license to experiment and his ability to deal with situations involving great uncertainty by trial and error remained intact.

Second, and perhaps more important, the private-sector notion of accountability allowed O'Keefe and EG&G's top management to insulate ongoing technocratic work from the uncertainty of the broader environment. Although technocratic routines and operations are often dismissed as unimaginative and bureaucratic, they allow for certain crucial organizational functions to be performed. It is from the known rules and routines and the division of labor according to expertise and specialization that members of organizations get their notions of due process and fairness. Organizations without this ongoing "constitution" are easily subject to politicization and competition for control. At EG&G, the fact that Freed's technocratic side of the organization was stable and flourished enhanced O'Keefe's ability to make the more "political" calls when they were necessary. In addition, the technocratic organization provided a mechanism for focusing the energy of many talented individuals on clear tasks and products: because by the rules of the accountability game, the company may be allowed to separate out the specialized capacity to deal with politics and technocratic issues, the chances for a sustained good performance of its legitimate functions are better than those confronting public-sector political entrepreneurs.

Politics and *politicians* have always been pejoratives in the vocabulary of American business. But political entrepreneurship such as Bernard O'Keefe's appears to be a central task that must be performed in any large organization that faces uncertainty. Many of the traits and activities that distinguish successful political entrepreneurs are characteristic of politically astute public- and private-sector executives alike: we need to learn how we can train managers to recognize and understand the tools and craft of politics. What is perhaps even more important, though, in ensuring the capacity of private-sector organizations to deal with the increasingly complex world both within and outside their boundaries, is the need to understand as legitimate the political tasks of top management. No notion of leadership is complete that does not acknowledge both that understanding politics is central to achieving goals in any large organization and that the practice of political statecraft, undertaken in behalf of the achievement of a common purpose, is often one of the central and crucial functions of the chief executive.

Notes

1. Joseph Bower, *The Two Faces of Management* (Boston: Houghton Mifflin, 1983). EG&G is the company's proper name; as indicated in the text below, this name is based on the last names of the firm's three founders—Edgerton, Germeshausen, and Grier.

2. See Joseph Bower and Martha Weinberg, "Statecraft, Strategy, and Corporate Leadership," Harvard Business School Working Paper, 1985. The literature to support the argument that the non-market-driven behaviors of the firm are significant is vast. See, for example, Chester Barnard, *The Functions of the Executive* (Cambridge: Harvard University Press, 1971); Philip Selznick, *Leadership in Administration: A Sociological Interpretation* (New York: Harper & Row, 1957; paperback Berkeley and Los Angeles: University of California Press, 1984); and Richard Cyert and James March, *A Behavioral Theory of the Firm* (Englewood Cliffs, N.J.: Prentice-Hall, 1963).

3. *Forbes*, 3 January 1983.

4. EG&G, Inc. (A), Harvard Business School case 9-377-027, revised August 1981.

5. O'Keefe chronicles his educational and professional experience in his book,

Nuclear Hostages (Boston: Houghton Mifflin, 1983). Much of the following description of his career is drawn from this source.

6. Bernard O'Keefe, interview by the author, 11 November 1983.

7. O'Keefe, *Nuclear Hostages*, 203.

8. O'Keefe interview, 11 November 1983.

9. Ibid.

10. O'Keefe, interview by the author, 15 February 1984.

11. Gordon Donaldson and Jay Lorsch, *Decision Making at the Top* (New York: Basic Books, 1983).

12. Jameson W. Doig, " 'If I See a Murderous Fellow Sharpening a Knife Cleverly . . .': The Wilsonian Dichotomy and the Public Authority Tradition," *Public Administration Review* 43 (1983): 298.

13. O'Keefe, interview by the author, 11 January 1984.

14. O'Keefe, interview 11 November 1983.

15. Charles Francisco, interview by the author, 23 January 1984.

16. Dean Freed, interview by the author, 21 December 1983.

17. O'Keefe interview, 11 January 1984.

18. Ibid.

19. O'Keefe, interview by the author, 5 November 1984.

20. Ibid.

21. David Beaubien, interview by the author, 15 February 1984.

22. Massachusetts state government official, interview by the author, 19 October 1984. Note that outsiders refer to O'Keefe as Bernie, while EG&G insiders call him Barney.

23. O'Keefe, interview by the author, 15 November 1984.

24. John Kucharski, interview by the author, 13 January 1984.

25. O'Keefe interview, 15 November 1984.

26. Erwin C. Hargrove, "The Task of Leadership: The Board Chairmen," in *TVA: Fifty Years of Grassroots Bureaucracy*, ed. Erwin C. Hargrove and Paul K. Conkin (Urbana: University of Illinois Press, 1983), 89.

27. William Pounds, interview by the author, 18 June 1984.

12

James Forrestal: The Tragic End of a Successful Entrepreneur

Cecilia Stiles Cornell and Melvyn P. Leffler

O n 23 May 1949, James V. Forrestal jumped out a sixteenth-floor window of Bethesda Naval Hospital. His suicide came two months after President Harry S. Truman had requested his resignation from the cabinet. Having made a fortune as an investment banker, having served with distinction as under secretary and then secretary of the navy, and having designed many of the key components of the National Security Act of 1947, Forrestal found himself overwhelmed by the responsibilities of the office of secretary of defense. His last months in office were filled with anxiety, frustration, and disappointment. Always a workaholic, he drove himself even more relentlessly; always insecure, he was increasingly conscious of his declining stature within the administration; always inspired by a sense of duty and loyalty to his country, he now anguished that he was falling short.

As one of the wartime and postwar leaders of the nation's defense establishment, he thought his mission was to convince the American people to assume the responsibilities of a world power, to project American influence around the globe, to contain Soviet-directed world communism, to stabilize the international economy along democratic capitalist lines, to augment American military capabilities, and most of all, to effect a better coordination of political, military, and economic policy at the highest echelons of the executive branch. Few of Forrestal's colleagues differed with him about these goals, but they did dispute his priorities. Air Force and naval officers fought one another and clamored for additional military funding; Treasury and Budget Bureau (BOB) personnel demanded fiscal restraint, if not a contraction of the defense establishment; and State Department spokesmen insisted that foreign economic assistance take precedence over military expenditures. As secretary of defense, Forrestal was beleaguered by these conflicting pressures. He viewed himself as a man of reason and compromise, seeking not only to reconcile the demands of service officers with the fiscal imperatives of BOB but also to develop the military capabilities necessary to implement the multiplying commitments incurred by the State Department.

His managerial style was predicated upon the assumption that men of ability, foresight, and good will would be able to reach consensus. But as secretary of defense he could not generate this consensus. Because the authority of the service secretaries had been preserved under the National Security Act, his ability to impose agreement on the warring services was limited; because he was sincerely committed to a consensual style of management, he was personally disinclined to demand obeisance from his colleagues. Caught in the internecine strife between the Air Force and the Navy and urging moderation on both, he found himself without an internal constituency. Viewed with suspicion by the White House, rebuffed by his friends at Foggy Bottom, rejected by many of his former allies on Capitol Hill, and subject to growing criticism in the press, he lost his external constituency. Despite an intensely loyal group of personal aides, Forrestal found himself alone, isolated, and unappreciated. As he anguished over many decisions, he grew increasingly indecisive and irresolute.

The irony that compounded Forrestal's personal tragedy was that he, more than anyone else, was responsible for the decision-making processes that proved so unworkable under his style of leadership. The man who had worked so hard to fashion the postwar global mission of the United States and who had so persistently beckoned for closer political, military, and economic coordination became one of the first casualties of the cold war.

Rapid Rise on Wall Street

James Vincent Forrestal took great pride in the Irish immigrant tradition in which he was reared. He was born in 1892 in Matteawan, New York, the youngest of three boys. His father James had emigrated from County Cork to the United States in 1857 at the age of nine. By the age of twenty-seven he had established his own construction company. An active Democrat, the elder Forrestal was appointed postmaster in 1894, a post he held for four years. The young James experienced his first taste of politics when his father participated in Franklin D. Roosevelt's 1910 campaign for the Senate. Forrestal's mother, Mary Toohey Forrestal, was from a well-established New York farming family with a strong Catholic background. She was devoted to the church and to music.[1]

Despite his mother's desire that he become a priest and his father's hope that he enter the prospering family construction business, Forrestal became a newspaper reporter when he graduated from high school at age sixteen. Journalism captured Forrestal's imagination. In 1947, after twenty-four years as an investment banker and seven years as a public servant, he proclaimed journalism "the most interesting business there is" and revealed his desire to start a weekly newspaper when he retired from the government. As a young reporter, Forrestal wrote for the *Matteawan Journal* and the *Mt. Vernon Argus*, and at age eighteen he became news editor of the *Poughkeepsie News Press*. In 1911 he enrolled in Dartmouth College, where he hoped to refine his writing skills. His academic performance was poor. The following year he transferred to Princeton University, where he developed a strong school loyalty that continued until his death. Forrestal joined the staff of the student newspaper, the *Daily Princetonian*. He developed a close friendship with the editor of the paper, Ferdinand Eberstadt, with whom he later worked on Wall Street and in Washington. According to Eberstadt's account, Forrestal labored hard to promote himself on the newspaper. He was "serious," "quiet," and "determined." Other staff members were often surprised to find that this "obscure" person had been awarded the plum assignments. Forrestal made it a habit to study the old news files to determine which important stories recurred regularly and signed up for them in advance. Eberstadt cited this as an example of Forrestal's foresight and planning ability.[2]

It was no surprise that Forrestal was appointed editor of the paper his senior year. That same year he and James Bruce, president of the Association of Eastern College Newspapers, edited a book on college journalism. The future looked promising for the young Forrestal, whose classmates voted him "Most Likely to Succeed." But during his college years he had evidently become alienated from the Catholic church and somewhat estranged from his family. The second development may well have been linked to the first. The independent Forrestal also disliked having to rely upon his family for support while he attended college. His reluctance to accept further financial aid from his parents, as well as academic problems in an English course, seem to have prompted his decision to withdraw from Princeton only six weeks before his scheduled graduation.[3]

Undecided about his future, Forrestal held several jobs during 1915 and 1916, including those of clerk for the New Jersey Zinc Company, salesman for the American Tobacco Company, and financial reporter for the *New York World*. In 1916 he joined the investment banking firm of William A. Read and Company, soon to become Dillon, Read, and Company. There is little evidence concerning why Forrestal abandoned his dream of a journalism career to pursue a career in sales, but financial considerations may have played a role in the decision. Forrestal made both his fortune and his reputation with Dillon, Read. He began work as the sole bond salesman in the Albany district. He proved so successful that the company established a branch office in that city and named Forrestal district manager. By 1919 he was head of the sales department in the main office; by 1923, a partner in the new firm; and by 1926, vice president.

Eberstadt attributed his friend's rapid climb within the company to his "thoroughness and energy." His greatest asset was his "ability to choose good men, to give them leadership and inspiration, and to give them their heads as well as to back them up even when they make mistakes."[4] Forrestal's success in the investment banking world continued during the late 1920s and the 1930s. He played a major role in the rapid expansion of Dillon, Read, which increased vastly its business in Europe, particularly Germany. The most famous deal Forrestal negotiated was the company's acquisition of the controlling stock of Dodge Brothers automobile company. He facilitated its merger with Chrysler in 1928. In 1938, at age forty-six, Forrestal was appointed president of Dillon, Read.

Despite his great success with the firm, Forrestal remained a modest man devoted to personal obscurity, according to Eberstadt. He revealed little about his personal life. Some of his closest friends were surprised by his marriage to *Vogue* editor Josephine Ogden in 1926. Many had assumed Forrestal to be a confirmed bachelor at age thirty-four. From the beginning it was a marriage of two very different personalities who would eventually lead rather independent lives. Their two sons, Michael Vincent and Peter Ogden, were born in 1927 and 1930.[5]

Forrestal's tenure as president of Dillon, Read was short. President Franklin D. Roosevelt had already embarked upon a program of defense preparedness in the face of the war in Europe. In 1940 Thomas Corcoran, William O. Douglas, and Harry Hopkins suggested to the president that Forrestal be named to one of the administrative assistant posts created in the Executive Office the previous year. The men remembered that Forrestal, a Democrat who did not support the New Deal, had cooperated in efforts to reform the banking and securities industries in the 1930s. Most of the financial community had proven hostile to governmental regulation. The Roosevelt administration was attracted to Forrestal because of his popularity on Wall Street, his administrative talents, and his support for the president's defense program. Corcoran was particularly impressed by Forrestal's ability to recruit the right man for a specific job. Forrestal had had a great deal of experience in selecting managers for operations being financed by Dillon, Read. Corcoran believed that this talent would be useful in recruiting men to direct the government's industrial mobilization efforts. Forrestal, however, initially was reluctant to accept the position. He suggested that Robert Lovett, a close friend and Wall Street colleague who would later serve in the War, State, and Defense departments, would be a better candidate for the job. The serious need for defense mobilization, however, convinced Forrestal to accept the position. On 23 June 1940 he became the fourth administrative assistant to the president. He left Wall Street at the height of his financial career, taking a salary cut from an estimated $190,000 per year to only $10,000.[6]

Ambivalence characterized Forrestal's attitude toward government service throughout his career. Although he remained a public servant for almost nine years, he shunned the celebrity that accompanied his position, much as he had at Dillon, Read. He repeatedly expressed a determination to return to the private sector as soon as his services were no longer needed. In his eighth year with the government, he still listed investment banking as his career and claimed that his Washington address was temporary. Public office was too much an invasion of Forrestal's privacy. Although he was mentioned as a possible candidate for the governorship of New York or the vice presidency, Forrestal concluded, "I am glad that the shadow of Rome and of Wall Street foreclose any continuation of my political career."[7]

But the tradition of service had been ingrained deeply within Forrestal by his father. He felt obligated to serve his country at a time when the world order seemed to be deteriorating rapidly. When President Harry S. Truman offered him the position of secretary of defense in 1947, Forrestal wrote that he expected much trouble and little happiness in the job, yet he could not refuse, because "the country is more important that [sic] I am." Naval aide William R. Smedberg testified to this attitude, stating that Forrestal "worked harder for the United States with less thought of his own person and personal interests than anybody I've ever met." In addition to his desire to serve the country, Forrestal also felt an obligation to the Democratic party. He greatly admired Al Smith and Woodrow Wilson, and he supported the Democratic goal to "prevent radicalism by a vigorous, progressive legislative program," despite his lack of enthusiasm for much of the legislation of the New Deal.[8]

The classic image of Forrestal the bureaucrat was recorded by Robert Cutler: "If you had seen Forrestal once," he wrote, "you were likely to remember him: the trim, taut figure of a fighter, the nose flattened in boxing, the mouth a straight unyielding line gripping tight a brier pipe, the aggressive look somewhat belied by a quiet voice." Forrestal projected the image of a tough, self-confident, rather hard man, but he was actually sensitive, reflective, and somewhat insecure. In comparing Forrestal with Secretary of War Robert Patterson, Bernard Baruch wrote that the two shared an intense dedication to their jobs. Forrestal, however, was "perhaps more sensitive, and certainly a more tortured man," but "these very characteristics made him the highly conscientious, single-minded public servant that he was." Forrestal was somewhat shy, which may help explain his reluctance to discuss his personal life.[9]

Work was apparently an arena where Forrestal tried to compensate for his personal insecurities. "Jim had a compulsion to work," according to Cutler. Work was his hobby, and he was happiest when on the job, according to Smedberg. Forrestal usually worked from early morning to late evening and did not seem cognizant of weekends or holidays. One classic anecdote tells how Forrestal as secretary of defense worked his staff seven days straight. When he left his office at 10:30 P.M. on Sunday, he told them to have a nice weekend. In another incident, Forrestal dictated several letters into his machine at midnight. When he arrived at 7:30 A.M. the next day, he asked why the finished copies were not yet on his desk. Secretary of State James F. Byrnes, after being awakened by one of Forrestal's late-night phone calls, concluded, "When Secretary Forrestal is really interested in a cause, he doesn't sleep, and he doesn't let others sleep."[10]

Such a schedule was at times hard on those who worked with Forrestal. Smedberg found his boss lacking in compassion for the private lives of his employees. Forrestal was a "tough fellow to work for," because one was always on call. Adm. Robert Lee Dennison, who served as assistant chief of naval operations (CNO) for political military affairs, characterized Forrestal as "extremely selfish and thoughtless." But Smedberg nonetheless confessed an admiration for Forrestal and praised him as a strong secretary of the navy. Marx Leva had only praise for his boss, to whom he wrote a touching tribute in which he concluded that Forrestal "quite literally worked himself to death in the service of the country he loved." Leva and his counterparts in the Office of the Secretary of Defense shared a strong loyalty to Forrestal.[11]

Forrestal was renowned for exercising as hard as he worked. He scheduled regular exercise sessions several times a week. During his days on Wall Street this usually included gymnastics, weight lifting, and boxing. Later he turned to calisthenics, tennis, and golf. Eberstadt noted that Forrestal's golfing partners complained that "instead of sauntering around the course, he usually goes through the eighteen holes at practically a dog trot." This view was confirmed by Floyd Parks, who after playing eighteen holes with Forrestal concluded that his partner did it more "for exercise than for fun." Parks wrote that while Forrestal did not have a warm personality, he was nonetheless "very pleasant and agreeable" on the golf course, though unable to forget his work. Despite these frequent recreational activities, Forrestal seldom took vacations while in government service. Those he did take were working vacations that included visits to naval installations. He wrote in August 1947 that he had not had a real holiday since entering the government seven years earlier.[12]

The War Years

The United States was supplying material aid to the Western democracies and beginning to strengthen its own defenses when Forrestal entered government service in 1940. His major task as administrative assistant was to use his business skills to improve hemispheric defense in the face of the Nazi threat. He feared German inroads into Latin American markets and wanted to block Nazi access to the raw materials of that region. Forrestal worked to safeguard those raw material resources for American war production and to maintain open markets in Latin America. He was willing to use some governmental control over marketing and exports in the hemisphere in order to achieve these goals.[13]

Although Forrestal believed that top priority should be given to hemispheric defense, he quickly grew bored with his work, or the lack thereof. The Roosevelt administration already was considering him for the position of under secretary of the navy, which had been established as part of the Naval Reorganization Act of 1940. Forrestal had some familiarity with the Navy Department, having served during World War I as a naval aviator and for a short time in the Aviation Division of the Office of the CNO. Corcoran and Douglas once again played a central role in securing a Forrestal appointment. Secretary of the Navy Frank Knox later stated that he selected Forrestal because he was a "shrewd, competent businessman."[14]

As under secretary of the navy from 1940 to 1944, Forrestal directed his energies primarily toward defense preparedness, industrial mobilization, and naval procurement. He reorganized the Navy to meet the material requirements of the war by applying many of the organizational principles he had learned on Wall Street. He encouraged close cooperation between government and business, bringing into the Navy Department experts from the private sector and relying upon his personal contacts in the business world to speed production. During his years as under secretary and throughout his career, Forrestal employed a consensual style of leadership. He did not like to make unilateral decisions, preferring instead to work with a team of associates. This was consistent with the self-effacing personality Eberstadt described. Once broad objectives were agreed upon, Forrestal hesitated to take sides in policy discussions; rather, he encouraged the expression of different points of view and guided the group toward consensus, often by asking a series of questions. Dennison found it "almost impossible to ever get an opinion out of him." This type of decision making allowed broad participation and avoided sharp conflicts. It was well suited to an organization with common goals. Members of Forrestal's team might disagree over the means for achieving those goals, but they were united in their dedication to a strong Navy and to the seapower theories of Alfred Thayer Mahan.[15]

The 1940 legislation specified no statutory duties for the under secretary of the navy. Knox assigned Forrestal responsibility for contracts, legal matters, relations with government agencies (other than the Army, BOB, and labor agencies), and supervision of the Office of the Judge Advocate General (OJAG) and several Navy boards. Forrestal took office during the largest peacetime naval expansion program in American history; yet the Navy was unprepared for war. He subsequently wrote that at the onset of the war "we operated . . . on a shoe string and held by the thinnest kind of a hair. I doubt if anybody back here will ever really comprehend how close we were to disaster." Forrestal found many problems hampering naval operations. There was little cooperation among the Navy's branches; there was little coordination between strategic and logistical planning; there was an inadequate supply program. The most serious problem was the lack of a direct line of command over the bureaus. The bureau chiefs had become too independent. The under secretary concluded that the Navy suffered from an excessive decentralization of policy making, and he was determined to solve its organizational problems.[16]

Forrestal's first task was to select personnel and organize his office. In order to maintain civilian control of the Navy, Forrestal needed to know what was happening within his department on a daily basis. He needed to garner that information from sources who were loyal to him and independent from the bureaus and the admirals. To achieve this goal, Forrestal introduced an unprecedented number of civilian specialists into the Navy Department. He most often hired men from the private sector whose work he knew from his Wall Street days. He liked the fact that men in the private sector had been accountable to show a profit on the job. Forrestal preferred to surround himself with men who he knew possessed "responsibility and integrity" rather than with political appointments. He wanted independent men who could "stand on their own feet rather than lean on him." As under secretary, instead of relying upon the traditional single naval aide, Forrestal appointed a staff of three specialized assistants. Among his most important assistants during his early years in office were Charles F. Detmar, Jr., legal aide; Eugene S. Duffield, public relations aide; and John Gingrich, naval aide. In addition to his regular staff, he hired more than forty special assistants during his career with the Navy.[17]

Forrestal and his assistants moved quickly in 1940–41 to reorganize the Navy Department in order to accelerate war production. His general pattern of problem solving emerged during these early months in office. He identified a problem, offered possible solutions, and then hired an outside specialist to make an in-depth study and to suggest action. The usual solution was to create a new agency within Forrestal's office. The new agencies were customarily staffed by civilian specialists, who implemented policies at lower levels, leaving Forrestal free to oversee general mobilization efforts and to coordinate naval policy with other departments. Forrestal followed this pattern when he established the Certification Supervisory Unit in the Office of the Under Secretary in January 1941. He hired civilian lawyers Struve Hensel and John Kenney to study the process whereby the Navy reviewed tax amortization applications from war manufacturers. The two men concluded that the review of such applications, which previously had been conducted in the individual Navy bureaus, should be centralized within the Office of the Under Secretary and should be reviewed by civilian lawyers who had experience with business contracts rather than by the Navy lawyers in the OJAG.[18]

Forrestal used the same approach to modify the Navy's procedures for approving business contracts. When he took office, he found an astonishing lack of uniformity in contracting. While he was responsible for signing some contracts, the bureau chiefs signed others. Contracts for millions of dollars might not even cross his desk. Forrestal also was frustrated at being asked to sign large contracts that neither he nor his staff had reviewed. The OJAG reviewed the legality of the contracts but did not attempt to determine whether the Navy was making a sound business deal. Relying once again upon a study by Hensel, Forrestal established the Procurement Legal Division (PLD) in his own office on 10 September 1941. The bureaus continued to determine what goods should be purchased, but contracts were prepared and coordinated by the civilian attorneys of the PLD. This procedure allowed Forrestal and his staff to supervise the contracting process in its early and crucial stages, when changes in the contracts still could be negotiated. Under this new system, the technical, business, and legal aspects of each contract were reviewed by the appropriate specialists. Naval historian Robert Connery concludes that the establishment of the PLD was "radical" in that it was "the first time that a Secretary had succeeded in placing his agents at the working level, the first time, in fact, that a Secretary had made effective arrangements to acquire knowledge of a particular field so that he might exercise his authority intelligently." Forrestal sought to establish an internal constituency within the Navy by placing in the bureau independent specialists responsible and loyal to him.[19]

Recognizing the immediate need to match strategic plans with production capabilities and to coordinate Navy requirements with the demands and capabilities of other military and civilian agencies, Forrestal established the Office of Procurement and Management (OP&M) in December 1941. He viewed this initiative as his major contribution to naval mobilization, because the new office saved the Navy "millions" of dollars. The purpose of the OP&M was to help translate war plans into materiel requirements, to establish standard procurement procedures, to coordinate naval requirements with those of other government offices, and to plan for future materiel needs. Naval historians Connery and Robert Greenhalgh Albion characterize the agency's establishment as a "master stroke" that was crucial to the Navy's ability to meet wartime production demands.[20]

Forrestal further attempted to coordinate Navy production efforts with those of other departments through the Army-Navy Munitions Board (ANMB). He and Under Secretary of War Patterson served as joint chairmen of the board. The two men worked closely with Eberstadt, who first served as a consultant to the board and then became its chairman after the attack on Pearl Harbor. Under the leadership of these three men, the ANMB tried to fill gaps in mobilization planning by developing a controlled materials plan, conducting a study of problems in machine tool production, and pressing for a more rapid conversion to a wartime economy.[21]

Forrestal's efforts to reorganize the Navy Department were challenged from both within and without. The chiefs of the Navy bureaus worried, with good reason, that the under secretary was trying to undermine their independence and to limit their power. They were reluctant to allow Forrestal's civilian specialists inside their respective domains. Both the OJAG and members of the House Naval Affairs Committee asked Forrestal why he preferred civilian lawyers to Navy lawyers. They worried that the under secretary was usurping the authority of the OJAG and causing costly and unnecessary duplications. Forrestal also came into conflict with Donald Nelson and Leon Henderson when he lobbied for military exemption from the jurisdictions of the War Production Board and the Office of Price Administration. Forrestal feared that excessive price regulation would slow conversion from peacetime to wartime production. He secured Nelson's cooperation by suggesting that Nelson put his own representatives inside military agencies, much as Forrestal had done in the Navy. He was less successful in his efforts to persuade Henderson that price ceilings on military goods would hinder rapid procurement and discourage industries from converting to war production. The Control Act of January 1942 placed price ceilings on a large number of military goods. Forrestal and Patterson, however, did win a partial victory in July of that year when Henderson agreed to exempt the services from additional restrictions, provided they succeeded in curbing inflation by controlling profits and wages.[22]

Chief of Naval Operations Adm. Ernest King occasionally challenged Forrestal's plans for the Navy Department. The secretary's reorganization efforts emphasized civilian control. From King's perspective, these changes threatened the CNO's control of logistics. He responded by proposing his own plans to increase military control of the bureaus and to establish within the Navy a strong general staff much like that of the Army. The conflict of interests between the two men was exacerbated by a conflict of personalities. King tended to be decisive, while Forrestal preferred to consider each side of an issue before reaching a decision. Smedberg found the two "at crosspoints a great deal." King openly acknowledged this friction in his autobiography, but Forrestal, displaying a characteristic distaste for conflict, refused to concede that any animosity existed between them.[23]

Forrestal's success in meeting these challenges to his leadership can be attributed primarily to the urgent requirements of the mobilization effort. The undefined nature of his office gave him great flexibility, and during the wartime emergency, Knox and Roosevelt allowed him to use that flexibility to speed production and supply. Forrestal's proven record of success in the private sector made it difficult to challenge his methods, particularly as they began to yield results in naval production and procurement. Even Admiral King temporarily abandoned his efforts at reorganization when the president directed him to concentrate upon waging war. In those areas where Forrestal was less successful, particularly in his attempts to gain exemption from economic regulation, it was because the needs of the Navy had to be weighed against the larger demands of the general economy and because of a lack of clear mobilization policy during the early years of the conflict. It was remarkable that Forrestal was able to gain any concessions from Nelson and Henderson, who had more power than the under secretary.[24]

Forrestal's record as under secretary was one of success. Naval tonnage increased from 1.3 million in July 1940 to 2 million in September 1943; combat tonnage jumped 3.5 times by the end of 1944; the number of naval planes multiplied tenfold between July 1940 and September 1943; and the number of aircraft carriers doubled between the end of 1941 and the end of 1943. Although he alone was not responsible for these achievements, he justly prided himself on the establishment of the OP&M, the modernization of naval logistics, and the acceleration of the production of destroyer escorts and landing craft. He coordinated materiel activities above the bureau level by establishing new agencies in the Office of the Under Secretary. These new agencies standardized purchasing procedures and centralized the review of those procedures. These changes helped reduce duplication among the bureaus and allowed Forrestal's staff to compile a large body of production statistics. The latter strengthened civilian control of mobilization by giving the secretary and the under secretary increased access to the information needed to make administrative decisions. Finally, Forrestal established a permanent role for the Office of the Under Secretary, which originally had been conceived as a temporary war measure. Arnold Rogow concludes that "under different leadership the Under Secretaryship might have become a relatively minor adjunct of the Office of Navy Secretary. Under Forrestal, the Undersecretaryship functioned as the powerful right arm of the Secretary with a reach that extended well beyond the field of industrial mobilization."[25]

Planning for National Security

Forrestal's role in the Navy changed slowly but markedly in 1944 as he began to shoulder more responsibility after Secretary Knox became ill. He seemed the natural choice to succeed Knox when the secretary died in April. The men had worked together closely for more than three years. Knox had been supportive of Forrestal's reorganization efforts and had spoken highly of his work in mobilization. The under secretary was intimately familiar with Navy production and had worked with Patterson, Nelson, Henderson, and the admirals. He could provide a necessary continuity of leadership in the midst of war. Furthermore, Forrestal had many friends in Congress, particularly among the members of the House and Senate Naval Affairs Committees. In 1942 Knox asked his assistants to list those in Congress to whom they could go on behalf of the Navy. Forrestal listed seventy-six names, more than twice as many as any other aide. Among the senators on Forrestal's list were Harry Byrd, Robert LaFollette, Jr., Robert Taft, Harry Truman, Robert Wagner, and David Walsh. Lyndon Johnson, Sam Rayburn, and Carl Vinson were among the congressmen listed. There were, however, some liabilities to a Forrestal nomination. He was not personally close to Roosevelt, and he would be the fourth New Yorker in the cabinet. Baruch evidently played an important role in persuading the president to appoint Forrestal. The Senate unanimously confirmed the nomination on 9 May. Forrestal was extremely pleased by the news. His personal secretary, Katherine Foley, said that this was the only time she ever saw her boss express emotion.[26]

Forrestal's succession to the secretaryship brought no immediate changes within the department. He continued his policy of working with three civilian assistants and employing specialists to determine how the Navy could operate more efficiently. It was left to Forrestal to implement the recommendations of a study on naval organization begun while Knox was secretary by T. P. Archer, vice president of General Motors, and G. W. Wolf, president of U.S Steel, Export. Following the recommendations of the study, in November 1944 Forrestal created the Top Policy Group, comprising the Navy's top civilian and military personnel. Its purpose was to act as a "board of directors" for the Navy, making decisions about conflicts in organizational policy that arose between the military and civilian components of the service. Forrestal established the Organizational Planning and Procedure Unit to implement the decisions made by the Top Policy Group. The Archer-Wolf Report also pointed to the need to coordinate fiscal accounting procedures among the agencies of the Navy. Forrestal appointed Wilfred J. McNeil as the new fiscal director. He would later serve the same function in Forrestal's Office of the Secretary of Defense.

As secretary of the navy, Forrestal continued to work to strengthen civilian control of his service. He won a major victory in September 1945 when Executive Order 1645 finally made the commander in chief of the navy specifically responsible to the secretary of the navy as well as to the president. He gained a second significant victory in January 1946 with General Order No. 230, which more carefully defined the responsibilities for logistics within the department. Professional naval officers would continue to determine what materials were needed for naval operations, but the civilian authorities would determine how best to procure those materials. Forrestal's OP&M became a permanent part of the Navy Department under this order.[27]

Forrestal's first goal as secretary of the navy was to win the war, but as victory seemed assured, he broadened his agenda. First, he wanted to define a new role and mission for a strong postwar Navy. Second, he hoped to persuade U.S. officials that the nation's interests were now global in nature and that the United States had to accept the responsibilities of leadership in a postwar world that seemed increasingly less secure. These objectives were closely related to Forrestal's third goal, to thwart the Army's unification plan and to reorganize the government in order to facilitate the close coordination of military, foreign, and economic policies.

In his new position Forrestal was charged not only with the responsibility of equipping his service for war but with establishing and implementing organizational goals. He and his colleagues faced a rapidly changing world in 1944 and 1945. The development of perhaps the greatest importance to the Navy was the new weapons technology, which challenged old conceptions of security, particularly the sea-power theories of Mahan. An increased emphasis upon air power and strategic bombing, as well as the development of atomic weaponry, threatened to make obsolete the role of the Navy. Even before the war ended, Forrestal organized a defense of the role and mission of his service and prepared to use the new technologies to enhance the Navy's capabilities.

Forrestal struggled to maintain a strong postwar fleet. The United States needed a large Navy to maintain control of the sea approaches to the continent and of the air lanes above those approaches. The U.S. Navy had to be superior to any potential enemy or combination of enemies in the western Atlantic or the Pacific Ocean. It had to have sufficient capabilities to defend U.S. global interests, to enforce peace treaties, to implement U.N. decisions, to support U.S. troops in any future land war, and to conduct routine training. A strong Navy also required a worldwide system of bases from which to project power rapidly to any area of the world. Forrestal also believed that the machinery for military mobilization established during World War II must be kept intact. He also championed a system of universal military training (UMT) to provide the Navy with a sufficient supply of manpower. From his perspective, the surprise attack on Pearl Harbor had demonstrated that the United States could no longer rely upon its geographic isolation from major power centers. Modern technology had removed the nation's invulnerability to attack from across the oceans. In the future the nation would have little time to mobilize for war.[28]

Organizational imperatives reinforced Forrestal's anxieties about the nation's security. He had worked to mobilize the Navy for war and to reorganize it along more rational and efficient lines. Although Forrestal believed that the Navy's postwar mission required a careful balancing of its sea, land, and air components, in 1945 he began to put particular emphasis upon the latter. He feared that the growing importance of strategic bombing and the increased prominence of the Army Air Forces threatened the Navy's traditional place of favor in the budgeting process. "The Navy," he wrote, "if it is to keep pace with the public mind and the changing character of war, must be an *air* Navy." He emphasized that although battleships, cruisers, and destroyers would be necessary complements to the aircraft carrier, "we must get across to the public that our striking power is *air*." Such an emphasis would also give the Navy a "legitimate and well-founded participation" in the use of atomic weapons. The development of an air mission became even more important in 1946, as Forrestal and the Truman administration came to define the Soviet Union as the prospective enemy. Traditional naval power would be of little use against a primarily landlocked nation with only a negligible navy.[29]

Forrestal helped to breathe life into a Navy that was in many ways still committed to the sea-power theories of Mahan. In addition to emphasizing air power, he pressed the admirals to develop more comprehensive plans for the postwar era. When he became dissatisfied with the pace of planning in the spring of 1945, Forrestal appointed Hensel, now assistant secretary, to head a special committee to coordinate planning. Forrestal's active role was a departure in the traditional relationship between naval officers and the civilian secretary, but he was able to win the loyalty of most officers through his wholehearted support of the Navy. Forrestal took his campaign for a strong postwar Navy based upon air power throughout the country in a series of speeches. He used his contacts in Congress and the press to preach this gospel. His tactics helped him to build strong internal and external constituencies.[30]

Forrestal also sought to cultivate external constituencies on behalf of the administration's efforts to contain Soviet-directed world communism. He was one of the first high officials to focus systematic attention on Soviet intentions and capabilities. He worried not only about the possibility of outright Soviet aggression but also about the prospects of communist subversion in areas plagued by postwar economic and political instability. In late 1945, Forrestal asked Professor Edward Willett, on leave from Smith College, to study the sources of Soviet foreign policy. When Willett concluded that the Soviets still were committed to world revolution and that conflict with the Kremlin was inevitable, Forrestal circulated the professor's findings among friends and colleagues. Similarly, Forrestal was greatly impressed by George Kennan's "Long Telegram" in February 1946. Subsequently, he helped to facilitate the publication of Kennan's "X" article in *Foreign Affairs*. "In my opinion," Forrestal wrote a close friend in April 1946, "we are facing now a far more serious business than we ever faced in the 30s." Within policy-making circles he continually reminded colleagues of the need to mobilize public opinion on behalf of the administration's initiatives to contain Soviet power. As a result of his early interest in journalism and his close ties with prominent publishers and journalists, he recognized the prospective impact of the mass media on American attitudes. "I believe that the press should be an instrument of our foreign policy," Forrestal emphasized to Secretary of State Byrnes.[31]

As part of the nation's global responsibilities, Forrestal urged his colleagues to expedite the economic rehabilitation of Germany and Japan. Aware of the power vacuums created by the defeat of the Axis powers, conscious of worldwide economic deprivation, and frightened by revolutionary turmoil throughout the Eurasian land mass, he believed that the quick economic rejuvenation of Germany and Japan would help to counter political and social instability in Europe and the Far East, to revive world trade, and to resuscitate the international economy. These ideas were in keeping with Forrestal's experiences in international banking during the 1920s and 1930s, when he had become impressed with the economic interdependence of nations. These views also accorded with the lessons learned from his economic mobilization efforts during World War II. The victory of the Allies had been made possible by the superior resources they could mobilize in wartime. For Forrestal, this meant that the United States had to thwart the spread of postwar communism in Europe and East Asia in order to deny the Kremlin the capability of utilizing the resources of Western Europe, Germany, or Japan in the event of another global conflict. Forrestal feared that indigenous communists, should they win or capture power, might align their countries with the Soviet Union or offer strategic or economic assistance to the Kremlin that might substantially augment the latter's ability to wage war.[32]

The postwar mission Forrestal envisioned for the United States was predicated upon its ability to project U.S. power and influence around the globe. The financial resources of the United States and the U.S. occupation presence in Germany, Japan, Italy, Austria, and Korea constituted potential levers for influencing postwar developments. But Forrestal was equally interested in developing an effective system of overseas bases. Before World War II was over, he differed with the State Department over the future status of the mandated islands in the Pacific (the Carolines, the Marshalls, and some of the Marianas) that had been under the control of Japan. State Department officials believed the islands should be made trusteeships under the United Nations. Forrestal contended that they should remain firmly under U.S. control as part of a worldwide system of bases. That system was needed to protect the approaches to the American continent, to defend the Philippines, to support the open-door policy in China, to retain access to the raw materials of Southeast Asia, and to project U.S. air power should war erupt. Forrestal's efforts finally succeeded when the United Nations declared that the mandates would become a strategic trust territory of the United States. Okinawa, too, became one element in a worldwide system of overseas bases.[33]

Forrestal also played a key role in projecting American influence into the Eastern Mediterranean and the Middle East. During late 1945 and early 1946, when Britain was curtailing her commitments in that area, the secretary was concerned about Soviet intentions in Iran, Greece, and Turkey. The strategic importance of the Mediterranean, the oil reserves of the Middle East, and the unfolding Iranian crisis led Forrestal to press for the establishment of a U.S. naval presence in the region. He hoped that presence could be used to foster stability, curb communism, and contain Soviet influence. In February 1946, Forrestal strongly supported a proposal by Adm. Forrest Sherman to return to Istanbul the body of the late Turkish ambassador aboard the USS *Missouri* rather than by plane. This seemed an opportune time to introduce U.S. ships into the Mediterranean. Later that month, Forrestal asked Secretary of State Byrnes to authorize a naval task force to the area. Byrnes suggested that such a force accompany the *Missouri* to Turkey, but plans for the task force collapsed because of a shortage of manpower due to rapid demobilization and a great demand for naval forces in the Far East. Yet Forrestal refused to abandon his goal. He used the escalating tensions of the Trieste and Dardanelles crises in mid-1946 as an opportunity to send additional ships to the Mediterranean. The USS *Roosevelt* and two American destroyers visited Greek ports in September. He then secured the permission of the State Department and the White House and announced that a U.S. naval force would be stationed permanently in the Mediterranean to support Allied operations and to protect U.S. interests. Initially, it was a small force, but by late February 1947 American ships had visited more than forty ports in the Mediterranean Sea, and American war planners were counting on utilizing British bases in the Cairo/Suez region as a springboard for the strategic air offensive against the Soviet Union should war erupt. With the declaration of the Truman Doctrine in March 1947, Forrestal could feel gratified that a permanent role for the United States in the Eastern Mediterranean and Middle East had been demarcated.[34]

Whereas Forrestal's success as under secretary of the navy might be measured easily in terms of production, his overall influence as secretary is more difficult to calculate. He continued the reorganization of the Navy Department, centralized policy making in the Top Policy Group, and envisioned greater cooperation between the Navy's military and civilian leaders. Moreover, as secretary, Forrestal further strengthened civilian control of the department. In 1944 and 1945 he emerged as the principal public spokesman for the Navy through his speeches, interviews, contacts on Capitol Hill, and personal involvement in the Navy's public relations program. He reformulated the goals of his organization to meet new challenges. As the traditional emphasis on battleships appeared obsolete, Forrestal helped define a new air mission for his service. He also tried to expand the role of the Navy in the formulation and implementation of foreign policy by seeking to match the capabilities of the Navy with the goals of the State Department. His efforts were a natural outgrowth of his global vision, which in turn provided a justification for increased naval expenditures in the postwar era. As one admiral put it, Forrestal was "the first real, positive Secretary of the Navy that we had, and he took charge."[35]

The Unification Controversy

The greatest challenge Forrestal faced as secretary of the navy was the battle over military unification. The War Department proposed to create three coequal services and to merge them into a single department of defense, which would be administered by a civilian secretary of defense and a military chief of staff. Army officials feared that the Navy and the Air Force might receive a disproportionately large share of the postwar military budget, and they viewed unification as a way to secure adequate funding for their own service. Air Force officers, meanwhile, supported unification as a means to gain autonomy and equality with the Navy and the Army. President Truman and many congressmen wanted unification in order to improve the efficiency of the services, reduce duplication, and cut expenditures.[36] But for Forrestal, unification not only challenged the organizational integrity of the Navy and its influence in the defense establishment but also diverted attention from the more important task of coordinating policy among the different offices of the executive branch.

From the beginning, Forrestal strongly opposed unification. He feared that the newly appointed secretary of defense and chief of staff might not understand the mission and tradition of the Navy. According to Forrestal, War Department officials were tied to a land strategy. They did not "view the world from the same global standpoint as the Navy." They understood neither naval operations and logistics nor the importance of controlling the seas. Furthermore, Forrestal worried that the secretary of the navy might be denied a seat in the cabinet, as well as direct access to the president, BOB, and Congress. The Navy would lose its chief civilian advocate.

Unification proposals also threatened the organizational integrity of the Navy. The Navy's marine arm might be incorporated into the Army, and its air arm into an independent Air Force. These losses would greatly impair the Navy's ability to seize advance bases and to conduct antisubmarine warfare and long-range reconnaisance, which were vital to maintaining control of the seas. Forrestal feared "that the Navy would be denied the use of the means to carry out the missions which only it fully comprehended." Worse yet, the Air Force could capture the public imagination and be given priority in the funding process.[37]

Forrestal also worried about the size of a unified defense establishment. He feared that a dangerous amount of power would be vested in the hands of the secretary of defense and the chief of staff. He also doubted that unification would result in significant savings, although this was clearly a secondary concern for him. He believed unification was contrary to established organizational principles. The new department would not be more efficient; it would be susceptible to the "inertia of size" and fall victim to the law of diminishing returns. A unified defense establishment would prove resistant to change and more difficult to motivate. It was unlikely to inspire organizational loyalty or the esprit de corps that was essential to a successful organization.[38]

But Forrestal's opposition to unification was also prompted by his view that the proponents of unification were addressing the wrong problem. For Forrestal, the key task was to effect a better coordination of economic, political, and military policies. As early as November 1944 he told Harry Hopkins that there was "nothing more important in the coming four years" than establishing mechanisms for effective interagency coordination. The national security was simply "too vast a concern to be assured by *any* single department." Deeply affected by the country's unpreparedness for war in 1941 and convinced that the nation's foreign and defense policies in the Far East had been poorly coordinated, he endeavored to ensure that such mistakes would not recur. He sought to integrate political and military policies, to reconcile strategic objectives with logistical capabilities, and to harmonize fiscal and defense imperatives. He contemplated a civilian body equivalent to the Joint Chiefs of Staff (JCS) and expected it to work like the British cabinet system. Representatives of the various government departments would meet to present the views of their respective organizations, to reconcile their differences on behalf of the overall imperatives of national interest, and to monitor the implementation of national policy. Forrestal hoped that a complementary body would be established to oversee the acquisition of the raw materials needed to implement the nation's security policies and war plans. To further improve the policy process, Forrestal wanted to establish a layer of permanent, experienced civil servants who would become specialists within their departments and who would provide continuity.[39]

In June 1945, Forrestal asked Eberstadt to undertake a comprehensive study of the Army's proposals and to determine whether unification would enhance U.S. national security. This strategy was typical of Forrestal, who often proposed broad ideas and relied upon Eberstadt or aides such as Hensel to give them structure. Eberstadt concluded his report in September. Like Forrestal, he opposed military unification under a single department, and he called for a greater degree of coordination among military, foreign, and domestic policies. Eberstadt, however, did recommend autonomy for the Army Air Forces, which he considered inevitable.

The Eberstadt Plan called for the establishment of a "Council of Common Defense" composed of the president, the secretaries of state, war, navy, and air, and the chairman of the National Security Resources Board (NSRB). A representative of the JCS and others invited by the president would also attend meetings. The primary purpose of the council, later named the National Security Council (NSC), would be to coordinate decision making among the civilian and military departments of the executive branch. Military strength would be tied more closely to the objectives of foreign policy and to the capabilities of the domestic economy. The council would be complemented by the NSRB, which would be charged with the responsibility of overseeing the supply of raw materials and planning for industrial mobilization during wartime. In this way Forrestal and Eberstadt sought to create the institutional structures needed to achieve the global mission Forrestal outlined for the nation.

Eberstadt also proposed that the JCS structure developed during the war be made statutory. The JCS would be responsible for strategic planning and for outlining the logistical requirements for implementing war plans. The chief of each service would be able to present his position but would be compelled to convince the others of its soundness before an action would be approved. Forrestal believed that the airing of conflicting opinions had been beneficial during World War II and would be crucial in a postwar era of conflicting objectives and limited budgets. He and Eberstadt contended that the creation of a permanent JCS would enhance the coordination of strategic planning and logistics, a goal toward which Forrestal had worked during the war.[40]

The Eberstadt Plan appeared well suited to Forrestal's personality and style of leadership. Policy making would be coordinated at the highest levels by officials from each major department. A diversity of opinions would be represented in the decision-making process, and consensus would precede action. Yet the administration of the military forces would remain firmly in the hands of the individual services and their respective secretaries. Forrestal's introduction of the Eberstadt Plan into the unification debate gave the Navy added bargaining power and temporarily allowed it to gain the initiative by calling for much broader changes than those proposed by the War Department.[41]

The chief obstacle to the implementation of the Eberstadt Plan was neither the War Department nor Congress, but President Truman. Truman believed that the establishment of a single department of defense would reduce duplication among the services, thereby saving money, as well as increase the efficiency of U.S. forces. As a cabinet member, Forrestal was in the awkward situation of opposing the president's policies. He sought to defend the best interests of the country and the Navy, as he perceived them, without appearing insubordinate and jeopardizing his position. This task became increasingly difficult in 1946 as the conflict between the War and Navy departments intensified during a series of congressional hearings. Forrestal emphasized that he supported the larger goal of improving the national defense, although he disagreed with the president over the tactics to be employed to achieve that goal. As the controversy persisted, it caused Forrestal much discomfiture. He wrote Congressman Carl Vinson, chairman of the House Naval Affairs Committee, that the unification battle was "troubling and embarrassing," for he could not "successfully play hypocrisy." At times Forrestal considered resigning, but in general he fought the Army's plan with great tenacity.[42]

Truman grew tired of Forrestal's intransigence and of the internecine battles between the services. In mid-May 1946 the president summoned top civilian and military leaders to the White House and insisted that they settle their differences. During the ensuing two weeks, Forrestal and Secretary of War Patterson agreed to establish joint agencies for research, procurement and supply, and training and education. Patterson acquiesced to Forrestal's opposition to a single chief of staff and accepted Forrestal's mechanisms for coordinating economic, political, and defense policies among civilian and military agencies. In turn, Forrestal acquiesced to a separate and coequal Air Force.[43]

Having elicited significant concessions from the War Department, Forrestal now shifted his emphasis and sought to preserve substantial autonomy for the individual services and for their secretaries within the framework of a unified defense establishment. He especially concentrated his energies on curbing the proposed powers of the secretary of defense. While War Department officials desired a strong secretary of defense who would have powers in the areas of policy coordination and administration, Forrestal insisted that the secretary's powers should be limited to the general oversight of the military establishment. The secretary would coordinate the policies of the three services and resolve disputes in areas such as missions, commands, and composition of forces, but the day-to-day administration of the three departments would remain in the hands of the respective service secretaries. Forrestal did not believe that the secretary should have the authority to fire a Navy bureau chief or an Army branch head. At a meeting with the president on unification, Forrestal announced that he would not be able to give public support to a unification bill that gave broader powers to the secretary of defense, and he threatened to resign. He also continued to insist on an air mission for the Navy and on its retention of the marines.[44]

Forrestal and Secretary of War Patterson reached a compromise in January 1947. Both men recognized that the disagreements between their departments had become counterproductive to the common goal of enhancing national security. Patterson agreed to limit the powers of the secretary of defense and to recognize the marine and air components of the Navy. These concessions were incorporated into the National Security Act and its accompanying executive order.

The National Security Act of July 1947 represented a compromise between the military departments. Forrestal did accept the autonomy of the Air Force and the unification of the services under a secretary of defense, but his own ideas provided the foundation for much of the legislation. The NSC was designed to coordinate military and civilian policies above the departmental level, while the NSRB was supposed to monitor an integrated effort to acquire strategic materials and to plan for their use. The secretary of defense would head not a unified department of defense but a confederation of services within the newly created national military establishment (NME). The Army, Navy, and Air Force would constitute separate departments under three secretaries, each of whom possessed cabinet rank and was guaranteed access to the president. The powers of the secretary of defense were circumscribed, and he was to focus on the coordination of policy within the NME. His staff was small, limited to three special civilian assistants. Strategic decisions fell within the purview of the JCS; official military advice could not be proffered to the secretary of defense without accommodating the demands of each of the services.[45]

Using Eberstadt's detailed study, Forrestal transformed unification from a threat to the postwar Navy into an opportunity to implement his views regarding the proper coordination of policy within the executive branch. As secretary of the navy, he safeguarded the interests of his internal constituency, advocated a global presence for the United States, cultivated external constituencies to support this new role, and worked tirelessly to create a more effective policy-making apparatus. His mission, as he defined it, was to create decision-making mechanisms that could effectively integrate defense and foreign policy, ensure military capabilities commensurate with diplomatic commitments, and reconcile the costs of defense with the fiscal imperatives of a sound economic policy.[46] The National Security Act, notwithstanding its latent weaknesses, attested to Forrestal's ability as a skillful manager who protected the Navy's organizational interests and as a governmental entrepreneur who succeeded in reshaping military unification into a restructuring of the entire national security decision-making apparatus. The tragedy was that he could not make that apparatus work.

The First Secretary of Defense

It was ironic that Truman named Forrestal the first secretary of defense after Patterson declined the position. Forrestal's opposition to unification had been exasperating to the president. Forrestal had mobilized opposition to unification within the Navy and among his friends in Congress, the press, and the business world. He had risked his position in the cabinet first to oppose unification and then to limit the powers of the office he now was to occupy. But Forrestal personally was enthusiastic about the national security apparatus. He believed it provided the framework whereby the United States could "marshall the full power of our human, material, and spiritual resources in defense of our security." He called the legislation "the most effective force for the maintenance of peace in our own—and I dare say—in the world's history." But he was characteristically pessimistic about his ability to fulfill his responsibilities as secretary of defense. In many respects his pessimism was well-founded, for he faced a number of difficult choices—between fiscal conservatism and military expenditures, foreign aid and domestic rearmament, service autonomy and an integrated defense.[47]

In establishing his new office, Forrestal employed the administrative techniques that had proven so successful during his tenure with the Navy. The national security legislation provided for the appointment of three civilian assistants. Forrestal once again selected specialists with experience in the business sector as well as in the military sphere. From the Navy Department he brought Marx Leva to handle legislative and legal matters and Wilfred McNeil to handle fiscal matters. He also recruited John Ohly, formerly an assistant to Patterson, to handle all other matters. The organization of the Office of the Secretary of Defense was primarily horizontal rather than vertical, and the lines of authority were initially blurred. The assistants worked well together because of a mutual respect and friendship and an intense loyalty to Forrestal. Forrestal also appointed three military assistants: Robert Wood, Army; Jerry Page, Air Force; and Herbert D. Riley, Navy. These men were to give Forrestal military advice independent of that offered by their service chiefs. This was another way in which Forrestal attempted to widen his channels of information in order to increase civilian control.[48]

Forrestal continued to rely upon a consensual style of decision making. The War Council, comprising the secretary of defense, the service secretaries and chiefs, and invited guests, met on a regular basis to discuss major policy issues. While Forrestal had the power of decision within that body, he preferred to work toward consensus. Forrestal also created the Committee of Four, consisting of himself and the service secretaries, which met to discuss more confidential matters. The secretary looked to the JCS, the NSRB, the Munitions Board, the Research and Development Board, and even the NSC as referral agencies. He often asked these groups to address specific problems and to make recommendations to him.[49]

As he had done with the Navy, the new secretary of defense brought civilian specialists into his office on a temporary basis to address specific problems. In the spring of 1948, for example, he hired the New York management consulting firm of Cresap, McCormick and Paget to study the organization of the office. Forrestal implemented most of the recommendations of the study: he clarified responsibilities and lines of authority within the office, and he hired additional staff support. He used the same technique in March 1948 when he asked William R. Mathews, publisher of the *Arizona Star*, and Frank Kluckhohn, a reporter for the *New York Times*, to study how to coordinate the public relations of the individual services and how to suppress news leaks. Forrestal also relied upon a number of ad hoc committees drawn from the business sector and the services to study important issues such as service pay, education programs, recreation for personnel, and military reserves. According to Stephen Rearden, this systematic use of committees "lessened the burdens on his office, which could not have handled all of these matters; it brought the services into 'grass roots' contact with one another on matters of common concern; it furthered his efforts to save money. Moreover, this practice accorded with Forrestal's concept of policy coordination. Since the committees reported directly to him, no intermediate layers of bureaucracy intruded."[50]

Forrestal's major goal as secretary of defense was to augment the nation's military strength in order to develop the means to implement its escalating foreign-policy commitments. His anxiety over the instability in Europe, the Mediterranean, the Middle East, and the Far East convinced him that it was more important to increase military capabilities than to scale back commitments or to redefine interests. During 1946 and 1947 he had favored taking the "calculated risk" of giving priority to foreign economic and military aid over U.S. rearmament. This priority was illustrated by his support of the Truman Doctrine and the Marshall Plan. A series of foreign-policy crises in early 1948, however, including the communist coup in Czechoslovakia, leftist threats in Greece and Italy, tensions arising from the creation of a Jewish homeland in Palestine, and controversies over German currency reform and access to Berlin, impelled Forrestal to seek additional military funding. He still did not expect a war with the Soviet Union, but he did believe that U.S. military forces were inadequate to respond to a major crisis in Italy, Greece, or Palestine. In his view, deploying more than one division of men to any of these areas in order to preserve stability or thwart a communist takeover would require partial mobilization.[51]

Several factors contributed to this military weakness. The services demobilized rapidly after World War II; equipment quickly became obsolete; and Truman placed a ceiling of $15.5 billion on the fiscal-year (FY) 1949 military budget. The president feared that higher levels of spending would wreak havoc with the domestic economy, accentuate inflationary pressures, and cause a recession, a development he could ill afford as the 1948 presidential election approached. Forrestal himself was also a fiscal conservative who acknowledged that "we can spend ourselves into defeat just as successfully as we can lose a war in battle." But he believed that it was impossible to safeguard American interests within the budget ceiling Truman had established. During early 1948 the secretary of defense called more stridently for increased military budgets, reactivation of the Selective Service System, and enactment of a program of UMT.[52]

Truman's budget ceiling enormously complicated Forrestal's efforts to develop a feasible strategic plan that was compatible with the role each of the services demanded. Discord over budgetary allocations, therefore, became inextricably linked to the vehement disagreements over roles and missions. Each service wanted additional funds to fulfill its mission, which each believed vital to U.S. security. Conversely, each service wanted to expand that mission in order to justify increased expenditures. Conflict intensified between the Navy and the Air Force soon after Forrestal took office. The postwar mission of the Navy, as Forrestal had helped define it, encompassed air power for reconnaissance, antisubmarine warfare, and the possible delivery of atomic weapons. The Navy wanted funds to build large aircraft carriers and high-altitude planes. The Air Force, on the other hand, wanted control of all strategic warfare. Air Force officers translated this desire into demands for a seventy-group air force and for mass production of the B-36 bomber. Forrestal realized that the desires of both services could not be met within the confines of the Truman budget. He acknowledged that developing a single integrated budget for the military was the "greatest central problem of unification."[53]

Forrestal took two approaches to the problems he faced. He encouraged the service chiefs and secretaries to agree upon a definition of roles and missions as the indispensable prerequisite to a rational division of funds within the Truman budget ceiling. Always committed to a consensual style of leadership, Forrestal believed that reasonable men could reach agreement through discussion, particularly if they were removed from the political atmosphere of Washington. He arranged a meeting of the JCS in Key West, Florida, in early March 1948. He hoped to resolve the disputes over roles and missions. The paper that resulted from the conference, "Functions of the Armed Forces and the Joint Chiefs of Staff," suggested that the service chiefs had reached a compromise. The Air Force would possess primary responsibility for strategic air power, while the Navy would have the responsibility for all air operations essential to conducting a naval campaign. It soon became clear, however, that neither the Air Force nor the Navy was satisfied with the results of the conference. The Air Force was angered because the paper failed to endorse a seventy-group air force, gave the Navy permission to develop a heavy aircraft carrier and high-altitude planes, and did not proscribe a naval role in the future use of atomic weapons. The Navy, on the other hand, believed that the Air Force wanted control over all air power and was seeking to deprive the Navy of a role in strategic bombing. Less than a month after the conference, Forrestal admitted that he was making "no progress" in defining roles and missions.[54]

Forrestal's other approach to the budget problem was to persuade Truman to raise the budget ceiling. The escalating tensions in Soviet-American relations during early 1948 played into Forrestal's hands. Truman himself appeared before a joint session of Congress and called for the reenactment of the Selective Service System, the passage of UMT legislation, and support for the European Recovery Program. The president also was prepared to consider requests for additional military funding and endorsed a supplemental bill totaling a little over $3 billion. Forrestal felt that he was making progress toward educating the president about the needs of the NME when Air Force Secretary Stuart Symington and Air Force Chief of Staff Carl Spaatz went behind his back and persuaded Congress to approve an additional $822 million to fund the seventy-group air force. This maneuver angered and humiliated Forrestal. He believed in a balance of forces and saw little utility in building up the Air Force disproportionately if there were no provision to provide the additional support elements from the Army and the Navy. Moreover, Forrestal felt that Symington's initiative discredited the defense secretary's stature and credibility at the White House and undermined his ability to request additional yet measured increases in military spending. Truman, in fact, was so infuriated that he refused to allow the expenditure of the extra funds allocated for the seventy groups.[55]

The conflict over the FY 1949 supplementary budget was the initial act in an unfolding drama. The FY 1950 budget constituted the first attempt to prepare a unified military budget. In July 1948 the president announced that the working military budget for 1950 would be $14.4 billion. The services, however, submitted separate requests totaling $29 billion. The JCS could not agree upon a strategic plan that could be implemented within Truman's budget, particularly when they lacked guidance from the NSC and the State Department on the priorities of U.S. foreign policy. Forrestal realized that continuing discord over roles and missions contributed to the incapacity of the JCS to agree on a strategic plan within budgetary confines. He again tried to reach a compromise on the role of each service by meeting with the JCS in Newport, Rhode Island, in August 1948. After many heated exchanges, the service chiefs grudgingly agreed to assign to the Air Force primary control over atomic warfare and to grant the Navy some undefined role in strategic bombing.[56]

Increasingly beleaguered by the acrimony among the services, Forrestal asked the JCS to appoint a special board to determine the division of funds within the budget ceiling. The board was composed of Gen. Joseph T. McNarney of the Air Force, Maj. Gen. George J. Richards of the Army, and Vice Adm. Robert B. Carney. Beginning in August, the board met for seven weeks with scores of witnesses, and eventually it proposed a budget of $23.6 billion. Although this sum exceeded Truman's ceiling by about $9 billion, the McNarney Board did correlate the service requests into one budget proposal instead of three. But military planners and budget officers still insisted that the minimum war plan, including a strategic air offensive from Britain and some effort to hold open the lines of communication in the Mediterranean, required a minimum budget of $23.6 billion. As a result, the JCS could not allocate sufficient resources to each of the services within the $14.4 billion limit, and the Navy and Air Force resumed their vehement attacks upon one another. In late October, Forrestal directed the JCS to submit a recommended allocation of funds for budgets of $14.4 billion and $16.9 billion. The JCS complied with Forrestal's request but warned that both figures were too low to provide adequate military strength.[57]

Forrestal was faced with two choices: either to accept the $14.4 billion budget or to persuade Truman, BOB, and Congress to raise that ceiling. Forrestal himself was increasingly skeptical of the military's ability to protect U.S. interests, support diplomatic commitments, and fulfill the most basic undertakings of the war plans without a sizable increase in military outlays. He therefore sought to enlist external constituencies on behalf of a larger military budget. He asked Under Secretary of State Robert Lovett and Policy Planning Staff Director George Kennan to conduct a comprehensive reappraisal of the relations between the nation's foreign-policy objectives and its military capabilities, but the final NSC study on this subject in the fall of 1948 did not satisfy Forrestal. He then asked Secretary of State George C. Marshall to agree that the international climate necessitated increased military expenditures. Marshall, however, was concerned primarily with U.S. attempts to provide economic aid to Western Europe. Moreover, neither he nor his colleagues at Foggy Bottom considered war likely, and they did not see a need to augment domestic military expenditures given the conflicting demands on the budget. The secretary of defense then tried to persuade Truman and BOB to accept a compromise between the $14.4 billion ceiling and the McNarney proposal. But the president refused to budge. His concerns were primarily fiscal and economic. Yet Forrestal's failure to mobilize support from other executive agencies and his inability to secure agreement among the services hurt the defense secretary's case for rearmament.[58]

Forrestal did not achieve his major goals as secretary of defense. He was unable to enhance military capabilities to match foreign-policy commitments. Furthermore, the Key West and Newport agreements represented only temporary compromises on the postwar roles and missions of the services. The inherent weakness of the Office of the Secretary of Defense, which he had insisted upon, was a key factor accounting for his failure. Strong-willed service secretaries like Symington had the institutionalized power to defy Forrestal. Moreover, the secretary of defense did not have the authority to compel agreement among the chiefs of staff. The assumption that the three services would hammer out compromises, as they had during World War II, proved fallacious. And without the cooperation of the three services, the small staff in the Office of the Secretary of Defense, which Forrestal also had insisted upon, could not possibly handle the jobs of collecting statistical data, mobilizing internal and external constituencies, securing effective coordination of policy, and overseeing the implementation of decisions.[59]

Forrestal's personal style of administration compounded his difficulties. He considered his task to be "the negotiation of consensus within the military establishment," and he believed that he should coordinate rather than dictate policy. But in the absence of a wartime emergency, this consensual style of management broke down. Forrestal wrote an associate in November 1948 that "you can multiply the problems of war ... by a multiple of about ten to get the picture now." The task of reconciling the demands of the NME with the needs of the peacetime domestic economy overwhelmed Forrestal. On occasion, he expressed his pent-up frustrations. "The Army Air people," he charged, "have been aggressive, ruthless, and, in my opinion, somewhat indifferent to the broader interests of national security." Usually, however, Forrestal controlled his rage, even when Symington's behavior appalled Forrestal's assistants and even when naval officers like Arthur Radford aggressively challenged Forrestal's attempts to arrange a compromise over the definitions of the roles and missions of the Air Force and the Navy.[60]

Forrestal's attempts to mediate the differences among the services and to cajole the JCS to operate within Truman's budgetary guidelines left him without an internal constituency. Although he believed that more money should be allocated to the NME, he also shared the conviction that military profligacy could fuel the inflationary cycle, undermine the domestic economy, and thwart the economic reconstruction of Western Europe and Japan. At times, he pleaded with the service secretaries and the JCS to recognize the overall economic context in which the NME had to function and to appreciate the socioeconomic causes of unrest abroad that constituted the most serious of all challenges to U.S. foreign-policy objectives. But such appeals often convinced Navy and Air Force leaders that Forrestal was an adversary and an agent of the White House rather than an advocate of the military services. They resented his efforts to align budget requests more closely with Truman's ceiling. The situation called for Forrestal to exercise his authority, but he was reluctant to use fully even those powers that he possessed. As he was torn between compliance with the president's wishes, maintenance of a balanced budget, and increased military strength, he appeared more and more irresolute.[61]

Neither the president nor his assistants possessed any sympathy for Forrestal's plight. His tenacity during the grueling debates over unification legislation and his prior record as a ceaseless proponent of larger naval expenditures made his motives suspect at the White House. From the moment he took the job as the first secretary of defense, Truman's aides, such as Clark Clifford and George Elsey, believed that Forrestal sought to use the NSC to impose a military stamp on the nation's foreign policy. They tried desperately to protect the president's authority, to circumscribe the powers of the NSC, and to diminish Forrestal's influence by placing the secretary of state at the head of the NSC in the president's absence. Truman's civilian advisers seemed unaware of the extent to which Forrestal always had emphasized civilian leadership in the Navy Department, even at the cost of angering career officers. Likewise, Truman's budget officers believed that Forrestal was doing all he could to punch holes in their budget ceiling. They denounced his budgetary demands, decried his inability to control the services, remonstrated over his irresolution, and often maneuvered for State Department support against Forrestal. Driven by their own organizational imperatives, they had little understanding of the pressures that engulfed Forrestal, and they cared little about his desire to match military capabilities and diplomatic commitments. They did not think that For restal shared their fiscal concerns; they did not believe that he wanted to secure military compliance with their wishes; and they did not credit his willingness (in 1949) to remove the service secretaries from the NSC, a recommendation that was incompatible with their presumption that he sought to effect military domination of the policy process. From the perspective of Truman's advisers in the White House, Forrestal was a sincere patriot, driven by a sense of duty, but wrongly obsessed with building up military capabilities to the exclusion of other considerations. They had only a limited understanding of Forrestal the man, the administrator, and the defense secretary.[62]

As Forrestal's relations with the White House staff deteriorated, his public image also grew more tarnished. Columnists like Drew Pearson and Walter Winchell criticized his business connections, his attitudes toward Israel, his inability to control the military services, and his alleged desire to ensure military control of national policy making. When Forrestal became secretary of defense, he noted that the job "not only has to be well done, but the public has to be convinced that it is being well done." Forrestal had succeeded in accomplishing this goal as secretary of the navy, but he failed to mobilize public support and to win an external constituency as secretary of defense.[63]

Forrestal was acutely aware of the sources of his problems. During 1948 he identified several weaknesses within the new defense establishment. He advocated increasing the power of the secretary of defense and establishing clearer lines of authority within the NME. He recommended the appointment of an under secretary of defense and the hiring of a larger staff for his own office. He proposed to separate the Joint Chiefs from their respective services in order to enable them to devote their full attention to overseeing the military establishment rather than promoting the interests of their individual services. Forrestal also came to support a chairman for the JCS who would guide that body toward decisions. He attempted to implement this proposal on a temporary basis in January 1949 when he asked retired Gen. Dwight D. Eisenhower to serve as unofficial chairman of the JCS. In March 1949 he recommended to the Senate Committee on the Armed Services that the powers of the service secretaries be circumscribed and that they no longer be allowed to sit on the NSC. Forrestal discussed these suggestions with Eberstadt's task force, which was studying the NME as part of the Hoover Commission on the Organization of the Executive Branch. As Forrestal phrased it, it was time "to convert the military establishment from a confederacy to a federation."[64]

Forrestal's plans for reorganization suggested that he expected to remain secretary of defense in Truman's second administration. Although his relations with Truman were never close, and although he was the subject of ridicule throughout the White House, Forrestal mistakenly believed that his job was secure. While he possessed a grudging admiration for Truman's fiscal conservatism, Forrestal did not realize how his own incapacity to control the demands of the NME exasperated the president. In mid-1948 Truman bluntly instructed Forrestal to get the services to agree on a program within the budget ceiling. "It seems to me that is your responsibility." Thereafter, Forrestal's refusal to take an active part in the 1948 presidential campaign against Thomas E. Dewey agitated Truman. Forrestal claimed that a defense secretary should be above politics. Truman, however, suspected that Forrestal was maneuvering to take a seat in Dewey's administration should the Republican candidate win. After the election, Truman saw no reason to retain anyone in his cabinet whom he suspected of disloyalty. In March 1949 the president requested Forrestal's resignation and designated Louis E. Johnson as secretary of defense.[65]

The loss of his job evidently contributed to Forrestal's severe mental collapse. A few days after leaving office he was admitted to Bethesda Naval Hospital. Several weeks later he took his own life. Although many of his acquaintances subsequently claimed that they had foreseen his psychological breakdown, those individuals who worked most closely with Forrestal, like Wilfred McNeil and Marx Leva, did not see his emotional unraveling. Instead they watched a man working indefatigably yet ineffectually to deal with the problems within his organization. They also knew that Forrestal was his own worst critic. He believed he was failing as secretary of defense, and he took the failure personally. Moreover, he was wounded by the professional conflicts with Symington and by the personal attacks in the newspapers. He increasingly lost perspective on the problems he faced; according to Eberstadt, details began to "assume a disproportionate size." He could not make decisions. "You know from personal experience what an unceasing strain this job is," he wrote a former colleague in November 1948. And the problems ahead appeared even more formidable. "There are some problems that almost seem insoluble: China, the Middle East, and France. . . ." He feared that he had not sufficiently alerted the American people to these future dangers. Eberstadt advised his friend to take a long vacation and urged him to resign before he was fired. But it was all to no avail.[66]

The Forrestal Legacy

Although Forrestal's career ended in failure and tragedy, during his years at the helm of the Navy Department he exemplified the characteristics of a successful entrepreneur in government. He was more than an administrator; he was an innovator. He reorganized the department to speed naval defense mobilization and to increase civilian control. He decisively shaped the Navy's postwar goals, recognized the implications of new technology for the Navy's future, underscored its air mission, and linked it to the global objectives of U.S. foreign policy. During the unification battle, he scanned the environment, identified adversaries, mobilized internal and external constituencies, and assumed the initiative. Against great odds, he successfully defended the integrity of his institution. What is even more important, he seized upon unification to reform the entire policy-making apparatus of the government as it pertained to national security. His major goal was to bring about a better coordination of political, economic, military, and diplomatic policies. He was the major proponent of institutionalized interagency cooperation through such new bodies as the NSC and the NSRB. Forrestal more than any other single individual shaped the National Security Act of 1947.

But the apparatus he designed was not nearly as effective as he expected it to be. The policy-making machinery was geared to a consensual style of management, which Forrestal cherished but which foundered upon the absence of a consensus within the NME and between the NME and other executive agencies. Interservice rivalry prevented Forrestal from ever securing a lasting agreement on roles and missions. Likewise, discord over the relative importance of a balanced budget, foreign economic assistance, and military rearmament embittered Forrestal's relations with the White House and distanced him from friends at the State Department. In this context, he needed to take charge, to exert more authority, and to mobilize external constituencies. But he frowned upon the exercise of personal power, and he disliked personal acrimony. As a result, he never succeeded at imposing discipline upon and eliciting cooperation from the services.

For similar reasons, he also failed to convince his colleagues at the White House and the State Department of the need to reconcile military capabilities and diplomatic goals. Capabilities were not enlarged, nor commitments narrowed. Indeed, the gap between goals and tactics widened until the nation's military unpreparedness and diplomatic ineptness were exposed by the outbreak of hostilities in Korea. By then, of course, Forrestal was dead. While he lived, his protests sounded shrill, and his leadership style in the NME proved ineffective. Yet his plea for effective interagency coordination and his call for a proper integration of military, economic, and diplomatic policies still echo through the corridors of the Pentagon, the State Department, and the White House.

Notes

1. Forrestal, speech to New York Rubber Corporation, 18 October 1943, Papers of James V. Forrestal, box 5, Princeton University, Seeley G. Mudd Library (hereafter cited as JFP). For additional details about Forrestal's early years see Arnold A. Rogow, *James Forrestal: A Study of Personality, Politics, and Power* (New York: Macmillan, 1963), 49–88. Rogow's account includes few attributed citations. For biographical sketches of Forrestal see Robert Greenhalgh Albion and Robert Howe Connery with Jennie Barnes Pope, *Forrestal and the Navy* (New York: Columbia University Press, 1962), 1–28; and Walter Millis with Eugene Duffield, eds., *The Forrestal Diaries* (New York: Viking Press, 1951), xvi–xxiv.

2. Forrestal to Warren Leslie III, 13 August 1947, JFP, box 75; Forrestal to George E. Allen, 12 August 1947, ibid., box 92; Albion and Connery, *Forrestal and the Navy*, 23; Ferdinand Eberstadt to George Fielding Eliot, 7 August 1947, Papers of Ferdinand Eberstadt, Forrestal Files, box 4, Princeton University, Seeley G. Mudd Library (hereafter cited as FEP).

3. Rogow, *James Forrestal*, 61–65. The book was *College Journalism*, published by Princeton University Press in 1914.

4. Eberstadt to Eliot, 7 August 1947.

5. Ibid.; Rogow, *James Forrestal*, 71–73. For other accounts of Forrestal's relationship with his wife see "Reminiscences of Hanson Weightman Baldwin, U.S. Navy, Ret.," U.S. Naval Institute, Annapolis, 1976, interview 5 by John T. Mason, Jr., 28 July 1975, transcript at Operational Archives, Washington Navy Yard, Washington, D.C.; and "Reminiscences of Vice Admiral William R. Smedberg III, U.S. Navy, Ret.," U.S. Naval Institute, Annapolis, July 1979, interview 3 by John T. Mason, Jr., 9 June 1976, ibid.

6. Albion and Connery, *Forrestal and the Navy*, 2–4; Rogow, *James Forrestal*, 89–92.

7. Unpublished diaries of James Forrestal, 4 November 1944, 1:52, and 8 December 1944, 1:85, Naval History Division, Washington Navy Yard, (hereafter cited as Diaries). Forrestal to C. C. Felton, 12 September 1944, box 60; Forrestal to Douglas Dillon, 17 June 1941, box 54; Forrestal to Robert D. Elder, 19 July 1944, box 60; Forrestal to Henry R. Luce, 11 May and 26 November 1944, box 61; Forrestal to Robert Matter, 20 April 1945, box 88—all in JFP. Carl W. Borklund, *Men of the Pentagon: From Forrestal to McNamara* (New York: Frederick A. Praeger, 1966), 42–43.

8. Albion and Connery, *Forrestal and the Navy*, 1, 4–5; Rogow, *James Forrestal*, 90. Forrestal, speech to Wednesday Law Club, 26 May 1945, box 5; Forrestal, speech to New York Rubber Corporation, 18 October 1943, box 5; Forrestal to Abe Fortas, 12 August 1947, box 73; Forrestal to Gordon Hardwick, 31 July 1947, box 74; Forrestal to Jouette Shouse, 25 July 1947, box 76; Forrestal to Ralph Bard, 20 November 1948, box 78—all in JFP. "Reminiscences of Vice Admiral Smedberg." Forrestal to Edmond Hanrahan, 21 October 1947, JFP, box 74; Forrestal memo, 15 March 1946, ibid., box 41.

9. Robert Cutler, *No Time for Rest* (Boston: Little, Brown, 1965), 242; "Reminiscences of Vice Admiral Felix L. Johnson, U.S. Navy, Ret.," U.S. Naval Institute, Annapolis, 1974, interview 5 by John T. Mason, Jr., 10 February 1972, transcript at Operational Archives, Washington Navy Yard; Forrestal to Adrian St. John, 9 October 1947, JFP, box 76; Bernard M. Baruch, *The Public Years* (New York: Holt, Rinehart & Winston, 1960), 296–98.

10. Cutler, *No Time for Rest*, 243; "Reminiscences of Vice Admiral Smedberg";

Borklund, *Men of the Pentagon*, 15, 42; James F. Byrnes, *Speaking Frankly* (Westport, Conn.: Greenwood Press, 1974), 212.

11. "Reminiscences of Vice Admiral Smedberg"; "Reminiscences of Admiral Robert Lee Dennison, U.S. Navy, Ret.," U.S. Naval Institute, Annapolis, 1975, interview 3 by John T. Mason Jr., 17 January 1973, transcript at Operational Archives, Washington Navy Yard; Marx Leva, "The Most Unforgettable Character I Have Ever Met," FEP, Forrestal Files, box 5; Stephen L. Rearden, *History of the Office of the Secretary of Defense: The Formative Years, 1947–1950* (Washington, D.C.: Historical Office, Office of the Secretary of Defense, 1984), 63.

12. Eberstadt to Eliot, 7 August 1947; Floyd Parks to V.A.M et al., 5 April 1948, Floyd Parks Papers (1947–48), box 5, Dwight David Eisenhower Library, Abilene, Kans.; Forrestal to Ernest Havemann, 29 August 1947, JFP, box 74.

13. Forrestal memo, 24 March 1941, JFP, box 41; Forrestal, undated memo enclosed in letter to Bernard Baruch, 26 July 1940, Papers of Bernard Baruch, vol. 47, Princeton University, Seeley G. Mudd Library.

14. Albion and Connery, *Forrestal and the Navy*, 5–8; Rogow, *James Forrestal*, 91–92; U.S. Congress, House, Committee on Appropriations, *Navy Department Appropriations Bill for 1943: Hearings before the Subcommittee of the Committee on Appropriations*, 78th Cong., 1st sess., 8 February 1943, 49.

15. "Reminiscences of Admiral Dennison."

16. Forrestal to William A. Read, 18 May 1943, JFP, box 59; Forrestal memo, 28 October 1944, National Archives (NA), RG 80, General Records of the Department of the Navy, Secretary of the Navy Files, box 120, 70–1–22 (hereafter cited as Secretary of the Navy Files); Forrestal memo, 24 May 1945, JFP, box 42.

17. H. Struve Hensel, "Changes inside the Pentagon," *Harvard Business Review* 32 (January–February 1954): 100; Forrestal speech, "*Herald Tribune* Forum," 16 November 1943, JFP, box 5; James Forrestal et al., *The Navy: A Study in Administration* (Chicago: Public Administration Service, 1946), 2; Diaries, 20 January 1945, 1:131; Cutler, *No Time for Rest*, 244.

18. Robert H. Connery, *The Navy and the Industrial Mobilization in World War II* (Princeton: Princeton University Press, 1949), 59–61.

19. Forrestal to Harry R. Sheppard, 30 January 1943, JFP, box 42; Albion and Connery, *Forrestal and the Navy*, 63–78; U.S. Congress, House, Committee on Appropriations, *Supplemental Navy Department Appropriations Bill for 1943: Hearings before the Subcommittee of the Committee on Appropriations*, 78th Cong., 1st sess., 8 February 1943, 61; Connery, *The Navy and the Industrial Mobilization*, 61–64, 69–75.

20. Albion and Connery, *Forrestal and the Navy*, 94–96.

21. Connery, *The Navy and the Industrial Mobilization*, 156–62, 178; Albion and Connery, *Forrestal and the Navy*, 77, 94.

22. Albion and Connery, *Forrestal and the Navy*, 66–67, 93–94, 113–115.

23. Ibid., 90–93, 124–127; "Reminiscences of Vice Admiral Smedberg"; Ernest J. King and Walter M. Whitehill, *Fleet Admiral King: A Naval Record* (New York: W. W. Norton & Co., 1952), 629–37.

24. Albion and Connery, *Forrestal and the Navy*, 96–103.

25. Forrestal speech, Third War Loan Drive, 9 September 1943, JFP, box 5; Albion and Connery, *Forrestal and the Navy*, 233, 122; Rogow, *James Forrestal*, 118.

26. Knox memo to Forrestal, 10 November 1942, and Forrestal reply, 11 November, RG 80, General Records of the Department of the Navy, Secretary of the Navy General Correspondence, Undersecretary of the Navy Files, 1940–44, box 169; Albion and Connery, *Forrestal and the Navy*, 10–13.

27. Minutes of Top Policy Group meeting #1, 13 November 1944, RG 80, General Records of the Department of the Navy, Top Secret Forrestal Files, box 1; Albion and Connery, *Forrestal and the Navy*, 234–41.

28. Forrestal to W. Douglas Burden, 19 November 1945, JFP, box 89; A. D. Douglas to Eugene S. Duffield, 6 April 1945, Diaries, 2: 247.

29. Forrestal to J. K. Vardaman, 14 September 1945, JFP, box 100; Forrestal, memo to L. L. Strauss, 7 November 1945, RG 80, Secretary of the Navy Files, box 71, 39–1–37; Forrestal to E. Palmer Hoyt, 1 November 1945, JFP, box 63.

30. Forrestal memo, 1 November 1945, revised 9 November, FEP, Forrestal Files, box 2; Vincent Davis, *Postwar Defense Policy and the U.S. Navy, 1943–1946* (Chapel Hill: University of North Carolina Press, 1962), 115, 123, 208, 87, 65, 227.

31. Lloyd G. Gardner, *Architects of Illusion: Men and Ideas in Foreign Policy* (Chicago: Quadrangle Books, 1970), 270–300; Forrestal to Clarence Dillon, 11 April 1946, JFP, box 101; Forrestal, memorandum for the secretary of state, 8 March 1946, ibid., box 68; Forrestal to Byrnes, 25 April 1946, ibid.; Millis, *Forrestal Diaries*, 14, 52–53, 57.

32. Diaries, 16 January 1945, 1: 121; Forrestal to Sen. Homer Ferguson, 14 May 1945, JFP, box 62; Diaries, 1 May 1945, 2: 322; Forrestal, notes for address to Phillips Exeter Academy, 10 June 1945, JFP, box 29; Forrestal, memo of phone conversation with Paul Shields, 20 March 1947, ibid., box 91.

33. Forrestal, memo to Ernest J. King, 8 February 1945, JFP, box 88; Forrestal, memo to Roosevelt, 9 April 1945, ibid., box 88; Forrestal, draft memo on bases, 17 April 1945, RG 80, Secretary of the Navy Files, Subject Files, 1942–48, box 2, Bases and Trusteeships File; "Will We Choose Naval Suicide Again?" prepared for *Saturday Evening Post*, 27 April 1944, ibid., Eugene S. Duffield Files, 1942–44; Diaries, 7 July 1944, 1: 7; Forrestal, speech on trusteeships, not delivered, JFP, box 34; Diaries, 17 April 1945, 2: 298–300; Albion and Connery, *Forrestal and the Navy*, 169–72. For overseas base planning see also NA, RG 218, Records of the Joint Chiefs of Staff, Combined Chiefs of Staff (CCS) 360 (12–9–42).

34. Millis, *Forrestal Diaries*, 141, 144–45, 171, 184, 196, 211; Davis, *Postwar Defense Policy*, 223; Albion and Connery, *Forrestal and the Navy*, 186–88; Leva, "The Most Unforgettable Character." For the importance of the Cairo/Suez area see Melvyn P. Leffler, "Strategy, Diplomacy, and the Cold War: The United States, Turkey, and NATO, 1945–1952," *Journal of American History* 71 (March 1985): 813–16.

35. Davis, *Postwar Defense Policy*, 65; Albion and Connery, *Forrestal and the Navy*, 228; "Reminiscences of Vice Admiral Smedberg."

36. For a detailed discussion of the unification battle see Demetrios Caraley, *The Politics of Military Unification: A Study of Conflict and the Policy Process* (New York: Columbia University Press, 1966).

37. For Forrestal's opposition to unification see, for example, Millis, *Forrestal Diaries*, 167, 205; Forrestal, memo to the president, 4 June 1946, RG 80, General Records of the Department of the Navy, Forrestal Papers, General Correspondence, box 24, 8–1–3; and Diaries, 19 January 1945, 1: 123.

38. Millis, *Forrestal Diaries*, 159–170; Forrestal, draft of statement before Woodrum Committee, 28 April 1944, RG 80, General Records of the Department of the Navy, Forrestal Papers, General Correspondence, box 22, 8–1–3; Forrestal to Harold Smith, 12 March 1945, ibid., box 27, 8–1–3.

39. Forrestal to Sheldon Clark, 24 September 1945, JFP, box 62; Forrestal to William A. Read, 18 May 1943; Forrestal to Frank White Hearned, 7 May 1945, JFP, box 88; Diaries, 13 June 1945, 2: 366; Millis, *Forrestal Diaries*, 19; Forrestal to Walter Lippmann, 27 November 1945, RG 80, General Records of the Department of the

Navy, Forrestal Papers, General Correspondence, box 107, 60–1–3.

40. Forrestal, memo to Russell, for King, 20 October 1945, JFP, box 89; "Summary of Report to Honorable James Forrestal . . . from F. Eberstadt," [October 1945,] FEP, box 29; Eberstadt, memorandum for Forrestal, 5 July 1945, ibid.

41. Forrestal to Chester W. Nimitz, 6 September 1944, JFP, box 48; Forrestal to Edward B. Germain, 15 September 1944, ibid., box 60; Forrestal to William M. Chadbourne, 22 December 1945, ibid., box 62; Caraley, *Politics of Military Unification*, 38–44.

42. Diaries, 13 June 1945, 2: 366; ibid., 30 July 1945, 2: 415; Forrestal to Douglas Dillon, 9 December 1946, JFP, box 68; Forrestal to Ralph Bard, 9 December 1945, ibid.; Forrestal to Truman, [17 April 1946?], RG 80, General Records of the Department of the Navy, Forrestal Papers, General Correspondence, box 24, 8–1–3; Millis, *Forrestal Diaries*, 160–70. For the quotation see Forrestal to Vinson, 24 June 1946, JFP, box 71.

43. Alfred J. Sander, "Truman and the National Security Council, 1945–47," *Journal of American History* 59 (September 1972): 374–77; Caraley, *Politics of Military Unification*, 125–52; Herman S. Wolk, *Planning and Organizing the Postwar Air Force, 1943–1947* (Washington, D.C.: Office of Air Force History, 1984), 149–55; Millis, *Forrestal Diaries*, 165–70.

44. Millis, *Forrestal Diaries*, 200–206, 221–31; Forrestal to Clark Clifford, 7 September 1946, JFP, box 68.

45. For the Patterson-Forrestal compromise and the subsequent legislation and executive order see Wolk, *Postwar Air Force* 161–78; and Caraley, *Politics of Military Unification*, 153–82, 251–63.

46. Forrestal to Harold S. Vanderbilt, 29 March 1946, JFP, box 71; Forrestal to Douglas Dillon, 9 December 1946; Forrestal to Clifford, 7 September 1946, Clark Clifford Papers, box 16, Harry S. Truman Library, Independence, Mo. (HSTL); U.S. Congress, Senate, Committee of the Armed Services, *National Defense Establishment: Unification of the Armed Services*, Hearings, 80th Cong., 1st sess., 20 March 1947, 23.

47. U.S. Congress, Senate, Committee on Naval Affairs, *Unification of the Armed Forces*, Hearings, 79th Cong. 2d sess., 1 May 1946, 49–50; Millis, *Forrestal Diaries*, 298–300; *New York Times*, 29 August 1947; Forrestal to Sen. Albert W. Hawkes, 30 July 1947, JFP, box 74; "Reminiscences of Vice Admiral Smedberg"; Forrestal to Clifford, 28 July 1947, Clifford Papers, box 16.

48. Rearden, *The Formative Years*, 63; Paolo E. Coletta, *The United States Navy and Defense Unification, 1947–1953* (Newark: University of Delaware Press, 1981), 35.

49. Rearden, *The Formative Years*, 33–35.

50. Ibid., 63, 79–80, 86–87.

51. Millis, *Forrestal Diaries*, 349–51, 373–79; Melvyn P. Leffler, "The American Conception of National Security and the Beginnings of the Cold War, 1945–1948." *American Historical Review* 89 (April 1984): 369–78.

52. For the quotation see Forrestal's prepared statement for the Naval Subcommittee of the House Committee on Approprriations, 11 January 1947, JFP, box 6; see also Rearden, *The Formative Years*, 316–30.

53. Forrestal, speech to Economic Club of New York, 25 February 1947, JFP, box 6; Forrestal, speech to National War College, 22 June 1948, ibid.; Forrestal to Baldwin, 16 June 1948, ibid., box 78.

54. "Functions of the Armed Forces and the Joint Chiefs of Staff," RG 330, Records of the Secretary of Defense, CD 25–1–40, box 107; Millis, *Forrestal Diaries*,

389–97; Outline of remarks for Luncheon of American Society of Newspaper Editors, 17 April 1948, JFP, box 113; Forrestal to Eisenhower, 21 February 1948, ibid., box 79; Rearden, *The Formative Years*, 385–97; Daniel Yergin, *Shattered Peace: The Origins of the Cold War and the National Security State* (Boston: Houghton-Mifflin, 1977), 336–65; Wilfred J. McNeil, Oral History, HSTL, 61–65.

55. Warner R. Schilling, Paul Y. Hammond, and Glenn H. Snyder, *Strategy, Politics, and Defense Budgets* (New York: Columbia University Press, 1962), 41–46; Rearden, *The Formative Years*, 309–34; Marx Leva, Oral History, HSTL, 53–56.

56. Rearden, *The Formative Years*, 335–41, 397–402; Millis, *Forrestal Diaries*, 476–78; "Agreed Final Version of Newport Meetings, 20–22 Aug. 1948," Washington Navy Yard, Records of the Chief of Naval Operations (CNO), Double Zero Files, box 1 (Newport Meetings).

57. Schilling, Hammond, and Snyder, *Strategy, Politics, and Defense Budgets*, 47, 159–62; Rearden, *The Formative Years*, 335–60; Millis, *Forrestal Diaries*, 450.

58. Forrestal to Marshall, 31 October 1948, and Marshall, telegram to Forrestal, 8 November 1948, both in RG 330, Records of the Secretary of Defense, CD 5–1–25, box 18; Rearden, *The Formative Years*, 347–51; Leffler, "American Conception of National Security," 376–78.

59. Forrestal had misgivings from the beginning about Symington's appointment as secretary of the Air Force (See Millis, *Forrestal Diaries*, 295, 462–65; and "Reminiscences of Hanson Weightman Baldwin").

60. Paul Y. Hammond, *Organizing for Defense: The American Military Establishment in the Twentieth Century* (Princeton: Princeton University Press, 1961), 232; Eugene S. Duffield, "Organizing for Defense," *Harvard Business Review* 31 (September/October 1953): 29–42; Forrestal to Ralph Bard, 20 November 1948; Forrestal to Baldwin, 28 March 1948, JFP, box 68; Leva, Oral History, 53–56; Eugene M. Zuckert, Oral History, HSTL, 18–19; Minutes of Newport Meetings, 21 August 1948, Records of the CNO, Double Zero Files, box 1.

61. For Forrestal's concerns with fiscal and economic considerations see, for example, Excerpt of Phone Conversation between Forrestal and C. E. Wilson, 2 April 1948, JFP, box 48; Excerpt of Phone Conversation between Forrestal and Clarence Cannon, 9 April 1948, ibid.; "Approved Transcript of Meeting Held in the Pentagon Auditorium" 24 August 1948, Records of the CNO, Double Zero Files, box 1 (Newport Meeting); Forrestal to Truman, 20 November 1948, RG 330, Records of the Secretary of Defense, CD 5–1–25, box 18; Rearden, *The Formative Years*, 43.

62. See the many documents in the George Elsey Papers, boxes 83 and 84, HSTL; see also documents in Clifford Papers, box 16. James Webb, director of BOB often sought Under Secretary of State Lovett's assistance to contain military expenditures. See, for example, entries of 16 December 1947, 5 and 15 January 1948, and 21 April 1948, Robert Lovett Diaries, New York Historical Society; see also Sander, "Truman and the National Security Council," 376–88; and Anna Kasten Nelson, "President Truman and the Evolution of the National Security Council," *Journal of American History* 72 (September 1985): 360–66. For Forrestal's recommendation to the Hoover Commission in 1949 see U.S. Congress, Senate, Committee on Armed Services. *National Security Act Amendments of 1949*, hearing, 81st Cong., 1st sess., 24 March 1949, 8–9.

63. Millis, *Forrestal Diaries*, 546–47, 300; "Reminiscences of Hanson Weightman Baldwin"; Rogow, *James Forrestal*, 26–31, 310–11; Borklund, *Men of the Pentagon*, 59–61.

64. Millis, *Forrestal Diaries*, 433, 465, 497–98; Forrestal to Walter G. Andrews,

13 December 1948, JFP, box 78; excerpt of phone conversation between Leva and Forrestal, 16 September 1948, ibid., box 48.

65. Forrestal to Bard, 20 November 1948; Forrestal to Andrews, 13 December 1948; Truman to Forrestal, 13 July 1948, RG 330, Records of the Secretary of Defense, CD 5–1–20, box 18; Eberstadt to Duffield, 28 February 1951, FEP, box 5, Forrestal Files; Rearden, *The Formative Years*, 43–45.

66. McNeil, Oral History, 100–102; Cutler, *No Time for Rest*, 244; Eberstadt to Thomas R. Armstrong, 28 February 1949, FEP, box 5, Forrestal Files; Eberstadt to Forrestal, 16 February 1949, ibid.; Eberstadt to Duffield, 28 February 1951, ibid.; "Reminiscences of Admiral Dennison"; Forrestal to Bard, 20 November 1948; Forrestal to Andrews, 13 December 1948. For comments of individuals who claimed they could foresee Forrestal's breakdown see, for example, "Reminiscences of Hanson Weightman Baldwin" and "Reminiscences of Vice Admiral Smedberg."

13

Robert McNamara: Success and Failure

Deborah Shapley

A textbook example of an outstanding public servant" was how President Lyndon B. Johnson characterized Secretary of Defense Robert S. McNamara as they stood under a black umbrella in the drizzling rain in front of the Pentagon on 29 February 1968 at farewell ceremonies for the departing secretary of defense. "This place has been called a puzzle palace. Bob McNamara may be the only man who found the secret to the puzzle and he is taking it with him," the president said as McNamara stood at his elbow, pale, shadow-faced from the strain of his final months in office, particularly from the inner tensions of managing the Vietnam War.[1]

The president's remark, like so many Johnsonisms, was crude and apt. For seven years, longer than any defense secretary before or since, McNamara had presided over the largest single institution in the United States, in peace and in war, with a degree of control over its activities unparalleled in the annals of federal management.

His example is remarkable in the sometimes revolutionary fashion with which he dealt with defense issues—such as nuclear weapons policy, the Pentagon budget, and how the U.S. defense establishment communicates its aims and purposes to the outside world.

However, McNamara's career has a tragic side, for the country and for himself, since this management expert also managed the U.S. war effort in Vietnam. His public advocacy of the war mired him in controversy, so that by the time he left office, and for years after, he remained one of the most controversial, and in some quarters one of the most mistrusted, figures in modern public life.

He was criticized sharply by the left for having helped the United States into the war and, once the country was in, for not doing more to get us out, since he was rumored to be the only high official actually running the war who was disillusioned with it. Meanwhile, the right castigated him for having prevented the military from using much greater force, which they believed would have brought victory, or at least a decisive conclusion, sooner. Today, almost twenty years after McNamara's departure, many in both camps remain as adamant in their views of him as they were on the day he left office. And the supposed lesson of McNamara's mistakes—that U.S. armed forces should never be sent to fight abroad without overwhelming prior public support—stamps U.S. foreign policy today.

Within the defense community, McNamara's primary legacy is the precedent he established for control over policy and budgets by the secretary of defense and his immediate staff, including the comptroller and the assistant secretary of defense for international security affairs. Aided by these offices and their management tools, McNamara exerted control over the military to an extent not tried by anyone in that office before or since. However, as some of the cases discussed below illustrate, his control was not as great as admirers and critics claimed, and it was sometimes counterproductive.

McNamara has another legacy, this one in the area of strategic nuclear doctrine and arms control. On this count, he was highly innovative in using the "bully pulpit" of his office to educate the public about the destructiveness of nuclear weapons and about the various strategic doctrines he put forward.

This chapter opens with a discussion of McNamara's education and his professional experience during fourteen years at the Ford Motor Company, where he rose to the presidency in 1960. It then discusses two domestic defense issues, strategic nuclear policy and Pentagon budgeting. The chapter concludes with a discussion of McNamara's handling of the war, including his management of the military entry into Vietnam and his later unsuccessful attempt to limit the American commitment. I show how the same executive style marked all these cases, leading to success on some issues and failure on others.

Early Professional Experience

Education and World War II

When he stepped onto the national stage in January 1961, McNamara had a well-developed executive style in which he had complete confidence. He had been rewarded in monetary and professional terms during the previous fourteen years at the Ford Motor Company, where he had perfected a particular brand of management based on statistical analysis. This executive style was rooted deeply in his personality and education and in his experience in the war and at Ford.

Though his parents had little formal education, McNamara excelled as a student, and at the University of California at Berkeley he was elected to Phi Beta Kappa and narrowly missed a Rhodes scholarship.[2] As a student at the Harvard Business School (1937–39), where analysis and verbal exposition of cases were the currency of success, in his first year McNamara achieved the highest grades of any student to that time.

McNamara was noticed by the faculty because he was articulate and adept at logical argument. He was unusually effective in using statistics to support his arguments. One classmate recalls, "It was terribly tempting for the rest of us to let Bob do all the work."[3] Perhaps the teaching style at the school, which gave individual students a chance to shine in group discussion, also contributed to his success.

In the 1930s the Harvard Business School was in the grip of an important revolution. This was the development of the field of "financial control," pioneered by Ross Graham Walker and others in the school's accounting department and based in part on Alfred P. Sloan's innovations at General Motors in the 1920s. One course, which explored ways to organize corporate budgets in order to reflect the organization's existing goals and then monitor changes as the organization moved toward different goals, made a particular impression on McNamara. As a student and then a junior instructor (1940–43), McNamara also became enthusiastic about the broader perspective suggested by Walker's approach: that the chief executive of a large organization could build rational models of most aspects of its activities. These models could be the basis for drawing up plans and holding those at lower levels responsible for carrying them out. Thus, if centrally controlled and properly managed, even very large organizations could be brought under control and redirected to whatever goal the executive sought: more profits, different products, different markets, or a different posture toward a rival.

These new methodologies reflected the educational philosophy of the Harvard Business School, which was that business administration was a field unto itself. The school had decided earlier in the century *not* to have separate departments for railroads, banking, or utilities, but to train its students as generalists, fit to run any enterprise on more or less the same principles.[4] So McNamara and his fellow future managers were schooled in management as a skill *apart* from the content of the business being managed. McNamara often endorsed these views in later years, and his career—spanning the auto industry, government agencies, and international banking—can be seen as an expression of this principle in practice.[5]

McNamara's first application of these lessons came in World War II; his wartime experience, following on the heels of his schooling, probably convinced him that good management had a place even in war. A pivotal figure in McNamara's early career was an equally ambitious young man, Charles Bates ("Tex") Thornton, who would later build Litton Industries into a worldwide conglomerate. In the early 1940s, Thornton was the right-hand aide to Secretary of War for Air Robert Lovett. Lovett gave Thornton the job of making weekly reports on the status of airplanes, crews, and equipment in all theaters—to be modeled on the daily investment-portfolio reports that Lovett had demanded as a banker with Brown Brothers, Harriman.[6] In 1943 Thornton hired McNamara, who spent much of the next two years devising reporting systems for the Air Corps to use in keeping track of its equipment and in assuring the proper flows from the States to combat areas. Sent to the field to work under combat commanders, McNamara gained respect there in advising generals on the efficiency of their operations. For example, in Calcutta he figured out how to maximize the amount of fuel flown over the Hump from India into China to be available for the B-29 campaign against Japan.[7] And while he came away from the war impressed with the high-precision operations carried out by some field commanders, he also concluded that one did not need combat experience to be able to manage military operations. This view helped to shape his behavior as defense secretary fifteen years later.

The Years at Ford

After the war, Thornton persuaded Henry Ford II, who at age twenty-eight had just taken over his grandfather's ailing company, to hire him and nine other young "stat control" officers, including McNamara, as a management team to help run the company. Thornton left in 1947; he was too dynamic and ambitious for the straight-laced promotional prospects Ford offered. But McNamara was more careful, more willing to please superiors, and more suited to remain with the company for the long term. He and most of the statistical control team stayed. McNamara was the group's natural leader after Thornton; and he was the first of the group to make it to the top as president, although several also became vice presidents.[8]

How did McNamara's Ford experience shape his management style? With hindsight, we can see at least four aspects of that experience that may have had a bearing on how he behaved at Defense.

First, he found bosses at Ford who encouraged his proclivities toward the use of innovative control strategies. Young Henry Ford knew he could not take over the company and turn it into a prosperous enterprise without senior executives who knew the business. The Thornton group, however bright and well-educated, knew nothing about car manufacturing. So Ford recruited Ernest Breech and Lewis Crusoe from his bigger, better-run rival empire, General Motors; they deserve much of the credit for the company's success in the postwar years.

In the 1930s and 1940s, General Motors was considered a model of a "scientifically" managed company and was held up as a model at the Harvard Business School. Alfred P. Sloan had rescued GM from failure in the 1920s using management techniques that Breech and Crusoe understood. They knew from real life what McNamara and the other stat control officers had learned only through their schooling and their experience with the Air Corps. If McNamara was lucky once to have been discovered by Thornton, he was lucky a second time to have the GM men, and young Henry Ford, as patrons at Ford. McNamara put what he had learned at Harvard into practice with a vengeance, in time becoming comptroller and using that office to affect decisions companywide.

Second, it is hard to overstate the rigid conformity demanded of subordinates in the auto industry and the absolute power of the chief executive. Perhaps McNamara's executive style would have been authoritarian in any event; certainly he "grew up," professionally speaking, in an environment where the chief executive could demand and expect absolute obedience. To this day the auto companies have rigid dress codes; in several, no employee may drive a rival manufacturer's car, not even as a rented car on business trips. If word of such infractions reaches higher authority, a young man's chances for promotion can be ruined.[9] This background may help to explain why McNamara demanded lock-step obedience to his decisions as defense secretary—and why he was so dismayed and frustrated when the military departments legally under his control sometimes worked to nullify his decisions.

A third aspect of his Ford experience was the market for U.S. automobiles in the late 1940s and early 1950s. In the 1950s, Americans were earning more and buying more consumer goods; the highway system was expanding; suburbs were springing up all over the country. It seemed as if American consumers would buy anything Detroit produced. The auto executive's job, therefore, was to produce more models to appeal to an ever-widening range of consumer tastes.[10] Today, we can see that this situation drove U.S. auto companies away from the features that later would attract U.S. buyers to imported cars: precision engineering, fuel economy, smaller size, safety. But in the 1950s the market was ripe for an almost mechanistic approach to car production: build more cars at the lowest possible production cost; squeeze more and more profit out of every production line; make more models through efficient use of existing production lines; optimize scheduling; maximize efficient use of resources at every level for a proportionately large gain. And Mc-Namara was very successful at getting record profits and sales from a company that not only produced machines but, with respect to the market, ran like a machine.

A fourth aspect of the Ford experience should be noted.[11] McNamara and his colleagues entered an ailing, money-losing, irrationally run company. Fourteen years later, he was the president of a company widely publicized as a model of modern scientific management. McNamara's rise in industry was not a scramble up a predesignated corporate ladder, though there were elements of this in the demands for conformity, loyalty, and obedience. It was also a drama of corporate transformation, of the very kind of institutional goal-setting and redirection he had learned about at the Harvard Business School. His success at Ford had an element of entrepreneurship to it that anticipated the kind of reforms he would undertake later at the Department of Defense.

To summarize: As a young man, McNamara entered a field for which he was unusually gifted. He had his first work experience in three institutional settings—the Harvard Business School, the military, and Ford—that badly needed his skills. He became adroit at working for a single boss and following his wishes, and at anticipating them. He learned to expect that the chief executive could exert absolute control; and he developed a belief in the power of his particular statistical methodology to institute large-scale organizational change, to redirect organizations for "rational" purposes. His chain of successes was basically unbroken, with no major setbacks.

Managing the Department of Defense

In November 1960, McNamara was named president of the Ford Motor Company, but a few weeks later he resigned, heeding President John F. Kennedy's request that he join the new administration as secretary of defense. As defense secretary from 1961 to 1968 McNamara dealt with many issues; in this section two are discussed.

The first is the evolution of strategic nuclear policy, which illustrates McNamara's entrepreneurship regarding U.S. nuclear weapons and policy. That he was drawn to the issues of nuclear war and peace, that he became expert in analysis and exposition, should be no surprise: as we have seen McNamara was strong in the areas of analysis and exposition, and perhaps of all the issues he addressed, nuclear policy had the largest component of these. It was also uniquely suited to quantitative analysis, another McNamara strength. However, there is an operational side of the nuclear issue: the secretary of defense is responsible to the president for the actual deployment and use of nuclear forces in times of crisis or war. On this operational side McNamara's impact was less important.

The Planning Programming Budgeting System (PPBS) illustrates how financial control can organize and track defense programs. However, the success of PPBS and its famous and notorious adjunct, systems analysis, was not due only to their intrinsic merits. They worked because McNamara insisted on making decisions and following up with implementation; he was personally suited to making strong and combative use of the information that PPBS and systems analysis gave him.

Strategic Nuclear Policy

On the spectrum from success to failure McNamara's handling of strategic nuclear weapons policy stands out as a success, though as with each of the cases discussed in this paper, success and failure are intermixed. The less successful part of his performance was on the operational side: the actual planning and targeting of nuclear forces, which required him to reach deep into the Pentagon bureaucracy. His success came in leading the revolution in public thinking about nuclear weapons; that important change in the 1960s to a large extent resulted from a fortunate confluence of McNamara's personality with the needs of the era.

Disarray is a mild term to describe the state of U.S. policy for strategic nuclear war at the close of the Eisenhower administration— if there was a policy at all. One of McNamara's earliest and most urgent assignments from President-elect Kennedy was to investigate and make recommendations to alter the nuclear-force posture and policies of the Eisenhower administration, which had been the focus of Democratic criticisms, including Kennedy's, of the incumbent during the 1960 presidential campaign.[12] McNamara's analytic skills helped in this: he plunged into the complexities of the issue with relish.

McNamara had a mandate from the president to "get the country moving again" with respect to nuclear weaponry. In response he might simply have built up the entire U.S. nuclear force. McNamara certainly did this; within two months of taking office he decided to double production of the Minuteman land-based ICBM (intercontinental ballistic missile) and to accelerate the schedules for delivery of Polaris submarines. All this was in step with his president's campaign pledges.

However, McNamara soon asserted a degree of independence. When he discovered that there was no "missile gap" putting the United States behind the Soviets in ICBMs, McNamara informed the press bluntly— despite the fact that Kennedy probably owed some of his narrow victory margin to his repeated charge that there was such a gap. Similarly, McNamara quickly decided that bombers, the Air Force's most cherished weapon, were less cost-effective than missiles and so began cutting back the prospective bomber force.

Though these moves were significant, they were only the beginning of McNamara's complicated odyssey into the nuclear terrain. Working his way through a range of complex issues during the next three years, McNamara had by 1964 created some sort of order: he had won agreement on ceilings on nuclear delivery systems and was winning public and governmental acceptance for a doctrine called "assured destruction," which had the potential of stabilizing the arms race and building a foundation for arms control.

McNamara's efforts are notable in part because they contrasted sharply with the inactivity of his predecessors. Previous secretaries of defense had not played an important role in strategic nuclear policy. In the Eisenhower administration the key public pronouncements had been made by the secretary of state, John Foster Dulles, a man oddly willing to talk about how readily the United States would use nuclear weapons (with the implication that we would use *all* our nuclear weapons), while remaining deliberately ignorant of the characteristics of the weapons and of existing war plans.[13] Previous secretaries of defense had been concerned primarily with Pentagon budgets, which in those days were divorced from military strategy or policy. Reaching beyond the budgetary realm, McNamara used the office of the secretary of defense as a platform to educate his fellow government officials and the broader public about U.S. nuclear policy.

One important reason why McNamara engaged the nuclear issue so actively was that his president was concerned about it too. In 1961 Kennedy was hawkish about U.S. nuclear might; the Democrats were hawkish, Washington was hawkish. The right-wing in Congress constantly hit at the administration for not doing enough. However, Kennedy and McNamara—and aides at the White House, including science adviser Jerome B. Wiesner and Carl Kaysen, special assistant to the national security adviser—soon began to see that all these nuclear weapons were too dangerous, that the arms race was getting out of control.[14]

Kennedy was one of the few people McNamara could talk with regarding his growing concern about the arms race and about the dangers of accidental nuclear war. Thus, we see two characteristics of McNamara's personality that drove his interest in the issue: first, his responsiveness to his boss, and second, his own private agenda of concern, which he dared not discuss too publicly for fear of bringing a storm of criticism on himself and the president. We will see the same pattern again in Vietnam.

But if McNamara was an activist in developing coherent themes for nuclear policy, his reforms on the operational side were less effective. The operational heart of U.S. nuclear posture is the SIOP, or Single Integrated Operating Plan, which is basically a huge set of timetables run on computers that dictate when each missile is to be fired, which target it will be aimed at, and how those weapons that are not sent right away will be directed after the system has information on the nature of the enemy attack.[15] Appalled by the levels of all-out destruction in the SIOP he inherited, in the summer of 1961 McNamara ordered the SIOP changed. The process took more than a year; at the end of that time the options available to the president had only been increased in the crudest fashion; now, for example, he could "withhold" forces so as not to *automatically* knock out the Soviet Union, China, and Eastern Europe all in one blow![16]

McNamara held office for six more years, while the relevant technology advanced, permitting more controlled patterns of action and escalation. And during those years, McNamara publicly promulgated changes in nuclear-war doctrine. But in fact, the operational plan for the nuclear forces changed little, mainly because of the resistance of the Strategic Air Command and other parts of the defense bureaucracy.[17]

The Planning Programming Budgeting System

McNamara's management style leaned heavily on his control over organization budgets, as might be expected from his accounting emphasis at the Harvard Business School and the Ford Motor Company. To help him take control of the complex Defense Department budget, McNamara selected Charles Hitch as Pentagon controller. Hitch was one of the few economists at that time who had tried to assign economic values to defense activities. Though professorial in manner, Hitch was tough enough for the challenging assignment McNamara gave him. He had had lots of experience with the military during a dozen years on the staff of the Rand Corporation, which worked for the Air Force, and he enjoyed a commanding lead in his profession.

In the early 1960s Hitch was seen as a guru of modern management techniques. He was also the employer and patron, at the Pentagon, of dozens of young "whiz kids" hired to overhaul U.S. military budgets, force posture, and strategy. And to the opposition that predictably galvanized within the Pentagon, Hitch was an almost sinister figure, the "godfather" or "dark angel" of these untidy, intellectual minions who roamed the building making a travesty—some officers thought—of the military's right to conduct its own affairs.

However, the pace, style, and impact of Hitch's work were crucially linked to McNamara's personality. Years later, Hitch recalled his first experiences at the Pentagon. He and his staff had worked hard to devise a way to institute program budgeting for the strategic forces on a trial basis; they thought implementation would require at least a year. At an early meeting, Hitch outlined the plan to McNamara. McNamara banged his hand on the table and said that that was exactly what he wanted Hitch to do—and to install the system not only for the strategic forces but for *all* military forces. And he wanted it installed inside of a year. Hitch was stunned at the magnitude of the task. When he went back and told his staff what McNamara wanted, they too were amazed.[18]

Some military officers admitted that tough decisions and reforms were long overdue. But so controversial were the McNamara-Hitch reformers that officers who worked with them were at times regarded by their parent services as disloyal. "The building shook" with tension, as one then-young lawyer says of the atmosphere in the Pentagon in the early 1960s.[19]

McNamara and Hitch's reforms centering on the budget and entailing an accompanying use of systems analysis were widely publicized outside. They started a vogue elsewhere, in government and industry, for their Planning Programming Budgeting System (PPBS). Much was made of PPBS as a methodology in its own right, an almost magic cure-all for all kinds of organizational ills (though Hitch and others warned that it was not). As a result, defense budgeting, particularly defense budgeting in the McNamara years, is a well-studied subject which enjoys a rich specialized literature.[20]

In brief, PPBS was a means of producing *explicit criteria* for decision making on defense issues, criteria that the Office of the Secretary of Defense (OSD) considered to be in the national interest, as distinct from other factors—tradition, habit, and the narrower perspective of individual armed services. To establish these criteria, the controller's office entered into a dialogue, in effect, with all parts of the defense organization—including the armed services and the many staff agencies. Each activity or subactivity was characterized by mission. In this way, the controller's office could discover cases of duplicative systems for meeting a given requirement, or where requirements were inadequately met.

The purpose of PPBS was not merely to find gaps and duplication within the defense system; it aimed at nothing less than a complete, thoroughly rational statement of all U.S. military force requirements and all associated costs, with a projection of these at least five years into the future. For example, the OSD could use the data Hitch's people had gathered in order to define the basic building blocks of U.S. defenses, which they called "program elements." Each of these elements was classified according to the basic military requirements it was intended to meet. The cost of a given program element—for example, the Air

Force's proposed B-70 bomber force—could be projected over five years (or over the lifetime of the projected force). Then McNamara and his aides could examine the cost of meeting this requirement (which in the case of the B-70 bombers was long-range nuclear attack of predesignated Soviet targets) together with other ways to achieve the same result, such as ICBMs and the existing B-52 bomber force. Other considerations could also be analyzed. To continue the example, these might be the comparative vulnerabilities of bombers and ICBMs and the comparative costs of reducing these vulnerabilities. Once there was an "agreed" statement of the requirement the whole force was to meet, highly "rational" decisions could, in theory, be made.[21]

The purpose of the system was to maximize the quality of American defenses at the lowest cost and, more basically, to obtain a clearer understanding of what American defenses were trying to do. Thus, McNamara saw PPBS as an essential element in an approach that began with the explicit goals of U.S. foreign policy and its global commitments, progressing next to the resulting needs for U.S. defense forces, and then deducing how to get that capability at the minimum cost and maximum effectiveness. The system also permitted the OSD to have close control over the annual budget cycle, to discuss prospective spending with the individual services, and to ratchet budgets up and down to make them conform to policy.

It also permitted a complete annual statement of what DOD thought it was doing. The classified versions of these were the Draft Presidential Memorandums (DPMs), which were circulated and commented upon within DOD, generating statements of opposing positions, before McNamara sent them to the president. By the time McNamara left office, there were DPMs for sixteen force missions, ranging from amphibious forces to nuclear weapons and materials requirements.

The public form of these statements was the *Annual Report* of the secretary, which was in effect a declassified version of the DPMs with supporting documentation and argument. The *Annual Report* was published each January when the overall administration budget was submitted to Congress. Under McNamara's predecessors the report had included little more than brief statements by each of the services and the secretary, on the threats the world posed and what forces the United States had. Under McNamara, it became an elaborate volume of analysis, more than two hundred pages in length, with many additional pages of detailed tables.

PPBS was better at getting a good understanding—and hence control—of some issues than others. McNamara aides Enthoven and Smith, in their definitive description of the method, admit that they never got a good handle on the problem of land-warfare force readiness, because this was difficult to measure. They do claim that their system "shook out" the issues in the strategic nuclear field very well, and they take credit for elucidating the "assured destruction" nuclear doctrine. Also, these analytical techniques became the basis for canceling numerous weapons systems and accelerating others.

As PPBS evolved at the Pentagon, it was shaped by the needs of its principal consumer, Robert McNamara. While very much Hitch's in conception and execution, the system was built around McNamara (right down to the preference for tables over graphs in all writing and reports because tables, not graphs, were the kind of data that McNamara preferred to read). As we have seen, his training and disposition gave McNamara an unshakeable faith in the importance of financial controls, in the "truth" as discoverable through statistics, and in the importance of using this kind of information as the basis for organizational planning and control.

Thus, McNamara was impelled to involve himself deeply in the analytical details. He asked each of his key civilian aides to come to his office once a week, same day and time, for the next installment in their particular study area—tactical forces, land warfare, strategic nuclear forces, military pay scales. He would hover over the analyses, fascinated by how they were coming out. He would sketch on paper additional prospective tables for the analysts to fill in. Often he gave these "whiz kids" specific new assignments, and sometimes he conjectured accurately how the analysis would come out. He was intellectually engaged at many levels with his subordinates' use of PPBS.

This active involvement enabled him to function quickly and efficiently, to make decisions rapidly, one at each meeting, no meeting longer than half an hour—an hour at most—and to maintain the image of tight control over the vast organization beneath. It also shifted the terms of discussion of defense issues to the statistical analytic grounds at which he and his aides excelled, thus putting others—foreign policy hands from the State Department, generals and admirals unable to adapt to his lingo—at a disadvantage in debate. And it saved time, illustrating that to McNamara speed was as important a criterion of decision making as the content of the decision.

Committees, in McNamara's view, were useless for garnering consensus. They were too fuzzy a mechanism; indeed, they could be seen as the antithesis of the rational quantification of PPBS. In November 1961, in the journal *Armed Forces Management*, McNamara wrote that committees were inefficient as a way to run an organization; he boasted that he had eliminated 424 committees and scheduled another 129 for deactivation. The important thing, he explained, was speed. Decisions at his department were not being made fast enough, said this monarch of decision making.[22]

With his penchant—and even passion—for analysis, personal involvement, and quick decisions, McNamara was able to function effectively in a system that tossed up the issues to him in a highly structured form, ready for his particular style of intervention. As PPBS was instituted in other government departments and spread in the private sector, it often proved less useful in meeting the organization's problems, especially when the boss's personality was different from McNamara's. As Thomas C. Schelling wrote in 1968:

> Systems analysis and other modern techniques of evaluation require a consumer, some responsible person or body that wants an orderly technique for bringing judgment to bear on a decision. PPBS works best for an aggressive master; and where there is no master, or where the master wants the machinery to produce his decisions without his own participation, the value of PPBS is likely to be modest and, depending on the people, may even be negative.[23]

The Uses and Limitations of an Analytic Style

From the foregoing cases, we can identify the attributes of McNamara's executive style at Ford and DOD and relate them to the idea of public-sector entrepreneurship described in this volume.

First, McNamara implemented a deep personal belief that the responsibility of the leader was to make decisions, to set overall goals for the institution, and to redirect the institution to work toward those goals. This concept of leadership was buttressed by his skills in abstract reasoning, his ability to formulate problems in quantitative terms, and his fondness for argument and exposition.

In 1946, the Ford Motor Company desperately needed strong central organization and executives determined to follow through on decisions and to discipline the sprawling feudal enterprise. McNamara and the other new executives hired in 1946–47 had these skills; in particular, their use of statistical techniques was well suited to solve the many problems the company faced at that time. We saw how the method of reform depended on cadres of subordinates trained in financial control to carry reform into the larger company. McNamara's personal traits— his loyalty to his boss, his willingness to shoulder responsibility to protect his boss, and his skilled, combative wielding of executive power— helped his rise.

At DOD, McNamara used these same qualities. On nuclear policy, from the morass of ideas about nuclear strategy and force structure floating around Rand and the universities in the late 1950s, McNamara identified specific doctrines and policy. His appetite for detailed rational exposition spurred him to put forward these concepts inside government and before Congress, the public, and the press. It was part of the idea of getting everyone to agree on common goals, and common policy, an educative process not unlike what he and the others had done at Ford. He showed on this issue the traits associated with public-sector entrepreneurship: creating a program, explaining it, gathering constituencies, and ridding the organization of elements contrary to the program.

His installation of PPBS and systems analysis sprang from these same traits: he seized on new tools, in this case the Rand work on budgeting for program control and his own background in financial control, and used them to define objectives, compare alternative strategies, and select the defense packages that he concluded would be most effective. However, if McNamara had had a different personality—if he had been less adept at abstract and statistical methods, less stubborn or combative—his reforms would not have gone so far.

But we also saw the negative side of his style, which bred resistance and backlash. With PPBS and the nuclear question, the success of reform depended upon cadres of people (mostly civilian analysts) who understood his goals and carried them forward into the military bureaucracies. But these bureaucracies sometimes resented being reformed; many of their members felt they were victims, rather than beneficiaries, of McNamara's plans. Thus, adversary relationships sprang up between the civilian cadres and military men, with contrary views based on their own analyses and traditions. McNamara's leadership style bred opposition between the leaders and the led.[24] And because the civilians seemed to disregard the military's tradition, lore, and accepted wisdom, opposition widened and deepened.

McNamara's analytic strengths were coupled with a limited personal capacity to understand and empathize with the culture and traditions of the organizations he commanded. In the 1960s, the military press often repeated a criticism heard in the officer corps—that McNamara rarely attended awards ceremonies or service academy commencements. His spokesmen would answer that McNamara believed it more important to spend the time in his office making decisions and managing the department. Moreover, those who watched him on ceremonial occasions saw that he seemed personally uncomfortable.

Many military careerists were strongly attached to the tradition and pomp of these events, and they wanted his participation as an indication that he understood and appreciated their values. But McNamara conveyed little interest in their ceremonies and their traditions.

Had he been able to reach out in these ways, his capacity to gain effective control and lead the organization might have been greater.

Managing the Vietnam War

While deeply engaged in efforts to "reform the Pentagon," McNamara also took on a major role in shaping America's involvement in Vietnam. In his first years as secretary of defense, McNamara attempted to shape the way the military conducted the war against a background of huge self-confidence in his powers of executive control (massive arrogance, his critics later said). Later, as he saw that the original plans were not working, he tried to reshape the commitment against a backdrop of traumatic military failure in the field.

This discussion does not, of course, assume that McNamara was solely responsible for the war; the decisions were made by the president with the advice of many advisers. Still, McNamara was possibly the most influential of these aides, and the way in which the war was managed from Washington reflected McNamara's management style.

The Early Years

During his first years in office, McNamara conveyed to others, and probably felt, great confidence that the political and military turbulence in Vietnam could be quelled through proper management. Testifying before Congress on the foreign aid request in 1961, he assured the House Foreign Affairs Committee that South Vietnam would not fall to the Communists. But the South Vietnamese government would require increased U.S. aid in the form of training and equipment to deal with the guerrillas coming from the North.[25]

McNamara began managing the Vietnam problem in 1961 by flying regularly to Honolulu, where he scheduled monthly meetings of top U.S. civilian and military leaders. This followed the pattern he had set in Washington, where he held regular meetings with officials who had specific tasks in order to review their work and guide the next phase. By 1962, McNamara's visits included the famous flying trips to Vietnam—leave on Wednesday, back on Saturday, for example—where he would be shown around by the military brass, listen to briefings, meet with the U.S. ambassador and the South Vietnamese leaders, wave, give a brief press statement, and step back onto the plane to Washington.[26]

These trips resulted in regular—and optimistic—statements about the progress his activist management was bringing about. After the March 1962 Honolulu meeting, for example, he said: "I am pleased to learn that the armed forces of Vietnam are taking the offensive throughout the country, carrying the war to the Viet Cong, inflicting higher casualty rates, and capturing Viet Cong weapons and supplies in greater numbers. . . . We must not, of course, expect miracles overnight." After the first of his trips to Saigon, in May of that year, McNamara said, "Every quantitative measurement . . . shows that we are winning the war."[27]

Later, the statistics McNamara used to document the U.S. success there would symbolize Washington's lack of understanding of the situation in Vietnam.[28] But in the early days, McNamara's use of statistics was seen as another earmark of his effective management style. This was "hands on" management by central authority, formulating plans, watching over implementation—the trusted supermanager in action.

The fate of the counterinsurgency strategy. In the discussion of domestic defense issues, we saw that McNamara's control over the organizations did not always extend to the operational level. Indeed, in the middle levels of these organizations there was often resistance, some of it to change in general, some of it to the style in which change was being imposed from above.

Another example of this resistance occurred in South Vietnam, when President Kennedy, early in 1961, asked that the military use the Vietnam conflict as a test case for a new kind of ground warfare, counterinsurgency war. It was McNamara's job to see that Kennedy's wish was carried out. Ironically, McNamara the supermanager who loyally carried out presidential orders, who took pride in his control over the bureaucracy, was unable to implement President Kennedy's orders on counterinsurgency warfare. For McNamara to have carried out this task, he would have needed a good understanding of military fighting strategy and tradition. But this kind of knowledge was not McNamara's forte.

In brief, the story is this: Kennedy believed that communism would challenge the West by wars of national liberation in the developing world. At his first National Security Council meeting on 1 February 1961, he instructed McNamara to have the Pentagon put more emphasis on counterinsurgency war (CI). The president publicized his personal interest in CI in 1961 and 1962. He attended exercises by the 82d Airborne light-mobile division at Fort Bragg, North Carolina, the home of the Special Warfare Division. In January 1962 he set up a White House task force on CI.

The military responded by expanding the Army Special Forces, and the president himself decided they should wear distinctive green berets as symbols of their elite status (such distinctions being, however, anathema to the traditional military). And the Special Forces indeed were sent to Vietnam to "test" CI theories in the field. The bureaucracy even had statistics showing that more officers were receiving CI training at military schools and academies.

But CI was very different from what military scholar Andrew Krepinevich terms the "Army Concept" of war, which consists of set-piece battles for territory using mechanized units and high firepower in a setting like that of Europe.[29] The military had little heart for CI, or for CI training. It largely went its own way, training the South Vietnamese to fight in traditional ways and when regular U.S. troops entered the war in large numbers, it emphasized traditional concepts in training them as well.

McNamara is important to this story as the watchdog in the Sherlock Holmes tale: he didn't bark. He appointed his deputy, Roswell Gilpatric, to chair an interagency task force on Vietnam. And his statements emphasized the need to simplify battlefield weapons and to train soldiers to work in companies and squads rather than battle groups. But McNamara never appeared interested in digging deeply into the issue or in learning about military strategy and culture so that he could explore meaningful steps to turn the CI concept into operational reality.[30]

Escalation in 1965

Public-sector entrepreneurs organize institutions and programs to run along new, often original, lines; one way these leaders make their mark is by modifying the behavior of institutions so they will fulfill new programs. McNamara, as we have seen, believed that the formulation of goals and modifying of institutional behavior to meet those goals were the essence of his role as an executive.

McNamara's behavior on the question of escalation in early 1965 followed the same pattern of entrepreneurial leadership identified in the domestic defense issues described earlier. At the end of 1964 there was a vacuum in U.S. policy for South Vietnam. The official policy was to encourage the South Vietnamese to fight ever more effectively themselves so that U.S. advisers could be withdrawn, but this policy had been less and less viable as governments came and went in Saigon and as weakness in the capital encouraged Viet Cong successes in the countryside.

In McNamara's view, the policy vacuum called for decisive action. He consulted with McGeorge Bundy, the president's national security adviser, who wrote to Johnson in late January on behalf of himself and McNamara, urging that the present, uncertain course be replaced with clearer policy. Then they held a private meeting with the president to press for a firm military commitment by the United States, arguing that South Vietnam's failures were the result of a perceived lack of American will. In most accounts these steps mark the beginning of McNamara and Bundy's push to get the president to intervene.[31]

By February they had succeeded: Johnson authorized reprisal bombing attacks on North Vietnam that would gradually phase into sustained bombing. McNamara then asked the Joint Chiefs of Staff to lay out an eight-week program of gradually escalating bombing pressures. It quickly became clear to the Joint Chiefs, however, that the president and McNamara would maintain tight operational control over the ways in which air power would be used. Target selection began to be made by LBJ, McNamara, and their close aides.[32] Their plan was to bomb selectively, then reduce bombing while threatening to escalate the devastation if the North did not cease its efforts in the South, and then escalate the bombing again if the lull failed to bring about the desired change.[33]

The plan did not work; North Vietnam's leaders did not respond according to the McNamara tenets of rationality. Captured by their own logic, LBJ and McNamara felt they had no choice but to escalate a little further in the hope that increased pressure would change Hanoi's stance. In the end, huge tonnages of bombs were dropped, but with few discernible results.

Meanwhile, the McNamara style of direct management control (in this case, over the bombing) and the unwillingness of McNamara and his boss to "unleash" the military bred deep resentment among the military advocates of the "sharp knock." Let us bomb our way—all ninety-four key targets at once—and you will see results, they argued in the councils of state. Such arguments were made publicly by congressmen and senators who also objected to the "micromanaging" of the bombing from Washington. What McNamara and Johnson saw as necessary and responsible restraints on the use of military power increasingly became a political liability as critics charged that American power was being withheld and the war "needlessly" prolonged.[34]

Changing Course Again

Having modified the military's preferred institutional repertoires when the United States went into Vietnam, McNamara tried to shape the character of the military involvement once again, in 1966 and 1967, as he realized that the North Vietnamese could force the U.S. side to escalate the ground and air war almost indefinitely. Gradually, he took a series of positions in favor of limiting the bombing, and he argued for limiting U.S. ground commitments, even as the commanding general, William Westmoreland, demanded more and more troops.

A major trait of McNamara's management style—his analytic

bent—shaped his ability to see that his previous policy course was headed for disaster. If in the early 1960s he was blinded by the statistical reporting from Vietnam, which reported growing enemy body counts and battlefield victories, and so believed the United States was winning, by 1966 he was aware that what the statistics really meant was that continued escalation would cost the United States more, in dollars and domestic controversy, than the country could afford.[35] In a series of memos, McNamara laid out the case for a leveling off of the commitment—much to the anger of the Joint Chiefs, who favored escalation as a means of getting the war over with more quickly, they said. McNamara was simply too good an analyst himself to ignore the reality that the statistics only partially described. He thus became something of a loner in the inner circle, for Dean Rusk, National Security Adviser Walt W. Rostow, and even the president favored the existing course.[36]

McNamara finally began using his cadres of analysts in Vietnam in 1966–67. At Ford, in his management reforms at DOD, and in strategic nuclear policy, having his analytic teams was crucial to his success. And in late 1966 the Office of Systems Analysis was turned loose on the war, analyzing the strategy of attrition that Westmoreland was following and finding it to be counterproductive; analyzing the bombing and documenting its failure.

If McNamara was drawing on his earlier strengths as a manager, why did he fail to turn policy his way? There are many reasons, the most obvious one being that the situation was, by 1966–67, beyond his control: the president was driven to widen the bombing for reasons that McNamara could not change; anyone in the inner circle who opposed expanding the bombing was bound to fall from favor. Similarly, to limit the ground commitment to a holding action for the long haul would have required a massive change in Westmoreland's strategy—and possibly the removal of Westmoreland himself. Again, the political forces were too large for McNamara to change. As with his bombing recommendations, his proposal for limiting the ground war only backfired on him.

At the personal level, McNamara's failure to redirect the war effort in 1966–67 also stemmed from the weaknesses of his style as an executive. Much of his success was based on his ability to loyally serve a single boss—Henry Ford II, John Kennedy, or Lyndon Johnson. He was very loyal, very obedient—and therefore not a skilled dissenter. McNamara's memos to the president of 19 May and 1 November 1967, on the need to limit the war and ways to do it are models of apparent logic and clarity.[37] They show that McNamara, true to form, was trying to persuade by exposition, logic, and the facts. But Johnson was a political animal. In 1967 there was a climactic debate over enlarging the bombing that was the culmination of many earlier debates in which the Joint Chiefs wanted more targets authorized and McNamara argued that the additions would make no difference; now the president began yielding to pressures from inside and outside to widen the bombing and began moving closer to the Chiefs and away from the once-trusted McNamara. McNamara, seeking to strengthen the hand of those opposed to the bombing, went public with his arguments against adding more targets to the list. Johnson was furious and soon after decided to move McNamara out of his job to be president of the World Bank. The change was announced in November, leading to the ceremony at the Pentagon the 29th of February.

But in defeat McNamara found victory. To insulate himself from criticisms of the kind pressed by McNamara, Johnson appointed a known hawk, the veteran Washington attorney Clark Clifford, to succeed him. McNamara assigned various analysts the job of briefing his successor on the war in Vietnam, and the result was one of the most remarkable turnarounds in American political history.[38] Within a month of taking office, not only was Clifford persuaded that the policy was wrong, that the bombing was accomplishing nothing, but he had so persuaded the president. And Lyndon Johnson decided on a partial bombing halt, and not to seek reelection—in other words, to let the American people elect a new president who could make the fresh decisions on the war that he could not. It was a startling, dramatic conclusion to a beleagured presidency.

Why did Clifford succeed where McNamara had apparently failed? McNamara's style was expository and argumentative, while Clifford had become famous—and rich—for his subtlety and shrewdness in dealing with the Washington power structure. Yet Clifford could not have been persuaded himself, nor could he have persuaded Johnson, if McNamara had not commissioned the analysis, sifted from the mass of data the key arguments for a different program, and laid them out lucidly in his own memoranda. McNamara prepared the ground and planted the seeds of a different perspective on the war, one that was to persuade Clifford and then the president.

Conclusion

McNamara's farewell ceremony in the drizzling rain outside the Pentagon in February 1968 symbolized the mixed record of his seven years as secretary of defense. No secretary of defense, before or since, had made as significant a contribution to defense management or U.S. nuclear policy. On the other hand, his role in the Vietnam War discredited him in the eyes of the left and the right.

The characteristics of McNamara's management style shaped his success at Ford and his mixed record of success in the two domestic defense issues examined. We have seen how his confidence in the power of the executive led him to assume vast responsibility for the war, including the detailed management of its military aspects, particularly the bombing. The skills honed throughout his previous career made him the valued manager of the war.

But these very qualities made McNamara less effective when he tried to redirect the commitment again, after he realized that the original program for the war would not work. His loyalty prevented him from resigning in protest or speaking out more openly. His preference for logical exposition made his dissenting memos targets for those who opposed his proposed course of action. His management revolution had brought change, but it had also bred resentment and resistance within the armed services, so that when his original strategy of gradualism did not work, the military were unwilling to credit any new strategy he might propose. Instead of drawing the military and their civilian leaders together, the war drove them more and more apart, and worsened the antagonisms that were already present.

It is useful also to think of what would have happened if someone else had held the defense secretary's job during this period. Another person might have felt that his job was to let the military fight the war their way, that, as a civilian, he was unqualified to second guess their requirements. Would this have led to a more violent war? Would a more violent war—such as the "sharp knock" bombing campaign the Chiefs originally wanted—have been more successful? Or would the military's recommendations, not modified by a defense secretary trying to limit and shape them, have so appalled the president that he would have declined to fight in Vietnam at all? If these questions are unanswerable, they nonetheless illuminate the critical role of the personality of the secretary of defense in shaping U.S. military options and the choices of the president in war.

But institutions, as well as the personality of the secretary of defense, shaped the president's choices and, even more, shaped events. The drama of McNamara's case is not only a personal one of his strengths and weaknesses as an executive; it is also the drama of the military services, each of which tried to fight the Vietnam War according to its preferred institutional roles. The services then found themselves in a war very different from the one they had expected to fight and so faced the trauma of changing course in the midst of failure in the field and conflict with civilian superiors.

Thomas Carlyle wrote that the history of what man has accomplished "is at bottom the History of the Great Men. . . . They were the leaders of men . . . and in a wide sense creators, of whatsoever the general mass of men contrived to do or to attain."[39] But the McNamara case reminds us that institutions, as well as the leader's personality, shape the history of any era. And as more documents come out, as the institutional histories of the war are published, we will gradually get the full story of the Defense Department's response to McNamara's domestic reforms and to his management of the Vietnam War. This tension between executive and institution, so evident in the McNamara case, is at the heart of the concept of public-sector entrepreneurship.

Notes

1. The quotations are from ABC News film of the Pentagon farewell ceremony, 28 February 1968 (Grindberg Film Research Libraries, New York, N.Y.).

2. Henry Trewhitt, *McNamara: His Ordeal in the Pentagon* (New York: Harper & Row, 1971), 26–31.

3. Quoted in ibid., 35.

4. See Melvin T. Copeland, *And Mark An Era* (Boston: Little, Brown, 1958), generally for the early philosophy of the Harvard Business School; Walker's accounting teaching is discussed on p. 158.

5. McNamara's generation would lead the postwar era in American business; they can also be seen as forerunners of the later generation of Harvard Business School graduates of the 1950s and 1960s, who sparked the still further evolution in business doctrine and made their fortunes by running businesses exclusively by profit-and-loss criteria, to the neglect of content and craft.

6. Beirne Lay, Jr., *Someone Has to Make It Happen: The Inside Story of Tex Thornton, the Man Who Built Litton Industries* (Englewood Cliffs, N.J.: Prentice-Hall, 1969), 52–76.

7. Trewhitt, *McNamara*, 36–39.

8. Allan Nevins and Frank Ernst Hill, *Ford, Decline and Rebirth, 1933–1962* (New York: Charles Scribners Sons, 1963), 252, 254, 294, 307–31.

9. Brock Yates, *The Decline and Fall of the American Automobile Industry* (New York: Empire Books, 1983); David Lewis, interview with the author, 1985, Ann Arbor, Mich.

10. Author interviews, 1985.

11. David Halberstam, *The Best and the Brightest* (New York: Random House, 1972), 229–39.

12. Arthur M. Schlesinger, Jr., *A Thousand Days* (Cambridge, Mass.: Houghton Mifflin Co., 1965), 315–19; Desmond Ball, *Politics and Force Levels* (Berkeley and Los Angeles: University of California Press, 1980), 3–40.

13. Townsend Hoopes, *The Devil and John Foster Dulles* (Boston: Atlantic Monthly Press, 1973), 126, 196–200.

14. Ball, *Politics and Force Levels*, 84–87; Halberstam, *The Best and the Brightest*, 241–45. See also Gregg Herken, *Counsels of War* (New York: Alfred A. Knopf, 1985), 161; and author interviews, 1984.

15. David Alan Rosenberg, "The Origins of Overkill: Nuclear Weapons and American Strategy, 1945–1960," *International Security* 7 (Spring 1983): 4–8; author interviews, 1984.

16. Ball, *Politics and Force Levels*, 190–92; Herken, *Counsels of War*, 156, 259; Rosenberg, "Origins of Overkill," 67–71.

17. See Rosenberg, "Origins of Overkill," 68.

18. Author interview material.

19. Ibid.

20. See Alain C. Enthoven and C. Wayne Smith, *How Much Is Enough? Shaping the Defense Program, 1961–69* (New York: Harper & Row, 1971); William W. Kaufmann, *The McNamara Strategy* (New York: Harper & Row, 1964); and Stephen Enke, ed., *Defense Management* (Englewood Cliffs, N.J.: Prentice-Hall, 1967).

21. Enthoven and Smith, *How Much Is Enough?* 32–35, 40, 41, 53–60, 199, 243.

22. Robert S. McNamara, "Committees Are of Value Only for Exchanging Ideas," *Armed Forces Management*, November 1961, 22–23.

23. Thomas C. Schelling, "PPBS and Foreign Affairs," *The Public Interest*, Spring 1968, 27. See also John Wayne Fuller, "Congress and the Defense Budget: A Study of the McNamara Years" (Ph.D. diss., Princeton University, 1972), 52–56, 72–78.

24. An interesting argument to the effect that managers stressing "control" of the kind taught by the Harvard Business School create resistance in the institutions beneath them is found in Abraham Zaleznik, "Managers and Leaders: Are They Different?" *Harvard Business Review* 55 (May–June 1971): 67–78.

25. "McNamara Says Viet Nam Will Not Fall," *New York Herald Tribune*, 9 June 1961.

26. Trewhitt, *McNamara*, 197–202; Roger Hilsman, *To Move a Nation* (Garden City, N.Y.: Doubleday, 1967), 507.

27. Trewhitt, *McNamara*, 199–200.

28. Stanley Karnow, *Vietnam: A History* (New York: Viking, 1983), 254.

29. Andrew F. Krepinevich, Jr., "The Army Concept and Vietnam: A Case Study in Organizational Failure" (Ph.D. diss., Harvard University, 1983), 131–88, passim; Arthur M. Schlesinger, Jr., *Robert Kennedy and His Times* (Boston: Houghton Mifflin, 1978), 465–67.

30. See Kaufmann, *The McNamara Strategy*, 77, 79, and Roswell Gilpatric, interview with Dennis J. O'Brien, 5 May 1970, Roswell Gilpatric Oral History, Boston: John F. Kennedy Library, 36.

31. McGeorge Bundy, "Memorandum for the President, Re: Basic Policy in Vietnam," 27 January 1965, National Security File, NSC History File, box 40, File Folder "Deployment of Major U.S. Forces, Vol. II, tabs 120–140," Lyndon B. Johnson Library, Austin, Texas.

32. *United States–Vietnam Relations, 1945–1967: Study Prepared by the Department of Defense* [Pentagon Papers] (Washington, D.C.: GPO, 1971), vol. 4, bk. IV.C.3, 35–73.

33. That McNamara was thinking along the lines of graduated military pressure bringing desirable outcomes at minimal risk shows in the language of the memos of his chief aide on the issue, John T. McNaughton, and in his own memoranda to the president in this period (see, for example, Larry Berman, *Planning a Tragedy: The Americanization of the War in Vietnam* [New York: W. W. Norton & Co., 1982], 79, 101–3).

34. The literature on this is extensive. See, for example, Ulysses G. Sharp, *Strategy for Defeat: Vietnam in Retrospect* (San Rafael, Calif.: Presidio Press, 1978). See also U.S. Congress, Senate, *Air War against North Vietnam: Hearings before the Preparedness Investigating Subcommittee of the Committee on Armed Services*, 90th Cong., 1st sess., 25 August 1967.

35. Robert S. McNamara, "Memorandum for the President, Subject: Actions

Recommended for Vietnam," 14 October 1966, National Security File, NSC Meetings File, box 2, File Folder "NSC Meetings, Vol. 4, Tab 47, 10/14/66," LBJ Library.

36. Trewhitt, *McNamara*, 272–76.

37. See Robert S. McNamara, "Draft Memorandum for the President, Subject: Future Action in Viet Nam," 19 May 1967, and "Memorandum for the President, Subject: A Fifteen Month Program for Military Operations in Southeast Asia," 1 November 1967, both in National Security File, Country File, Vietnam, boxes 74 and 75, File Folder "Vietnam 2 EE 1965–67," LBJ Library.

38. See, generally, Herbert V. Schandler, *The Unmaking of a President: Lyndon Johnson and Vietnam* (Princeton, N.J.: Princeton University Press, 1977).

39. Thomas Carlyle, *On Heroes, Hero-Worship, and the Heroic in History* (1840), 1.

Notes on Contributors

JOHN MILTON COOPER, JR., is professor of history at the University of Wisconsin, Madison. He is the author of *Walter Hines Page: The Southerner as American* and *The Warrior and the Priest*, and he is a member of the Editorial Advisory Committee to the Papers of Woodrow Wilson.

CECILIA STILES CORNELL studied American history at Vanderbilt University and is completing a dissertation on James Forrestal. She has held positions as research associate for The Correspondence of James K. Polk, 1983–85; as instructor at George Mason University, 1984; and as dissertation fellow at the Office of Air Force History, 1982–83.

JAMESON W. DOIG is professor of politics and public affairs at Princeton University. He is author of *Metropolitan Transportation Politics and the New York Region*, coauthor of *The Assistant Secretaries, Men Who Govern*, and *New York: The Politics of Urban Regional Development*, and editor and coauthor of *Criminal Corrections: Ideals and Realities*.

PHILIP V. FELLMAN is a graduate student in the Department of Government at Cornell University, where he is studying international relations and security policy. In 1986 he received a master's degree in public and private management from Yale's School of Organization and Management. For four years prior to attending Yale, Fellman was a member of the president's staff at the Chevron Shipping Company.

ERWIN C. HARGROVE is professor of political science at Vanderbilt University. He is the author of *Presidential Leadership* and *The Power of the Modern Presidency* and coauthor of *Presidents, Politics and Policy*. He coedited *The President and the Council of Economic Advisers* and

TVA: Fifty Years of Grass Roots Bureaucracy, and he has recently completed a study of policy making in the Carter administration.

DONALD F. KETTL is associate professor of government and foreign affairs at the University of Virginia. He is the author of *Leadership at the Fed*, a study of the Federal Reserve Board, and *Government by Proxy*, a study of public management and varying policy strategies, such as contracting, grants, regulation, loan programs, and tax preferences.

W. HENRY LAMBRIGHT is professor of political science and public administration at the Maxwell School, Syracuse University, and director of the Science and Technology Policy Center, Syracuse Research Corporation. He is author of *Presidential Management of Science and Technology: The Johnson Presidency, Educating the Innovative Public Manager* (with Samuel I. Doctors and Donald C. Stone), *Technology Transfer to Cities*, and *Governing Science and Technology*. He served as a special assistant with the National Aeronautics and Space Administration in Washington, D.C.

MELVYN P. LEFFLER is professor of history at the University of Virginia. He is the author of *The Elusive Quest: America's Pursuit of European Stability and French Security, 1919–1933* and of articles published in the *American Historical Review*, the *Journal of American History*, *International Security*, and *Diplomatic History*.

EUGENE LEWIS is professor of political science at New College of the University of South Florida. He has served as provost of New College and Hamilton College. His writings include *Public Entrepreneurship: Toward a Theory of Bureaucratic Political Power, Urban America* (with F. M. Anechiarico), *American Politics in a Bureaucratic Age: Citizens, Constituents, Clients and Victims*, and *The Urban Political System*.

THEODORE R. MARMOR is professor of public management and political science at Yale University. He is author of *The Politics of Medicare* and *Political Analysis and American Medical Care* and editor and contributor to *National Health Insurance: Conflicting Goals and Policy Choices*. He was editor of the *Journal of Health Policy, Politics and Law* in 1980–84 and has served on presidential commissions on income maintenance and health planning issues.

DEBORAH SHAPLEY is the author of *Lost at the Frontier: U.S. Science and Technology Policy Adrift* and *The Seventh Continent: Antarctica in a Resource Age*. Previously a staff writer for *Science* and *Nature* magazines, she has published in *Daedalus*, the *New Republic*, the *New York Times*, the *Washington Post*, and the *Christian Science Monitor* and has contributed chapters in several academic books.

WALLACE EARL WALKER is an Army lieutenant colonel and permanent associate professor in the Department of Social Sciences at West Point, New York. He has written articles on bureaucratic and organizational politics, Congress, and the presidency, and his book *Changing Organizational Culture* was published in 1986. In 1980–81, as a White House fellow, he served in the Department of Energy and later in the White House Office of Policy Development.

MARTHA WAGNER WEINBERG is adjunct professor of public policy and American institutions at Brown University. She has been on the faculty at MIT and the Graduate School of Business at Harvard, where she focused her research on similarities and differences in public- and private-sector management. Her books include *Managing the State* and (with W. D. Burnham) *American Politics and Public Policy*.

MARGARET JANE WYSZOMIRSKI is director of the Graduate Program in Public Policy at Georgetown University. She has published articles on presidential leadership and advisory systems, and she collaborated in editing and contributing to *Art, Ideology and Politics* (1985).

Index

Leadership and Innovation: A Biographical Perspective on Entrepreneurs in Government

Designed by Martha Farlow.

Composed by EPS Group, Inc., in Century Schoolbook (condensed).

Printed by the Maple Press Company on 50-lb. Sebago Eggshell Cream offset and bound in Joanna Arrestox A with Rainbow Antique endsheets.